# INDIGENOUS MEXICAN MIGRANTS IN THE UNITED STATES

CENTER FOR U.S.-MEXICAN STUDIES AND
CENTER FOR COMPARATIVE IMMIGRATION STUDIES
UNIVERSITY OF CALIFORNIA, SAN DIEGO

## Contributors

Warren D. Anderson
Patricia Artía Rodríguez
Bonnie Bade
Federico Besserer
Garance Burke
Isidro Cerda
María Crummett
Yolanda Cruz
Guillermo Delgado-P.
Rufino Domínguez Santos
Luis Escala Rabadán
Jonathan Fox
Ulises García
Javier Huizar Murillo
Ilene J. Jacobs
Paul Johnston
Michael Kearney
Edward Kissam
Felipe H. López
Filemón López
Centolia Maldonado
Jesús Martínez-Saldaña
Alejandrina Ricárdez
Gaspar Rivera-Salgado
Liliana Rivera-Sánchez
Sergio Robles Camacho
David Runsten
Gustavo Santiago Márquez
Ella Schmidt
Lynn Stephen
Laura Velasco Ortiz
María Cristina Velásquez C.

# INDIGENOUS MEXICAN MIGRANTS

# IN THE UNITED STATES

*Edited by*

Jonathan Fox and Gaspar Rivera-Salgado

LA JOLLA, CALIFORNIA

CENTER FOR U.S.-MEXICAN STUDIES, UCSD
CENTER FOR COMPARATIVE IMMIGRATION STUDIES, UCSD

Printed in the United States of America

Library of Congress Cataloging-in-Publication Data

Indigenous Mexican migrants in the United States / edited by Jonathan Fox
and Gaspar Rivera-Salgado.
 p. cm.
 Based on papers from a conference hosted by the University of Santa Cruz,
Latin American and Latino Studies Dept., with co-sponsorship from the Frente
Indígena Oaxaqueño Binacional and two UCSC research centers.
 Includes bibliographical references.
 ISBN 1-878367-50-1 (pbk.)
 1. Mexican Americans—Social conditions—Congresses. 2. Immigrants—
United States—Social conditions—Congresses. 3. Indigenous peoples—
Mexico—Congresses. 4. Mexican Americans—Ethnic identity—Congresses.
5. United States—Emigration and immigration—Congresses. 6. Mexico—
Emigration and immigration—Congresses. I. Fox, Jonathan, 1958-  II. Rivera-
Salgado, Gaspar.

E184.M5I455 2004
2004045753

# CONTENTS

## Part III. Social and Economic Processes

## Part IV. Comparative Perspectives: Ethnic and Geographic Diversity

# Acknowledgments

We are very grateful to the many people who helped to make this volume possible. First, we would like to thank the participants in the University of California, Santa Cruz conference entitled "Indigenous Mexican Migrants in the US: Building Bridges between Researchers and Community Leaders." The conference was hosted by the UCSC Latin American and Latino Studies Department, with cosponsorship from the Frente Indígena Oaxaqueño Binacional (FIOB) and two UCSC research centers, the Chicano Latino Research Center and the Center for Justice, Tolerance, and Community.

Many of the conference participants are represented in this volume, but we would also like to recognize the following other panelists for sharing their experiences and insights, in order of appearance: Víctor López and Candelaria Domínguez (MayaVISION, Maya Various Interpreting Services and Indigenous Organizing Network, Los Angeles), Olga Nájera Ramírez (Anthropology and Chicano Latino Research Center, UCSC), Luin Goldring (Sociology, York University), Fred Krissman (Center for U.S.-Mexican Studies, University of California, San Diego), Raúl Hinojosa-Ojeda (North American Integration and Development Center, University of California, Los Angeles), Eduardo Stanley (independent journalist, Fresno), Marisol Ayala and Rick Mines (California Institute for Rural Studies, Davis), Eric Popkin (Sociology, Colorado College), Ireneo Rojas Hernández (Centro de Investigación de la Cultura P'urhepecha, Universidad Michoacana de San Nicolás de Hidalgo), Fernando Melo Farrera (Trasparencia, Oaxaca), Romualdo Juan Gutiérrez Cortés (Oaxaca Regional Coordinator, FIOB), Pat Zavella (Latin American and Latino Studies and Chicano Latino Research Center, UCSC), Carol Zabin (Center for Labor Research and Education, University of California, Berkeley), Sergio Guzmán (United Farm Workers, Watsonville), David Bacon (independent journalist, Berkeley), Hugo Morales (Radio Bilingüe, Fresno), Myrna Martínez (American Friends Service Committee, Fresno), Angélica Salas (Coalition for Humane

Immigrant Rights of Los Angeles), and Manuel Pastor (LALS and Center for Justice, Tolerance, and Community, UCSC).

We are very grateful for the highly professional organizational and diplomatic skills of UCSC Latin American and Latino Studies and Politics student (now alumna) Emma Lukin, without whom the conference and follow-up would not have been possible. Ramona Kolman-Leland, then LALS department manager, also made a major contribution, including the design of the bilingual conference Web site (www.lals.ucsc.edu/conference). We would like to recognize the following current and former UCSC graduate and undergraduate students for their support during the conference itself: John Ackerman, Roxana Aguilar, Lorena Alvarado, Aaron Bobrow-Strain, Alejandra Castañeda, Roberto I. De la Rosa, Breanna George, Sandino Gómez, Dianna Guzmán, Simon Keegan, Tony Lopreste, Diana Reveles, Riccardo Rivera, Irma Sandoval Ballesteros, and Robin Shuett-Hames. Thanks also to the Barrios Unidos video team for the use of their equipment. We are very grateful to Omar Monterrubio Sosa of *El Oaxaqueño* newspaper for his creative contribution to the design of the poster, program, and book cover. Thanks also go to the conference interpreters, Oscar Ríos and Carlos Landaverry.

We would like to express our gratitude to Robert Bach, then at the Rockefeller Foundation, and to Rubén Puentes of the Rockefeller Foundation's Transnational Communities Program. Their timely and generous grant made possible both the conference and the book. Thanks also to Manuel Pastor for strategic support at an early stage. UC MEXUS supported Oaxaca-based research and participation. The LALS/CLRC Hemispheric Dialogues two research projects also contributed by making possible Centolia Maldonado's extended research visit to UC Santa Cruz (http://lals.ucsc.edu/hemispheric_dialogues/). In addition, grants from Larry Gonzales at the California Endowment, from the University of California's Institute for Labor and Employment, and from the Ford Foundation allowed us to support conference follow-up and dissemination of the research findings. We are also grateful to Gisela Richards for her able administrative support.

Thanks also go to Professor Wayne Cornelius and Sandra del Castillo, at the University of California, San Diego, for their consistent support in the publication process. Our goal of producing both English and Spanish versions of this book proved to be a major challenge. Thanks very much to our translators, including Naomi Adelson, Stuyvesant Bearns, Adam Critchley, Ana Elena González Treviño, María Socorro Gutiérrez, Odette

León Martínez, Felipe López, and Natalia Pérez García, as well as to Garance Burke for facilitating the process. The completion of the full Spanish version of the manuscript was made possible by the superb quality and consistency of Luis Escala Rabadán's editorial and translation support, for which we are very grateful.

Finally, we would like to thank all of the authors who appear in this volume, for their contributions and for their patience. This diverse group of activists, academics, and applied researchers has inspired us with their words and with their example.

Jonathan Fox and Gaspar Rivera-Salgado
Santa Cruz and Los Angeles
December 2003

# 1

# Building Civil Society among Indigenous Migrants

## Jonathan Fox and Gaspar Rivera-Salgado

Mexican migrants in the United States are still widely assumed to be an ethnically homogeneous population. Historically, most Mexican migrants did share many common characteristics, coming primarily from rural communities in the central-western part of the country. Over the last two decades, however, the Mexican migrant population has diversified dramatically, both socially and geographically. Their regions of origin now include a more diverse range of states as well as large cities.[1] For example, the Los Angeles area now has federations of hometown associations from at least thirteen different Mexican states, and eleven statewide federations are active in Chicago. Regions of migrant settlement in the United States are becoming similarly diverse—researchers recently found license plates from thirty-seven different U.S. states just along the main road of San Juan Mixtepec, Oaxaca.[2]

Thanks very much to Luis Escala Rabadán, Luin Goldring, Michael Kearney, Lynn Stephen, and Laura Velasco Ortiz for especially insightful, constructive, and timely comments on an earlier version of this introduction. The authors bear sole responsibility for what follows. This volume will be published in Spanish by the Universidad Autónoma de Zacatecas/Miguel Ángel Porrúa.

[1] On the variation in state-to-state cross-border migration patterns, see the maps in Cano 2002. See also CONAPO 2000; Durand 1998; Durand and Massey 2003.

[2] See López and Runsten, this volume. Besserer documented that this municipality received remittances from 171 locations scattered across seven states in Mexico and fifteen states in the United States (2003: 67–69).

The Mexican migrant population is not only growing more geographically diverse, it is also increasingly multiethnic. Some Mexican indigenous peoples have many decades of experience with migration to the United States, dating back to the Bracero Program (1942–1964), such as the P'urépechas of Michoacán and Oaxaca's Mixtecs and Zapotecs. This binational government program also recruited Nahuas, as revealed in the recent account of a rare (successful) strike by braceros in the late 1950s. As one participant reported, "We spoke in *mexicano* [Náhuatl] and they didn't understand us, that's how we were able to organize even though it was prohibited and we fought for fair pay. We did the strike in *mexicano*."[3]

Historically, however, most indigenous migrants went to large cities or agribusiness jobs within Mexico. Until the 1980s, their relative share of the overall cross-border migrant population was relatively low. More recently, the indigenous proportion of the Mexican migrant population has grown significantly, most notably in both urban and rural California and increasingly in Texas, Florida, New York, and Oregon. As the public debate within Mexico continues over the nation's multiethnic character and indigenous rights, the growing presence of indigenous migrants has also raised this issue within Mexican migrant communities in the United States.

To provide context, it is important to keep in mind that, in absolute terms, Mexico's national indigenous population is the largest in the hemisphere, with approximately one-quarter of the Indians in the Americas as a whole.[4] In relative terms, at least one-tenth of the Mexican population is of indigenous origin, according to the government's relatively strict criterion of indigenous language use (though the most recent national census allows for ethnic self-identification for the first time). In other words, despite five centuries of pressure to assimilate, at least one in ten Mexicans reports to their national census that an indigenous language is spoken in their household.[5]

---

[3] Testimony of Florencio Martínez Hernández, from Tlaxcala, cited in Ramírez Cuevas 2003. Authors' translation.

[4] In terms of the relative sizes of national indigenous populations in Latin America, Mexico is followed by Peru, Guatemala, Bolivia, and Ecuador (Dossier Courrier International 2003). See also Varese 1991.

[5] The National Indigenous Institute's (INI) most recent estimates of the national indigenous population range between 10.3 and 12.7 million people, depending on the criteria. See Serrano Carreto, Embriz Osorio, and Fernández Ham 2002 for details on the 2000 census. For background on the census and indigenous peoples in Mexico, see Valdés 1995; Lartigue and Quensel 2003. For analyses of indigenous

The future projected by Mexico's dominant economic model has little place for indigenous peoples other than their joining the urban and agro-export workforce.[6] Because the majority of Mexico's indigenous population depends on agriculture, their livelihood prospects are highly sensitive to governmental policies toward that sector. Two decades ago, the government abandoned its previously on-again/off-again commitment to make family farming economically viable.[7] Since the 1980s, peasant agriculture became a target of welfare policy rather than production support, a shift that weakened the economic base of indigenous communities.[8] Since implementation of the North American Free Trade Agreement (NAFTA), the government's rural development strategy has been based on the assumption that a large proportion of the rural poor would move either to the cities or to the United States.[9] Indeed, Mexico City's population of urban Indians in the hemisphere is officially estimated by the city government at half a million in the Federal District and one million in the greater metropolitan area.[10] The long-term crisis of the peasant economy has been exac-

---

migration by the INI, see Rubio et al. 2000 for an overview, as well as Atilano Flores 2000 and Valencia Rojas 2000. For background, see Molinari Soriano 1979.

[6] The widespread perception of systematic social exclusion by the dominant economic model was summed up by Subcomandante Marcos's widely repeated prediction that NAFTA would be "a death sentence" for Mexico's indigenous people. It is no coincidence that the Zapatista rebellion became, in effect, the "shot heard 'round the world" in the spreading concern with what later became known as economic globalization.

[7] On the history of government policies toward peasant grain production, see Fox 1992.

[8] According to the government's National Population Council (CONAPO), poverty worsened in 30 percent of the predominantly indigenous municipalities during the 1990–2002 period (cited in Urrutia 2002).

[9] See the explicit 1992 predictions of then Undersecretary of Agriculture Luis Téllez that the rural proportion of the national population would (and should) fall from 26 percent to 16 percent over the following decade or two (cited in Fox 1994: 224). According to the logic of these neoliberal policy makers, if agriculture accounts for only 7 or 8 percent of gross domestic product (GDP), then that is the appropriate share of the population that should remain in the countryside. They implicitly regard the rest of the rural population as surplus that should move to the cities (thereby keeping industrial wages down to attract foreign investment).

[10] This is the official estimate of the Government of the Federal District (personal communication, Pablo Yanes, Dirección de Atención a los Pueblos Indígenas, June 2003). For details on ethnicity and the most recent census in the Mexico City context, see Yanes Rizo 2002, as well as Anzaldo Meneses 1999; Dirección de Atención a los Pueblos Indígenas 2001; Gobierno del Distrito Federal 2000. For

erbated in recent years by the persistent collapse of the international price of coffee, which is the principal cash crop for many of Mexico's indigenous farmers.[11]

Both in the United States and in Mexico, indigenous migrants find themselves excluded—economically, socially, and politically—both as migrants and as indigenous people. Economically, they work in ethnically segmented labor markets that relegate them to the bottom rungs. In the social sphere, in addition to the well-known set of obstacles that confront cross-border migrants, especially those without documentation, they also face entrenched racist attitudes and discrimination from other Mexicans as well as from the dominant society in the United States. In the civic-political arena, most cross-border migrants are excluded from full citizenship rights in either country. On the one hand, the U.S. government resists proposals to regularize the status of millions of workers. On the other hand, by 2003 the Mexican government had yet to comply either with the 1996 constitutional reform that recognized migrants' right to vote or with the 1996 San Andrés Accords on Indigenous Rights and Culture which had promised a modest form of indigenous autonomy.[12] In addition, lack of effective absentee ballot provisions also prevents many migrants within Mexico from

---

background on the Assembly of Indian Migrants of Mexico City, see www. indigenasdf.org.mx/.

[11] For background on the coffee crisis, see Aranda 2003; Oxfam 2002; and many Internet resources linked to a recent PBS documentary: www.pbs.org/ frontlineworld/stories/guatemala.mexico/. On NAFTA's impact on Mexico-U.S. migration, see Cornelius 2002. On corn and NAFTA, see Nadal 2000. On the role of U.S. policy in Mexico's corn economy, see Oxfam 2003.

[12] For background on the right-to-vote issue, see Martínez-Saldaña and Ross Pineda 2002. On the San Andrés Accords and their context, see Hernández Navarro and Vera Herrera 1998. For essays by Mexican indigenous rights advocates in English, see the spring 1999 thematic issue of *Cultural Survival Quarterly*. Mexico's movement against second-class citizenship for indigenous peoples has had a significant impact on national political culture and has made public racism increasingly "politically incorrect." Nevertheless, some Mexico City cultural elites, ranging from television network managers to prominent intellectuals, persist in reproducing racist bias. For example, noted historian and public intellectual Enrique Krauze recently declared that "Mexico has many problems, but an Indian problem or ethnic violence is not one of them" (Authers and Silver 2003). This formulation implies that the "Indian problem" would only really count if it expressed itself through ethnic violence, while erasing the alternative frame which would define the main "problem" in terms of systematic patterns of political exclusion, biased public policies that reinforce structural poverty, and discriminatory social attitudes.

voting. In the less tangible arena of the dominant national political culture, both indigenous peoples and migrants have long been seen, especially by Mexico City political elites, as less than full citizens—a powerful historical inheritance that only began to change substantially within Mexico by the mid-1990s. Like other migrants, indigenous Mexicans bring with them a wide range of experiences with collective action for community development, social justice, and political democratization, and these repertoires influence their decisions about who to work with and how to build their own organizations in the United States.[13]

## REFRAMING MEXICAN MIGRATION AS A MULTIETHNIC PROCESS

The past and the future of the Mexican nation can be seen in the faces of the tens of thousands of indigenous people who each year set out on their voyages to the north, as well as the many others who decide to settle in countless communities within the United States. To study indigenous Mexican migrants in the United States today requires a binational lens, taking into account basic changes in the way Mexican society is understood as the twenty-first century begins. On the one hand, Mexico is increasingly recognized to be a nation of migrants, a society whose fate is intimately linked with the economy and culture of the United States. On the other hand, the experiences specific to indigenous migrants require understanding Mexico as a multiethnic society in which basic questions of indigenous rights are finally on the national agenda but remain fundamentally unresolved.

Historically, different indigenous peoples in Mexico have pursued different migration paths. Note, for example, that there is no direct correlation between the relative size of the populations of Mexico's different indigenous peoples and their respective tendencies to migrate to the United States. Until recently, Mexico's two largest indigenous ethnolinguistic groups, the Nahua and the Maya, did not tend to cross the border in large numbers.[14] Even within the state of Oaxaca, there is no direct correlation

---

13 For overviews of Mexico's patchwork quilt of widely varying degrees of political space and conflict in indigenous regions following more than two decades of contestation over rural democratization, see Fox 1996 and Cornelius, Eisenstadt, and Hindley 1999, among others.

14 In terms of the relative sizes of these populations in Mexico, according to the INI's analysis of the 2000 population census, the fifteen largest indigenous language groups include: Náhuatl (1,771,000), Maya (1,149,000), Zapoteco (546,000), Mixteco (534,000), Tzotzil (445,000), Otomí (427,000), Tzeltal (349,000), Totonaco (289,000),

between the lowest-income municipalities and those with the most out-migration.[15] In contrast to the predominance of Oaxacans among migrants to Baja California and the United States, the groups with the largest presence in Mexico City are of Nahua and Hñahñu (Otomí) origin, representing approximately 27 percent and 17 percent, respectively.[16] However, as the economic and social dynamics that encourage migration spread more deeply throughout the Mexican countryside, indigenous peoples who did not have a history of migration outside of their regions are coming to the United States.[17] For example, Mayans from Yucatán and Chiapas are now working in California and Texas, both Hñahñus and Nahuas from central Mexico are coming to the Midwest and Texas, and Mixtecs from Puebla are settling in the New York area, followed more recently by Hñahñus from neighboring Veracruz.[18] Mixtecs and Nahuas are also coming to the United

Mazahua (256,000), Mazateco (224,000), Huasteco (186,000), Chol (174,000), Chinanteco (157,000), Purépecha (141,000), and Tlapaneco (98,000) (Serrano Carreto, Embriz Osorio, and Fernández Ham 2003: 73–74).

[15] For a different comparative approach, see the state maps of differing migration rates and poverty levels in Dirección General de Población de Oaxaca 2002. Notably, the southern Sierra is one of the state's poorest regions, yet so far few from this area migrate to the United States. Note also that Oaxacan migration to the United States includes urbanized mestizos. See, for example, Grimes's study of the impact of migration from Putla on local identities. Atlantic City, New Jersey, is one of the main areas of U.S. settlement for this group (Grimes 1998: 58).

[16] In Mexico City, Mixtecs and Zapotecs come in third and fourth place, with 14 percent and 13.5 percent, respectively, followed by Mazahuas with 4.2 percent. See Dirección de Atención a los Pueblos Indígenas 2001: 2.

[17] In 1994, of the 803 municipalities considered by the INI to be predominantly indigenous, 25 percent were considered to "expel farmworkers." By 1998–1999, 38 percent of indigenous municipalities fell into this category (cited in Barrón 2003). Approximately 40 percent of Mexico's farmworker population is indigenous, with Guerrero now ahead of Oaxaca as the leading source (Barrón 2003: 49). Barrón's report notes, "More than ten years ago, farmworkers of Nahua origin from the Huasteca region of Hidalgo began to work in the cane fields of the Huasteca regions of San Luis Potosí and Veracruz. Currently, an important proportion of farmworkers working in the fields of Sonora and Sinaloa come from the Huasteca region of Hidalgo.... Also, farmworkers from Chiapas and indigenous Coras and Huicholes from Nayarit, who before only migrated from the mountains to the valleys of Nayarit, now go to Sonora and Sinaloa" (Barrón 2003: 15; authors' translation). A longtime Huasteca-based community organizer confirms this pattern, reporting that Nahua migration from the region goes mainly to central and northern Mexico to take the place of workers who migrate (personal email communication, Juan Felipe Cisneros Sánchez, San Luis Potosí, September 2003).

[18] For example, from the largely Hñahñu municipality of Texcatepec, in the Huasteca region of Veracruz, an estimated 400 to 500 young men are now working in

States from Guerrero, a Mexican state whose migration patterns have received little research attention so far.[19] As newer arrivals coming with different traditions of community organization back home, these indigenous migrants have experiences that differ from those of the Oaxacans. To improve our understanding of these new groups and their regions of origin and settlement, researchers will need to broaden the exchange between those who study indigenous communities and those who study migration, as well as between those who focus on domestic versus international Mexican migration.[20]

While this volume focuses primarily on the Oaxaca-California experience, it also includes several studies of other indigenous Mexican migrant groups. It is important to recognize that not all migrants have formed satel-

---

the New York City area, out of a local population of approximately 9,000. According to a Jesuit priest from the region who travels regularly from Veracruz to see them, they live and work together based on "the natural organization of their community," though they are not sufficiently settled to produce formal organizations that send collective remittances. Even though the local community of Amazac recovered their ancestral land from violent rancher elites after decades of agrarian struggle in 1994, large-scale migration to the north began in 1995. The members of the agrarian community were unable to access the capital needed to convert the ranchland to more job-creating crops. Out-migration was reportedly further accelerated by NAFTA's opening to meat imports, which drove down the price of their cattle, and coffee is no longer a viable alternative. After the terrorist attacks of September 11, 2001, some of these migrants branched out to New Jersey, North Carolina, and Florida, where Hñahñus from the Valle del Mezquital, Hidalgo, have been going for two decades. In contrast, Totonacos from Veracruz, being closer to the coast, tend to cross at Matamoros and work in Texas (author interview with Alfredo Zepeda, S.J., Huayacocotla, Veracruz, October 2003). Hñahñu migrants from Hidalgo have now reached almost 15 percent of the population of Clearwater, Florida. See Schmidt and Crummett, this volume.

[19] See, however, Boruchoff 1999; Boruchoff and Johnston 2003; García Ortega 2002, 2003. García Ortega's study of both national and international Nahua migration from the Alto Balsas region of Guerrero finds an important local role of the Bracero Program. She also reports a 2001 community census from the village of Ahuelican that found that migrants made up 38 percent of the total population of 760 (2002: 112 ff). Most were working in the United States, including in Atlanta, Dallas, Denver, Houston, Las Vegas, Los Angeles, and Ontario, California. A recent front-page story on the growing tendency of migrant farmworkers to settle in the United States for the long term (Porter 2003) profiled a migrant from Guerrero who is of Nahua origin (personal email communication, Eduardo Porter, October 2003).

[20] For one of the few studies that focus specifically on the interaction between national and international Mexican migration, see Lozano-Ascencio, Roberts, and Bean 1999.

lite communities in the United States, which is a key precondition for organizing along hometown lines, and even fewer have formed ethnic, regional, or pan-ethnic organizations. Some indigenous Mexican migrants organize as members of ethnically mixed groups, whether along religious lines, as in the case of New York's Tepeyac Association, or along class lines, as in the case of Oregon's Northwest Treeplanters and Farmworkers United (PCUN) or Florida's Coalition of Immokolee Workers (CIW).[21] Indigenous migrant organizations also vary in terms of their degree of interest in collaboration with other kinds of groups, whether they be organizations of other kinds of migrants or U.S.-focused civic and social organizations. In Los Angeles, for example, the Oaxacan Federation works closely both with other Mexican organizations and with trade unions and civil rights organizations on issues such as access to driver licenses for undocumented workers.

Because of cultural, political, and language differences between groups of Mexicans, any efforts to communicate or build coalitions among these groups must take these differences into account. Advocacy efforts by U.S. groups on behalf of indigenous migrants face major challenges in terms of building trust and cross-cultural communication.[22] Various incipient cross-sectoral coalition-building efforts have not coalesced, leading to some skepticism as well as suggesting the need for greater mutual understanding to facilitate the process of finding the common ground needed to sustain balanced multicultural coalitions.[23]

## THE EXPERIENCE OF OAXACAN INDIGENOUS MIGRATION

Historically, most indigenous migrants to the United States were temporary, but the increased risk and cost of crossing the border without docu-

---

[21] On the Tepeyac Association, see Rivera-Sánchez, this volume; Galvez 2003. On the PCUN, see Stephen, this volume. On the CIW, see Bowe 2003; Cockburn 2003; Payne 2000; and www.ciw-online.org. The CIW's struggle is especially notable because they actually managed to convict violent labor contractors on criminal charges of slavery. Founded in 1994, CIW works to empower low-wage workers in southwest Florida, and its members include Latinos, Haitians, and indigenous migrants from Mexico and Guatemala.

[22] For one precedent-setting case, see Paul Johnston's study of the community-based coalition defense and public debate against the 2001 INS roundup of Triqui men in Greenfield, California (this volume).

[23] On related issues of identity formation and organizational strategy in coalition-building processes, see the classic study by Nagengast and Kearney 1990. See also Rivera-Salgado 1999, 2002; Fox 2001a, 2002.

ments has led more of these immigrants to settle in the United States for the long term. This is possible in part because their networks have matured over the past two decades.[24] In addition to the cross-border workers in the Bracero Program, the first travels of Oaxacan villagers in search of employment began back in the 1930s, taking them to Oaxaca City, the sugarcane fields of Veracruz, and later to the growing neighborhoods in Ciudad Nezahualcóyotl on the periphery of Mexico City. Then labor contractors supplying the agribusinesses of the northwestern state of Sinaloa began recruiting, especially in the Mixteca region. These south-to-north flows later extended to the Valley of San Quintín in northern Baja California. By the early 1980s, indigenous migrants reached further north, to California, Oregon, and Washington.[25]

Early migrants were able to regularize their status and settle down in the United States following the 1986 immigration policy reform (the Immigration Reform and Control Act, or IRCA). Within California, Oaxacans have long-established communities in the San Joaquin Valley, the Los Angeles metropolitan area, and northern San Diego County.[26] Within a relatively short time, these indigenous migrants went from invisibility to outsiders to attracting media attention and becoming a subject of both academic research and progressive activism.[27]

Oaxacan migration took off by the end of the 1980s, with the extensive incorporation of Zapotecs in urban services and Mixtecs in farm labor—

---

[24] On the concept of migratory networks, see Wilson 1998.

[25] On the history of Oaxacan migration to the United States, see Aguilar Medina 1979; Besserer 1999a, 1999b, 2003; Corbett et al. 1992; Escárcega and Varese n.d.; Guidi 1992; López and Runsten, this volume; Molinari Soriano 1979; Mountz and Wright 1996; Rivera-Salgado 1999; Stephen, this volume; Varese 2000; Velasco Ortiz 2002; Wright 1990; Zabin and Hughes 1995—as well as the citations in notes 23 and 26. By the late 1990s the Mexican government–sponsored survey of migrants to the border heading further north considered 7.6 percent of those surveyed to be speakers of indigenous languages (CONAPO 2001: 4). On the historical patterns of migration from Oaxaca to Mexico City, see Orellana 1973; Hirabayashi 1993; Sánchez G. 1995. For a comparison of urban migrant associations across Latin America, see Altamirano and Hirabayashi 1997.

[26] See Zabin 1997; Zabin, ed. 1992a, 1992b; Zabin, Kearney, et al. 1993; Runsten and Kearney 1994; Huizar Murillo and Cerda, this volume.

[27] For example, the first New York Times coverage of Mixtec migrants to California appeared in Mydans 1989.

often in the most difficult and lowest-paid jobs.[28] The IRCA reforms permitted millions of earlier migrants to regularize their status, allowing them to move up in the labor force, leaving open bottom rungs in the social ladder for newer indigenous migrants. Employers of low-wage workers have been more than willing to continue their long tradition of encouraging ethnic segmentation in labor markets. As a conservative scholar and farmer summed up the employers' view, "they will tell you, 'don't bring anybody onto the cement crew who speaks English' because the second generation will not work like the people from Oaxaca."[29] Indigenous workers also draw on ethnic difference to position themselves in the labor market. As one informant reported to Guidi: "Of course we speak Mixteco! [in the United States]. Sometimes we speak to each other in *dialecto* in front of the [Chicano] contractor so that we can come to an agreement about our wages. And they get mad because they don't understand us."[30]

By the early 1990s, an estimated 45,000 to 55,000 Mixtecs worked in agriculture in California's Central Valley, and 50,000 to 60,000 Zapotecs had settled in Los Angeles, mainly in the central neighborhoods of Koreatown, Pico Union, and South Central.[31] The proportion of predominantly indigenous migrants from southern Mexico in California farm labor almost doubled during the 1990s, from 6.1 percent (1993–1996) to 10.9 percent (1997–2000), spurring researcher Edward Kissam to project that indigenous migrants will represent more than 20 percent of California's farmworkers by 2010.[32]

---

[28] On the disparities in wages and working conditions between mestizo and indigenous migrants, see Zabin, Kearney, et al. 1993. See also, for example, the excellent account in Schlosser 1995.

[29] Victor Davis Hanson, California State University, Fresno, cited in "Mexifornia: A State of Becoming," Panel Discussion Transcript, August 19, 2003, National Press Club, Washington, D.C., at www.cis.org/articles/200e/mexiforniapanel.html. For analysis of the active roles played by employers and labor contractors in the ethnic segmentation of agricultural labor markets, see Krissman 1996, 2002.

[30] Cited in Guidi 1992: 162. Note that the use of the term "dialect" instead of words for "language" indicates the still widespread self-denigration of indigenous culture.

[31] See Runsten and Kearney 1994; Zabin and Escala Rabadán 1998; López and Runsten, this volume. On specifically Zapotec migration to California, see Caballero and Ríos Morales n.d.; Cruz Manjarraz 2001; Hulshof 1991; Klaver 1997; López 1999; Montes 2000; Mountz and Wright 1996; Rivera-Salgado 1999; Robles Camacho, this volume. On Zapotec migration to Mexico City, see Hirabayashi 1993; Sánchez G. 1995.

[32] See Kissam 2003a: 1. This trend is corroborated by a 1998–1999 anthropological field survey of migrant farmworkers in Napa and Sonoma counties, which found

The parallel process of long-term settlement and geographic concentration has led to the creation of a "critical mass" of indigenous Oaxacans, especially in California. This has permitted the emergence of distinctive forms of social organization and cultural expression, especially among Mixtecs and Zapotecs. Their collective initiatives draw on ancestral cultural legacies to build new branches of their home communities. Their public expressions range from building civic-political organizations to the public celebration of religious holidays, basketball tournaments involving dozens of teams, the regular mass celebration of traditional Oaxacan music and dance festivals such as the Guelaguetza, and the formation of village-based bands, some of which return to play in their hometown fiestas, as in the case of the Zapotec community of Zoogocho. Their cultural and political projects also include the revival of traditional weaving workshops, the publication of binational newspapers, indigenous- and Spanish-language radio programs, and efforts to provide translation services and preserve indigenous languages, as well as the emergence of writers and visual artists with cross-border sensibilities.

This collection explores these migration processes and their social, cultural, and civic impacts in the United States and in Mexico. The studies come from diverse perspectives, but they share a concern with how sustained migration and the emergence of organizations of indigenous migrants influence social and community identity, both in the United States and in Mexico. These studies also focus on how the creation and re-creation of collective ethnic identities among indigenous migrants influences their economic, social, and political relationships in the United States.

## ETHNIC IDENTITY AND COLLECTIVE ACTION

Our understanding of the relationship between Mexican migration, collective action, and the formation of ethnic identities has been greatly influenced by the research of Michael Kearney, who pioneered the study of Mixtec migration to the United States.[33] His work provides detailed descriptions of the transformative impact of migration on the ethnic identities

---

that Oaxacans represented 11.9 percent of the sample (n = 252). See Sánchez G. 2000, n.d.1, n.d.2, n.d.3: 7. Oaxacans were the third largest group, after migrants from Michoacán (47.2 percent) and Jalisco (15.1 percent).

[33] See Stuart and Kearney 1981; Kearney 1986, 1988, 1994, 1995a, 1995b, 1996, 2000, 2002; Kearney and Nagengast 1989; Nagengast and Kearney 1990; Nagengast, Stavenhagen, and Kearney 1992; Runsten and Kearney 1994. See also Wright's comprehensive early study (1990).

of indigenous Oaxacan workers. The process of racist discrimination and exclusion, both in northern Mexico and in the United States—though not completely new for Oaxacan indigenous people—was sharpened in the agricultural fields of Sinaloa, Baja California, and California's San Joaquin Valley. Vividly represented by the widespread use of derogatory terms such as "*oaxaquitas*" (little Oaxacans) and "*indios sucios*" (dirty Indians), this process of racialization led to a new ethnic identity for many migrants. Not only does this experience intensify their sense of ethnic difference, Kearney goes further to suggest that the process of migration to a new social context generates a new, broader ethnic identity that brings together migrants from communities that would not necessarily have shared identities back in Oaxaca. "This experience of discrimination outside of Oaxaca was a major stimulus for indigenous migrants to appropriate the labels—*mixteco*, *zapoteco*, and *indígena*—that formerly had only been used by linguists, anthropologists, and government officials, and to put them to work in organizing along ethnic lines."[34]

The newly appropriated ethnic identities that emerge in the process of migration created new opportunities for collective action that were expressed through the emergence of a diverse array of civic and political organizations in the United States and northern Mexico. These organizations differed from those in the communities of origin, where cross-community solidarity was often blocked by persistent legacies of intervillage conflict.[35] Kearney argues that workers from communities that might have been rivals in Oaxaca came to develop a sense of solidarity through their shared experiences of class and racial oppression as migrants. The resulting pan-Mixteco, pan-Zapoteco, and, later, pan-indigenous Oaxacan identi-

---

[34] Personal communication, Michael Kearney, July 2003. Ethnic slurs used against indigenous migrants from Guerrero include: "nacos, güancos, huarachudos, montañeros, piojosos, indios pata rajada, calzonudos, comaleros, sombrerudos, sin razón, paisanitos, indio bajado a tamborazos de la Montaña, Metlatontos (de Metlatónoc), Tlapanacos (Tlapanecos), son de Tlapa de me conformo (Tlapa de Comonfort), tu no savi, tu sí savi (tu no sabes, tu sí sabes), mixtequillo, indiorante (ignorante), paisa, mixterco (mixteco terco)" (cited in García Leyva 2003).

[35] For a full discussion on intercommunity land conflict in Oaxaca, see Dennis 1987. Dennis finds that government agencies deliberately allowed such disputes to fester for decades, thereby focusing political conflict inward and preventing the emergence of broader, cross-community coalitions. For an analysis of one of the first political openings—subtle but systematic—that permitted widespread regional, cross-community coalition building in Oaxaca, see Fox 1992. See also Fox 1996 on the dynamics of scaling up indigenous organizations from local to regional levels.

ties made possible broader pan-ethnic organizing among migrants for the first time.[36] This interpretation has been confirmed by recent developments within the Oaxacan Indigenous Binational Front (FIOB), which include a collaborative agreement with a newly organized P'urépecha community in Madera, California.[37] Of the six elected leaders of the FIOB's Baja California branch, one is Mixtec from Guerrero and the vice-coordinator is P'uré-pecha from Michoacán. This partial shift from a pan-Oaxacan frame to a broader pan-indigenous base has initiated an internal discussion over whether to drop "Oaxacan" from the organization's name, possibly to become the "Indigenous Binational Front."[38]

These insights about how migration and racialization influence collective identities provide the context in which migrants are understood in this volume. Here, migrants are framed as social actors rather than as either passive victims or faceless flows of amorphous masses. In contrast to idealized views of migrants, whether as "heroes" or "*pochos*," this collection focuses on their efforts to create new lives, to build their own organizations, and above all to represent themselves in a process of building an indigenous migrant civil society that can help face the challenges of the future.

Despite the adverse conditions that indigenous migrants encounter, they have nevertheless managed to create a wide range of civic, social, and political organizations that are notable for the diversity of their strategies and goals. Within this indigenous migrant civil society, two main kinds of organizations stand out. The first includes the large number of hometown associations, known in Spanish as "*organizaciones de pueblo*," "*clubes de oriundos*," or "*clubes sociales comunitarios*." They are composed of migrants from specific communities who come together mainly to support their commu-

---

[36] It would be useful to compare this process with others in which localized collective identities become transformed, through bottom-up antiracist struggle and contact with outside allies, into ethnic and pan-ethnic collective identities. Note Pallares's study of the Ecuadorian experience with this process (2002).

[37] They are primarily from Angahuan, Uruapan, and the membership is primarily female. The October 9, 2003, "*convenio de trabajo*" with the FIOB states: "Knowing that we are two indigenous peoples with different languages and cultures [Oaxaca and Michoacán], we affirm that we are brothers and sisters from one single country. In our condition as indigenous migrants in the United States, we face the same issues of human and labor rights, and therefore we want to work together to improve the living conditions in our community and to continue maintaining our culture amongst ourselves, our children, and our young people, with gender equality" (authors' translation).

[38] Author interview with Rufino Domínguez, Fresno, November 2003.

nity of origin, most notably by raising funds for local public works such as road or bridge building, water systems, electrification, or public spaces such as town squares, sports fields, schools, churches, or community halls.[39]

The second main kind of indigenous migrant associations includes coalition-building projects that draw on hometown, "translocal" ties but bring people together from a broader, regional ethnogeographic sphere. The most consolidated coalitions include the Oaxacan Indigenous Binational Front (FIOB), the Oaxacan Regional Organization (ORO), the Union of Highland Communities of Oaxaca (UCSO), the Coalition of Indigenous Communities of Oaxaca (COCIO), the International Indigenous Network of Oaxaca (RIIO), and the recently formed Oaxacan Federation of Indigenous Communities and Organizations in California (FOCOICA), whose affiliates include most Oaxacan organizations in that state.

Both kinds of organizations have created spaces within which indigenous migrants can engage in collective action and cultural sustenance. These organizations open up spaces within which social identities are created and re-created through the institutionalization of collective practices in which migrants are recognized as Oaxacans and as indigenous people. That is, these diverse collective practices generate discourses that recognize their specific cultural, social, and political identities. The real and imagined space in which they develop these practices is called "Oaxacalifornia," a transnationalized space in which migrants bring together their lives in California with their communities of origin more than 2,500 miles away.[40]

Note, for example, the wide range of names chosen for the organizations that bring together indigenous migrants from different regions and political backgrounds. These names reflect the previous political experiences of some of the leaders, who were able to channel the members' col-

---

[39] On Oaxaca hometown collective remittances, see de la Garza and Lowell 2002; Girón Cruz and Reyes Morales 2003; López, Escala-Rabadán, and Hinojosa-Ojeda 2001; Molina Ramírez 2003; Runsten 2003; Tucker, Díaz McConnell, and Van Wey 2003. For a study that compares community development initiatives in a Oaxacan community in terms of the degree to which they emerge internally or externally, see Gil Martínez de Escobar 2003. On Mexican hometown collective remittances more generally, see, among others, Alarcón 2002; Bada 2001; Corona Vásquez 2000; García Zamora 2002, 2003; García Zamora, ed. 2002; Goldring 1998a, 1998b, 2001, 2003a; López Espinosa 2002; Lozano-Ascencio 1993, 2003; Orozco, González, and Díaz de Cossío 2003; Suro et al. 2002.

[40] The term "Oaxacalifornia" was coined by Michael Kearney and Carole Nagengast, to refer to the deterritorialized community from which new forms of organization and political expression emerged. See their seminal articles: Kearney and Nagengast 1989; Nagengast and Kearney 1990.

lective efforts to recognize themselves as social actors with specific political roots. The use of *frente* in FIOB reflects the previous activism of some of the founding leaders in leftist causes and organizations in Mexico. Some of the FIOB's founding members were active, for example, in the class-based Independent Central of Agricultural Workers and Peasants (CIOAC), the leading independent farmworker union in Mexico during the 1970s and 1980s (and especially active in Sinaloa).[41] Several key leaders were teachers and veterans of Oaxaca's movement to democratize the official union.[42] Since the 1930s, this tendency within the teachers' union encouraged members to commit themselves to "serving the people."[43]

In this context, the concept of *frente* referred to a coalition that could coordinate the actions of independent groups desiring to join their efforts in a common cause, all the while maintaining their own autonomy. When FIOB was founded as the Mixteco-Zapoteco Binational Front (FM-ZB) in late 1991, its main goal was to coordinate the indigenous campaigns of the nine original founding organizations that were opposing celebration of the quincentenary of the "Discovery of the Americas." These organizations did not want to dissolve their organizations and create a new one for this purpose; rather, they wanted to coordinate their efforts temporarily in a "front" that would serve as an umbrella organization for this very specific goal. After this first joint campaign, some of the founding organizations merged in what became the FIOB in 1994; others withdrew from the process and remained independent.[44] Notably, the shift in the organization's name reflected a more inclusive, pan-Oaxacan identity (the state has sixteen distinct ethnic groups).

---

[41] The CIOAC was originally affiliated with the Mexican Communist Party (PCM), which later merged with moderate left-wing groups to form the Unified Socialist Party of Mexico (PSUM). See López Monjardín 1991.

[42] For a history of Oaxaca's teachers' movement, see Cook 1996.

[43] Dating from the 1950s, the political influence of radical teachers' movement leader Othón Salazar in the Montaña region of Guerrero was felt in the neighboring Mixteca region of Oaxaca.

[44] On the history of the FIOB, see Domínguez Santos n.d. and his chapter in this volume; Rivera-Salgado 1999, 2002; Hernández Díaz 2001; Kearney 2001; Leal 2001; López Mercado 1998; Ramírez Romero 2000; Robles Camacho, this volume. As per an official November 5, 1992, "circular" of what was then called the Frente Mixteco-Zapoteco Binacional, the member organizations at that time included the CCPM, ORO, COTLA, OPEO, ACBJ, OPAM, YEB, YEA, and Tlacochahuaya. When the FM-ZB became the FIOB in 1994, the ACBJ left, as did some but not all members of ORO.

The names of the Oaxacan migrant organizations also offer clues about their members' political orientation. The name of the Organization of Exploited and Oppressed People (OPEO) clearly emphasizes its members' shared sense of both class identity ("exploited") and racial identity ("oppressed"), though the members also share a strong territorial identity since they come from the same community of origin. Other groups chose to highlight different dimensions of their identity. "Civic," for example, in the Mexican context of the 1960s through the 1980s (before electoral democracy was on the agenda) was a relatively nonconfrontational way of referring to the struggle for respect for citizens' rights and for clean government (especially at the local level), and it sometimes provided cover for a radical democratic agenda.[45] "Civic" also had the advantage of suggesting a nonpartisan approach in a context in which explicitly "political" opposition was severely sanctioned by the state. The term "popular" in the Mixteco Popular Civic Committee (CCPM) suggested a broad class identity, bridging workers, peasants, and small entrepreneurs with both a civic and an ethnic (Mixtec) identity. Inherent in the name of the CCPM is the ideological dilemma facing members as to whether to organize along class lines, or as Mixtecs, or both. Yet either approach implicitly required a fight for democracy; hence the term "civic." In practice, however, the organization's membership was primarily hometown-based.

The name of the Benito Juárez Civic Association (ACBJ) also identifies it with the cause of democracy and good government implied by "civic." The reference to Benito Juárez combines an implicit call for the rule of law with the ethnic/national pride symbolized by Mexico's "indigenous Abraham Lincoln." This name choice also sent an implicitly pan-ethnic signal; because the ACBJ's base was primarily Mixtec while Juárez was Zapotec, the name underscored shared Oaxacan identity. The names of the primarily Zapotec Oaxaca Regional Organization and the Tlacolula Community in Los Angeles (COTLA) illustrate the use of more politically neutral descriptive terms, reflecting their primarily cultural goals as well as their members' shared territorial identities.[46]

---

[45] Recall the case of Guerrero's Civic Association of the 1960s, which government repression later provoked into becoming the Revolutionary National Civic Association (ACNR).

[46] The ORO's member organizations as of a decade ago included COTLA, OPAM, Yatzachi El Bajo, Yatzachi El Alto, and Tlacochahuaya, though in the process of working together in the Mixteco-Zapoteco Binational Front, COTLA and OPAM were represented directly rather than through ORO.

Despite the wide variety of political backgrounds of indigenous migrants that are reflected in the nature of the different organizations, all emphasize public activities and mobilizations that reaffirm their collective identities as indigenous peoples. As a consequence, the migrant organizations' wide range of public cultural events nourishes the multicultural experience of its citizens. The Guelaguetza festivals of music and dance are among the most important Oaxacan cultural events, and at least four Guelaguetzas are now celebrated annually in California within the context of a broader pan-ethnic Oaxacan indigenous identity.[47]

The Oaxacan Regional Organization pioneered the celebration of these festivals in the United States in 1987 and has been holding them in a park in the Pico Union neighborhood of Los Angeles. The festivals bring together two thousand people each year. In 2003 the XVI Guelaguetza featured two of the oldest musical bands of migrants in Los Angeles—Yatzachi El Bajo and Zoochina—as well as six community-based dance troupes (Huaxyacac, Yalálag, OPAM, Nueva Antequera, Centeotl, and COTLA; see *El Oaxaqueño* 2003a).

The Coalition of Indigenous Communities of Oaxaca, based in northern San Diego County, also holds an annual Guelaguetza festival, this one on the campus of California State University, San Marcos, in association with the leading Chicano student organization (MEChA) and other university- and community-based organizations. COCIO's Guelaguetza is unique in that it draws on organized support from the region's broader Latino and university community, in addition to the Oaxacan immigrant community.[48] COCIO 's festival, begun in 1994, is the second oldest in the state. Its organ-

---

[47] Guelaguetza is a Zapotec word that refers to reciprocity or mutual aid, but its meaning now refers to dance and musical exchanges. The festival centers on a series of dances associated with Oaxaca's ethnically distinct regions, each with its own music and costumes. In Oaxaca City, the state-sponsored Guelaguetza is the most important annual tourist event, but grassroots organizations also organize their own Guelaguetza festivals on special occasions. For historical context that underscores the role of the state government in structuring officially acceptable regional identities, beginning in the 1930s, see Poole 2002, 2004.

[48] The flyer distributed by COCIO announcing the 2003 Guelaguetza included the support of the following organizations and community groups: CSUSM-MEChA, CSUSM-Center for Border Studies, CSUSM-Latino Association of Faculty and Staff, Grupo Folklórico Zaachila, Grupo Folklórico Guelaguetza, Grupo Folklórico Renovación Oaxaqueña, Banda Tlapacoyam, Banda de Yatzachi El Bajo, San Pedro del Rincón, El Trapiche, Ayoquesco de Aldama, Santiago Yucuyachi, Nieves Ixpantepec, and Rosario Nuevo Tezoatlan.

izers report that more than four thousand people have participated.[49] Since 2001, northern San Diego County's Oaxacan organizations have also participated in a broad, multisectoral, officially sponsored public celebration of the Day of the Dead in downtown Oceanside, which draws thousands of people to a community otherwise known for its social polarization.

In the city of Fresno, in California's Central Valley, the Oaxacan Indigenous Binational Front has held a Guelaguetza annually since 2000, drawing on newly formed local dance troupes and also on larger, more consolidated Los Angeles–based dance and music groups. In 2002 this Guelaguetza opened with music from a local Native American group, and in 2003 with traditional Mixtec dances (*chilenas y diablitos*) performed by the Madera-based Grupo Folklórico Cultural Se'e Savi. Public interest groups and civic groups in the region are invited, with outreach activities that range from disseminating information about political causes to culturally appropriate public health education.

More recently, FOCOICA has since 2002 celebrated a Guelaguetza in the Los Angeles Sports Arena (former home of the Lakers basketball team), cosponsored by the Oaxaca state government, local trade unions, and the Spanish-language media (see García 2003a). FOCOICA's Guelaguetza draws between six and ten thousand people, mainly Oaxacan immigrants in Southern California, as well as a large number of Mexicans from other states. This event also promotes Oaxacan imports (ranging from traditional arts and crafts to mescal, chocolate, and so on) brought by entrepreneurs trying to gain a foothold in the large immigrant market.

Sports competitions are also important public events for Oaxacans, with basketball more popular than soccer.[50] One of the most important tournaments is the Los Angeles "Juárez Cup," organized by the Union of Highland Communities of Oaxaca each March for the past six years. Some

---

[49] Author interview, Miguel Morales, COCIO, San Diego, November 2003. See also *El Oaxaqueño* 2003b.

[50] For detailed accounts of the role of basketball in Oaxacan migrant communities, see Quiñones and Mittelstaedt 2000; Quiñones 2001. See also the new film *Oaxacan Hoops*, by Olga Rodríguez (www.oaxacanhoops.com). The game's popularity in the northern Sierra region is due in part to the very limited availability of flat space, which makes basketball courts easier to build than the larger soccer fields. On the key role of basketball among Nahua migrants from Guerrero, see García Ortega 2002; this author finds the game incorporated into village rituals.

sixty-five teams participate, representing more than forty Oaxacan communities.[51]

Some Mixtecs and Zapotecs in California also play a pre-Columbian ball game.[52] "Mixtec ball" is played in some very unlikely places—a parking lot in Los Angeles's Griffith Park, a lot adjacent to a farm in Selma, a high school sports field in the agroindustrial city of Watsonville. The resurgence of this game among immigrants is culturally important because, according to a recent report in *El Oaxaqueño*, the number of players of the game has decreased in Oaxaca as appropriate open spaces have disappeared.[53] As many as twelve different teams meet in an annual statewide tournament in Los Angeles. According to one player, many "play this game from childhood for fun. This is a tradition, a custom that we carry in the blood, and we do it for the sheer pleasure of the game" (see García 2003c). As in the case of many other Oaxacan migrant cultural activities—dances, music, food—Mixtec ball has generated a demand for traditional equipment, creating jobs for the artisans back home who make the gloves and balls.

Public religious celebrations among indigenous migrants in California have emerged much more recently. The "community calendar" section of *El Oaxaqueño* newspaper is very revealing. For example, the July 28, 2001, issue listed a number of fund-raising events organized by various Los Angeles–based Oaxacan hometown associations, including a dance organized by the Commission for the Restoration of the Santiago Mayor Apostol Church in Villa Hidalgo, Yalálag, to raise money for major repairs to the community's church. The Club Pro-Santos Fiscales from San Francisco Cajonos was organizing a dance to support their efforts to get two local

---

[51] In many Oaxacan villages, basketball courts are central public spaces. Historically, they were often among the few paved surfaces and therefore filled many village needs, from keeping coffee clean while drying to protecting participants in community dances from mud or dust. For a study of Oaxacan rural community decisions about how to prioritize different kinds of infrastructure investments based on a representative statewide sample of municipalities, see Fox and Aranda 1996.

[52] The game is played in two different ways, both with a *guante* (glove) and *pelota de forro* (wrapped ball). The gloved version, also known as "fastball," is played by migrants from Oaxaca's Central Valleys, especially those from Ejutla de Crespo. This particular version is played with a heavy glove that can weigh up to six kilos.

  Migrants from the Mixteca Baja, especially those from the Juxtlahuaca District, play with the *pelota de forro*. The ball is made of cloth and leather, and its weight (about 200 grams) makes this version of the game much slower.

[53] See García 2003b. This report mentions that at present there is only one ball court in the entire city of Oaxaca, compared to ten courts that existed just a few years ago.

"martyrs" declared "saints." After some twenty years, the Oaxacan Archdiocese had sent the case for canonization to the Vatican for consideration.[54] The association from the town of Santa María Xochixtepec was announcing a "traditional fiesta" honoring the Virgen del Rosario. And
finally, the association from San Miguel Cajonos was organizing a dance
honoring their community's patron saint, San Miguel Arcángel. In addition
to these fund-raising events, announcements reminded readers about the
monthly "oaxaqueño" mass every third Sunday in a Catholic church in
South Central Los Angeles. This "oaxaqueño" mass, accompanied by a Oaxacan dance troupe and a 25-piece Zapotec brass band, reflects a high degree of community participation. This crowded calendar of religious happenings is typical among indigenous Oaxacan immigrants in Los Angeles,
with events spread evenly throughout the year. In fact, Oaxacan hometown associations in Los Angeles often compete for available venues in
which to hold their dances.

A more public example of faith-based collective action was the procession of the Virgen de la Soledad, organized by a group of immigrants who
call themselves the Oaxacan Catholic Community of Los Angeles (Comunidad Católica Oaxaqueña). The procession drew more than a thousand
participants on December 16, 2002.[55] On this Sunday the Oaxacan community celebrated finding a permanent home for the Virgin, the patron Saint
of Oaxaca City and a special religious symbol for oaxaqueños in general. The
statue of the Virgin that led the procession had been brought from Oaxaca
City by the Oaxacan Catholic Community, who had lobbied the Oaxacan
Archdiocese for a statue of the Virgin and then traveled to Oaxaca to bring
it back to Los Angeles. The procession began at the intersection of Nor-
mandie and San Marino in Koreatown. The mood was very festive, with
Oaxacan dancers leading the procession and a brass band playing traditional jarabes serranos. Auxiliary Bishop of Los Angeles Edward Clark declared, "the Virgen de la Soledad is your patron saint; she is your mother.

---

[54] During the Pope's visit to Mexico City in 2002, he beatified the Santos Fiscales,
with the participation of many people from San Francisco Cajonos (see Rendón
2002). At ORO's Guelaguetza festival that summer, reactions were divided, with
some of the faithful overjoyed at the result of their years of campaigning, while
others were more skeptical about honoring some of the early leaders of the cultural assimilation process. One volunteer organizer went so far as to declare them
"traitors" (author interviews, Los Angeles, August 2002).

[55] See El Oaxaqueño, January 19, 2002, pp.18–19.

She has come here, to be beside you, so that you do not feel alone far away from home."[56]

This procession, organized by Oaxacan immigrants, culminated a series of actions begun about four years earlier when Oaxacans from different communities had decided to set aside their differences and organize as Catholics and as *oaxaqueños*. Both the religious procession itself and the formation of the Oaxacan Catholic Community can be explained in part by Hirabayashi's concept of *paisanazgo* (see Hirabayashi 1993). It is true that Oaxacan immigrants draw on the social solidarity prescribed by *paisano* relations to form village-based migrant associations. However, the formation of the Oaxacan Catholic Community as a Oaxaca-wide religious organization had to transcend village-based social relations through the development of a strategy that would provide the basis for a Oaxacan identity, bringing immigrants from dozens of villages in the Mixe, Mixtec, and Zapotec regions of Oaxaca together in a single collective organization. This is a good illustration of the interconnectedness between religious practices and ethnic identity.

The dense web of social, civic, and political organizations—as well as their performances and "public rituals"—creates an environment in which preexisting collective identities come through in a new context, in the process transforming the actors themselves. These organizations create a dual identity. First, they are vehicles for reinforcing collective practices that affirm broader ethnic identities emerging from the migrant experience. Second, these organizations—above all the hometown associations— encourage community building, cultural exchange, and the flow of information. Both processes are crucial for sustaining the links that connect communities of origin with their satellite communities spread beyond their traditional homeland.

The use of alternative media also plays a central role in building migrant civil society. Notably, the biweekly newspaper *El Oaxaqueño*, "the voice of Oaxacans in the United States," is one of the few professional Mexican newspapers with a binational circulation. The paper was launched by Fernando López Mateos, a successful Zapotec migrant entrepreneur and native of Matatlán. It has published more than 117 issues since its founding in 1999. Its content is developed binationally; graphic design work is done in Oaxaca and then the job is sent to Los Angeles for printing. The paper's coverage includes civic, political, social, sports, and cultural issues that affect Oaxacan communities in both Mexico and the United

---

[56] His words were published in Spanish in the January 19, 2002, issue of *El Oaxaqueño*.

States. Reports range from local village conflicts and the campaign to block construction of a McDonald's on the main square in Oaxaca City, to the binational activities of hometown associations and California-focused coalition building for immigrants' right to obtain driver licenses and against cutbacks in health services. The press run of 35,000 copies is distributed free of charge throughout California and in other migrant communities in the United States, as well as in Oaxaca.[57] *El Oaxaqueño* is made available at public events and through community institutions and local businesses (as well as given to arrivals at the Oaxaca City airport). This groundbreaking effort in community media remains largely invisible outside of the Oaxacan community.

Oaxaca's indigenous migrants are also using radio and electronic media in the United States. Filemón López, a native of the Mixtec community of San Juan Mixtepec, has for the last six years anchored *La Hora Mixteca*, a bilingual (Mixtec-Spanish) weekly program broadcast on the Radio Bilingüe network founded by Hugo Morales, another Oaxacan migrant from the Mixteca. Radio Bilingüe recently obtained a Rockefeller Foundation grant for a satellite link that will enable it to transmit its programming to listeners in Oaxaca and Baja California.[58] As another example, in 2001 the FIOB and New California Media jointly produced a one-hour news show, *Nuestro Foro*, on local community radio in Fresno (KFCF-88.1 FM). In addition, FIOB has published a monthly newsletter, *El Tequio*, since 1991 and introduced an on-line version two years ago, allowing its binational membership to share news on local activities and maintain a sense of unity across the U.S.-Mexico border.[59] Since these migrant-run mass media also report systematically on other community initiatives, they promote "virtuous circles" of institution building within indigenous migrant civil society, each reinforcing the other.

The effort to sustain the use of indigenous languages has become a collective activity, both as part of the political struggle for rights and as an endeavor in cultural survival. Indigenous migrants who do not speak

---

[57] Personal communication, Fernando López Mateos (president, *El Oaxaqueño*), November 13, 2003. Of a press run of 35,000 copies, 20,000 are distributed in the United States (70 percent in the Los Angeles area, with the rest distributed throughout California and in Seattle, Columbus, Nashville, and Las Vegas). The other 15,000 copies are distributed across Oaxaca, through migrant organizations, money transfer agencies, and municipal authorities.

[58] See Magagnini 2002. For more on Radio Bilingüe's programming, see www.radiobilingue.org. On radio and migrants, see also Besserer 2002; Reyes 2002.

[59] To access *El Tequio* newsletter, see www.laneta.apc.org/fiob.

Spanish well experience intense language discrimination on a daily basis at the workplace and also in their interactions with legal, educational, and health institutions. Long-standing Mexican cultural prejudices, symbolized by the use of the term "dialect" to describe indigenous languages, are widespread in immigrant communities in the United States. Ayala and Mines (2002) documented a classic example involving mestizo discrimination against P'urépechas in California's Coachella Valley:

> The son of a *mayordomo* [crew manager] coined the term *chaca*
> to describe the P'urépecha. One man described the origin of
> this derogatory phrase in this way: "The *mayordomo* asked
> me, 'Hey, you guys sure talk a lot. All of this chaca, chaca,
> chaca and I don't understand anything! What are you say-
> ing?'" That's how it started—at that moment. They say,
> "You're a chaca because you guys say *chaca, chaca, chaca,*
> *chaca* like a washing machine" [authors' translation].

In at least two well-known cases in the 1980s, indigenous-language speakers were incarcerated in Oregon, unable to offer any defense because they did not speak either Spanish or English. The first victim was Adolfo Ruiz Álvarez, a Triqui, who was confined to a mental hospital and kept sedated for two years before being released (see Davis 2002). The second, Mixtec Santiago Ventura Morales, was jailed for more than four years for murder before his conviction was overturned.[60]

This situation began to change when California Rural Legal Assistance (CRLA), in a precedent-setting move, hired the first Mixteco-speaking outreach worker in 1993 (see Olivera 2003). Migrant organizations have also responded to the need by creating their own translation services in Mixteco, Zapoteco, and Triqui to help people responding to criminal charges or trying to access health care and other public services. Interpreters for the Binational Center for Indigenous Oaxacan Development (CBDIO) work throughout California as well in other states.[61] The Madera School

---

[60] Ventura Morales is now a trilingual community organizer. See his own account (2000), as well as De León's analysis of the role of linguistic disconnects in the trial (1999).

[61] CBDIO currently has a roster of fourteen trained translators (see contact informa- tion at www.laneta.apc.org/fiob). In 1999, twelve indigenous migrants were pro- fessionally trained in translation at the Monterey Institute of International Stud- ies, with support from a grant from Oxfam America. The content of the training included code of ethics, types of translation, medical translating, and translating

District has hired a Mixtec community outreach worker to communicate with the hundreds of Mixtec parents who send their children to the public schools of this farming community in the heart of California's Central Valley. The Oaxaca-based Academy of the Mixtec Language recently began conducting workshops in the Central Valley to teach the writing of the Mixtec language.[62] At the same time, the Mexican government's Adult Education Agency, which is already active in eighteen U.S. states, recently launched an outreach project specifically for indigenous migrants (see Poy Solano 2003). These various initiatives have been reinforced by the use of CD-ROM teaching materials in English and Spanish that provide accessible introductions to many dimensions of Mixtec history and culture, from analysis of little-known codices to contemporary issues of land and identity (see Bakewell and Hamann 2001).

Indigenous immigrant organizations face a huge challenge with the coming of age of the second generation. As thousands of indigenous immigrant families settle for the long term, the rising number of their children born and raised in the United States poses the risk of losing the indigenous languages. In some cases, migrant youth become trilingual, and hence are a crucial resource for the migrant community. For example, FIOB has employed several trilingual organizers in strategic positions, encouraging leadership development. Nevertheless, these cases are the exception. More often, second-generation indigenous youths are not unlike other migrant groups, and they often show low levels of retention of fluency in their parents' first language.[63]

---

during immigration proceedings, along with applications to serve as Berlitz International translators.

[62] "A written script for Mixtec will help inhabitants from different villages communicate with one another, since the creation of a standardized vocabulary will smooth over linguistic variants [from] the rugged countryside where the language originated," according to the Academy of the Mixtec Language (Stanley 2003a).

[63] For example, Cruz Manjarrez's ethnographic study of the reproduction of highland Zapotec culture in Los Angeles reports, "although most immigrants continue to speak Zapotec for everyday use, most Yalaltecos born in the U.S. just understand it. I have observed that American Yalaltecos generally speak Spanish with their parents and relatives, and usually switch from English to Spanish when they are with friends of their own age. Immigrant Yalaltecos consider it more important for their descendents to learn Spanish than Zapotec" (2001: 49).

Gender roles are also changing the terms of community membership.[64] Some migrant women experience changes in the division of labor when they begin to earn wages. In the less isolated new areas of settlement, the women are exposed to different customs and institutions, and they sometimes enter into contact with U.S.-based social actors promoting gender equality. Note, for example, the active role of Líderes Campesinas in making domestic violence a public issue for the first time in many small towns of rural California, challenging the widely held view that such violence is strictly a private matter and cannot be changed.[65] Women are also taking on public leadership roles in mixed-gender migrant organizations in the United States.[66] At the same time, migration from many indigenous communities remains primarily male, affecting the women who remain in at least two ways; on the one hand, their workload is increased, but on the other they often gain greater access to the local public sphere. In some communities of origin, women are participating more in assemblies, creating their own organizations, and fulfilling their husbands' community obligations (in a context in which local citizenship often remains explicitly reserved for men) (see Maldonado and Artía Rodríguez, Robles Camacho, and Velásquez C., all in this volume). Women often undertake their increased public role in the name of their absent spouse, making this a form of "indirect citizenship." Much more research is needed to enhance our understanding of the diverse patterns of change in gender relations, both in communities of origin and in settlement areas.

---

[64] For gendered analyses of women's participation in Mexican migrant organizations, see Goldring 2001, 2003a, 2003b. For one of the few analyses of indigenous migrants that bring together ethnicity and gender, see Sánchez G. n.d.2.

[65] Líderes Campesinas is a California-based women's membership organization that is mestiza-led but includes indigenous migrant women as well. It is the first organization in this country founded by and for farmworker women. It is assisting nascent organizations in other states, including Arizona, Iowa, Oregon, Texas, and Washington.

[66] See Martínez-Saldaña, this volume, and Maceda et al. 2003. As Fresno-based FIOB organizer Oralia Maceda put it, "There have been many changes within our culture.... Now there is more of our participation, as women, in community organizations or participating in meetings.... These are positive [changes] that are happening in our lives, as indigenous women, because it's always been that the honors and everything that has to do with the community were under men's control" (remarks at the panel discussion "Cambio, cultura, y migración: las indígenas oaxaqueñas en California," Chicano Latino Research Center, University of California, Santa Cruz, May 1, 2003; authors' translation). For context, see Mejía Flores 2003.

This nascent process in which migrants are creating their own public spaces and membership organizations is built on the foundation of what are increasingly referred to as "transnational communities," a concept that refers to groups of migrants whose daily lives, work, and social relationships extend across national borders.[67] The existence of transnational communities is a precondition for, but is not the same as, an emerging migrant civil society, which also must involve the construction of public spaces and representative social and civic organizations.

Some analysts use the concept of "cultural citizenship" to describe cases where migrant collective action has transformed the public sphere in the United States. This term "names a range of social practices which, taken together, claim and establish a distinct social space for Latinos in this country [the United States]" and serves as "a vehicle to better understand community formation.... It involves the right to retain difference, while also attaining membership in society."[68] This process may or may not be linked to membership in a territorially based community, either in the home country or in the United States. Instead, it may be driven by other kinds of shared collective identities, such as racialized and gendered class identities as Latina or Latino workers. The idea of cultural citizenship is complementary to but quite distinct from the notion of transnational community, which both focuses on a specific kind of collective identity and emphasizes sustained *bi*national community membership.

The research presented in this collection also speaks to a third way of conceptualizing migrants as social actors, which is the process of constructing a de facto form of *"translocal community citizenship."* This term refers to

---

[67] For a comprehensive literature review, see Fletcher and Margold 2003. Studies that deal with Mexican transnational communities include, among others, Bada 2001, 2003; A. Castañeda 2003; Espinoza 1999; de la Garza and Hazan 2003; Fitzgerald 2000, n.d.; Fletcher 1999; Gledhill 1995; Goldring 1998b, 2002; Leiken 2000; Moctezuma Longoria 2003a, 2003b; Portes, Guarnizo, and Landolt 1999; Portes and Fernández Kelly 2003; Rivera-Salgado 1999; Roberts, Frank, and Lozano-Ascencio 1999; Rouse 1992; R. Smith 1995, 2003; M. Smith and Guarnizo 1998; Zabin and Escala Rabadán 1998. Fitzgerald n.d. suggests that relationships that are often called transnational are actually more translocal, observing: "Migrants' strongest cross-border links are often highly *localistic* ties between particular sending areas and their satellites in the receiving country.... Transborder local connections are embedded in macro structures, but the specifically 'national' element cannot be assumed."

[68] See Flores and Benmayor 1997: 1; Flores 1997: 255, 262. See also Stephen 2003. Johnston 2001 applies the concept of "transnational citizenship" to refer to similar struggles for inclusion with empowerment.

the process through which indigenous migrants are becoming active members of both their communities of settlement and their communities of origin.[69] Like the idea of transnational community, translocal community citizenship refers to the cross-border extension of the boundaries of an existing social sphere, but the term "citizenship" differs from "community" in at least two ways. First, it involves much more precise criteria for determining membership rights and obligations. Second, it refers explicitly to membership in a public sphere. The idea of "translocal community citizenship" therefore involves much more explicit boundaries of membership in the public affairs of a community that is geographically dispersed or, in Kearney's terms, "deterritorialized."

Like cultural citizenship, the term "community citizenship" refers to a socially constructed sense of membership, often built through collective action, but it differs in at least three ways. First, community "citizenship" incorporates the term *that is actually used by the social actors themselves* to name their experience of membership. In indigenous communities throughout rural Mexico, a member in good standing—one who fulfills specific obligations and therefore can exercise specific rights—is called a "citizen" of that community.[70] In contrast, it is not clear whether the idea of cultural citizenship has been appropriated by those to whom it refers. Second, the idea of translocal community specifies the public space within which membership is exercised, whereas "cultural citizenship" is deliberately open-ended as to the *arena* of inclusion (local, regional, or national? territorial or sectoral?). Third, the concept of cultural citizenship focuses, quite appropriately given its goals, on the contested process of negotiating new terms of incorporation *into U.S. society*, in contrast to the emphasis embedded in the idea of translocal community citizenship on the challenge of sustaining binational membership in a cross-border community.

The concept of translocal community citizenship has its own limits as well. It does not capture the broader, rights-based perspective that transcends membership in specific territorially based (or deterritorialized)

---

[69] In some cases this process could be called "dual community citizenship," but since many migrant communities are "multi-local," or "multi-sited," it is more inclusive to use a more open-ended term.

[70] Note that this use of the term "citizen" for full membership in local communities *predates* the widespread usage of the term by national and international civil society organizations. Its use appears to be widespread within indigenous Mexico. On its use in Oaxaca, see Robles Camacho, this volume; in Nahua communities in Guerrero, see García Ortega 2002; and in Hñahñu communities, see Schmidt and Crummett, this volume.

communities, such as the broad-based migrant movement for Mexican voting rights abroad, or the FIOB's emphasis on pan-ethnic collective identities and indigenous and human rights. These collective identities are shared beyond specific communities. The idea of translocal is also limited insofar as it does not capture the frequently *multilevel* process of engagement between migrant membership organizations and the Mexican state at national and state as well as local levels.

These different concepts for describing migrants as social actors are all complementary, and each reflects important dimensions of the process. Each one refers to social processes of migrant identity and organization that may overlap but are distinct, both in theory and in practice. At the same time, they do not capture the full range of migrant collective identities. The broader idea of *"migrant civil society"* provides an umbrella concept for describing diverse patterns of collective action.

The collective and individual practices that are beginning to constitute a specifically indigenous migrant civil society show us a positive side of what would otherwise be an unrelentingly devastating process for Mexico's indigenous communities — their abrupt insertion into globalized capitalism through international migration in search of wage labor. In spite of their dispersion throughout different points along the migrant path, at least some indigenous communities manage to sustain the social and cultural networks that give them cohesion and continuity. In some cases, the migratory experience has both broadened and transformed collective ethnic identities.

This open-ended process serves as a reference point for rethinking what it means to be indigenous in the twenty-first century. Notably, "long-distance membership" in home communities, as well as the construction of new kinds of organizations not based on ties to the land, raises questions about the classic close association between land, territory, and indigenous identity. Within Mexico, the national debate over how institutions and social actors could or should build indigenous autonomy has yet to fully grapple with this dilemma.

In this context, one analytical puzzle that emerges from the studies that follow is why, in spite of the challenges posed by migration, some communities, within some ethnic groups, manage better than others to sustain themselves as a group and create their own public spaces as organized migrants. Note, for example, the case of Nahua migrants to the United States. Though they represent the largest indigenous group in Mexico and some have been coming for many years, their migrants have not sustained visible membership organizations in the United States. Yet this does not mean that they are not organized or capable of cross-border collective action. On the contrary, it turns out that Nahua transnational communities from the state of Guerrero supported a pioneering and highly successful public interest advocacy campaign in defense of their villages against a planned hydroelectric dam in 1991. The project threatened to displace an estimated forty thousand people in the Alto Balsas Valley, damage a critical ecosystem, and flood a newly discovered major archaeological site. Local communities drew on existing cross-village social ties and local marketing networks to quickly build a cohesive regional movement, gaining national and international leverage in the context of the pending quincentenary of the Conquest. Migrants not only contributed funds, drawing on their traditional quota system for village fiestas, but they were also involved in campaign strategy and tactics. Migrants bought video cameras to tape the movement's mass direct actions in a state known for intense repression. This tactic not only served to inform *paisanos* in the United States; it also inaugurated what became the Mexican indigenous movement's now widespread use of video to deter police violence. Migrant protests in California also drew the attention of Spanish-language television, which led to the first TV coverage of the Alto Balsas movement within Mexico itself.[71] With their combination of regionwide, national-level, and transnational organizing crosscut by multisectoral alliances with environmentalists, anthropologists, and human rights activists, these migrants pioneered what could be called a "vertically integrated" approach to public interest campaigns.[72]

## PRESENTING THE COLLECTION

This collection is the result of collaboration between the two coeditors and Rufino Domínguez Santos, general coordinator of the FIOB since 2001. The three jointly convened the conference where these essays were first presented. The gathering was entitled "Indigenous Mexican Migrants in the US: Building Bridges between Researchers and Community Leaders." It was hosted by the University of California, Santa Cruz's Department of Latin American and Latino Studies and cosponsored by the FIOB and UCSC's Chicano Latino Research Center. The conference included eighteen indigenous migrant leaders of Mixtec, Zapotec, Triqui, P'urépecha, Chat-

---

[71] See Good 1992. See also Díaz de Jesús et al. 1996; García Ortega 2000; Hindley 1999.

[72] On the vertical integration of civil society policy advocacy, see Fox 2001b.

ina, and Mayan origin, as well as academics, applied researchers, journalists, trade unionists, local civic leaders, lawyers, and foundation representatives. The chapters that follow are organized into themes, beginning with perspectives of diverse indigenous migrant leaders, followed by sections on social and civic participation, social and economic processes, and ethnic and geographic diversity among indigenous migrants. The volume concludes with analyses of some of the binational dimensions of migration in communities of origin.

This initiative follows in a tradition pioneered by the first meeting between indigenous migrant leaders, scholars, and other potential allies, which was held at the University of California, San Diego's Center for U.S.-Mexican Studies in 1988 (see Zabin, ed. 1992a, 1992b; Runsten and Kearney 1994). This process encouraged what would become the California Rural Legal Assistance's Mixtec farmworker outreach project, as well as key benchmark studies of migrant farmworkers and campaigns to reduce the census undercount. This effort was followed by a 1994 meeting in Mexico that presented the state of the art of research on Mixtec migration (see Varese and Escárcega n.d.).

This collection broadens the scope from what started as a primary focus on Mixtecs in rural California to address indigenous migrants in the United States more generally. Studies here focus on "Oaxacalifornia" but also include research from Oregon, Illinois, Florida, and New York, as well as Baja California, Michoacán, Puebla, Hidalgo, Yucatán, Chiapas, and Oaxaca itself. Major research gaps remain, especially on the increased diversity of indigenous migrants and their regions of origin and settlement.

## Migrant Leaders' Perspectives

This collection begins with indigenous Oaxacan migrant leaders holding the floor. The first is Rufino Domínguez Santos, general coordinator of the Oaxacan Indigenous Binational Front, whose lifelong commitment to social justice began when, as a young man, he challenged violent boss rule in his home village. Domínguez Santos followed the path known as the "*ruta mixteca*," migrating first to the fields of Sinaloa and then to San Quintín, Baja California, before coming to the United States.[73] His essay combines a

---

[73] For more on the "*ruta mixteca*," see Atilano Flores 2000; Besserer 1999a, 1999b, 2003, n.d.; Varese and Escárcega n.d.; Zabin, ed. 1992a, 1992b; Zabin, Kearney, et al. 1993. For background on this migration process analyzed through the lens of the changing agricultural and environmental context, see Wright 1990. On the relationship between regional agricultural problems and out-migration from the

personal and organizational history of one of the most broad-based bina-tional Mexican migrant organizations, including a frank discussion of the difficult process of building leadership accountability. The FIOB is distinc-tive for at least two reasons. First, the organization has promoted a broad pan-ethnic understanding of indigenous identity and indigenous rights. Second, while migrant communities in the United States are brimming with a wide range of hometown clubs and home state federations, the FIOB is among the relatively few with close ties to broad-based *counterpart* membership organizations in their communities, regions, and states of origin.[74] FIOB is active in three very different arenas at once, including within its membership active base committees and statewide structures of representation in California, Baja California, and Oaxaca.

Migrant leader Gustavo Santiago Márquez's testimony follows; he shares his experience as the first president of the Oaxacan Federation of Indigenous Communities and Organizations in California, an umbrella group that brings together both hometown clubs and regional organiza-tions from across different ethnic groups. Following mixed results from the first round of efforts to come together in the early 1990s, for most of that decade Oaxacan migrant organizations each tended to follow their own paths. Some focused more on cultural activities, preserving Oaxacan music and dance traditions in the United States; some prioritized their hometown community development efforts; and still others pursued a more activist rights agenda. In this context, the FOCOICA's emergence in 2001 reflects the work of many Oaxacan organizers to overcome past differences and find common ground. The FOCOICA's work has focused on issues of shared concern, including dialogue with the governor of Oaxaca on issues such as matching funds for collective remittance investments in commu-nity development projects back home, large-scale cultural activities such as the Guelaguetza, cross-sectoral coalitions for driver licenses for migrants and campaigns for migrants' right to vote in Mexico, as well as networking on an equal footing with other long-standing state-based Mexican migrant organizations in California, such as those from Zacatecas and Jalisco.[75]

---

Mixteca, see Simon 1997: chap. 2; García Barrios and García Barrios 1992, 1994. For an analysis of farmworker union organizing in northwestern Mexico, see López Monjardín 1991.

[74] For discussions of issues of balance within binational coalitions and networks, as well as the concept of counterparts, see Fox 2002.

[75] For detailed coverage of the activities of the FOCOICA and its affiliates, see *El Oaxaqueño*.

Mixtec community organizer and radio show host Filemón López is a co-founder of one of the first Oaxacan migrant organizations in the United States, the Benito Juárez Civic Association (ACBJ).[76] He is also the host of one of the single most important mass media outlets for indigenous Oaxacans in the United States, the *Mixtec Hour* radio show, broadcast over the Radio Bilingüe network. This show reaches most of California for two hours at midday on Sundays.[77] In addition to broadcasting music and messages to community and family, this radio show also includes interviews and call-in discussions with guests who address a wide range of issues confronting Mixtec, Zapotec, Triqui, and other Mexican indigenous peoples. The show was launched in 1997, and López is now training Zapotec and Triqui DJs, so that they too can launch their own shows.

Chatina migrant videographer Yolanda Cruz is playing a leading role as a cultural interlocutor between indigenous migrant communities and other social and intellectual sectors in the United States. Her videos document the binational social and cultural dynamics of the migration process. She portrays the universal immigrant story, through the eyes and experiences of her subjects, to help U.S. and Mexican decision makers and scholars understand the challenges and unique position of indigenous Mexican migrants. Her work also attempts to provoke conversations among different indigenous migrant communities, to learn from each other's experiences. As she put it, "if Chatino migrants see the development of the Mixtecos in the United States they will be inspired to organize strong community organizations in their hometowns and abroad. And when Mixtecos see their stories and the story of the Chatinos, they will identify with the same experience. They can feel good about their accomplishments and continue to work at improving their organizations."[78] Her work also contributes to broader video efforts to reach across cultural boundaries, such as the recent binational "Video México Indígena/Video Native Mexico" tour of the United States, organized by the Smithsonian National Museum of the American Indian.[79]

---

[76] For an oral history of one of the other founders of this organization, who later became mayor of his home municipality, see Besserer 1999a. See also Besserer 2003, n.d.

[77] Radio Bilingüe's regular listeners include "about 60% of the Spanish-dominant, predominantly immigrant population in the rural communities in the 11-county areas of California" served by the network (Kissam 2003b: 4).

[78] Personal communication, July 9, 2003.

[79] See www.nativenetworks.si.edu (English) and www.redesindigenas.si.edu (Spanish).

Ulises García is vice president of FOCOICA and a leader of the Union of Highland Communities of Oaxaca (UCSO), an association of Zapotec communities from the Sierra de Juárez that includes five hometown clubs. His testimony sheds light on the process through which their community service traditions are reproduced in the United States. He focuses on how sports and cultural activities bring migrants together across both communities of origin and generations. Inspiring migrant youths to continue to identify with their ancestral homes and traditions despite crosscutting U.S. cultural influences is easier said than done. For the first time, gangs of Oaxacan young people are beginning to emerge in Los Angeles, which underscores the importance of García's efforts to bring young Oaxacans, the U.S.-born sons and daughters of migrant families, into their community sports networks.[80]

Quechua anthropologist Guillermo Delgado shares his reflections on indigenous Mexican migrants in the broader context of indigenous rights movements in the hemisphere. For more than two decades, indigenous activists from throughout the Americas have been entering the international arena, both to find counterparts and to influence national and international authorities. Within the United States, indigenous migrants have come together across their different community and ethnic identities. For example, a growing pan-Indian network is emerging in the San Francisco Bay Area among migrants of Shuar (Ecuador), Quechua, Lenca (El Salvador), Maya, Triqui, and Yurok (California) origin.[81] As an explicitly pan-ethnic organization, the FIOB in California also includes—in addition to its main base of Mixtecs from Oaxaca—Mixtecs from Guerrero, Zapotecs, Chatinos, Triquis, P'urépechas from Michoacán, and mestizos.[82]

---

[80] For example, Cruz Manjarraz reports that a community leader estimated that there are between four and six thousand people who identify with Yalálag, a Zapotec highland village, but only just over two thousand now live in Yalálag. "This estimate includes not only the immigrant population, but also Yalaltecos born in the U.S. Some Yalaltecos consider that the 30% of Yalaltecos are immigrants, whereas 70% are Yalaltecos born in the U.S. They also suggest that among the 30% of immigrants, 25% of them are legal residents" (2001: 48).

[81] Personal communication, Robin Maria Delugan, Anthropology Department, University of California, Berkeley, May 7, 2003. Los Angeles also has a pan-ethnic network, the Los Angeles Indigenous People's Alliance (LAIPA), which was launched in 1991 to address the Quincentenary. LAIPA is an affiliate of the International Xicano Human Rights Council, a working group from the International Indian Treaty Council. See www.laipa.net.

[82] Personal email communication, Rufino Domínguez Santos, June 4, 2003. The approximately one thousand members in California are affiliated through their

Concluding this roundtable discussion, conference participant Alejandrina Ricárdez, a migrant from Oaxaca's Central Valleys and urban planner trained at the University of California, Los Angeles, shares her insights into the need to rethink what "traditions" mean from the point of view of indigenous women. She also underscores the challenge that indigenous intellectuals face in their efforts to translate knowledge into specific practices that benefit their communities. Her experience illustrates the challenges that young migrants face, as those who grew up in the United States increasingly serve as cultural bridges between very different worlds — and must, in the process, balance often conflicting social and cultural demands.[83]

## Social and Civic Participation

Anthropologist Laura Velasco Ortiz's study of indigenous organizations in Baja California opens the section of chapters on indigenous migrant organizations. Though this collection focuses primarily on migrants in the United States, one cannot understand the social processes that generate both indigenous migration and migrant organization without taking into account the Baja California arena. This border region is both a major center of long-term indigenous migrant settlement and a staging area for migration between southern Mexico and the United States.[84] After years of campaign and public debate, the reproduction of ethnic identity is increasingly institutionalized in Tijuana, including active roles for the migrants' own organizations, the local media, human rights organizations, and bilingual schools and teachers, as well as specialized government agencies such as the National Indigenous Institute (INI). As part of Tijuana's own approach to reinforcing national identity in the shadow of the United States, the local

---

eight base committees, located in Santa Rosa, Livingston, Madera, Fresno, Selma, Lamont/Arvin, Santa Maria, and Vista/Oceanside. Organizers in Oaxaca estimate the membership there at approximately five thousand families, mainly in the Mixteca Baja but also in the Chatino region, as well as almost five hundred new members in the Central Valleys, mainly at the edge of Oaxaca City. The FIOB's urban *colono* base is multiethnic, made up of migrants to the city who have few relatives in the United States (Jonathan Fox, field interviews in six Oaxaca urban *colonias*, May 2003).

[83] On issues facing second-generation indigenous women, see also Stanley 2003b.

[84] See also Velasco Ortiz 2002. On the process of building community and ethnic identity among Oaxacan farmworkers in San Quintín, Baja California, see Bacon 2004: chap. 5; Garduño, García, and Morán 1990; Garduño 1998, n.d; Quiñones 2001: chap. 5.

municipal authorities—not known for their ethnic sensitivity—celebrated "Indian Day."[85]

Velasco Ortiz's work underscores Baja California's powerful symbolic importance to binational organizations. For example, the FIOB's 2001 binational assembly, held in Tijuana, was inaugurated with a multiethnic chorus of schoolchildren singing the national anthem in Mixteco—surprising the dozens of community delegates who had traveled from Oaxaca, most of whom had never before heard the anthem sung in an indigenous language. The International Indigenous Network of Oaxaca (RIIO) held its binational assembly in San Quintín. Velasco Ortiz's study focuses on the diversity and consolidation of indigenous migrant organizations, comparing the urban experience in Tijuana with the agribusiness zone of San Quintín and highlighting the role of women. She finds that Oaxacan migration itself integrates California and Baja California, making possible the exchange of experiences across the border. In addition, on both sides of the line migrant organizations face the challenge of bringing together urban and rural-based groups. In the process, women's organizing has encouraged a "redefinition or incorporation of new interests, more associated with the private sphere, into the plans and actions of these organizations, and has been enriched by cross-border interactions between women in organizations on both sides of the border."[86]

Jesús Martínez-Saldaña, veteran analyst of migrant history, culture, and organization, shares his analysis of the texture of local participation in indigenous migrant organizations in California. He takes as his case study the local community–based committees of the FIOB in the Fresno area, comparing their participation in both cultural and civic action. He frames this in broad historical context, reaching back to recall major national figures in Mexican social change who were themselves migrants of indigenous origin, such a Benito Juárez and Ricardo Flores Magón. Martínez-Saldaña highlights the migrant's multiple identities—with the capacity to simultaneously be seen as a low-profile, low-status worker in one context while playing major leadership roles in other arenas. Who would have thought, looking at Benito Juárez rolling cigars in a New Orleans factory while in exile, that he would go on to become one of his country's leading political figures? Martínez-Saldaña also analyzes one of the most innovative public spaces so far in terms of the emergence of a distinctive migrant civil society. In 1999 the Zapatistas and their allies in Mexico organized a

[85] See Lestage 2002, 1998, 1999. See also Clark Alfaro 1991; Young 1994.
[86] Personal communication, Laura Velasco Ortiz, July 28, 2003.

national referendum in support of constitutional recognition of indigenous rights and "true peace through dialogue" in Chiapas. The voting was also carried out in Mexican communities throughout the United States. The FIOB organized polling places both in Oaxaca and in California.[87]

Sociologists Gaspar Rivera-Salgado and Luis Escala Rabadán shift the level of analysis of organization building from local forms of grassroots participation to broader forms of representation, through statewide migrant federations.[88] Their study examines the similarities and differences among the federations of migrants from Zacatecas, Jalisco, and Oaxaca. By focusing on these different "territorially based" organizations in the Los Angeles area, they are able to "hold constant" the role of other factors that might explain their organizational dynamics, such as the role of the Mexican government presence through the local consulate office (in the Mexican context, the Los Angeles consulate is one of the single most important and active diplomatic posts). In each case, the statewide federations take on the structure and look of Mexico-based civic associations since they emerge primarily as counterparts to deal with their respective state governments. At the same time, the Oaxaca umbrella group organizes in its own distinctive way, combining the hometown club base similar to the *zacatecanos* and *jaliscienses* with the regional and pan-ethnic associations specific to Oaxaca.

Lynn Stephen, an anthropologist with extensive field experience in Oaxacan communities in both Mexico and Oregon, compares the histories and dynamics of two different kinds of Mixtec collective action in Oregon. One form of participation involves the defense of their rights as workers and migrants through Oregon's main farmworker organization, Northwest Treeplanters and Farmworkers United (PCUN), founded in 1985.[89] The other form of organization comes together around a shared community of

---

[87] The Zapatista Army of National Liberation (EZLN) sent more than five thousand delegates to do outreach throughout Mexico in support of the referendum, and in Oaxaca the FIOB was assigned twenty-six Zapatistas to cover thirteen municipalities in the Mixteca region. The FIOB organized four polling places in California, in the cities of Fresno, Watsonville/Santa Cruz, Los Angeles, and Vista. The voter participation was highest in Fresno, registering 1,627 votes. See Rivera-Salgado 1999.

[88] For further discussion of statewide federations of hometown associations, see, among others, Bada 2001, 2003; de la Garza and Hazan 2003; Espinoza 1999; Goldring 2002; R. Smith 2003. For a contrasting discussion of less formal expressions of Mexican transnational communities, see Fitzgerald 2000; Fletcher 1999.

[89] See their Web site at www.pcun.org and Stephen 2001, 2003. On the history of Mixtec migration to Oregon, see De León 1995.

origin and ethnic identity, San Agustín Atenango, which has ten different hometown clubs spread throughout the United States. Stephen finds that many Mixtec farmworkers participate in both organizations, pursuing their class and ethno-local goals through different forms of practice.

## Social and Economic Processes

Medical anthropologist Bonnie Bade contributes to cross-cultural understanding with her ethnographic account of the health challenges facing Mixtec migrants in California. These challenges include both the health risks and the difficulty of accessing health services that are specific to their class, ethnic, and legal positions in U.S. society. Bade's research helps us to understand the dramatic differences in basic frames of reference about health, including ethnically specific beliefs and practices regarding health and illness.[90] She also shows the ways in which Mixtec migrants cope with this situation, outlining a series of alternative health care strategies they have developed, in the context of difficult and limited access to mainstream health care. These strategies include the use of the "Mixtec medical culture" to treat ordinary and ethnic-specific illness through medicinal plants, *temascales* (steam baths), massages, and healing ceremonies. These ethno-specific healing practices reaffirm the patients' ethnic identity and sense of belonging to a specific community. Bade contends that these practices complement, but do not replace, the need for mainstream medical care.

The study by urban planner Felipe López and economist David Runsten provides cutting-edge documentation of important differences in migration patterns, both across and within ethnic groups. They document the notable differences in migration patterns between Mixtec and Zapotec communities from Oaxaca's Central Valleys. They find that Mixtecs consistently migrate to rural areas of California (as well as Oregon and Washington) to work in agriculture, while Zapotecs tend to move to large cities, such as Los Angeles, and work primarily in services. In addition, Mixtec migration originated as a step process, via northwestern Mexico, whereas Zapotec migration, in addition to a long tradition of going to Mexico City,

---

[90] Note that nonindigenous Mexican migrants of rural origin also report "ethno-specific diseases," such as *nervios, empacho, susto,* and *mal de ojo.* See Mines, Mullenax, and Saca 2001. On Mixtec migrant health issues, see also Grieshop 1997; McGuire 2001. On farmworker health in California more generally, see Villarejo et al. 2000.

has tended to go straight to California. López and Runsten explore a range of hypotheses that might explain these differences.

Researchers Javier Huizar Murillo and Isidro Cerda present a very original set of data on where indigenous migrants are settling in California. They draw on the 2000 U.S. census to document the presence of the new category of "Hispanic American Indians" — that is, people who choose to identify *both* as Hispanic or Latino as their ethnicity, *and* as American Indian as their race.[91] The overlapping category that emerges primarily reflects indigenous migrants from Latin America, primarily from Mexico, but also including Guatemalan Mayans, especially in the Los Angeles area.[92] The absolute numbers show that this self-identified population now numbers at least 400,000 in the United States as a whole, including more than 150,000 in California alone. Other major receiving states include Texas, New York, and Florida, though preliminary research suggests that the magnitude of the undercount of indigenous migrants may vary by state, depending on the unevenness of outreach efforts undertaken in the 1990s. Because of the persistence of the undercount, the absolute census numbers must be interpreted with a great deal of caution. At the same time, the relative data are very suggestive since they produce a revealing pattern of geographic distribution, at least within California. The findings summarized visually by these maps reinforce the data presented by López and Runsten, showing the principal population concentrations both in agribusiness regions of Southern California and California's Central Valley, as well as a strong presence in the Los Angeles metropolitan area.

Independent researcher Edward Kissam and attorney Ilene Jacobs's study describes with unusual detail and precision the nature and mechanisms of the U.S. census undercount of rural indigenous migrants. After the widely criticized undercount of 1990, California public officials worked with community-based organizations in California to develop more effective outreach strategies. Some progress was made, insofar as some of the most egregious patterns of exclusion were reduced (though they probably

---

[91] On race, ethnicity, and Latinos in the U.S. census, see, among others, C. Rodríguez 2000; Yanow 2003. The most recent research on Latino responses to the race and ethnicity questions in 2000 finds that, based on the widespread response of "other" to the race question, the ethnic Latino category is treated as a de facto racial category. See Navarro 2003; Tafoya 2003; Crece and Ramírez 2003.

[92] There is a substantial literature on Guatemalan Mayan migrants in the United States. See Burns 1993; Castañeda, Manz, and Davenport 2002; Fink 2003; Hagen 1994; Loucky and Moors 2000; Popkin 1999; N. Rodríguez 2000; N. Rodríguez and Jonas n.d.

persist in other states). At the same time, Kissam and Jacobs's ethnographic community studies, when contrasted with official census data, provide clear evidence that the census undercount persists in California, though through more subtle mechanisms. Only further research, adapted to urban settings, will be able to tell us whether similar patterns of undercount are a serious problem affecting urban indigenous migrant populations as well.

## Ethnic and Geographic Diversity among Indigenous Migrants

Journalist Garance Burke's study sheds light on the challenges facing Mexican indigenous peoples who have joined the migrant stream most recently. Historically, Yucatecan and Chiapan Mayas limited their travels for work to southeastern Mexico, as in the case of Chiapan migration to lowland agroexport estates and to wage labor when the oil industry was being built in Tabasco.[93] It may not be a coincidence that the people who rose up in the Zapatista rebellion lived in one of Mexico's regions with the least likelihood of migrating to the cities and to the United States. Yet many of the lowland Chiapas communities that took up arms for their cause and have since built autonomous local governments are also themselves migrant communities — homesteaders who came down from crowded highland villages only a generation or two before. Burke's study documents the experiences of those Mayas who made their way to the Bay Area of California.[94] Like other migrants, they form their own informal support networks. Like other indigenous migrants, they face discrimination from within the migrant community, which reinforces their own social solidarity.

Anthropologist Warren Anderson focuses on Cobden, Illinois, a small town in the rural Midwest that has become a classic satellite community of the town of Cherán, in the P'urépecha highlands of Michoacán.[95] Though P'urépecha migrants have been coming to the United States for at least as

---

[93] The first published documentation of Chiapan migration to the United States focuses on communities near San Cristóbal and traces its beginnings back to the late 1980s. See Rus and Guzmán López 1996. On the new travel industry from Chiapas to the northern border, see Ross 2002. See Balkan 2001 for an unusual study of the determinants of *non*-migration in two Chiapas communities.

[94] See Adelson 2002 on one of the first Yucatecan Mayan migrants to San Francisco. Najar (2003) reports that Mayans in Quintana Roo gain service work experience in the tourism industry, which prepares them to find related jobs as migrants in the United States.

[95] See also Rubén Martínez's richly nuanced journalistic portrait of Cherán's migration process (2001).

long as the Oaxacans, so far they have attracted less research attention.[96] Anderson's ethnographic case study provides a detailed portrait of the growing wave of migration to rural U.S. communities that until recently had no history of receiving migrants. Though lacking a legacy of progressive cultural and racial attitudes, the community of Cobden has "tolerated and coped."[97] Anderson's approach stresses the interaction between individual agency and binational social context, focusing on how migrants also "tolerate and cope."

Sociologist and community organizer Paul Johnston analyzes an important case of multisectoral solidarity with a Triqui community in southern Monterey County that had been targeted for a raid by the U.S. Immigration and Naturalization Service (INS).[98] The Triqui people come from western Oaxaca, and though they have a long tradition of migrating within Mexico, they are increasingly coming to the United States.[99] The capacity of community-based organizations to rally in their support was unusual in part because the Triquis tend to be more socially isolated in the United States than other Oaxacan migrant groups, in part due to their more limited command of Spanish. Some compare their situation to that of Mixtec migrants two decades ago. Previous cycles of Latino political enfranchisement and empowerment in the small town of Greenfield made the campaign possible, and the INS proved to be unusually vulnerable to public

---

[96] On P'urépechas in the United States, see also Anderson 1997; Ayala and Mines 2002; Krissman 2002. For background on ethnic politics in the P'urépecha highlands, see Vásquez León 1992; Zárate Hernández 2000.

[97] Perhaps the arrival of migrants in communities that were not previously socially polarized into a caste system (as in the case for much of rural California) allows for creative adaptation. For example, it is common for Cobden farmers to know all the names of as many as a hundred of their Mexican workers (Warren Anderson, comment at the University of California, Santa Cruz conference, October 11, 2002). Rubén Martínez's journalistic study of Cherán migrants in a small Wisconsin meatpacking town finds a similar local flexibility (2001).

[98] The Triqui community in Greenfield, currently numbering about five hundred, is in part a waystation to other destinations within the United States, including Oregon and New York (author interview, visiting Mexican scholar María Dolores París Pombo, also adviser to Las Mujeres de Sur, a Triqui artisan cooperative in Greenfield, Santa Cruz, June 2003). See also París Pombo 2003a, 2003b.

[99] In contrast to most Mexican migrants, a significant number of Triquis leave home in fear of the high level of political violence in the region. For details, see París Pombo 2003b: 13. For background, see López Bárcenas 2002. The collapse of the price of coffee is also a key factor.

criticism in the process.[100] Since then, Triqui community leaders have forged a sustained partnership with the local branch of the United Farm Workers, using their hall for assemblies held in the Triqui language.[101]

Sociologist Liliana Rivera-Sánchez's chapter focuses on a pattern of migrant social organization that is very different from the cases that draw from the Oaxacalifornia experience. She documents the origins and dynamics of New York City's Tepeyac Association, a Catholic Church–sponsored association of local faith-based committees of migrants, mainly from the state of Puebla. Tepeyac has quickly become a major activist voice for the growing Mexican community in New York City, now referred to as "Puebla York."[102] The Mexican population of New York City tripled over the decade of the 1990s, reaching an estimated 300,000—the vast majority from Puebla.[103] Many come from the Mixteca region within Puebla, and a minority of them are of indigenous Mixtec ancestry.[104] They sometimes

---

[100] For background on the Citizenship Project, which led the coalition in defense of the Greenfield Triquis, see www.newcitizen.org.

[101] Author interview, París Pombo, Santa Cruz, June 2003.

[102] Tepeyac has consistently focused on raising the media profile of the immigrant rights agenda. Note, for example, their annual collective run from Mexico to New York in honor of the Virgin of Gualalupe (Galvez 2003; Najar 2002; Solís 2001, 2002). See www.tepeyac.org. The other main activist Mexican migrant organization in New York City is Casa México/Asociación de Trabajadores Mexicano Americanos, which "spearheaded the organizing drive that culminated with a landmark agreement between Korean greengrocers and Mexican workers [an estimated forty thousand in the New York region work for the greengrocers]"; David Brooks, personal email communication, June 4, 2003.

[103] Kamber 2001a, citing Robert Smith. See also Binford and D'Aubeterre 2000; Kamber 2001b, 2001c; López Ángel 2000a, 2000b, 2003a, 2003b; Najar 2002; R. Smith 1995, 1996. For a recent video documentary on a Puebla hometown association based just north of New York City, see "The Sixth Section," at www.sixthsection.com. For another example of this kind of organization, note the case of two hundred migrants from the community of Axutla, "in the heart of the Mixteca Poblana," who raised US$80,000 to build a bridge for which they had been lobbying the government for more than four decades (it is now known as the "Mixteco Bridge"). The majority of the community of 2,800 now lives in New Jersey (Juárez Galindo 2002).

[104] This dual usage of the term Mixteco to refer both to the region and to the ethnic group leads to a persistent ambiguity in discussions of the ethnicity identity of *poblano* migrants to the New York area. Note also the role of Casa Puebla, a community outreach center sponsored by the Puebla state government, whose goal is to create "a single regional identity, that of *poblanos*, among a fractured community composed of people from the very different ethnic groups that inhabit the different *municipios* of the state of Puebla" (Sevy Fua 2000: 13).

refer to New York City as "Ñuu York"; "ñuu" means "land" in Mixteco. Unlike in California, these migrants do not organize or publicly identify in terms of their indigenous roots, but rather come together through either their hometown associations or their religious identities, through communities of faith called "Comités Guadalupanos."[105]

Sociologists Ella Schmidt and María Crummett add a new dimension to our understanding of Mexicans' ethnic and geographic diversity in the United States, focusing on the growing community of Hñahñu migrants from Ixmiquilpan, Hidalgo, now working on the Florida gulf coast. Hidalgo is one of Mexico's lowest-income states and has recently experienced one of the country's highest rates of increase in out-migration. The process began to take off in the mid-1990s and also leads migrants to Las Vegas, Atlanta, and North Carolina. Migrants from Hidalgo now account for approximately 15 percent of the population of Clearwater, Florida, where they have revitalized the downtown area and own more than fifty businesses. This chapter explores how the Hñahñu's historical and cultural legacies in Mexico have shaped their contemporary forms of civic organization, both in Hidalgo and in Florida, embodied in the partnership between the Supreme Hñahñu Council and the Mexican Council of Tampa Bay.

## Binational Dimensions of Migration in Communities of Origin

Michael Kearney and Federico Besserer's study focuses on the interaction between migration and Oaxaca's key institutions of local governance, the municipality and *agencias* (distinct self-governing communities within municipalities). These local governments are much smaller in scale and more politically autonomous than in most of the rest of rural Mexico. More than 400 of Oaxaca's 570 municipalities, including thousands of smaller

---

[105] Many of those Puebla migrants who organize through hometown clubs in New York or California tend to triangulate their hometown relationship through Mexico City–based migrant associations, which end up orienting the more recently formed clubs in Tijuana or New York. Personal email communication, anthropologist Gustavo López Ángel, November 19, 2002. For example, "the Asociación Micaltepecana, based in Barrio de Santiago of Iztapalapa in Mexico City, is responsible for convening the association of paisanos who live in New York and California." López Ángel added that the following indigenous communities in the Mixteca Poblana have hometown clubs in New York or California: San Baltasar Atlimeyaya (Valle de Atlixco), Rosario Micaltepec, Santa Ana Tepejillo, Xayacatlán de Bravo, Piaxtla, Chinantla, Tehuitzingo, and Petlalcingo. See also López Ángel 2000a, 2000b, 2003a, 2003b.

villages, are governed by community assemblies rather than Western-style voting for political parties. These participatory local institutions are organized around rotating, unpaid service commitments, which are a requirement for community membership. High rates of out-migration make it difficult to fill many of these jobs, putting these local institutions under stress. Besserer and Kearney have led a long-term anthropological field research team, based at the Iztapalapa campus of Mexico's Autonomous Metropolitan University (UAM-Iztapalapa), that is analyzing the diverse community responses to this challenge. In the process, they have developed alternative policy proposals that could help institutions of local governance adapt to the realities of widespread migration.

Zapotec civic leader Sergio Robles Camacho reflects on his experience as a returning migrant and the challenges that migration poses to traditions of community governance and civic participation. Communities in his region of the northern Sierra have a long tradition of migration in search of personal development and education—what he calls the "*tradición juarista.*" Their first hometown associations emerged at the end of the 1950s, in Mexico City and Oaxaca. Migration became widespread in the 1970s, "in the face of the increasingly acute loss of food self-sufficiency," and they formed the first hometown associations in Los Angeles. Today, the community association from Robles's hometown of Zoogocho reports more than four hundred members, including the second generation.[106] Back home, community governance structures adjust by electing migrants to municipal leadership positions, although this owes more to the scarcity of candidates than to a recognition of the migrants' citizenship rights. Indeed, local community citizenship rights are traditionally limited to *resident* adult males. Organized migrants have encouraged Sierra communities to become more flexible about the terms of membership, and they have reacted in diverse ways. Some communities have remained firm, requiring migrants to return to perform the obligatory unpaid leadership service required of all local citizens.[107] Other communities, especially those with a

---

[106] See García 2003d. In addition, after twenty years of effort, the Zoogocho hometown associations in Los Angeles, Mexico City, and Oaxaca City completed their project of building a "Casa del Migrante Zoogochense" just outside Oaxaca City.

[107] For a vivid case study of a northern Oaxaca community that tries to discourage out-migration through strict minimum standards for reincorporation, see Mutersbaugh 2002. Mutersbaugh documents the concept of "civic death"—the expulsion of those who do not make their economic and leadership contributions. García Ortega finds similar responses among Nahua communities in Guerrero (2002). See also Tucker, Díaz McConnell, and Van Wey 2003 for a comparison of

longer tradition of migration, have reassessed their definitions of membership in an effort to reconcile both local leadership and migrant needs.[108]
Robles's own trajectory—he eventually returned and drew on his extensive
professional experience to become both a municipal and a regionwide civic
leader—reflects the commitment of even long-term migrants to provide
diverse forms of community service over decades.

Anthropologist María Cristina Velásquez points out that, despite the
widespread impression that indigenous women are always excluded from
participation in community self-governance in rural Mexico, in Oaxaca the
panorama is quite diverse. Though women are increasingly migrating,
men still leave in widely disproportionate numbers, which renders many
home communities majority-female.[109] This dramatic demographic shift
does not by itself change the local gender balance of power. Social and
cultural changes, encouraged in some communities by deliberate empowerment strategies, are also key to increasing women's direct participation
and representation in both civic and *cargo* responsibility systems. Velásquez's study, based on extensive statewide field research, shows that actual practices range from complete exclusion to "*voz con voto*" (the right to
speak and to vote), "*voz sin voto*" (the right to speak but not vote), and the
right to be elected to community leadership positions.[110] At the same time,

---

different local Oaxaca community efforts to negotiate their terms of engagement
with migrants.

[108] For example, the northern Zapotec community of San Juan Tabaá, which spent
four years putting its community governance processes in writing, details the
distinctions between "*comuneros ausentes (activos en cooperacion)*" and "*ausentes definitivos.*" Their governance structure officially includes participation in "*organizaciones de paisanos*" in Oaxaca, Mexico City, and Los Angeles as a form of community membership, though sustaining full citizenship still requires paying
annual taxes and, eventually, fulfilling leadership service. In contrast, "*ausentes
definitivos*" ("*paisanos que están totalmente olvidados de su comunidad de origen*") risk
losing their property and must pay thirty-four days of the local minimum wage
in order to visit the community. See the "Estatuto comunitario de San Juan Tabaá, Villa Alta," published in *Hora Cero, Suplemento Especial*, June 20, 2001.

[109] On the increasing tendency of indigenous women to migrate, see Poy Solano
2003. For data on rural women's migration, including indigenous women, see
INEGI 2002.

[110] According to the statewide 1997 "Catálogo Municipal de Usos y Costumbres" of
the Oaxaca Electoral Institute, in 10 percent of the state's 418 municipalities governed by *usos y costumbres*, women are not allowed to vote nor to hold local office
(referring to *tequios*). In 9 percent of the cases they cannot vote in local elections
but can hold local office. In 21 percent of the municipalities, women can vote but
cannot hold local office. In 60 percent of the cases, women can both vote in local

Velásquez finds that some kinds of women's participation in the local public sphere have contradictory implications, as in the frequent case when a woman participates indirectly, in the place of her absent spouse, constituting a kind of second-class citizenship as well as additional work obligations. From a long-term point of view, Oaxaca's indigenous communities are in the midst of an uneven transition that is still little understood. The current patchwork-quilt pattern of varied but limited female access to the local public sphere is quite different from the complete exclusion of women two decades ago, but it is still far from a system in which women have full rights to citizenship in local community governance.

The chapter by Centolia Maldonado, the FIOB's leading women's organizer in the Mixteca region, and anthropologist Patricia Artía Rodríguez builds on Velásquez's overview by offering a participant's perspective on women's activism in a high out-migration region. In this case the presence of a regional social organization has encouraged the women of the region to create their own social, economic, and civic organizations. As with most mixed-gender poor people's organizations, the women of the FIOB participate in the group's mass mobilizations for political change, as well as for community development demands such as local projects and to gain access to the government community development funds that are ostensibly targeted to them. In addition, however, they are organizing to create their own savings clubs, alternative productive projects, and *artesanía* marketing, and in some cases they are demanding their rights to participate as full citizens in local community governance.

## CONCLUSIONS

This collection seeks to make existing research on indigenous Mexican migrants in the United States more widely available. Hopefully, this will encourage further collaborative initiatives among researchers to help fill the many gaps that remain, as well as among other social and civic actors concerned with building sustainable bridges across multiple cultural divides. This will require rethinking Mexican migration in terms of the diversity of different ethnic, gender, and regional experiences. This recognition has very practical implications. First, it can help to inform potential

---

elections and hold local office (cited in Velásquez 2002). See also Velásquez 2000, 2001, 2003, as well as Bonfil Sánchez 2002; Dalton 2003; Ibarra Templos 2003; EDUCA 2003. For background on Oaxaca state policy toward indigenous local governance, see Fox and Aranda 1996; Hernández Navarro 1999.

strategies through which indigenous migrants can bolster their own capacity for self-representation. Second, this recognition of diversity is crucial for broadening and deepening coalitions with other social actors, both in the United States and in Mexico.

To illustrate the potential for coalition-building experiences, consider two recent initiatives in the domain of symbolic politics. The historic memory of Benito Juárez continues to resonate powerfully among Oaxacan migrant communities, as noted above. As a result, migrant organizations took initiatives that raised statues in his honor in prominent public places in March 2003, on the 197th anniversary of his birth (Stanley 2003c). Independently, both the FOCOICA in Los Angeles (Lynwood) and the FIOB in Fresno launched campaigns to forge the broad coalitions necessary to build and install the statues, coalitions that involved policy makers in both countries as well as organized sectors of U.S. society. In the Lynwood case, the FOCOICA first persuaded the governor of Oaxaca to donate the statue. They then persuaded the mayor of Lynwood (a migrant born in Michoacán) to authorize its placement, and they convinced a Korean migrant businessman to donate a location in his shopping center (including funding the pedestal). The FOCOICA also gained the support of the Council of Federations in Los Angeles, which represents Mexican migrant federations from fourteen different states (see *El Oaxaqueño* 2003c).

In Fresno, the FIOB followed a similar strategy, gaining support from the governor of Oaxaca, local elected officials, businesses, and public interest groups to inaugurate a statue of Juárez, right next to a statue honoring the bracero workers. As County Supervisor Juan Arámbula put it, the statue was in an especially appropriate location, "because it is between two symbols of justice, the State Court on one side, and the Federal Court [under construction] on the other" (cited in N. Martínez 2003). Juárez's most famous phrase bound his legacy to the principles of self-determination: "between nations as between individuals, respect for the rights of others means peace." This message gave the two statues an unforeseen but powerful added meaning in the midst of the U.S. war in Iraq. Indeed, just two weeks before the inaugural ceremony in Fresno's main square, the FIOB's leadership released a communiqué addressed to the presidents of the United States and Mexico, entitled "No to the United States' unilateral and hegemonic war!" (FIOB 2003).

Juárez is a symbol not only of pan-Oaxacan unity but also of a more diverse Mexican identity as well. The installation of the statues was only possible because of the multisectoral and cross-border coalitions that Oaxacan migrant organizations in the United States have built over more than a decade. The statues' incorporation into the public landscapes of Los Angeles and Fresno also symbolizes the coming of age of a new phase of Mexican migration, one in which indigenous migrants are taking their place in the collectively imagined Mexico outside of Mexico. To sum up, indigenous Mexican migrants' organizational initiatives and rich collective cultural practices open a window on their efforts to build new lives in the United States while remaining who they are and remembering where they come from. This is the challenge they face.

## References

Adelson, Naomi. 2002. "Los mayas de San Francisco," *Masiosare (La Jornada)* 255 (November 10).

Aguilar Medina, José Íñigo. 1979. "La mixteca oaxaqueña, una zona de emigración." In *Aspectos sociales de la migración en México,* edited by Margarita Nolasco Armas. Mexico City: Departamento de Proyectos Especiales de Investigación, Instituto Nacional de Antropología e Historia.

Alarcón, Rafael. 2002. "The Development of the Hometown Associations in the United States and the Use of Social Remittances in Mexico." In *Sending Money Home: Hispanic Remittances and Community Development*, edited by Rodolfo O. de la Garza and Briant Lindsay Lowell. Lanham, Md.: Rowman and Littlefield.

Altamirano, Teófilo, and Lane Ryo Hirabayashi, eds. 1997. *Migrants, Regional Identities and Latin American Cities*. Washington, D.C.: Society for Latin American Anthropology/American Anthropological Association.

Anderson, Warren. 1997. "Ethnic Identity and Migration among Mexican Wage Laborers in Southern Illinois." PhD dissertation, Southern Illinois University at Carbondale.

Anzaldo Meneses, Juan, ed. 1999. "Indígenas en la ciudad de México,"*Ce-Acatl* 101 (Summer).

Aranda, Josefina. 2003. "Peasant Farmers in the Global Economy: The State Coalition of Coffee Producers of Oaxaca." In *Confronting Globalization: Economic Integration and Popular Resistance in Mexico*, edited by Timothy Wise, Hilda Salazar, and Laura Carlsen. West Hartford, Conn.: Kumarian.

Atilano Flores, Juan José. 2000. *Entre lo propio y lo ajeno: la identidad étnico-local de los jornaleros mixtecos*. Serie Migración Indígena. Mexico City: Instituto Nacional Indigenista/United Nations Development Programme.

Authers, John, and Sara Silver. 2003. "Mid-term Poll May Add to Fox's Woes," *Financial Times*, July 1.

Ayala, Marisol, and Richard Mines. 2002. "Patterns of Community Cross Border Migration from a Purépecha Town: Dispersion of a People and a Culture."

Presented at the conference "Mexican Indigenous Migrants in the US: Building Bridges between Researchers and Community Leaders," University of California, Santa Cruz, October. At www.lals.ucsc.edu/conference/index.html.

Bacon, David. 2004. *The Children of NAFTA: Labor Wars on the U.S./Mexico Border*. Berkeley: University of California Press.

Bada, Xochitl. 2001. "Collective Remittances, Culture and National Identity: The Reconstruction of Identities among Michoacano Hometown Associations in the Chicago Area." Master's thesis, University of Chicago.

———. 2003. "Mexican Hometown Associations," *Citizen Action in the Americas* 5 (March). At www.americaspolicy.org.

Bakewell, Liza, and Byron Hamann. 2001. *Mesolore: Exploring Mesoamerican Culture* (CD-ROM). Providence, R.I.: Brown University/Prolarti. At www.mesolore.com.

Balkan, Jennifer Lynn. 2001. "Why Not Migrate? A Case Study of Two Rural Villages in Chiapas, Mexico." PhD dissertation, University of Texas at Austin.

Barrón, María Antonieta. 2003. "Evaluación del Programa de Atención a Jornaleros Agrícolas, impacto en 2001, comportamiento en 2002 y un análisis comparativo entre 2001 y 2002." Mexico City: Departamento de Economía, Universidad Nacional Autónoma de México. Manuscript.

Besserer, Federico. 1999a. *Moisés Cruz: historia de un transmigrante*. Culiacán: Universidad Autónoma de Sinaloa/Universidad Autónoma Metropolitana-Iztapalapa.

———. 1999b. "Estudios transnacionales y ciudadanía transnacional." In *Fronteras fragmentadas*, edited by Gail Mummert. Zamora: El Colegio de Michoacán.

———. 2002. "Política cuántica: el uso de la radio por comunidades transnacionales," *Nueva Antropología* 25, no. 57.

———. 2003. "Contesting Community: Cultural Struggles of a Mixtec Transnational Community." PhD dissertation, Stanford University.

———. n.d. *Topografías transnacionales: hacia una geografía de las comunidades transnacionales de origen mixteco*. Mexico City: Universidad Autónoma Metropolitana–Iztapalapa/Plaza y Valdés. Forthcoming.

Binford, Leigh, and María Eugenia D'Aubeterre, eds. 2000. *Conflictos migratorios transnacionales y respuestas comunitarias*. Puebla: Gobierno del Estado de Puebla.

Bonfil Sánchez, Paloma. 2002. "Las mujeres indígenas y su participación política: un movimiento contra la desmemoria y la injusticia." In *Participación política de las mujeres y gobiernos locales en México*, edited by Delia Barrera Bassols. Mexico: GIMTRAP.

Boruchoff, Judith A. 1999. "Creating Continuity across Borders: Reconfiguring the Spaces of Community, State, and Culture in Guerrero, Mexico and Chicago." PhD dissertation, University of Chicago.

Boruchoff, Judith A., and Jennifer Johnston. 2003. "Reconfiguring the Mexican State from the Inside Out and the Outside In: Impacts of Community Action within and beyond Guerrero." Presented at the International Congress of the Latin American Studies Association, Dallas, March.

Bowe, John. 2003. "Nobodies: Slavery in Agricultural Industries of South Florida," *New Yorker* 79 (April 21).

Burns, Allan F. 1993. *Maya in Exile: Guatemalans in Florida.* Philadelphia, Penn.: Temple University Press.

Caballero, Juan Julián, and Manual Ríos Morales. n.d. "Impacto de la migración transnacional entre los *Nuu Savi* (Mixtecos) y los *Bene Xhon* (Zapotecos de la Sierra Norte) de Oaxaca." In *La ruta mixteca: el impacto etnopolítico de la migración transnacional en los pueblos indígenas de México*, edited by Stefano Varese and Sylvia Escárcega. Mexico City: Universidad Nacional Autónoma de México. Forthcoming.

Cano, Arturo. 2002. "Paisanos en Estados Unidos: cuántos, cómo, dónde. Hacia una geografía del otro México," *Masiosare (La Jornada)* 235 (June 23).

Castañeda, Alejandra. 2003. "The Politics of Citizenship: Mexican Migrants in the U.S." PhD dissertation, University of California, Santa Cruz.

Castañeda, Xochitl, Beatriz Manz, and Allison Davenport. 2002. "Mexicanization: A Survival Strategy for Guatemalan Mayas in the San Francisco Bay Area," *Migraciones Internacionales* 1, no. 3 (July–December): 103–23.

Clark Alfaro, Víctor, 1991. "Los mixtecos en la frontera (Tijuana), sus mujeres y el turismo," *Cuadernos de Ciencias Sociales* (Universidad Autónoma de Baja California) 4, no. 10.

Cockburn, Andrew. 2003. "21st Century Slaves," *National Geographic* 204, no. 3 (September): 2–28.

CONAPO (Consejo Nacional de Población). 2000. *Índices de intensidad migratoria, Mexico–Estados Unidos.* Mexico City: CONAPO. At www.conapo.gob.mx.

———. 2001. "Población indígena en la migración temporal a Estados Unidos," *Migración Internacional* 5, no. 14. At www.conapo.gob.mx.

Cook, Maria Lorena. 1996. *Organizing Dissent: Unions, the State and the Democratic Teachers' Movement in Mexico.* University Park, Penn.: Pennsylvania State University Press.

Corbett, Jack, Murad A. Musalem Marhey, Othón Ríos Vásquez, and Héctor A. Vásquez Hernández, eds. 1992. *Migración y etnicidad en Oaxaca.* Nashville, Tenn.: Vanderbilt University.

Cornelius, Wayne A. 2002. "Impacts of NAFTA on Mexico-U.S. Migration." In *NAFTA in the New Millennium*, edited by Edward Chambers and Peter H. Smith. La Jolla: Center for U.S.-Mexican Studies, University of California, San Diego/University of Alberta Press.

Cornelius, Wayne A., Todd Eisenstadt, and Jane Hindley, eds. 1999. *Subnational Politics and Democratization in Mexico.* La Jolla: Center for U.S.-Mexican Studies, University of California, San Diego.

Corona Vásquez, Rodolfo. 2000. "Monto y uso de las remesas en México." In *Migración Mexico–Estados Unidos, opciones de política,* edited by Rodolfo Tuirán. Mexico City: CONAPO/SEGOB/SRE.

Crece, Arthur R., and Roberto R. Ramírez. 2003. *Analysis of General Hispanic Responses in Census 2000.* Population Division Working Paper Series, no. 27. Washington, D.C.: Population Division, U.S. Census Bureau.

Cruz Manjarrez García, Guadalupe Adriana. 2001. "Performance, Ethnicity and Migration: Dance and Music in the Continuation of Ethnic Identity among Immigrant Zapotecs from the Oaxaca Highland Village of Villa Hidalgo, Yalalag to Los Angeles." Master's thesis, University of California, Los Angeles.

Dalton, Margarita. 2003. "Las presidentas municipales en Oaxaca y los usos y costumbres." In *El municipio: un reto para la igualdad de oportunidades entre hombres y mujeres,* edited by Dalia Barrera Bassols and Alejandra Massolo. Mexico: Instituto Nacional de las Mujeres/UNDP/GIMTRAP.

Davis, Alex. 2002. "Unusual Woodburn Office Helps Indigenous Mexicans," *Associated Press Newswires,* October 28.

De la Garza, Rodolfo O., and Myriam Hazan. 2003. *Looking Backward, Moving Forward: Mexican Organizations in the U.S. as Agents of Incorporation and Dissociation.* Claremont, Calif.: Tomás Rivera Policy Institute. At www.trpi.org.

De la Garza, Rodolfo O., and Briant Lindsay Lowell, eds. 2002. *Sending Money Home: Hispanic Remittances and Community Development.* Lanham, Md.: Rowman and Littlefield.

De León, Lourdes. 1995. "The Mixtecs' Annual 3,000-Mile Journey." In *Nosotros: The Hispanic People of Oregon,* edited by Erasmo Gamboa and Carolyn M. Buan. Portland: Oregon Council for the Humanities.

———. 1999. "'Si' Means 'Yes': Lenguaje y poder en el juicio a un mixteco en EUA." In *Mirando … ¿hacia afuera? Experiencias de investigación,* edited by Gabriela Vargas Cetina. Mexico City: Centro de Investigaciones y Estudios Superiores en Antropología Social.

Dennis, Philip. 1987. *Intervillage Conflict in Oaxaca.* New Brunswick, N.J.: Rutgers University Press.

Díaz de Jesús, Marcelino, Guillermo Álvarez Nicanor, Pedro de Jesús Alejandro, Hipólito Morales Ramírez, Gilberto Remegio Román, Sabino Estrada Guadalupe, and Gerardo Pineda Gerónimo, eds. 1996. *Alto Balsas: pueblos nahuas en lucha por la autonomía, desarrollo y defensa de nuestra cultura y territorio.* Mexico City: Consejo de Pueblos Nahuas del Alto Balsas, Guerrero/ Consejo Guerrense "500 Años de Resistencia Indígena."

Dirección de Atención a los Pueblos Indígenas del Distrito Federal. 2001. "Situación de pueblos indígenas originarios y poblaciones indígenas radicadas en el Distrito Federal: elementos para un diagnóstico," June. At www.equidad.df.gob.mx/cuerop/indigenas/diag/htm.

Dirección General de Población de Oaxaca. 2002. *Marginación municipal: Oaxaca 2000*. Oaxaca: DIGEPO.

Domínguez Santos, Rufino. n.d. "Migración y organización de los indígenas oaxaqueños. " In *La ruta mixteca: el impacto etnopolítico de la migración transnacional en los pueblos indígenas de Mexico*, edited by Stefano Varese and Sylvia Escárcega. Mexico City: Universidad Nacional Autónoma de México. Forthcoming.

Dossier Courrier International. 2003. "Les Indiens aux portes du pouvoir. 44 Millions d'Indiens en Amérique Latine," *Courrier International* 668 (August 21).

Durand, Jorge. 1998. "Nuevas regiones migratorias." In *Población, Desarrollo, y Globalización: V Reunión de Investigación Sociodemográfica en México*, edited by René M. Centeno. Mexico City: SOMEDE/COLEF.

Durand, Jorge, and Douglas Massey. 2003. *Clandestinos: migración México–Estados Unidos en lo albores del Siglo XXI*. Mexico: Miguel Ángel Porrúa/Univerersidad Autónoma de Zacatecas.

EDUCA (Servicios para una Educación Alternativa). 2003. *El camino a la equidad: un estudio de género en municipios indígenas de Oaxaca*. Oaxaca: EDUCA.

*El Oaxaqueño*. 2003a. "La Guelaguetza de ORO en su cúspide," August 9.

———. 2003b. "Guelaguetza en San Marcos," August 9.

———. 2003c. "Oaxaqueños reivindian principios juaristas," March 29.

Escárcega, Sylvia, and Stefano Varese. n.d. "Introducción retrospectiva a la migración transnacional mixteca." In *La ruta mixteca: el impacto etnopolítico de la migración transnacional en los pueblos indígenas de México*, edited by Stefano Varese and Sylvia Escárcega. Mexico City: Universidad Nacional Autónoma de México. Forthcoming.

Espinoza, Víctor. 1999. *The Federation of Michoacán Clubs in Illinois*. The Chicago-Michoacan Project Report, Heartland Alliance, September.

Fink, Leon. 2003. *The Maya of Morganton: Work and Community in the Nuevo New South*. Chapel Hill: University of North Carolina Press.

FIOB (Frente Indígena Oaxaqueño Binacional). 2003. "Comunicado: Frente Indígena Oaxaqueño Binacional, Coordinación Estatal Baja California, Asamblea Estatal," March 2.

Fitzgerald, David. 2000. *Negotiating Extra-Territorial Citizenship: Mexican Migration and the Transnational Politics of Community*. La Jolla: Center for Comparative Immigration Studies, University of California, San Diego.

———. n.d. "Beyond 'Transnationalism': Mexican Hometown Politics at an American Labor Union," *Ethnic and Racial Studies*. Forthcoming.

Fletcher, Peri. 1999. *"La Casa de Mis Sueños": Dreams of Home in a Transnational Migrant Community*. Boulder, Colo.: Westview.

Fletcher, Peri, and Jane Margold. 2003. "Transnational Communities," *Rural Mexico Research Review* 1. At www.reap.ucdavis.edu/rural_review.html.

Flores, William V. 1997. "Citizens vs. Citizenry: Undocumented Workers and Latino Cultural Citizenship." In *Latino Cultural Citizenship: Claiming Identity, Space, and Rights*, edited by William V. Flores and Rina Benmayor. Boston, Mass.: Beacon.

Flores, William V., and Rina Benmayor. 1997. "Constructing Cultural Citizenship." In *Latino Cultural Citizenship: Claiming Identity, Space, and Rights*, edited by William V. Flores and Rina Benmayor. Boston, Mass.: Beacon.

Fox, Jonathan. 1992. *The Politics of Food in Mexico*. Ithaca, N.Y.: Cornell University Press.

———. 1994. "The Politics of Mexico's New Peasant Economy." In *The Politics of Economic Restructuring: State-Society Relations and Regime Change in Mexico*, edited by Maria Lorena Cook, Kevin J. Middlebrook, and Juan Molinar Horcasitas. La Jolla: Center for U.S.-Mexican Studies, University of California, San Diego.

———. 1996. "How Does Civil Society Thicken? The Political Construction of Social Capital in Rural Mexico," *World Development* 24, no. 6 (June): 1089–1104.

———. 2001a. "Evaluación de las coaliciones binacionales de la sociedad civil a partir de la experiencia México–Estados Unidos," *Revista Mexicana de Sociología* 63, no. 3 (July–September).

———. 2001b. "Vertically Integrated Policy Monitoring: A Tool for Civil Society Policy Advocacy," *Nonprofit and Voluntary Sector Quarterly* 30, no. 3 (September).

———. 2002. "Lessons from Mexico-U.S. Civil Society Coalitions." In *Cross-Border Dialogues: U.S.-Mexico Social Movement Networking*, edited by David Brooks and Jonathan Fox. La Jolla: Center for U.S.-Mexican Studies, University of California, San Diego.

Fox, Jonathan, and Josefina Aranda. 1996. *Decentralization and Rural Development in Mexico: Community Participation in Oaxaca's Municipal Funds Program*. La Jolla: Center for U.S.-Mexican Studies, University of California, San Diego.

Galvez, Alyshia. 2003. "'I Too Was an Immigrant': The Transformation of Affinities and Identity through Time in a Mexican Migrant Devotional Organization in the South Bronx." Presented at the meeting of the American Anthropological Association, November.

García, Martín Alejandro. 2003a. "Guelaguetza en Los Angeles," *El Oaxaqueño*, April 26.

———. 2003b. "La pelota mixteca: una tradición milenaria," *El Oaxaqueño*, May 24.

———. 2003c. "Rescate de un juego milenario: pelota mixteca de forro," *El Oaxaqueño*, August 9.

———. 2003d. "Instituyen Día del Migrante Zoogochense," *El Oaxaqueño*, August 23.

García Barrios, Raúl, and Luis García Barrios. 1992. "Subsistencia maicera y dependencia monetaria en el agro semiproletarizado: una comunidad rural mixteca." In *Reestructuración económica y subsistencia rural: el maíz y la crisis de los ochenta*, edited by Cynthia Hewitt de Alcántara. Mexico City: El Colegio de Mexico/Centro Tepoztlán/UNRISD.

——. 1994. "The Remnants of Community: Migration, Corn Supply and Social Transformation in the Mixteca Alta of Oaxaca." In *Economic Restructuring and Rural Subsistence in Mexico: Corn and the Crisis of the 1980s*, edited by Cynthia Hewitt de Alcántara. La Jolla: Center for U.S.-Mexican Studies, University of California, San Diego/United Nations Research Institute for Social Development.

García Leyva, Jaime. 2003. "Por los caminos del sur indígena," *Ojarasca (La Jornada)* 79 (November).

García Ortega, Martha. 2000. "El Consejo de Pueblos Nahuas del Alto Balsas contra la construcción de la presa hidroeléctrica San Juan Tetelcingo, Guerrero (1990–1992)." Bachelor's thesis, Escuela Nacional de Antropología e Historia.

——. 2002. "Nómadas, viajeros y migrantes: la comunidad sin límites de la región nahua del Alto Balsas, Guerrero." Master's thesis, Escuela Nacional de Antropología e Historia.

——. 2003. "Desarrollo indígena, migración y autonomía." Presented at the "Primer Coloquio Internacional sobre Migración y Desarrollo: Transnacionalismo y Nuevas Perspectivas de Integración," Universidad Autónoma de Zacatecas, October 23–25. At www.migracionydesarrollo.org.

García Zamora, Rodolfo. 2002. "Los proyectos productivos de los migrantes en México hoy." Presented at the "Segundo Coloquio sobre Migración Internacional: Mexico-California," University of California, Berkeley, March.

——. 2003. "Migración, remesas y desarrollo local." PhD dissertation, Universidad Autonóma de Zacatecas.

García Zamora, Rodolfo, ed. 2002. *Seminario internacional sobre la transferencia y uso de las remesas: proyectos productivos y de ahorro*. Mexico: CEPAL/Universidad Autónoma de Zacatecas/Sin Fronteras.

Garduño, Everardo. 1998. "Applying Anthropology among Migrant Indians in San Quintín, Mexico," *Practicing Anthropology* 20, no. 4 (Fall): 34–38.

——. n.d. "San Quintín, Baja California, en la ruta indígena." In *La ruta mixteca: el impacto etnopolítico de la migración transnacional en los pueblos indígenas de Mexico*, edited by Stefano Varese and Sylvia Escárcega. Mexico City: Universidad Nacional Autónoma de México. Forthcoming.

Garduño, Everardo, Efraín García, and Patricia Morán. 1990. *Mixtecos en Baja California: el caso de San Quintín*. Mexico: Universidad Autónoma de Baja California/Museo Regional Universitario.

Gil Martínez de Escobar, Rocío. 2003. "Estrategias de desarrollo transnacional de una comunidad indígena oaxaqueña: Santa Maria Tindú." Presented at the "Primer Coloquio Internacional sobre Migración y Desarrollo: Transnacionalismo y Nuevas Perspectivas de Integración," Universidad Autónoma de Zacatecas, October 23–25. At www.migracionydesarrollo.org.

Girón Cruz, Alicia Sylvia, and Rafael G. Reyes Morales. 2003. "Impactos de la migración en el desarrollo de las comunidades indígenas de Oaxaca." Presented at the International Congress of the Latin American Studies Association, Dallas, March.

Gledhill, John. 1995. *Neoliberalism, Transnationalization and Rural Poverty: A Case Study of Michoacán, Mexico.* Boulder, Colo.: Westview.

Gobierno del Distrito Federal. 2000. *Memoria de los encuentros sobre presencia indígena en la ciudad de México.* Mexico City: Dirección General de Equidad y Desarrollo, Gobierno del Distrito Federal.

Goldring, Luin. 1998a. "From Market Membership to Transnational Citizenship? The Changing Politicization of Transnational Social Spaces," *L'Ordinaire Latino-Americaine* 173–174 (July–December).

———. 1998b. "The Power of Status in Transnational Social Fields." In *Transnationalism from Below,* edited by Michael Peter Smith and Luis Eduardo Guarnizo. New Brunswick, N.J.: Transaction.

———. 2001. "The Gender and Geography of Citizenship in U.S.-Mexico Transnational Spaces," *Identities* 7, no. 4: 501–37.

———. 2002. "The Mexican State and Transmigrant Organizations: Negotiating the Boundaries of Membership and Participation," *Latin American Research Review* 37, no. 3: 55–100.

———. 2003a. "Rethinking Remittances: Social and Political Dimensions of Individual and Collective Remittances." CERLAC Working Paper. At www.yorku.ca/cerlac/ABSTRACTS.htm#Goldring.

———. 2003b. "Gender, Status and the State in Transnational Spaces: The Gendering of Political Participation and Mexican Hometown Associations." In *Gender and U.S. Immigration: Contemporary Trends,* edited by Pierrette Hondagneu-Sotelo. Berkeley: University of California Press.

Good, Catherine. 1992. "'Making the Struggle, One Big One': Nahuatl Resistance to the San Juan Dam, Mexico." Presented to the Agrarian Studies Colloquium, Yale University, October 30.

Grieshop, James I. 1997. "Transnational and Transformational: Mixtec Immigration and Health Beliefs," *Human Organization* 56, no. 4: 400–407.

Grimes, Kimberly. 1998. *Crossing Borders: Changing Social Identities in Southern Mexico.* Tucson: University of Arizona Press.

Guidi, Marta. 1992. *Estigma y prestigio: la tradición de migrar en San Juan Mixtepec (Oaxaca/Mexico).* Bonn: Holos Verlag.

Hagen, Jaqueline Maria. 1994. *Deciding to Be Legal: A Maya Community in Houston.* Philadelphia, Penn.: Temple University Press.

Hernández Díaz, Jorge. 2001. *Reclamos de la identidad: la formación de las organizaciones indígenas en Oaxaca.* Mexico City: Miguel Ángel Porrúa/Universidad Autónoma "Benito Juárez" de Oaxaca.

Hernández Navarro, Luis. 1999. "Reaffirming Ethnic Identity and Reconstitut-
ing Politics in Oaxaca." In *Subnational Politics and Democratization in Mexico*,
edited by Wayne A. Cornelius, Todd A. Eisenstadt, and Jane Hindley. La
Jolla: Center for U.S.-Mexican Studies, University of California, San Diego.

Hernández Navarro, Luis, and Ramón Vera Herrera, eds. 1998. *Acuerdos de San
Andrés*. Mexico City: Era.

Hindley, Jane. 1999. "Indigenous Mobilization, Development, and Democratization in Guerrero: The Nahua People vs. the Tetelcingo Dam." In *Subnational Politics and Democratization in Mexico*, edited by Wayne A. Cornelius,
Todd A. Eisenstadt, and Jane Hindley. La Jolla: Center for U.S.-Mexican
Studies, University of California, San Diego.

Hirabayashi, Lane Ryo. 1993. *Cultural Capital: Mountain Zapotec Migrant Associations in Mexico City*. Tucson: University of Arizona Press.

Hulshof, Marije. 1991. *Zapotec Moves, Networks and Remittances of U.S.-Bound
Migrants from Oaxaca, Mexico*. Amsterdam: Koninklijk Nederlands
Aardrijkskundig Genootschap.

Ibarra Templos, Yuribi Mayek. 2003. "Espacios alternativas de poder: la participación de las mujeres en una comunidad transnacional." Bachelor's thesis, Universidad Autónoma Metropolitana–Iztapalapa.

INEGI (Instituto Nacional de Estadística, Geografía e Informática). 2002. *Las
mujeres en el México rural*. Aguascalientes, Mexico: INEGI/SAGARPA/PA.

Johnston, Paul. 2001. "The Emergence of Transnational Citizenship among
Mexican Immigrants in California." In *Citizenship Today: Global Perspectives
and Practices*, edited by T. Alexander Aleinikoff and Douglas Klusmeyer.
Washington D.C.: Carnegie Endowment for International Peace.

Juárez Galindo, Ignacio. 2002. "Inauguran el puente mixteco en Axutla; fue
construido con dinero de los migrantes," *La Jornada de Oriente*, January 9.

Kamber, Michael. 2001a. "A Link in the Chain," *Village Voice*, April 11.

———. 2001b. "Deadly Game," *Village Voice*, April 18.

———. 2001c. "Toil and Temptation," *Village Voice*, April 24.

Kearney, Michael. 1986. "Integration of the Mixteca and the Western U.S.-
Mexican Border Region via Migratory Wage Labor." In *Regional Impacts of
U.S.-Mexican Relations*, edited by Ina Rosenthal Urey. La Jolla: Center for
U.S.-Mexican Studies, University of California, San Diego.

———. 1988. "Mixtec Political Consciousness: From Passive to Active Resistance." In *Rural Revolt in Mexico and U.S. Intervention*, edited by Daniel Nu-
gent. La Jolla: Center for U.S.-Mexican Studies, University of California, San
Diego.

———. 1994. "Desde el indigenismo a los derechos humanos: etnicidad y
política más allá de la mixteca," *Nueva Antropología* 14, no. 46: 49–67.

———. 1995a. "The Effects of Transnational Culture, Economy, and Migration
on Mixtec Identity in Oaxacalifornia." In *The Bubbling Cauldron: Race, Eth-*

*nicity, and the Urban Crisis,* edited by Michael Peter Smith and Joe R. Feagin. Minneapolis: University of Minnesota Press.

———. 1995b. "The Local and the Global: The Anthropology of Globalization and Transnationalism," *Annual Review of Anthropology* 24: 547–65.

———. 1996. "Indigenous Ethnicity and Mobilization in Latin America," *Latin American Perspectives* 23: 5–16.

———. 2000. "Transnational Oaxacan Indigenous Identity: The Case of Mixtecs and Zapotecs," *Identities* 7, no. 2: 173–95.

———. 2001. "Struggle and Difference: The Jiujitsu of Transnational Indigenous Resistance and Domination." In *History in Person: Enduring Struggles and Identities in Practice,* edited by D. Holland and J. Lave. Santa Fe, N.M.: School of American Research Press.

———. 2002. "Transnational Migration from Oaxaca: The Agrarian Question and the Politics of Indigenous Peoples," *Oesterreichische Zeitschrift für Geschichtswissenschaften* 13: 4.

Kearney, Michael, and Carole Nagengast. 1989. "Anthropological Perspectives on Transnational Communities in Rural California." Davis: Working Group on Farm Labor and Rural Poverty, California Institute for Rural Studies.

Kissam, Edward. 2003a. "Trends in the Ethnic Composition of the California Farm Labor Force." Memo to the Agricultural Worker Health Initiative Policy Advisory Group, July 1.

———. 2003b. "Transformation of Civic and Political Life in Rural California Communities." Presented at the conference "The Changing Face of Rural California," Asilomar, California, May.

Klaver, Jeanine. 1997. *From the Land of the Sun to the City of Los Angeles: The Migration Process of Zapotec Indians from Oaxaca, Mexico to Los Angeles, California.* Netherlands Geographical Studies, no. 228. Utrecht, Amsterdam: Dutch Geographical Society.

Krissman, Fred. 1996. "Californian Agribusiness and Mexican Farm Workers, 1942–1992." PhD dissertation, University of California, Santa Barbara.

———. 2002. "Apples and Oranges? Recruiting Indigenous Mexicans to Divide Farm Labor Markets in the Western U.S." Presented at the conference "Mexican Indigenous Migrants in the US: Building Bridges between Researchers and Community Leaders," University of California, Santa Cruz, October. Available at www.lals.ucsc.edu/conference/index/html.

Lartigue, Francois, and André Quesnel, eds. 2003. *Las dinámicas de la población indígena: cuestiones y debates actuales en México.* Mexico City: Centro de Investigaciones y Estudios Superiores en Antropología Social/Institut de Recherche pour le Developement/Miguel Ángel Porrúa.

Leal, Alejandra. 2001. "La identidad mixteca en la migración al norte: el caso del Frente Indígena Oaxaqueño Binacional," *Cahier ALHIM, Amérique Latine Histoire et Mémoire* 2: 237–55.

Leiken, Robert. 2000. *The Melting Border: Mexico and Mexican Communities in the United States*. Washington, D.C.: Center for Equal Opportunity.

Lestage, Francoise. 1998. "Apuntes sobre los mecanismos de reconstrucción de la identidad entre los migrantes: los mixtecos de las Californias." In *Encuentros Antropológicos: Power, Identity and Mobility in Mexican Society*, edited by Valentina Napolitano and Xochitl Leyva. London: Institute of Latin America Studies, University of London.

———. 1999. "Diseñando nuevas identidades: las uniones matrimoniales entre los migrantes mixtecos en Tijuana, B.C." In *Fronteras fragmentadas*, edited by Gail Mummert. Zamora: El Colegio de Michoacán.

———. 2002. "La emergencia de 'neocomunidades' étnicas en Tijuana." In *Migración internacional e identidades cambiantes*, edited by María Eugenia Anguiano Téllez and Miguel J. Hernández Madrid. Zamora: El Colegio de Michoacán/El Colegio de la Frontera Norte.

López, Felipe, Luis Escala-Rabadán, and Raúl Hinojosa-Ojeda. 2001. "Migrant Associations, Remittances and Regional Development between Los Angeles and Oaxaca, Mexico." Los Angeles: North American Integration and Development Center, University of California, Los Angeles. At www.naid. sppsr.ucla.edu/pubs&news.

López, Francisco H. 1999. "The Re-invention and Re-adaptation of *Mayordomía*: The Case of Tlacolula, Oaxaca and Los Angeles, California." Bachelor's thesis, University of California, Santa Cruz.

López Ángel, Gustavo. 2000a. "Mixteca internacional: la fuerza de la ausencia," *Ojarasca (La Jornada)*, July.

———. 2000b. "Mixtecos: lengua, migración y procesos organizativos." In *Conflictos migratorios transnacionales y respuestas comunitarias*, edited by Leigh Binford and María Eugenia D'Aubeterre. Puebla: Gobierno del Estado de Puebla.

———. 2003a. "Organizaciones de migrantes en la mixteca poblana: membresía transnacional o exclusión de la ciudadanía multicultural." Manuscript.

———. 2003b. "Membresía e identidad en procesos migratorios translocales: la experiencia de la Asociación Micaltepecana." Presented at the "Primer Coloquio Internacional sobre Migración y Desarrollo: Transnacionalismo y Nuevas Perspectivas de Integración," Zacatecas, October. At www. migracionydesarrollo.org.

López Bárcenas, Francisco. 2002. *Muertes sin fin: crónica de represión en la región mixteca oaxaqueña*. Serie Derechos Indígenas, no. 2. Mexico: Ce-Atl.

López Espinosa, Mario. 2002. "Remesas de mexicanos en el exterior y su vinculación con el desarrollo económico, social y cultural de sus comunidades de origen," *Estudios sobre Migraciones Internacionales* (International Labour Organization) 59.

López Mercado, Alejandro. 1998. "La defensa de los derechos colectivos de los pueblos indígenas en México: los casos del FIOB, la UCIHJ y la Comunidad de Santa Ana Zirosto," *Cuadernos Agrarios* 16, nueva época: 174–98.

López Monjardín, Adriana. 1991. "Organization and Struggle among Agricultural Workers in Mexico." In *Unions, Workers, and the State in Mexico*, edited by Kevin J. Middlebrook. La Jolla: Center for U.S.-Mexican Studies, University of California, San Diego.

Loucky, James, and Marilyn M. Moors, eds. 2000. *The Maya Diaspora: Guatemalan Roots, New American Lives*. Philadelphia, Penn.: Temple University Press.

Lozano-Ascencio, Fernando. 1993. *Bringing It Back Home: Remittances to Mexico from Migrant Workers in the United States*. La Jolla: Center for U.S.-Mexican Studies, University of California, San Diego.

———. 2003. "Discurso oficial, remesas y desarrollo en Mexico," *Migración y Desarrollo* 1 (October).

Lozano-Ascencio, Fernando, Bryan Roberts, and Frank Bean. 1999. "The Interconnections of Internal and International Migration: The Case of the United States and Mexico." In *Migration and Transnational Social Spaces*, edited by Ludger Pries. Aldershot: Ashgate.

Maceda, Oralia, Rosa López, Fidelina Espinosa, Martha Moreno, Julia Hernández, Concepción Pacheco, May Lee, Lee Lor, Sally Yang, Pai Yang, and Vilaysouk Vee Inthaly. 2003. *Immigrant Women: A Road to the Future / Mujeres inmigrantes: camino al futuro*. Fresno, Calif.: Pan-Valley Institute/American Friends Service Committee.

Magagnini, Stephen. 2002. "Radio Gives Mixtecs Their Own Voice: 'La Hora Mixteca' Reaches Out across California," *Sacramento Bee*, October 20.

Martínez, Nayamín. 2003. "El Benemérito de las Américas habita en el corazón de Fresno," *El Tequio*, March–April. At www.laneta.apc.org/fiob/teqmarz03/indicemarz03.html.

Martínez, Rubén. 2001. *Crossing Over: A Mexican Family on the Migrant Trail*. New York: Henry Holt.

Martínez-Saldaña, Jesús, and Raúl Ross Pineda. 2002. "Suffrage for Mexicans Residing Abroad." In *Cross-Border Dialogues: U.S.-Mexico Social Movement Networking*, edited by David Brooks and Jonathan Fox. La Jolla: Center for U.S.-Mexican Studies, University of California, San Diego.

McGuire, Sharon Ann. 2001. "Crossing Myriad Borders: A Dimensional Analysis of the Migration and Health Experiences of Indigenous Oaxacan Women." PhD dissertation, University of San Diego.

Mejía Flores, Susana. 2003. "Mujer indígena y violencia," *México Indígena* 2, no. 5 (September): 41–47.

Mines, Richard, Nancy Mullenax, and Lisettte Saca. 2001. "The Binational Farmworker Health Survey: An In-depth Study of Agricultural Worker Health in Mexico and the United States." Davis: California Institute for Rural Studies/California Endowment, June.

Moctezuma Longoria, Miguel. 2003a. "The Migrant Club El Remolino: A Binational Community Experience." In *Confronting Globalization: Economic Integration and Popular Resistance in Mexico*, edited by Timothy Wise, Hilda Salazar, and Laura Carlsen. West Hartford, Conn.: Kumarian.

————. 2003b. "Territorialidad de los clubes de zacatecanos en Estados Unidos," *Migración y Desarrollo* 1 (October).

Molina Ramírez, Tania. 2003. "El sueño de frenar la migración," *Masiosare (La Jornada)* 307 (November 9).

Molinari Soriano, Sara. 1979. "La migración indígena en México." In *Aspectos sociales de la migración en México*, edited by Margarita Nolasco Armas. Mexico City: Departamento de Proyectos Especiales de Investigación, Instituto Nacional de Antropología e Historia.

Montes, Olga. 2000. "Cultura, etnicidad y migración: los zapotecos en Los Angeles," *Cuadernos Agrarios* 19–20: 49–67.

Mountz, Alison, and Richard Wright. 1996. "Daily Life in the Transnational Migrant Community of San Agustín, Oaxaca and Poughkeepsie, New York," *Diaspora* 5, no. 3.

Mutersbaugh, Ted. 2002. "Migration, Common Property and Communal Labor: Cultural Politics and Agency in a Mexican Village," *Political Geography* 21 (June).

Mydans, Seth. 1989. "Strawberry Fields Bear a New Immigrant Crop," *New York Times*, May 22.

Nadal, Alejandro. 2000. "The Environmental and Social Impacts of Economic Liberalization on Corn Production in Mexico." Oxford: Oxfam, Great Britain/World Wide Fund for Nature.

Nagengast, Carole, and Michael Kearney. 1990. "Mixtec Ethnicity: Social Identity, Political Consciousness and Political Activism," *Latin American Research Review* 25, no. 2.

Nagengast, Carole, Rodolfo Stavenhagen, and Michael Kearney. 1992. *Human Rights and Indigenous Workers: The Mixtecs in Mexico and the United States*. La Jolla: Center for U.S.-Mexican Studies, University of California, San Diego.

Najar, Alberto. 2002. "La carrera México–Nueva York de los migrantes: en busca del milagro," *Masiosare (La Jornada)* 255 (November 10).

————. 2003. "Después del free-way maya, todo es Cuautitlán," *Masiosare (La Jornada)* 294 (August 11).

Navarro, Mireya. 2003. "Going Beyond Black and White, Hispanics in Census Pick 'Other,'" *New York Times*, November 9.

Olivera, Mireya. 2003. "Festeja CRLA proyecto mixteco," *El Oaxaqueño*, November 15.

Orellana, Carlos. 1973. "Mixtec Migrants in Mexico City: A Case Study of Urbanization," *Human Organization* 32, no. 3 (Fall).

Orozco, Graciela, Esther González, and Roger Díaz de Cossío. 2003. *Las organizaciones mexicano-americanas, hispanas y mexicanas en Estados Unidos*. 2d rev.

ed. Mexico: Centro de Estudios Migratorios/Fundación Solidaridad Mexicano-Americana.

Oxfam. 2002. *Mugged: Poverty in Your Coffee Cup*. Boston, Mass.: Oxfam America. At wwwmaketradefair.com.

———. 2003. "Dumping without Borders: How US Agricultural Policies Are Destroying the Livelihoods of Mexican Corn Farmers." Oxfam Briefing Paper No. 50, August. At www.maketradefair.com/assets/english/corn_dumping.pdf.

Pallares, Amalia. 2002. *From Peasant Struggles to Indian Resistance: The Ecuadorian Andes in the Late Twentieth Century*. Norman: University of Oklahoma Press.

París Pombo, María Dolores. 2003a. "Género y etnicidad entre los migrantes triquis al Valle de Salinas, California." Presented at the "Seminario Permanente sobre Migración Internacional," El Colegio de la Frontera Norte, Tijuana, July.

———. 2003b. "Derechos humanos de los y las migrantes triquis en California." Presented at the "Seminario Permanente sobre Migración Internacional," El Colegio de la Frontera Norte, Tijuana, July.

Payne, Brian. 2000. "Taking Back the Reins of Identity Formation: The Evolution of a Grassroots Organization in a South Florida Migrant Farm Working Community." Master's thesis, University of Florida.

Poole, Deborah. 2002. "Mestizaje, Distinction and the Political Language of Culture in Oaxaca." Presented at the conference "Mestizaje in the Andes and Central America," University of Iowa, October.

———. 2004. "An Image of 'Our Indian': Type Photographs and Racial Sentiments in Oaxaca, 1920–1940," *Hispanic American Historical Review* 84, no. 1 (February): 37–82.

Popkin, Eric. 1999. "Guatemalan Mayan Migration to Los Angeles: Constructing Transnational Linkages in the Context of the Settlement Process," *Ethnic and Racial Studies* 22, no. 2 (March).

Porter, Eduardo. 2003. "Once Migrant, Farm Workers Now Settle in California," *Wall St. Journal*, October 10.

Portes, Alejandro, and Patricia M. Fernández-Kelly. 2003. "Subversion and Compliance in Transnational Communities: Implications for Social Justice." In *Struggles for Social Rights in Latin America*, edited by Susan Eva Eckstein and Timothy P. Wickham-Crowley. New York: Routledge.

Portes, Alejandro, Luis E. Guarnizo, and Patricia Landolt. 1999. "The Study of Transnationalism: Pitfalls and Promise of an Emergent Research Field," *Ethnic and Racial Studies* 22, no. 2 (March): 217–37.

Poy Solano, Laura. 2003. "Aplicará el INEA proyecto educativo para los indígenas mexicanos en EU," *La Jornada*, October 19.

Quiñones, Sam. 2001. *True Tales from Another Mexico*. Albuquerque: University of New Mexico Press.

Quiñones, Sam, and Alan Mittelstaedt. 2000. "A League of Their Own: How a Team of Oaxacan Busboys Is Redefining L.A. Basketball," *LA Weekly*, February 4–10. At www.laweekly.com/ink/00/11/features-mittelstaedt.php.

Ramírez Cuevas, Jesús. 2003. "Cuando los braceros se fueron de huelga en California," *Masiosare (La Jornada)* 304 (October 19).

Ramírez Romero, Silvia Jaquelina. 2000. "Identidad política y derechos de los pueblos indígenas: la reconstrucción de la identidad política del Frente Indígena Oaxaqueño Binacional." Master's thesis, Instituto de Investigaciones Dr. José María Mora.

Rendón, Iván. 2002. "Toca banda oaxaqueña para el Papa," *Reforma*, July 8.

Reyes, Alma. 2002. "El papel que juega la radio en las comunidades transnacionales." Bachelor's thesis, Universidad Autónoma Metropolitana–Iztapalapa.

Rivera-Salgado, Gaspar. 1999. "Migration and Political Activism: Mexican Transnational Indigenous Communities in a Comparative Perspective." PhD dissertation, University of California, Santa Cruz.

———. 2002. "Cross-border Grassroots Organizations and the Indigenous Migrant Experience." In *Cross-Border Dialogues: U.S.-Mexico Social Movement Networking*, edited by David Brooks and Jonathan Fox. La Jolla: Center for U.S.-Mexican Studies, University of California, San Diego.

Roberts, Bryan R., Reanne Frank, and Fernando Lozano-Ascencio. 1999. "Transnational Migrant Communities and Mexican Migration to the US," *Ethnic and Racial Studies* 22, no. 2 (March): 238–66.

Rodríguez, Clara E. 2000. *Changing Race: Latinos, the Census, and the History of Ethnicity in the United States.* New York: New York University Press.

Rodríguez, Néstor. 2000. "Maya Urban Villagers in Houston: The Formation of a Migrant Community from San Cristóbal Totonicapan." In *The Maya Diaspora: Guatemalan Roots, New American Lives*, edited by James Loucky and Marilyn M. Moors. Philadelphia, Penn.: Temple University Press.

Rodríguez, Néstor, and Susanne Jonas. n.d. *Guatemalan Migrant Communities in a Changing Tri-national Region.* Austin: University of Texas Press. Forthcoming.

Ross, John. 2002. "Confronting Chiapas' Migration Woes," *Crossborder Updater*, August 6. At www.americaspolicy.org.

Rouse, Roger. 1992. "Making Sense of Settlement: Class Transformation, Cultural Struggle, and Transnationalism among Mexican Migrants in the United States," *Annals of the New York Academy of Sciences* 645.

Rubio, Miguel Ángel, et al. 2000. "Desarrollo, marginalidad y migración." In *Estado del desarrollo económico y social de los pueblos indígenas de Mexico, 1996–1997*, edited by Carlos Zolla and Miguel Ángel Rubio. Mexico City: Instituto Nacional Indigenista/Programa de las Naciones Unidas para el Desarrollo.

Runsten, David. 2003. "Migration and Rural Development: Further Notes." Presented at the International Congress of the Latin American Studies Association, Dallas, March.

Runsten, David, and Michael Kearney. 1994. *A Survey of Oaxacan Village Networks in California Agriculture.* Davis: California Institute for Rural Studies.

Rus, Jan, and Salvador Guzmán López, eds. 1996. *Jchi'iltak ta Slumal California/Chamulas en California: el testimonio de Santos, Mariano y Juan Gómez López.* San Cristóbal: Instituto de Asesoría Antropológica para la Región Maya, A.C. (INAREMAC).

Sánchez G., Martha Judith. 1995. "Comunidades sin límites territoriales: estudio sobre la reproducción de la identidad étnica de migrantes zapotecos asentados en el área metropolitana de la ciudad de México." PhD dissertation, El Colegio de México.

———. 2000. "Identidad y migración: oaxaqueños en Napa y Sonoma, California," *Cuadernos Agrarios* 19/20.

———. n.d.1. "Caracterización sociodemográfica de los mexicanos que trabajan en la agricultura en los condados de Napa y Sonoma, California." Mexico City: Instituto de Investigaciones Sociales, Universidad Nacional Autónoma de México. Manuscript.

———. n.d.2. "Comunidades sin límites territoriales: fortalecimiento y redefinición de identidades étnicas y genéricas de la migración de mexicanos hacia Estados Unidos." In *Simposio sobre la Emigración Latinoamericana, 2002.* Osaka: Japan Center for Area Studies. Forthcoming.

———. n.d.3. "Migración indígena y nuevas formas de organización política: retos para la literatura existente," *México Indígena.* Forthcoming.

Schlosser, Eric. 1995. "In the Strawberry Fields," *Atlantic Monthly*, November. At www.theatlantic.com/issues/95nov/strawber.htm.

Serrano Carreto, Enrique, Arnulfo Embriz Osorio, and Patricia Fernández Ham, eds. 2003. *Indicadores socioeconómicos de los pueblos indígenas, 2002.* Mexico: Instituto Nacional Indigenista/Programa de las Naciones Unidas para el Desarrollo. At www/ini.gob.mx.

Sevy Fua, Rosa María. 2000. "Casa Puebla: An Organizational Ethnography." Master's thesis, University of British Columbia.

Simon, Joel. 1997. *Endangered Mexico: An Environment on the Edge.* San Francisco, Calif.: Sierra Club Books.

Smith, Michael Peter, and Luis Guarnizo, eds. 1998. *Transnationalism from Below.* New Brunswick, N.J.: Transaction.

Smith, Robert C. 1995. "Los Ausentes Siempre Presentes: The Imagining, Making and Politics of a Transnational Migrant Community between Ticuani, Puebla, Mexico and New York City." PhD dissertation, Columbia University.

———. 1996. "Mexicans in New York City: Membership and Incorporation of a New Immigrant Group." In *Latinos in New York*, edited by Gabriel Haslip Viera and Sherrie Baver. Notre Dame, Ind.: University of Notre Dame Press.

———. 2001. "Mexicans: Social, Educational, Economic and Political Problems and Prospects in New York." In *New Immigrants in New York*, edited by Nancy Foner. New York: Columbia University Press.

———. 2003. "Migrant Membership as an Instituted Process: Transnationalization, the State and the Extra-Territorial Conduct of Mexican Politics," *International Migration Review* 37, no. 2 (Summer).

Solís, Jacqueline. 2001. "Immigration Status and Identity: Undocumented Mexicans in New York." In *Mambo Montage: The Latinization of New York*, edited by Agustín Laó Montes and Arlene Dávila. New York: Columbia University Press.

———. 2002. "The (Trans) formation of Illegality as an Identity: A Study of the Organization of Undocumented Mexican Immigrants and Their Children in New York City." PhD dissertation, City University of New York.

Stanley, Eduardo. 2003a. "Mixtec Revival: Mexican Indigenous Language on the Rise," *Pacific News Service*, September 16. At http://news.pacificnews.org/news/.

———. 2003b. "A Mixtec's Story: From the Onion Fields to College," *Pacific News Service*, October 31. At http://news.ncmonline.com/news/.

———. 2003c. "Homenaje a Juárez refleja el crecimiento oaxaqueño en California," *El Oaxaqueño*, March 29.

Stephen, Lynn. 2001. "Globalization, the State, and the Creation of Flexible Indigenous Workers: Mixtec Farmworkers in Oregon," *Urban Anthropology and Studies of Cultural Systems and World Economic Development* 30, nos. 2–3 (Summer–Fall): 189–214.

———. 2003. "Cultural Citizenship and Labor Rights for Oregon Farmworkers: The Case of Pineros y Campesinos Unidos del Noroeste (PCUN)," *Human Organization* 62, no. 1 (Spring).

Stuart, James, and Michael Kearney. 1981. "Causes and Effects of Agricultural Labor Migration from the Mixteca of Oaxaca to California." Working Paper No. 28. La Jolla: Center for U.S.-Mexican Studies, University of California, San Diego.

Suro, Robert, Sergio Bendixen, B. Lindsay Lowell, and Dulce Benavides. 2002. *Billions in Motion: Latino Immigrants, Remittances and Banking.* Los Angeles: Pew Hispanic Center/Multilateral Investment Facility, Inter-American Development Bank. At www.pewhispanic.org.

Tafoya, Sonya M. 2003. "Latinos and Racial Identification in California," *California Counts* 4, no. 4 (May). At www.ppic.org.

Tucker, Catherine M., Eileen Díaz McConnell, and Leah Van Wey. 2003. "The Role of Local Organization in Migration, Remittances and Community Development in the Sierra Juárez, Oaxaca, Mexico." Presented at the International Congress of the Latin American Studies Association, Dallas, March.

Urrutia, Alonso. 2002. "Aumentó la pobreza en una de cada tres poblaciones indígenas," *La Jornada*, August 9.

Valdés, Luz María. 1995. *Los indios en los censos de población*. Mexico City: Universidad Nacional Autónoma de México.

Valencia Rojas, Alberto. 2000. *La migración indígena a las ciudades*. Mexico City: Instituto Nacional Indigenista/Programa de las Naciones Unidas para el Desarrollo.

Varese, Stefano. 1991. "How Many Native People," *Report on the Americas* 25, no. 3 (December).

———. 2000. "Migrantes indígenas mexicanos en los Estados Unidos: nuevos derechos contra viejos abusos," *Cuadernos Agrarios* 19–20: 49–67.

Varese, Stefano, and Sylvia Escárcega, eds. n.d. *La ruta mixteca: el impacto etnopolítico de la migración transnacional en los pueblos indígenas de México*. Mexico City: Universidad Nacional Autónoma de México. Forthcoming.

Vásquez León, Luis. 1992. *Ser indio otra vez: la purepechización de los tarascos serranos*. Mexico City: Consejo Nacional para la Cultura y las Artes.

Velasco Ortiz, Laura. 2002. *El regreso de la comunidad: migración indígena y agentes étnicos (Los mixtecos en la frontera Mexico–Estados Unidos)*. Mexico: El Colegio de México/El Colegio de la Frontera Norte.

Velásquez, María Cristina. 2000. *El nombramiento: las elecciones por usos y costumbres en Oaxaca*. Oaxaca: Instituto Electoral de Oaxaca.

———. 2001. "Frontiers of Municipal Governability in Oaxaca, Mexico: The Legal Recognition of *Usos y Costumbres* in the Election of Indigenous Authorities." In *The Challenge of Diversity: Indigenous Peoples and Reform of the State in Latin America*, edited by Willem Assies, Gemma van der Haar, and Andre Hoekama. Amsterdam: Thela Thesis.

———. 2002. "Discriminación por género y participación en los sistemas normativos de gobierno indígena: contrastes y paradojas." Manuscript.

———. 2003. "¿Mujeres indígenas gobernando en municipios de Oaxaca?" *México Indígena* 2, no. 5 (September): 24–29.

Ventura Morales, Santiago. 2000. "Condena injusto por prejuicio cultural," *El Tequio*, January. At www.laneta.apc.org/fiob/condena.html.

Villarejo, Don, David Lighthall, Daniel Williams, Ann Souter, Richard Mines, Bonnie Bade, and Steve Samuels and Steven McCurdy. 2000. *Suffering in Silence: A Report on the Health of California's Agricultural Workers*. Woodland Hills: California Endowment/California Institute for Rural Studies, November. At www.calendow.org/pub/publications/AgrWorkersSurveyver012301.pdf.

Wilson, Tamar Diana. 1998. "Weak Ties, Strong Ties: Network Principles in Mexican Migration," *Human Organization* 57, no. 4.

Wright, Angus. 1990. *The Death of Ramón González: The Modern Agricultural Dilemma*. Austin: University of Texas Press.

Yanes Rizo, Pablo. 2002. "Urbanización de los pueblos indígenas y la etnicización de la ciudad." Presented at the "Seminario Permanente 'Ciudad, Pueblos Indígenas y Etnicidad,'" July 9. At www.equidad.df.gob.mx.

Yanow, Dvora. 2003. *Constructing "Race" and "Ethnicity" in America: Category-Making in Public Policy and Administration.* Armonk, N.Y.: M.E. Sharpe.

Young, Emily. 1994. "The Impact of IRCA on Settlement Patterns among Mixtec Migrants in Tijuana, Mexico," *Journal of Borderlands Studies* 9, no. 2.

Zabin, Carol. 1997. "U.S.-Mexico Economic Integration: Labor Relations and the Organization of Work in California and Baja California Agriculture," *Economic Geography* 73, no. 3 (July).

Zabin, Carol, ed. 1992a. "Mixtec Migrant Farm Workers in California Agriculture." Working Paper No. 9. Davis: California Institute for Rural Studies.

———. 1992b. *Migración oaxaqueña a los campos agrícolas de California.* La Jolla: Center for U.S.-Mexican Studies, University of California, San Diego.

Zabin, Carol, and Luis Escala Rabadán. 1998. "Mexican Hometown Associations and Mexican Immigrant Political Empowerment in Los Angeles." Working Paper. Washington, D.C.: Nonprofit Sector Research Fund.

Zabin, Carol, and Sallie Hughes. 1995. "Economic Integration and Labor Flows: Stage Migration in Farm Labor Markets in Mexico and the United States," *International Migration Review* 29, no. 2 (Summer).

Zabin, Carol, Michael Kearney, Anna García, David Runsten, and Carole Nagengast. 1993. *Mixtec Migrants in California Agriculture: A New Cycle of Poverty.* Davis: California Institute for Rural Studies.

Zárate Hernández, José Eduardo. 2000. "The Reconstruction of the Purépecha Nation and the Process of Autonomy in Michoacán, Mexico." In *The Challenge of Diversity: Indigenous Peoples and Reform of the State in Latin America*, edited by Willem Assies, Gemma van der Haar, and Andre Hoekema. Amsterdam: Thela Thesis.

# PART I

# Transnational Indigenous Organizers: Lessons from the Past and Challenges for the Future

# 2

# The FIOB Experience: Internal Crisis and Future Challenges

RUFINO DOMÍNGUEZ SANTOS

> *In memory of my father, Primo Domínguez Tapia, a traditional healer. Thanks to him, I am what I am today.*

Throughout my childhood, I worked in the fields with my father, tending livestock or carrying firewood on my back, carrying water, grinding corn. I also went to the primary school in my village. In 1979 I began attending secondary school in Juxtlahuaca. It was a long way from home, so I boarded with the Hermanos Maristas, a group of Catholic monks who offered me housing, food, and financial help toward my studies. There were thirty of us in my cohort, youngsters from the Mixteco and Triqui ethnic groups.

The monks taught us many things, from household chores to how to live a responsible life. We studied the Bible every day with a sense of social awareness, attempting to understand the injustices our communities were suffering. The Maristas also taught us liberation theology, and I participated in several works of the "theater of awareness." What I am today I owe in large part to them and to my father, because that is how I began to organize people in my village to fight for change.

---

Translation by Adam Critchley.

In 1980 Deputy for Communal Property Gregorio Platón Gil began to abuse his power. He imposed fines on migrants who did not live in the village, and if they refused to pay they were incarcerated, expelled from the village, even threatened with death. He ordered the rape of women and burned down the houses of his opponents. I had to organize people so that we could change this.

On October 30, 1983, after a year of organizing efforts, we decided to peacefully take over the municipal offices and force Platón Gil to resign. Unfortunately, he was armed. Along with several of his supporters, he managed to force me and two of my companions into the municipal building, where we were detained and tortured for almost four hours. I thought I was going to be killed. Then my father arrived, accompanied by virtually the entire village — men and women alike — to rescue us.

This is when the idea arose to create a Village General Assembly to depose this cacique; the assembly came into being in February 1983. In April 1984 I fled to Sinaloa State after receiving death threats. In Sinaloa, we founded the Organization of Exploited and Oppressed People (OPEO) with the counsel of Benito García Sánchez, leader of the Independent Central of Agricultural Workers and Peasants (CIOAC). I then traveled to Valle de San Quintín, Baja California. Although my original intention had been to cross the border into the United States, I stayed in San Quintín and participated in major mobilizations and strikes alongside CIOAC. I finally reached Madera, California, in November 1984, and since then I have been organizing migrant communities.

## CITIZEN RIGHTS BEYOND THE BORDER

Inhabitants of Oaxaca have long migrated to other parts of Mexico to seek a better life. Nonetheless, the economic crisis of the 1980s hit the state particularly hard, obliging entire families to move further afield, across the border into the United States, particularly to California, where a large number of Oaxacan indigenous migrants began to establish themselves and, over time, brought their families as well. This migratory process is easy to understand if one takes into account the poverty of Oaxacan indigenous communities as well as these communities' strong social networks and the mutual support their members give one another.

Solidarity among Oaxacan migrants is not limited to those in the United States; it has a binational dimension. Proof of this is that Oaxacan migrants in the United States are called to participate in meetings with their fellow citizens in Oaxaca regarding the *tequio* (communal community labor) and all affairs related to community development. In the same way, Oaxacans living in the United States have been called on to serve our people by working in municipal agencies or as police. Thus a system of binational civic participation was born; it transcends the local and national circumscription of state laws and breaks through borders in order to attend to the communities' needs in these changing times. We continue to this day with our own method of electing authorities and of governing and organizing ourselves.

## THE FIRST BINATIONAL ORGANIZATION

In the mid-1980s, organizations of Oaxacans began to emerge in California, spurred by a number of factors: the human rights violations indigenous migrants suffer, both in our own country and in the United States; discrimination; racism; unjust wages; our inability to communicate in languages other than our indigenous tongue; and our general lack of information regarding available social resources and our legal rights. Over time, one of the biggest challenges proved to be how to unite these organizations into a single organization that could best assist indigenous Oaxacan migrants.

To this end, the central leaders from different indigenous organizations—Zapotecs César Sánchez Liébana and Rodrigo Ruiz, and Mixtecs Filemón López, Juan Lita, and myself—met in Los Angeles in October 1991 and founded the first coalition organization, the Mixteco-Zapoteco Binational Front (FM-ZB). FM-ZB was intended to coordinate with other indigenous organizations in opposition to official celebrations marking the quincentenary of Christopher Columbus's arrival in the Americas.

After achieving substantial success toward this first goal, in late 1992 we decided to undertake other projects. Among these was a labor training and education project, presented to California Rural Legal Assistance (CRLA), which we planned to staff with indigenous speakers of native languages. The project was implemented in September 1993 in all areas of California where there were high concentrations of Oaxacan indigenous people. Also in 1993 we traveled to Oaxaca and Baja California to organize the communities, based on the experiences of the Comités de los Pueblos. That is how the organization emerged, attending to Oaxacan migrants' problems in the places where we live and work and, for the first time, assuming a truly binational scope.

The FM-ZB soon began to grow and extend to other indigenous villages, including those of the Triqui and Mixe, who called for a change in the organization's name. A Binational General Assembly was convened in Tijuana in September 1994, which was attended by a hundred delegates from the states of Oaxaca, Baja California, México, and California. The assembly participants agreed to call the new organization the Oaxacan Indigenous Binational Front (FIOB), with no reference to any specific indigenous group.

FIOB's organizational structure has several levels. The highest authority is the Binational General Assembly (AGB), which convenes every three years. The AGB elects the Central Binational Council (CCB), composed of ten members from Oaxaca, Baja California, and California; the CCB also has a group of advisers. The State Assembly is made up of members of the State Council and meets before the Binational General Assembly in each of the states mentioned above. The Regional Assembly in each state elects regional and district councils within that state. At the local level, local committees elect a Community Assembly. We currently have three offices in Oaxaca, two in Baja California, and two in California, all with modern communication technologies (email, fax, telephone, and Internet) to support coordination of our binational activities.

## BINATIONAL-LEVEL FIOB PROJECTS

Over the last eleven years, many FIOB projects have been implemented in the three states where we work. Among the most recent and important for Mexico is the Education and Training on Human Rights, Organizational Work, and Law Project, which is financed by a three-year, $180,000 grant from the MacArthur Foundation. We are also receiving support from Mexico's National Indigenous Institute (INI), which provided over 260,000 pesos to complement and consolidate the project. Thanks to these resources, ten people—men and women from the communities—are working to promote justice and dignity for Oaxacan indigenous migrants, both in their communities of origin and in the communities to which they migrate. Specifically, the project aims to reinforce the FIOB's consolidation and institutionalization in Oaxaca and Baja California and to support its activities in Mexico on national and international human rights education and training.

In the United States, we have implemented the Health Project for Indigenous Migrants, which focuses on organizing training workshops on health issues affecting the community and on promoting medical examination sessions to facilitate the diagnosis of diabetes, tuberculosis, HIV, and so on. Although we initially focused on California's Central Valley, we extended the project to Los Angeles in July 2002 in collaboration with the Oaxacan Federation of Indigenous Communities and Organizations in California (FOCOICA). This project, which has four staffers, has been financed for a two-year period with $479,000 in grants from the California Endowment and the Wellness Foundation.

Another important initiative is the Civic Participation Project, through which we organize training workshops on the organization and operation of schools and local government, collaboration with other community-based organizations, and civic participation (see also Martínez-Saldaña's chapter in this volume). The goal is to raise awareness about our responsibility to carry out political, social, cultural, and educational actions for the community and, through collective action, to facilitate social change that benefits us all. Twenty-five people have been trained in Fresno and Madera counties, and, thanks to a two-year, $160,000 grant from the James Irvine Foundation, the project has been expanded to include Kern and Merced counties.[1]

## INTERNAL PROBLEMS OF THE ORGANIZATION

We have logged some successes, but we have also experienced failures. History demonstrates that community organizations are vulnerable to problems of corruption, arrogance, and authoritarianism. Leaders of organizations often forget the Zapatista admonition to "give orders while obeying orders" — that is, before giving orders good leaders should lead by good example and practice what they preach.

Leaders of a financially successful organization may, however, be tempted to misappropriate the organization's resources, especially if these leaders lack the wherewithal to support their families. There are many honest leaders, but we must also recognize that there is also corruption and the abuse of authority, and we must speak out as a first step toward finding a solution to this problem. Accountability, decision making by consensus, teamwork, and delegation of responsibilities are the sacred principles that guide authorities in indigenous communities, and these are the prac-

---

[1] We took receipt of these grants through the Binational Center for Oaxacan Indigenous Development, Inc. (CBDIO, INC.), a nonprofit organization under U.S. and California law 501(c)(3). FIOB established CBDIO in December 1993 with the objective of collecting funds to support implementation of specific projects. CBDIO has its own board of directors, people from the Oaxacan community who are elected every three years and registered with the Internal Revenue Service as the individuals legally responsible for handling these resources.

tices that must prevail in indigenous organizations. Part of being account-able to the bases is informing the community in writing about the leaders' and staffers' activities and the overall plan of work.

## FIOB'S INTERNAL CRISIS

FIOB's first chief coordinator was Juan Martínez, who headed the organi-zation until May 1992, at which time his authoritarianism and dishonest management prompted the General Assembly in Los Angeles to dismiss him. Arturo Pimentel Salas served as provisional chief coordinator until December 1992, when the second congress ratified him as head of FIOB on both sides of the border. Much work was done in that second congress to record the organization's basic documents: its Declaration of Principles, Program of Action, and Statutes, which list the members' responsibilities, obligations, rights, and duties across all levels of membership. Article 14 of the Statutes addresses the risk of abuse of internal power: "Sanctions will be imposed upon organizations, communities, groups, and individuals that betray FIOB principles and policies, promote divisions or slander, act without discipline, or abuse their authority."

Pimentel Salas was to have served as FIOB's chief coordinator for three years (until December 1996), but in the Binational General Assembly held in Tijuana in September 1994 his term was extended to September 1997. After he completed this term, members of the Central Binational Commit-tee began trying to set a date for the next AGB but were met with a series of excuses: there were too many activities, the political situation in Oaxaca was not right for the assembly, and we did not have sufficient money to hold such an event. The coordinator was designated to find additional funding, but this never materialized.

In the state legislative elections of August 1998, an alliance between the FIOB and the left-leaning opposition Party of the Democratic Revolution (PRD) helped achieve the first-ever defeat of a candidate from the Institu-tional Revolutionary Party (PRI) when Professor Romualdo Juan Gutiérrez Cortés was elected local congressional representative for the twenty-first district of Juxtlahuaca/Silacayoapan in the Mixteca region, a position he held until 2001. Arturo Pimentel Salas, then serving as chief coordinator of FIOB, portrayed this electoral achievement as a personal victory, failing to acknowledge Gutiérrez Cortés's work and that of other FIOB leaders, as well as the will of the citizens who exercised their votes en masse to defeat the PRI candidate.

Gutiérrez Cortés's electoral victory attracted many new members to the FIOB and gave it a national and binational political presence. At the same time, FIOB began to receive economic support (approximately US$184,700 between 1998 and 2001) from U.S. foundations for projects in Oaxaca and Baja California. The MacArthur Foundation gave $90,000; the Public Welfare Foundation, $25,000; and the National Endowment for Democracy, $22,000. Funds also came in from the Oaxaca state government, the National Indigenous Institute, and Deputy Gutiérrez Cortés himself. Unfortunately, not all resources were used correctly; materials were diverted to the construction of Pimentel Salas's house. Nobody questioned how Pimentel Salas survived without a salary. Only a handful of his close associates knew the extent of the monies that had come to FIOB, and most FIOB members did not know that Pimentel himself was in charge of implementing projects in Oaxaca.

This situation continued until the next state congressional election. When Pimentel Salas was named the FIOB/PRD candidate for the twenty-first district, the Central Binational Council first congratulated him for his political success and then asked him to resign his FIOB position while he ran his campaign, as stipulated in the organization's statutes. He refused, maintaining that he was both a candidate for the local congressional seat and president of the Binational Center for Oaxacan Indigenous Development (CBDIO), a FIOB project established to receive funds in Mexico and whose board of directors Pimentel Salas had secretly stacked with his relatives.

The majority of Central Binational Council members decided to give Pimentel Salas two options: (1) resign as binational chief coordinator and dedicate himself full-time to his campaign, with full FIOB support, or (2) continue to resist stepping down, in which case all FIOB members would publicly disavow him. Pimentel Salas chose the second option, even after a commission of twelve leaders met with him prior to the opening of his campaign to convince him to rethink his choice. Pimentel Salas did his utmost to avoid meeting with the commission, but they waited at his home (a very elegant two-story building with an untold number of rooms) until he finally received them. They asked one last time that he respect the majority's opinion. He replied, "I'm not going to resign as chief coordinator because this position helps me in the campaign. Moreover, this organization is mine; I have sacrificed for it. You haven't. Go and do what you like. I don't care."

The commission conveyed Pimentel Salas's response to the more than five hundred FIOB members who were prepared to march with the candidate. Meanwhile, we held our public meeting and withdrew our recognition of candidate Pimentel. After we explained our reasons, everyone supported the decision and pledged to visit FIOB communities to inform the bases about what had happened.

After ten days spent visiting over twenty communities, we agreed to hold an event in Oaxaca City to publicly denounce Pimentel Salas's actions and, at the same time, pressure the government to comply with the communities' demands. The event took place on May 29, 2001; over eight hundred people attended, including a dozen municipal authorities. I was named provisional chief coordinator until a Binational General Assembly could be held. A Provisional Policy Commission was also named to coordinate activities in Oaxaca; heading this commission were ten colleagues who had shown outstanding talent and leadership.

Since then, Pimentel Salas has repeatedly attacked the FIOB, using his political and economic power to intimidate our members—all done with the tacit permission of the authorities. The following are some of the incidents we have documented: On August 3, 2001, a day after the FIOB Political Commission[2] denounced Pimentel, Deputy Romualdo Juan Gutiérrez Cortés's office began to receive death threats against members of the Political Commission. On August 13, a manipulated group stormed the state government offices in Santiago Juxtlahuaca on the pretext of pressuring the government to comply with the communities' demands, thus demonstrating their frustration at losing their regional influence. The local government offices in Huajuapan de León were also taken over, as were—ironically—the offices of FIOB, which were sprayed with graffiti. On April 26, 2002, unknown assailants tried to kill Marcelino Ramírez Pérez, a Triqui and a member of FIOB.

These incidents were made public and communicated directly to José Murat Casab, the governor of Oaxaca, through letters and in two private meetings in Los Angeles in May 2002. The governor agreed to issue arrest warrants for Pimentel Salas, but he remains free—and armed—and he continues to intimidate FIOB members and leaders. The government of Oaxaca, meanwhile, has done nothing.

Regrettably, the state and federal governments and their institutions continue to finance Pimentel Salas, despite our proof of his theft of thou-

---

[2] The commission was headed by Gaspar Rivera, the former financial and special projects coordinator of the CCB.

sands of dollars and thousands of pesos. The INI approved financing for two FIOB-related projects, one in the name of FIOB itself, with Pimentel Salas serving as chief adviser, and another in the name of the Binational Center for Oaxacan Indigenous Development, A.C., of which Pimentel Salas is president. We learned of these funded projects via the national newspapers, including *La Jornada* and *Excélsior*, and were pained to see these FIOB organizational names so misused. In 2002, FIOB received a grant of 180,000 pesos for a project on the human rights of indigenous migrants in Baja California. Unlike in Mexico, in the United States there has been a clean break between Pimentel Salas and the foundations and organizations he directed; funding streams to those organizations have been frozen.

On May 13, 2002, in a meeting between FIOB's Binational Council and Xóchitl Gálvez Ruiz, head of the Office for Development of Indigenous Peoples,[3] we submitted proof of Pimentel Salas's embezzlement of funds and his violence against FIOB members. Gálvez Ruiz responded that these were internal problems within FIOB and that nothing could be done. I disagree; in my opinion, fighting corruption and arresting those who violate human rights is the duty of every level of government and of society in general. Without such a response, corruption continues and there is no rule of law.

Even though governments and government institutions may fail to comprehend their responsibility, democratic indigenous organizations cannot close their eyes to their leaders' treachery and deception. For these organizations, which fight for social change and full rights for indigenous people, it would be both unjust and unacceptable to cover up misdeeds in our own ranks. If we are not willing to acknowledge and address serious accusations, at the end of the day we are undermining the very sacrifices that we make for our cause.

On December 13–15, 2001, the fourth Binational General Assembly of the FIOB was held in Tijuana, with over a hundred delegates attending from Oaxaca, Baja California, and California. In addition to electing a new Central Binational Council, participants introduced important changes to the statutes, effectively decentralizing the CCB by creating state coordinators who also form part of the CCB. This modification aims to avoid centralizing power in one person and to ensure that leaders do not remain in their posts beyond three years. We also determined to name in the statutes

---

[3] The meeting was held at Los Pinos, the official residence of the Mexican president.

the agencies through which we gather funds through the law for nonprofit organizations 501(c)(3) in the United States and for *asociaciones civiles* in Mexico.

Of special note, the Assembly voted unanimously to expel Pimentel Salas from the FIOB and demanded that he return the organization's property and funds. Pimentel Salas had been sent a written invitation to state his case at the Assembly, but he did not accept.

Because of FIOB's experience with Pimentel Salas, we decided to register the organization in order to defend its name, history, and objectives. On February 2, 2002, the Frente Indígena Oaxaqueño Binacional, A.C. was formally recognized by the Mexican Foreign Ministry (SRE) and the Treasury (SHCP). Decision making is now by consensus, resources are invested in developing our young leaders, responsibilities are delegated, and there is broad consultation with the bases.

## CHALLENGES FOR INDIGENOUS ORGANIZATIONS

The experiences described here are not unique; other organizations have also trusted leaders who took advantage of their positions. To avoid similar occurrences in the future, we must consider the following:

- Organizations must impose severe internal sanctions on leaders who abuse their positions, and these sanctions should be applied in every appropriate case. Imposition of sanctions should be made public, and organizations that report on such problems should feel neither fear nor pity in doing so.

- All levels of government, all kinds of social organizations (indigenous, human rights, and so on), and society in general must close ranks in a united front against corruption so that such incidents do not recur.

- All state and federal government institutions in Mexico should carefully review organizations' histories and their leaders' backgrounds to prevent corrupt people from receiving financial and political support.

- New laws are needed to punish leaders who divert community funds. Their actions cannot be met with impunity; they must be punished by legal means, and the guilty parties must be made to return misappropriated monies and property.

- Government and foundation support for nongovernmental organizations (NGOs) constitutes the backbone of NGO successes. Nonetheless, such resources must be administered properly and with utmost transparency. Without transparency and proper administration, the result is more problems within community organizations. There is no place among indigenous peoples for illicit enrichment at the expense of the communities. We have long suffered manipulation by the government, and we will not tolerate it from our leaders.

FIOB's current challenge is to continue working binationally to develop its general and specific goals — in countries with different laws, political systems, languages, cultures, and community problems. However, we are confident that we can continue to do our work, as we have done since the foundation of our organization.

Another challenge we face is economic. Despite the fact that our budget in the United States has reached $500,000, foundations are reluctant to give more because they question our capacity to handle such amounts. Nevertheless, we are confident that an audit will give us greater financial credibility and that we will be able to implement longer-term projects with increased budgetary support.

## CONCLUSION

Although the FIOB has enjoyed important successes, we need to move ahead with much more ambitious projects on both sides of the border. Admittedly, FIOB has not escaped the corruption, authoritarianism, arrogance, and manipulation that we so often criticize. Yet these ills are not inherent to our indigenous culture; they are the product of mestizo political culture. Therefore, it is vitally important to "decolonize" our thoughts and practices — both individually and within our communities, organizations, and municipalities. By doing so, we can demonstrate how to govern with justice, humility, honesty, and accountability and work toward greater transparency. It is up to all members of an organization and its communities to question their leaders without fear and to evaluate their daily work. An organization's leaders must be prepared to answer any question; our organizations must be composed not of "untouchable bosses" but of indigenous brothers and sisters who share a common struggle. Finally, we need to deal with each other as equals, acknowledging the capacity and moral authority of each person in their own particular role.

# 3

# Cross-Border Indigenous Organizers: Lessons from the Past, Challenges for the Future

This chapter presents the reflections of Oaxacan migrant leaders in California. Their roundtable discussion led off with Gustavo Santiago of the Oaxacan Federation of Indigenous Communities and Organizations in California (FOCOICA), Ulises García from the Union of Highland Communities of Oaxaca (UCSO), Yolanda Cruz from Petate Productions, and Filemón López from the Benito Juárez Civic Association (ACBJ). Their comments are followed by Andean activist anthropologist Guillermo Delgado's discussant remarks and a comment from the floor by Alejandrina Ricárdez, a leader of the Coalition of Indigenous Communities of Oaxaca (COCIO). These diverse testimonies reflect extemporaneous deliberations that combine historical memories with critical contemporary analysis, seen from the trenches of social change. The roundtable combined representatives of pioneer groups, such as the ACBJ, with more recent organizations such as the UCSO and FOCOICA. This chapter opens an important window on the perspectives of the actors themselves.

## THE OAXACAN FEDERATION OF INDIGENOUS COMMUNITIES AND ORGANIZATIONS IN CALIFORNIA

### Gustavo Santiago Márquez

Somewhere around 1973, when we arrived in the United States, we saw the conditions under which the immigrant community lived. That situation

---

Translations by Stuyvesant Bearns.

has changed somewhat since then, thanks to the Oaxacan community's years of working and organizing here in the United States. My community in Oaxaca, Santo Domingo Yanhuitlán, has been represented in the Los Angeles area for over forty years. As early as the 1950s, our community became aware of the organization of *oaxaqueños* here. Throughout this time we wanted to participate in the struggle of the Oaxacan community, particularly in places like California. When I returned to the United States, I was invited to serve on the board of directors of my organization. I had already been involved in similar activities back in Mexico and had pledged never to become involved again, because we know what this means in terms of dedication and commitment. We know the responsibility that this implies. But one day, a day we weren't doing anything in particular, we said, "Let's just go and see what happens; it's a get-together of *paisanos*; we'll meet some of our friends there." We attended the meeting and I ended up leaving as vice president of the Santo Domingo Yanhuitlán, Oaxaca Association in Los Angeles. Just two months later they invited us to participate in an effort to organize a network among all of the different Oaxacan associations.

I think we should set aside the problems we've encountered during our organizing struggles. We all knew that it would take a tremendous effort to build an organization like this. I just want to share with you some of the positive experiences of this work. Well, we came to the constitutional congress of the Oaxacan Federation of Indigenous Communities and Organizations in California. Interestingly, even the name of the organization was debated with a fervor that is typical of us, the people of Oaxaca. That meeting energized us. Then we attended meetings at the University of Southern California on February 18, 2001; we brought delegates from thirty-two Oaxacan community organizations all the way from San Diego up to Fresno. We also had representatives of the Oaxacan state government and from the Mexican consulate in Los Angeles, community leaders from various Mexican organizations, and representatives from nongovernmental organizations. We left that meeting as officials elected to chair a leadership committee of fourteen people—fourteen people who do their work with passion, fourteen people who, first and foremost, are committed to working for the Oaxacan community and then for the Mexican community as a whole. We left the meeting convinced that we had to work very diligently on this endeavor that had been taking shape for a long time: the unification of all *oaxaqueños* in the United States, starting with California. What was our goal? The goal was simple—to gain a voice, a strong voice that would

be heard wherever there are Oaxacans, and to promote the institutionalization of projects undertaken by these organizations. We have accomplished
many things, but much remains to be done. We know that we are on the
right path. We also set about establishing the "Casa del Oaxaqueño"
(House of the Oaxacan) as a means of preserving our Oaxacan culture. But
perhaps the most important pillar of support for our indigenous people is
civic participation in their community, side by side with those organizations that fight for full rights for immigrants on both sides of the border.

We began our work as FOCOICA's board of directors by establishing a
relationship of mutual respect with the Oaxacan state government. This is
an area where we know we must continue to break down barriers. You all
know the reasons why we left our communities of origin. We recognize
that we have been misused, that we have been diminished. And for those
reasons, we must keep on working, we will keep on working with our
organizations and our *paisanos*. Just because we are sitting at the table with
the governments of Mexico and California does not mean that we are collaborating with them or supporting their agendas. Our participation is a
matter of mutual respect. In every forum where we participate, we state
that we want to be partners, not clients, in projects. We are willing to sit at
the table with anyone who wants, as our motto states, to work for the unity
and advancement of the Oaxacan people. We began this relationship of
mutual respect with the Oaxaca state government, and after much debate
within the organization, we invited the governor to come and visit us. We
wanted him to come and formalize an agreement with us specifying that
all of the projects we have been undertaking for some time now would be
done professionally, with a view to the long term. "To professionalize the
projects" is how we refer to it. As you all know, we are working on a variety of projects in our communities of origin. It was time, however, to give
these works a longer scope, to make them lasting, to ensure that they are
done in a professional manner. This is what we have proposed and have
set out to accomplish.

On July 7, 2001, once again at the University of Southern California, we
signed an agreement with the government of Oaxaca to formally institute
the "Three for One" program. We have also undertaken other important
efforts for our communities of origin. The first such work undertaken by
FOCOICA was in Jaltianguis; it was completed in December of this past
year. Let me tell you, this was one of the best possible experiences, because
after such a long and torturous road, it has not been easy to bring these
projects to fruition.

Before I talk about some cultural issues, I'd first like to say that these kinds of organizations — not just Oaxacan organizations, but all Mexican organizations of this type — have been stereotyped. It has been said that these organizations are only concerned with bringing well-being to our communities of origin, a little bit of the well-being we have found here in the United States. This is the stereotype that exists about our organizations in the United States. However, we don't just concern ourselves with our communities of origin; we also concern ourselves with our people here — our children, the children of our children, the ones who will have a very difficult time returning to their communities of origin. We also organize many activities here in the United States that people are unaware of. In that sense, we Oaxacans worry a lot about preserving our roots.

We celebrate the Guelaguetza, a symbol of our culture, wherever we find ourselves. In Oaxaca this is a grand event. In the United States, all the organizations that carry out the Guelaguetza, no matter where the actual event is occurring, execute it with dignity and respect. We promoted the celebration of the last Guelaguetza at the level that we had envisioned for it and in a setting we had pictured for it. Not because it was undignified for it to occur in any other place, but because the Guelaguetza had to be held in a place, in a setting, where all the great events of Los Angeles take place. We had to overcome a lot of negativism in the process. It was difficult to imagine that the Guelaguetza, a magical festival of dance and music, could fill the Los Angeles Sports Arena. Luckily, FOCOICA, or at least its board members, believed that it could happen, and on May 26 of this year, the Guelaguetza filled the Sports Arena. This was the starting point. This Guelaguetza was the point when Oaxacans began to leave their anonymity behind and, at least in Los Angeles, began to establish themselves within the context of the Mexican community as a whole.

From my point of view, Oaxacans gained real respect from the rest of the Mexican community as a result of this event. Of course, there have been many other factors that have contributed in this, but I believe that this event is what propelled Oaxaca into the community as a whole. Bringing together more than ten thousand people in that arena caused the rest of the Mexican community to think differently. They now think about preserving and fighting for our culture so that we don't lose our roots. They are also realizing that our culture can be demonstrated at any event, even at the world-class level. And they are doing it.

This also gave us a starting point for venturing, now whole-heartedly, into the political arena. We are working hard, among other things, to promote the Council of Presidents of Mexican Federations representing Mexican nationals here in the United States. But that's another story. I want to speak with you about FOCOICA's various projects. What are we doing in the United States for the Oaxacan community? We have educational programs. We are helping children through an organization, through Oaxacan professionals who have graduated from university and can help children from grades one through twelve with any academic problems they encounter. We are working with high school and college-level youth through the Oaxacan regional student committee. We encourage our high school students to attend universities. We are working very intensely with this and have, in each one of these offices, people who are passionate and committed to their work.

We are also working on health care. For over a year now we have had to create our own history in relation to this type of work. FOCOICA has made a strong foray in this field and it has done it with very little funding—US$10,000 with which to start a health education program in the Los Angeles area. This is because of the needs in that respect—health, education, the legal aspects of immigration;... well, you already know them in depth. With those $10,000 we started the health education program. And we are now in the midst of a great effort. They have just renewed our grant—and that of the Oaxacan Indigenous Binational Front, or FIOB—for this project, and we now have $120,000 for Los Angeles. This is shared with FIOB, which has the same amount for the San Joaquin Valley. We want funds, and we are working hard to bring them in to cover the many expenses of our community.

We want to be a different type of organization. We want to change what I believe to be the mistaken stereotypes that exist of these types of organizations. It is crucial that the community understand that we have arrived in this country and that we are just as important to this country as we are to Mexico. That at one specific moment, all of these types of organizations will have the financial stability to make an impression and aid our community, so that they may all learn their rights and responsibilities. We take into account that FOCOICA's work has just begun; we have been engaged in this type of work for only a year and eight months. We have achieved very important things, but we know there is still a long road ahead. We are here not only to share our experiences but also to share our needs. We want to make researchers, academics, and politicians aware of our cause. We want to tell them that we need each other. The community wants to work, the community needs you, and we know you need us too.

## RADIO BILINGÜE/BENITO JUÁREZ CIVIC ASSOCIATION
### Filemón López

Many of you are friends who have known me for some time, but we also see many new faces here, and this forum has allowed us to get to know one another. I want first to thank all the people who made this event possible, giving us an opportunity to share our humble organizational experiences, experiences of people coming from very marginalized areas that lack schools and educational opportunities. But based on our sacrifices, humiliations, and exploitation—all the problems we have encountered along the way after leaving our towns—we have been compelled to do something to better our situation. And that "something" is a source of pride to each and every one of the representatives of all the different organizations that are present. Their pride gives me pride, and I very much value the work that is being done. I know it's not easy; our community is a bit of a behemoth, and it's very difficult to please everyone. And if we only help Oaxacans, other groups complain. They say, "What about us, the Mexicans from Michoacán, Guanajuato? Why do you only pay attention to the Mixtecs?" That's one thing that makes this struggle difficult, and we recognize the work that every one of you has contributed. I'm very pleased to see my Mixtec *paisanos,* such as Gaspar Rivera, a university professor, and others who have long been by our side on the path. We applaud their work and all that the students, the young people, and especially our *paisanos* are contributing to our cause. Since we may be too old to go back to school, you are the ones who will represent us in the future, helping us claim our pensions and so on. Thank you.

I'm going to share a brief personal recollection with you. I grew up in a *rancho* deep in the Mixteca. As a kid, I herded goats to earn a living. I chopped wood for bread to eat. This was no game, and we all wish we could have gone to school. But our parents, out of ignorance, said that only lazy people go to school, and they wouldn't let us go. Here we are today, unable to read or write, and with only a little Spanish. Well, maybe a bit more Spanish, because once we left our hometowns we learned a little bit here and a little bit there. That's why I so admire those who study, because they are the ones who have a good understanding of things.

In 1971 I left my hometown and went to the state of Sinaloa. There we were discriminated against because we did not speak Spanish. Later on, I worked in Sonora, Baja California, Chiapas, and Mexico City. In 1980 I was inspired by the work of Benito García Sánchez, who worked with Rufino Domínguez and another *compañero* in San Juan Mixtepec. Benito was probably one of the first of us to do organizing in Sinaloa—hard work, as all of you know. As I was saying, his work inspired me, and in 1980 I began organizing, bringing together more than 150 people in La Paz, Baja California. Within six months, we got rid of the exploitative work contracts and also freed the workers from the obligation to buy only from the company store. That same year, with no knowledge of the United States and no English, I crossed the border looking for a better life.

In 1981, fifteen of us from San Juan Mixtepec joined a farmworker organization in Bartow, Florida. It was managed by a Texan named Benito López, who helped us get identification papers. Even back then we felt a need to do something, but we had no idea how to go about it. In 1982 I came to Madera, California, where the working conditions were even worse. We were forced to pay for rides to work, to the store, and so on. The labor contractors and foremen forced the workers to live in horrendous conditions. When the job ended, we followed the harvest season to Oregon. In July 1984, there were more than a hundred *paisanos*, mostly Oaxacan and mostly Mixtecs, living on a farm in Oregon, where the labor contractor stole from us by paying less than ten cents per pound of picked strawberries. After this occurred, we organized into two commissions and left for the town in search of legal help. That is how we found the Oregon Legal Services office in Woodburn. Attorney Mary Lewis helped us file a lawsuit against the farmer and the labor contractor on behalf of eighty *paisanos*; we won the suit a year later. Out of this battle emerged a committee to maintain contact with the lawyers, and this was the committee that went on to organize the Benito Juárez Civic Association.

On the advice of Mary Lewis, when we returned to California we sought out California Rural Legal Assistance (CRLA). That is how we began to organize our legal battles. We came to learn that even though we were undocumented immigrants, as workers we still had rights under the law. Over the following five years, we filed about fifteen lawsuits against farmers, job foremen, and labor contractors in California and Oregon for failure to pay minimum wage, failure to pay earned wages, and failure to provide humane living conditions. We won every case covering workers who were forced to live outside under the trees, workers fired without justification, and workers threatened on the job. All these battles spurred us to form an association in Fresno. There the organizing committee found a lot of support. We contacted the board of directors of Radio Bilingüe, who advised us on strategy, and we also opened communication with several organizations, including the Congreso de Igualdad. We established committees in Fresno, Madera, Arvin, and Woodburn, Oregon. We spoke in parks and community centers to raise consciousness about our labor and housing rights, our health and education rights, and our civil and human rights. We also won support from a group of friends in Los Angeles who helped us establish a house of refuge in Mexicali, Baja California, where *paisanos* who had been deported could stay. These friends distributed a flyer telling our *paisanos* that, if deported, they could find shelter and food there.

In those days we had conversations with important organizers from César Chávez's United Farm Workers (UFW). They invited us to join their union, but we preferred an association that reflected our own culture and where Mixteco was the language spoken. In mid-1986 we held a press conference in the Fresno public library, where we announced the establishment of the Benito Juárez Civic Association. Our first order of business was to educate our *paisanos* about the Immigration Reform and Control Act of 1986 (IRCA) and how they could benefit from the amnesty provisions it contained. At the time, there was a lot of fear, distrust, and confusion, which we countered by organizing meetings in people's homes and community-wide conferences with immigration lawyers. We helped *paisanos* write letters and contact their bosses to get verification of their employment. We received a small foundation grant and set up a loan fund from which *paisanos* could borrow to cover the costs of getting their documents in order. The majority of them were eventually legalized.

Over time, the ACBJ was able to establish an office in the San Joaquin Valley. Later we opened a house in downtown Fresno to give shelter to *paisanos* who were migrating from Mexico to Alaska. This house would later be named the "Casa del Mixteco" (House of the Mixtec), and it was here that many musical groups were formed (*cheleneros*, with guitar and violin) and cultural activities were organized. The house also served as a center for fund-raising. In 1988 the committee in Arvin, headed by Moisés Cruz Sánchez, asked for help for the many migrant families that were living outdoors during the harvest season. The committee met with some county leaders, and a few days later shelter, food, and clothing appeared for the families of the Mixtec workers.

In 1989 Radio Bilingüe announced the death of Ismael Ramírez, a young Oaxacan who had been arrested by the *migra*, agents of the U.S. Immigration and Naturalization Service (INS) in Madera, California. The ACBJ and other organizations in the San Joaquin Valley organized a joint press conference and called for an investigation into this injustice. This was the origin of a coalition of organizations demanding an end to INS raids and calling for a general amnesty and for justice to be served in the death of Ismael Ramírez. A few years later, the attorneys in the case obtained a settlement for Ismael's family.

One night in 1992, INS agents entered the homes of Mixtec families and a bar in Farmersville, California, arresting some household heads and deporting others, and causing the families widespread pain, fear, and humiliation. A group of young Mixtecs contacted the ACBJ about these events, and our association organizers helped facilitate communication with the press and the consulate, and also helped obtain legal assistance. This effort, spearheaded by young Mixtec university students, won widespread support among organizations and, after several months, also gained the backing of the local government against INS raids and against the trampling of people's rights. There have been no further roundups of undocumented workers in Farmersville since that time.

The ACBJ has also helped communities in Oaxaca. For example, in 1986 the association organized a support committee for the food cooperative in San Juan Mixtepec. In Río Timbre, where I am from, the *paisanos* earmarked their *tequio* contributions (collective community work) for the cooperative. The co-op stores are still selling their products cheaply and dedicating the profits to community services like electrification and drinking water for the town.

The ACBJ also helped organize public forums in Madera, attended by Oaxaca's Governor Heladio Ramírez López in 1989 and Governor Diódoro Carrasco Altamirano in 1993. At the 1989 forum, the ACBJ and the Oaxacan Mixtec Popular Defense Committee petitioned Heladio Ramírez to intervene in boundary disputes between the Mixtec community of San Juan Mixtepec and the Triqui community of San Martín Ituyoso, hostilities that had already claimed the lives of fifteen people. Ramírez was also asked to support indigenous Oaxacans who were encountering problems when trying to sell their artisanal work in Nogales; the problems were resolved with the government's help. In the 1993 forum, participants asked Diódoro for help in returning to Mexico the bodies of *paisanos* who had died in the United States. They also asked him to provide economic support to some communities in Oaxaca and to help halt the police brutality against indigenous *oaxaqueños* that was occurring in bus stations in Mexico City and Oaxaca. Thanks to these forums, representatives of the state government of Oaxaca were brought into close communication with leaders of indigenous migrant organizations in California.

In 1991 the ACBJ convened several meetings with the Popular Civic Committee of San Diego and the Oaxaca Regional Organization of Los Angeles. These discussions led to the naming of the Mixteco-Zapoteco Binational Front (FM-ZB), which Rufino just mentioned. Later, other Oaxacan organizations joined; the associations got together. The Benito Juárez Civic Association, one of the founders, left the Front a year later.

In 1996, the leaders of a sister organization, the Center for Indigenous Regional Development (CEDRI), asked for our support after their president, Felipe Sánchez Rojas, was abducted by heavily armed men. In a press conference and in a later meeting with functionaries from the Oaxaca state government, the ACBJ and Radio Bilingüe demanded Sánchez Rojas's return, as well as an end to the militarization of Oaxaca and all hostilities against community leaders there. After a week of being held hostage (during which time he was threatened and tortured), Felipe Sánchez was set free along a highway in Oaxaca, worse for the experience but alive. No one was ever charged with his kidnapping, but he has not been victimized again.

The year 1999 was one of continued conversations and meetings with several Mixtec, Triqui, and Zapotec organizations, directed toward forming a new front, the International Indigenous Network of Oaxaca (RIIO). By exerting pressure on the federal and state governments, RIIO has succeeded in obtaining development funds for the communities that make up the San Quintín Oaxacan Network. Many of the ACBJ's current projects in California and Oaxaca are collaborative efforts with RIIO.


## A CHATINO MIGRANT PERSPECTIVE ON CULTURAL PRODUCTION
### Yolanda Cruz

We Chatinos are a small community. We are one of the sixteen indigenous groups of Oaxaca, and we are located in the coastal Sierra. We are best known for our district, the District of Juquila. All other communities in the region know about Juquila because it is where the Virgin of Juquila, famous for her miracles, appeared. We Chatinos, however, do not see it as a miraculous place but as a place of humiliation and repression directed against our communities. I was born in San Juan Quiahije Cieneguilla, eight hours from Oaxaca City. My father helped found this place. My father was a sexton in San Juan Quiahije when a priest arrived one day and told him that progress would never come to San Juan because it is in the highlands. The priest's words troubled my father; as a young man of twenty, he wanted very much to live in a modern place. So he and other young people of the village, who felt that the priest spoke the truth, decided to go and settle in the Valley of Cieneguilla. The older people remained in San Juan. The priest helped the young people contact some recent engineering graduates from Mexico's National University, who came and drew up the plans for a modern town. I am one of the first citizens of that new town, Cieneguilla, a town that continues to pursue modernity.

My family moved to Juquila when I was five years old to join my father, who was a community worker for Mexico's National Indigenous Institute (INI). As a result I grew up among anthropologists and sociologists who had come to "study" — I might say "to be studied," since my family got a great deal of enjoyment watching them learning to cope in our environment. I grew up bilingual, a skill that has helped me to enter two largely incompatible cultures at will. Mine is a world that is both extremely complicated but also very stimulating, as people from two different cultures try to live side by side.

A few years later my father got a new job, and we moved to Oaxaca City. Several young people from San Juan Cieneguilla joined us there, and we all went to find work as house servants. Many of us were lucky and got to go to school as well. Others were less lucky and ended up eating only scraps and suffering physical abuse in the households that employed them — becoming virtual slaves there. After a few years in the city, my father built a house and it became an unofficial community center for Chatinos. The young people would visit on Sundays; some would tell funny stories, others would ask for help in escaping from an abusive employer. The house was always buzzing.

In 1989, my father was assassinated, and this brought a great change to my family. I immigrated to the United States. As Filemón already mentioned, we always had the idea that school was only for lazy people, but when I first arrived I decided I wanted to learn English. So I enrolled in school and I have been going to school for over ten years. While at the university, I was involved in several organizations, helping plan events like this roundtable, or going to Mexico to gather information and disseminate it here. I've always liked to participate in information exchanges.

I've had many choices in my career path. I graduated from Evergreen College, a liberal arts school in Washington State, where I was exposed to a range of different subjects — poetry, political science, some photography. I became interested in informing the community about government injustices. I believe that we can make a better world if everyone becomes informed, but this means making information accessible. I eventually decided that film was the key that opened the communication door. I came to Los Angeles four years ago to complete a master's degree at UCLA, which has a very competitive film school and is close to Hollywood.

My work as an indigenous professional compels me to inhabit different cultures. This often complicates matters, but it has also helped me understand that information must be creative and never boring. Film work has opened many doors for me and my community. Film has a very complicated history in relation to the portrayal of indigenous people, and that is what my first short film, "Entre Sueños," is about. It deals with television's influence on the psyche of a person who is suffering, in this case a young indigenous woman. I am at ease conversing with people, and I think that really helps me.

As a result of my interviews and other work, I am included in "Oaxacalifornia," an exhibit to be mounted in Paris. This exhibit was prepared to showcase the artistic creations of indigenous people from Chiapas, Oaxaca, and Guerrero. Thanks to the involvement of Gaspar Rivera, we have conducted interviews that will present the "voices" of Oaxacalifornia.

As I complete my studies, I want to move toward working with community organizations. I want to document the different kinds of work done in our communities, to make documentaries about successful projects and those that work less well. My hope is that these documentaries will be shown widely so that the communities can learn something about themselves and also learn from the experiences of other organizations.

I have a strong interest in giving honest representations, and I think ethnographic film is the most honest way to portray people. But my perspective is more that of the "people under study" than that of those who are doing the "studying." Ultimately, my goal is to make films that entertain but also to use film as a tool with which to construct a more just society.

## THE UNION OF HIGHLAND COMMUNITIES OF OAXACA
### Ulises García

I am Zapotec. I was born in the Sierra Juárez in northern Oaxaca, and I came to the United States in 1990. I never participated in any events of the Zapotec community here because of a resentment I had been fostering for many years. But once at a celebration in my community in Oaxaca I promised a *compañera* that I would come to a Sunday get-together in Los Angeles and, well, I had to keep my promise. That same day the assembly named me head of the sports club of my community. Well, the first need I saw for my community was that we had no public bathrooms. When we would go to community events, my family and I, my daughters would ask to go to the bathroom, and I would wonder where I could take them, where I could get permission so they could use a bathroom. So that was in my mind when it was my turn to do something—to install a public bathroom, not just for my daughters but for all of us in the community. I had the opportunity after being named head of the sports club, and we worked very hard.

We organized many events. Macuiltianguis has always been a community that stages huge events. It had a lot of funds; it still does. But I noticed that they were always trying to collect more money. If they raised $10,000 the previous year, the committee would try to double that. So at one assembly I asked them, "Hey, what are we working for? Why should I work so hard if these resources aren't benefiting our community?" And then I said, "Why don't we invest some of that money in the community and still leave a little bit here? Keep 30 percent, but invest 70 percent. This is what we are working for." Well, I guess they liked what I had to say, because they listened to me and that is how we invested in the community. We built bathrooms near the chapel. We paved some streets. We bought supplies for the children because our community is very poor; most of us can't afford pencils or notebooks, and this lack causes some of us to drop out of school. So that was one of our proposals for the money—to buy notebooks, pencils, whatever our children needed for school.

It worked, and I was invited to a meeting of the Union of Highland Communities of Oaxaca, which was just beginning to take shape, to be an organization. I attended the meeting as the head of our sports club; my community was asked to send two delegates and they chose me as one of them. The first thing I heard when I got there was the UCSO's history, which I will read to you now.

> The Union of Highland Communities of Oaxaca originated in January 1996 as the result of an initiative by the leadership committees of Santa María Macuiltianguis, and San Pablo, here in Los Angeles. A few months later the towns of San Juan Analco, San Juan Uvina, and Santiago Comaltepec joined as well. In 1997 the communities of Benito Juárez, San Juan Atepec, and San Pedro Jolox were added, and Nativi-

dad joined in April 1998. All of these communities are in the
District of Ixtlán de Juárez.

I came to the meeting with some new ideas, and because I talked about
them so much, I got named president of the UCSO for the year. I told them
right off that I didn't know the first thing about sports, that I had never
been interested in them. But they said it didn't matter, that the secretaries
would help, that they are the ones who know about sports. That's why we
are all here, to help each other. So I told them that, in that case, I'd be de-
lighted to accept the position and would give it my best effort. That is how
my work began; this was from 1999 to 2000.

UCSO's primary objective is to promote unity through sports among
people of the Sierra Juárez who are living in Los Angeles. It organizes huge
basketball tournaments. In 2000 we brought eighty-five teams together, a
number never seen before. That was a huge accomplishment, and I'm
pleased that it happened during my time as president. We've done other
things along those lines. One thing that I'm very proud of is that we've
been able to include children; in the past the events had all been for young
adults. Since we had to charge an entrance fee as a way of building up a
fund, the games only attracted the players, their wives, and their friends.
But I had this vision, and I told the committee that if what we were doing
was to raise funds to give mutual support among our communities, we
had to include the children. And so we began with three kids' teams, and it
turned out really well because the children brought their parents. So we
started with three teams and now we have twelve or fifteen. This has
brought in a lot of people. The number of people showing up for games
has doubled. And I have noticed that sports are one of the most important
vehicles for building unity, not just among Oaxacans but among all Mexicans and people from every country. Sports provide entertainment for the
whole family.

I was invited to be part of a group that wanted something different for
Oaxacans. I remember one of the first meetings we had, when I told them,
"I'm tired of our own countrymen seeing us on the street and saying, 'hey,
look, there goes a *oaxaquita.*'" That's what spurred me to get involved. I am
one of the people who's been here from the start and I want to be here until
the end. But it's been really, really hard. It's been a lot of work. My family
bore the brunt because I was never home. My daughters always asked me
why I went to so many places and never took them. I would always promise to take them one day. When I finally brought one of them with me, she
was so bored that she said, "never again." But my wife has been very sup-

portive; she has tried to understand how important this work is for me. This is very important; we have to consider our wives in this, because if they don't understand, then none of this will work. That's why we must include them. When the federation was formed, we took this into account, and that is why the UDMO, the Union of Oaxacan Women, was formed.

I will listen and learn, and share what I learn with my *compañeros* so that they will be energized to advance the struggle and so that our cause will continue. As for FOCOICA, I have given my full support to its office-holders. My general task has been to cover logistics. I have learned a lot and continue to learn, and I am very grateful for this opportunity.

## COMPARATIVE REFLECTIONS
### Guillermo Delgado-P.

*Aruskipaxipjañanakasakipunirapispawa...*

I have welcomed you in Aymara, a language I am learning and one that is spoken by a million people in the Andes. This Aymara welcome says that we must speak with one another, that as humans we cannot choose not to communicate.

Like Rufino, we have learned that the concept of democracy held in the United States is incomplete. But the activities of our organizations are redefining it and making it tangible. The experiences that redefine our understanding of social reality also advance our efforts to redefine, to perfect, democracy. The interactions between indigenous peoples, their leaders, their militants, and the academy are compelling us, as activists and as people searching for knowledge, to seek new ways to make these ideas matter. One example might be a redefinition of the university. Rufino also reminds us about the redefinition of the nation-state, the need to redefine it in terms of the problems we face. This does not apply only to the transnational area defined by the North American Free Trade Agreement. It is happening everywhere that indigenous peoples survive: the Pacific Islands, all of the Americas, parts of Australia. In this sense, this is a truly transnational movement, and the cases we have discussed are part of a much broader process.

Gustavo has reminded us of the practices of de-colonization proposed by indigenous peoples as a possible response to severe poverty and out-migration. He also spoke about the redefinition of space, the ways in which we define whatever spaces we inhabit. And we know why we are here

today. As indigenous peoples we are entering a time of great remembering — a word that means to recall. But if we look at the word's component
parts — re-membering — it also implies reconnecting, reknitting our communities, reconstructing our dismembered bodies and rebuilding ourselves as a whole, "re-membering." Our history tells us that our indigenous peoples have been under continuous attack. We have seen our
numbers reduced, our leaders cut down. The pattern has repeated over
and over again, not only in the distant past, as recorded five hundred years
ago, but to this day, as collected in the stories of abuse and violence re-
counted by those present here.

Just a month ago three Mayan Indians were murdered in Oakland for
no reason but the killers' desire to do violence. The police have no leads, no
idea of who carried out this horrendous crime or why. They only know
that the victims were Mayas.

Filemón, of Radio Bilingüe, gives us the media's perspective. Over time
indigenous peoples have learned to use technology to advance our interests and protect our rights. Filemón calls on us to question how wealth is
created and how it is controlled. How much of this wealth makes its way
into workers' paychecks in this system that we call capitalism? But under
these circumstances and given our experiences, the law of capitalism is not
self-evident. As we learn more about the nature of capitalism, we find that
it is most evident in the abuse and exploitation of the workforce, the radi-
calism of violence.

Yolanda spoke to us about the consequences of a history of colonization
but also about the processes of de-colonization. Her words remind me of
all the anthropological research that has been done, especially in the
Americas, research that rarely holds much value for solving real problems.
When I read anthropological studies, I sometimes read them solely as literature. Yolanda also talked about actions — both overt and covert — against
indigenous peoples, but also about the value of technology to create our
own versions of history, "honest representations" that are essential in determining who controls our interpretation of history and who frames historical images. To create our own images is to de-colonize the images, to
wrest control from those who would create false images of us.

And last, Ulises offered his view of personal de-colonization, his understanding of who we are and why we are here. In the face of radical economic power, he has demonstrated his determination and his commitment
to community building through his work with children. Racism exists
everywhere — in the Andes, Central America, Mesoamerica, the United

States — and we have long felt its impact. Indigenous peoples have no difficulty identifying racism. Our history, of a people continually uprooted, continually displaced, that these presentations have brought to mind remind me of a saying popular with the Aymara women of the Andes: "The men cannot do it on their own." That is why they configure their work to be done in pairs. The women say that you can't just change one side; you must change both.

As I see it, the labors and actions described in these presentations by transnational indigenous organizers focus very clearly on this view of organization. We are trying to shape new visions, new perspectives, new projects — but in a different manner than before. And these efforts will also redefine the nation-state, not only in the United States but also in Latin America. They will redefine democracy, justice, human rights. We will set aside the notion of individual human rights to embrace that of collective human rights. The experiences and entreaties of indigenous peoples throughout the Americas reflect an advancement. The experiences of these conference participants and indigenous organizers resonate with what is happening in other parts of the globe, with indigenous people around the world.

## FROM THE COALITION OF INDIGENOUS COMMUNITIES OF OAXACA: BETWEEN CULTURES
### Alejandrina Ricárdez

I am a master's student in urban planning at the University of California, Los Angeles, but I have also been a community organizer in San Diego for the past ten years and am co-founder of the Coalition of Indigenous Communities of Oaxaca. For me, one of the challenges we face as organizers is to define what it means to be an indigenous person, to specify what we mean by tradition, and to determine what role women can play and want to play within our definition of tradition. As we work within our organization, we also come across the challenge of a wide range of social problems.

As we try to conduct our research projects and fit them within a development framework, we are encountering nearly insurmountable challenges. Part of the problem is attributable to the outmoded infrastructure of our political systems. But equally to blame are concrete issues such as generational and gender differences and, within these, problems of alcoholism and domestic violence.

What have we learned thus far? First, that the Oaxacan community is not homogenous. We are not all alike. We have different histories, we have different patterns of migration, and we need to learn more about what these differences are. We are beginning to understand these differences. This is one of the goals of COCIO, and I believe that it is also part of our experiences in San Diego with COCIO, where I am the only woman involved in this type of organization. The challenges we face are daunting because, at the same time, we are also learning a second lesson—that this is also a redefinition of our culture. As transnational actors, we need to determine what transnationalism means for us, for indigenous peoples; whether, as indigenous peoples, we are one with all migrants.

My biggest challenge from an academic perspective is to identify a framework within which to contemplate transnational theories, writings— to develop my project and write my thesis as elegantly as possible. But I also must commit to finding a theory with practical application, right? I share the view that much of the work of anthropologists and sociologists in our field is fascinating from a theoretical perspective. And yet the problems in Oaxaca persist. We haven't seen any decrease in out-migration. Even more worrisome are the problems that we confront on a daily basis. So those are the challenges we face in COCIO. How do we, as a migrating population, a population on the move, fit in? How do we see ourselves within the overall image of community? And in what ways have we joined—or not joined—the mainstream community?

What I find most stimulating is to exist in this world of *oaxaqueños* and simultaneously in the academic world, playing a role in each of the two worlds where one may be seen as an outsider. You are no longer seen as fully Oaxacan because you no longer speak the indigenous language and because you are a woman challenging the system.

# PART II

# Indigenous Migrant Civic and Social Organizations

# 4

## Organizational Experiences and Female Participation among Indigenous Oaxaqueños in Baja California

### LAURA VELASCO ORTIZ

The diverse points of origin for Mexican migrants to Baja California[1] have not prevented these migrants from re-creating regional or ethnic links in Baja California through the formation of associations or organizations. Here, as in other parts of the world with significant migration flows, people from the same place tend to group around their common interests.[2]

This is the case for organizations founded in Baja California by indigenous people from Oaxaca State, whose experiences in northwestern Mexico are interwoven with events in their hometowns and across the border, in California. The institutionalization of these organizations has been accompanied by transformations in migratory currents in the border region (Velasco 2002). One of the most important such transformations over the past two decades has been a change in the ethnic and gender composition of the migratory flow.

---

Much of the information and argument presented in this chapter appears in Velasco 2002. This chapter updates results from fieldwork in the Valle de San Quintín in 2001 in an attempt to advance the study of local people's role in the formation of organizations and the participation of women in these organizations. Translation by Adam Critchley.

[1] In 2000, 43.6 percent of the people in Baja California had been born elsewhere in Mexico (INEGI 2000).

[2] For a discussion of other locations displaying this pattern, see Jenkins 1986; Rex, Joly, and Wilpert 1987; Roosens 1994; Goss and Lindquist 1994; Zabin and Escala Rabadán 2002; Hirabayashi 1985.

This chapter continues previous work (Velasco 1996) on the types of activities undertaken by Mixtec migrant organizations and especially the participation of indigenous women in these organizations. On this occasion the goal is to place these organizations within the context of Baja California and discover their specific local characteristics. For present purposes, migrant organizations are considered as collective agents defined simultaneously by ethnic, gender, and generational heterogeneity. The conjunction of these factors, as well as an organization's collective identity, distinguishes the forms of participation of their members.

Keeping in mind the analytical difficulties implied by the articulation of transnational processes in Oaxacan indigenous migration to Baja California, I focus my study on the role of women within these organizations in the two local scenarios where the large subcurrents of indigenous Oaxacan migration in Baja California concentrate: one rural — the Valle de San Quintín — and the other urban — Tijuana. This responds to the hypothesis that transnational forces find their concrete expression in local formations of state capital and power, creating the tangible structural frameworks in which options to act individually or collectively are framed. In particular, I focus on the prospects for women to act within these local scenarios in relation to their participation in organizations.

The chapter concludes with some reflections on the role that these organizations can play in introducing changes at the community and family levels in order to promote women's participation.

## ORGANIZATIONS AND GENDER RELATIONS IN LOCAL CONTEXTS

By definition, the members of indigenous migrant organizations in Baja California share territories of origin and define themselves as indigenous. Within this definition, their universe of action can be very broad, from an orientation toward their place of origin to one focused on employment and living conditions in the places to which the members migrate. The definition of indigenous migrant associations as ethnic agents capable of generating collective action agreed upon by articulating interests and resources from distinct territories (Velasco 2002: 369) can be usefully applied to the study of women's participation.

The literature on migrant associations in various parts of the world presents several hypotheses on the conditions that make strategic action possible (see, for example, Orellana 1973; Hirabayashi 1985: 580–81; Roosens 1994; Rex, Joly, and Wilpert 1991: 73). These can be summarized as an intense communal tradition, the politicization of social networks, and links with the political system in the places of origin, a combination of elements that can be viewed against the backdrop of the historicity of the ethnic agent and, as a result, its identity project. Central features of such a project are the gender ideology and practices that differentiate spaces of participation according to gender.

It is difficult to study women's participation in organizations without considering the ideology pertaining to appropriate spaces for women's action and the changes that migration can bring to that ideological order. Studies of female migration in Mexico and the United States in the 1980s and 1990s (González et al. 1996; Hondagneu-Sotelo 1994; Malkin 1997; Grieco and Boyd 1998; Mummert 1999; Woo Morales 2001; Barrera Bassols and Oehmichen Bazán 2000) produced a series of findings regarding the kinds of changes that occurred in the condition of women as a result of migration. This literature gave more attention to family contexts and migrant networks, and less attention to the role of women in community life as part of the settlement process (Pardo 1998).

However, understanding the way in which the system of patriarchal relations operates in the family context and in migrant networks—as some works on women's participation in employment or political life in Mexico have done; see Massolo 1994; Tarrés 1989—allows us to postulate a correlation between the changes in the various spheres of social life: family, migrant networks, community, political organizations, and political parties. As a case study of indigenous street vendors in Tijuana showed (Velasco 1996), the changes between women's various spaces for action are neither unidirectional nor concurrent. This fact led me to make analytical distinctions between women's different spaces for action and then observe the patterns of change in each one in order to identify the modes of operation of women's subordination and resistance.

For this reason, it is virtually impossible to talk about women's participation in migrant organizations without reference to the gender division of labor in specific times and places, which harks back to the local construction of the contexts of subordination and resistance. This is related, in turn, to the difficulty of conceptualizing "public" and "private" in any universal way. The task, then, is to document how, in concrete situations, these two arenas—public and private—are transformed and defined within migration, even in communities that share the same historical and territorial origin, as is the case for the indigenous migrants from Oaxaca.

In the case of the Mixtecs, we can hypothesize that their migrant organizations maintain a certain continuity with the form of community life

based on the civic-religious *cargo* system of their towns of origin and with
political processes in the town, where women have a specific role in the
division of labor and specific spheres for action. Yet these organizations
have assimilated new interests, resources, and action strategies as a result
of their accumulated migratory experience and their insertion into new
political systems such as California or Baja California. In this sense they
represent new forms in the terrain of politics and identity, including new
definitions of their members' spaces of action according to gender or age.

Among the multiple threads that intertwine to weave an ideology of a
division of labor by gender, a central one is male authority. Assuming that
this principle is fairly universal, the challenge is to identify ways in which
to subvert that authority and spaces in which it is possible to do so within
specific local contexts. Given women's identification with the private
sphere, women's presence in organizations initially led us to suppose an
immediate subversion. However, by analyzing the role of women in decision making within those same organizations, the change in gender relations was less clear (Laguna 1992; Foweraker 1995; Zárate Vidal 2000).

Conceptualizing a human being as a social agent highlights that person's capacity to transform the relations of power that produce subordination and places special emphasis on the decision-making process within
frameworks of tangible options. The structural frameworks within which
indigenous women can exercise this capacity function with a double system of subordination, which is based, in both practical and ideological
terms, on their exclusion from decision making in the framework of patriarchal relations and also in the framework of the Mexican nation-state.

As Pettman (1996: 2) points out for Australia, both women and ethnic
minorities have been excluded from the definition of what is debated in
public spaces, characterized as "political." The case for Mexico is no different; indigenous policies have basically been "cultural," and policies toward
women have generally been directed toward "the family." The historical
exclusion of indigenous peoples and women from the construction of public spaces was accompanied by self-definitions of indigenous and feminine
identities in Mexico, with "indigenous" relegated to the rural and cultural
spheres and "feminine" relegated to domestic life.

This allows us to consider the spaces of everyday life—family, community, and organizations—as politicized spaces and spaces of resistance. The
theme of decision making by the subordinated members of a community
relates to the theme of citizenship. As Jelin (1996: 116) points out, citizenship refers to conflictive practices linked to power that reflect the struggles

regarding who will be able to decide what in the process of defining common problems and determining how they will be addressed. The daily negotiations of women as they move between different social spaces can reveal some of the mechanisms of subordination that operate in daily life and limit indigenous women's constructions of citizenship.

The following section provides a brief description of the local contexts in which indigenous women in Baja California organize their everyday lives.

## PUBLIC AND PRIVATE IN THE LIVES OF INDIGENOUS WOMEN MIGRANTS IN BAJA CALIFORNIA

Migration from various towns in the Mixteca region of Oaxaca to Mexico's northwestern border region has a long history. Mixtec migration to Baja California began with the development of the agricultural regions of northwestern Mexico, the growth of Baja California's urban centers, and the expansion of agriculture in California. Mixtecs participated in the Bracero Program in California in the 1940s, and the first indigenous migrants arrived in the Valle de San Quintín in the late 1950s. Their presence in the cities of Baja California is more recent, dating from the early 1970s. Tijuana appears to have been one of the first border cities to receive migrants from the Mixteca of Oaxaca. Although other indigenous groups appeared, including Triquis and Zapotecs, Mixtecs remain the majority in Tijuana and constitute the most numerous indigenous group along Mexico's entire border with the United States (INEGI 2000). Many Mixtec migrants to northern Mexico, though born in the Mixteca, grew up in Baja California, and many formed families or had children there. As the migratory flow continued, a process of settlement developed, drawing migrants toward areas where others were already settling. From the 1980s onwards this settlement process was accompanied by the emergence of a series of organizations—Mixtec, Triqui, and Zapotec. Their struggles have differed depending on local living conditions, which are associated, in turn, with agricultural labor markets versus urban labor markets in services and tourism.

The rural and the urban zones on the border—especially San Quintín and Tijuana—reflect Mexico's economic and social interactions with the United States. One must view the urban settlement of Oaxacan Mixtecs in connection with the labor market associated with transborder tourism. And Mixtecs' rural residency in San Quintín draws our attention to the evolution of the agroindustrial market for fruits and vegetables and its connection with consumer demand in the United States. Both labor markets—urban and rural—seem to contextualize in different ways the settlement process of Oaxacan indigenous groups, characterizing the local conditions that constrict women's participation and define their public and private spaces.

## THE RURAL BORDER: AGRIGULTURAL WORK IN SAN QUINTÍN

The Valle de San Quintín has been a major receiving area for Mixtec, Triqui, and Zapotec migrants to Baja California. The evolution of the agricultural export market defined not only the demand for manual labor but also the principal forms of migrant residence. Between 1989 and 1999 the number of agricultural workers in the valley almost tripled, reaching 63,250 (PRONJAG 1999). A change in migrants' residency patterns also occurred (see table 4.1). In 1989, 66.7 percent of the workers lived in camps and 33.3 percent in colonias; by 1999 the pattern had reversed, with 56.5 percent of the workers living in colonias. Rooming houses (*cuarterías*)[3] had appeared as an additional option and were housing a little more than a tenth of the workers (PRONJAG 1999).

Table 4.1. Population of Agricultural Workers in San Quintín, 1989–1999

|  | 1989 | | 1999 | |
|---|---|---|---|---|
|  | N | Percent | N | Percent |
| Population living in camps | 16,234 | 66.7 | 20,800 | 33.0 |
| Population living in colonias (including 3,380 living on common land) | 8,120 | 33.3 | 35,820 | 56.5 |
| Population living in rooming houses | — | — | 6,650 | 10.5 |
| Total day laborer population | 24,354 | 100.0 | 63,270 | 100.0 |

*Sources*: INI 1989; PRONJAG 1999.

Camps were the pioneering form of residence in the Valle de San Quintín. Their existence responded to the establishment of agricultural export firms, which rely on workers brought in from other parts of Mexico. According to the National Program of Agricultural Workers, in 2000 there were twenty-three camps in the valley, and they housed a population of 10,711 inhabitants.

---

[3] *Cuarterías* are rooms built by colonia inhabitants and rented to other migrant workers.

Daily life in the camps is organized around the routines and seasons of agricultural work. The migrants, who generally arrive in the valley through their own means, live in camps owned by the firm that hires them; these camps are usually associated with a ranch. An agricultural firm may own several ranches and several workers' camps, access to which is often controlled by guards. The interests of the ranchers or owners define the use of sleeping and eating spaces. In general, it is uncommon to see women alone in the camp; they are usually accompanied by a male relative. The most common kind of camp in Valle de San Quintín comprises large rooms divided into smaller rooms, with communal bathrooms, washrooms, and laundry facilities. A single room can house two families or a group of people, depending on the firm's labor needs in each agricultural season.

As noted above, domestic life and community life in San Quintín are structured in close relationship to agricultural work. This is seen in community personages such as the "*campero*," who is charged with organizing and supervising everyday life in the camp, the use of space, and the needs of its inhabitants. The *campero* is the owner's representative in the camp, just as the *mayordomo*[4] represents the owner in the field.

Despite the restrictions implicit in camp living, family and community life is established very quickly, with gender differences clearly apparent. When the men return to camp from the fields, they play basketball, chat with friends, and, on weekends, drink alcohol and go to town. Men rarely do any domestic tasks during their stay in the camp, and it is common for single men to pay a migrant woman to cook his food or wash his clothes.

In contrast, the majority of women I interviewed speak of other activities outside of agricultural work, such as washing other people's clothes, cooking, selling fruits and candies, carrying water, and making handicrafts (usually embroidery, textiles, or woven palm). Women wash clothes and look after the children, as well as working in the fields.

In the productive process there are two forms of differentiation among migrants: by age and gender in the agricultural camps, and by ethnic condition (indigenous or nonindigenous) in the packing process. In the field, adult men carry out the heaviest tasks, such as placing stakes, fumigating, irrigating, or working as *mayordomo*, *campero*, or driver. The women and children work at picking or collecting. Mestiza women from Sinaloa State are generally hired to pack the fruits and vegetables. Childcare facilities

---

[4] *Mayordomo* also is used for someone with an important responsibility in the civic-religious *cargo* system in an indigenous community.

were installed in some camps in the 1990s, along with elementary schools and chapels. These are frequently maintained by the women.

Despite the fact that the camps are generally near highways, their inhabitants make little use of these roads because of the lack of public transport. Services and shops are usually at least a kilometer away, and this distance would have to be traversed on foot. Therefore, the camp generally has self-contained stores for food and some medicines. Transportation from the camp to the fields is by vehicles — school buses, trucks, trailers — belonging to the owner.[5]

In the 1980s a series of settlements of agricultural workers started to grow up around the camps. Some developed as small nuclei of residents who built small, improvised houses around the fields (Ramírez Morales 2000). The majority, however, appeared when agricultural workers invaded common lands and developed colonias, under the protection of organizations and unions such as CIOAC or SINGOA. This settlement process was driven by the migrants in their search for a better standard of living, and also by the ranch owners' interest in stimulating the settlement of a manual labor force in the region.

According to the information in table 4.1 on the evolution in residence types in San Quintín in the 1980s and 1990s, there was an increase in the number of people living in colonias. Displaced agricultural workers founded thirteen colonias in the valley in 1989; by 1999 there were forty-three.[6] This shift in residence patterns is linked to the appearance of ethnic organizations and their transformations in terms of demands and forms of mobilization.

What is of interest here how this change from the restrictions of camp life affected the spaces of female action. That is, what possibilities did life in the colonias established in San Quintín during the 1980s and 1990s offer women? For the bulk of the population — people linked to agricultural work — the move to colonias brought some changes, which we will examine solely from the perspective of the women's routines. For example, there was a clearer separation between the space of domestic/community life

---

[5] Nevertheless, camp residents, especially men, manage to get access to alcohol, as reported by *camperos*, camp owners, women, and outside institutional observers. Alcohol abuse is associated with two problems: community violence arising from arguments between neighbors in the camp, and domestic violence against children and women.

[6] Despite the fact that agricultural workers founded the colonias, other activities, such as trade and services, appeared over time.

and that of work in the fields. By leaving the camps for the colonias, women were able to organize domestic space independently, to raise chickens and pigs, and to plant and tend small vegetable gardens. While many routines were still associated with agricultural work, by the end of 1990 certain changes had emerged in the models of mobility and consumption once workers were established in the colonias or elsewhere outside the camps.[7]

Whether they work in carrots, flowers, or tomatoes, field hands are driven from the colonias to the fields. Women leave their colonias between 5:30 and 6:00 a.m. and work from 7:00 a.m. to 4 p.m., with an hour lunch. Workers in the carrot and tomato fields are generally paid piecework, which sets the work pace. Carrots, for example, pay 10 pesos per five-pound bag. An average worker digs twenty bags of carrots per day, for a daily average of 200 pesos. Tomatoes pay 2.50 pesos per box; a worker who picks an average of 33 boxes a day would receive 82.5 pesos. If we add two hours of transport time to an average eight-hour day in the fields, we get an average paid workday of ten hours. For women, we must add four to five hours of domestic work, such as food preparation, housecleaning, and provisioning the household with food, water, and so on.

The mobility that colonia living brings involves a greater expenditure of energy in order to organize domestic life. Yet domestic work in the colonias also offers novel advantages absent in the camps. Women in colonias report using domestic appliances—blenders, irons, washing machines—and may even have access to an automobile. They also highlight the free time gained because they no longer have to grind corn and collect firewood.[8] Another innovation is their access to childcare facilities, which appeared concurrently with the establishment of colonias outside the camps. In 1991 there were three childcare centers, and by 1995 there were eight, maintained by the Mexican Social Security Institute (IMSS) and the National Agricultural Day Laborers Program (PRONJAG) and funded through the Inter-American Development Bank.[9]

---

[7] See Hernández 2000 for a detailed description of changes in the consumption patterns that are taking place in the colonias founded by agricultural day laborers in San Quintín.

[8] This change is due in part to the addition of flour tortillas (or tortillas made with both corn and flour) to the diet. This change is also reported in Maier 2000: 235 and Ramírez Morales 2000: 93.

[9] Author interview with Lourdes Brenes, head of the PRONJAG office, Valle de San Quintín, 2001.

Community life has also altered as a result of the agricultural workers' shift to life in colonias. Residents' organizations have emerged that mobilize to demand water, electricity, transportation, and medical and educational services. Many of the demands that mobilized workers in the 1980s — such as access to medical services — have now been taken up by the colonia inhabitants.[10] Women have played a fundamental role in these mobilizations, including in land invasions and carrying protests to government offices. Clearly the change in settlement pattern has brought a new definition of the spaces that women occupy. In the colonias, we can see a marked difference in the domestic environment for women who participate in the informal sector and are forging an incipient relationship with the state, while life in the camps remains completely subject to the work environment and to the contractual relationship with the owner.

The experiences of Doña Ana clearly illustrate this new state of affairs (see Ramírez Morales 2000: 46). Because she lives outside the camps, she can take a job packing vegetables during the months when there is little work in the tomato fields, without needing to move. She can stay in her own home until tomato production peaks again. This advantage was echoed in interviews with men living in rooming houses,[11] who noted that they could be hired by different bosses at different times of the year without having to depend on the relationship with the boss in order to have a place to live.

## THE URBAN BORDER: TIJUANA'S INFORMAL LABOR SECTOR

In the personal and family stories of migration to Mexico's northwestern border, Tijuana appears as a strategic geographical point for mobility to the agricultural zones of Baja California and across the border to the southwestern United States.[12] The flows from Tijuana to the U.S. side, which are driven by work and/or consumption needs, contrast sharply with the southbound flow into Tijuana, which consists almost entirely of tourists.

Tijuana is the spot where the first nucleus of Mixtec migrants formed; it was on its streets that the first indigenous street vendors appeared in the

---

[10] The Social Security Law was modified in 1997 to incorporate the protection of agricultural day laborers.

[11] Interview with Florencio Hernández, president of the "13 de Mayo" colonia, 2001.

[12] Half of all border crossings along the Mexico-U.S. border take place in Tijuana. Tourism and migration have been the two main components of this city's dynamic growth since the 1960s (Klagsbrunn 1988: 16).

tourist areas and the first groups of indigenous gardeners gathered in middle-class neighborhoods. In the 1980s Tijuana was a place where families stayed while they arranged the documents necessary to enter the United States. It was the decade of the Immigration Reform and Control Act of 1986 (IRCA) and the advent of Oaxacan Mixtecs who migrated to Tijuana and crossed the border daily to work (Velasco 1996). By the 1990s, Mixtecs from Guerrero State had joined those from Oaxaca in this border city. Nuclei of Mixtecs had also appeared in other cities of northwestern Mexico, including Ensenada, Nogales, and Mexicali (Rubio and Millán 2000).

Colonia Obrera was the first Mixtec indigenous settlement in Tijuana.[13] In 1989, most of the Mixtec families who had settled this neighborhood had already been there for over four years and owned their land. Their homes recalled the general aspect of the towns of the Mixteca Baja—small houses on hillsides, winding roads across canyons. But the Mixtecs have introduced an architectonic novelty in this urban landscape, with stairs and walls made of old tires, typical of the working-class neighborhoods of Tijuana.

Many families living in Colonia Obrera in 1989 had at least one family member working in the United States (43.7 percent) and a number of more distant relatives living there (Velasco 1996: 55). The presence of Mixtec families residing on this border is linked to both international migration and the region's flourishing tourism sector. The search for work, a place to live, and services—especially schools—defines the settlement process of the migrants in Colonia Obrera.

Women played a definitive role in this settlement process, especially given that a large portion of the male population was absent for long days of work locally or for even longer periods for those working in the United States. Most Mixtec women in Tijuana are employed in informal jobs, such as street vending and domestic work, while the men "commute" to greenhouses in California or to residential gardens or construction sites in Tijuana. This urban-border scenario presents employment opportunities for the women, who can construct their spaces for social action differently than women in the agricultural environment of the Valle de San Quintín, whether in camps or colonias. It is possible to discern in the lives of these "urban" women clearly differentiated social spaces—the house (children, husband, domestic work); the community (the school, childcare center,

---

[13] There are now other settlements of Mixtecs from Oaxaca and Guerrero in Lomas Taurinas and Valle Verde.

market); and work, which is inscribed in public space (street or park, trade union organization, and the political relationship with government authorities).

The different work spaces for men and women, especially work "on the other side," and the nature of informal work present challenges to women, who must exercise their capacity for action in order to get work and to improve their standard of living in the community. For street vendors the challenge is heightened by relationships with other competing vendors, with tourists, and with government officials.

Despite the fact that in cities the line between domestic and outside work is clearer than in San Quintín, much of women's domestic work is affected by their working life and calls for collective organization. A part of their response has been to "domesticate" the work space by taking many domestic activities—childcare, meal preparation, supervision of children's homework—to the street (Velasco 1996).

A study carried out in Tijuana's Plaza Santa Cecilia in 1999 (Wight 2000: 51) enabled me to update many of my findings from 1994 (Velasco 1996). The majority of women involved in street vending in the plaza had come from Oaxaca, were married, had an average of three children, and spoke Mixteco as their first language. The length of their residence in Tijuana confirms that they formed part of an in-migration of Mixtec families that populated several working-class neighborhoods of Tijuana in the 1980s. The family arrangement of informal work reported for the early 1990s still prevailed at the end of the decade.

The workday of women street vendors begins around 6 a.m. Most start the day by tending to their children and husband so that these family members can go about their daily activities of work or school. The women then must go to collect a cart and merchandise to sell during the day, a task with which older children help during school vacations. Selling begins between 9 and 10 a.m. and ends between 7 and 9 p.m., depending on the season and day of the week. The workday is longer in summer, when daylight lasts into the evening and the tourist flow is heaviest. On weekends, when sales are highest, entire families typically go to sell on the street and tend the stalls. The vendors concentrate in Tijuana's tourist zone, along Revolution Avenue near the San Ysidro border crossing. In the 1980s and the first half of the 1990s, indigenous street vendors concentrated along Revolution Avenue and the streets around Plaza Santa Cecilia. By the end of the 1990s, they had spread along the full length of the tourist route that runs from the San Ysidro border gate to Revolution Avenue. The new additions to the vendor populations were Mixtec migrants from Guerrero

State who came to Tijuana in 1993 and established the Valle Verde neighborhood, after the "El Niño" weather phenomenon worsened their chances for survival in Guerrero and forced them into migration.

Because street vending is informal by definition, it is difficult to calculate income earned from this activity. Income and expenditure are organized day to day depending on family needs, such as food, school materials, transportation, and medicines. The vendors' costs include acquisition of necessary permits, payments toward the maintenance of the vending area, and outlays for "help" that is demanded by the officials who patrol public spaces.

Unlike the women in San Quintín, the women street vendors in urban areas have not been able to establish childcare facilities in places close to their work areas.[14] However, the nature of the informal sector allows them to bring their children with them to work without encountering undue resistance, although government officials do object to the children being on the street.

And unlike women in San Quintín, these urban women do not work for a boss—although the spaces they occupy on the street require permits provided by the incumbent government. Recognizing this, the women typically establish a relationship with whichever party is in power—whether it be the Institutional Revolutionary Party (PRI) or the National Action Party (PAN).

## WOMEN'S ORGANIZATIONS AND PARTICIPATION

Since the early 1980s a series of Oaxacan migrant organizations has emerged in Baja California. These organizations—of Mixtecs, Zapotecs, and Triquis—cannot be separated from events under way in Oaxaca or from Oaxacan migration to California. Their immediate antecedents are the migrants' hometown associations, which have their origin in the civic-religious associations of their home communities in southern Mexico. However, the experience of migration itself and the increasing activism of indigenous migrants is altering the profile of migrants' organizations in the border region. One fundamental element in this change is the intrinsic relationship that exists between the type of organization and the local context.

---

[14] The only childcare facility, which has existed in Colonia Obrera since the 1980s, services the entire community.

This relationship to the local context reflects the organizations' initial focus on the daily needs of the migrants, and forms such as mutual service institutions laid the foundation for the emergence of new associative forms that broadened the focus to include the working and living conditions of migrants, agricultural workers, colonia residents, and street vendors. The 1990s witnessed the emergence of fronts, coordinating groups, and coalitions. Although not all have achieved the same level of success, they represent a new organizational stage because they articulate regional, national, and — in the case of the Oaxacan Indigenous Binational Front (FIOB) — even transnational demands.

Until 2000, Oaxaca-origin organizations in Baja California could be divided into three broad categories according to their main interest: labor, residents' rights, and human rights. The organizations were concentrated in three key locations: Tijuana, Maneadero, and the Valle de San Quintín (see table 4.2). The organizations also separated broadly along a rural-urban divide — that is, the agricultural sector versus the informal sector. Although these organizations are not explicitly monoethnic or multiethnic, in Tijuana they are predominantly Mixtec and in San Quintín and Maneadero they are ethnically more diverse. These organizations also differ by social base. Some are composed of activists who have intermittent relations with migrant groups. Others have a mixed membership and work to coordinate the actions of local committees. And still others are constituted around a nucleus of indigenous peoples; being a Oaxacan indigenous agricultural worker appears to be the basis of organizations in San Quintín and Maneadero, whereas in Tijuana it is working as a street vendor.

The residents' and agricultural workers' organizations in San Quintín have been the most successful at building transnational linkages, an area in which the urban organizations have lagged. At the beginning of the 1990s, one street vendors' organization was incorporated into the recently established FIOB, but the relationship foundered when, according to Felipa Reyes, leader of the street vendors in Tijuana, the (male) FIOB leadership demanded that she yield spaces to vendors from Ensenada. When she refused, she was accused of failing to support the organization, which the vendors then left. This conflict between two leaders, one male and one female, leads us directly to the topic of women's participation in organizations.

Women's participation in indigenous organizations differs dramatically depending on whether they are urban or rural as well as by the type of organization in question. Women dominate the street vendors' organizations, both at the grassroots and in some leadership positions. In one case, in fact, the entire leadership is female. In the agricultural workers' and residents' organizations in San Quintín and Maneadero, in contrast, there are few cases of women in leadership positions, and even then the women occupy lesser posts—such as treasurer, head of women's actions, or one of the newly created positions responsible for local organizing activities. Men control nearly all leadership positions in the agricultural organizations and, to a lesser degree, in the organizations of rural and urban residents and in one street vendors' organization.

This difference in participation by gender appears to be related to the way in which local context defines the spaces of female action, as discussed above. Men's and women's stories of migration, work, and political participation reveal that men reconstruct their migration and political participation biographies with little attention to what goes on in the spaces of personal life. The conflict between political life, what they call "commitments to the people," and their family life as partner and parent is resolved in their discourse through the evaluation of their role as a good provider.

In these stories, men negatively evaluate certain vital events, such as the separation of the family, in terms of the need to migrate or fulfill political tasks, but I never found a man who would have left the organization for family reasons. In reconstructing the dilemmas of the life of the organization and domestic life (home life with the wife and children), male leaders displayed differences depending on the intensity of their political participation, which was usually associated with their hierarchical position in the organization.

On the other hand, Mixtec women's stories of migration, work, and political participation show a marked fluidity between the personal, domestic, labor, community, urban, and political spaces—the latter apparently constructed as the space for confrontation with government institutions. The ties of life at home—the everyday schooling of the children, their feeding, their health problems, and even their ethical formation—occupy a large part of their biographical narratives and are constantly connected with the women's presence in community life and work. Unlike the men, these women do not speak of major events in national life, including those that helped build a foundation for the emergence of indigenous migrants' organizations in the region (the 1968 student movement, the teachers' movement in Oaxaca in the 1970s, and the trade union movements of day laborers in the Mexican northwest, also in the 1970s), or about the protagonists that are reconstructed in history as allies or enemies (bosses, local government, the federal government, mestizos, caciques).

Table 4.2. Oaxacan Migrant Organizations in Baja California by Ethnic Composition, Social Base, and Objectives

| Organizations[a]/Location | Ethnic Composition | Social Base | Objectives |
|---|---|---|---|
| Unión de Vendedores Ambulantes y Anexos Carlos Salinas de Gortari (UVAMA CS), Tijuana | Mixtecs | Street vendors | Labor permits, work spaces, ending police abuse of authority |
| Unión de Comerciantes "Benito Juárez" (UCBJ), Tijuana | Mixtecs | Street vendors | Labor permits, work spaces, and ending police abuse of authority |
| Movimiento Unificado de Jornaleros Indígenas (MUJI), San Quintín | Mixtecs, Zapotecs, Mestizos | Activists and agricultural workers | Land, housing construction, attention to migrants |
| Central Independiente de Obreros Agrícolas y Campesinos (CIOAC), San Quintín | Mixtecs, Triquis, Mestizos | Agricultural workers and residents | Residential and urban services |
| Organización del Pueblo Triqui (OPT), San Quintín | Triquis, Mixtecs, Zapotecs | Agricultural workers and communities | Residential and urban services |
| Organizations of Colonia Residents "La Colonia Primero de Mayo," San Quintín | Triquis, Mixtecs, Zapotecs, Mestizos | Residents of working-class colonias | Residential and urban services |
| Coordinadora de Comités con Jornaleros Agrícolas y Migrantes Indígenas A.C. | Triquis, Mixtecs, Zapotecs | Residents of working-class colonias | Residential and urban services; medical services for workers (Social Security) |

| Organization | Ethnic group | Members | Activities |
|---|---|---|---|
| Unión de Alianza de Huitepec (UAH), Maneadero | Mixtecs | Communities | Allocation of residential lots and urban services |
| Movimiento Independiente de Unificación de la Lucha Indígena (MIULI), Maneadero | Triquis, Mixtecs | Agricultural workers and residents | Allocation of residential lots and urban services |
| Frente Indígena Oaxaqueño Binacional (FIOB), California, Baja California, Oaxaca | Mixtecs, Triquis, Zapotecs | Organizations, academics, activists | Implementation of political actions |
| Alianza Indígena A.C., San Quintín | Mixtecs | Activists | Legal defense in labor issues and abuses of authority |
| Alianza Huitepec, El Arenal, Ensenada | Mixtecs | Community | Mutual help, support to hometown, transport of deceased, and collections for community |

a I have omitted two organizations—the Frente Independiente de Lucha Triqui (FILT) and Zapotecos Unidos—due to the fact that, although they have been mentioned by other leaders or have been registered by government institutions, I was un able to confirm their existence during my fieldwork. I have also omitted labor organizations, such as the CTM (Confederation of Mexican Workers), CROC (Revolutionary Confederation of Workers and Peasants), COR (Confederation of Revolutionary Workers), and CROM (Mexican Regional Labor Confederation). These are active statewide, but I found no indigenous migrant or activist who identified them as Oaxacan indigenous organizations, even though they sometimes influenced itinerant vendors in Tijuana. Since the National Action Party's entry into government, these organizations have lost stature with the itinerant vendors' organizations.

This difference in spheres of concern, together with the men's partisan participation, casts women as being oriented toward local scenarios, on a community and family scale, in their involvement in political life,[15] raising the possibility of tensions arising between the demands of their family lives as mothers and wives, and their lives as workers, migrants, and members of political communities.

This tension, which appears to be generalized among indigenous migrant women, is specific to the local conditions in which their participation occurs. Women's life in the camps offers few options for mobilization, but gender does not seem to be the key factor here. A more likely explanation is their condition of class and ethnicity; they are part of families whose livelihood depends on intensive and seasonal agricultural work.

These conditions appear to change when families move from camps to colonias or neighborhoods in San Quintín. Women's participation has been a central part of the process of urbanization in the Valle de San Quintín, but thus far there have been no women in a top leadership position within a colonia. That is, women mobilize, not as women, but as agricultural workers trying to settle and have land and a house to live in. The case of the street vendors allows us to compare the impact of local conditions — the labor market based on border tourism — on collective action among indigenous women, the majority of whom are from Oaxaca. These women have managed to achieve a direct relationship with government officials and have developed linguistic and political skills that remove them from the domestic sphere.

If these local conditions function as structural constraints that define how women participate in organizations, there are also other, ideological constraints that serve to highlight their condition of gender subordination and which act on women's movement between the domestic and external spheres. Such ideological constraints continue to function even when women participate fully and continuously or assume a degree of responsibility within the organizations.

These constraining mechanisms find expression in the women's need to seek permission from a male authority, which appears to be a pillar of the sexual division of labor. In order to work outside the home, or even within the home, a woman must have her husband's approval and explicit permission. This permission becomes even more important for women's participation in political life. Women require permission to attend meetings, to

---

[15] An exception is Felipa Reyes, the only woman leader among the organizations of itinerant vendors in Tijuana.

carry out organizational tasks, to be absent from the home, to extend the length of the workday. Women leaving the home can win their partners' approval but only as long as they do not neglect their domestic chores. That is, permission to work or participate politically outside the home is not equivalent to a redistribution of household tasks; it is merely "the husband's consent that the woman be outside the house as long as she does not neglect her obligations as a woman."

Moreover, there is supervision to ensure that the norm is being observed; some family member, typically the husband's mother, would be the observer whose keen eye guaranteed compliance with the norms defining gender roles in the home. But the involvement of mothers-in-law in this role means that the women not only have to overcome opposition from "the husband," who could be excused because he was "a man," but it can also breed conflict toward figures of the same sex. And for single women, in both the rural and urban cases, the entire community becomes the overseer of their behavior outside the home. One agricultural worker, a mother and separated from her husband, told how she was called a "tramp" by members of her community because she had left the house after returning from the fields.

The degree of "license" granted to a woman will depend on her stage, and her family's stage, in the life cycle, although these two factors are not determinant on their own. That is, permission for participation in activities outside the home is more likely to be given to an older woman whose children are grown than to a young woman with small children in the household. And stage in the life cycle and the associated domestic situation also influence how willing women are to press for the freedom to involve themselves in activities outside the home.

Men in leadership positions frequently mention women's lack of participation as an organizational problem, noting that women cannot give the organization their full attention because they must attend to the duties of home and family. They attribute this difficulty to "macho husbands who won't let their wives participate."[16] Similarly, the women I interviewed identified their partners' withholding of permission as an obstacle to their participation in organizations.

This ideology of gender-differentiated spaces of action responds to the same logic that underlies the ideology of a gender division of labor anywhere outside the domestic sphere—including in the workplace and in indigenous migrants' organizations. The solution that women in indige-

---

[16] During my field interviews, I was found no wife or partner of a leader who was an activist or had a leadership position within any of the organizations studied.

nous organizations and committees and in street vendors' associations have hit upon, one that is seconded by the male leaders of indigenous migrant organizations, is not to question the legitimacy of the prevailing order, in which male authority dominates. Rather, the solution is to encourage men to give this permission so that women can temporarily leave the domestic sphere to participate in the workplace and in organizations.

Leaders and representatives of indigenous migrant organizations have advocated for women's involvement, calling on their fellow *paisanos* to allow their wives to participate. As these organizations have become increasingly institutionalized, the male leaderships have gained legitimacy. According to the women I interviewed, they have also begun heeding the calls of the women in the organizations. The leaders of these organizations frequently mediate family conflicts, including problems that arise when a husband is unwilling to allow his wife to leave the house in order to participate in the organization, but also in cases of domestic violence toward women and children. The politicization of these themes at the heart of the organizations is clearly visible in transnational organizations, but it has been less obvious in organizations with a more local character.

Most of the spaces that have opened to women have come within the framework of alliances between interethnic and transnational organizations.[17] Although few in number and somewhat isolated from one another, these openings are of great importance because they have brought to the political arena issues that have generally been considered private. At the same time, transnational links between organizations have allowed experiences of participation to be transferred from different political systems, such as the U.S. system, presenting new challenges and opportunities for local-level organizations. In bringing issues such as domestic violence and women's dependence on their husbands' permission to participate in activities outside the home, we can see a questioning of the kind of community identity, in ethnic terms, that is being constructed in the organizations.

---

[17] One example of a space that opened for reflection on these themes in Baja California within the framework of transnational relations with organizations in the United States is the Women's Meeting of the Mixteco-Zapoteco Binational Front, on September 2, 1994, in Tijuana, on the eve of the formation of the FIOB. Further, with the FIOB's support, a workshop was created for training promoters of reproductive health in Maneadero. The workshop was part of an action-research project carried out by a research center in Tijuana. Six community promoters were trained in reproductive health (Maier n.d.).

## SOME CONCLUSIONS

The local conditions in which domestic, labor, community, and political spaces are constructed are fundamental to our understanding of indigenous migrants' organizational forms and indigenous migrant women's participation. Local conditions consolidate global processes—such as capital investment and conditions for the reproduction of the workforce—in the lives of these migrants, constituting a framework of constraint in social and gender relations.

In addition to restrictions inherent in the local context, female participation in Oaxacan indigenous organizations is subject to mechanisms of gender subordination, which operate in the domain of male authority over women's spaces of action. In the case of Oaxacan indigenous women, this mechanism is expressed in the permission women must seek from the male authorities in the family, the community, and the organizations themselves.

Therefore, the framework of possibilities and options for women is even more constricted, resulting in a double limitation on their participation. We can view the permission requirement as a mechanism of power over women; it expresses a social order in which spaces in which people in migrant communities can act are differentiated by gender. It appears that the need to obtain permission expresses the ideological nucleus upon which gender relations in these communities are based and in which male authority is internalized as legitimate as much by women as by men, in the house, in the street, and in the organizations.

Women's participation in various spaces of action is continuously conditioned by their life stage. Marriage and the birth of children mark a period of absence from community and organizational spaces. As their children grow up, women's possibilities for participation increase, although this expanded range of action can be reversed once a mother's children have children and she is again needed to provide help in the domestic sphere. In this sense, the domestic sphere must be viewed as a source of inequality in terms of the workload for women.

Despite the fact that migrants' organizations are actively promoting and trying to facilitate female leadership, these same organizations never question the social order that legitimizes male authority over women. Negotiations take place with the male authority to gain recognition of the importance of women's participation, but the gender division of labor that assigns greater workloads to women and works to ensure that women comply with control mechanisms like the permission requirement is not questioned. Nevertheless, the collective discussions that women have had within the indigenous migrants' organizations about the permission requirement have brought to light other high-profile issues in the transnational political arena—such as alcoholism, unequal workloads within the family, and domestic violence. These discussions, and their implicit questioning of social relations in domestic life, acknowledge such issues as negative emblems of ethnicity and allow for forms of action to be proposed that are not necessarily directed against "others" who are different but rather are focused on taking action within the community itself.

## References

Barrera Bassols, Dalia, and Cristina Oehmichen Bazán, eds. 2000. *Migración y relaciones de género en México*. Mexico City: GIMTRAP, A.C/Instituto de Investigaciones Antropológicas, Universidad Nacional Autónoma de México.

Foweraker, Joe. 1995. *Theorizing Social Movements*. London: Pluto.

González, Soledad, Olivia Ruiz, Laura Velasco, and Ofelia Woo. 1996. *Mujeres, migración y maquila en la frontera norte de México*. Mexico City: El Colegio de México/El Colegio de la Frontera Norte.

Goss, John, and Bruce Lindquist. 1994. "Conceptualizing International Labor Migration: A Structuration Perspective," *International Migration Review* 39, no. 2: 317–51.

Grieco, Elizabeth, and Monica Boyd. 1998. *Women and Migration: Incorporating Gender into International Migration Theory*. Tallahassee, Fl.: Center for the Study of Population, Florida State University.

Hernández, Cuitlahuac. 2000. "Prácticas ambientales y migración indígena en el Valle de San Quintín, B.C." Master's thesis, El Colegio de la Frontera Norte.

Hirabayashi, Lane. 1985. "Formación de asociaciones de pueblos de migrantes a México: mixtecos y zapotecos," *América Indígena* 14, no. 3 (July–September): 579–98.

Hondagneu-Sotelo, Pierrette. 1994. *Gendered Transitions: Mexican Experience of Immigration*. Berkeley: University of California Press.

INEGI (Instituto Nacional de Estadística, Geografía e Informática). 2000. *XII Censo General de Población y Vivienda*. Mexico: Dirección General de Estadística.

INI (Instituto Nacional Indigenista). 1989. *Reporte del módulo operativo del Instituto Nacional Indigenista*. Mexico.

Jelin, Elizabeth. 1996. "La construcción de la ciudadanía: entre la solidaridad y la responsabilidad." In *Construir la democracia: derechos humanos, ciudadanía y sociedad en América Latina*, edited by Elizabeth Jelin and Eric Hirshberg. Caracas, Venezuela: Nueva Sociedad.

Jenkins, Shirley. 1986. *Ethnic Associations and the Welfare State*. New York: Columbia University Press.

Klagsbrunn, Víctor. 1988. *Tijuana, cambio social y migración*. Tijuana: El Colegio de la Frontera Norte.

Laguna, Maetzin. 1992. "Bases, activistas y dirigentas: mujeres de la Unión de Colonos de Xalpa." In *Mujeres y ciudades: participación social, vivienda y vida cotidiana*. Mexico City: El Colegio de México.

Maier, Elizabeth. 2000. "La migración como mediación en las relaciones de género: de obreras agrícolas indígenas de Oaxaca a residentes en Baja California." In *Migración y relaciones de género en México*, edited by Dalia Barrera Bassols and Cristina Oehmichen Bazán. Mexico City: GIMTRAP, A.C/Instituto de Investigaciones Antropológicas, Universidad Nacional Autónoma de México.

———. n.d. "Encuentros, empoderamiento y construcción de análisis a través de la investigación acción." In *Investigación-acción en salud reproductiva: lecciones de la frontera México-Estados Unidos*, edited by Catalina A. Denman, Janice Monk, and Norma Ojeda de la Peña. Tucson, Ariz.: Southwest Institute for Research on Women/El Colegio de Sonora. Forthcoming.

Malkin, Victoria. 1997. "Reproduction of Gender Relations in the Mexican Community of New Rochelle, N.Y." Presented at the Colloquium of Regional Anthropology and History, El Colegio de Michoacán, Zamora, October 22–24.

Massolo, Alejandra. 1994. "Política y mujeres: una peculiar relación." In *Los medios y los modos: participación política y acción colectiva de las mujeres*, edited by Alejandra Massolo. Mexico City: El Colegio de México.

Mummert, Gail, ed. 1999. *Fronteras fragmentadas*. Zamora: El Colegio de Michoacán.

Orellana, Carlos. 1973. "Mixtec Migrants in Mexico City. A Case Study of Urbanization," *Human Organization* 32: 273–83.

Pardo, Mary S. 1998. *Mexican American Women Activists: Identity and Resistance in Two Los Angeles Communities*. Philadelphia, Penn.: Temple University Press.

Pettman, Jan Jindy. 1996. "Second-Class Citizens? Nationalism, Identity and Difference in Australia." In *Gender, Politics and Citizenship in the 1990s*, edited by Barbara Sullivan and Gillian Whitehouse. Sydney, Australia: University of New South Wales Press.

PRONJAG (Programa Nacional de Jornaleros Agrícolas). 1999. *Panorámica general de la problemática de los jornaleros agrícolas en el valle de San Quintín, Baja California*. Ensenada, B.C., April.

Ramírez Morales, César. 2000. *Buscando la vida: mujeres indígenas migrantes*. Mexico City: Instituto Nacional Indigenista/Programa de las Naciones Unidas para el Desarrollo.

Rex, John, Daniéle Joly, and Czarina Wilpert, eds. 1987. *Immigrant Associations in Europe*. Aldershot, U.K.: Gower.

Roosens, Eugeen. 1994. "The Primordial Nature of Origins in Migrant Ethnicity." In *The Anthropology of Ethnicity: Beyond "Ethnic Groups and Boundaries,"* edited by Hans Vermeulen and Cora Govers. Amsterdam: Het Spinhuis.

Rubio, Miguel Ángel, and Saúl Millán. 2000. "Migrantes mixtecos en Baja California." In *La migración indígena en México: estado de desarrollo económico y social de los pueblos indígenas de México*, edited by Miguel Ángel Rubio, Saúl Millán, and Javier Gutiérrez. Mexico: Instituto Nacional Indigenista/ Programa de las Naciones Unidas para el Desarrollo.

Tarrés, María Luisa. 1989. "Más allá de lo público y privado: reflexiones sobre la participación social y política de las mujeres de clase media en Ciudad Satélite." In *Trabajo, poder y sexualidad*, edited by Orlandina de Oliveira. Mexico City: El Colegio de México.

Velasco Ortiz, Laura. 1996. "La conquista de la frontera norte: vendedoras ambulantes indígenas." In *Estudiar a la familia, comprender a la sociedad*. Mexico City: PUEG/CONAPO/DIF/Universidad Autónoma Metropolitana-Azcapotzalco.

———. 2002. *El regreso de la comunidad: migración indígena y agentes étnicos: los mixtecos en la frontera México–Estados Unidos*. Tijuana: El Colegio de la Frontera Norte.

Wight, Heather. 2000. "Mixtecas en la Frontera: Migrant Women, Informal Work, and Household Strategies in Tijuana." Master's thesis, Western Washington University.

Woo Morales, Ofelia. 2001. *Las mujeres también nos vamos al norte*. Guadalajara: Universidad de Guadalajara.

Zabin, Carol, and Luis Escala Rabadán. 2002. "From Civic Association to Political Participation: Mexican Hometown Associations and Mexican Immigrant Political Empowerment in Los Angeles," *Frontera Norte* 14 (January–June): 7–43.

Zárate Vidal, Margarita. 2000. "Participación política, migración y mujer en Michoacán." In *Migración y relaciones de género en México*, edited by Dalia Barrera Bassols and Cristina Oechmichen Bazán. Mexico City: GIMTRAP, A.C./Instituto de Investigaciones Antropológias, Universidad Nacional Autónoma de México.

# 5

# Building the Future: The FIOB and Civic Participation of Mexican Immigrants in Fresno, California

JESÚS MARTÍNEZ-SALDAÑA

This chapter analyzes the civic role of immigrants from Oaxaca State who live in the metropolitan area of Fresno, California. Fresno lies in the heart of the San Joaquin Valley, the most important agricultural region of the United States and home to a large concentration of Mexican immigrants. I specifically analyze the local activities of the Oaxacan Indigenous Binational Front (FIOB). This organization, which was founded in 1991, has a strong organizational presence in both Mexico and the United States. Before I begin, it is important to point out the limits of this essay; it is not my intention to cover the totality of what other researchers have called the transnational political space of international migrants (see, for example, Rivera-Salgado 1999) or to examine the achievements of other important institutions created by *oaxaqueños* in the Fresno area, such as Radio Bilingüe and the Benito Juárez Civic Association (ACBJ).

My principal argument is that FIOB's local history is evidence of a long trajectory of political participation that transcends models of liberal citizenship found in Mexico and the United States. With their everyday activities, migrant workers affiliated with this organization and its leaders perform multiple and simultaneous roles that come close to what Soysal (1994) has called "postnational citizenship." In doing so, an organization such as FIOB challenges widely held stereotypes of Mexican and *oaxaqueño* migrants. This organization's activities have transformed the local community and paved the way for the possibility of a more inclusive social order better equipped to represent social diversity.

The FIOB's daily activities change the local meaning of community membership. This involves working to help *oaxaqueño* immigrants gain access to the public and private resources available to other social sectors, as well as promoting the rights and interests linked to Mexican indigenous identity. To do so, FIOB frequently organizes activities that help to preserve and celebrate indigenous and *oaxaqueño* interests. In various ways, organizations such as FIOB invite us to broaden the meaning of democracy and community membership to take into account contemporary migration.

## MIGRANT POPULATIONS AND THEIR CONTRIBUTION TO THE MEXICAN NATION

*Oaxaqueño* migration forms part of Mexican migration to the United States, a phenomenon that produced a massive migration stream during the twentieth century. Over this period, Mexican migrants made important and valuable contributions to Mexico by defending its political and economic sovereignty and promoting reforms that have advanced the development of the Mexican people. Sadly, this part of Mexican history is unknown to much of the population and ignored by the nation's privileged sectors.

Attempting to correct this blind spot, Juan Gómez-Quiñónes and others have worked to document the historic relationship between Mexico and its neighbor to the north (see Gómez-Quiñones 1994). Ann Craig has shown that, following the Mexican Revolution, most leaders of the *agrarista* movement in Los Altos, Jalisco, had some experience of migration to the United States (Craig 1983). In a current research project I found proof of the incredible support, on the part of Mexicans in the United States, for the oil expropriation carried out by President Lázaro Cárdenas in 1938, an act that has been widely seen as an ultimate expression of Mexican national sovereignty. Not only did migrants support the presidential decrees of March 18, 1938, but they also contributed funds to cover the debt that arose from this act, thereby helping to strengthen the country's economic independence (see Martínez-Saldaña 1999a).

Migrant participation was also crucial during the 1910–1920 Mexican Revolution. Francisco I. Madero issued his call to arms from the United States, where the Mexican community offered him—and many other revolutionary and counterrevolutionary forces—shelter and support. An outstanding case involves the Flores Magón brothers, originally from Oaxaca, who were forced into exile for fighting against the Porfirista dictatorship.

The brothers, while in the United States, became important precursors of the Mexican Revolution (Raat 1993). The support offered by their followers, known as *magonistas*, established an important precedent, creating support for Madero and his overthrow of Porfirio Díaz, who was also from Oaxaca.

Before, during, and after the revolution, migrants clearly were concerned with the events that took place in their homeland. The long-standing importance of the links between migrants and Mexico can be seen in the creation of mutualist organizations, frequently named after national heroes, that promoted solidarity among Mexicans. In many ways, love for their country and the desire to contribute to its development have been inherited and reproduced by the numerous migrant clubs that currently exist in the United States.

Included in the migrant sector are people who are not normally associated with the migration process but who were forced to leave Mexico for economic reasons or to protect their personal safety during periods of political change. Among these is a figure who is the very symbol of constitutionality and sovereignty in Mexico, a leader who represents liberal ideology and principles still evoked by contemporary political forces: the *zapoteco* Benito Juárez. Juárez had been governor of Oaxaca and was director of the Oaxaca Institute for Science and Arts in 1853, when Antonio López de Santa Ana took office and began an attack against liberal leaders. Juárez was banished and went into exile in New Orleans, where he met other liberals, including Melchor Ocampo, Ponciano Arriaga, and José María Mata. As has been noted by many researchers, Juárez arrived in New Orleans without money or knowledge of English. He worked in a cigar factory, and, like other migrants who labored to improve their situation, Juárez seems to have had an "unbreakable faith" that helped him overcome the "adverse circumstances" he faced when forced to leave Mexico (Fernández Ruiz 1986: 69–71).

While in exile, Juárez and his circle tried to keep up with events in Mexico and to establish contact with other liberal forces, such as Juan Álvarez. Juárez's contributions upon his return to Mexico in 1855 are immense and of undeniable historical value. Yet who could have imagined the magnitude of these contributions when Juárez was carrying out his role as a *zapoteco* worker in New Orleans? How many women and children are in similar situations and struggle daily to improve themselves as human beings and citizens? How many migrants are forced to carry out multiple and contrasting social roles so as to allow their personal aspirations to coincide with the material needs that must be addressed on a day-to-day basis?

Fresno and other regions with large migrant communities offer countless examples of the effort to make human potential coincide with daily reality. Concepción Pacheco provides a concrete example of the multiple and sometimes contrasting social roles that *oaxaqueño* migrants play. She served as master of ceremonies during the Guelaguetza 2002 ceremonies that took place in a high school auditorium in Fresno on August 18, 2002. Drawing more than a thousand people from northern and southern California, the event, the fourth of its kind, was the region's largest and most important *oaxaqueño* celebration. During the event, Concepción moved with ease on stage, demonstrating charisma, talent, and a capacity to improvise. She went through several costume changes, transmitting through her attire additional evidence of the artistic contributions made by *oaxaqueños*.

On stage at the microphone, Concepción was an eloquent and dignified representative of the local *oaxaqueño* community. Someone observing her in the role of master of ceremonies would be hard-pressed to visualize Concepción in her daily life, where she earns her living as a cleaning lady in the Fresno area. In much the same way, those who see her cleaning homes would be unlikely to view Concepción as vital for the success of one of the most important cultural celebrations for the *oaxaqueño* community in California. At first sight many might find it hard to believe that a domestic worker like Concepción is becoming a protagonist of the historical changes created by *oaxaqueño* migrants in areas like Fresno.

Like Concepción, there are other Oaxacan migrants in Fresno who daily prove their capacity to make notable contributions to the region's social, cultural, and political development:

- Leoncio Vásquez came to the United States as a child. He now works as operations chief for the Binational Center for Indigenous Oaxacan Development (CBDIO), a nonprofit organization created by FIOB to carry out social programs. He also edits the *El Tequio* bulletin and travels throughout California as a trilingual interpreter (Spanish, English, Mixteco), helping Mixtecs gain access to adequate services in courts, hospitals, and other private and public institutions.

- Oralia Maceda, also a young staffer at CBDIO, has developed multiple projects for FIOB. She has played an active part in increasing the role of women within the organization and in society in general, and is at ease dealing with parents, authorities, businesspeople, and the media.

- Rosa López, a young wife and mother, has played an outstanding role as part of the local FIOB committee in Madera. She has carried out intensive fund-raising and works with local authorities to improve the institutional services offered to migrants from Oaxaca. She also works to keep *oaxaqueño* migrants in Madera informed and organized.

- Irma Luna, a longtime member of FIOB, has done important organizing and fund-raising. She also offers trilingual interpreting services and holds an outreach job with the California Rural Legal Assistance office in Fresno.

- Jorge Sanjuan is a young member of the CBDIO board of directors. He works in the construction industry and is also a poet who celebrates his *oaxaqueño* heritage. Jorge became a pioneer in the arts with the establishment of a folk dance group that trains young people to preserve and celebrate traditional dance and music from their native country.

In their own way, the members of FIOB are trying to build spaces that will allow for the development of their individual and collective potential by strengthening their links to their ethnic group, their home state, the Mexican American community, and American society. Their activities are transforming Fresno and have redefined the concept of local and national community in Mexico and the United States.

## MEMBERSHIP AND MIGRATION: THE DEBATE AMONG MIGRANTS

Not all migrants conceive of their relationship with Mexico and the United States in the same way. This has forced FIOB and its leaders to become involved in the debates surrounding naturalization laws and the fight for political rights for Mexican migrants. This became evident on June 17, 1995, when *La Opinión*, California's leading Spanish-language newspaper, published two letters to the editor from Mexican migrants on the issue of a possible constitutional reform in Mexico that would allow citizens based in the United States to hold dual citizenship. This debate had gained momentum after California voters passed Proposition 187 in November 1994.

What followed was a proposal, advanced by Mexican intellectuals and officials, for the non-loss of Mexican nationality. The alleged aim of this reform was to make it easier for Mexican migrants in the United States to naturalize as U.S. citizens and thus be better able to protect migrants' rights in their host country (Bustamante 1995). On the other side of this debate, a number of migrant organizations revived the idea of allowing

Mexicans abroad to vote in presidential elections in Mexico. This was the main axis of a different dual citizenship proposal, one that would explicitly include political rights. The letters published in *La Opinión* summarized the discussions taking place on both sides of the border.

In his letter, migrant Héctor García offered a view that reflected an orthodox stand in relation to citizenship. He seemed unwilling to accept the possibility of carrying out a dual political membership:

> Are we here or aren't we? What is the deal with dual citizen-
> ship? Some people want to work both sides. I don't think
> things should work this way, since those who work here take
> the place of others who also need work. And vice versa. I
> don't think things should be this way. When we raise a flag,
> it is sacred. It is like someone standing on a fence, they are
> not on one side or on the other. Like something neutral. One
> is or one isn't…. We are in the United States for many rea-
> sons, but if we want to change things, we have to stand to-
> gether. We can't be on two sides at the same time (H. García
> 1995).

Of course, the ideas of the migrant community are not monolithic or uniform. In the second letter published by *La Opinion*, Rufino Domínguez Santos, then executive vice-coordinator of FIOB, described his participation weeks before in the "Border Workshop for the Analysis of Nationality Issues," organized by the Mexican Congress and held at El Colegio de la Frontera Norte (COLEF) in Tijuana. Domínguez Santos pointed to the ab-sence of what he called independent migrant organizations and described well-known figures' opposition to granting the right to vote to Mexicans living in the United States. He denounced the Mexican Foreign Ministry's (SRE) inability to address the problems facing the migrant population. He also argued that the struggle for the vote is an old one and that the double nationality or inalienable nationality is limited and unacceptable. Before concluding with the suggestion that events like the COLEF workshop should take place on American soil, Domínguez Santos stressed what citi-zenship means to him and to people like him:

> Indigenous people from Oaxaca have been practicing dual
> citizenship for years, without complications or fear of facing
> the true problem. Many of us return to govern our home-
> towns as the townspeople mandate, and we continue to help
> out with the *tequio* [collective community work], and this

gives us the right to be called citizens of the place where we
were born, where we work, and where all our dead are buried. We surpassed this issue many years ago. Whatever happens in the Mexican Congress, the government will not be
able to limit these legitimate rights, which are part of indigenous autonomy (Domínguez Santos 1995).

Although these two letters reflect important aspects of the polarization
on dual citizenship, even more important is the fact that the debate took
place at all, a fact that can only be understood in the context of a specific
moment in national history. This debate demonstrates the migrant community's interest in political issues, calls attention to their ties to Mexico,
and states their intention to find the best stand possible within the difficult
binational context created by their incorporation into international migration processes. Letters such as these demonstrate the contributions of individuals like Domínguez Santos and García, who wish to help resolve the
controversy.

Even if Héctor García's comments state the contrary, these letters confirm that migrants are playing an important part in Mexico's transformation and in defining the country's relationship to the Mexican population
outside its borders. Migrants like Domínguez Santos and García are fighting to be included in a political struggle that in the past has been in the
hands of others—federal authorities, the mass media, the private sector,
and political parties. Migrants are refusing to be excluded from the political struggle, and they are working to defend their interests and make their
respective ideas heard. Even before they have achieved the right to vote
abroad, Mexican migrants' political attitudes and behaviors can only be
thought of as elements of multiple and simultaneous political membership.

The case of Rufino Domínguez is especially significant. Domínguez,
who has lived in the San Joaquin Valley for almost twenty years, or almost
all of his adult life, has risen to the post of general coordinator for FIOB. In
his leadership role he has helped define the path that FIOB has taken, and
he has influenced the way in which other social sectors view this organization and *oaxaqueño* migrants. Domínguez has gained recognition from regional agricultural workers and from authorities and political actors on
both sides of the border. As part of his leadership responsibilities, Domínguez travels regularly to agricultural regions in Fresno County, to California's legislative offices, to the offices of the Mexican presidency and Congress, as well as to Washington, D.C., and to rural communities in the
Mixteco area of Oaxaca. His weekly itinerary is the embodiment of trasna-

tionality, as he pursues issues that affect *oaxaqueño* immigrant workers on both sides of the border. The transnational mobility that characterizes Domínguez's work is essential in the promotion of FIOB members' interests. To limit his work to issues related to only one nation-state would be both inconceivable and absurd.

## ZURUMUATOS AND OAXAQUEÑOS: POOR UNCULTURED MEXICANS?

To better appreciate *oaxaqueño* migration to the United States and the role played by actors such as Rufino Domínguez, a few comparative references are useful. In this case, our point of departure is observations on Mexican migration at the beginning of the twentieth century. In *Desert Immigrants*, (1981), which documents the impact of Mexican migration on El Paso, Texas, over the 1880–1920 period, Chicano historian Mario García outlines the problems faced by the period's recently arrived immigrants in their contact with labor contractors (*enganchadores*). According to García, an article published by *El Clarín del Norte* in 1906 reported instances of contractors who mistreated and abused "poor *surumatos*,"[1] who are further portrayed as "poor, uncultured Mexicans."

No one would dispute that the migrants of the time were poor or that there was an exploitative relationship between contractors and recently arrived migrants. Nevertheless, the reference in García's book hides a very complex and rich reality. The migrants alluded to cannot be described merely as "poor, uncultured Mexicans." These migrants were campesinos, the majority of indigenous origin. Most were from the Zurumuato Hacienda (now known as Pastor Ortiz) in the Bajío region of Michoacán State. More than a century ago, campesinos from this region began migrating to the United States, driven by the socioeconomic conditions prevailing during the Porfiriato and seduced by American labor demand and the promises made by labor contractors. Migration rose with the construction of a railroad linking the Bajío with other regions of Mexico and with El Paso.

Far from being "uncultured Mexicans" or defenseless victims exploited by labor contractors on U.S. soil, among these migrants were important figures such as Benito Canales, a campesino-turned-*agrarista*-leader during the revolution. Before he went on to earn fame as a rebel leader, Canales had fled to the United States after killing a work foreman with whom he had had a series of conflicts. While in the United States, Canales apparently

---

[1] García reproduced an erroneous spelling of *zurumuato*.

was in contact with *magonistas* who had settled in Los Angeles, a connection that may have contributed to Canales's politicization. Another migrant later informed on him, and Canales was arrested by the Los Angeles police. After extradition to Mexico he was jailed in the city of Morelia, but escaped from prison and became a celebrated revolutionary figure in Michoacán. He eventually turned himself in and was executed, but his legend continues to be sung in ballads (*corridos*) in Michoacán and elsewhere in Mexico. The examples set by Canales and other revolutionaries point up the need to examine current interpretations with care in order to construct a more faithful history of Mexican migration from Oaxaca.

*Oaxaqueño* migrants of today report high poverty levels. This is to be expected given their concentration in agricultural jobs or low-paid urban employment. It is also true that many migrants have been exploited by people smugglers (*coyotes*), employers, labor contractors, drivers who transport workers to the workplace (*raiteros*), landlords, and others who inhabit the world of recent immigrants. Yet, just as in the case of the *zurumuatos*, these migrants' condition as exploited workers is only one aspect of their lives as migrants. These men and women come to the United States with their own personal and collective history. They have previously carried out roles as citizens, consumers, artists, poets, athletes, parents, *compadres*, students, community leaders, healers, catechists, seminarians, businesspeople, farmers, holders of religious/community service positions (*cargueros*), members of political parties, neo-Zapatista sympathizers, union leaders, communal land commissioners, professionals, and even public officials. Interpretations that portray *oaxaqueño* migrants solely as victims do not do justice to their creative and organizational capacity, and they perpetuate the belief that solutions to the problems this group faces can only come from outside.

## LOCAL CONTEXT

The Fresno metropolitan area, which includes Fresno and Madera counties, has a high and growing presence of people of Mexican origin. The region also has one of the largest concentrations of *oaxaqueños* in the United States. In 2000, according to the population census, the Fresno metropolitan area had 922,516 inhabitants, of whom 44 percent (406,151) were Latinos and 37.8 percent (349,109) were of Mexican origin (U.S. Census Bureau 2001: 11, 21, 1143). In 1970 Fresno and Madera counties reported only 455,500 inhabitants, so demographic growth over past decades has clearly been considerable (California Department of Finance 2001: 13).

Fresno's Mexican-origin population did not have access to political power through the vote until 1972, when students from the Fresno campus of California State University launched a campaign to take control of the government in Parlier, a small rural community south of Fresno. According to Adaljiza Sosa Riddell and Robert Aguallo, Jr., Parlier only had 2,000 inhabitants at the time. Although 85 percent were of Latino origin (mainly Mexican farmworkers), white farmers controlled the local government. In fact, from 1921 to 1972 no Mexican was elected to local office. The struggle to take control of the government began when two university students — Arcadio Viveros (an immigrant) and Andrew Benites — attended city government meetings held to name a new police chief. In the face of government opposition to naming a Mexican American to the post, the Mexican community united and undertook a number of political strategies that yielded an electoral victory in April 1972 and gave them a majority on the city council. The Parlier victory was historic: it was the first case of a Mexican American community winning an electoral victory in local government in the contemporary history of California. It also marked the starting point for reversing a political exclusion and marginalization that had prevailed since the United States' conquest of previously Mexican territory during the mid-nineteenth century (see Sosa Riddell and Aguallo 1972: 1–19).

In some instances, such as in Madera County, the political incorporation of Mexicans has been limited and uneven. In the city of Madera there was no Mexican representation until 1978, when Marge Esquibel, a Mexican American born to immigrant parents from Jalisco, was elected to the city council. Madera County did not have any Mexican elected official until 1980, when Jess López, also Mexican American and also born to immigrant parents from Jalisco, was elected to the county board of supervisors. Esquibel and López remained in their offices until 1994 and 1997, respectively. Unfortunately, today there are almost no Mexicans in similar positions; the single exception is a Mexican American representative on the Madera school district board. The absence of Mexicans in high-ranking administrative posts in local government is also notable.

Mexicans' lack of political power in Madera has contributed to a deterioration of public services, especially in education. The Madera Unified School District (MUSD) has reported a serious shortage of classrooms and other services for a growing student population composed mostly of children of Mexican origin. Deficient access to education limits future generations' social mobility. Despite over-enrollment in the district's schools, the local electorate — mainly citizens of European descent and largely uninterested in investing in the education of a predominantly Mexican student body—had refused to approve new taxes to finance local school construction and renovation. In November 2002, however, in a historic move the Madera electorate approved Measure B, a $46 million bond for education projects. Just over 63 percent of voters supported the initiative, casting aside the long history of neglect that had characterized local education. Not all sectors were pleased with the result. In the days following the election, a group of residents from the county's rural areas denounced the new tax as unfair to rural property owners and announced a campaign to separate these areas from the school district.

Post-election events further reflect the difficulties of bringing about change in a community like Madera. Under California election law, when a school bond is issued, local authorities must create a commission to supervise the use of these funds. In the case of Madera, MUSD authorities created a commission of nine local citizens, all white. The Mexican community—along with African Americans, Asians, and citizens of Middle Eastern descent—were excluded. When Dennis Meisner, a local farmer who had headed the separatist movement after the November election, was offered a seat on the commission, there was a surge in public pressure to increase representation within the commission, but most commission members are still of European descent.

Political incorporation has been more successful in Fresno. On two separate occasions, a Mexican American has been appointed to the county board of supervisors, and people of Mexican origin recently held a majority on the city council. One element that helps explain the greater electoral success in Fresno is this city's district electoral system, versus Madera's "at large" electoral system, in which all citizens vote for all candidates. The former system facilitates the electoral representation of the Mexican American population (Flores 1992: 181–200).

Changes in patterns of political participation influence the local political context in which FIOB operates. The relationship between FIOB and local Fresno authorities has been limited but surprisingly productive. FIOB has established good relations with Supervisor Juan Arámbula, a Mexican American from Jalisco who has amply demonstrated his concern for the problems that Mexican immigrants encounter. Thanks to his collaboration, FIOB has been able to promote important initiatives, including development of the Casas San Miguel housing project, created in cooperation with a number of local, state, and federal agencies. The Casas San Miguel project will provide housing for the more than fifty families who formerly lived in the Tall Trees Trailer Park in Málaga, which oil companies had transformed into a toxic waste site.

Also thanks to its relationship with local contacts like Supervisor Arámbula, FIOB has learned how to navigate local bureaucracy, positioning the organization to support health projects, civic participation, and symbolically important issues such as erecting a statue of Benito Juárez in downtown Fresno. The inauguration of the statue in spring 2003 confirmed the permanence of the *oaxaqueño* community in Fresno, as well as the importance of working with like-minded political forces.

## THE GUELAGUETZA AND THE REAFFIRMATION OF OAXAQUEÑO IDENTITY

FIOB has established a recognized public presence in Fresno by building strong working relationships with public officials, government agencies, nongovernmental organizations, activist networks, businesspeople, English and Spanish-language media, educational institutions, hospitals and health centers, and immigrants from Oaxaca and other states in Mexico. Over the years, FIOB has garnered many awards for its efforts. In 2001 it received the Advocacy Institute/Ford Foundation's New Community Leadership award and a recognition award from State Assemblywoman Sarah Reyes, and in 2002 it received an award from the KVPT public television station.

Among immigrants from Oaxaca, FIOB has played the role of community development promoter, offering social services, cultural activities, and political leadership that benefit thousands of people every year. For example, during the celebration of the IV Guelaguetza Oaxaqueña 2002, Antonio Rodríguez, a 53-year-old immigrant from Oaxaca, praised FIOB for its promotion of Oaxacan culture and for the recent creation of "Se'e Savi," a folk group of Fresno teenagers interested in preserving the cultural legacy of their ancestors. Rodríguez expressed his excitement in the weekly *El Oaxaqueño*: "I am so happy. This is incredible; every year I come here [to the Guelaguetza] and remember my homeland when I see the dancers and listen to the music that is played in my hometown" (Rodríguez 2002).

The Guelaguetza is a Oaxacan celebration dating from pre-Columbian times. Today this celebration takes place in Cerro del Fortín in Oaxaca City, as well as in regions of the United States with high concentrations of Oaxacan immigrants. Los Angeles and Fresno are two such locations, where thousands gather each year to celebrate their heritage through music, dance, food, and interaction with their fellow *oaxaqueños*. The celebration is an important element in strengthening their links with their home state.

The first Guelaguetza in California, in 1987, was organized by the Oaxacan Regional Organization (ORO). In 1999 FIOB organized a Guelaguetza in the heart of the San Joaquin Valley, filling the Veterans Memorial Auditorium in Fresno to capacity with *oaxaqueños* from Livingston, Madera, Arvin, Lamont, Farmersville, Selma, Kerman, and Orange Cove.

The following year the event was held in the much larger Roosevelt High School auditorium. More than a thousand people, mostly *oaxaqueños*, gathered to watch folk dances by "Huaxyacac" and hear music performed by the woodwind band "Xochistepec." Attendance rose even further in the 2003 Guelaguetza in Fresno, to 1,500 people. Each year the Guelaguetza offers thousands of people the opportunity to rediscover their traditions and their fellow *paisanos*, to savor a *tlayuda* or *pan de yema*, to join with a thousand other voices to sing "Canción Mixteca" or "Mi Lindo Oaxaca." The Guelaguetza creates an environment in which migrants can leave concerns and worries behind and, in a pan-ethnic collective, unite to enjoy the culture that brings them together as *oaxaqueños*.

In addition to its cultural symbolism, the Fresno Guelaguetza is also an expression of civic participation. The event is made possible by the volunteer work of FIOB committees in Madera, Fresno, and Selma. FIOB members meet over many months to plan when and where the Guelaguetza will be held. They promote the event by word of mouth or through radio and television interviews as tickets go on sale. On the day of the Guelaguetza, these volunteers serve as masters of ceremonies; sell tickets, food, and folk art; and even fill in as security. Clearly an event of this magnitude is only possible thanks to the efforts and goodwill of these volunteers.

The Guelaguetza has also enabled FIOB to organize and promote other projects. During the last Guelaguetza, for example, FIOB, in collaboration with a local hospital, offered diabetes testing as part of their ongoing regional health project. And during the last four celebrations, FIOB has provided information on health and labor rights. Cultural celebrations such as the Guelaguetza evoke ties to the homeland, strengthen state and ethnic identity, and promote individual and collective pride among *oaxaqueño* residents in the Fresno area.

## THE CIVIC PARTICIPATION PROJECT

Through its Civic Participation Project (Proyecto de Participación Cívica), FIOB has been able to formalize its long-standing leadership and civic participation work. This pilot project was launched in August 2001, after months of meetings with directors of the James Irvine Foundation, who expressed interest in FIOB activities. As its name indicates, the project aims to promote *oaxaqueños'* participation in mainstream institutions and activities. Specifically, the project was designed to train between twenty and twenty-five activists in the Fresno and Madera area.

The project's underlying purpose is to involve outstanding members of local FIOB committees or individuals who are not FIOB members but who have a history of activism in their community. These people are invited to training workshops on the organization and practice in schools, organization and practice in local government, cooperation with community organizations, and the importance of different forms of civic participation.

FIOB determined that a project of this kind is necessary because, although migrants from Oaxaca have a history of traditional organization and volunteer work which goes back to their home communities, when they come to the United States they experience culture shock, not only because of the differences in language and customs but also because of the difference in organization between American society and society in Oaxaca. These differences impede their participation; even people who have a talent for organization and community work need help in understanding how U.S. society functions.

The Civic Participation Project proposes to educate these activists about the functioning of important institutions — schools, local government, and community organizations — and offer concrete examples of civic participation. This training provides the tools to increase the effectiveness of the activists' work in the community. The FIOB leaders' decision to pursue the Civic Participation Project grew out of decades of experience working with migrants from Oaxaca and day-to-day encounters with members of the Oaxacan community.

The FIOB faced many challenges in implementing the project. Initial interest was tepid. Once under way, it was challenging to ensure the activists' continued participation, given that many migrants return home or relocate at the end of the year, when there is no work in the San Joaquin Valley. Bad weather was also a problem. Nevertheless, 80 percent of the twenty-five activist participants attended at least four of the five workshops.

Beyond the quantitative aspect of workshop participation, it is important to point out the qualitative aspects of the environment created by the project. Initially, participants were shy when answering questions, but they slowly gained confidence until they were able to participate actively. A favorite activity was dividing into groups to discuss hypothetical problems and come up with solutions. For example, during one of the workshops dealing with the schools' organization and practice, the participants were instructed on the structure behind decision making and on their rights as parents. They were then divided into four groups, given a set of problems affecting a public school, and asked to identify the key problems and to offer some possible solutions. Although all the groups received the same information, each approached the problem differently. Some concentrated on the need to improve classroom cleanliness and maintenance; others emphasized the need to increase the number of bilingual teachers. Nevertheless, since the majority of the participants were parents, all identified with the hypothetical problems, which resembled the situations they face with their own children. In this way the discussion was influenced by everyday experience. After the workshop, many of the participants spontaneously began sharing experiences and discussing the importance of the information received during the day.

A *oaxaqueño* mother living in Madera described how her daughter was harassed by her classmates and had refused to go to school. The woman told her daughter to ask her teacher for help; when the teacher ignored the problem, the mother told her daughter to defend herself. The child did so and was expelled from school. Although the situation was ultimately resolved, the girl's parents felt powerless since they did not know their rights as parents or where to turn for help. "If I had had the information I got today, I could have avoided some bad moments and found a solution sooner," the mother said at the end of the workshop. Testimonies like this one reflect the value and usefulness of the workshops and the ways in which participants can apply the new knowledge in their daily lives.

FIOB has used questionnaires to track how well participants assimilate the information presented in the workshops. Further, the organization has documented examples of increased community activism among participants. For example, Plácido Rivera, who lives in Selma, is now a school-board member at his children's school. Teresa Calvo and Concepción Pacheco, members of the local FIOB committees in Madera and Fresno, respectively, participate in community projects with other organizations. Teresa is a health promoter for Campesina Leaders (Líderes Campesinas); Concepción is a promoter for a movement that fosters art education for Mexican and Mexican American children in Fresno.

The Civic Participation Project is an example of how FIOB not only helps *oaxaqueños* solve specific problems but also tries to attack the root of the problem and find strategies to encourage a more critical, responsible, and active citizenry.

## THE ZAPATISTA REFERENDUM

Many Mexican migrants come from indigenous communities or rural areas that maintain certain traditions of Mesoamerican civilizations (Bonfil Batalla 1994). According to the pioneering work of Manuel Gamio (1971), a large proportion of Mexicans who immigrated to the United States early in the twentieth century were indigenous people or mestizos. These migration patterns that were established a century ago continue today.

Successive waves of migrants have created large Mexican-origin communities in the United States, and these communities were deeply affected by the Zapatista movement that broke out on January 1, 1994. Witness the many protests that migrant organizations staged outside Mexican consulates. Subsequently, groups of Mexicans and Chicanos traveled to Chiapas to express their solidarity with the Zapatista Army of National Liberation (EZLN).

The link between migrants and Zapatistas was strengthened when the EZLN included in its March 1999 referendum — on the "Recognition of the Rights of Indigenous People and for the End of the Extermination War" — a question on the right of Mexican migrant workers to vote in Mexican elections (see Martínez-Saldaña 1999b). The question, one of a total of five, read: "Do you agree that Mexicans living abroad should play an active part in creating a new Mexico and have the right to vote in the elections?"

Booths were set up in many U.S. cities with large migrant populations, and Mexicans abroad were encouraged to vote in the referendum, a civic action that received enthusiastic support from migrant and Chicano organizations. Thousands of Mexicans voted in the United States, thereby expressing their support for the Zapatista movement. The majority replied in the affirmative to the question on the right to vote of Mexicans residing abroad. According to the La Jornada newspaper, 190 brigades were created to promote the Zapatista referendum in the United States (Cason and Brooks 1999), and FIOB was among the most active participants.

The referendum's inclusion of Mexicans in the United States offered hope to people who felt excluded and rejected. A representative from the New York Brigade expressed the importance of the EZLN's struggle for migrants and other groups:

> The EZLN's vision and struggle is a glimmer of hope for all Mexican people in the Americas ... for immigrants, women, men, lesbians, homosexuals, transgendered bisexuals, the disabled, children, the elderly, those who have been exploited, all indigenous people, everyone who has been forced to leave Mexico in search of dignity, all Chicanos looking for their spirit, all people of Mexican heritage who remember and those who have been forced to forget. The EZLN brings hope to all marginalized people of the world. The EZLN's vision and struggle is a new dawn—a dawn that pierces the enormous darkness of persecution and sadness that exists in the world.

A report from the Bay Area described the successful referendum:

> We are really tired of talking and explaining, but also really happy. People responded really well, including some people from the underworld of who knows what world. Our brigade, from San Francisco and named after Remedios Varo, set up booths in Redwood City, South City, and Oakland, a total of four booths.... All in all it's been a good day, the kind the heart needs once in a while. I'll talk to you more later; now we are exhausted.

FIOB reported that 1,627 people voted in Fresno, and most answered "yes" to all five questions. The referendum in Fresno was organized by the Fresno Committee for Justice in Mexico, California State University–Fresno, Club Azteca 2000, and the Fresno Committee for the Poor. Besides Fresno and Madera, booths were set up in Tulare, Selma, and Huron.

Convincing 1,627 people to participate in a referendum that had only symbolic value speaks to the well-developed organizational capacity of FIOB and other local Fresno organizations. This strength has carried over into mobilizations in which FIOB has participated—demanding fair U.S. migration laws, the vote for Mexicans abroad, and Mexican government recognition of and adherence to the San Andrés Accords on indigenous rights and culture. It is through actions such as these that FIOB has gained recognition as one of the few organizations in the Fresno area that can bring together large numbers of migrants and attract print and electronic media coverage of migrant issues. This, in turn, has influenced both local perceptions of the migrant experience and the attention that government and society give to the *oaxaqueño* population. The causes supported by

FIOB have transformed the political context, giving immediacy and local significance to issues that might otherwise seem external and distant.

## CONCLUSION

In working to represent Mexican migrants in the United States, FIOB has contributed to the construction of membership models that are inclusive and that allow for the political incorporation of *oaxaqueño* migrants and the Mexican population in general. The fact that the growing *oaxaqueño* community in Fresno and elsewhere in the United States is a relatively young social sector, with low levels of formal education, low income, and, in many cases, irregular migration status, has imposed limits on the work that FIOB is able to carry out. Yet despite these difficulties, FIOB is establishing an impressive track record. Fresno's *oaxaqueño* community is maturing, in a region in which Mexican-origin citizens are increasing their political importance — though not yet at a level commensurate with their demographic presence. The groundbreaking work of organizations like FIOB is fundamental to the creation of a more inclusive and democratic future.

## References

Bonfil Batalla, Guillermo. 1994. *México profundo: una civilización negada*. Mexico City: Grijalbo.

Bustamante, Jorge A. 1995. "Como luchar contra los Wilsons," *Excélsior*, March 27.

California Department of Finance, *California Statistical Abstract: 2001*. Sacramento, Calif.: Dept. of Finance.

Cason, Jim, and David Brooks. 1999. "Promovieron la consulta casi 200 brigadas," *La Jornada*, March 22.

Craig, Ann L. 1983. *The First Agraristas: An Oral History of a Mexican Agrarian Reform Movement*. Berkeley: University of California Press.

Domínguez Santos, Rufino. 1995. Letter to *La Opinión*, December 17.

Fernández Ruiz, Jorge. 1986. *Juárez y sus contemporáneos*. Mexico City: Universidad Nacional Autónoma de México.

Flores, William V. 1992. "Chicano Empowerment and the Politics of At-Large Elections in California: A Tale of Two Cities." In *Community Empowerment and Chicano Scholarship: Selected Proceedings*, edited by Mary Romero and Cordelia Candelaria. Houston: National Association for Chicano Studies.

Gamio, Manuel. 1971. *Mexican Immigration to the United States: A Study of Human Migration and Adjustment*. New York: Dover.

García, Héctor. 1995. Letter to *La Opinión*, December 17.

García, Mario T. 1981. *Desert Immigrants: The Mexicans of El Paso, 1880–1920*. New Haven, Conn.: Yale University Press.

Gómez-Quiñones, Juan. 1994. *Roots of Chicano Politics, 1600–1940*. Albuquerque: University of New Mexico Press.

Martínez-Saldaña, Jesús. 1999a. "Los primeros dólares de Pemex," *La Jornada*, March 14.

———. 1999b. "Propuesta a Marcos," *La Jornada*, January 23.

Raat, William Dirk. 1993. *Los revoltosos: rebeldes mexicanos en los Estados Unidos, 1903–1923*. Mexico City: Fondo de Cultura Económica.

Rivera-Salgado, Gaspar. 1999. "Migration and Political Activism: Mexican Transnational Indigenous Communities in a Comparative Perspective." PhD dissertation, University of California, Santa Cruz.

Rodríguez, Antonio. 2002. "El resplandor de la Guelaguetza," *El Oaxaqueño*, August 31.

Sosa Riddell, Adaljiza, and Robert Aguallo, Jr. 1972. "A Case of Chicano Politics: Parlier, California," *Aztlán* 9, nos. 1–2 (Spring–Fall).

Soysal, Yasemin Nuhoglu. 1994. *The Limits of Citizenship: Migrants and Post-national Membership in Europe*. Chicago: University of Chicago Press.

U.S. Census Bureau 2001. *Profiles of General Demographic Characteristics, 2000 Census of Population and Housing, California*. Washington, D.C.: U.S. Government Printing Office, May.

# 6

# Collective Identity and Organizational Strategies of Indigenous and Mestizo Mexican Migrants

GASPAR RIVERA-SALGADO AND LUIS ESCALA RABADÁN

Grassroots organizations formed by Mexican migrants in the United States have proliferated since the early 1980s, especially in the metropolitan area of Los Angeles. Although indigenous and mestizo migrants forged different kinds of organizations — including committees, fronts, and coalitions — through which to pursue their diverse goals, by the end of the 1990s hometown associations and home state federations had become the most prevalent organizational forms for both migrant communities. In fact, we find hometown associations (which appear under various names, including civic clubs, social clubs, and committees) and federations of hometown associations among Mexican groups with a long migratory tradition, such as *zacatecanos* (natives of Zacatecas) and *jaliscienses* (natives of Jalisco), as well as among groups who come from regions with a more recent migratory history, as is the case of Oaxacan migrants.

This chapter compares the organizations of indigenous Oaxacan migrants that belong to the Oaxacan Federation of Indigenous Communities and Organizations in California (FOCOICA) with those of mestizo migrant groups that belong to the Jalisco and Zacatecas federations in the Los Angeles area. Our analysis follows two lines of research. First, while at the level of federations their organizational strategies look similar, we find

---

Translation by Stuyvesant Bearns.

mestizo-indigenous differences in terms of the forms and strategies of their respective base organizations. Second, we find differences in the identity discourse that indigenous and mestizo migrants deploy at both the hometown association level and the federation level. We will focus particularly on explaining how the ethnic and regional identities prevalent among Oaxacan indigenous migrants differ from those of mestizo organizations, where the identity discourse centers more around the notion of the *la patria chica* (literally "the little homeland").

Our main argument regarding Oaxacan indigenous organizations' decision to adopt certain features of the organizational model pioneered by mestizo migrants is that this decision was not limited to the socialization value of home state federations. Instead, the explanation lies with the ability of indigenous migrants to become political actors and, in the process, adapt traditional forms of community organization to a new social and political environment. The new political environment is characterized by a growing relationship between organized migrants and the state and federal levels of the Mexican government.

This trend has produced two fundamental changes in the profiles of both indigenous and mestizo Mexican migrant organizations. On the one hand, unlike the relative informality and political isolation that characterized them in the mid-1990s,[1] these associations have now consolidated their organizational structures. Notably, the philanthropic activities they carry out for their communities of origin have changed significantly. While these projects were infrequent and haphazardly organized in the past, cross-border fund-raising and investments in home community infrastructure have grown substantially in scale and become much more formalized and systematic. This "scaling up" has increased the federations' visibility, leading to a growing recognition of them in both the public and political spheres, which in turn has encouraged extended dialogue between them and all levels of the Mexican government: federal, state, and municipal.

On the other hand, these changes are not limited to the associations' internal structure but also involve their environment. In recent years, different Mexican state representatives from all levels of government have forged important relationships with the associations, relationships that both civil society and state actors consider to be real partnerships, at least

---

[1] Zabin and Escala Rabadán (1998) found a high level of political isolation among the federations and the more prominent Latino politicians in the Los Angeles area, especially with regard to their very limited participation in the movement against California's Proposition 187 in 1994.

in the case of organized migrants in Los Angeles who have come from Oaxaca, Zacatecas, Jalisco, and, more recently, Michoacán.

Politicians, researchers, and activists in both Mexico and the United States have noted the growing importance of these migrant groups and highlighted their significance—and the significance of their organizations—as bridges between the two nations. What is needed now is a better understanding of indigenous migrant organizations' internal dynamics, including their differences and similarities with mestizo organizations, in order to evaluate their effectiveness and binational impact on local political processes in their communities of origin and in their communities of settlement in California. In short, although migrants from throughout Mexico have adopted hometown associations and federations as organizational models, significant differences may lie behind their similarities in form. This chapter analyzes the trajectories of the "classic" mestizo migrant organizations from Jalisco and Zacatecas, and those of more recent migrants to California—Zapotecs and Mixtecs from Oaxaca.

## MEXICAN MIGRANT ASSOCIATIONS IN THE UNITED STATES

The consolidation of strong social networks between specific regions in Mexico and the United States has encouraged the emergence of both indigenous and mestizo *paisano* organizations that base themselves in their locality, municipality, ethnic group, or state of origin. These associations, which represent Mexican migrants' first attempts to formalize their organizations, can trace their origins to informal networks of migrant *paisanos* based on their respective hometowns.[2] From the 1970s onward, there was a proliferation of Mexican clubs and associations, with varied social and ethnic compositions and distinct levels of organization.[3]

A key element in the emergence and development of these associations is the strengthening of ties between migrants and their towns in rural Mexico, which transform hometowns into powerful reference points for creating a collective identity among migrants from the same community or region. The "*paisano* connection" becomes an essential part of the migrants'

---

[2] For the historical evolution of Mexican migrant associations, see, for example, Díaz de Cossío, Orozco, and González 1997. There is an extensive literature on the importance of social networks in the Mexico-U.S. migratory process; see, among others, Mines 1981; Massey et al. 1987; Zabin et al. 1993.

[3] For a more detailed analysis of the emergence of these migrant associations in the United States, see Goldring 1995; Smith 1995; Espinoza 1999; Rivera-Salgado 1999.

social organization, akin to the ties that bind family and friends. Ties with the "little homeland," far from weakening or disappearing with distance, are strengthened and transformed into *paisano* networks that eventually lead to the construction of associations as a privileged way of "translocal" belonging. In this context, working together in the United States as an organized group allows migrants to promote and consolidate a feeling of cultural identity.[4]

The following description, offered by a migrant from Pegueros, Jalisco, who now resides in the Los Angeles area, illustrates one typical way in which these associations take shape:

> In the beginning we [people from Pegueros] often got together for events, especially sporting events.... I brought my family to the soccer and baseball games I played in, and the majority of the players did the same. It was not only our families there; there were a lot of other people who came as spectators, because wherever we went we were always the group with the largest cheering section. It was after getting together at these sporting events that it occurred to us to establish an association that would fulfill other needs, above all to confront the necessities our people in Pegueros were facing. In fact, our first project was the donation of an ambulance to our town.[5]

Literally hundreds of these associations now exist across the United States. In many cases they are informal groups known only to their members and have little contact with other groups in either Mexico or the United States. This early structure is sometimes the first step toward organizational formalization, which then allows for the integration of migrants' communities in the United States by linking them not only through kinship relations but also through *paisano* relations based on town and region of

---

[4] The importance of these Mexican migrant associations in constructing a local/national identity can also be found in the historical evidence. According to some historians, Mexican groups formed in California in the second half of the nineteenth century to promote celebrations of national events. In so doing, they also developed an ethnic consciousness among Mexicans in the United States. This organizational tradition extended into the early decades of the twentieth century (with, for example, the founding of the "Independence Club" in Los Angeles). See Taylor 1997.

[5] Interview with Rafael Gutiérrez, founding member of the Club Pegueros, Los Angeles, February 1997.

origin in Mexico. The main activities of these groups are fund-raising events to finance philanthropic projects in their towns in Mexico. They hold dances, dinners, raffles, *charreadas* (Mexican rodeos), beauty contests, and other cultural and social activities throughout the year. These events serve two important objectives: they enable the associations to finance projects in their home communities in Mexico, and they create a sense of community by strengthening the ties among migrant *paisanos*. In this sense, the founding of these associations is an important element for the consolidation of relations among Mexican communities on both sides of the border.[6]

Although there are no data on the exact number of Mexican migrant clubs or associations in the United States, Mexican consulates in the United States have created a registry of them. As noted in table 6.1, by 2002 there were nearly seven hundred migrant clubs or associations in the United States, concentrated primarily in California (with over half of the total), Illinois, and Texas.

**Table 6.1. Mexican Migrant Associations in the United States by State of Origin, 2002**

| Mexican State of Origin of Members | U.S. State Where Association Formed | | | | |
|---|---|---|---|---|---|
| | California | Illinois | Texas | Other | Total |
| Michoacán | 19 | 17 | 0 | 4 | 40 |
| Guanajuato | 17 | 17 | 13 | 7 | 54 |
| Oaxaca | 24 | 3 | 1 | 4 | 32 |
| Jalisco | 75 | 25 | 3 | 8 | 111 |
| Guerrero | 2 | 35 | 2 | 4 | 43 |
| Durango | 14 | 6 | 4 | 2 | 26 |
| Zacatecas | 126 | 37 | 12 | 5 | 180 |
| Other (states with lower levels of out-migration) | 97 | 21 | 49 | 25 | 192 |
| Total | 374 | 161 | 84 | 59 | 678 |

*Source*: Authors' estimates, based on data in Orozco, González, and Díaz de Cossío 2003.

---

[6] For a detailed analysis of the associations' internal dynamics, see Goldring 1992; González Gutiérrez 1995; Zabin and Escala Rabadán 1998; Rivera-Salgado 1999.

The emergence and growth of these formal examples of organization among Mexican migrants led to the creation of an additional organizational level—the federation—that unites clubs or associations. The first of these amalgamations was the Federation of United Mexican Clubs (Federación de Clubes Mexicanos Unidos) in Los Angeles, established in 1972 with eight migrant clubs from Jalisco, Chihuahua, Michoacán, Guanajuato, and Zacatecas. Its main objective was to extend social links between similar associations and to support the philanthropic projects of the associations in a more decisive way.

The success of this organizational model of hometown clubs and unifying federations supported Mexican migrant communities in the United States throughout the 1970s and 1980s as the migrant population became more numerous and more permanent, the latter largely as a result of the amnesty provisions in the Immigration Reform and Control Act of 1986 (IRCA). During this period, contact with Mexican government agencies— with the federal government through consulates in the United States and with Mexican state governments—was largely sporadic and informal.

By the second half of the 1980s, however, a number of factors led to a strengthening of these contacts. For example, with the gradual addition over time of Zacatecan clubs, the Federation of United Mexican Clubs became the Federation of Zacatecan Clubs of Southern California—and the model for federations based on state of origin in Mexico. At the same time, the Zacatecan government was seeking increased contact with migrant communities in the United States, particularly with Zacatecan clubs in the Los Angeles area. These efforts evolved into a gradual formalization of the relationship between the migrant associations and the state government, which led, in turn, to the implementation of more social projects in Zacatecas. This coming together of the Zacatecas state government and Mexican migrant organizations was a seminal experience in the Mexican government's broader outreach strategy with Mexican communities in the United States.[7] The following sections analyze in detail the formation and consolidation of federations from Oaxaca, Zacatecas, and Jalisco, in order to illustrate the diverse processes in the experience of indigenous and mestizo migrants.

---

[7] For a more detailed analysis of the participation of different Mexican agencies and these associations, see González Gutiérrez 1993, 1995; Zabin and Escala Rabadán 1998; Espinoza 1999; Rivera-Salgado 1999.

## INDIGENOUS OAXACANS IN THE MIGRATORY PROCESS

The migration of Oaxacans is a bifurcated process involving two ethnic groups with large migratory flows—Mixtecs and Zapotecs. The Mixtecs have tended to work in agriculture, both in northern Mexico and in the United States. They have worked in the Culiacán Valley of Sinaloa since the early 1970s and in Baja California's San Quintín Valley since the early 1980s. Their migratory route in the United States covers the most important agricultural sectors of California (the Central Valley, northern San Diego County, Napa Valley, Cochella Valley, Pajaro Valley), as well as Oregon, Washington, Florida, North Carolina, New Jersey, and New York (Rivera-Salgado 1999, 2000; Zabin et al. 1993).

Zapotec migration, by contrast, goes primarily to urban areas (Hirabayashi 1993; Bartolomé and Barabás 1986). This is especially true for communities in Oaxaca's Central Valleys and northern Sierra region, which have sent substantial numbers of migrants to Oaxaca City and Mexico City since at least the mid-1950s (Hirabayashi 1993; López and Runsten, this volume). Zapotec migration to the United States dates from the Bracero Program (1942–1964). This early migration precipitated a flow that, though initially small, made an impact on the early migrant-sending communities. In our interviews with people over age 65 in the Mixtec and Zapotec region, it became clear that the flow in the mid-1950s drew from very remote communities. In a group interview with the municipal council of Macuiltianguis in the Zapotec northern Sierra region, five of the eight members present had come to the United States under the Bracero Program. All of them had worked as laborers in Oaxaca City and Mexico City.[8]

Oaxacan migrants, especially Zapotecs from the Central Valleys and northern Sierra, have been migrating to Los Angeles since the early 1970s. One participant in this early migration stream was Constantino Vásquez, who migrated from the Zapotec community of San Francisco Cajonos to Los Angeles in 1973. Mr. Vásquez told us about the difficulties he encountered when, having no contacts in the city, he set about trying to find a job:

> I came directly here to Los Angeles. When we left our town, everyone felt sad about leaving. We didn't know when we were going to come back. When I got to Los Angeles there

---

[8] Interview with Priciliano Cortez, San Pablo Macuiltianguis, Oaxaca, March 1997. In a collective interview with other council members, Mr. Cortez narrated his experience as a bracero in the late 1950s and early 1970s, when he worked as an agricultural laborer in Texas and California.

were eleven or twelve of us here from the town—just a handful. We didn't all have work; there wasn't enough work for
us. Some worked two, three days a week, and we took any
job we could find. Some were dishwashers, others worked as
gardeners, or sewing, or cleaning houses. I went without
work for eighty days and then I found a job cleaning a school
with a Texan contractor. That's when I finally got a handle
[on things]. I earned very little, ten dollars a day, and that
was only by working all day. I left at six in the morning and
came back at nine or ten at night.[9]

Zapotec migrants like Constantino were pioneers in a migratory process of Oaxacans to Los Angeles that began only thirty years ago. During
the 1970s, it was rare to see Oaxacans in Los Angeles. By the end of the
1990s, however, the presence of the Oaxacan migrant community was notable, especially in neighborhoods like Pico Union, Koreatown, Santa
Monica, Venice, and El Sereno, and in the nearby cities of Lynwood and
South Gate. Researchers at the North American Integration and Development Center of the University of California, Los Angeles have documented
the presence of migrants from at least eighty-two communities from three
districts in Oaxaca, two in the northern Sierra (Ixtlán and Villa Alta) and
one from the Central Valleys (Tlacolula) (López, Escala-Rabadán, and
Hinojosa-Ojeda 2001). Although this study limited its interviews to migrants from the District of Tlacolula, it reveals the dramatic increase in the
number of Zapotec migrants living in the Los Angeles metropolitan area.

The indigenous migrants who began coming to Los Angeles in the early
1970s and whose presence increased dramatically in the mid-1980s are part
of a much larger change in Mexico's migratory patterns. From the 1980s
onward, Mexican communities with little or no history of migration became incorporated into the migratory flow to the United States, which had
already existed for nearly a hundred years. Mexico's traditional migrant-
sending areas had been its midwestern states: Zacatecas, Jalisco, Guanajuato, Durango, and Michoacán (Massey et al. 1987; Cornelius 1988). The
new sending areas are the south-central parts of the country and rural
communities in the southern states of Puebla, Guerrero, Oaxaca, and, more

---

[9] Interview with Constantino Vásquez, Los Angeles, December 2001. Mr. Vásquez
has lived in Los Angeles continuously since 1973. He currently works as a conci-
erge at a Catholic school in the Pico Union neighborhood. Mr. Vásquez participated in a collective interview with other members of the Club Social y Cultural
San Francisco Cajonos.

recently, Chiapas. Notably, much of this new flow comes from large cities, including Mexico City, Ciudad Nezahualcóyotl, and Puebla City.

Three characteristics distinguish indigenous Oaxacan migration from the predominantly mestizo migration that originates in central-western Mexico. First, indigenous Oaxacan migration to the United States increased substantially in the mid-1980s, when Zapotecs and Mixtecs began crossing the border in large numbers. Second, despite incorporating into the labor market at the lowest level (agriculture for the Mixtecs, urban services for the Zapotecs), these migrants have been able to build solid grassroots organizations to confront the challenges they face on both sides of the border. And third, these indigenous migrants are culturally and socially different from the mestizo migrants that make up the majority of the population in the enclaves in which they settle.

## The Formation of Oaxacan Migrant Associations

The process through which Oaxacan migrants form associations and community sports clubs is similar in many ways to that of mestizo migrants from Jalisco and Zacatecas. There are two major incentives to organize such an association or club. The first is to systematize the mutual support among migrants from the same community who find themselves confronting the same challenges as they adapt to their new environment. Constantino Vásquez illustrates the benefits for Zapotecs of forming the Club Social y Cultural San Francisco Cajonos:

> I came here to Los Angeles in 1973, and I was the first president of the organization. When I came here, well, we came in bad shape and we didn't have anyone to turn to.... I owed a little money—125 dollars—which was a lot at the time, so I was looking for someone to lend it to me. But since no one knew us, it wasn't easy to get someone to give us a loan. That is until I found the daughter of a cousin of mine who had money [because] they were already organized.... The husband is from Yatzachi El Bajo and the wife was from Zoogocho, so I don't know which one of them had the money, but the point is that they had the money to give and that's where I got the idea that we had to have an organization to be able to support each other, or to support the others that would come later.[10]

---

[10] Interview with Constantino Vázquez, December 2001.

The second incentive for migrants to form an association or club is the impetus that exists to help their communities of origin, perceived as a "moral obligation." Héctor Mata, outgoing president of the Club Social y Cultural San Francisco Cajonos, expressed this sentiment:

> When the idea came up of forming a committee to help the community [San Francisco Cajonos], one of my relatives said that the community living here [Los Angeles] would have more clarity because we all know that our communities have been independent of the government—marginalized in a certain way. So we felt a moral obligation to continue working together with them, with the *tequios* (collective community labor), the contributions, and with all the projects that are lacking in a small town like ours. We have to look out for our interests: schools, streets, the municipal building, lighting, and a list of other things that are plenty of work for a small community. Thanks to the loyalty of the *paisanos* who have been here, we have been able to tackle these necessities. But that is not to say that the work is done, because there is still a lot to do. Now we are working on the streets. They are installing cobblestone paving. We are working on the San Antonio Chapel—they are investing a large sum there—because, as I said, we feel responsible for meeting the needs as citizens of the town, and that is what we do.[11]

Although Oaxacan associations and community sports clubs have always had a strong local focus—their main goal is financing community infrastructure projects similar to those of the "classic" migrants from Jalisco and Zacatecas—they have also adapted diverse indigenous community practices for their organizations. Among these are *tequio* (collective community work, which is more or less obligatory), the *cargo* system (the practice of rotating community leadership positions), and customary law (which involves convening community assemblies for the election of local authorities and making consensual decisions on issues concerning the community as a whole). Another member of the Club Social and Cultural San Francisco Cajonos, Porfirio Hernández Ruiz, who was elected to the

---

11 Interview with Héctor Mata, Los Angeles, December 2001. Mr. Mata is from San Francisco Cajonos and has lived in Los Angeles for thirty years. He has a small gardening business with six employees. He is also the owner of two apartment complexes, which he rents. Mr. Mata participated in a collective interview with other members of the Club Social y Cultural San Francisco Cajonos.

municipal council of his home community even though he has been a resident of Los Angeles since he came from Oaxaca in 1973, articulates this point:

> I am leaving this month to serve a full year there in the town. I have a lot of love for my town and I want to set an example in Oaxaca. The post they have assigned me is First Administrator, which is like the vice president here [in the United States].... I should have served this year, but they [the authorities] didn't accept the people I wanted to pay [to take my place]. Now they require someone to serve there so that they have a better idea of how to impart justice in case there are serious problems. I can see that the older people want those who will serve in the future to prepare themselves and have an idea of what is happening in the municipality. I feel pretty honored that they have appointed me to this post, and, with God's help, I will do the best I can.[12]

Adapting these community institutions to the migratory process has allowed the direct incorporation of indigenous migrants into the political processes of their communities of origin. In many cases this participation comes not as a voluntary act but under pressure from local authorities who have decided to make the migrants' participation in community leadership posts obligatory. As a result, migrants often maintain strong translocal ties, to the point that the role and structure of *paisano* associations may be regulated by local authorities in the community of origin, who give official titles to people who live thousands of miles away.

## The Formation of the Oaxacan Federation

On February 18, 2001, with Oaxacan *paisanos* filling an auditorium at the University of Southern California, Don Telésforo Cruz, of the northern Sierra Zapotec community of Lachitaa, led the elected board of directors of the recently created FOCOICA in their solemn oath. Before an audience of more than four hundred people, he asked the thirteen members of the

---

12 Interview with Porfirio Hernández Ruiz, Los Angeles, December 2001. Mr. Hernández is from San Francisco Cajonos and has lived in Los Angeles since 1973. He is employed as an independent contractor in building maintenance. This is a family business employing four people, including Porfirio's wife. He participated in a collective interview with other members of the Club Social y Cultural San Francisco Cajonos.

board of directors, "Do you swear to respect, and ensure that others respect, the statutes and principles of the Oaxacan Federation?" Standing,
they raised their right hands and replied in unison, "Yes, I do." Don Telésforo responded: "May it thus be, and if not, may the people who are present demand it." No sooner were these words uttered than the audience
erupted in applause, followed by cheers of "Viva la Federación Oaxaqueña!"
This act culminated a string of attempts, on many different occasions and
under many different leaderships, to bring the Oaxacan migrant associations in California together in a single organization.

The formation of FOCOICA became public at the end of January 2001,
when the *El Oaxaqueño* newspaper printed a public invitation issued by the
organizing committee of the First Congress of the Oaxacan Federation; part
of that text (in translation) appears in figure 6.1.

What is distinctive about this invitation is that it calls on "all Oaxacan
communities and organizations," not only the hometown associations or
community clubs. This issue was discussed during the preliminary meetings, when a member of a regional Zapotec organization noted that the
organizations that Oaxacan migrants had formed were very diverse and
that they should give everyone who wanted to promote Oaxacan unity an
opportunity to participate. This observation gave rise to the motto that the
Federation eventually adopted: "For the Unity and Advancement of Oaxacans," which joins the concept of federation (which suggests a centralized
organization of similar peer organizations) to the concept of coalition
(which brings to mind an alliance of more or less dissimilar organizations
that work together toward common objectives).

The creation of a coalition of different kinds of organizations with varied historical and organizational experiences under the leadership of a
board of directors gives FOCOICA an organizational character that differs
somewhat from the Zacatecas and Jalisco federations. This distinction was
made clear when a Mixtec leader with a long trajectory in political organizations of indigenous migrants questioned whether a "Oaxacan federation" should even be formed, arguing that "this was copying mestizo migrants from other states." In the end, those favoring the formation of a
federation prevailed, as reflected in the words of Gustavo Santiago, from
the Mixtec community of Yanhuitlán: "[this is] the precise moment to give
the Oaxacan community the organization it deserves, one that speaks for
all Oaxacans together, once and for all."[13]

---

[13] These and following quotes come from notes taken at a meeting of the FOCOICA
promotion committee, Los Angeles, November 17, 2000.

**Figure 6.1. Invitation to the First Congress of the Oaxacan Federation**

---

SUMMONS

to all OAXACANS to participate in the

FIRST CONGRESS OF THE OAXACAN FEDERATION

To be held in the city of Los Angeles on Sunday, February 18, 2001, under the following rules:

**FIRST**: All Oaxacan communities and organizations can participate....

**SECOND**: All communities and organizations can participate with THREE delegates with the right to a voice and a vote, as well as an unlimited number of guests they wish to invite.

**THIRD**: All applications for accreditation should contain the name of the community or organization, the authorization of their board of directors (with signature and seal), and the names of the delegates with a voice and a vote that they nominate for the Congress....

**FIFTH**: The board of directors of the Federation will be elected by applications that are supported by EIGHT communities or organizations.... The positions for the governing board that should fill the application are: 1- President; 2- Vice President; 3- Secretary of Organization; 4- Under Secretary of Organization; 5- Treasurer; 6-Secretary of Projects; 7- Secretary of Political Relations; 8- Under Secretary of Communications; 9- Secretary of Women's Issues; 10- Secretary of Culture; 11- Secretary of Sports; 12- Secretary of Youth Action; 13- Coordinator of Advisers....

**SEVENTH**: Each delegate with a voice and a vote will obtain a numbered ballot to emit his or her individual and secret vote. The application that obtains the majority of votes will be the winner....

---

On November 17, 2001, a key meeting took place at which the participants addressed the question of what type of organization should be endorsed. One proposal, advanced and supported by several political organizations, was to form a more or less wide and flexible network of organizations, given that there already were several strong organizations working in different places in California. Among these were the Oaxacan Indigenous Binational Front (FIOB), based in Fresno; the Coalition of Indigenous Communities of Oaxaca (COCIO), from north San Diego County;

the Oaxacan Regional Organization (ORO); and the Union of Highland Communities of Oaxaca (UCSO), from Los Angeles. Another proposal, backed by several organizations, was to create a federation with a large, centralized governing board, so that it could support the communities' projects. This proposal gained momentum because the Oaxacan associations in Los Angeles wanted to participate in a dialogue with government policy makers, as had other state-level Mexican migrant organizations, and this would require some kind of federation.

The agreement that ultimately came out of the debate over the "character" of the organization to be created was to adopt the organizational form of a federation (that could work for the communities, not solely as a political organization) and to define it as an indigenous organization (since this was the members' ethnic identification and should be proudly displayed). Once this agreement was negotiated, the meeting participants quickly reached consensus on the Federation's motto and message: "For the Unity and Advancement of Oaxacans."

## FOCOICA's Member Organizations

As noted above, approximately four hundred people attended the Oaxacan Federation's organizational congress; they represented its thirty-two founding member organizations. The delegates with the right to a voice and a vote and who registered to participate and become federation members included:

- Nineteen community associations and sports clubs that registered with their respective delegates. All but two of these organizations were linked to Zapotec communities; one was Mixtec (Yanhuitlán) and one was Chinantec (Temextitlán). The majority of the Zapotec communities were from *municipio* headtowns in Oaxaca (municipal seats of government).

- Five regional groupings that could be classified as political organizations. Three were Mixtec: FIOB, the New Oaxacan Alliance (NAO), and the International Indigenous Network of Oaxaca (RIIO). UCSO was Zapotec. And COCIO had a mixed Zapotec/Mixtec membership.

- Eight cultural and educational organizations. Two were dance troupes: Huaxyacac and Danza de los Rubios. Four were community education organizations: Union of Oaxacan Women (UDMO); Regional Student Committee of Oaxaca (Comité Regional Estudiantil de

Oaxaca); the Benito Juárez Educational Center (Centro Educativo Benito Juárez); and United Mixtecs (Mixtecos Unidos). Two were cultural associations from specific communities: Mixtecos Unidos and the Organization for Macuiltianguis Community Support (OPAM).

Thus FOCOICA's creation in February 2001 came as a result of the unification of three different kinds of organizations formed by Oaxacans in California: community associations and sports clubs; regional groupings and political organizations; and cultural and educational organizations.[14]

## FOCOICA's Leadership

FOCOICA's leadership structure is rather traditional: a president, vice president, executive secretary and assistant secretary of organization, treasurer, secretary of projects, secretary of political relations, assistant secretary of communications, secretary of women's issues, secretary of culture, secretary of sports, secretary of youth action, and coordinator of advisers. This structure is similar to that of the Jalisco and Zacatecas federations in that the organization's public representation and leadership is concentrated in the presidency. This configuration has proved healthy for the organizational life of the Zacatecas Federation (discussed below); in contrast, the Jalisco Federation, which has had a highly centralized presidency since its formation, has encountered some difficulty alternating leaders. In the Oaxacan case, the leadership that was elected during FOCOICA's first congress is quite heterogeneous and representative of the ethnic and social diversity of Oaxacan migrants (see table 6.2).

Although the majority on the governing board are Zapotec men, its first president is Mixtec, and two women hold leadership positions. The board represents a wide range of organizations, and their social and economic profiles are equally diverse. Owners of small businesses are not as overrepresented as they are in the leadership of the mestizo federations. The challenge for a team as diverse as this, however, will be to strengthen FOCOICA's future and see that a leadership succession occurs in 2004, when a new board of directors will be elected.

---

[14] See the chapter appendix for a list of FOCOICA's member organizations.

Table 6.2. Characteristics of the Oaxacan Federation's Board of Directors

| | |
|---|---|
| Total | 13 members |
| Organizational origins | 13 different organizations |
| Gender | 2 women, 11 men |
| Ethnicity | 3 Mixtecs |
| | 8 Zapotecs |
| | 1 Chinantec |
| | 1 Chatina |
| Education | 6 with a bachelor's degree or higher in the United States |
| | 1 with university studies in Mexico |
| | 1 with high school diploma in Mexico |
| | 5 with primary school in Mexico |
| Profession and employment | 1 full-time organizer |
| | 2 students |
| | 1 supervisor |
| | 1 worker in research and video |
| | 1 physician |
| | 1 university professor |
| | 2 business owners |
| | 4 workers |

## MESTIZO MIGRANTS: THE CASES OF ZACATECAS AND JALISCO

In the early 1960s, the various communities of Mexican migrants in key destinations like Los Angeles were already organized into so-called social clubs. These organizations sometimes formed because the members came from the same town or region in Mexico, and other times simply because the members were Mexican. "We had a lot of fun, there was a lot of sharing," commented one founder of such a group. "All the families held dances or picnics in the countryside, and we spent some really nice time together." Some years later, in 1972, several of these social clubs, with members from different states in Mexico, decided to organize within the Federation of United Mexican Clubs in order to encourage friendship and solidarity among their members and to carry out occasional philanthropic projects. At that time, there did not seem to be a marked differentiation between the various groups of Mexican migrants, and, generally speaking, relations with the various Mexican government agencies were scarce and weak. This would change in years to come.

In the 1990s the growing presence of associations within Mexican migrant communities in California, along with the Mexican government's outreach campaign (led by the Program for Mexican Communities Abroad, or PCME), encouraged the further expansion of migrant associations via the organizational model of clubs and federations. Those communities that had a long migratory and organizational tradition managed to take advantage of this new circumstance to consolidate their organizational networks, especially those from Jalisco and Zacatecas (see table 6.3).[15]

Table 6.3. Mexican Migrant Clubs and Federations in Los Angeles, 1998–2003

| State of Origin | Number of Clubs | | Federation | |
|---|---|---|---|---|
| | 1998 | 2003 | 1998 | 2003 |
| Jalisco | 49 | 82 | Yes | Yes |
| Michoacán | 11 | 16 | No | Yes |
| Zacatecas | 51 | 52 | Yes | Yes |
| Guanajuato | 1 | 4 | No | Yes |
| Federal District | 0 | 0 | No | No |
| Sinaloa | 11 | 6 | Yes | Yes |
| Durango | 4 | 3 | Yes | Yes |
| Nayarit | 9 | 16 | Yes | Yes |
| Guerrero | 1 | 2 | No | No |
| Puebla | 5 | 4 | No | No |
| Oaxaca | 8 | 41 | No | Yes |
| Other | 20 | 49 | – | – |
| Total | 170 | 275 | 5 | 8 |

*Sources*: Zabin and Escala Rabadán 1998, and authors' estimates based on information from the Mexican consulate in Los Angeles and from interviews with federation leaders, 1998 and 2002.

Jalisco is the home state of the largest Mexican migrant communities living in the United States. This western Mexican state has in the past been the largest single source of Mexican migration to the United States, which explains the consolidation of Jalisco's migrant communities in different

---

15 Most of the literature on Mexican clubs and federations in the United States focuses on migrants from both regions. For seminal work on migrants from Zacatecas, see Goldring 1992, 1995; Moctezuma 1999; Mestries 1998. For the case of Jalisco, see Morán 1998.

areas of northern and southern California, the central arrival points for these migrants. Networks of Jalisco *paisanos* living in the Los Angeles area led to the emergence of their associations years ago. For example, migrants from Pegueros, in the municipality of Tepatitlán in the highlands of Jalisco, have been migrating and settling in the northern and western areas of Los Angeles for decades.[16] During the 1960s and 1970s, they began to form sports teams from their locality and later decided to adopt the organizational model already common in other migrant communities. The Club Pegueros, formally established in Los Angeles in 1981 as a result of these initial steps, then allowed its members to make official the implementation of philanthropic projects they had been carrying out for years.

The sports leagues and migrant clubs from Jalisco that had existed throughout the 1970s and 1980s received a significant boost when the PCME was established in 1990. The Mexican consulate in Los Angeles was particularly active in developing these clubs; and because of its past experiences, the community of Jalisco migrants was especially receptive. The consulate developed a very effective strategy that involved arranging meetings between municipal presidents from Jalisco and their *paisanos* in Los Angeles. The consulate could identify the place of origin for migrants in Los Angeles (and their local addresses and telephone numbers) by consulting the consular identification cards kept on file at the consulate. Invitations would then go out to migrants, asking them to attend a meeting with *paisanos* and local authorities and emphasizing the advantage of having an organization to represent their interests. Local authorities simultaneously underlined the importance of having their "absent children" support their communities of origin by organizing and aiding in their home communities' development.[17]

This strategy was so successful that by 1991 there were enough Jalisco clubs to establish a federation. The Federation of Jalisco Clubs (Federación de Clubes Jaliscienses) was created that year in Los Angeles; through its collaboration with the Mexican consulate in Los Angeles, it was able to increase the number of member clubs to about fifty by the end of the decade. The inclusion of so many associations within a single federation over

---

[16] There are a significant number of studies on migration from Jalisco to the United States in general, and to California in particular. See, for example, Castillo and Ríos 1989; Davis 1990; Fábregas 1986; Escobar et al. 1987; Arroyo Alejandre, de León Arias, and Valenzuela Varela 1991.

[17] For a more detailed discussion of the Mexican consulate in Los Angeles's implementation of these mechanisms, see Zabin and Escala Rabadán 1998.

such a short period represents a remarkable achievement on the part of the Jalisco migrant community.

The Zacatecas migratory tradition also dates from the early twentieth century. By the late 1950s and early 1960s, Zacatecans had already created the Fresnillo, Zacatecano, Guadalupe Victoria, and Yahualica clubs in the Los Angeles area, so their organizational structures have already been tested for decades. As with similar associations, these clubs were the starting point for the development of two central organizational aims: the creation and strengthening of ties between *paisanos* from the same community, and a philanthropic orientation with regard to their towns of origin. This is clearly demonstrated in the following narrative told by one of the founders of these clubs:

> In 1962 we became concerned and met with a group of people from the town to install potable water there, which was very much needed. This group started to get together, and we held small parties at homes and started to provide support and we managed to install the water. After that I told them: "Well, why don't we unify and establish a structured club?" That is where the Club Social Guadalupe Victoria came from; that's the name of the town in Zacatecas.... It was very pleasing; it was a beautiful moment of sharing because there were no personal interests.... We shared because we wanted to. We made good friends, the family spent time together, and most of the time we also went to the other clubs' events and kept in contact with each other.[18]

Due to their large numbers, Zacatecan clubs became the most visible nucleus within the Federation of United Mexican Clubs in the early 1970s; as a result of their continuing growth, the name of this federation had changed to the Federation of Zacatecas Clubs by the mid-1980s, as noted earlier. The organizational tradition of the Zacatecan migrant community would be further strengthened by support from the Zacatecas state government, which, with the Los Angeles visit of the state's governor in 1986, sought to fortify its ties with the migrant communities. These two elements — the continuation of an organizational tradition and the consolidation of mutually cooperative mechanisms with the state

---

[18] Interview with Gregorio Casillas, Club Guadalupe Victoria de Jerez, Los Angeles, February 2001.

government—explain the sustained growth of Zacatecan migrant associations in the United States.[19]

## Leadership: Federations from Zacatecas and Jalisco

A determining factor in the development of the Zacatecas and Jalisco federations has been the existence of leaders capable of promoting their emergence and consolidation. These leaders tend to have common socioeconomic characteristics (most are successful small and medium-size business owners, whose income, education level, and years of residence in the United States exceed those of the average Mexican migrant), and the federation model that the Jalisco and Zacatecas clubs promoted is apparently similar in terms of numbers and functions. Nevertheless, there are marked differences between them, and these can be explained by their different leadership styles.

In theory, the Federation of Jalisco Clubs has a decentralized leadership represented by the various committees that constitute the board of directors, rotated every two years. In practice, however, leadership has been markedly centralized in the presidency. For example, the board of directors was chosen by the president, not by the federation's members. Further, the president has extended his term in office since the foundation of the federation, reelecting himself periodically until early 2002, except for a two-year period when, according to federation statutes, he had to step down. During that period, he served as vice president of the federation, and the presidency was occupied by his wife (another founding member of the federation), which allowed for his return to the presidency at the end of the two-year period (Zabin and Escala Rabadán 1998).

The centralized leadership of the Federation of Jalisco Clubs is also visible in its internal practices. The president wrote the agenda and chose the discussion topics for its regular business meetings, and decisions were made with little or no discussion. The president generally dominated the discussion and often took on most of the important tasks instead of delegating them to others. This centralism restricted the formation and development of new leaders, despite the growing number of member clubs.

---

[19] Although there are several Zacatecan federations throughout the United States, grouping hundreds of these clubs, the Federation of Zacatecan Clubs in Los Angeles appears to be the "poster child" for studies conducted on Mexican migrant associations in the United States, as many of the works cited demonstrate. However, we should remember that this organization's prominence owes much to the Zacatecan migrants' long organizational experience.

The long organizational tradition of the Zacatecas Federation, by contrast, has supported the formation of a number of capable leaders over the years. These individuals have held different leadership roles within the federation, as well as in other migrant organizations such as the Mexican Charity Committee (Comité de Beneficencia Mexicana) and Mexican Civic Patriotic Committee (Comité Mexicano Cívico Patriótico). The federation has developed a highly effective organizational structure, with an extensive division of labor represented by the various committees that make up the board of directors, elected annually by federation members. This decentralization of responsibilities is an important factor in the internal dynamic of the federation itself. For example, discussions at regular business meetings routinely involve different viewpoints, and the voice of the president, although important, does not determine outcomes. The importance of this deliberative dynamic is clearly evident in the *comisario* position on the board of directors; the *comisario*'s main responsibility is to regulate participation in federation meetings (Zabin and Escala Rabadán 1998).

## COMPARING INDIGENOUS AND MESTIZO FEDERATIONS

Despite their differences, the Jalisco and Zacatecas federations exemplify the unification of the organizational traditions of their respective migrant communities and the effects of the Mexican government's new policies to strengthen contacts with their communities abroad. The consolidation of this organizational model—the creation of "pan-state" federations—eventually became the most visible form of representation of the distinct organized communities.

As for indigenous Oaxacan migrants, whose organized presence in California dates from the 1970s, their various organizations did not manage to consolidate a federation comparable to those of Jalisco and Zacatecas until February 2001. The establishment of the Oaxacan Federation as a statewide organization allowed indigenous migrants to overcome multiple ethnic, regional, and political divisions that had blocked the creation of an organization large enough and representative enough to serve as an interlocutor with the state government. The following comparative analysis of federation leadership structures and styles draws on data from the authors' ethnographic fieldwork in Los Angeles from June 2002 to September 2003.

The Jalisco and Zacatecas federations have employed a basic organizational structure from the time of their formation until today. There is a board of directors made up of different committees, which include members of the various member clubs, and headed by the federation president.

Interestingly, FOCOICA adopted a very similar organizational structure, though with certain modifications, including the creation of committees for women's action, youth action, and coordination of consultants. Yet, although the three federations are all represented by a president, the ways in which specific committees are filled are different. In the case of the Oaxacans, the members of the board of directors (and the president) are elected by slates; in the case of the Jalisco Federation, the current president appoints his governing board; and in the Zacatecas Federation, members vote separately for each committee.

The creation of the Jalisco and Zacatecas federations involved their establishment as nonprofit organizations in the United States, which allowed them to fund-raise for their operations. These federations also became an important source of support for the philanthropic work of their member clubs, whether in project initiation, project implementation, or problem solving related to community projects.[20] FOCOICA followed this same model; it also registered as a nonprofit organization, except that it specifically used this status to obtain funding from public and private foundations to implement community projects.[21]

The ability of these three federations to relate to different political and social actors in both Mexico and the United States gives their members access to information and resources that they would have difficulty obtaining as isolated groups. One example is the information that representatives of the organizations receive in their monthly meetings—information from the Mexican consulate and state and federal governments, as well as from other members on the board of directors. This information is then conveyed to the membership of each club during their respective meetings. The federations have been able to provide diverse, reliable information to their member associations on issues ranging from changes in immigration law to requirements for compliance with U.S. tax law or information about new Mexican government programs (such as the medical insurance pro-

---

[20] Some of the literature on these associations has analyzed their internal dynamics in detail. See, for example, Goldring 1992, 1995; Moctezuma 1999, 2000.

[21] FOCOICA obtained its first grant from a U.S. foundation, the California Wellness Foundation, in November 2001, for a community health project for the Oaxacan migrant community in Los Angeles. The grant was renewed in July 2002 for two years. This project was funded due to FOCOICA's collaboration with the Centro Binacional de Desarrollo Indígena Oaxaqueño, a nonprofit based in Fresno, California, which was founded by Mixtec members of FOCOICA and has more than six years of experience in developing and implementing community projects, mainly in the San Joaquin Valley.

gram for migrants' families in Mexico). Another example of the kinds of resources that can be accessed through this process is businesses' involvement in the federations. Federation presidents or other federation leaders regularly invite company representatives to offer their products and services to federation members, thereby enabling the associations to garner additional funds. For example, a Mexican construction company (Construmex) has negotiated an agreement with the three federations to sponsor several of their fund-raising events—dances, sports tournaments, and their participation in the Independence Day parade. In exchange, the company gains access to the board of directors, to whom it can sell its construction materials. These materials are then delivered directly to the home communities in Mexico for use in the infrastructure projects financed by the clubs via the "Three for One" program.[22] Yet another example is that federation meetings also serve as forums for petitions for philanthropic support (for example, requests for support from religious orders in their states of origin or for *paisanos* who are in dire need in the United States) (see Zabin and Escala Rabadán 1998).

## Indigenous and Mestizo Migrants and the Mexican Government

The increasing importance of indigenous and mestizo migrant clubs and federations, as well as the implementation of new policies pertaining to migrants, has led the Mexican government, at the state and federal levels, to implement programs to facilitate relations between communities on both sides of the border and to optimize the material and financial resources provided by the different groups. Not only have these programs been useful for channeling resources from organized migrants to their places of origin, but they have also created a structure through which migrant associations can interact with local, state, and federal governments in Mexico.

The result has been a sometimes comfortable, sometimes conflictive, relationship between these associations and the various levels of government. For example, for several years now the state governments of Oaxaca, Zacatecas, and Jalisco have operated liaison offices for their migrant communities. In Oaxaca, the State Coordinating Office for Oaxacan Migrant Affairs (CEAMO) is in constant contact with FOCOICA. The Zacatecas state government's representative in the United States, a former president of the Zacatecas Federation, has permanent offices in Los Angeles. Migrant liai-

---

[22] Under this program, the federal, state, and municipal governments each match the funding coming from migrant associations in the United States.

son agencies coordinate with the federations and other organizations to implement the "Three for One" co-investment program, to access emergency funds (mainly to transport home the bodies of migrants who die in the United States), to coordinate Mexican governors' visits to the United States, and to organize state government–sponsored cultural events (such as the Oaxacans' Guelaguetza and, for Zacatecas and Jalisco, the election of beauty queens).

Although the migrant communities themselves laid the foundations for their new organizational structures, Mexican government involvement, particularly in the 1990s, has been crucial in consolidating the federation of clubs as an organizational model.[23] Almost all Mexican migrant associations have adopted this model, probably because of the advantages it offers in the interaction between government influences and the migrant associations' assertion of political independence. On the one hand, federations are better able to interact with other agencies in Mexico, particularly with municipal and state governments, as well as with Mexican consulates in areas like Los Angeles, a fact that enables them to better support the objectives and initiatives of their member clubs. On the other hand, the various Mexican government agencies find it more productive to work with the federations, which can negotiate agreements and more easily overcome any obstacles that emerge.[24]

The internal dynamic of the Jalisco Federation in Los Angeles, which added a substantial number of clubs during the 1990s, has limited its role as mediator. Although this federation has become a legitimate representative of the interests of communities of Jalisco migrants in Los Angeles, its achievements have been restricted by two factors. The first is the fact that it lacks a decentralized leadership that can provide optimal support to its member clubs' initiatives; second, even though the Jalisco state government recognizes the federation's role as interlocutor, state support has been tepid. Despite Jalisco's long history of out-migration, the state gov-

---

[23] An extensive literature on "transnational communities" set the basis for "transnational studies" or, simply, "transnationalism." See, for example, the classic collection compiled by Schiller, Basch, and Blanc-Szanton (1992). A more recent work in this fruitful analytical field is Levitt 2001. However, this perspective has also been subject to criticism; see for example Weber 1999; Fitzgerald 2002.

[24] Much of the literature on this issue has emphasized the Mexican government's role in this relationship and analyzed its importance. See, for example, Goldring 1992, 1995; Moctezuma 1999, 2000; Smith 1995. See also Guarnizo's comparative work on Mexican and Dominican migrants and the policies of their respective governments (1998).

ernment has been very slow to implement policies that attend to the needs of its communities in the United States, which is one reason for its limited cooperation with the federation (Escala Rabadán 2001).

In contrast, the Zacatecas Federation has been able to build a solid relationship with Mexican government officials, particularly state government officials. These links, along with the federation's organizational history, have made it an important intermediary between its member clubs and government agencies in Mexico. The Zacatecas clubs in California have taken extensive advantage of this effective intermediation to implement infrastructure projects in their communities of origin. Through the "Two for One" program, established in 1992, and the "Three for One" program created in 1999 (under the former program, federal and state governments match every dollar the clubs provide for social infrastructure projects; the latter adds a match from municipal governments), the Zacatecas Federation has generated more investment funding and implemented more infrastructure projects than any other federation. The programs to match migrants' investments in their home communities grew out of the relationship between this migrant organization and the Zacatecas state government, attesting to the federation's ability to create effective intermediation between its member associations and communities of origin in Mexico.[25]

Because of its more recent creation, FOCOICA has been able to draw upon the experiences of the other, earlier federations, particularly the Zacatecas Federation, in order to consolidate quickly as the interlocutor for Oaxacan migrants vis-à-vis Mexico's state and federal governments. In fact, FOCOICA's earliest supporters promoted this organizational project as a platform for unifying the different voices of the Oaxacan community in order to establish a co-investment program similar to the "Three for One" program that had proved so successful for the Zacatecas Federation.

In this sense, by its very existence the Oaxacan Federation supports the hypothesis that such organizations facilitate dialogue and bargaining between migrant communities and their respective state governments and, to a lesser degree, the federal government. Only five months after FOCOICA was formed, Oaxaca's governor, José Murat, visited Los Angeles with the sole purpose of signing an agreement to implement the "Three for One" program in Oaxaca. This was the beginning of a powerful working rela-

---

[25] Practically all writings about the Zacatecas Federation and clubs in Los Angeles have underlined the achievements of cooperative mechanisms as an indicator of their solidity. In addition to the works already cited, see Esparza 2000; García Zamora 2000, 2001.

tionship that went on to address issues such as a youth cultural exchange program, establishment of a emergency fund for migrants in need, celebration of a Guelaguetza in Los Angeles, and the donation of a statue of Benito Juárez, which was erected in the Plaza México in Lynwood.

Due to FOCOICA's short existence, it is difficult to evaluate the efficacy of its leadership and its capacity to generate new leaders. One thing is evident, however: a radical change has occurred in the relationship between the Oaxacan migrant community and their state government. The intensification of this relationship is a direct result of the formation of the Oaxacan Federation, which gave the current governor a counterpart in the Oaxacan migrant community, an option that the state's two previous governors, who also wanted to reach out to the migrant community, did not have.

## CONCLUSION

The formation of immigrant-led federations shows how Mexican migrants, far from being passive victims of the discriminatory and exploitative conditions they face in the United States, have responded creatively, building grassroots organizations that make collective action possible in their communities of origin and in the communities they have established along their migratory circuit in the United States. These federations demonstrate Mexican migrants' capacity to build transnational organizations and social spaces over the long term; their efforts even predate the Mexican government's various attempts to incorporate Mexicans abroad. Indeed, these migrant organizations, based on their states of origin, have leveraged their power as counterparts of political authorities in Mexico and the United States, thereby reinforcing their members' sense of identity and empowerment.[26] However, as we can see from the experience of the Oaxacan Federation, statewide *indigenous* migrant organizations, with their strong eth-

---

[26] This is consistent with arguments by Luin Goldring and Robert Smith, prominent analysts of Mexican transnational organizations. In their recent theoretical works, Goldring (2002) and Smith (2003) examine the relationship between the Mexican state and transmigrant organizations. While both highlight the somewhat clientelistic relationship between some federations and the Mexican government, our orientation and findings are closer to Goldring's, who emphasizes the importance of probing the specific dynamics between these organizations and Mexican political authorities, particularly state governments. This perspective makes it possible to look beyond the state-led or immigrant organization–led transnational dilemma and highlights the importance of the subnational level in capturing the relationship between federations and the Mexican state, as well as in explaining the different outcomes in terms of bargaining power among these groups.

nic identity component, stand in sharp contrast to the less overtly ethnic and more localistic identities developed by the village-based organizations that mestizo migrants from Jalisco and Zacatecas have developed.

Comparing the experiences of indigenous and mestizo Mexican migrants can further our understanding of how ethnicity shapes the migratory experience and incorporation patterns of Mexican migrants. It also sheds light on the intensification of ethnicity among Oaxacan indigenous migrants and "*paisano* identity" among mestizos from Jalisco and Zacatecas, which leads to the counterintuitive proposition that long-term transnational migration is increasing, not reducing, self-identification by ethnicity. This new identity is an important force in the formation of hometown associations and federations among both indigenous and mestizo Mexican migrants.

The political practices of Oaxacan indigenous migrants' organizations are shaped by the political context in which they take place. Indigenous migrant organizations like FOCOICA respond to the strong political presence of the Zacatecas and Jalisco federations in Los Angeles. In this respect, the organizational space of Mexican migration to the United States— exemplified by migrant clubs and federations—has been consolidated in recent years as a result of the many experiences generated by migrant networks and by the exponential growth in their interaction with political actors at different levels of the Mexican and U.S. governments.

For example, the creation in July 2002 of the Council of Presidents of Mexican Federations of Los Angeles (which includes the heads of all thirteen Mexican federations in the region) has given the migrant associations an even stronger political voice.[27] In January 2004 the Council of Presidents of Mexican Federations participated in two key political events. First, responding to an invitation from the Bush administration, the council sent a member to the White House to attend the January 7 announcement of a new immigration reform initiative. Second, on January 20, at the offices of the Mexican consulate in Los Angeles, the council hosted a delegation of five Mexican governors (representing the Mexican Conference of Governors) who came to discuss the right to vote of Mexicans living abroad and President Bush's immigration proposal and its implications for the Mexican immigrant community.

The Council of Presidents of Mexican Federations has also collaborated closely with unions and immigration advocates to lobby for driver licenses

---

[27] The Council of Presidents claims to represent almost 300,000 Mexican immigrant families in California; see Wides 2004.

for undocumented workers. Further, it sent six participants to the recent Immigrant Workers Freedom Ride to Washington, D.C. This new political activism stands in sharp contrast to the general political disengagement of hometown associations in the mid-1990s, when anti-immigrant Proposition 187 was being debated in California. These activities show how the consolidation of Mexican migrant organizations has permitted the emergence of a dense transnational communications network linking migrants with their communities and with Mexico's municipal, state, and federal governments. This expanding communications network has now come to incorporate political and social actors in the United States as well.

Another important achievement of the migrant clubs and federations is an increased socialization among migrants across ethnic and regional identity boundaries. A central objective of this essay was to illustrate how indigenous and mestizo migrants—despite their many ethnic, political, and social differences—have adopted similar models for their statewide organizations. In the Los Angeles area, clubs and federations have become an important component of the social networks of both indigenous and mestizo migrants.

Despite their achievements, these associations now face a broad array of challenges. The first is the increasing competition between immigrant-led organizations that claim to represent the Mexican immigrant community. The Council of Presidents of Mexican Federations of Los Angeles has emerged as a very strong voice in this debate, but it is not the only one.[28] In the fall of 2003, the Mexican government created an Advisory Council to the Institute of Mexicans Abroad (a governmental entity within the Foreign Ministry). This council includes one hundred Mexican migrants from different walks of life—from activists to lawyers and business owners.[29] Officially, the Mexican federal government created this council to serve as the main conduit for its relations with Mexican immigrants in the United States. Clearly, the emergence and institutionalization of immigrant-led organizations has allowed for the creation and strengthening of ties that link migrant communities in the United States to their home communities

---

[28] Other organizations vying to position themselves as representatives of Mexicans in the United States include the Coalición por los Derechos Políticos de los Mexicanos en el Exterior (CDPME), the Frente Cívico Zacatecano (FCZ), the Coalición Internacional de Mexicanos en el Extranjero (CIME), and the Asociación Mundial de Mexicanos en el Exterior (AMME).

[29] For an excellent account of the process of electing council members in different U.S. cities, see Cano, Molina, and Najar 2002.

in Mexico and to the different levels of the Mexican government. We expect that this trend will not only continue but will expand dramatically in the near future.

## References

Arroyo Alejandre, Jesús, Adrián de León Arias, and M. Basilia Valenzuela Varela. 1991. *Migración rural hacia Estados Unidos: un estudio regional en Jalisco.* Mexico City: Conaculta.

Bartolomé, Miguel A., and Alicia Barabás. 1986. "Los migrantes étnicos de Oaxaca," *México Indígena* 2, no. 18: 23–25.

Cano, Arturo, Tania Molina, and Alberto Najar. 2002. "El consejo de migrantes nace bajo fuego: lista, la representación de los mexicanos en EU," *Masiosare* (*La Jornada*), December 1.

Castillo, Pedro, and Antonio Ríos. 1989. *México en Los Angeles: una historia social y cultural, 1781–1985.* Mexico City: Alianza/Conaculta.

Cornelius, Wayne A. 1988. *The Changing Profile of Mexican Labor Migration to California in the 1980s.* La Jolla: Center for U.S.-Mexican Studies, University of California, San Diego.

Davis, Marilyn. 1990. *Mexican Voices/American Dreams: An Oral History of Mexican Immigration to the United States.* New York: Henry Holt and Co.

Díaz de Cossío, Roger, Graciela Orozco, and Esther González. 1997. *Los mexicanos en Estados Unidos.* Mexico City: Sistemas Técnicos de Edición.

Escala Rabadán, Luis. 2001. "Migrants' Associations in California, Collective Remittances, and Productive Investment in Mexico: The Case of Jalisco." Presented at the workshop "Mexican Migration, Remittances, and Regional Economic Development," University of California, Los Angeles.

Escobar, Agustín, et al. 1987. "Migración, mercados de trabajo y economía internacional: Jalisco y los Estados Unidos," *Encuentro* (El Colegio de Jalisco) 16, vol. 4, no. 4.

Esparza, Armando. 2000. "Evaluación del Programa 'Tres por Uno.'" In *Memorias del Foro Sivilla-Fundación Produce sobre Temas de Migración,* edited by Miguel Moctezuma. Zacatecas, Mexico.

Espinoza, Víctor. 1999. "La Federación de Clubes Michoacanos en Illinois: historia y perspectivas a futuro de una organización civil mexicana en Estados Unidos." Report of the Chicago-Michoacán Project, Heartland Alliance.

Fábregas, Andrés. 1986. *La formación histórica de una región: Los Altos de Jalisco.* Mexico City: Centro de Investigaciones y Estudios Superiores en Antropología Social.

Fitzgerald, David S. 2002. "Rethinking the 'Local': Cross-Border Politics and Hometown Networks in a Mexican Immigrant Union." Presented at the

Second Colloquium on International Migration, Mexico-California, University of California, Berkeley, March.

García Zamora, Rodolfo. 2000. *Agricultura, migración y desarrollo regional.* Zacatecas: Universidad Autónoma de Zacatecas.

———. 2001. "Migración internacional y desarrollo local: una propuesta para Zacatecas, México." Zacatecas: Universidad Autónoma de Zacatecas.

Goldring, Luin. 1992. "La migración México-EUA y la transnacionalización del espacio político y social: perspectivas desde el México rural," *Estudios Sociológicos* 10.

———. 1995. "Blurring Borders: Constructing Transnational Community Process of Mexico-U.S. Migration," *Research in Community Sociology* 6.

———. 2002. "The Mexican State and Transmigrant Organizations: Negotiating the Boundaries of Membership and Participation," *Latin American Research Review* 37, no. 3.

González Gutiérrez, Carlos. 1993. "The Mexican Diaspora in California: The Limits and Possibilities of the Mexican Government." In *The California-Mexico Connection*, edited by Abraham Lowenthal and Katrina Burgess. Palo Alto, Calif.: Stanford: Stanford University Press.

———. 1995. "La organización de los inmigrantes mexicanos en Los Angeles: la lealtad de los oriundos," *Revista Mexicana de Política Exterior* 46: 59–101.

Guarnizo, Luis. 1998. "The Rise of Transnational Social Formations: Mexican and Dominican State Responses to Transnational Migration," *Political Power and Social Theory* 12: 45–94.

Hirabayashi, Lane Ryo. 1993. *Cultural Capital: Mountain Zapotec Migrant Associations in Mexico City.* Tucson: Arizona University Press.

Levitt, Peggy. 2001. *The Transnational Villagers.* Berkeley: University of California Press.

López, Felipe, Luis Escala-Rabadán, and Raúl Hinojosa-Ojeda. 2001. "Migrant Associations, Remittances, and Regional Development between Los Angeles and Oaxaca, Mexico." Los Angeles: North American Integration and Development Center, University of California, Los Angeles.

Massey, Douglas, Rafael Alarcón, Jorge Durand, and Humberto González. 1987. *Return to Aztlan. The Social Process of International Migration from Western Mexico.* Berkeley: University of California Press.

Mestries, Francis. 1998. "Tradición migratoria y organización comunitaria: el caso de Zacatecas." In *Población, desarrollo y globalización*, edited by René Zenteno. Mexico: SOMEDE/El Colegio de la Frontera Norte.

Mines, Richard. 1981. *Developing a Community Tradition of Migration: A Field Study in Rural Zacatecas, Mexico and California Settlement Areas.* La Jolla: Center for U.S.-Mexican Studies, University of California, San Diego.

Moctezuma, Miguel. 1999. "Redes sociales, comunidades filiales, familias y clubes migrantes." PhD dissertation, El Colegio de la Frontera Norte.

————. 2000. "Coinversión en servicios e infraestructura comunitaria impulsados por los migrantes y el gobierno de Zacatecas." In *Memorias del Foro Sivilla-Fundación Produce sobre Temas de Migración*, edited by Miguel Moctezuma. Zacatecas, Mexico.

Morán, Luis Rodolfo. 1998. "Los sentidos de la transición: migrantes internacionales y cultura regional." PhD dissertation, El Colegio de la Frontera Norte.

Orozco, Graciela, Esther González, and Roger Díaz de Cossío. 2003. *Las organizaciones mexicano-americanas, hispanas y mexicanas en Estados Unidos.* Mexico City: Centro de Estudios Migratorios (Instituto Nacional de Migración)/Fundación Solidaridad Mexicano Americana.

Rivera-Salgado, Gaspar. 1999. "Migration and Political Activism: Mexican Transnational Indigenous Communities in a Comparative Perspective." PhD dissertation, University of California, Santa Cruz.

————. 2000. "Transnational Political Strategies: The Case of Mexican Indigenous Migrants." In *Immigration Research for a New Century: Multidisciplinary Perspectives*, edited by Nancy Foner, Rubén Rumbaut, and Steven Gold. New York: Russell Sage Foundation.

Schiller, Nina Glick, Linda Basch, and Cristina Blanc-Szanton, eds. 1992. *Towards a Transnational Perspective on Migration. Race, Class, Ethnicity, and Nationalism Reconsidered.* New York: New York Academy of Sciences.

Smith, Robert. 1995. "Los Ausentes Siempre Presentes: The Imagining, Making and Politics of a Transnational Migrant Community between Ticuani, Puebla, Mexico and New York City." PhD dissertation, Columbia University.

————. 2003. "Migrant Membership as an Instituted Process: Transnationalization, the State and the Extra-Territorial Conduct of Mexican Politics," *International Migration Review* 37, no. 2 (Summer).

Taylor, Lawrence. 1997. "Las fiestas patrias y la preservación de la identidad cultural mexicana en California: una visión histórica," *Frontera Norte* 9, no. 18.

Weber, Devra. 1999. "Historical Perspectives on Mexican Transnationalism," *Social Justice* 26, no. 3.

Wides, Laura. 2004. "Immigrant Mexican Philanthropic Groups Turn toward Politics," Associated Press, January 19. At http://www.sfgate.com/cgibin/article.cgi?file=/news/archive/2004/01/19/state1445EST0047.DTL.

Zabin, Carol, and Luis Escala Rabadán. 1998. "Mexican Hometown Associations and Mexican Immigrant Political Empowerment in Los Angeles." Working Paper Series. Washington, D.C.: The Aspen Institute.

Zabin, Carol, Michael Kearney, Anna García, Dave Runsten, and Carole Nagengast. 1993. *Mixtec Migrants in California Agriculture: A New Cycle of Poverty.* Davis: California Institute for Rural Studies.

## APPENDIX: FEDERATION MEMBERSHIPS

### Founding Organizations of the Oaxacan Federation of Indigenous Communities and Organizations in California (FOCOICA)

Ayoquezco
Asociación Santo Domingo Yanhuitlán, Oaxaca en Los Angeles
Centro Educativo Benito Juárez
Unión de Comunidades Serranas de Oaxaca (UCSO)
Club Deportivo Atepec
Santa María Jaltianguis
San Juan Luvina
Comunidad Tlacolulense en Los Angeles (COTLA)
Comité Regional Estudiantil Oaxaqueño (CREO)
Círculo Unido para el Progreso de Lachitaa
Comunidad Benito Juárez
Frente Indígena Oaxaqueño Binacional (FIOB)
El Trapiche
Grupo Folclórico Huaxyacac
Ejutla Libre
Rosario Temextitlán
Nueva Alianza Oaxaqueña (NAO)
Red Internacional Indígena Oaxaqueña (RIIO)
Paisanos Unidos de Santiago Matatlán
Unión de Mujeres Oaxaqueñas (UDMO)
Organización de Comunidades Indígenas de Oaxaca (COCIO)
Santa Ana Tlapacoya
Organización de Profesionales Oaxaqueños
Danza de Los Rubios del Condado Norte de San Diego
San Pedro el Rincón Tlapacoya
Organización Zapoteca de Teotitlán del Valle
Organización Pro-mejoramiento de San Pedro Cajonos
Organización Quiaviní
Mixtecos Unidos
Santo Tomás Tecolotitlán
Club LA Temex
Organización Para la Ayuda Macuiltianguense (OPAM)

## Member Clubs of the Zacatecas Federation of Southern California
(as of October 2002)

Club Amigos La Pitahaya
Club Campesinos Remolino
Club Deportivo Santa Juana
Club Ermita de los Correa
Club Fraternidad las Ánimas
Club Hermandad Latina
Club Jomulquillo
Club Las Ánimas
Club Comité San Cristobal
   Magallanes Momax
Club Cultural Adjuntas del
   Refugio
Club Deportivo San Vicente
Club Familias Unidas de
   Tepechitlán
Club Grupo El Remolino
Club Huanusquenses
Club Miguel Auza
Club Asociación de Apoyo
   Tlaltenanguense
Club Del Pueblo Susticacán
Club Deportivo Valparaíso
Club Familias Unidas por Jalpa
Club Hermandad Jalpense
Club Jagüeyense
Club Milpillas de la Sierra
Club El Nochistlense
Club Raíces Zacatecanas
Club Ranchos Unidos Atolinga
Club San Ignacio

Club Social El Cargadero
Club Social La Luz de California
   en U.S.A.
Club Social Tepechitlán
Club Tres Brincos
Club Unión Juvenil de la
   F.C.Z.S.C.
Club Rancho los Cuervos
Club Ranchos Unidos de Luis
   Moya
Club San Juan del Centro
Club Social Caxcanes de Moyahua,
   Zacatecas
Club Social Momax
Club Social Villanueva
Club Unidad Social y Cultural
Club La Villita
Club El Puerto
Club Rancho el Pedregal
Club Rieleros
Club Social Atolinga
Club Social Chacuiloca
Club Tlachichila
Club Unidos por los de Nava
Club Zacatecas, Zacatecas
Club San José de la Era
Club Piñón Gigante de Juchipila,
   Zacatecas
Club San José de Mesillas

## Member Clubs in the Jalisco Federation in Los Angeles
(as of May 2003)

Club San Pedro Itzicán
Club Rancho Los Sotoles
Club San Andrés
Club San Buenaventura

Club Sin Fronteras Chiquilistlán
Club Unión de Tula
Club Poncitlán
Club San Isidro Mazatepec

Club Sta. María del Valle
Club Teocuitatlán
Club Tequesquitlán
Club Tonalá
Club Unidos Solidarios
Club Chapala
Club San Sebastián
Club Capilla de Guadalupe
Club San Marcos Evangelista
Club El Rincón
Club Santa María de L.A.
Club San Martín de Bolaños
Club Temaca
Club Encarnación de Díaz
Club Tonayense
Club San Gabriel
Club San Ignacio Cerro Gordo
Club La Barca
Club Autlán de la Grana
Club Santa Rosa y Santa Gertrudis
Club Tepatitlán
Club Trigo de Alteñas
Club Sacalco de Torres
Club Etzatlán
Club Mezcala de la Asunción
Club Ajijic
Club Hijos Ausentes de Soyatlán
    de Oro

Club Hijos Ausentes de Mazatepec
Club Hijos Ausentes de San
    Antonio
Club Huejúcar
Club Ixtlahuacán del Río
Club Jamay
Club Jilotlán
Club Cocula
Club Comunitario Tepehuaje
Club Las Palmas de Ejutla
Club Potrerillos
Club Autlense
Club Mezquitic
Club Pegueros
Club Quila Jalisco
Club Guadalajara
Club Hacienda del Cabezón
Club Soyotlán de Oro
Club Talpa de Allende
Club Tecalitlán
Club Tecolotlán
Club Temastián
Club Tenamaztlán
Club Juanacatlán
Club Juchitlán
Club Asociación de Hijos Ausentes
    de Oconahua
Club Villa Guerrero

# 7

# Mixtec Farmworkers in Oregon: Linking Labor and Ethnicity through Farmworker Unions and Hometown Associations

LYNN STEPHEN

Beginning in the early 1980s, the Mexican immigrant farmworker population in Oregon began to reflect the emergent pattern in California: its composition was increasingly indigenous. By the mid-1980s, Mixtec farmworkers were a significant presence in the state and were among those who received legal residency in the United States through the Special Agricultural Workers (SAW) program of the Immigration Reform and Control Act of 1986 (IRCA). Since that time, family members of amnestied workers and others have joined the population of indigenous immigrants in Oregon. By 2002, indigenous immigrants accounted for a significant part of the state's temporary and permanent farmworker population and had moved into other sectors as well, including canneries, nurseries, construction, home care and child care, and other service and food-related industries.

As their numbers grew, Mixtec workers became a significant constituency for Oregon's farmworker union, Northwest Treeplanters and Farmworkers United (PCUN). The union was able to attract Mixtec members initially through its Immigration Service Center and through organizing campaigns in the growing season that targeted farms with significant numbers of Mixtec workers. The multiple legal statuses that Mixtec workers and their family members held (undocumented, legal resident, citizen), as well as their position as low-wage agricultural workers, were significant facets of the Mixtec experience that the union supported.

For many Mixtec farmworkers, the ethnic dimensions of their identity and experience in Oregon came to be realized through family networks and through participation in hometown associations such as the San Agustín Atenango Improvements Committee (Comité Pro-Obras de San Agustín Atenango), which has branches in Chicago and Las Vegas; in Madera, Oxnard, Santa Maria, Vista, and Santa Elena, California; in Portland and Salem, Oregon;[1] and in Grand Canyon, Arizona. Such associations can provide a social framework for men and women to come together and work toward a common goal in relation to their communities of origin. They also help maintain the rights and obligations that members of a particular community have, to institutionalize political practices that allow community members to engage in collective projects to benefit their hometown, and to engage in information exchange and practices that stretch across national boundaries and rework the concept of community in a transnational space (Rivera-Salgado 1998). The cultural and even physical sense of "place" or "community of origin" is accommodated to the realities of individuals and families who live their lives in several locations simultaneously and have done so for quite some time (see Rouse 1992; Kearney 1998). In the process of participating in hometown associations, the pan-Mixtec and local (community-of-origin) dimensions of their ethnic identity are often reinforced.

This chapter takes an ethnographic approach to understanding the multiple ways that Mixtec farmworker men and women have organized collectively in the state of Oregon, and how their participation in multiple organizations works to validate the different dimensions of their experience living and working in Oregon. I focus in particular on Mixtec participation in the PCUN and in one hometown association branch in Salem. Because of their unique position as indigenous persons within the Mexican immigrant population and the institutionalized racism against indigenous peoples, in both Mexico and the United States, in combination with their (often undocumented) status as low-wage workers, Mixtecs in Oregon and elsewhere have developed survival strategies that defend, maintain, and strengthen their ethnicity as well as their status as workers. In a state where indigenous politics refers to the original native peoples of Oregon (Coquille, Grand Round, Siletz, and others), being Mixtec is not part of the "native peoples map." On the other hand, when "diversity" is discussed in terms of the state's population, the categories of "Latino" or "Mexican" are

---

[1] The Salem branch began in October 2001.

often used to identify Mixtec immigrants, thus erasing their ethnic identity through Mexican nationalism or a pan-Latino identity. As discussed by Kearney (1998), hometown associations can act as visible forms of Mixtec self-differentiation—distinguishing them from U.S. Native Americans and Latinos. They thus serve as a focal point for ethnicity and for what we might call a public self-consciousness about ethnicity. As discussed here, participation in such ethnically identified and constituted organizations can occur simultaneously with people's participation in class-based forms of organization such as labor unions.

## THE MIXTEC PATH TO OREGON

Oregon Mixtec farmworker life-history narratives reveal a migration pattern similar to the one documented for California (Runsten and Kearney 1994; Kearney 1995; Rivera-Salgado 1998; Zabin and Hughes 1995). Many workers now in their 40s describe childhoods spent in the Mexican state of Sinaloa, where they went to harvest tomatoes, returning occasionally to their home communities for annual fiestas or for a family life-cycle event. Some have few memories of being children in Oaxaca. Delfina Cruz Vera,[2] forty years of age and now a resident in Salem, Oregon, describes her childhood as primarily taking place in Sinaloa.

> My parents worked in Sinaloa. We went to Culiacán and worked picking tomatoes, cucumbers, and peppers. My parents would leave in September and stay in Sinaloa until May. As kids, we almost always stayed in Sinaloa. Sometimes my father would go back to Oaxaca to check up on the house. I never went to school.... In Sinaloa there were whole families working in the fields. There were no restrictions on how old you had to be to work there. Everyone worked.

Delfina met her husband when she returned at twenty years of age to her natal community of San Agustín Atenango, Oaxaca.

From Sinaloa, some Mixtec workers who eventually came to Oregon went to Baja California, following the commercialization in the 1970s of tomato and strawberry crops for the North American market. Many spent

---

[2] This and all other names are pseudonyms unless otherwise specified. Interviews cited in this chapter were conducted from 2000 to 2002 in the Willamette Valley region of Oregon, primarily through two projects supported by grants from the Wayne Morse Center for Law and Politics in collaboration with PCUN.

time as fieldworkers in San Quintín, Baja California, and have family members who own small homes and land there.

Reina Bautista was born near Juxtlahuaca, Oaxaca, in 1975 but moved with her parents to Sinaloa when she was a year old. When she was six years old, her family arrived in San Quintín, where her father was already living. She remembers moving around quite a bit before arriving in San Quintín, where she went to school for several years. After leaving school and working for six years in San Quintín, Reina followed the path of an older sister and came directly to Woodburn, Oregon:

> When I was very small my parents left Oaxaca and went to Sinaloa. They were working there, and when the work ran out I remember that we went all over the place. We went to Culiacán and other places, and then when we got to Baja California, to San Quintín, we stayed there. We didn't move, and I got to go to school for three years.... I used to work during school vacations, and then when I got out of school at age nine or ten I started working all of the time.... We worked in tomatoes, potatoes, peas, whatever there was.... All the kids began to work when they were nine or ten years old. We worked all day long.... My parents bought a little piece of land and put up a small house.... I stayed there until I was sixteen, when I came to the United States. We were there with a lot of kids from the town where I was from.

> [What memories do you have from San Quintín?]

> Well, on the one hand it's a little sad because I would have liked to have studied more, but I didn't have the opportunity. The only nice memory I have is being together with my parents.

> [Did your whole family stay, or did some of them come to the United States?]

> My oldest sister came first, and afterward she sent for my father, my other sister, and then for me.

> [Where did they go in the United States?]

> Well, they went to San Bernardino and then to Fresno. Then in 1991 one of my sisters came here to Woodburn, Oregon, and she stayed. Then she sent for the rest of us. In 1991 we came directly to Woodburn from San Quintín.

While women like Reina were likely to come directly to Oregon from Mexico to reunite with family members who had already established themselves, many male migrants now over the age of forty first crossed into the United States from Baja California to work in California. They later moved to Oregon as part of circular migration routes. If they received legal U.S. residency as a result of IRCA, they eventually brought their families to Oregon. In the 1970s these men began to cross the border into California to work in berry and tomato fields near San Diego and Oxnard. From there they went on to harvest grapes in Fresno and often to other parts of California as well. As a part of that circuit, they began to arrive in Oregon in the late 1970s and early 1980s, usually brought by labor contractors.

Rodolfo Contreras first crossed the border near Tijuana in 1979 to work in Carlsbad and Oceanside, California. Like many migrants in San Diego County at the time (and to this day), he lived under ground in a hidden camp he and others fashioned to avoid detection by the U.S. Immigration and Naturalization Service (INS) — and to save on rent. He went from there to Madera, California, where he got to know a labor contractor who brought him to Oregon and Washington to work in a variety of crops, from strawberries to Christmas trees. Around 1987 he received amnesty through papers supplied by the labor contractor, and he became a legal permanent resident. He then brought his wife to Oregon directly from Oaxaca in the late 1980s. As he recalls:

> I came over to this side by Tijuana and San Ysidro. It was cheap then. I paid a coyote $100 there in Tijuana, and I arrived in Carlsbad and Oceanside. There were other people from my town there as well. Some of them had come from San Quintín. After I got here I built my house … but I made it under ground. We dug under the ground and made it deep enough so we could fit fifteen or twenty people. We made it there because we didn't want anyone to see us. We used a green branch and would pull it over the opening for our door. We slept there. That was how I started out when I first came here.

> [How did you get to Oregon?]

> Well, first we were in Madera, California. I got to know a *señora* who rented us rooms for $2 per night. That is where we got to know Miguel. He asked us if we wanted to plant pine trees and cut them down. So we went with him to

Klammath Falls, Medford, even to Washington State.... He
wasn't so good because of the way he would treat us.... We
worked with him all year. We worked in the Christmas trees
and then in strawberries and wheat.... I did my amnesty
with Miguel in 1988. Before that, when we first got to this
country, we didn't have anything and we were really afraid.
When you don't have papers, you don't go into the street.
You stay inside so that no one from the *migra* [INS] will get
you.... That's how we were when we came to Oregon.

## FROM SINGLE MEN TO FAMILIES AND BACK AGAIN

The majority of the agricultural workers granted legal residence through
the SAW provisions of IRCA were men. Overall, approximately a million
people were legalized under the SAW. In Oregon, 23,736 Mexicans received permanent residency. While this statistic reflects the number who
applied and completed the SAW program in Oregon, a figure between
40,000 and 50,000 may be more realistic because many workers who now
reside in Oregon completed the SAW program in California. Although it is
not clear how many of those legalized under the SAW were Mixtec, informed estimates put the current permanent Mixtec population in Oregon
at about 10,000 and the circulating population at between 20,000 and
30,000. In their 1994 survey of Oaxacan village networks in California,
Runsten and Kearney found that about "one-half of U.S. migrants from
Oaxaca were legalized by IRCA" (1994: viii). There are no similar statistics
for Oregon. It might be reasonable to assume, however, that about half of
the Mixtec workers (primarily men) who were seasonal workers in Oregon
in the mid-1980s received amnesty.

Because many Mixtec migrant men would return to their communities
of origin at least once a year in the 1980s—and sometimes had to stay
longer in order to fill community service roles (*cargos*)—not everyone who
was an agricultural worker in the mid-1980s was able to apply for amnesty
at the right time and receive legal residency. Nonetheless, some workers
who were not in the United States during the period specified in the SAW
were nevertheless able to receive amnesty. Further, it is widely acknowledged that the number of people who received amnesty was far greater
than the number probably employed in agriculture. The SAW program
was expected to grant legal status to 350,000 undocumented immigrants.
More than 1.3 million applied, and about a million eventually received
legal permanent residence (Schlosser 1995: 6). A significant number se-

cured amnesty using letters they had purchased from labor contractors and/or growers—whether or not the applicants technically met the SAW qualifications. Such letters were important in helping a significant number of people secure legal residency. Some growers and labor contractors also used letters like these to secure laborers in 1987.

From the late 1980s to the mid-1990s, Oregon's Mixtec farmworker population changed significantly in two ways. First, many of the men who became legal permanent residents sent for their wives and children. Second, once their families arrived, they settled more permanently and, in communities like Salem, came to form significant clusters of people from the same community. These clusters were often built around groups of siblings who established families or who brought their nuclear families with them from Oaxaca, San Quintín, or sometimes California. For example, most of the twenty or so nuclear families that compose a cluster of natives from San Agustín Atenango in Salem, and that now have their own branch hometown association, arrived in the late 1980s and early 1990s. Most of these families were established by about 1994, and they have children, both undocumented and U.S. citizens, now working their way through the public school system and, in some cases, junior college. While many families continue to have some "undocumented" members, all of these people have documents of a kind and are working. As Schlosser (1995) noted, "Counterfeit green cards, Social Security cards, driver licenses, SAW work histories—the documents necessary to obtain employment as a farmworker—can be easily obtained in rural California for $50.00. The process usually takes about an hour." This continues to be the case in Oregon as well.

The pattern of men coming to Oregon to work, attempting to receive amnesty, and then sending for their wives and children was not without consequences for the women left behind in Oaxaca. María de la Luz Contreras was married in her hometown of San Agustín Atenango in 1980. Immediately after the wedding her new husband returned to Oregon, and she spent seven years living with her in-laws. During that time her husband visited sporadically. As she recalls:

> I lived with my mother-in-law ... for seven years. Seven years and then I came here in 1987 when Enrique sent for me. All of this time I was in my hometown.

> [So your husband returned to the United States right after you got married?]

Yes. He was only around for fifteen days after we were married, and he came back to the United States and didn't come back for another ten months. He stayed another two weeks and then went back to the United States. And there was one time when he left me for four years in our village—with nothing to live on, without anything. I had to live with a lot of doubts for four years.... It was really hard for me to be there for those four years.... For the first two years, Enrique wrote to us and sent us money, but during the last two years he was very distant.... I had to wash and iron clothes and sell tortillas in order to earn money for food and to help out my mother-in-law.

[Were there other women in your community who had this same experience of being left for four years incommunicado?]

There were a lot of women in this situation. I wasn't the only one. There were a number of women who were in this situation and others whose husbands never returned. Their husbands got together with another woman on this side of the border, and they completely abandoned their wives at home.

In September 1987, Luz's husband sent for her and her two children, and they came directly from San Agustín to Salem, where he had rented an apartment. Luz's husband had been working in Oregon since 1984. She began working in the strawberry harvests the following summer while she was pregnant. In 1989 she started working in the local canneries as well as in the fields. She had two more children in the United States; her oldest two are now in junior college. Luz continues to work in two local canneries and frozen food plants, as does her husband. They work on opposite shifts so that someone can always be home with the younger children. Luz and her husband both became active in Oregon's PCUN farmworker union.

While undocumented relatives of established Mixtec families continue to come to Oregon, over the past four to five years new waves of young men have come to occupy an important niche in the state's seasonal berry and other harvests. The trend of family settlement and female migration has slowed considerably, and once again seasonal workers tend to be lone men, often young (see McConahay 2001). They are found primarily in labor camps and are brought by labor contractors who work them through a circuit encompassing California, Oregon, and Washington. As in the past, some are Mixtec, but recruiters are reaching into Triqui communities and

Veracruz State as well. Kissam, Intili, and García note this trend, particularly emphasizing the recruitment of teenagers as farmworkers:

> In 2000, we find that indigenous ethnic minorities within a Latino farm labor force are making up a greater and greater proportion of the local farm labor force throughout the country.... Along the entire length of the Eastern Seaboard, there are increasing numbers of Guatemalan and Mexican Maya, Zapotec workers from central Oaxaca state and smaller numbers of Mixtec and Triqui migrants from western Oaxaca state and the eastern areas of the state of Guerrero which adjoins the leading sending regions of Juxtlahuaca and Silacoyoapan. Along the Pacific Seaboard, there is an equally dramatic increase in the numbers of indigenous farmworkers but dominant networks are the Mixtec and Triqui ones; interestingly the ethnic composition of the labor force of working teenagers in California and Oregon is now very similar to that of Baja California in the late 1980s (Kissam, Intili, and García 2001: 6).

Lorenzo Morales, a forty-five-year-old Mixtec farmworker who was a labor organizer for PCUN, spoke with me in 2000 about how contractors work in his home region of the Mixteca in Oaxaca. Part of Lorenzo's organizing work has taken him to visit workers during the off-season in their home communities in Mexico, often in the marginalized regions of Oaxaca, Guerrero, and Veracruz. Lorenzo has followed the path of contractors for quite some time as well, as he explained:

> Well, I will tell you a little bit about how the system actually works, because there are more indigenous immigrants coming now.... The reason why more and more people are coming from the furthest places, like Oaxaca, Guerrero, and parts of Veracruz, is that the growers are using this kind of tactic to control the workers.... The growers have their contractors, and the contractors have connections to the *coyotes*, the ones who transport the workers.
>
> [And who are the contractors?]
>
> The majority are Mexicans, but they can also be Chicanos. They have their connections with the smugglers, the *polleros*. They use these *coyotes* to bring people here, but the people

they are bringing don't know anything about their rights and they often can't even speak Spanish. So these contractors bring them here and really control them.... We spoke with some recent immigrants who came from Mexico to a labor camp, and they started to tell us that the *coyotes* said "Come with us, there is plenty of work, there is free housing, even washing machines." Well as you know, there is housing, but it isn't free. At that camp they charge workers $4 per day. So the *coyotes* tell this to people in Mexico, and they come here and then the contractors and *coyotes* control the workers. When they bring people who are more and more marginalized in Mexico, they know less and less what their rights are. In the last years of the 1990s, they began to bring people from the most marginalized areas of Oaxaca and Guerrero.

[Where are the contractors going?]

They are going to Copala, Jutla ... indigenous regions.

[So contractors are going to the corners of Mexico and collaborating with coyotes and others. So contractors are important?]

Well, the growers are the key part of this system because it stems from them. They say, "How can we dominate the workers? How can we do this if all of those people who already came have rebelled against the conditions? Well, we have to bring more new people." And that is what they have been doing all of these years. They are trying to bring new people every time who are more and more marginalized so that they [the growers] can maintain their position.

[Do you think that with time the workers come to realize some of what goes on?]

They are seeing part of what goes on, but at the same time they think that maybe the contractors did them a favor. The contractors tell them that they did them a favor by bringing them. The contractors tell them this, as if they were doing them a favor by charging them $1,500 for bringing them and giving them work.

[How much would it cost me to come from Copala now?]

About $2,000 to $2,500. And since the indigenous person or worker doesn't have the money to pay this up front, there is an agreement between them and the labor contractor that they have to work here and the contractor takes the money out of their checks. And so the worker has to at least finish the season with the grower in order to be free of this debt ... to be free of the "favor" the contractor did for him.

[Is it possible to come and work for four months and go back to Mexico with nothing?]

Exactly; with nothing. A lot of workers come with the idea that they will stay for four months, but they end up staying for a year or more in order to cover their expenses and to save a little bit of money to be able to return to Mexico.

Increasingly, as Mixtec families have settled in Oregon, they have moved out of the seasonal farm labor sector and into other kinds of agricultural work, primarily in nurseries. Some continue to work in food-processing and freezing plants, but as they age they prefer to stay out of the fields. Children of Mixtec migrants who settled in Oregon between 1988 and 1994 are employed primarily in the service sector, in jobs at K-Mart, gas stations, KFC, and the like. Meanwhile, berries and other field crops are increasingly being picked by young, male, indigenous recruits.

## PCUN AND MIXTEC FARMWORKERS

Oregon's farmworker union—Northwest Treeplanters and Farmworkers United, or PCUN—has its origins in the 1970s, when several organizers, inspired by the work of César Chávez, envisioned a social movement of Mexican immigrants and farmworkers in Oregon. Their initial organizing strategies were influenced by the hostile attitudes toward Mexican immigrant farmworkers in the Willamette Valley at the time. In May 1977, the Willamette Valley Immigration Project (WVIP) opened to provide legal representation for undocumented workers, first in Portland. In 1978, WVIP moved permanently to Woodburn. WVIP staff and organizers went on to facilitate the creation of PCUN in 1985, with the initial goal of changing working conditions for tree planters and farmworkers. The eight-year track record already established by the WVIP was key to gaining the trust of the farmworker/tree planter community and enabling an open discussion of a farmworker union. During the 1990s the union engaged in a series of actions aimed at opening up political and cultural space for immigrant Mexican farmworkers and raising farmworker wages. It was also at this time that PCUN negotiated its first contracts with small organic growers. In the summer of 2002 the union was finalizing negotiations with NORPAK, a large cooperative of growers which had been the focus of a ten-year boycott (see Stephen 2001).

## Securing Amnesty for Oregon Farmworkers

Most Mixtec farmworkers and tree planters first came in contact with the union in the mid-1980s. Some of them were living in labor camps targeted by PCUN for organizing. The vast majority, however, came to know the union through help they received in processing their amnesty cases in 1986 and 1987. Within days of IRCA's enactment in November 1986, PCUN held a number of forums that were attended by more than eight hundred people in Woodburn, Salem, Independence, and other locations in Oregon.

The first meetings focused on the various ways that undocumented people could apply for U.S. residency under the 1986 law. PCUN staff also warned about potential discrimination against Latino workers because of the employer sanctions included in the IRCA legislation. During 1987, staff from PCUN and the Farmworker Service Center (CSC) devoted a great deal of time to working with those seeking amnesty through the IRCA and SAW. Between June 1987 and June 1988, the combined staffs of PCUN and CSC (just ten people) managed to process 1,300 legalization cases, at that point representing more than 10 percent of the total number of amnesty cases in the state. Their work significantly increased the union membership; from October 1986 to June 1988, PCUN signed up nearly two thousand new members, about a third of whom were probably Mixtecs (mostly men but also a few women). When these men later brought their wives and children from Mexico, some of these family members went to the CSC for assistance in petitioning for their residency. Since 1986 the immigration services that the union offered have been a key reason why Mixtec workers continue to relate actively to PCUN. Mixtec workers were deeply involved in negotiating the first PCUN contracts, have been recruited as labor organizers, and have come to occupy key spots on the union's governing board and in a spin-off women's organization.

## Improving Conditions for Mixtec Farmworkers and Others

For Mixtecs who had been working in Oregon for up to six years without documents, PCUN's assistance in securing legal residence was—and is—greatly appreciated. After the union's membership grew dramatically in

1987, it began to concentrate on the struggle for collective bargaining. In 1991 PCUN began the first union-organized strike in the history of Oregon farm labor, and in 1992 it intensified the pressure on key growers by initiating a boycott of the NORPAK grower cooperative, which included growers that workers had strongly criticized. In 1995, PCUN began a massive organizing campaign to honor their tenth anniversary and to raise the wages of strawberry workers.

During the campaign, PCUN broadcast trilingual radio spots in Spanish, Mixtec, and Triqui. It also sent organizers to Madera, California, to alert workers headed to Oregon about the campaign.[3] In this campaign, the union self-consciously acknowledged the indigenous ethnicity of a significant fraction of the workers they sought to represent. Many of these Mixtec and Triqui workers spoke little or no Spanish and were completely under the thumb of labor contractors. In order to communicate with them, the union used—and still uses—multilingual organizers and radio broadcasts.

Lorenzo Morales began working as a union organizer in 1997 and was still active in this role in April 2002. He exemplifies the union's efforts to reach out to Mixtec workers. During the winters of 2000, 2001, and 2002, he spent several months in Mexico visiting workers in their home communities in Oaxaca, Guerrero, and Veracruz. During these visits he warned potential workers about the kinds of "come-ons" contractors would use, and he told them about the real working conditions and about the union. For two years he was able to track some workers from labor camps in Oregon back to their home communities. Visits to workers in these three states were an important part of the union's effort to build support on a particular farm to which some of the same workers returned year after year.

The final years of the 1990s brought PCUN a historic victory when it signed Oregon's first farmworker collective bargaining agreement, with Nature's Fountains Farms. Three other agreements were signed later. These agreements provided more than a dozen rights and protections for farmworkers not afforded by law, including seniority, grievance procedures, overtime, paid breaks, and recognition of their union. María de la Luz Contreras, a Mixtec immigrant worker introduced earlier in this chapter, led one of the negotiating teams that worked on the first PCUN contracts. For her, the contracts were an important step toward better treatment and working conditions. In the fall of 2000 she discussed what the contracts meant to her:

---

[3] Madera is a stopping point for many Mixtec migrants who come seasonally to Oregon to work. Some have now moved permanently from Madera to Woodburn, Oregon.

> [What were working conditions like when you had the con-
> tract? Were they different than before?]

> They were not the same [with the contract]. We had clean
> bathrooms, we had fresh water to drink, we each had a glass
> with our own name on it for water. We got our break, and
> we got to eat lunch. We never got this before. In the other
> places, the bathrooms were filthy, they gave us warm water
> to drink. And we never even drank water, took breaks, or ate
> lunch because we had to keep picking in competition with
> others or we wouldn't have enough work. In other places
> where I worked, if you didn't get to the fields early and keep
> working in a big hurry, you wouldn't even earn enough
> money to pay for your food.... Under our contract they paid
> us the minimum and guaranteed eight hours of work per
> day.

For Mixtec immigrant workers like Luz and Lorenzo, PCUN offered
legal assistance at a crucial time (following the IRCA and SAW legislation).
By demonstrating that the union had the resources and skills to help people gain legal residency in the United States, PCUN staff won their confidence and began to talk to them about their working conditions as low-
wage workers in the fields. Lorenzo and Luz became involved in union
activities and eventually became key parts of the organization and important links to its growing Mixtec membership. In helping workers like Luz
and Lorenzo meet two of their primary needs—legal residency and improved working conditions—PCUN was able to engage with them along
two dimensions of their experience of marginality in the United States.

Participation in a hometown association offers a different form for organizing Mixtec immigrant workers. In contrast to the union, hometown
associations allow these workers to focus more centrally on their links to
Oaxaca, linguistic and cultural identity, and transnational status.

## STAYING CONNECTED IN HOMETOWN ASSOCIATIONS: THE COMITÉ PRO OBRAS DE SAN AGUSTÍN ATENAGO

> It's really nice having this Mixteco language. But a time is go-
> ing to come when this language will be lost, when it will be
> forgotten. Our children do not want to speak it. I tell them
> that it would be good for them to learn a little bit of Mixteco.
> But they don't listen to me. I tell them that it is important to

have this Mixteco language and that they shouldn't forget it. For my generation, speaking Mixteco makes me think about my youth and the kids I knew growing up. We used to speak Mixteco in school. We had a teacher who told us that we shouldn't speak Mixteco, that we should speak Spanish among ourselves. That is what he said. But we didn't know how to speak Spanish. Our parents spoke pure Mixteco. My mother and father didn't know how to speak Spanish. That is why I couldn't speak Spanish growing up. Now, speaking Mixteco reminds me of where I come from. When I get together with other men here and talk in Mixteco, I feel different (Víctor León Gómez, age fifty-five).

Víctor León Gómez first arrived in Oregon in 1979 from Ensenada, where he worked a circuit picking berries. He returned to Oregon in 1981 and again in 1988. From 1981 until 1986, he served as communal land commissioner in his home community in Oaxaca, a position of local leadership that later pushed him to the forefront of his hometown association. He brought his wife and older children to Oregon in 1994. He has been unable to legalize his residency, and his entire family remains undocumented. Víctor is a member of PCUN and sometimes attends union events, though his passion is the hometown association, which he helps to lead, along with his involvement with other migrants from his town and their efforts to raise money for expanding the community cemetery.

Víctor's hometown, San Agustín Atenango, has contributed sister populations to many parts of California. There are approximately a hundred families from San Agustín in Vista, California, another fifty in Santa Maria, California, and about twenty in Salem, Oregon. Other clusters are found elsewhere in California and in Chicago, Arizona, and Las Vegas. In the fall of 2001, San Agustín's mayor (*presidente municipal*) sent an official letter to his townspeople living in Salem, an event that Víctor describes:

> On October 19th, we received an official letter from Baltazar Ávila Arena, our town authority, telling us that there was a piece of land for sale…. Baltazar's letter said the owner was willing to sell this land to the community for our cemetery. After we got the letter, we called all the people from our town living here. We had a big meeting in a nearby park to see who was interested. Whole families came to the meeting. We asked if they wanted to help out in purchasing the land. They said yes, they agreed. So they named some of us to a

> committee. It had a president, secretary, treasurer, and two
> *vocales*. Everyone nominated us. And they voted. We were
> named to the committee. I am the president.

During this informal interview, Víctor asked another friend (also in the committee's leadership) to bring the list of names. His friend Lorenzo (introduced above) returned with a computerized list in tiny, six-point type. He and Lorenzo counted the names and announced that there were eighty people in total, including children and even single mothers. Víctor then continued describing the committee.

> The work we do is really important. We worked hard on this
> because it is about the needs of the town. Every person gave
> $200, and we raised $7,899 right here in Salem. We were in
> contact with all of the other committees, and we had a big
> meeting in Santa Maria. We rented a hall and had a meal.
> Then we began to report on our money.

Lorenzo became increasingly animated as Víctor talked, and he began adding details about the get-together in Santa Maria, the phone calls to other committees, and their ideas for new projects.

By the fall of 2002, more than $60,000 had been raised from all branches of the San Agustín Atenango Improvements Committee. The money was taken to the community, and when the original parcel of land became unavailable, a different one was purchased for the cemetery expansion. Through the fall and winter of 2002–2003, community members contributed volunteer labor (*tequio*) to build a wall around the acquired land. Lorenzo returned to San Agustín from October to March and served as an *alcalde* in the town's civil *cargo* system, a job he has filled on a rotating basis with a colleague.[4] When his term was over, Lorenzo returned to work in Salem's fruit and vegetable freezing and packing industry.

For Víctor, Lorenzo, and others, their participation in the Improvements Committee has been rejuvenating, largely because it provides ongoing contact with others from their community. One male member described the committee as being "like a community," and the men involved in the committee have clearly found it to be an important cultural and

---

[4] In many Mixtec communities, the local governance system is run by pairs of men—and now sometimes women—who rotate in and out of *cargo* positions for four- to six-month periods. This division of labor allows transnational families to move back and forth between the hometown and the United States.

social space. While they report that most meetings are conducted in Spanish—"because the young people don't speak *dialecto* [Mixteco]"—the committee leaders often switch to Mixteco when they get together to plan for larger meetings. This, they stated, reminded them of how community assemblies were run at home in Oaxaca: "There we have to speak in Spanish and Mixteco," reported Víctor. "There are old people who don't speak Spanish and now young people who don't speak much Mixteco. So we need both languages."

For the men from San Agustín (particularly for those between the ages of thirty and sixty), many of whom also belong to PCUN, the hometown association seems to have opened up an important cultural space where they can reconnect with the Mixteco language, with the governance structure of their community, and with their childhood memories and experiences. The emergence of the Improvements Committee has also connected them with other clusters of *paisanos* and increased their feeling of interconnectedness in the United States.[5] Community is thus reconstituted not only in specific locales but also through networks in the United States and in Mexico, transnationally, as described by Kearney (1995: 232) and others. For Mixtecs in Salem, Oregon, the Comité Pro-Obras has provided an ethnically based mode of organization.

## MIXTEC WOMEN'S POLITICAL PARTICIPATION: WOMEN-ONLY ORGANIZATIONS AND LEADERSHIP SKILL DEVELOPMENT

Although women attend meetings and vote in the San Agustín Improvements Committee in Salem, none was named to a leadership position on the committee. This mirrors the dynamics of community assemblies in San Agustín, where women now can attend meetings but have not yet been named to *cargo* positions. Community leaders used to be chosen by those present in the assemblies, but ever since the Party of the Democratic Revolution (PRD) began to campaign actively in the community in the early 1990s, civil *cargos* have been elected through political parties. While this process can take partial credit for the inclusion of women in local meetings, it has not resulted in their election to leadership positions. In the context of the hometown association in Salem, women are present but not particu-

---

[5] As pointed out by López, Escala-Rabadán, and Hinojosa-Ojeda (2001), hometown associations can also provide collective remittances that are used to build shared community infrastructure and collectively engage migrants in efforts to develop their communities.

larly vocal or central to the activities of the committee beyond paying their quotas and discussing projects. The San Agustín hometown association does not appear to be a mechanism for expanding women's political participation, and it may even serve to preserve and strengthen male-dominated political culture in the United States (see Goldring 1996).

An important question when evaluating the gender dynamics of hometown associations is whether they are an appropriate or likely space for women to expand their roles in political participation and leadership. Two recent experiences—in Oregon and California—suggest other possibilities.

In the 1990s, PCUN began to respond to the increasing number of women migrating from Mexico to Oregon, often following husbands who had been legalized in the mid-1980s. The women's needs were different than the men's, and they demanded a different kind of organizational space. Women Fighting for Progress (Mujeres Luchadoras Progresistas) was formed in 1997 to provide a place for women who came from communities in Mexico where they seldom attended public meetings or expressed opinions outside of extended family gatherings. Begun as a women's income-producing project, which each year sells hundreds of Christmas wreaths (nearly 1,200 in 2002), the group also provides farmworker women with an opportunity to foster pride and mutual support, and to learn new skills in public speaking and leadership. The group provides a refuge for women, and members describe its meetings as having a "family feeling." Mixtec women have played a prominent role in the development of the group and its leadership.

One Mixtec participant in the women's project, Francisca López, first came to the CSC at PCUN in 1997 in order to straighten out an auto insurance claim. She joined the women's project and eventually became very involved. The space this group of women has created provides many new arrivals—who are often socially isolated, lonely, and missing their extended families in Mexico—with a haven for sharing their feelings and working collectively to resolve common issues. Having a women-only space also gives women the confidence to speak up. Once they have gained self-confidence within the women's group and are comfortable taking positions and speaking up in public, they can translate these skills to other arenas, including union leadership slots, local political forums such as PTA meetings and city council meetings, and renegotiation of domestic roles. As Francisca stated:

> A lot of women who come to the group have lived in poverty.... They have families where the husband works, but it

isn't enough to maintain the children and also pay rent. We also have single mothers who don't have anyone to help them. They come to the group, and we help them. They come here and work and earn a little money.... And when they come here with us, they begin to talk. It feels like coming to visit your family. When women come to be with us, they feel comfortable and they begin to talk, and it really helps. We can help women who want to talk about their problems.... It's different here. Women won't talk about things this way in a group of men. But this is a group of women, and they come and talk about their personal lives.... They talk about what they have done, what kind of suffering they are going through, and we help each other.

In 2002, Mujeres became independent of PCUN. Union activists and the women in Mujeres both view this as a success, an indication of the women's capacity to be self-supporting and run their own organization. The women's group has been the source of many up-and-coming leaders in the union and the community of Woodburn. Through having a "women-only" space, Mixtec women were able to cultivate political skills that they might not have been able to develop in the hometown associations.

A second recent development, this one in California, also suggests the importance of women-only spaces in allowing Mixtec women to consolidate their political skills and leadership. At the October 2003 conference on "Indigenous Mexican Immigrants in the US," held at the University of California, Santa Cruz, Mixtec and Triqui women announced the formation of a network of Oaxacan indigenous women leaders. In the discussion preceding their decision to form the network, the women considered the different organizational spaces in which they operated—hometown associations, broader women's organizations, and multiethnic immigrant rights organizations—and concluded that they needed to form their own organization. "There are a lot of general organizations for women, but they don't know the particular problems of indigenous women," commented Oralia Maceda of the Oaxacan Indigenous Binational Front (FIOB) (Meléndez 2002).

The women commented about their great difficulty in getting their issues integrated into the priorities of hometown associations and federations of such associations. The issues they named included: how to provide for their families, discrimination against them as indigenous women workers (sometimes expressed as subtle sexual harassment by contractors), monolingualism, lack of education, and very early marriage ages for girls (thirteen to fifteen). They also acknowledged that some organizations, such as the Oaxacan Indigenous Binational Front, had made progress in integrating women into their leadership structures. Nevertheless, the women felt the need to form their own network, independent of both transnational indigenous organizations and U.S. feminist organizers and academics, in order to formulate their own agenda and priorities. Since the formation of the network, its members have held several California-wide meetings and workshops.

The recent experiences of Mujeres in Oregon and the formation of the network of Oaxacan Indigenous Women Leaders in California suggest that hometown associations may not be the best place for women to develop political participation and leadership skills. Women-only organizations can be an important resource for helping to expand women's confidence, skills, and analysis in ways that, further down the line, may enable them to be more active in hometown associations if they so desire.

Leaders such as Centolia Maldonado of the FIOB have commented on the progress women have made in their home communities in Oaxaca as they moved to fill the vacuum in local political participation and leadership opened by migrating men:

> Migration has forced indigenous women to open up spaces in community assemblies and other local political arenas.... At first there was conflict with the husband, the father, and local authorities and between the women themselves.... Leaving the house and conquering their fear of speaking up, meeting with other women who share the same situation and ambitions, obligated them to reflect and change perceptions about some local customs (Stanley 2002).

Such changes are significant and may eventually influence how immigrant Mixtec women participate politically in the United States. When organizations like hometown associations follow traditional patterns of political participation that largely exclude women or render them voiceless, then it makes more sense for women to hone their political skills and organize around issues unique to their position in other kinds of organizations, such as the network created in California. As women gain confidence and experience, they may want to continue working in women-only organizations, but they can also expand their roles in hometown associations, federations, and other types of organizations. A factor limiting the political participation of many indigenous migrant women, however, is their continuing responsibility in the areas of housework, cooking, shopping, and childcare.

## LINKING LABOR, ETHNICITY, AND GENDER THROUGH FARMWORKER UNIONS AND HOMETOWN ASSOCIATIONS

My interest in this chapter has been in exploring the experiences of Mixtec men and women who have worked as farmworkers in Oregon and have participated in two specific organizational forms, the PCUN farmworker union and the recently formed San Agustín Atenango hometown association in Salem. The farmworker union originally captivated people's attention and enthusiasm through its legal services center, which played a pivotal role in helping undocumented workers receive amnesty in the mid-1980s, and through campaigns to raise wages for strawberry workers and others. Since that time, Mixtec workers have played key roles in negotiating contracts and providing leadership in field organizing efforts. Because the union is primarily focused on labor relations, immigration, and broad defense of Latino immigrants' rights, Mixtecs have valued the union's assistance and commitment. Apart from their significant participation in the union, Mixtec workers have also formed hometown association committees that provide a cultural and organizational space for expressing specific local ethnic identities that span the U.S.-Mexico border. Through a series of networked committees, Mixtecs are able to draw unity from their links to a single community in Oaxaca.

Although the Salem-based hometown association includes women in its membership and meetings, men dominate its organizational structure by carrying out most of the national and international networking aspects of the committee (see Goldring 1996). Thus, while Mixtec men in Oregon have found a way to participate organizationally in multiple spheres that validate the various aspects of their identity and experience in the United States—as Mixtecs, low-wage workers, and, sometimes, undocumented workers—women have not found an equivalent outlet in which to express their cultural identity and connections to their home community. For a small number of Mixtec women, Mujeres Luchadoras Progresistas has provided support for key issues in these women's lives and offered a chance to develop leadership and organizing skills. This women-only venue has been quite successful in raising women's confidence and participation levels, not only in the PCUN union but in other venues as well.

The patterns of organizational participation I have documented in this chapter suggest that the concerns of transnational Mixtec migrants remain focused on a range of issues: the relations of production, the politics of immigration and immigrant rights, culturally based issues like language and local cultural expression and maintenance, collective memory and connection to communities of origin, the creation of community across borders and through networks, raising family income, and the gendered dynamics of immigration, work, and home life. This list of concerns certainly suggests that Mixtec migrants are not assimilating into "mainstream" U.S. culture and that they continue to cultivate ethnic distinctiveness in relation to both people of Mexican descent in the United States and Native Americans. They have created transnational communities that operate in multiple sites and social fields (see Goldring 1999). This finding concurs with the work of Kearney (1996, 1998), Rivera-Salgado (1998, 1999), Smith (1999), and others.

Based on my work with Mixtec migrants, I offer the following suggestions for strengthening the organizational structures in which Mixtec workers participate and for promoting dialogue across organizational spaces.

- Given the fact that many states' farmworker populations are increasingly indigenous, farmworker unions can continue looking at how indigenous ethnicity among farmworkers might affect their organizing strategies. Farmworker unions necessarily retain a focus on improving the working and living conditions of all farmworkers. Working to represent the diversity within the farmworker population is an ongoing challenge, and many organizations are making significant efforts in this direction. Such efforts should be supported.

- The presence of significant numbers of Mixtec farmworkers who participate simultaneously in farmworker union activities and in a hometown association suggests the importance of exploring the possibilities for collaboration between these two organizational spaces. Hometown associations can provide a link to workers who may not be aware of union activities, and can also provide advice and assistance to farmworker unions that are interested in developing a more central focus on ethnicity, specifically Mexican indigenous ethnicities, in their work. Unions can provide important information on labor rights, immigration rights, and other issues. Within such a dialogue, a special place must be reserved for the plight of undocumented workers and the struggles of families whose members hold different legal statuses—that is, undocumented, citizen, resident (see Stephen 2001).

- While some Mixtec men appear to have found a satisfying way to re-member, maintain, and further Mixtec cultural identity at local levels and through networks of hometown association committees, Mixtec women have been somewhat marginalized in these processes. Within farmworker unions such as PCUN, women have been encouraged through special projects and leadership training to take on more active roles. Hometown associations, federations, and farmworker unions can support, encourage, and collaborate with women-only organizational spaces in their efforts to focus on issues particular to indigenous women migrants and to develop organizing and leadership skills.

Farmworker unions and hometown associations have much to share and much to learn from one another. The fact that the same population is often participating in both kinds of organizations simultaneously suggests the importance of making institutional links — and personal ones — between the two. As global competition for cheap rural labor heightens, indigenous workers leaving rural Mexico are likely to remain the dominant source of farm labor in the United States. Dialogue and collaboration between unions and hometown associations will be an important part of the process in continuing to defend the rights of Mixtec workers.

## References

Goldring, Luin. 1996. "Gendered Memory: Reconstructions of Rurality among Mexican Transnational Migrants." In *Creating the Countryside: The Politics of Rural and Environmental Discourse*, edited by Melanie DuPuis and Peter Vandergest. Philadelphia, Penn.: Temple University Press.

———. 1999. "The Power of Status in Transnational Social Fields." In *Transnationalism from Below*, edited by Michael Peter Smith and Luis Eduardo Guarnizo. New Brunswick, N.J.: Transaction.

Kearney, Michael. 1995. "The Effects of Transnational Culture, Economy, and Migration on Mixtec Identity in Oaxacalifornia." In *The Bubbling Cauldron: Race, Ethnicity, and the Urban Crisis*, edited by Michael Peter Smith and Joe R. Feagin. Minneapolis: University of Minnesota Press.

———. 1998. "Transnationalism in California at End of Empire." In *Border Identities: Nation and State at International Frontiers*, edited by Thomas Wilson and Hasting Donnan. Cambridge: Cambridge University Press.

Kissam, Edward, Jo Ann Intili, and Anna García. 2001. "The Emergence of a Binational Mexico-U.S. Workforce: Implications for Farm Labor Workforce Security." Presented at the conference "America's Workforce Network Research," U.S. Department of Labor, Washington, D.C., June 26–27.

López, Felipe H., Luis Escala-Rabadán, and Raúl Hinojosa-Ojeda. 2001. "Migrant Associations, Remittances, and Regional Development between Los Angeles and Oaxaca, Mexico." Research Report Series, no. 10. Los Angeles: North American Integration and Development Center, University of California, Los Angeles. At http://naid.sppsr.ucla.edu.

McConahay, Mary Jo. 2001. "The New Face of Farm Labor—Indian Teens from Mexico, Guatemala." San Francisco, Pacific News Service, August 27. At http://www.pacificnews.org/content/pns/2001/aug/0287farmlabor.html.

Meléndez, Claudia S. 2002. "Mujeres indígenas formarán red de apoyo," *Nuevo Mundo*, October 18.

Rivera-Salgado, Gaspar. 1998. "Radiografía de Oaxacalifornia," *Masiosare (La Jornada)*, August 9. At http:/www.jornada.unam.mx/1998/ago98/980809/mas-rivera.html.

———. 1999. "Migration and Political Activism: Mexican Transnational Indigenous Communities in a Comparative Perspective." PhD dissertation, University of California, Santa Cruz.

Rouse, Roger. 1992. "Making Sense of Settlement: Class Transformation, Cultural Struggle, and Transnationalism among Mexican Migrants in the United States," *Annals of the New York Academy of Sciences* 645 (July): 25–52.

Runsten, David, and Michael Kearney. 1994. *A Survey of Oaxacan Village Networks in California Agriculture*. Davis: California Institute for Rural Studies.

Schlosser, Eric. 1995. "In the Strawberry Fields," *Atlantic Monthly*, November. At http://www.theatlantic.com.issues.95nov/strawber.htm.

Smith, Robert C. 1999. "Transnational Localities: Community, Technology and the Politics of Membership within the Context of Mexico and U.S. Migration." In *Transnationalism from Below*, edited by Michael Peter Smith and Luis Eduardo Guarnizo. New Brunswick, N.J.: Transaction.

Stanley, Eduardo. 2002. "El despertar de las mujeres mixtecas," October 21. At http://www.lainsignia.org/2002/octubre/soc031.htm.

Stephen, Lynn. 2001. "Globalization, the State, and the Creation of Flexible Indigenous Workers: Mixtec Farmworkers in Oregon," *Urban Anthropology and Studies of Cultural Systems and World Economic Development* 30, nos. 2–3: 189–214.

Zabin, Carol, and Sallie Hughes. 1995. "Economic Integration and Labor Flows: Stage Migration in Farm Labor Markets in Mexico and the United States," *International Migration Review* 29, no. 2: 395–422.

# PART III

# Social and Economic Processes

# 8

# Alive and Well: Generating Alternatives to Biomedical Health Care by Mixtec Migrant Families in California

## BONNIE BADE

*Soledad lay on the soiled and torn couch, moaning softly and rubbing her abdomen gently. Her husband was outside talking to Don Sabio, the curandero who had come to the house to heal Soledad. Soledad and her family have lived in Madera, California, for ten years. Her husband works in the agricultural fields, bringing home $11,539 a year. Of the entire family of eight, only the two youngest daughters have legal status, having been born in Madera Community Hospital. As an "illegal alien," Soledad quali-*

Some of the material for this chapter, such as the section on working and living conditions, has been published previously in slightly different form in my writings that appear in the reference list to this chapter.

The research that produced the data and interpretations presented here began in 1987 and continues today. Initial funding came from the Ford Foundation; UC MEXUS; the California Institute for Rural Studies; the Center for Chicano Studies, University of California, Santa Barbara; the Department of Applied Behavioral Sciences, University of California, Davis; and the University of California, Riverside. Subsequent field research was supported by California State University, San Marcos; Minority International Research Training, San Diego State University; and the San Diego Museum of Man.

I dedicate this work to the Mixtec families in Mexico and California who have generously opened their lives and hearts to me. Without their kindness and patience, and collaborative support, none of the work presented here would have been possible.

*fies for a Medi-Cal card that covers her for "emergency and pregnancy-related" services only. Today Soledad was coughing up blood for the third time this month. She has already been to the emergency room at the hospital twice, sent away both times after receiving a five-minute examination and a prescription for Maalox. The doctor, who speaks neither Spanish nor Mixtec, does not attempt to tell her what is wrong. The pain continues, so she asked her husband to send for Don Sabio, a healer from her native village of Ñuu Chucún in the mountains of Oaxaca.*

*Don Sabio's hands are stained dark green from two months in the tomato fields of the San Joaquin Valley. He presses gently on Soledad's abdomen, reciting an oration in Mixtec to the spirits of the wind, rain, sun, and earth. He lights several candles and through prayer invokes the intervention of the saints and other nonmaterial powers on behalf of Soledad while Soledad drinks a tea of rue and chamomile. After a while Don Sabio puts rubbing alcohol in a glass and lights it on fire. After applying the juice of a cut piece of aloe vera to Soledad's belly, he places the rim of the glass onto her abdomen, just below her breastbone, extinguishing the fire and causing the skin to pull up into the glass in a mound. Soledad whimpers but says nothing. Don Sabio intends to remove the "mal" that is inside of her, an affliction sent to her by a jealous neighbor who is also from Ñuu Chucún.*

*In the tradition of Mixtec medical treatment, unlike clinical biomedicine, discovering the cause of an ailment is even more important than alleviating its symptoms. In this regard, the patient gains a sense of empowerment once the source of her suffering is known. It becomes merely a question of repelling the source with the appropriate means. For this reason, the clinical treatments that Soledad has received to this point, although beneficial toward relieving her pain, do nothing toward treating the cause of her illness. Only someone with the appropriate knowledge of how to deal with external cause – in this case Don Sabio's navigation and manipulation of the nonclinical forces involved in her ailment – can truly address Soledad's need. At the end of the two-hour healing ceremony, Soledad feels exhausted, but the pain inside is gone.*

For Mixtec families living in California, economic and social barriers act to limit access to and use of clinical health care. Expensive biomedical treatments, lack of health insurance, language barriers, transportation problems, and cultural differences concerning illness causation and treatment combine to marginalize Mixtec families from the mainstream biomedical health care culture. This study examines the ways that Mixtec families generate alternatives to clinical health care to meet their health care needs and the conditions under which such a practice is necessary.

Drawing upon fifteen years of qualitative and quantitative research, the findings presented here indicate that Mixtec medical culture, with its ancient roots of medical and plant knowledge, provides Mixtec families with the means to supplement insufficient access to clinical care in California. The generation of health care alternatives by Mixtec families represents an ethnically based self-defense strategy of unrecognized economic and political value. It is this practice of transmedical health care that maximizes health care treatment options because it involves crossing the boundaries and drawing upon the resources of distinct medical, linguistic, and cultural systems. Due to limited access to biomedical clinical treatments, Mixtec families therefore complement them with medicinal plants, sweat baths, massage, and ritual healing ceremonies to meet their health care needs. Mixtec cultural forms and practices thus combine with the social and economic marginalization of Mixtec communities, in both Mexico and the United States, to reaffirm community membership and identity and to enforce a cultural distinctness that defies "melting pot" assimilationist theories and provides increased alternatives for coping with health problems.

## THE MIXTECA

*Don Primo points to another plant with the end of his cane. "With the root from that one you can make a tea to treat people with diabetes," he says. "The milk from a broken stem of it can eliminate dark blotches on your hands," he adds. We wind our way down a trail in the mountains overlooking his small pueblo. The three botany students from the University of California scramble to take a digital image of the plant and then press it between pieces of cardboard to be dried and added to the collection. Don Primo has been directing the medicinal plant collection since we arrived in Ñuu Yucu two weeks ago. For Don Primo and myself, the presence of the students offers a refreshing twist to our own mentor-student relationship that began twelve years earlier. As the only person expressing interest in learning the medicinal concepts and practices employed by Don Primo, I had been assigned the duty of recording his knowledge to the best of my outsider, non-Mixtec ability. Forty years earlier Don Primo had been trained as a healer and herbalist by three men from neighboring villages. He had worked with them for years, learning the orations, diagnostic methods, and plant remedies while accompanying them during healing ceremo-*

*nies. The last time I had been in Ñuu Yucu with him, it became apparent that we had to systematically tackle the immense plant knowledge he had acquired. With some help from San Diego State University and the San Diego Museum of Man, the means to do an ethnobotanical study and plant collection materialized. "Now this one is good for women who are in labor," he said, indicating a small plant with yellow flowers. "It makes the baby come out faster." Again the students rush to capture the plant physically and digitally. Don Primo smiles.*

The civilization from which Don Primo draws his knowledge has been practicing medicine for thousands of years. Their books tell of a great warrior, Lord Eight Deer, born in 1063 A.D., who unified the coasts, mountains, and valleys of the Mixteca. Pre-Columbian Mixtec society based its economy on agriculture and long-distance trade. It distinguished itself by generating sophisticated forms of art, literature, architecture, religion, cosmology, and a complicated calendar based on mathematics and meticulous long-term observation of the celestial bodies.

Today, in mountains covered by pine and oak forest, small villages occupy valleys and hillsides where Mixtec farmers cultivate corn, beans, and squash on steep slopes and along arroyos. Agricultural production in the Mixteca still depends on the Spanish-introduced plow and oxen team, which replaced the pre-Columbian digging stick. Rugged mountains render mechanized agricultural production inappropriate. Steep slopes, the plow, goat herding, a thin layer of topsoil, and torrential rains have combined to accelerate the ecological devastation of the Mixteca. Since there are no natural gas systems available to the rural indigenous regions of Mexico like the Mixteca, the ecological loss of the area is furthered by the dependence on wood for household fuel.

Economically underdeveloped communities of the Mixteca frequently lack basic services such as potable water, roads, telecommunications, sanitation, natural gas, secondary schools, and often clinical health care. In light of the economic reality of farming in the Mixteca, Mixtec families practice infra-subsistence agriculture, producing on average enough corn to last four months out of the year (Bade 1994).

Employment opportunities in the Mixteca are limited; a significant feature of local Mixtec economies is that there is virtually no wage labor available. Small businesses that theoretically could provide employment are run by families and tend to be front-porch general stores with basic goods like sugar, coffee, toilet paper, and candles. Some families generate household income through petty capitalistic activities such as basket and hat weaving, furniture making, and selling surplus fruits and vegetables. These labor-intensive economic means pay poorly. For example, it takes an expert weaver eight hours to make two hats, which she can sell for $0.20 each. If she has a soda while she works she just breaks even.[1] Handmade wooden chairs sold in Juxtlahuaca take days to make and sell for $20.[2]

As a consequence of poverty, diminishing local resources, and Mexico's worsening economic crisis, many Mixtec families migrate to external labor markets to support themselves. Since the early 1980s, Mixtec families have increasingly become transnational migrants seeking work as farm laborers, construction day workers, gardeners, and factory workers in the north. Runsten and Kearney report that in 1994 more than 50,000 people from the Mixteca were residing in California. Madera, California, with a population of approximately 30,000 in 1993 and 45,000 in 2003, is experiencing a "Mixtecization" of its agricultural labor force as more than 5,000 Mixtec families from more than 38 communities of the Mixteca work and reside there (Bade 1994; Runsten and Kearney 1994).

## WORKING CONDITIONS IN CALIFORNIA

Although some Mixtec workers find labor in other sectors of the economy, the majority of migrant Mixtec families support themselves in California as hired farmworkers. Large concentrations of Mixtec families can thus be found in the agricultural regions of the state, including the Central Valley, San Diego County, the Salinas Valley, the Imperial Valley, the Sacramento Valley, and agricultural towns along the coast, such as Oxnard.

Agricultural workers in California are paid by one of two systems: hourly pay and piece rate. The most common wage system in California agriculture is hourly pay. California farmworkers earn an average of $5.69 an hour, up only 29 cents since the average in 1990–91.[3] Zabin et al. (1993) report widespread violation of minimum wage laws by those employing Mixtec workers.

Qualitative data from Madera and San Diego counties indicate that hourly pay is less desirable than the piece rate system because there is no way to earn more money by doing more work. However, while the piece rate system maximizes production, it also puts greater mental and physical

---

[1] Carole Nagengast and Michael Kearney, field notes, July 1987.

[2] Bade field notes Ñuu Yucu, November 1992.

[3] According to the 1995–1997 NAWS, 73 percent of California farmworkers are paid hourly (Rosenberg et al. 1998: 6).

stress on the workers. Due to their often desperate financial situation and the sporadic nature of employment as agricultural laborers, farmworkers are already under great pressure to maximize their earnings in a given work period. In addition, labor contractors are also often paid by the piece rate system (by tonnage, for example), greatly increasing pressure on the workers to work as fast and efficiently as possible. The piece rate system creates a situation in which laborers work at full capacity as long as possible, and considerations such as health and accident risk are often secondary to production.

Workers can be fired for not being able to maintain a fast and productive pace. The practice of eliminating slower workers especially affects older workers, who frequently suffer from health problems such as arthritis and rheumatism. One sixty-two-year-old worker said that he had not been able to hold a job in the tomato fields for more than a few days before he was asked not to come back: "I get so hot out there, and after a few hours my knee hurts real bad. The foreman says that if I sit down, then I can just go home and not bother to come back."

According to data from the 1995–1997 National Agricultural Workers Survey (NAWS), 61 percent of California farmworker families live in poverty.[4] California farmworkers are employed, on average, twenty-three weeks during the year and, when employed, average forty-two hours of work per week. The median annual personal income of California farmworkers is between $5,000 and $7,500, while the median total farmworker family income is between $7,500 and $10,000 (Villarejo et al. 2000; Rosenberg et al. 1998: 11–17).

Job security does not characterize the farmworker occupation. Thirty percent of farmworkers interviewed in the 1995–1997 NAWS survey held five or more jobs a year, 53 percent held between two and four jobs a year, and only 18 percent held one job all year.

If one looks only at the annual earnings of a farmworker, one gets an incomplete portrait of net farmworker income. An aspect of agricultural employment that is not commonly known to non-farmworkers is that the worker must pay for a number of services, such as transportation to and from the workplace, regardless of whether these services are needed.

Transportation to and from the fields, known as the *raitero* (or ride) system, is prevalent throughout California and in some areas is obligatory.

---

[4] Poverty is defined by the Federal Register (1997) as an annual income below $10,610 for two, below $13,330 for three, below $16,050 for four, below $18,770 for five, below $21,490 for six, below $24,210 for seven, and below $26,930 for eight.

The NAWS data reveal that half (52 percent) of California farmworkers pay for rides to work that are arranged by their employers (Rosenberg et al. 1998: 16). Recent research done by the California Agricultural Worker Health Survey (CAWHS) reveals a significant correlation[5] between the use of *raiteros* by an individual and both housing density in which the individual lives and the number of unrelated residents with whom the farmworker lives (Bade and Villarejo 2004). Cost for a *raitero* is $4 to $5 a day (Bade 1989: 46, 2000). The *raitero* system constitutes one of the primary sources of worker injury. Many of the vehicles have no windows, no seat belts, and are overcrowded. As one worker put it, "They pack us in there like we're sardines or something, and usually it's so hot and a lot of people get dizzy or sick." On August 9, 1999, thirteen people working the tomato harvest were killed on their way to work; the van in which they traveled had wooden benches bolted to the floor and no seatbelts. Several comparable incidents have occurred throughout the state since then.

Another on-the-job expense for workers is food. On a typical day a worker might get one or two breaks in which to rest and eat. Food in the fields is usually provided by a catering truck, or *lonchera*. Due to overcrowded or nonconventional housing accommodations in which many farmworkers must live, where there is no kitchen in which to prepare food, many workers cannot bring their lunches with them to work and therefore have no choice but to buy lunch from the catering truck. The available food—chips, sodas, and pastries—is generally overpriced and low in nutrition, although more solid items, such as burritos and tacos, are also available. A bag of chips and a soda can cost $5 (Bade 1989). Company store dominance contributes to elevated food prices. Workers in Madera report that the *lonchera* is usually owned by the labor contractor or one of his friends or relatives, and that competing food services are driven off the fields so that workers can only buy from one *lonchera*.

Often the agricultural work done in the fields requires special tools, such as clippers, knives, cartons, and gloves. The 1995–1997 NAWS data indicate that 89 percent of California farmworkers pay for all or some of the tools they use on the job (Rosenberg et al. 1998: 15), even though requiring workers who earn less than $11.50 per hour to buy work-related materials that are essential to performing the job is an illegal practice. In the garlic harvest, for example, the workers must buy clippers to cut the roots off the garlic bunches before placing them in the bins. A pair of clip-

---

[5] $p$ = .178 and $p$ = .235. Pearson's correlation coefficients significance of 0.01.

pers ranges from $18 to $30. Knives used in the grape harvest cost between $8 and $13, and buckets used in the olive harvest run between $10 and $15.

Many agricultural laborers in Madera, Merced, and Fresno counties report that they do not receive paychecks. Instead, they are charged a check-cashing fee and then paid in cash. According to the workers, this service, provided by the labor contractors, costs between $2 and 10 percent of the check's total value. The workers are then given a check stub on which deductions for Social Security, federal and state taxes, and unemployment are recorded. All agricultural employees pay for these private and public services, regardless of their legal status in the United States. As one migrant farm laborer put it:

> Since 1976 I've been picking tomatoes and grapes here and paying Social Security and unemployment and all that. The sad part of it is that even though I pay this money to be here, and even though they make me buy a permit, I still have to hide from the authorities because they still consider me illegal (Bade 1989: 36).

One of the greatest costs to California's seasonal farmworkers manifests itself in the form of harassment. For example, undocumented workers frequently suffer denial of pay for their work.[6] A group of workers in Arvin reported that more than a hundred workers had not been paid for a week's worth of labor in the grape harvest. According to Herminio, one of those who had been denied this pay, the labor contractor simply told them that he had never seen them before and that they had not worked for him. Not surprisingly, all of the workers who were refused their earned pay were undocumented and were using false permits. The labor contractor, who knew which of his employees were undocumented and therefore likely to avoid legal confrontation, decided not to pay them for their work. According to Herminio, the workers were eventually paid—but only after weeks of persistent complaining and camping out on the labor contractor's front lawn. Such occurrences represent an additional source of stress and financial hardship for undocumented workers.

A farm laborer's workday is long and tiring. During the tomato harvest, for example, the day begins at 3:30 or 4:00 a.m., when the *raitero* comes to

---

[6] According to data from the 2000 NAWS, 91 percent of workers are Mexico-born, and 42 percent are undocumented. Further, the majority of workers and their families arriving to the United States since 1987 are undocumented.

pick up the workers from houses, shacks, and fields, loading four to five workers at each stop. After about forty-five minutes of driving, the vehicles are filled and then head for the fields, sometimes traveling more than an hour before reaching the work site. Once in the fields, the workers begin filling five-gallon buckets, for each of which they earn between 33 and 45 cents.[7] By 9:00 a.m., the cool morning hours are over, and the average worker has filled between sixty and eighty buckets, hauling the full containers, now weighing twenty-five pounds each, to the tomato truck and lifting them head high to the person who will dump them into the truck trailer. Young and ambitious workers run all the while, racing to the *ponchera* to get their cards punched for each bucket filled, the tally that represents their earnings. By the time of the first twenty-minute break, about 10 a.m., the older workers are sweating and tired, and many complain of headaches and nausea. They complain quietly, however, out of fear of being overheard and dismissed.

Maintaining personal hygiene in the field is difficult. Hands become encrusted with a mixture of oil from the tomato plants, dirt, and chemicals. A dark green muck cakes under fingernails, on hands and forearms, and over shoes, ankles, and legs.

Posted information about the chemicals in use in the fields is rarely seen. Even the labor contractors do not know what pesticides are sprayed in the fields and when. They say it is the grower's responsibility to make sure the fields are safe to pick. As the heat builds to over 100 degrees at midday, the thick smell of chemicals becomes almost unbearable. One worker commented that he holds his breath while picking, breathing when he stands up and his face is farther from the ground. He admits, however, that this slows him down: "I'd probably make more money if I didn't worry so much about dying" (Bade 1989: 52).

By the end of the day, if it has been a good one, most workers will have picked between 175 and 200 buckets of tomatoes. They are exhausted and dirty, having had only one or two twenty-minute breaks all day. One older worker, who worries that his shoulder might not last another day, falls asleep during the ride back to Madera. Another keeps rubbing a red and swollen eye with the back of his green and grimy hand. He says his eye has been bothering him during the last few days, and his eyelids are puffy and infected.

---

[7] Although these data were originally gathered by the author in 1990, piece-rate pay for tomatoes had changed little by 2003.

## UNHEALTHFUL LIVING CONDITIONS

A dominant feature of the living conditions of California farmworker families is crowding due to the scarcity and high cost of housing. Several families often share a single unit, with entire families inhabiting single rooms in a house or apartment. In such situations, a household may have seven or eight women cooking and caring for fifteen or twenty children in the same living space. In one house in Madera, an older couple rented out rooms to migrant families and single men from their home village. One woman, Magdalena, reported that she and her husband and their three children lived in a 12-by-10-foot room off the kitchen. A tattered king-sized mattress, which served as the bed for the family, took up nearly all of the floor space. Food was stored in cardboard boxes in a corner. Another corner contained clothing and cardboard boxes and bags with personal items. Magdalena complained of a high, persistent fever that she had had intermittently for over a month. Two of the other women making tamales in the kitchen also had fevers. When asked what she had done to get well, Magdalena replied:

> I've taken a whole bunch of pills that I bought at the pharmacy, but nothing seems to help. I feel so tired all of the time, and when I cook hot things I get dizzy and need to sit down. That's why I'm not working. My husband can't find a job in the tomatoes because they told him they already have people. I need to work but I feel so sick. I want to just sleep but then who would watch the children and cook the food? Besides, my husband would get mad (Bade 1989: 47).

The shortage of affordable housing means that farm laborers find themselves in unhealthful living situations. Extreme crowding and a lack of basic needs such as beds and indoor plumbing characterize the home lives of California's seasonal farmworkers. In a house in the Central Valley, an elderly couple have more than twenty men staying in their living room. Other rooms in the house have at least one family in each, and more than thirty men and women live in the backyard and shed. All living space in the house is overcrowded, especially the kitchen and bathroom. The women with children generally stay home during the day, preparing food for their families and some of the other workers. The couple charges weekly rents of $10.00 for individuals and $15.00 for families.

For many of the more than 700,000 farmworkers employed in California, home is a shack or shed in someone's backyard (Villarejo 1999: 9).

When a farmworker family can rent a house, there are often twenty or thirty workers sleeping in the house's rooms, hallways, bathrooms, closets, and backyard. As one man who rents out space to workers put it:

> There isn't any place for my *paisanos* to live. They won't let the single men rent houses here because they always end up with fifty or so, all living under the same roof. I let these guys and couples stay here in my backyard because they don't have any other place to go. If they stay in the park, the cops chase them out. The ones with cars just park here in front of my house, they sleep in their cars. My wife won't let everyone in to use the bathroom because it would just be too much, so they all go to the San Joaquin River to bathe and clean up after work (Bade 1989: 42).

Sherman et al. (1997: 31) found that in Parlier a significant portion of the farmworker population lives in substandard and unofficial housing, such as shacks, trailers, sheds, and tents. Many seasonal farm laborers, usually lone males, live in garages, abandoned shacks, orchards, warehouses, caves, or beside a river. Some individuals find housing through their labor contractors. One group of four men converted an old refrigerator truck-trailer in a junkyard into living quarters with bunk beds. They made an outdoor shower of four corrugated tin walls with an elevated hose. When they got so enterprising as to run an extension cord from a power source in the yard, the owner of the property, who was their labor contractor, began to charge each of them an additional $20 a week to stay. In another case, there were thirty-seven men living in a garage behind a private home. There were no bathroom facilities, and the kitchen consisted of a board on two sawhorses and a water bucket. A portable electric grill served as a stove. The only water source for these men was a faucet around back, which was used for bathing, cooking, and clothes washing. The area beneath the faucet was perpetually muddy. Most lone male workers have no more than two or three changes of clothes, so after a couple of days in the same pants and shirt, a worker would wash his clothes under the faucet and hang them to dry on the barbed wire fence.

The farmworkers' inability to rid themselves of pesticide residue is compounded by their lack of space, water, and other basic facilities. Flea-ridden carpets, broken windows, makeshift bedding, and dirty clothing caked with sweat and chemicals all combine to make the living conditions of farm laborers a perpetual health hazard. These conditions exist not by choice but because of lack of choice. The shortage of low-income housing for farmworkers is one reason for workers' unhealthful living conditions. Other reasons lie in a rental system that fails to recognize the limiting factors that dictate the nature of the seasonal farmworker lifestyle. Since many workers follow the crops throughout California and into Washington and Oregon, they are not able to rent or lease living space for extended periods. Many landlords reported that short rental time was the main cause for their unwillingness to rent to farm laborers (Bade 1994). Second, since many farmworkers come to the United States as economic refugees, they do not have the necessary capital for the deposits required by owners of rental housing. As a result, the majority of the California agricultural labor force lives in substandard, crowded, and unhealthful living conditions.

In Mecca, California, during the grape harvest of May and June, workers live in their cars and rent parking spaces in parking lots owned by local merchants. The shortage of housing has produced a proliferation of unlicensed trailer parks, shacks, and sheds for farmworkers in backyards, as well as a swell of people living in the open in city parks and on city streets. Riverside County's efforts to control the situation by shutting down unlicensed trailer parks merely displaced hundreds of families to the streets.

The neighborhoods where farmworkers and their families live are poor and dangerous. Communities of migrants are usually located in low-income districts and ghettos, where housing is more affordable and available. These areas tend to have high crime rates and are often home to drug dealers and users. This environment is hostile and threatening, especially for women and young people. Qualitative data gathered between 1989 and 1999 in central and southern California reveal that women who are abused or raped in these areas are often afraid to seek help from authorities because they do not speak English or even Spanish, because they fear deportation, and because they do not trust legal authorities such as the police.

## HEALTH OF FARMWORKERS

Research that I and others conducted in 2000 in the first statewide study of farmworker health—the California Agricultural Worker Health Survey—indicates poor health for California's hired farmworkers. In the CAWHS we interviewed 971 farmworkers and performed 652 physical exams. The findings show that farmworkers suffer from high blood pressure, high serum cholesterol, obesity, anemia, and dental problems (Villarejo et al. 2000). The main findings of physical examination and blood chemistry data are as follows:

- Nearly one in five male subjects (18 percent) had at least two of three risk factors for chronic disease: high serum cholesterol, high blood pressure, or obesity.

- Both male and female subjects in the CAWHS sample show substantially greater incidence of high blood pressure as compared with the incidence of hypertension among U.S. adults.

- A significantly larger fraction of male subjects had high serum cholesterol as compared with the U.S. adult population.

- Eighty-one percent of male subjects and 76 percent of female subjects had unhealthful weight, as measured by Body Mass Index, with 28 percent of men and 37 percent of women obese.

- Both male and female subjects show evidence that they are more likely to suffer from iron deficiency anemia than is the case for U.S adults.

- More that one-third of subjects had at least one decayed tooth, and nearly four out of ten female subjects had at least one broken or missing tooth.

## BARRIERS TO CLINICAL HEALTH CARE

Health care is the outcome of the interaction between two fundamental processes — *access* and *utilization* — of health care services. An individual's ability to gain access to clinical diagnosis and treatment, coupled with that person's experience in the utilization of these gained services, determines the quality of health care. Access involves both the *ability to pay* for needed health services and the *availability* of those services. Cash, worker's compensation, Medi-Cal, Healthy Families, and other health programs provide access to health care services because they cover the costs, or part of the costs, of those services. The number of service providers in a given region (that is, the availability of health care) also promotes or hinders access to health care. Utilization can be defined as the individual's ability to employ health care services. The following discussions of maternal, child, occupational, and elderly health among Mixtec families in California inherently raise the primary issues of problems surrounding health care access and health service utilization.

The various factors that combine to present difficulties in accessing care for Mixtec farmworkers and their families include both the ability to pay for care and the availability of care. Fundamental to the ability to pay for health care in California is health insurance. Farmworker health studies in

McFarland found that 46 percent of all families and 64 percent of Spanish-speaking families did not have health insurance coverage (California Department of Health Services 1992). Similarly, Sherman et al. (1997) report that 61 percent of adults in Parlier lack any form of health insurance. Findings from the 2000 CAWHS reveal lack of insurance and underutilization of clinical services. Of the 971 farmworkers interviewed:

- 70 percent of all persons lacked any form of health insurance;

- 16.5 percent said their employer offered health insurance, but one-third of these same workers did not participate in the insurance plan that was offered because they could not afford the premiums or co-payments;

- 32 percent of male subjects said they had never been to a doctor or clinic;

- half of all male subjects and two-fifths of female subjects said they had never been to a dentist; and

- two-thirds of all subjects reported never having had an eye-care visit (Villarejo et al. 2000).

There are numerous health care programs that do offer access to health care for California's farmworkers and their families. General coverage, however, does not exist. Health care coverage for Mixtec farmworker families is limited to emergency/pregnancy-related care programs such as Medi-Cal, federal public health programs such as for tuberculosis treatment, disease-specific grant-funded sporadic programs such as diabetes or chlamydia treatment, or immigration status–specific programs such as Healthy Families. While these programs are invaluable sources of acute health care coverage for Mixtec farmworker families, many health conditions, such as chronic illness and primary care needs, do not receive clinical attention. Many individuals with health needs—such as an elder with arthritis, a worker with psoriasis, or a woman with an ulcer—do not meet the criteria for such limited programs and thus cannot access clinical care unless they can pay for it out of pocket.

Access to health care is also determined by its availability. The unavailability of health care services in areas where farmworkers in California live poses another barrier to accessing health care. According to numbers from the 1990 census and the Medical Service Study Areas database, maintained by the Department of Health Services, there are twice as many primary care physicians relative to population in urban areas of California than in

rural areas, where Mixtec families are concentrated.[8] Furthermore, 16 percent of the rural Medical Service Study Areas in California have *no* primary
physicians. The low-income rural agricultural towns in California where
Mixtec families largely reside, such as Mecca, Cutler, and Gonzalez, have
fewer resources available to attract potential providers, who need an in-
sured or economically comfortable clientele—illustrated by the fact that the
ten most affluent communities in California have an average of 498 residents per primary care physician, while the ten poorest communities have
an average of 3,548 residents per primary care physician (Villarejo 1999: 6).

Utilization of services refers to the ability of the person with the health
need to employ the existing services. The following case, which I recorded
in 1997, illustrates the ways in which access barriers combine to negatively
influence health service utilization.

*Angela is a nineteen-year-old undocumented Mixtec farmworker living in
the Central Valley. Along with her mother and four siblings, Angela arrived in California in 1990 to join her father, who has been a farmworker in
Fresno County since 1979. At twelve years of age Angela quit school to
work the tomatoes and grapes with her father. She had been attending the
local elementary school, but had decided that her family needed her help in
order to make ends meet.*

*At fifteen Angela met a young man from her hometown in Mexico. An-
tonio and Angela married and Angela had her first child within a year. She
continued to work the tomato and grape harvests, leaving her daughter
with her mother, who had two toddlers of her own, during the day. One
night while Angela and her husband drove through the barrio to the local
park to relax and watch their daughter play on the grass, a bullet pierced
the back windshield and killed Antonio immediately. Angela became a
widow at seventeen.*

*After a year of living with her parents and siblings, Angela met an-
other man from her hometown and the two became engaged. Angela didn't
realize that her boyfriend was already promised to another young woman,
only fifteen years old, from the hometown. The fifteen-year-old's parents
became enraged with the boyfriend, called the cops, and had him arrested*

---

[8] Medical Service Study Area (MSSA) is a concept developed by the Office of
Statewide Health Planning and Development. It refers to a small geographic area
in which residents seek health services. There are 487 Medical Service Study Areas
in California.

*for molesting a minor. Angela's boyfriend is currently serving a two-year sentence in the county jail.*

*Within days of his arrest, Angela discovered that she was pregnant. By the time of her second child's birth, Proposition 187 had passed in California. Angela, along with the rest of the undocumented portion of her family, avoided the local clinic since she had heard that she might be taken away by the migra, or immigration service, if she went there. By the fifth month of her pregnancy, Angela had still not sought prenatal care. In the sixth month she began to have pains and became extremely worried. She went to the local clinic, but they refused to see her; because she was past her first trimester and had had no prenatal care, she was considered to be "high-risk." The only health service provider around that sees high-risk pregnant women is the Medical Center in Fresno, a thirty-minute freeway ride from the small agricultural town in which Angela lives.*

*The clinic gave Angela a telephone number and told her to call the Medical Center and make an appointment. Since Angela did not have a phone, she had to use the public phone at the local convenience store to make the toll call to Fresno. After three unsuccessful communications with the Medical Center, Angela finally got an appointment for the following week. She had to take the day off from work. There is no regular public transportation available in this small agricultural town in California, so Angela had to round up a ride from neighbors and acquaintances. A young man across the street said he would take her for $20.*

*After wandering the halls for half an hour, Angela finally found the obstetrics division of the Medical Center. Another Spanish-speaking patient observed Angela's arrival and told her that she needed to sign in at the desk. The receptionist handed Angela a "medical history" form and told her to fill it out while she waited. Since Angela had completed only six years of school, she found the medical history form to be mostly incomprehensible. In addition, the medical conditions listed on the form, such as cervical cancer, lie outside of the illness categories of Angela's medical culture, which includes illnesses such as susto and evil eye. She spent the hour guessing which items to check or not check on the form and finally decided to leave it blank.*

*An hour later a bilingual medical assistant called Angela's name. Angela was weighed, her blood pressure taken, and a blood sample drawn before the medical assistant led her to an examination room and instructed her to remove her skirt and underpants. Angela sat on the vinyl and steel chair with the apron draped over her lap for over forty-five minutes before a non-Spanish-speaking nurse practitioner entered the room and proceeded to do a pelvic exam. Since the nurse practitioner did not speak Spanish, Angela was unable to tell her of the pains she had been experiencing. Later Angela had a sonogram, and the doctor assigned to her expressed concern over the size of the fetus. The bilingual medical assistant was not present, and thus the information was not communicated to Angela.*

*After determining that Angela was anemic, the medical staff gave her a prescription for iron pills and told her to go to another counter to make her next monthly appointment. When she walked out to the parking lot, her ride had long since left. Angela called her mother's house and waited for her mother to find a neighbor willing to go and get her. Angela sat in the parking lot of the Medical Center until after dark, when a van pulled up two hours later and gave her a $30 ride back to her house. Angela never made another prenatal appointment, became a "noncompliant" patient, and returned to the hospital four months later to give birth to a healthy baby boy.*

In Angela's case we see that health service utilization involves much more than availability and access. At play are the usual barriers that have been reported to negatively affect health service utilization since the early 1980s, such as lack of transportation, lack of child care, inconvenient service provider hours, and language difficulties (cf. Mines and Kearney 1982; Bade 1994; Diringer 1996). Several other obstacles arise in Angela's case. Bureaucratic labels, such as "high risk" and "noncompliance," determine Angela's health care options without consideration for her situation, placing added hardship on an already dire situation. If no attempts are made to explain biomedical illness categories such as cervical cancer, they become little more than esoteric jargon to the patient. Finally, what could be called a lack of bedside manner—Angela's waiting undressed in an examination room and not being given the opportunity to express her concerns—can negatively affect a Mixtec woman's decision to continue to pursue a particular course of clinical treatment.

Maternal and child health constitute a primary health need among Mixtec families. Data from a 1993 survey of 109 Mixtec women in Madera, California,[9] reveal that 39 percent of last visits to a clinic were to seek perinatal care, such as family planning, prenatal, delivery, and postnatal health

---

[9] Survey conducted by the author and financed by the University of California Agricultural Cooperative Extension with the support of James Grieshop of the University of California, Davis and Martha López of UC Cooperative Extension in Madera.

**Table 8.1. Monthly WIC Food Coupon Benefits for a Representative Migrant Farmworker Family**

| Week/Year | Product | | | | | | | Monthly |
|---|---|---|---|---|---|---|---|---|
| | Milk | Cereal | Beans | Eggs | Cheese | Juice | Formula | Total |
| July 20, 1992 | $3.74 | $9.57 | $0.79 | $2.46 | $5.26 | $11.66 | | $33.48 |
| Sept. 3, 1992 | $6.48 | $7.42 | $0.79 | $2.92 | $5.56 | $11.36 | | $34.53 |
| Sept. 9, 1992 | $7.86 | $10.07 | $0.79 | $2.92 | | $12.78 | | $34.42 |
| Oct. 14, 1992 | $9.89 | $7.42 | $0.79 | $2.86 | $4.07 | $11.34 | $37.80 | $74.17 |
| Total | $27.97 | $34.48 | $3.16 | $11.16 | $14.89 | $47.14 | $37.80 | |

care. Perinatal care needs function as a result of the youthfulness of the Mixtec migrant population. In the 1993 Madera study, the average age of first pregnancy among the 109 Mixtec women interviewed was 17.8 years, with 70 percent of pregnancies occurring between 15 and 19 years of age. However, utilization of perinatal services by Mixtec families also reflects the availability of federal, state, and local perinatal support programs, such as Medi-Cal and the Special Supplemental Food Program for Women, Infants, and Children (WIC). Data from the 1995–1997 NAWS indicate that although only 18 percent of farmworker households received any type of needs-based assistance from social service programs, the program that most frequently assists them is WIC, which is used by one in seven California farmworker households (Rosenberg et al. 1998: 8). The Madera survey I conducted in 1993 confirms that WIC is widely used by Mixtec farmworker families; in that survey 86 percent reported that they had participated in WIC with their children born in the United States. WIC's primary benefit to farmworker families takes the form of food coupons. Table 8.1 shows price totals of WIC food coupons from various months in 1992 for the family of Juan and Soledad (introduced earlier in this essay). Excluding baby formula, the average monthly value of the food coupons is $34.70. The items that a family can buy with WIC coupons are limited to specific quantities and brands of milk, cereal, beans, eggs, cheese, juice, and formula. The WIC coupons subsidize the insufficient wages of farmworker families, which for three-quarters of the farmworker population is below $10,000 per year.

As of the writing of this essay in 2003, Medi-Cal continued, despite recent legislation, to provide emergency and pregnancy-related health care benefits. For young farmworker families, these two benefits are indispensable. My 1993 Madera data show that 73 percent of the 109 women who responded sought prenatal care during their last pregnancy. The study also reveals, however, that prenatal care was sought *after* the first trimester of pregnancy, with a mean of 3.8 months for the first prenatal visit. This number is consistent with data gathered nearly *twenty years ago* in Tulare County by Mines and Kearney, who found that 18 percent of women interviewed had no prenatal care and over half did not have a prenatal exam during the first trimester (Mines and Kearney 1982: 74). Studies have shown that prenatal care after the first trimester creates a situation of high risk for both mother and child.

An obvious aspect that affects health service utilization by Mixtec families is patient/provider interface. During the 2000 CAWHS study, I conducted qualitative ethnographic research regarding patient/provider interface while acting as site coordinator in Vista, California. The following case illustrates the problems surrounding utilization of health care services by Mixtec farmworkers in the context of the medical clinic.

> *Lázaro waits daily on the corner of Vista Way and South Santa Fe Avenue for prospective employers to drive by and offer him a day's work. He had been working the cucumber harvest in Vista, but his job ended when there were no more cucumbers to pick. One of the CIRS [California Institute for Rural Studies] interviewers from the Vista community, assigned to randomly select farmworker participants at different outlying day laborer pickup sites, arranged for Lázaro's physical exam. Lázaro arrived at the clinic along with three other workers from a nearby nursery, who were also participating in the study. When greeted by the CIRS staff, he took the opportunity to tell the site coordinator about an acute pain he had been experiencing in his foot. The CIRS site coordinator communicated the complaint to the bilingual medical assistant, who said she would mention it to the doctor during the physical exam. When Lázaro returned to the waiting room after having had his physical, he told the CIRS staff that the doctor, who did not speak Spanish, had not mentioned his sore foot. Lázaro had not said anything to her about it for fear that she would not understand him. When Lázaro returned two weeks later for his follow-up appointment, lab results showed that his glucose level was alarmingly high. The medical assistant sat with Lázaro in one of the examination rooms to explain that he needed more tests because the doctor suspects he is diabetic. Lázaro refused to make another appointment because he could not afford it. He said he didn't trust the people at the clinic because they had not acknowledged his problem with his foot, which had worsened dramatically in the two weeks since his last visit. He told the CIRS staff that he had to leave his last job due to the pain in his foot and was headed to Mexico to "get injections" and some treatment for his foot.*

We learn several lessons from Lázaro's experience at the clinic. The lack of health delivery personnel who speak the patient's language creates a situation in which the patient cannot communicate his needs to the provider and the provider cannot communicate concerns to the patient. The lack of communication generates mistrust and fear, which affects both utilization and delivery of health care. Furthermore, the lack of communication allows treatable, preventive health conditions to escalate to full-blown health crises.

Farmwork obviously ranks as a highly stressful and dangerous occupation. Recently published data show that the 1994 accident rate among California hired farmworkers was 10,546 per 100,000 full-time employees (Villarejo 1999: 39). Accidents on the job and in vehicles transporting workers to and from work, pesticide and dust exposure, and heat, cold, and other environmental exposures that come with outdoor work are only some of the risks that farmworkers face daily in the agricultural fields of California.

*Eugenia's eyes wrinkled in delight as I ate the bowl of mole she placed before me. We sat alone in the kitchen in the late afternoon, the other men and families who occupy the house all out in the backyard cooling off after a long day in the tomato fields. "As I was telling you, guerita, my arm is so messed up I can't work anymore," she said as she cleaned the herbs her husband had found in the tomato field. She held out her hand and exclaimed, "look, guerita, look how this arm is so much shorter than the other. They used to be the same, you know."*

*Ever since Eugenia fell off a ladder while picking olives in Selma two years ago, things have not been the same. She still works, picking tomatoes with her husband. They work together under his name since the farm labor contractor won't hire Eugenia because she works too slowly. So all her tomatoes go in Francisco's bucket, earning them 34 cents for each five-gallon tub they fill. This helps Francisco keep his job as well, since he's old and moves slowly due to chronic knee pain. He goes to Mexico every six months to buy arthritis medicine that he himself injects while seated on the floor of the single bedroom the couple share in a two-bedroom house full of farmworkers and their families. The house rents for $650 a month, so many people live there to share the rent, including a family of five in the other bedroom and seventeen single men farmworkers who sleep in the living room. Another family lives in a makeshift shack behind the house, and migrating farmworkers frequently camp out in the backyard.*

*Eugenia has her legal documents, which she proudly waves under the noses of the local bureaucrats with whom she must deal in order to get compensation for her injury. She has been involved in a legal battle since her accident. A friend had told her about a lawyer in Fresno who would help her "get money" for her injury. Eugenia had been working the olives less than thirty days when she fell from the top of the ladder, smashing her arm against both the tree and the ladder and breaking the ulna in four places. She has a huge scar on her elbow where the bone broke through the skin. Her labor contractor drove her to the emergency room, and Medi-Cal covered the expenses of her initial treatment. Eugenia had heard of worker's compensation from a friend and had asked her employer about it. He claimed that since she had worked for him less than thirty days, she did not qualify for it. The injuries Eugenia suffered needed treatment beyond the emergency room. Physical therapy, as well as further surgery, would be necessary if Eugenia was to regain the full use of her arm.*

*"I can't get that employer to talk to me. He acts like he has never seen me," Eugenia says as she pulls a stack of papers and envelopes bound in a rubber band out of a plastic shopping bag she keeps stored under the mattress. "Here, can you read these to me, because I think they want me to go to court or something." Mixed in with notices from Medi-Cal and the Employment Development Department are a few letters from a public defender stating that Eugenia's case had been closed. As she pulls an x-ray of her arm out of the bag to show me, she exclaims, "Can you believe all those screws and nails they put in my arm? No wonder it hurts all the time." As I read through the legal documents, all written in English and full of incomprehensible jargon, I realized that the courts had determined that Eugenia suffered from no lasting effects of the fall and that she required no further treatment. "But how can they say that?" she said, showing me an arm at least two inches shorter than the other and covered with scars. "At night it really hurts, guerita. What can I do? That's how life is."*

Elderly workers, who tend to experience more health problems than younger workers as a consequence of the strenuous and stressful farmworker lifestyle, are in a particularly vulnerable position without health insurance. A case in point is Eliseo, a sixty-two-year-old Mixtec farmworker from Tepejillo, Oaxaca. Eliseo suffers from rheumatism in his left knee. He also broke his arm several years ago in the citrus harvest, and it frequently causes him severe pain when he does strenuous work. Work in the tomato fields has recently become quite difficult for him. The five-gallon buckets, which weigh up to twenty-five pounds when full, are too heavy for him to lift over his head for eight or ten consecutive hours. He also complains that he has trouble standing from the kneeling position required for picking and filling the buckets.

As noted previously, access to and utilization of health care are intimately related. The nature of access programs such as Medi-Cal can determine an individual's pattern of health service utilization. The very structure of Medi-Cal, the default health insurance for Mixtec farmworker families in California, directs individuals with health conditions to specific treatment "choices," including treatments that are covered by Medi-Cal and treatments that are not. Furthermore, Medi-Cal promotes use of emergency rooms by farmworker families seeking primary care. Figure 8.1 outlines the pathway to health care for farmworker families without medical insurance, whose access to clinical treatment is Medi-Cal dependent. The arrows represent the movement of individuals toward health care. The diagram does not include all available options, but focuses instead on those most commonly used by economically disadvantaged farmworkers and their families living in agricultural towns of California.

The pathway begins at "health condition" with a particular health situation occurring in California—for example, a Mixtec woman with prolonged uterine bleeding. She can seek clinical care at a local clinic, hospital, or private doctor (institutional care), or she can rely on self-treatment or perhaps a traditional healer, depending on her cultural background (noninstitutional care). If she chooses institutional care, she has two options for payment of services: cash or Medi-Cal. Her economic status limits cash-rendered services to affordable treatments, which in this case may be none. As her condition worsens, she seeks emergency care at a hospital, where she is given a series of tests and possibly prescribed something and/or operated on and released. If the condition persists after emergency treatment, which tends to treat symptoms and not causes of illness, she may turn to her own medical culture and knowledge in an attempt to alleviate the problem, which, if it recurs, will lead her back to the emergency room. The woman is forced into a treatment "loop," alternating between institutional emergency care and noninstitutional self- or traditional care as her condition persists or diminishes in severity. Her other health care treatment option is to go to Mexico, perhaps Tijuana, where she is familiar with both institutional and noninstitutional forms of treatment.

Two important points stand out in the pathway to health care for uninsured low-income individuals in California such as Mixtec farmworkers and their families. First, ailments that are not emergencies or pregnancy-related—such as general aches and pains, respiratory aliments, and gastrointestinal problems (vomiting, diarrhea)—as well as chronic illnesses like diabetes, arthritis, asthma, and high blood pressure either: (1) go untreated, (2) develop into emergency or urgent care situations, or (3) are diagnosed and treated using ethnospecific (folk) methods. Second, the bureaucratic structure of Medi-Cal imposes emergency care, one of the most expensive types of health care, upon individuals with nonemergency health needs who wish to receive clinical medical attention. In other words, if an uninsured Mixtec farmworker needs clinical care and cannot afford it, then that individual must seek emergency care.

**Figure 8.1. Pathway to Clinical Health Care Treatment for the Uninsured**

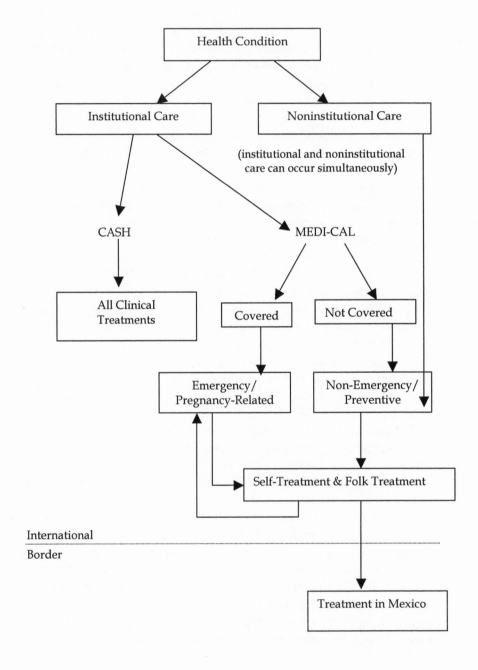

Quantitative data recorded in the 1993 study I conducted in Madera indicate that Mixtec families rely heavily on self- and ethnospecific treatment to meet health care needs. Tables 8.2 and 8.3 represent treatment choices reported for ethnospecific and clinical ailments. The ethnospecific illnesses (discussed in more detail below) refer to illnesses or ailments that are not formally recognized or diagnosed as illnesses by biomedical or clinical health care practitioners. The ethnospecific illnesses reported were *susto* (fright), *empacho* (constipation, stomach pains), *aire* (coldness), *caída de mollera* (fallen fontanel), *espinilla* (childhood illness of clammy skin), *mal de ojo* (evil eye), *mal puesto* (hex), and *látido* (stomach cramps), in order of descending frequency. The respondents were asked if they had sought clinical treatment (at a medical facility such as a clinic, hospital, or private doctor), ethnospecific treatment (seen a Mixtec healer), or self-administered pharmaceuticals or medicinal plants.

**Table 8.2. Treatment Choices for Reported Ethnospecific Illnesses**

| Illness | Reported Cases | Clinical Treatment | Ethnospecific Treatment | Self-Treatment[a] |
|---|---|---|---|---|
| *Susto/espanto* | 38 | 6 | 17 | 15 |
| *Empacho* | 20 | 4 | 3 | 13 |
| *Aire* | 12 | 2 | 7 | 3 |
| *Caída de mollera* | 9 | 5 | 2 | 2 |
| *Espinilla* | 4 | 1 | 3 | 0 |
| *Mal de ojo* | 6 | 2 | 1 | 3 |
| *Mal puesto* | 2 | 2 | 0 | 0 |
| Other[b] | 3 | 0 | 3 | 0 |
| All ethnospecific ailments | 94[c] | 22 (24%) | 36 (38%) | 36 (38%) |

[a] Self-treatment includes three options: no care sought, herbal treatment, pharmaceutical treatment.
[b] Stomachache, headache, and *látido* were included as ethnospecific illnesses reported.
[c] Total number of respondents = 109.

This same procedure was followed for the section on treatment choices for clinical ailments. These data are recorded in table 8.3. Respondents were asked if they suffered from a particular health condition, such as toothache, stomachache, diarrhea, weakness, and so on, and if so, what

**Table 8.3. Treatment Choices for Reported Clinically Recognized Health Conditions**

| Health Condition | Total | Average[a] | Clinical Treatment | Ethnospecific Treatment | Self-Treatment |
|---|---|---|---|---|---|
| Aches and pains (4)[b] | 211 | 53 | 38 (18%) | 13 (6%) | 160 (76%) |
| Mental/stress (6) | 150 | 25 | 15 (10%) | 10 (7%) | 125 (83%) |
| Dental (3) | 137 | 46 | 70 (51%) | 1 (1%) | 66 (48%) |
| Respiratory/allergy (4) | 88 | 22 | 28 (32%) | 4 (4%) | 56 (64%) |
| Gastrointestinal (3) | 39 | 13 | 9 (23%) | 2 (5%) | 28 (72%) |
| Menstrual/urinary (2) | 28 | 14 | 16 (57%) | 2 (7%) | 10 (36%) |
| Obesity (1) | 7 | 7 | 1 (14%) | 0 | 6 (86%) |
| All clinical ailments | 660 | | 177 (27%) | 32 (5%) | 451 (68%) |

[a] Average: reported cases of category divided by number of ailments per category.
[b] This indicates the number of ailments combined to form each category. In the cases of aches and pains, there is some ambiguity as to whether it referred to syndromes or symptoms.

type of treatment—clinical, ethnospecific, self-treatment—they had utilized. The categories "aches and pains," "mental/stress," "dental," "respiratory/allergy," "gastrointestinal," and "menstrual/urinary" are the result of grouping several related health conditions together. The aches and pains category, for example, consists of headaches, backaches, stomachaches, and chest pains; the mental/stress category includes lack of energy, sleeplessness, nervousness, depression, lack of appetite, and *coraje* (anger); the dental category comprises toothache, dental caries, and tooth loss; the respiratory/allergy category covers breathlessness, coughing, allergies, rashes; the gastrointestinal category encompasses diarrhea, vomiting, bowel problems; the menstrual covers urinary; and the obesity category corresponds to the one condition identified.

Tables 8.2 and 8.3 show the relationship between ailment type and treatment choice. Non-ethnospecific ailments (table 8.3) are more commonly reported then ethnospecific ailments (table 8.2). However, the patterns of treatment choices differ between clinical ailments and folk ailments and with respect to ethnospecific and self-treatment. Both tables confirm a considerable reliance on self- and ethnospecific treatment as compared to clinical treatment for all types of ailments—ethnospecific and clinical. For clinical ailments, however, table 8.3 shows that ethnospecific treatment is sought in only 5 percent of reported cases. The data also indicate that self-treatment, such as the use of herbs, sweat baths, and pharmaceuticals, plays an important role in the treatment of clinical illnesses, while folk treatment plays a more important role in the treatment of ethnospecific illnesses.

Figures 8.2 and 8.3 show the types of treatments chosen for both ethnospecific and clinical ailments. Clinical care was sought with more or less the same frequency for both ethnospecific (24 percent) and clinical ailments (27 percent). That is to say, regardless of the type of illness or health condition suffered—clinical or ethnospecific—only one-quarter of these cases are clinically treated. In contrast, close to three-quarters of all ailments, both ethnospecific (76 percent) and clinical (73 percent), are being treated with self- and ethnospecific care, meaning that the Mixtec rely heavily on their own resources, such as herbs, purchased pharmaceuticals, sweat baths, and healers, to confront their health problems.

Figure 8.2 represents reported treatment choices for ethnospecific ailments. A total of ninety-four ethnospecific ailments were reported by 109 respondents. Twenty-four percent (twenty-two) of the reported ethnospecific aliments were clinically treated; 38 percent (thirty-six) were treated ethnospecifically; and 38 percent (thirty-six) were self-treated. Figure 8.3

represents reported treatment choices for clinically recognized health conditions. A total of 660 health conditions were reported by the 109 respondents. Twenty-seven percent (177) of the reported clinical ailments were clinically treated; 5 percent (32) were treated ethnospecifically; and 68 percent (451) were self-treated.

**Figure 8.2. Treatment Choices for Ethnospecific Ailments**

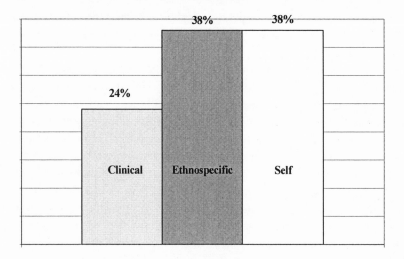

**Figure 8.3. Treatment Choices for Clinical Ailments**

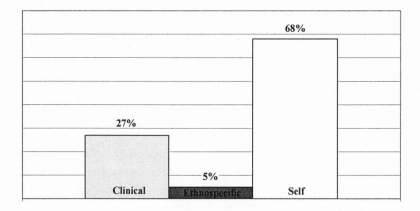

Differing patterns are revealed in comparing self- and ethnospecific treatment choices for confronting ethnospecific and clinical ailments. Figure 8.2 shows that ethnospecific and self-treatments equally provide health care options for ethnospecific, or folk, ailments, such as *susto* or *empacho*. In contrast, figure 8.3, or treatment choices for clinical ailments, shows that there is a higher dependency on self-treatment (68 percent) than on any other type of care to meet perceived health care needs. When comparing clinical, self-, and ethnospecific treatment choices for specific health conditions, such as dental or menstrual problems (tables 8.2 and 8.3), we see that clinical care is preferred over ethnospecific care. In summary, the data in the tables and figures reveal a pattern of high reliance on ethnospecific and self-treatment to meet health care needs for Mixtec women in Madera.

Regarding health care, Mixtec families, like anyone else, want "full coverage," which means having as many available treatment options as possible. For the political, economic, and social reasons discussed above (undocumented status, chronic poverty, ethnic status), clinical care for Mixtec families in California is limited. The quantitative Madera data indicate that clinical care actually meets only about 25 percent of Mixtec women's health care needs. To fill this gap and better meet their medical needs, Mixtec families supplement clinical care with indigenous care. The qualitative data reveal that Mixtec women adeptly exploit as many types of health care as deemed necessary or possible, ultimately alternating between self- and folk treatments such as herbs and sweat baths (discussed below) and clinical treatments, especially emergency room care. In addition, it is significant that some travel to Mexico to seek treatment that is unavailable or unaffordable in California. Mixtec women and their families move between distinct health care systems (with differing values, methods, languages, behaviors, and schedules) and along diverse pathways (with differing social relationships and behavioral expectations) to attend to their medical needs in California. This is the practice of "transmedical" health care. When Mixtec families practice health care in California, they move not only across, beyond, and between medical systems, but also across, beyond, and between social and linguistic barriers, cultural landscapes, and political borders. The movement implied by the term "trans" refers not only to the migrant nature of the Mixtec lifestyle but also to the complex systems—social, political, and economic—that Mixtec families navigate to achieve health care.

## CONTEMPORARY MIXTEC MEDICINE

In California, increasing numbers of indigenous people from southern Mexico and Guatemala bring with them nosologies (classifications of disease), etiologies (causation theories), diagnoses, therapies, and concepts of prevention that are markedly distinct from those of clinical biomedicine. Pre-Columbian indigenous medicine, fifteenth-century Spanish medicine, and some contemporary biomedical concepts and practices all inform contemporary Mixtec medicine.

For the Mixtec people, as with many other indigenous cultures, illness, health maintenance, religion, and social relations are all intimately interwoven. When an illness occurs, one's spiritual, social, and cosmic positions are considered to affect both cause and cure. In addition, the principle of equilibrium lies at the foundation of Mixtec medical beliefs and practices. Thus illness can occur when a healthy individual in balance has been exposed to a potentially disruptive force—be it physical, such a heat or cold, social, such as a relationship with a relative or neighbor, or spiritual, such as entities that occupy caves, roads, and rivers.

Mixtec worldview dictates the presence of outside forces—physical, social, and cosmic—that can threaten the equilibrium of an individual and create illness. In fact, some scholars have reported that malevolent actions of outside agents—supernatural, human, or nonhuman—form the cornerstone of Mixtec illness etiology (Aguirre Beltrán 1947: 115; Butterworth 1975: 109; Chiñas 1973: 87; Mak 1959: 127; Romney and Romney 1966: 72). Illness results, for example, when one has somehow let down his/her psychological or physical defenses and become exposed to attack. The causes of many illnesses are therefore attributed to offended spirits, the evil eye, sorcery, the dead, and violations of prescribed codes of social behavior. Several scholars have attributed this perception of the pervasiveness of threatening forces to the chronic poverty that characterizes Mexican indigenous communities. Theoretical models such as Foster's "image of limited good" (1967) and Kearney's "image of diminishing good" (1969) explain this fatalism in terms of competition between neighbors over "goods," such as land or food, that exist in limited quantities. Concepts of illness causation in the form of threatening malevolent forces thus stem from historic, economic, and social realities mandating defensive social forms and practices.

In accordance with the principle of equilibrium upon which Mixtec illness causation theories are founded, it is believed that strong emotions—such as fear, anger, or jealousy— can put one off balance and cause one to

absorb or transmit illness, depending on the conditions behind the experience (Foster and Anderson 1978; Kearney 1972; Rubel 1960). Young children in particular are believed to be extremely susceptible to potentially
disruptive forces like strong emotions, and they must be protected from
jealousy, anger, and fear if they are to avoid illness. For example, a nursing
Mixtec mother must maintain control over her emotions, particularly anger, lest she cause "anger sickness" (*cuehe canduu*) in her child (Mak 1959:
131).

Recent studies indicate that Mixtec families in California maintain and
cultivate ethnospecific medical beliefs. In table 8.4, data from the 1993
Madera study show that out of 107 women interviewed, 49 report having
suffered from *coraje*, which is characterized by feelings of frustration, pow-
erlessness, and general restlessness (Bade 2000: 30). Furthermore, 36 percent of these women reported suffering from *susto* (Spanish) or *kueniiyu'u*
(Mixtec). Literally "fright," this is an illness in which the soul separates
from or is taken from the body. It can result from a shocking experience
such as a fall. *Susto* can be caused by offending the spirits of the ground,
the cornfield, a river, a cave, the sweat bath, and so on (personal
communication with Don Primo, 1998; Dyk 1959: 87). Symptoms of *susto*
include loss of appetite, listlessness, and often diarrhea and vomiting.
These effects can be delayed, frequently appearing later in life. Often adults
suffering from prolonged symptoms of general fatigue, lack of appetite,
and listlessness that have not responded to self-treatment will attribute the
illness to a traumatic episode in their childhood in which they experienced
fear. Proper cure of soul loss due to *susto* involves appropriate ritual and
prayer, usually performed by a healer and often accompanied by the
administration of pharmaceuticals and/or herbs.

**Table 8.4. Ethnospecific Illnesses Experienced in Madera**

| Illness | Number of Cases | Percent of Sample |
|---|---|---|
| *Coraje* | 49 | 46.0% |
| *Susto* | 38 | 36.0 |
| *Empacho* | 19 | 18.0 |
| *Aire* | 11 | 10.0 |
| *Caída de mollera* | 9 | 8.5 |
| *Mal de ojo* | 6 | 5.6 |
| *Mal puesto* | 2 | 2.0 |

*Source*: Bade 1994.
Number of respondents = 107.

Nonclinical health care treatment in the Mixteca generally involves healing ceremonies of strong religious value in which divine intervention is sought. Offerings, in the form of sacrifice, food, or other valued items, serve to appease an offended spirit responsible for the illness, as well as to petition the assistance of benevolent spirits to aid in the cure (cf. González Villanueva 1989). Hens and roosters are common sacrificial offerings, highly valued in both symbolic and material senses.

Since for the Mixtec people many illnesses are attributed to indirect or supernatural causes, the role and function of the healer and the skills required to cure differ markedly from those of clinical health practitioners. Indeed, for illnesses of supernatural origin, the Mixtec healer must possess divinatory or prophetic skills to determine the cause and appropriate treatment. The sick person in such cases is a victim of malevolent forces— bad spirits or witchcraft—that must be neutralized or redirected with the aid of the healer. Diagnosis of the illness, therefore, holds great psychological value because it reveals not the immediate cause but rather who or what was the originating cause and why.

In contrast to the diagnostic methods of biomedical clinicians, the Mixtec healer rarely asks questions about symptoms, focusing instead on recent events in the individual's life that may have disturbed his or her physical, spiritual, or social balance. The skill of the healer is evaluated largely on the basis of his ability to use divination, pulsing, and other methods to diagnose an illness and determine where it seized the individual, which deities or supernatural entities are involved, which prayers are required for the cure, whether the patient's soul has been captured, whether the illness is spiritual or physical in nature, and whether strong emotions such as envy are at work. In addition, the healer must have intimate knowledge of the physical, symbolic, and religious attributes of medicinal plants and their proper preparation. Many healers combine modern pharmaceuticals, such as analgesics, antihistamines, and antibiotics, with nonbiomedical treatment. The following case describes Don Primo's use of the ancient diagnostic method called "*sacar tiempo*" (reckoning time).

*Don Primo led us over the log bridge to the other side of the river. The woman who had asked him to come and heal her child lived down in the cornfield by the path that ran to the caves. A plant with small yellow flowers grew by the side of the path. "That one is called* pericón, *it's used for stomachaches," he indicated as he turned onto the trail to Guadalupe's house. She waited for him at the door of her wood slat kitchen, the sick child in her arms. An older son brought us Pepsis, and it began to rain steadily.*

*In the kitchen Don Primo sat on the small chair on the dirt floor and examined the child, who began crying the minute his mother handed him to the healer. Snot ran from the child's nose, and his eyes showed the dull puffiness of fever. Don Primo rubbed his hands together and blew into his cupped palms. He then began an ancient Mixtec oration.[10]... While speaking, Don Primo took the pinky finger of his right hand and positioned it on the tip of his left elbow. With the pinky finger in place, the thumb of his right hand extended along the outer edge of his forearm toward his left hand. As he spoke, and keeping his thumb in place, he swung the pinky finger from his elbow up to the side of his left palm, noting where on the outer edge of the palm the finger landed. He did this several times, his eyes staring in a faraway, unfocused manner and his head at times rolling forward as if he were asleep. After a bit he stopped praying and looked at the woman. "Something has happened to frighten the boy," declared Don Primo. "Last week during the Todos Santos celebrations the fireworks in town woke him from sleeping, and he has been crying ever since," the woman replied while she resumed grinding chilies on her metate. "Do you have the items for the cure?" he asked, pulling his bible from the medicine bag slung over his shoulder. "We'll have to do the ceremony here in the kitchen, since it's raining so hard out there." The woman reached behind a large clay pot by the fire and pulled out a plastic tub containing flowers, candles, beer, cigarettes, eggs, and loose tobacco.*

Although certain elements of the above history are unquestionably contemporary, the medical knowledge possessed by Don Primo comes from an ancient and sophisticated civilization known for its complexity and grandeur. Employing pre-Hispanic cosmological concepts, such as the complex twenty-day sacred calendar and the thirteen levels of the upper world, Don Primo's oration and hand gestures, documented in 1998, are described in uncannily similar detail by Ruiz de Alarcón, who lived among the Aztecs and wrote about their culture in the seventeenth century. The ritual called "*sacar tiempo*" constitutes a complex diagnostic procedure that indicates to the healer what illness has seized the individual and how to proceed with treatment.

Extensive knowledge of the plant and animal worlds characterizes the information possessed by Mixtec healers and herbalists. Don Primo's knowledge about plant medicinal uses was vast. As referred to briefly

---

[10] See chapter appendix 1 for a transcription of this healing ritual.

above, in 1998 I and three research assistants conducted an ethnobotanical collection of 140 medicinal plants as indicated by Don Primo.[11] The study recorded the Mixtec name, Spanish name, scientific name, uses, preparations, harvesting procedures, and location of each one. This knowledge of medicinal plants has been transmitted orally for generations among Mixtec communities. In 2003, a Mixtec herbalist in Vista, California, supported by the Oaxacan Indigenous Binational Front (FIOB), grows medicinal herbs in a field donated by a local mental institution. He trades and sells these herbs to local Mixtec families who wish to use them medicinally.

In addition to the extensive knowledge of medicinal plants, Mixtec medical culture possesses several very effective and healthful treatment practices. Mixtec women throughout California use the sweat bath as a postpartum treatment. The sweat bath incorporates the use of medicinal plants as well as the use of a small structure in which the individuals receive treatment.

*It is nearly sunset and the 105-degree day in Madera finally begins to cool. Magdalena's husband, Ignacio, pokes at the fire pit, which is full of burning embers two feet deep. He built the wooden frame for the sweat bath, or ñi'i, several days ago, gathering willow branches down by the Fresno River. He then dug the pit and this afternoon began to burn wood so that by sunset there would be enough embers to provide the necessary heat for the sweat ritual. Having determined that the embers are ready, Ignacio covers them with a metal trashcan lid punctured with holes and then places rocks in a pile on the lid. He lays cardboard sheets on the ground inside the structure and then on the wooden frame itself. Ignacio covers the cardboard with several blankets, mostly the fuzzy acrylic ones with "Lion King" prints that you can get in Tijuana for $10. The sweat bath looks something like a makeshift two-person tent, with one end sloping down to the ground just beyond the enclosed fire pit and the other open end draped with blankets which must be pulled aside for entry. My* comadre *Magdalena and I had gone out earlier in the afternoon to gather the* yucu ni, *a special herb used for the sweat bath. Since true* yucu ni *grows only in Oaxaca, we settled for walnut branches, which we bunched up into small hand-held brooms. Magdalena says that when you get in the ñi'i, you gently slap the skin with the leaves of the brooms and this causes the blood to flow to the*

---

[11] Collaborative study with the San Diego Museum of Man and funded by San Diego State University's Minority International Research Training Program, supported by a Fogarty grant.

surface of the skin, which is one of the beneficial aspects of the sweat bath. Magdalena had asked me earlier if I would assist her in the sweat bath. She said that the woman who normally sweats with her had gone to Oregon with her husband to pick cherries. Magdalena had given birth to a daughter two weeks before and now needed to cleanse her body with the sweat. We would do four sweats over the next two weeks before the ritual was complete. With her other children running about the yard chasing the chicks that had hatched two days before, Magdalena and I crawled into the structure and removed our clothes, covering ourselves with a bed sheet. Ignacio went into the house to get a chair so that he could sit outside the sweat structure and monitor if we had any problems. As we lay side by side in the small wood and cardboard tent, Ignacio handed me the plastic five-gallon bucket of water, which he instructed me to place near the embers. Leaves of fresh rue (Ruta graveolens), another beneficial herb used in Oaxaca and grown in Magdalena's garden in Madera, floated on the water in the bucket. Ignacio dropped the blankets over the entrance, and Magdalena and I lay in darkness. When our eyes adjusted, Magdalena reached for the plastic bowl floating in the water and splashed a bowl full of water over the rocks in the trash can lid. Steam immediately enveloped us, searing my eyes so that I had to close them. I scrambled to remove a gold hoop earring I had forgotten as it burned a ring onto the skin below my ear. The heat entered our lungs and made breathing difficult. Magdalena instructed me to grab one of the brooms and slap it against her legs, making sure to cover every inch. The leaves became extremely hot. The small space we had to work in seemed even smaller with the oppressive heat and steam. Magdalena then used one of the brooms to slap my legs. The wet leaves burned against my skin, leaving red blotches. We lay there too exhausted to move and then she called to Ignacio to lift the blankets. Twenty minutes had passed, but it felt like an hour. I gasped at the fresh air, but Magdalena and Ignacio told me not to get out. After we refreshed ourselves for ten minutes or so, Ignacio again lowered the blankets and Magdalena and I repeated our actions, concentrating on the other parts of the body. I had become accustomed to the heat, and my body began to relax in a way I had never before experienced. After four sessions, we were finally done. I felt extremely relaxed, my skin was smooth, and my consciousness had entered an acutely aware state. We put our clothes back on, and Magdalena covered my head with a blanket and told me to keep covered for a few hours so that the aire, or cold air, wouldn't get into me and make me sick.

Obviously, illness or any other health condition involves a certain degree of emotional insecurity. Fear, uncertainty, denial, anxiety, and despair are among the most notable emotional states that may be associated with illness. Recognition of and attention to such feelings are notably absent from most clinical health care procedures. The impersonal, often cold approach to illness in medical clinics or county hospitals offers little reassurance to the individual that the illness will be cured through persistent and comprehensive efforts. Such clinical visits typically comprise a five-minute examination by a physician and a prescription for an expensive medicine with an unpronounceable name. Faith must be placed in the assumed skills of a stranger and the workings of science. In contrast, religious diagnostic and therapeutic methods that Mixtec healers employ (such as oration and elaborate ritual) combine with physical treatments such as the use of herbs, massage, sweat baths, and pharmaceuticals to give the patient the perceived emotional and "spiritual" support necessary to overcome illness. In such a context, the ill person may take comfort in the knowledge that several possible forces, rather than merely the physical forces, have been rallied in her defense.

## SOCIAL AND POLITICAL SIGNIFICANCE OF TRANSMEDICAL HEALTH CARE

A comprehensive study of health care for low-income foreign-born migrant workers in California must include such complex and volatile social and political issues as national immigration and border policies, U.S.-Mexico relations, national health policies, social services, civil rights, public education, and the economy. Many relevant support programs sponsored at local, state, and federal levels provide support to the poor and to women and children. Special programs to service the legal, educational, and health needs of ethnic migrants include California Rural Legal Assistance, Migrant Education, the Child Health Dental Program, and numerous local church and community organizations such as the Lion's Club and the Catholic Church.[12] Medi-Cal offers invaluable support in emergency and pregnancy-related situations. The WIC program provides material and social support by teaching dietary awareness, offering family planning consultation, and supplying infant formula and food coupons for staples

---

[12] Fortunately, it would be difficult to list here all of the many local, county, state, or federal programs that support the poor or migrant farmworker population.

such as milk, eggs, cheese, cereal, beans, and juice. Most of these and similar programs have recently lost invaluable funding.

Local private, county, state, and federally funded medical clinics constitute the primary source of clinical health care for migrant farmworker families in California. Most of these facilities offer flexible payment programs and fixed low-cost visitation fees, and employ Spanish-speaking personnel. Mixtec families living and working in California depend upon these facilities for treatment of serious conditions, such as fevers, infections, diarrhea, and skin irritations, as well as for reproductive health concerns.

Largely as a result of California's economic troubles, the current political environment for undocumented men, women, and children in the state continues to be hostile and threatening. High unemployment rates, crime, overpopulated schools, and overrun prisons and hospitals fuel fear and mistrust of noticeable migrant workers like the Mixtec. Recent legislation aims to further cut medical aid to the undocumented, denying emergency, prenatal, delivery, and postnatal services to thousands of taxpaying workers.

The structural relationship of mutual dependency between the economies of the Mixteca and California, as well as Oaxaca's economic and political situation, indicate that Mixtec families will continue to commute to work, traveling thousands of miles to the agricultural sectors of the United States (Kearney 1986; Runsten and Zabin 1989; Wright 1990). The social, political, and economic marginalization of the Mixtec, manifest in labor market segregation and the formation of Mixtec enclaves throughout California, has combined with their own cultural forms of distinct identity—inscribed in language, custom, and religious celebration—to defy "melting pot" assimilationist models of immigration. Long-term circular migration between the Mixteca and California will doubtlessly deepen the integration of Mixtec and California communities. However, for many social and cultural reasons, the Mixtec residing in California will continue to be ethnically distinct from mainstream culture. Problems in the delivery and consumption of health care services will be magnified not only by poverty, inaccessibility, and immigration status, but also by differences in the cultural construction of illness etiologies, health care treatments, and the functioning of the human body. Mixtecs, in contrast to other indigenous peasant immigrants to the United States such as the Khmer and Hmong, will continue to reinforce and refresh their ethnic identity and cultural forms through circular migration and continuous new migration to California from the Mixteca. For these reasons, policy makers cannot assume that the problems surrounding health care delivery to migrant ethnic groups like the Mixtec will be solved by assimilation, a paradigm that expects the Mixtecs' eventual adoption of the biomedical model of the human body and health simply by exposure. Mixtec families' reliance on their own medical system to treat illness possibly indicates some culturally related psychological benefits. However, this use of ethnomedical resources is best understood as supplementing insufficient clinical care.

The problems surrounding health care service utilization for Mixtec families in California are due in large part to the chronic poverty and political repression in Oaxaca, and they will continue until there is a considerable improvement in economic opportunities in Oaxaca. Any attempts to resolve health care service utilization and access problems in California, such as the promotion of indigenous health care practitioners and the employment of trilingual clinicians, must therefore include and link with both institutional and indigenous health care systems of the Mixteca.

## References

Aguirre Beltrán, Gonzalo. 1947. "La medicina indígena," *América Indígena* 7: 107–27.

Bade, Bonnie. 1989. "Migrant Farmworker Needs Assessment: A Report for the University of California Agricultural Cooperative Extension." Unpublished.

———. 1994. "Sweatbaths, Sacrifice, and Surgery: The Practice of Transmedical Health Care by Mixtec Migrant Families in California." PhD dissertation, University of California, Riverside.

———. 2000. "Is There a Doctor in the Field? Underlying Conditions Affecting Access to Health Care for California Farmworkers and Their Families." Sacramento: California Program on Access to Care, California Policy Research Center.

Bade, Bonnie, and Don Villarejo. 2004. "Housing and Health among California's Hired Farm Workers." Unpublished.

Butterworth, Douglas. 1975. *Tilantongo: communidad mixteca en transición.* Mexico City: Instituto Nacional Indigenista.

California Department of Health Services. 1992. "McFarland Child Health Screening Project." Draft report. Unpublished.

Chiñas, Beverly L. 1973. *The Isthmus Zapotecs: Women's Roles in Cultural Context.* New York: Holt, Rinehart and Winston.

Cornelius, Wayne A. 1982. "Interviewing Undocumented Immigrants: Methodological Reflections Based on Fieldwork in Mexico and the United States," *International Migration Review* 16: 378–411.

Diringer, Joel. 1996. *Hurting in the Heartland: Access to Health Care in the San Joaquin Valley. A Report and Recommendations.* San Luis Obispo, Calif.: Rural Health Advocacy Institute, California Rural Legal Assistance Foundation.

Dyk, Anne. 1959. *Mixteco Texts.* Norman, Okla.: [Summer Institute of Linguistics].

Foster, George. 1967. *Tzintzuntzan: Mexican Peasants in a Changing World.* Boston, Mass.: Little, Brown.

Foster, George, and Barbara G. Anderson. 1978. *Medical Anthropology.* New York: John Wiley & Sons.

González Villanueva, Pedro. 1989. *El sacrificio mixe: rumbos para una antropología religiosa indígena.* Mexico: Ediciones Don Bosco.

Kearney, Michael. 1969. "An Exception to the 'Image of Limited Good,'" *American Anthropologist* 71: 888–90.

———. 1972. *The Winds of Ixtepeji: World View and Society in a Zapotec Town.* New York: Holt, Rinehart and Winston.

———. 1986. "Integration of the Mixteca and the Western U.S.-Mexico Region via Migratory Wage Labor." In *Regional Impacts of U.S-Mexican Relations,* edited by Ina Rosenthal-Urey. La Jolla: Center for U.S.-Mexican Studies, University of California, San Diego.

Mak, Cornelia. 1959. "Mixtec Medical Beliefs and Practices," *América Indígena* 19: 125–50.

Mines, Richard, and Michael Kearney. 1982. "The Health of Tulare County Farmworkers: A Report of the 1981 Survey and Ethnographic Research for the Tulare County Department of Health." [Visalia, Calif.?]: The County.

Romney, Kimball, and Romaine Romney. 1966. *The Mixtecans of Juxtlahuaca, Mexico.* New York: John Wiley & Sons.

Rosenberg, Howard, Anne Stierman, Susan M. Gabbard, and Richard Mines. 1998. "Who Works on California's Farms? Demographic and Employment Findings from the National Agricultural Workers Survey." Agricultural and Natural Resources Publication 21583. Oakland: Agricultural Personnel Management Program, University of California.

Rubel, Arthur. 1960. "Concepts of Disease in Mexican-American Culture," *American Anthropologist* 62: 795–814.

Runsten, David, and Michael Kearney. 1994. *A Survey of Oaxacan Village Networks in California Agriculture.* Davis: California Institute for Rural Studies.

Runsten, David, and Carol Zabin. 1989. *Oaxacan Migrants in California Agriculture: A New Cycle of Poverty.* Davis: California Institute for Rural Studies.

Sherman, Jennifer, Don Villarejo, Anna García, Stephen McCurdy, Ketty Mobed, David Runsten, Cathy Saiki, Steven Samuels, and Marc B. Schenker. 1997. *Finding Invisible Farmworkers: The Parlier Survey.* Davis: California Institute for Rural Studies.

Villarejo, Don. 1999. "Health Care among California's Hired Farmworkers." Sacramento: California Program on Access to Care, California Policy Research Center.

Villarejo, Don, David Lighthall, Daniel Williams, Anne Souter, Richard Mines, Bonnie Bade, Steven Samuels, and Stephen McCurdy. 2000. "Suffering in Silence: A Report on the Health of California's Agricultural Workers." Davis: California Institute for Rural Studies.

Wright, Angus. 1990. *The Death of Ramon Gonzalez: The Modern Agricultural Dilemma.* Austin: University of Texas Press.

Zabin, Carol, Michael Kearney, Anna García, David Runsten, and Carole Nagengast. 1993. *Mixtec Migrants in California Agriculture: A New Cycle of Poverty.* Davis: California Institute for Rural Studies.

## APPENDIX 1: SACAR TIEMPO

The following is a transcription of "Sacar Tiempo,"[1] a Mixtec diagnostic healing ritual performed by Don Primo Domínguez Tapia, followed by translations in Spanish and English.

### MIXTEC

Biti ntaui stoyo, biti nda tiin siin ya cata, ya casiin, kaandanto kaankuiti ndo kaandanti kankuitiindo, indukaba indubatia Ndo. kaantando kaankuitindo siin yu tia yuba, tia sii. Tia kaui yubi tia kaui kivi. Tia kaui tiaii ishi naa, tia naa, kissi ña naan ñaan utbi kiui ushi iin, ushi ii ushi uñi.

Ita cua, ita ya antivi ushi uvi antivi ushi uñi, kaandanto kaankuitindo. Ñuun tun ñun yeeh yosokui, yoso ya, ña indaka mi yuku ann ntian indau Yaa tunñi nda, kaantaa kaankuitiuin taan kava taa kasiaun tan shitaun taa kaan shitun ña yuvi. Biti ndavi sto.

Kaandanto kaankuitindo siin yuu, kaanta tiakundo indukaba intubatia, kaandanto kaankuitindo siin yu tia yuba tia sii tia kavi yubi tia kavi tiaii, tia kavi yubi tia kavi tiai. Biti kaandanto, kaankuitindo, kaandanto kaankuitindo ntatiaku.

Tiin kiti canrââ, tiin kiin nticara

### SPANISH

¡O! Mi señor ahora ruego al todopoderoso, señor de los señores, ustedes que andan de día y de noche, ruego a ustedes que me den esa sabiduría para entender lo que yo quiero saber. Desde el camino de la tierra, de la sombra; ¡oye! Vino cosas extrañas, cosas del monte o del otro mundo. Porque esta situación parece ser dificil, este día once, este día doce, este día trece, ruego a las flores rojas y blancas, al cielo doce, trece.

Yo clamo que vengas a ayudarme para saber lo que yo pregunto. Ahora, fuego rojo, fuego brillante [the sun], valles verdes y blancos ¡o! yo clamo, adonde estás en la tierra del monte o adonde estás colgado.

---

[1] Recorded by Bonnie Bade and Deborah Small on July 13, 1998, in San Miguel Cuevas, Juxtlahuaca, Oaxaca.

Sabiduría de las palmas, de las manos, ahora ayúdame, tú que sueñas, tú que das vuelta, tú que sabes y proteges, ayúdame. Camino de sabiduría, esto es lo que pido humildemente ahora, a mi señor.

[Here he blows twice on his hands, then places his left hand along his right lower arm.]

Hablen con la verdad y más que la verdad ¿Me hablarán la verdad? No me rechazen, no se burlen de mí persona humilde. Háblenme con la verdad y más que la verdad conmigo, yo que soy más que honorable, yo que he sido más que ustedes. Por eso ahora hablen con la verdad y más que la verdad. Se oye, que todo hablo y que todo hablo.


ENGLISH

Oh my lord, I now pray to the all-powerful, lord of lords, you who walk in the day and in the night, I pray to you who give me the knowledge to understand that which I want to know. From the road of the earth, of the shadow; listen! Strange things have come, things of the mountain or of the other world. Because this situation seems to be difficult, this day eleven, this day twelve, this day thirteen, I pray to the red flowers, to the white flowers, to the twelfth heaven, to the thirteenth heaven.

I implore that you come to help me to know that which I ask. Now, red fire, brilliant fire [the sun], green valleys and white valleys, oh! I implore to where you are in the earth of the mountain, to where you are located.

Knowledge of the palms, of the hands, now help me, you who dream, you who turn about, you who know and who protect, help me. Road of knowledge, this is what I humbly ask you now, my lord.

[Here he blows twice on his hands, then places his left hand along his right lower arm.]

Speak the truth and more than the truth. Will you tell me the truth? Do not refuse me, do not make fun of this humble person. Speak to me with the truth and more than the truth, I who am honorable, I who have been more than you. For this, now speak the truth and more than the truth.
Listen to all I say, to all I say.

## APPENDIX 2: METHODOLOGY

The binational fieldwork on which this study is based began in 1987 and is ongoing. The primary ethnographic field method has been participant observation. In Oaxaca I have lived in two villages on and off for fifteen years, participating in civil and religious ceremonies, assisting in daily life chores, attending healing rituals with a local healer, and documenting Mixtec medical practices. Qualitative data recorded in California come primarily from participating in the daily lives of more than twenty women and their families. I have accompanied them to clinics, doctors' offices, grocery stores, schools, and other private, state, and local institutions and agencies for fifteen years. Assisting the women (and health service providers), by translating, filling out forms written in English and Spanish, providing rides, explaining clinical procedures and concepts, negotiating with officials, and offering general support in adapting to the complex and bureaucratic details of California social structure formed the basis for a bond of trust between myself and these women.

The data from the Madera study were gathered in summer 1993. Support from Dr. James Grieshop, of the Applied Behavioral Sciences Department at the University of California, Davis, and Dr. Martha López, of the University of California Cooperative Extension in Madera County, enabled the development and administration of a 159-question Spanish-language questionnaire[1] to 109 Mixtec women living in Madera, California. A sample of the Mixtec community was taken using various methods: "snowball" sampling (Cornelius 1982), lists of addresses of Migrant Education students at a local elementary school, contacts made through Mixtec self-help organizations, and *comadre* networks. Interviews were conducted by three Spanish-speaking women from the Madera community. Interviews averaged about two hours; families were compensated for their time with a ten-dollar gift certificate redeemable at a local supermarket. Relevant issues addressed in the questionnaire include barriers to health care, maternal health histories, illness history, including clinical and ethnospecific illnesses and their corresponding treatment choices, and some demographics.

---

[1] Spanish was chosen for the interview due to difficulties with written Mixtec, marked linguistic differences between Mixtec villages, and scarcity of Mixtec-speaking women with sufficient reading and writing skills to conduct interviews. I developed the questionnaire after more than three years' experience in the field. Parts of Mines and Kearney's study of the health of Tulare County Farm Workers (1982) provided a model for the section on health conditions.

# 9

# Mixtecs and Zapotecs Working in California: Rural and Urban Experiences

FELIPE H. LÓPEZ AND DAVID RUNSTEN

In 1994 David Runsten and Carol Zabin compared Mixtec migration to the received wisdom on Mexican migration more generally, which had been derived from sending regions in western Mexico. They found that, unlike the western Mexican migrants to the United States, Mixtecs had significant daughter communities in other states of Mexico, often arrived in the United States through a process of stage migration to northwest Mexico, relied on labor contractors to secure jobs, and had a higher propensity to migrate as families. The Mixtecs were found in most of the worst, short-term jobs in agriculture, and their access to jobs was generally controlled by mestizos. This led to speculation that their indigenousness—that is, the history of racism in Mexico—had something to do with the distinctive nature of the Mixtecs' migration experience.

In this chapter we compare the migration experience of two indigenous groups from Oaxaca: the Mixtec, who are primarily engaged in agricultural work, and Zapotecs from the Tlacolula District of Oaxaca, who mainly work in restaurants and other urban services in the Los Angeles area. Though both groups' migrations to the United States occurred in a similar timeframe, the outcomes and impacts of their migration have been very different.

A previous comparison of this type (Goldring 1990) looked at the migration experiences of workers from Las Ánimas, Zacatecas, and Gómez Farías, Michoacán, two villages that had long been sending migrants to

California and for which thorough studies existed (for example, Mines 1981; López Castro 1986). Although the two villages had different patterns of land tenure and different wage labor opportunities nearby, Goldring argued that the types of jobs taken by U.S.-bound migrants in the California labor market had been the greatest determinant of migration patterns, settlement in the United States, and the evolving use of the villages.

This important idea—that the type of work to which Mexican migrant labor networks find entry in the U.S. economy has differential effects on the villages of origin—has been little explored in the research literature. More attention has been given to the effects of such insertion on the outcomes for immigrant groups in the receiving country, which is the focus of this chapter as well. In fact, the research on immigrant small business has evolved toward a focus on how such work experiences condition the possibilities for entrepreneurship (Waldinger 1986). Though there are specific stories associated with how migrant networks started in specific industries and places, they are almost random occurrences, much as with the origins of many industries that locate in specific towns or regions (Krugman 1991, 1995). That someone from Las Ánimas found a job in south San Francisco, or, as we will see, that someone from Tlacolula found a job in a West Los Angeles restaurant, is not an occurrence that could be predicted from any prior history or cultural traits. Rather, it happened by chance. But just as with the cumulative effects that occur as an industry develops in an area, so the cumulative participation of migrants from a particular village in certain types of jobs has distinct impacts on the pattern and consequences of migration.

## OAXACAN MIGRATION

The pattern of migration from Mexico to the United States is shifting as more and more "nontraditional" Mexican migrants, such as indigenous people from the state of Oaxaca, find their way north, particularly to California. Compared to the mestizo population, indigenous migrants arrive in the United States with greater disadvantages: some are monolingual in their indigenous language or speak Spanish poorly, often their economic conditions are more difficult, and they are subject to racism by both Mexicans and Americans (Zabin et al. 1993).

Oaxaca is divided into eight regions and comprises at least sixteen ethnic groups, each with its own characteristics. The Zapotecs and Mixtecs are

the predominant ethnic groups in the state.[1] Although many different Oaxacan ethnic groups are migrating to the United States,[2] the Zapotecs and
Mixtecs are also the major groups found in California. We seek to understand the different migration and settlement patterns of these two groups,
especially as they are conditioned by participation in different labor markets.

Zapotecs tend to migrate to urban areas and work in the service industries. Depending mainly on social and familial networks to migrate and to
get access to jobs, they could be classified as having a "traditional" Mexican migration pattern, where members of families progressively migrate to
the United States. The Zapotec migration has not created many satellite
communities in areas within Mexico, with the exception of Mexico City
and Veracruz.

The Mixtecs, on the other hand, usually migrate to rural areas and work
in the agricultural sector. The Mixtec migration history is linked to enganchadores, or labor contractors. The Mixtec migrate and move in groups
often composed of families, and specific village networks have usually
arrived in the United States via stage migration to work in northwest Mexico. The long legacy of domestic mixteco migration in Mexico has left its
imprint; the Mixtecs are numerous in many Mexican states, particularly in
northwest Mexico and around Mexico City (Valdés 1995). Now we also
find Mixtec communities along the U.S.-Mexico border, especially in Tijuana, where some of them find temporary jobs in which they can earn
enough money to make the "jump" into the United States.

How can we begin to explain the differences in the migration experiences of these two groups? In this first attempt, we trace through the recent
migration histories of both groups and consider each group's participation
in the California economy and the cumulative consequences that have
arisen as a result.

For the purpose of this chapter we have chosen to focus on Zapotecs
from the district of Tlacolula and Mixtecs from the district of Juxtlahuaca
(figure 9.1).[3] The Tlacolula District is one of seven districts located in the

---

[1] In 1995 there were 355,000 speakers of Zapoteco (34 percent of the total Oaxacan
population) and 229,000 speakers of Mixteco (22 percent of the total Oaxacan
population) who were four years old and older (INEGI 1997: 23).

[2] Other groups, such as the Chinantecs, Chatinos, Mixes, Triquis, and Zoques, have
also begun to migrate to different parts of the United States.

[3] In addition to utilizing previous research, we interviewed a number of people
from each district. For Tlacolula, we interviewed immigrants from Díaz Ordaz,
San Pablo Güiilá, Abasolo, Tlacochayaya, Tlacolula, Matatlán, Santa Ana del

Central Valleys of Oaxaca.[4] The Tlacolula District, with twenty-five *municipios* (akin to U.S. counties), is one of the largest districts, covering about a third of the Central Valleys (Acevedo Conde and Restrepo 1991: 15), and it is the principal source of Zapotec migration to West Los Angeles (figure 9.2).

**Figure 9.1. State of Oaxaca**

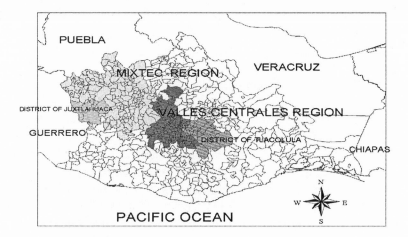

The district of Juxtlahuaca is one of seven districts in the Mixtec region,[5] which altogether encompasses 155 *municipios*. Juxtlahuaca has been one of the districts most affected by migration (Íñigo 1980: 176) (figure 9.3). In the 1991 census of Mixtecs in California, Juxtlahuaca, Silacayoapan, and Huajuapan accounted for 78 percent of the people counted, and Juxtlahuaca was the leading district (Runsten and Kearney 1994).

---

Valle, Teotitlán de Valle, San Bartolomé Quialana, San Lucas Quiaviní, and San Marcos Tlapazola. For Juxtlahuaca, we interviewed immigrants from San Juan Mixtepec, San Miguel Cuevas, Tlacotepec, San Martín Peras, and Santa María Teposlantongo.

[4] The others are Centro, Ejutla, Ocotlán, Etla, Zaachila, and Zimatlán.

[5] The others are Coixtlahuaca, Nochixtlán, Silacayoapan, Teposcolula, Tlaxiaco, and Huajuapan.

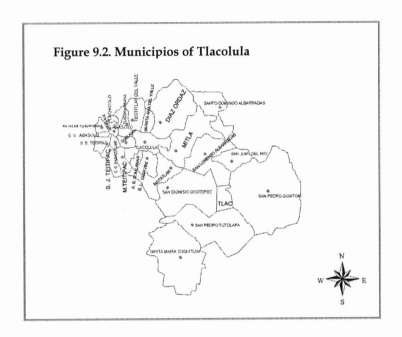

Figure 9.2. Municipios of Tlacolula

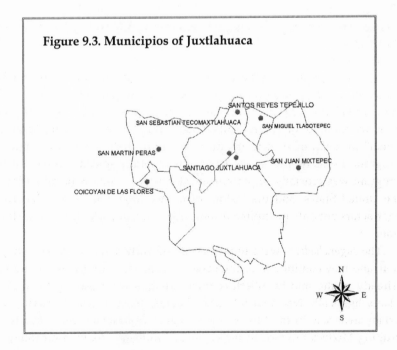

Figure 9.3. Municipios of Juxtlahuaca

## MIXTEC MIGRATION HISTORY

De la Peña (1950) contends that migration from the Mixtec region was caused by various factors, including land erosion and the demise of the livestock industry following the Mexican Revolution. The Mixtecs who first began emigrating were from communities where Spanish was the most commonly spoken language. Those who were monolingual Mixteco speakers usually did not migrate. As early as the first decades of the twentieth century, we also begin to see what De la Peña calls "interval" migration, or temporary migration for particular harvest seasons, a pattern that many Mixtecs continue today. During this period, Mixtecs were migrating by the thousands, leaving some villages virtually empty.

Butterworth (1990) classified these early stages of Mixtec migration into two types: the more permanent migration to urban areas and the circular migration to rural regions. However, Mixtec migration can be classified *a grosso modo* into three phases: (1) the early 1900s, when people migrated largely regionally, to Mexico City, Puebla, and Veracruz; (2) the mid-1900s, when migration focused on Mexico City, Oaxaca City, and the early migrations to northwest Mexico, especially Sinaloa (Ojeda Ramírez 2000; Garduño, García, and Morán 1989) and when some men participated in the Bracero Program (1942–1964); and (3) the 1970s, when there was a rapid increase and mass flow of migration to northwest Mexico (Sonora, Sinaloa, Baja California Sur, Baja California) and a constant migration flow to the United States.

Mixtec migration is embedded within the agricultural contract labor network, which perhaps partially explains the concentration of Mixtecs in rural areas both in Mexico and in the United States. Interestingly, this type of network migration is rarely taken into consideration within the "conventional" Mexican migration literature, except in discussions of the Bracero Program, a kind of *super-enganchador*. It is generally agreed that the Bracero Program was crucially important in establishing patterns of migration to the United States, and the history of Mixtec migration shows that labor contractors not only precipitated some migration but also dictated its direction.

The *enganchadores* were important in the early stages of Mixtec migration, and they continue to be important in contemporary Mixtec migration. Already in the mid-twentieth century, Mixtecs were leaving to work in places like Valle Nacional (Oaxaca), Puebla, Mexico City, Veracruz, and urban areas within the Mixtec region. Labor contractors were already recruiting Mixtecs to work in the sugarcane industry. As we find today, in order to recruit workers, these *enganchadores* promised good jobs, good wages, and good living conditions. They operated with verbal agreements and would give workers an advance so they could leave some money for their families while they traveled and could pay for their transportation to Veracruz or Valle Nacional (De la Peña 1950: 154).

After the midpoint of the 1900s, the Mixtec journey to northwest Mexico was very much linked to these *enganchadores*. According to Esteban Ojeda Ramírez, beginning in the 1940s ranch owners from Baja California Sur sent labor contractors to Sinaloa and Oaxaca to recruit workers. The recruiters who went to the Mixtec villages in Oaxaca offered good jobs and health and life insurance, and they promised to return the workers` back home. In many of these cases transportation ended up being only one way; seldom were these workers returned home, and most promises were never kept (Ojeda Ramírez 2000: 345–46). Over time, the recruiters ventured farther into remote regions of the Mixteca, from areas where Spanish was predominant to those where little Spanish was spoken.

By 1970 the migration that had begun in the 1940s to northwest Mexico had not only become a mass migration, but it had also begun to spill into the United States. By 1990 over eight thousand Mixtecs were residing in Baja California (Velasco Ortiz 1995: 114–15). Yet the number of Mixtecs in this region fluctuated according to the seasons; in peak season the Mixtec population was estimated to reach over twenty thousand (Zabin et al. 1993; Rubio and Millán 2000). Recruitment of farmworkers in the Mixteca reached into increasingly remote areas, encompassing new groups such as the Triqui. Surveying by Runsten and Zabin in San Quintín, Baja California, in 1990–1992 found migrants from fifty-five Oaxacan villages, of which twenty-five, including more remote areas such as Miahuatlán, were not found in California at the time (Runsten and Kearney 1994; Runsten et al. 1993; Zabin and Hughes 1995). And many Mixtecs were recruited from northwest Mexico by agents of farm labor contractors who operated in the United States. One grower in San Quintín, interviewed in the early 1990s, said that of the busloads of Mixtecs he brought up from Oaxaca, as many as half headed straightaway for the United States.

The constant recruitment of Mixtecs to Baja California led, of course, to settlement there. Víctor Clark Alfaro notes that Mixtecs had begun arriving in Tijuana by the end of the 1950s, settling in the Colonia Obrera, the city's marginal area (Clark Alfaro 1991: 12). Many of those who live in Tijuana now have become truly transnational migrants. In a survey conducted of Mixtecs in Tijuana in 1990, Emily Young found that 70 percent of those surveyed lived in Tijuana but worked in San Diego. These people obtained their U.S. residency through the amnesty provisions of the Immigration Reform and Control Act of 1986 (IRCA), established themselves in Tijuana, and commuted to work in the agricultural sector in Southern California (Young 1994).

Estimates vary, but the only attempt to actually count the Mixtec population in California gave a peak season estimate in 1991 of as many as fifty thousand (Runsten and Kearney 1994: vii). However, Mixtecs are not only found in California but all over the United States. In a 2002 trip to the Mixtec region, we observed in San Juan Mixtepec a multitude of car licenses from the United States. Just driving by houses on the main road, we counted license plates from thirty-seven U.S. states.

## Juxtlahuaca District

We can see how this history played itself out in the Juxtlahuaca villages. People from different pueblos — such as the *agencias* of San Lucas Tejocote in the *municipio* of Mixtepec, Juxtlahuaca District — began their migration process during the 1920s. These early migrants usually went to Veracruz to work in the sugarcane fields, walking as many as seven days to reach their destination (Edinger 1996: 132). Similarly, people from San Martín Peras also began to leave their community in order to look for better opportunities within the region. In the 1930s they began to journey outside of Oaxaca, going to places like Veracruz, also to work in sugarcane. As one San Martín Peras native noted:

> From Huajuapan the boss came to take us to work. In 1945 it was the first time that I left to work to Acatlán de Pérez, Veracruz.... I was working there, cutting sugarcane, coming and going for eight years. We worked in Veracruz in January and February and returned to the pueblo in March (Atilano Flores 2000: 62).

Atilano Flores contends that one of the main factors prompting people from San Martín Peras to migrate to northwest Mexico, instead of to Veracruz, was the arrival of labor contractors from the northwest. This migration began in the 1970s, especially for those who spoke some Spanish.

Some people from the Juxtlahuaca *municipio* have followed the same pattern. For example, one of our interviewees from Asunción Naranjos, Juxtlahuaca, contends that for as long as he remembers, people from his village have migrated. There were those who participated in the Bracero Program, some of them continuing to go to California after the program ended to work for the same ranchers. By 1969 people had begun to go work in Culiacán and Sonora. At the beginning, those who wanted to work in these states had to cover their own travel expenses, but in the 1980s buses were sent to Asunción to take them to the fields in Culiacán. Now one can find people from Asunción in various places in northwest Mexico—including Camalú, San Quintín, Colonia Guerrero, Lázaro Cárdenas, and El Rosario. Flows from Asunción to the United States began in 1977 when migrants came to work in the agricultural areas of Del Mar, Vista, and Oxnard, California. There are now about sixty families from Asunción in Oxnard; people from Asunción also migrate to Oregon, especially to Gresham.

The migration from Tlacotepec resembles the general migration pattern of the Mixteca region. For instance, although Algimiro Morales grew up in Tlacotepec, he was born in Veracruz,[6] where his mother formed part of the constant migration of people from Tlacotepec who worked in the sugarcane fields. Morales's migration history reflects that of other Mixtecs. He remembers always being on the road, to Veracruz, Mexico City, Culiacán, Baja California. Until he immigrated to the United States, however, "home" had been Tlacotepec. As a migrant to Sinaloa, Algimiro witnessed the unfair treatment of Oaxacans there and became involved in activism—activities for which he was jailed for two years. No longer feeling safe in Sinaloa, Algimiro saw Mexico City as a more stable option and a chance at a better life for his family. But when the 1980s economic crisis hit and he lost his job, he decided to come to the United States, where, he thought, he would make enough money to send some back home and also build a house in the village, something he did in 1986.

It is interesting that even though these communities may display similar patterns, some have concentrated their migration on urban areas. For example, people from Tlacotepec who have migrated to Vista, California (near San Diego) are mainly in construction, service, and factory work. According to Algimiro, although there are people from Tlacotepec in other communities as well—Madera, for instance, as well as in Oregon and Washington states—the main concentration of his pueblo is found in Vista,

---

[6] This is one of the principal problems in trying to count a migratory group like the Mixtec, who were born in many different states. Algimiro considers himself a Mixtec from a village in Oaxaca, yet the statistics would show him to be an immigrant from Veracruz.

where two hundred Tlacotepecan families reside, compared to eight families in the San Joaquin Valley. Algimiro points out that the new immigrants, mostly young men, look for jobs in urban areas, whereas the older immigrants tend to work in agriculture.

The pattern of Mixtec migration thus has been one of traveling ever further afield, with workers recruited by farm labor contractors. Regional migration gave way to migration to northwest Mexico, which led in turn to stage migration to California and beyond. Migration to the United States was facilitated by the experience some Mixtecs had had in the Bracero Program, but it was also due to active recruitment in northwest Mexico. In the early 1990s, Runsten and Zabin identified about 150 Mixtec villages that were sending migrants to California. Given this large number of villages, patterns of migration inevitably differed. Some villages had mainly back-and-forth migration. Some had families strewn around Mexico—in the Federal District, Sinaloa, or Baja California. Some had a lot of settlement in the United States and mostly empty villages. There were also stories of villages whose migrants had found their way into urban sectors. Migrants from certain villages in Huajuapan and Juxtlahuaca reported *paisanos* in restaurants in Reno, Santa Cruz, and New York, selling popsicles and working in factories in Santa Ana, in construction in San Bernardino, in aircraft maintenance in Los Angeles, in gardening in New York, in racetrack stables in Oceanside, and so on. Each of these might lead to distinct patterns of employment and business formation in the future, but up to now the Mixtecs have overwhelmingly continued to work in agriculture.

Mixtecs' participation in the agricultural labor market has shaped their living and working conditions. The average agricultural worker in the United States has employment for only six months a year and earns less than $10,000. Surveys have shown that, compared to the average farmworker, Mixtecs worked more in short-term jobs that paid less, migrated more, bore more side payments to labor market intermediaries, and were more often the victims of nonpayment of wages and other labor law violations (Zabin et al. 1993). These factors made it difficult for them to accumulate capital in the United States. Working on farms, they are often isolated from other labor markets. Upward mobility is limited, as there are few supervisory jobs, and these are tenaciously guarded by earlier groups of mestizo immigrants. Business formation is difficult in U.S. agriculture, which has become much more capital intensive with larger-scale farms.

The history of California agriculture—and, by extension, that of Sinaloa, Baja California, and Florida—is a history of the use of seasonal immigrant labor. It became apparent to successive immigrant groups in California that there was no future in farm labor, so they helped one another get into other work or start their own farms or businesses. This is proving more difficult for the Mixtec due to the structural conditions in place over the past thirty years.

## Mixtec Migration Experiences

Michael Kearney, whose reference group are the Mixtec, has long argued that the experience of migration creates a certain self-consciousness. As Mixtec migrants move from place to place in Mexico, suffer discrimination, and find they speak a different language, they develop an identity as Mixtec that is tied up with their ancestral land in Oaxaca. People who are born on the migrant trail and have never set foot in Tlacotepec may still identify themselves as from that village.

What are the implications for the Mixtecs as they move along with the harvest both in the United States and in Mexico? Why do they stay in agriculture despite the constant seasonal movement, the low-paying jobs, and the dangers that exist within the agricultural sector? We are struck by how many of them continue to encounter serious obstacles and hardships. It is more obvious in the rural areas, in both Mexico and the United States, where indigenous migrants face different types of abuses—such as discrimination by their mestizo counterparts or abuses from the Mexican authorities that lead to violations of human rights. Also, many find that their living conditions are not much better than they were at home (Clark Alfaro 1991; Nagengast, Stavenhagen, and Kearney 1992; Bacon 2002; Quiñones 1998; Zabin et al. 1993).

For many Mixtec farmworkers, abuses begin from the time they leave their community with the labor contractors who have come to recruit them. The promise of good jobs, decent pay, and adequate living conditions sometimes turns into nightmares (De la Peña 1959; Rubio and Millán 2000; Atilano Flores 2000; Álvarez 1995; Díaz-Romo and Salinas-Álvarez 1998). For example, one reporter, describing the living conditions of farmworkers in San Quintín, writes:

> The camp has no electricity. The rooms are four walls and roofs of corrugated tin. There's no place to cook and no beds, only hard-packed dirt for floors. When it rains, people at Francisco Villa sleep in mud (Quiñones 1998).

Additionally, many indigenous people are given worse treatment in Mexico than the local mestizos who work and live on the same ranch (Clark Alfaro 1991: 21–22).

The dismal living conditions for indigenous farmworkers are found in the United States as well (Chávez 1992; Zabin et al. 1993). In Malaga, California (near Fresno), for instance, over two hundred Mixtecs from Juxtlahuaca (most spoke neither English nor Spanish) were living in fifty-six trailers and cabins surrounded by an oil dump, a scrap metal heap, a wrecking yard, a manure plant, and a propane business. As a result of living in this toxic environment, there was a high rate of miscarriages and respiratory problems (Hanley 2000). The situation was so bad that the housing was torn down and relocated to a different area. Whether living in parked cars in Madera, in garages in Parlier, in the canyons of San Diego, or fifty people to a hotel room in Santa Maria, whenever the worst living conditions are found, it is now usually the Mixtec who are suffering them (Zabin et al. 1993; Runsten and Kearney 1994).

The incorporation of indigenous people into California's agricultural labor market puts them in direct competition with the more established Mexican mestizo workers. Further, because these new indigenous immigrants are more susceptible to abuses—having to pay for rides and tools, receiving cash wages, and so on—they have been increasingly preferred by farm labor contractors and growers, thus affecting the "conditions for all farmworkers as employers chose a more vulnerable group of workers over the longtime, settled farmworkers competing for the same job" (Zabin et al. 1993).

The Mixtecs' vulnerability is due to many factors, but an important one is language. Not only do many indigenous people from the Mixteca not speak English, they often do not speak fluent Spanish either. Although we do not have a clear idea of the number of Oaxacan rural immigrants who are monolingual or speak little Spanish, initiatives by Mixtec leaders in the United States and Mexico attest to the significance of the issue:

- In Tijuana, Mixtec community leaders have fought for bilingual education (Spanish-Mixteco) in local schools to fulfill the needs of the large Mixtec student population (Rubio and Millán 2000: 98; Golden 1996).

- In Madera, California, where there is a large Mixtec student population, a team from the University of California, Los Angles has begun to assist some people from San Mateo Tunuchi, Juxtlahuaca District, to develop written Mixteco materials,[7] "instructional materials which can be used by children and other community members who want to learn to read and write their language, and informational materials for teachers and others who interact with monolingual speakers" (Munro 2002).

- In Oxnard, California, two separate groups are offering adult Spanish programs for Mixtecs, most of whom are from San Martín Peras, Juxtlahuaca.

- The Santiago Ventura case, in which a farmworker from San Miguel Cuevas was wrongly incarcerated for murder in Oregon, led to demands for court interpreters for indigenous migrants, a campaign largely led by the Mixtec.

Apart from a few instances, in contrast, these have not been pressing issues for Zapotec immigrants. In this sense, the Mixtec often appear more culturally isolated and without access to U.S. institutions. Working for farm labor contractors, they are spatially and linguistically isolated. The main determinant of the difficult conditions the Mixtec have endured has been their continued employment in agriculture. Seasonal, often short-term jobs lead to considerable migration and instability, low incomes, and blocked mobility.

## HISTORY OF ZAPOTEC MIGRATION

The migration history of the Zapotec, as with the Mixtec, dates to the early 1900s. People from small villages in the Valley of Oaxaca began to leave to look for better opportunities regionally and outside of Oaxaca State (Cook 1982; Clarke 2000). Some people left to work in Oaxaca City and the many haciendas found within the Valley of Oaxaca at the turn of the 1900s (Ornelas López 1982: 150; Díaz Montes 1982: 65). Some began to go to Mexico City, Veracruz, and Tapachula, Chiapas; others had a short migration experience to Sinaloa and Sonora in the 1960s (Hulshof 1991). The lack of research on Valley Zapotec migrants in agriculture does not allow us to understand the nature of this rural phenomenon. An interesting question,

---

[7] According to Timoteo Mendoza, a Mixtec teacher at a local school, there is a great need for materials in Mixteco that people who work in the school's administration could use to learn basic Mixteco vocabulary in order to communicate with parents who speak neither Spanish nor English.

though, is why the Zapotec migration to Sinaloa and Sonora did not continue. For instance, Marije Hulshof reports that the community of San Bartolomé did participate in seasonal migration to northwest Mexico but the migrants "quickly returned shortly after arrival," dissatisfied with the conditions (Hulshof 1991: 3). Instead, the people from San Bartolomé redirected their migration to the United States.

We did not find much evidence that Zapotecs have settled in major numbers in the northern parts of Mexico. However, we do find some Valley Zapotec, especially people from Teotitlán del Valle, living in Tijuana (Clark Alfaro 1991). For the most part, Valley Zapotecs who have migrated within Mexico have chosen places such as Mexico City or Oaxaca City. Most of those who migrated did so due to the lack of job opportunities at home, but some left because of village conflicts and violence, which were factors in San Juan Teitipac (FAO 1999).

During the Bracero Program men from valley villages such as Tlacolula, Teotitlán del Valle, Santa Ana del Valle, San Lucas Quiaviní, and San Miguel del Valle participated. Though some remained in the United States, there seems to have been no immediate impact on international Zapotec migration. It was not until the 1970s that Valley Zapotecs began to migrate to the United States as a constant flow.

## Tlacolula District Migration

Tlacolula de Matamoros, the district head town, has played an important role by becoming the link to the United States for other small villages in the Tlacolula District. Tlacolula is a small city, and many people who live there consider themselves more "mestizo" than the people from the smaller villages. Less Zapotec is spoken, and the town has had a long history of migration, which many people tapped into.

Among the first immigrants to arrive from the Tlacolula District were three people who went to Los Angeles from the town of Tlacolula in 1956. Although there were some other Tlacolula immigrants who lived elsewhere in California, such as Santa Maria and Salinas, these three people in Los Angeles were instrumental in facilitating the subsequent Tlacolula District migration, according to Onofre Santiago, who came to Los Angeles in 1968.

In the late 1960s, people from other Tlacolula Valley villages began to arrive in Los Angeles. In 1968, Lucas Diego arrived from San Lucas at the invitation of his *compadre*, also from Tlacolula. He arrived in Santa Maria but felt it was not safe from migration officials and returned home. Eventually Lucas decided to go to Los Angeles to live with some friends from Tlacolula who had already established themselves there. With the help a Tlacolula *coyote* (people smuggler), he arrived in Los Angeles at the end of 1968, with no money and having been apprehended once during his journey. His friends housed him, and Onofre Santiago helped him get a job in a restaurant. Two years later, Lucas invited a younger brother, Melitón, who brought another brother, then a brother-in-law, and so forth.

Other surrounding villages also have their original connection via Tlacolula (Hulshof 1991). The *coyote* who brought many of these immigrants also came from Tlacolula. The fact that this *coyote* spoke some Zapoteco created a degree of trust between him and potential migrants, since many of those who first came to the United States spoke little or no Spanish.

The people who first tapped into the Tlacolula network were later sought out by people from neighboring villages that had no connection with Tlacolula. For instance, some early immigrants from San Marcos Tlapazola and Tanivet came with people from San Lucas.

The early Zapotec Valley migration to California seemed to be heading toward rural areas such as Santa Maria (natives from Tlacolula and Santa Ana del Valle) or Santa Ana (people from Teotitlán and San Bartolomé), yet today the majority are concentrated in urban areas, especially in Los Angeles. The initial return to the United States in the late 1960s and early 1970s was no doubt directed by contacts and experiences obtained in the Bracero Program. Unlike the Mixtec experience, however, the Zapotecs quickly shifted into urban jobs.

By the mid-1970s, there were about eighty people from San Lucas living in Los Angeles. Those who came early and had learned how to get an apartment, move around the city, and, most importantly, get a job, took advantage of the new arrivals. For instance, some earlier immigrants initially rented almost all of the apartments for the people from San Lucas, and they collected the rent. However, as more and more people from San Lucas arrived in Los Angeles, this practice tapered off and had all but disappeared by the end of the 1970s. Job accommodation among friends and families, however, continued. Today, of the more than eight hundred people from San Lucas that we estimate are living in Los Angeles, most work in restaurants.

According to Julio Ruiz, about twenty-five people from Teotitlán del Valle obtained legal U.S. residency after the Bracero Program (author interview). Some remained in Colorado; others moved to California, establishing themselves in Santa Ana (see Stephen 1991). Ruiz notes that these early immigrants had little influence on migration from their home community, and it was not until the 1980s that people from Teotitlán began to migrate as a constant flow. Nevertheless, these newer migrants are concentrated in Santa Ana and Moorpark (as well as in San Francisco, Stockton, and Oakland). Those who went to Santa Ana originally all worked in the agricultural sector, but today there are only twelve natives of Teotitlán who work in agriculture, while nearly three hundred work in the service industry.

Some people from Tlacochahuaya also stayed in California after the Bracero Program, according to Amador Sánchez (author interview), but the current U.S. migration from this community dates from the late 1980s. Although the majority of these immigrants are concentrated in Los Angeles, some have gone to New York, Chicago, Florida, and Michigan. Others have migrated domestically, principally to Mexico City. Similar to others from the Tlacolula Valley now residing in Los Angeles, the migrants from Tlacochahuaya are overwhelmingly concentrated in the restaurant sector. According to Amador Sánchez, more than 90 percent of the Tlacochahuayans in Los Angeles (more than four hundred people) work in restaurants.

More recent immigration from the Tlacolula District is coming from San Pablo Güilá, Santo Domingo Albarradas, and San Pedro Totolapa. People from the first two pueblos, as with the other communities from the Tlacolula District, are concentrated in the restaurant industry, but the small number of migrants from San Pedro Totolapa also work as day laborers. People from San Pablo Güilá began to migrate to the United States in 1990. According to one community leader, there are about 200 of these more recent immigrants living on the west side of Los Angeles, as many as 440 in Chicago, and about 50 in Atlanta. Those who live in Los Angeles are mostly young, single males; Moisés López noted that he knows of only one woman from his pueblo living in Los Angeles (author interview).

## Working in Restaurants

Zapotecs who come from the Tlacolula District are concentrated in the restaurant industry, a type of employment that historically has had positive consequences for immigrant groups. A person from Tlacolula, who came to Los Angeles in 1980 and now owns a restaurant, reports that as far back as he can remember, most people from his town have worked in restaurants. Before he came, his father and brothers had also worked in restaurants.

People from Tlacolula and San Lucas were already working in the restaurant sector in the late 1960s and may have started even earlier (López H. and Munro 1999, n.d.). Thus the growth of Zapotec employment in restaurants has occurred gradually, including over epochs of rapid growth in the industry. The Zapotecs' participation in the Los Angeles restaurant industry stems from a growing need for labor in a growing industry. For some Valley Zapotecs, the idea of working in a restaurant was strange, something they had never done before. A Zapotec migrant who came to Los Angeles in 1970 recalled: "They said 'a restaurant,' but over there [San Lucas] who's going to work in restaurants? So I worked in a restaurant washing dishes. Well, when a person doesn't know anything, he washes dishes. I did [it] fast, and people liked what I did."

Unlike the work in rural areas, the jobs that most people from Tlacolula have are stable. Those who work in restaurants usually start in entry-level positions, as dishwashers or janitors. Some eventually make their way up to a position as prep-person, lead cook, kitchen manager, *sous chef*, or even chef. For many, the money they earn washing dishes is not enough to pay rent (the minimum hourly wage in California in October 2002 was $6.75), so they tend to live with several friends and/or family members. And many have to work double shifts to cover their living expenses and still have money to send to their families in Mexico.

Most Zapotec immigrants find jobs through friends, family members, and *paisanos*. Some are incorporated into the restaurant business by agreeing to cover a worker's shifts while that person takes time off to visit family in Mexico. These absences vary from a few weeks or months to as long as a year. Workers who want to return to their jobs try to convince the restaurant owner or manager to allow them to train a friend or family member to cover their shifts while they are away. In this way, the person who fills in on the job gains experience and a possible reference for landing another job. And sometimes the owner accommodates both workers once the absentee worker returns.

It is not uncommon to find an entire restaurant kitchen crew all from the same pueblo. In such cases, the kitchen's dominant language might be Zapotec, and migrants would not have to speak English or Spanish to be able to get a job there. However, speaking Zapotec has created some tensions between indigenous and nonindigenous workers. Oaxacan immigrants who work on the "floor" work mostly as bus-persons or runners. A bus-person must have a good knowledge of restaurant vocabulary but need not necessarily be fluent in English (even though a bus-person might actually know more English than Spanish).

Most Zapotecs, with their limited English, are after busing jobs, which tend to involve shorter hours than a job as cook. Bus-persons can potentially earn more than cooks, even though cooks may be paid more per hour; tips may make up the difference. Furthermore, a bus-person has fewer responsibilities. In one restaurant in West Los Angeles, a bus-person was estimated to earn an average of about $60 a night, over and above the minimum wage; a waiter would make twice as much. In upscale restaurants, a bus-person might make as much as $100 a night plus minimum wage. However, both of these jobs are very physical and stressful, and they carry no health care or other benefits. One advantage of restaurant work is that workers may be provided with meals.

The urban Oaxacan indigenous immigrants in southern California, mostly Zapotecs, do not seem to confront the problems found in rural areas. However, the experiences with mestizos is similar in both settings. Many Valley Zapotecs have encountered discrimination from their fellow Mexicans, and many have denied their ethnicity because of this. Manuel Marcial, who experienced this kind of discrimination, points out that many members of his community, even members of his own family, rejected their "Indian-ness" by denying being from Oaxaca (author interview).

## From Restaurant Workers to Restaurant Owners

The research literature indicates that restaurant work is a typical entry point for immigrant groups and that the nature of the industry, with low barriers to entry, provides an opportunity for workers to start their own restaurants once they have gained sufficient skills (Waldinger 1986; Ram et al. 2000; Kesteloot and Mistiaen 1997; Rath and Kloosterman 2000; Herman 1979). As Herman notes, a job as dishwasher has more potential for self-employment than work in a mine, a lumber camp, or a steel mill (1979: 88). Immigrants who arrive with few skills and engage in manual labor have limited options for upward mobility, which often makes self-employment a goal (Waldinger 1986). As Bailey (1985) argued in his study of New York restaurants, immigrants are willing to gain skills that have a low return for native workers, because immigrants do not have better options. Any ethnic group with a distinctive cuisine has a natural advantage in running such restaurants (Ram et al. 2000), and the nature of network migration provides a ready labor force to staff the restaurant.

Because of the experience that Valley Zapotecs have had in the restaurant industry, there is an increasing number of Oaxacan restaurants all over the Los Angeles area. In surveying the Oaxacan restaurants, we find that almost all are owned by Valley Zapotecs. We were able to identify twenty-eight Oaxacan-owned restaurants in Los Angeles, only one of which has since closed (table 9.1).[8] The first restaurant that we know to have been opened by a Oaxacan immigrant was Nelly's Grill. It is owned by Gregorio Santiago, who came to the United States from Tlacolula in 1982, worked in various restaurants, and opened Nelly's in North Hollywood in 1989. Nelly's does not sell Oaxacan food. Gregorio subsequently opened the Chulada Grill in 1994, which has evolved from a pizza parlor to Mexican food to a somewhat Oaxacan restaurant, and in 1997 he opened the Tequila Grill in Costa Mesa. Gregorio has also owned a large maintenance company and has investments in a number of other businesses.

The first Oaxacan cuisine restaurant we know of was started in 1992 by four brothers from San Marcos Tlapazola, an *agencia municipal* of Tlacolula, who pooled their money to invest $30,000 in a restaurant on Lincoln Boulevard in Santa Monica, the Tlapazola Grill. All four had worked as cooks at upscale restaurants around West Los Angeles. One of the brothers, Celerino Cruz, had arrived in Los Angeles in 1978 and worked in an upscale restaurant in Venice, starting as a dishwasher and working his way up to cook. Noting the lack of high-quality traditional Mexican food in Los Angeles, Celerino believed that Los Angeles would embrace Oaxacan cuisine.

In the beginning, the new Oaxacan food was seen as "too authentic," and the restaurant had to adapt its food to the clientele. Thanks to a good review from a *Los Angeles Times* food critic, people flocked to the Tlapazola Grill. However, the restaurant was eventually forced to close because of rising rent and the landlord's refusal to do repairs to the building. In 1998, the brothers closed the restaurant and went to work for their former employers while they searched for a new location. In 2000 they reopened the restaurant in a mini-mall in West Los Angeles, and they now have fourteen employees, twelve of them from the Tlacolula area.

In 1994 two other Oaxacan restaurants opened, both owned by families from the Tlacolula District. El Texate, owned by the Marcial family from Tlacolula de Matamoros, opened in Santa Monica just blocks from the

---

[8] The Tlacolula restaurant was located off Vermont Avenue in Los Angeles and was owned by the proprietors of El Texate. They report that business was good, but they were repeatedly robbed after hours so they closed the restaurant. A number of restaurants have been sold to new owners, as noted in table 9.1.

**Table 9.1. Oaxacan-Owned Restaurants in Los Angeles**

| Restaurant | Year Established | Owner's Village | District of Oaxaca | Restaurant Location |
|---|---|---|---|---|
| Nelly's | 1989 | Tlacolula | Tlacolula | North Hollywood (LA) |
| Tlapazola Grill | 1992 | San Marcos Tlapazola | Tlacolula | West Los Angeles (LA) |
| Guelaguetza I | 1994 | Matatlán | Tlacolula | Los Angeles (LA) |
| El Texate | 1994 | Tlacolula | Tlacolula | Santa Monica |
| Chulada Grill[a] | 1994 | Tlacolula | Tlacolula | Los Angeles |
| Valle de Oaxaca Restaurant | 1996 | Santa Ana del Valle | Tlacolula | Mar Vista (LA) |
| Siete Regiones | 1996 | Tlacochahuaya | Tlacolula | Pico Union (LA) |
| Tlacolula (closed)[b] | 1996-98 | Tlacolula | Tlacolula | Los Angeles |
| Juquila | 1998 | Matatlán | Tlacolula | West Los Angeles (LA) |
| Guelaguetza II | 1998 | Matatlán | Tlacolula | West Los Angeles (LA) |
| El Sazón Oaxaqueño | 1998 | Matatlán | Tlacolula | Mar Vista (LA) |
| Tacomiendo | 1998 | San Lucas | Tlacolula | West Los Angeles (LA) |
| Tacos La Raza[c] | 1999 | Yavesia | Villa Alta | Los Angeles |
| Zapoteca Restaurant[d] | 1999 | Santa Ana del Valle | Tlacolula | West Los Angeles (LA) |
| El Danzante | 2000 | Yalalag | Villa Alta | Los Angeles (LA) |
| Guelaguetza III | 2000 | Matatlán | Tlacolula | Koreatown (LA) |
| Cristy's Restaurant | 2001 | Oaxaca City | Centro | Los Angeles |
| El Cántaro[e] | 2001 | San Lucas | Tlacolula | Hollywood (LA) |
| El Torito Oaxaqueño | 2001 | Yalalag | Villa Alta | Los Angeles |

| | | | | |
|---|---|---|---|---|
| Mi Lindo Oaxaca | 2002 | Talea de Castro | Villa Alta | Pico Union (LA) |
| Yalalag Restaurant | 2002 | Yalalag | Villa Alta | Pico Union (LA) |
| Clayuda, Café Oaxaqueño | 2002 | Yatee | Villa Alta | South-Central (LA) |
| La Chocita | 2002 | Teotitlán del Valle | Tlacolula | Los Angeles |
| Expresión Oaxaqueña | 2002 | San Francisco Yatee | Villa Alta | Los Angeles |
| La Casita de Oaxaca | 2003 | Talea de Castro | Villa Alta | Los Angeles |
| Lindo Oaxaca[f] | 2003 | San Miguel Cajonos | Villa Alta | Los Angeles |
| Oaxacalifornia | 2003 | Tlacolula | Tlacolula | Los Angeles |
| Rincón Oaxaqueño | 2003 | San Marcos Tlapazola | Tlacolula | Pico Union (LA) |

*Source:* Author interviews with restaurant owners.

*Note:* There are also other Oaxacan-owned restaurants in the Los Angeles region, for instance in Moorpark (La Calenda), San Bernardino (Pancho's and La Victoria), Westminster (Café Westminster), Costa Mesa (Yucatán), Santa Ana (Moctezuma), and Fullerton (El Fortín).

[a] This restaurant was first opened in 1994 on La Cienega but moved in 1998 to San Vicente Blvd.

[b] Another Oaxacan restaurant, El Tule in Hollywood, closed, but we do not have information about it.

[c] This restaurant was recently sold to a person from Puebla.

[d] The previous owner was from San Miguel del Valle, Tlacolula.

[e] It was recently sold to Oaxacans and is now called "Antequera de Oaxaca."

[f] The previous owner was from Zoogocho, Villa Alta, and it was sold in March 2003.

ocean. Although four brothers and sister run this restaurant, the idea came from their mother who, complaining of the lack of good Mexican food in Santa Monica, began to cook and sell food from her home in 1990. She became the cook for the new restaurant, and the children (one of whom had worked as manager at a Santa Monica upscale restaurant) ran the front of the house. They now employ seven people, all from Oaxaca. The other restaurant that opened in 1994, Guelaguetza, in Koreatown, was owned by a brother and a sister from Santiago Matatlán. This was the first of the three Guelaguetza restaurants in Los Angeles. Another sister also owns a restaurant in Fresno.

Of the twenty-eight restaurants for which we have information, eighteen are owned by Zapotecs from the Tlacolula District, nine by Zapotecs from the Villa Alta District, and one by people from Oaxaca City (table 9.1). We have mapped the locations of the restaurants in figure 9.4. They are basically clustered in two groups: along the 405 freeway on the west side, and in and around Pico Union. All of the west-side restaurants are owned by immigrants from Tlacolula; most of those further east are owned by immigrants from Villa Alta — dovetailing with the basic residential patterns of the two groups.

The two Zapotec groups[9] that are mostly found in Los Angeles are from the highlands (the northern Sierra) and the Tlacolula Valley. These groups are concentrated in specific areas of Los Angeles according to their region. For instance, the Highland Zapotecs have settled mainly in Pico Union but also in El Sereno and the San Gabriel Valley. The Valley Zapotecs, on the other hand, are concentrated on the west side of Los Angeles because of the labor niche they fill, working mostly in restaurants in West Los Angeles, Santa Monica, Venice, and Culver City. Recently, however, they have begun to move to the San Fernando Valley, Costa Mesa, and San Bernardino, among other areas.

Several of the early restaurants were oriented toward the *gringo* market, but the rest are selling to Oaxacan immigrants, with *gringos* a minor or nonexistent part of the clientele. The restaurants are thus mostly occupying the "ethnic niche" typical of such immigrant small businesses. They are also multiplying rapidly. Twelve restaurants have opened in the past thirty

---

[9] The Zapotec are usually divided into four major groups, Zapotecs from the Valley, Sierra Norte, Sierra Sur, and the Isthmus. In Los Angeles we also find a small group of Zapotecs from the Isthmus of Tehuantepec, especially from the community of Tequixtitlán, and at least one family of Zapotecs from the Sierra Sur, specifically from the conflicted area of the Loxichas.

months, and several more are about to open (six have closed or been sold). Their sheer numbers suggest a large population of Zapotecs in Los Angeles and a culture in which food is important.

**Figure 9.4. Oaxacan-owned Restaurants in Los Angeles**

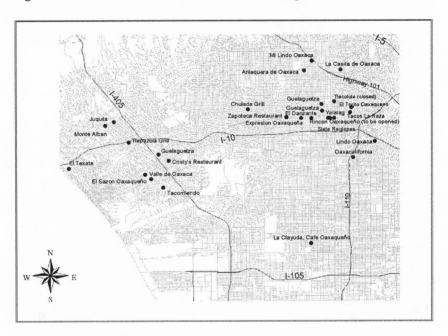

The growth of Oaxacan restaurants is facilitated by the presence of Oaxacan food merchants (butchers and bakers) in Los Angeles. Before Los Angeles had Oaxacan *carnicerías* (butcher shops) and *panaderías* (bakeries), a restaurant owner or family member would have to fly to Oaxaca to obtain essential food items — *tasajo, chorizo, cesina* — which were often brought as contraband and hence subject to confiscation at the border. Others would go to Tijuana to purchase ingredients. With the opening of the *carnicerías*, restaurant owners no longer need travel to Oaxaca or Tijuana. However, certain items — such as the Oaxacan *quesillo* or *chapulines* — are still not made locally. Restaurants that specialize in more regionally oriented food still have to make trips to Mexico or rely on someone from the home area to bring special items. Such is the case of one restaurant owner whose village's signature dish cannot be made without a specially prepared meat from her village in Oaxaca, and this item is offered only occasionally for the villagers residing in Los Angeles.

It took thirty-six years from the time that the first Tlacolula migrants settled in Los Angeles for someone to open a Oaxacan restaurant. Large-scale migration began in the 1970s, but it took another twenty years for a restaurant to appear. Why so long?

First, most of the immigrants were not wealthy, and they needed time to accumulate capital. The restaurant owners we interviewed said it took them ten to twenty years of work in the United States to reach that point. The Zapotecs have no history of rotating credit associations, so amassing sufficient capital was a family affair (a number of the restaurants were partnerships among family members). Second, because most of the restaurants cater to immigrants, they had to be preceded by a critical mass of Zapotec settlers. This immigrant market is always limited by the group's low incomes, so the passage of time allowed for people to obtain better jobs and have disposable income to spend in restaurants. Third, in order to rent business property and engage in other legal transactions, potential entrepreneurs needed legal status; most Zapotec immigration has been undocumented, but the 1986 amnesty under IRCA provided legal status for earlier immigrants. Fourth, business formation requires a certain permanence, settlement, and commitment to the receiving country. Piore (1979) emphasized the point that legal, settled immigrants with families would be more likely to form businesses than would temporary migrants who were remitting large amounts of money to their home countries. As Zapotec migration proceeded, male migrants were increasingly joined by mothers and wives, and in the cases we have studied it was often the impetus of the women that led to the establishment of the restaurants.

## POSSIBLE EXPLANATIONS FOR DIFFERENCES IN MIXTEC AND ZAPOTEC MIGRATION

Various explanations have been suggested for the differences between the Mixtec and Zapotec migration experiences, including why the Mixtec continue to work in agriculture and the Zapotec are concentrated in cities. We consider several such arguments.

### Language

*The location of Tlacolula in the Central Valleys, near Oaxaca City, led to greater use of Spanish, which facilitated access to distant labor markets without the need for labor contractors.*

In Juxtlahuaca, 73 percent of the total population speak an indigenous language, and 28 percent speak *only* an indigenous language. In Tlacolula, by contrast, 63 percent speak an indigenous language, and only 9 percent are monolingual in such a language (INEGI 2000). Thus there is clearly a higher proportion of monolingual speakers of an indigenous language in the Mixteca, which could lead to a certain cultural isolation and may explain the importance of contractors. Certainly agricultural work itself promotes isolation.

## Tourism

*Tlacolula's location close to Oaxaca City caused it to experience a rise in national and international tourism beginning in the 1930s, directed toward the sites of Mitla and Yagul and to the Tlacolula Sunday market. This tourism led to changes in occupational patterns to cater to tourists, such as rug weaving in Teotitlán del Valle, San Miguel del Valle, and Santa Ana del Valle, or the increasing production of commercial mescal in Matatlán.*

Already in the early 1960s, Tlacolula was being transformed into a commercial center (Diskin 1967). Proximity to Oaxaca City may have exposed the Zapotec population to urban service jobs. However, we have found no evidence that any of the Tlacolula migrants had prior experience working in restaurants.

## Education

*Tlacolula's population is more educated than Juxtlahuaca's.*

In Juxtlahuaca, 57 percent of the adult population is literate, whereas 77 percent are literate in Tlacolula. Of course, literacy is defined in Spanish, so the higher proportion of monolingual Mixtec speakers accounts for much of the difference.

## Enganchadores

*Labor contractors did not recruit farmworkers in the Central Valleys.*

This assertion is not strictly true. San Bartolomé Quialana sent people to Culiacán with *enganchadores* in the 1960s, but when they saw the bad conditions, they immediately returned to Oaxaca (Hulshof 1991). Also, almost every village in the Tlacolula area sent braceros to the United States. It is only after the Bracero Program ended that the migration patterns of the two groups diverge. Nevertheless, it is certainly true that labor contractors seeking workers for the fields in northwest Mexico delved further and further into the mountains of the Mixteca.

## CONCLUSION

Reflecting on the migration history of two indigenous groups from Oaxaca, we see that although both groups first migrated within southern Mexico to work in agriculture, both migrated to Mexico City, and both participated in the Bracero Program, they had significantly different migration patterns within Mexico in the last half of the twentieth century.

The Mixtecs have migrated in large numbers to northwest Mexico since the 1960s, creating settlements throughout the region. This migration was facilitated by *enganchadores* who recruited workers for northwest agribusinesses. Many Mixtecs then migrated to the United States in a form of stage migration, often recruited by contractors from the United States. In California, despite thirty years of experience, the Mixtecs continue to work mainly in agriculture and often in the worst jobs, though there is some movement into construction and services. There has been little small business formation by the Mixtecs in California. Some have become *mayordomos* crew bosses) or *raiteros* (crew drivers) — including the important early case of Rafael Morales in Sonoma (see Zabin 1992) — but these migrants' ability to accumulate capital has been limited by the low incomes from seasonal work, constant migration, the need to remit money to their villages, and the use of their savings to survive periods of unemployment and to travel to Oaxaca.

In contrast, Zapotecs from the Tlacolula area found work in Los Angeles restaurants in the 1960s, which led to a spreading pattern of network migration to Los Angeles from throughout the district. These networks became so predominant in West Los Angeles restaurants that a growing number of families have been able to open their own Oaxacan restaurants; they had the skills, the support of well-known restaurateurs, and capital pooled from the family members' permanent jobs. The restaurant owners we interviewed were focused on the United States and not on remitting money to Oaxaca.

The Zapotecs resisted contract agricultural work in northwest Mexico, but the Mixtecs participated. We hypothesize that these different trajectories over the past forty years were due in part to the different distances of the two groups from Oaxaca City and all it implied. The Zapotecs of Tlacolula experienced the influence of a more Spanish-speaking population, more commerce opportunities, and more tourism. In contrast, the Mixtecs were more remote, more monolingual, and had fewer business opportunities. Those who could speak Spanish were driven to migrate by deteriorating ecological conditions. And those who could not speak Spanish could still be recruited by the labor contractors who acted as intermediaries to the farm labor market. We hypothesize that language was a key differentiating factor and that it continues to be an important difference, as evidenced by Mixtec organizations' focus on linguistic and political issues. Further research is needed to ascertain the importance of these differences.

The principal difference between the groups' experiences lies in the different types of work they have undertaken in the United States. The Mixtecs' willingness to live and work under miserable conditions in large-scale agriculture in Mexico made them obvious candidates for recruitment by farm labor contractors for a similar purpose in the United States. The Tlacolula Zapotecs' rejection of such work led them to follow chance pioneers into Los Angeles restaurants, a type of employment that can have positive outcomes. Large-scale, labor-intensive agriculture in the United States has proven highly resistant to improvements in labor conditions over the past century, and it is hard to be optimistic that this will change. Like other immigrant groups before them, the Mixtec will have to find their way out of agricultural work and into urban jobs if they are to prosper in the United States.

## References

Acevedo Conde, María Luisa, and Iván Restrepo. 1991. *Los valles centrales de Oaxaca*. Mexico City: Centro de Ecodesarrollo, Gobierno de Oaxaca.

Álvarez, Fred. 1995. "The Mixtecs: A Grim Life in the Fields," *Los Angeles Times*, July 27.

Atilano Flores, Juan José. 2000. *Entre lo propio y lo ajeno: la identidad étnica-local de los jornaleros mixtecos*. Serie Migración Indígena. Mexico City: Instituto Nacional Indigenista.

Bacon, David. 2002. "Build a House, Go to Jail," *LA Weekly*, August 23.

Bailey, Thomas. 1985. "A Case Study of Immigrants in the Restaurant Industry," *Industrial Relations* 24, no. 2.

Butterworth, Douglas. 1990. *Tilantongo: comunidad mixteca en transición*. 2d ed. Mexico: Instituto Nacional Indigenista/Secretaría de Educación Pública.

Chávez, Leo R. 1992. *Shadowed Lives: Undocumented Immigrants in American Society*. Fort Worth, Tex.: Harcourt Brace Jovanovich.

Clark Alfaro, Víctor. 1991. *Los mixtecos en la frontera (Baja California)*. Cuadernos de Ciencias Sociales. Baja California: Universidad Autónoma de Baja California.

Cook, Scott. 1982. *Zapotec Stoneworkers: The Dynamics of Rural Simple Commodity Production in Modern Mexican Capitalism*. Washington, D.C.: University Press of America.

De la Peña, Moisés T. 1950. *Problemas sociales y económicos de las mixtecas*. Mexico: Instituto Nacional Indigenista.

Díaz Montes, Fausto. 1982. "La producción de mezcal en Oaxaca." In *Sociedad y política en Oaxaca, 1980*, edited by Raúl Benítez Zenteno. Oaxaca: Instituto de Investigaciones Sociológicas, Universidad Autónoma "Benito Juárez" de Oaxaca.

Diskin, Martin. 1967. "Economics and Society in Tlacolula, Mexico." Ph.D. dissertation, University of California, Los Angeles.

Edinger, Steven T. 1996. *The Road to Mixtepec: A Southern Mexican Town and the United States Economy*. Fresno, Calif.: Asociación Cívica Benito Juárez.

FAO (Food and Agriculture Organization). 1999. *Asociación de migrantes y desarrollo local*. Rome: SDAR/FAO.

Garduño, Everardo, Efraín García, and Patricia Morán. 1989. *Mixtecos en Baja California: el caso de San Quintín*. Serie Museo. Mexicali: Universidad Autónoma de Baja California.

Golden, Arthur. 1996. "Baja in Struggle to Preserve a Multitude of Native Tongues," *San Diego Union-Tribune*, March 11.

Goldring, Luin. 1990. *Development and Migration: A Comparative Analysis of Two Mexican Migrant Circuits*. Working Paper No. 37. Washington, D.C.: U.S. Commission for the Study of International Migration and Cooperative Economic Development.

Herman, Harry Vjekoslav. 1979. "Dishwashers and Proprietors: Macedonians in Toronto's Restaurant Trade." In *Ethnicity at Work*, edited by Sandra Wallman. London: MacMillan.

Hulshof, Marije. 1991. *Zapotec Moves: Networks and Remittances of U.S.-Bound Migrants from Oaxaca, Mexico*. Nederlandse Geografische Studies, 128. Amsterdam: Koninklijk Nederlands Aardrijkskundig Genootschap.

Kesteloot, Christian, and Pascale Mistiaen. 1997. "From Ethnic Minority Niche to Assimilation: Turkish Restaurants in Brussels," *Area* 29, no. 4.

Krugman, Paul. 1991. *Geography and Trade*. Cambridge, Mass.: MIT Press.

———. 1995. *Development, Geography, and Economic Theory*. Cambridge, Mass.: MIT Press.

López Castro, Gustavo. 1986. *La casa dividida: un estudio de caso sobre la migración a Estados Unidos en un pueblo michoacano*. Zamora: El Colegio de Michoacán.

López, Felipe H., and Pam Munro. 1999. "Zapotec Immigration: The San Lucas Quiaviní Experience," *Aztlan* 24, no. 1.

————. n.d. *X:a Mo'od bie'd ra buunny Sann Lu'uc Lohs Aa'nngl* (How People of San Lucas Came to Los Angeles). Zapotec Immigration Narratives. Los Angeles: Chicano Studies Research Center, University of California, Los Angeles. Forthcoming.

Mines, Richard. 1981. *Developing a Community Tradition of Migration to the United States: A Field Study in Rural Zacatecas, Mexico, and California Settlement Areas*. Monograph No. 3. La Jolla: Center for U.S.-Mexican Studies, University of California, San Diego.

Nagengast, Carole, Rodolfo Stavenhagen, and Michael Kearney. 1992. *Human Rights and Indigenous Workers: The Mixtec in Mexico and the United States*. La Jolla: Center for U.S.-Mexican Studies, University of California, San Diego.

Ornelas López, José Luz. 1982. "La migración en Santo Domingo del Valle, Tlacolula." In *Sociedad y política en Oaxaca, 1980*, edited by Raúl Benítez Zenteno. Oaxaca: Instituto de Investigaciones Sociológicas, Universidad Autónoma "Benito Juárez" de Oaxaca.

Piore, Michael J. 1979. *Birds of Passage: Migrant Labor and Industrial Societies*. Cambridge: Cambridge University Press.

Quiñones, Sam. 1998. "Migrant Life: Poverty and Exploitation," *San Francisco Examiner*, January 11. At http://sfgate.com/cgi-bin/article.cgi?file=/examiner/archive/1998/01/11/NEWS11736.dtl.

Ram, Monder, et al. 2000. "Ethnic Minority Business in Comparative Perspective: The Case of the Independent Restaurant Sector," *Journal of Ethnic and Migration Studies* 26, no. 3.

Rath, Jan, and Robert Kloosterman. 2000. "Outsiders' Business: A Critical Review of Research on Immigrant Entrepreneurship," *International Migration Review* 34, no. 3.

Rubio, Miguel Ángel, and Saúl Millán. 2000. "Migrantes mixtecos en Baja California." In *La migración indígena en México: estado del desarrollo económico y social de los pueblos indígenas de México*, edited by Saúl Millán, Javier Gutiérrez, and Miguel Ángel Rubio. Mexico: Instituto Nacional Indigenista.

Runsten, David, Roberta Cook, Anna García, and Don Villarejo. 1993. "The Tomato Industry in California and Baja California: Regional Labor Markets and IRCA." In *Report of the U.S. Commission on Agricultural Workers, Appendix I: Case Studies and Research Reports*. Washington, D.C.

Runsten, David, and Michael Kearney. 1994. *A Survey of Oaxacan Village Networks in California Agriculture*. Davis: California Institute for Rural Studies.

Runsten, David, and Carol Zabin. 1994. "A Regional Perspective on Mexican Migration to Rural California." Presented at the conference "The Changing Face of Rural America," Asilomar, California, June 12–14.

Stephen, Lynn. 1991. *Zapotec Women*. Austin: University of Texas Press.

Valdés, Luz María. 1995. *Los indios en los censos de población*. Mexico: Universidad Nacional Autónoma de México.

López and Runsten

Velasco Ortiz, Laura. 1995. "Entre el jornal y terruño: los migrantes mixtecos en la frontera noroeste de México," *Nueva Antropología* 14, vol. 10: 113–29.

Waldinger, Roger D. 1986. *Through the Eye of the Needle: Immigrants and Enterprise in New York's Garment Trades.* New York: New York University Press.

Young, Emily. 1994. "The Impact of IRCA on Settlement Patterns among Mixtec Migrants in Tijuana, Mexico," *Journal of Borderlands Studies* 9, no. 2.

Zabin, Carol, ed. 1992. *Migración oaxaqueña a los campos agrícolas de California: un diálogo.* Current Issue Brief No. 2. La Jolla: Center for U.S.-Mexican Studies, University of California, San Diego

Zabin, Carol, et al. 1993. *Mixtec Migrants in California Agriculture: A New Cycle of Poverty.* Davis: California Institute for Rural Studies.

# 10

## Indigenous Mexican Migrants in the 2000 U.S. Census: "Hispanic American Indians"

JAVIER HUIZAR MURILLO AND ISIDRO CERDA

The growing presence of indigenous Latin American migrants in the United States made the front page of the *San Jose Mercury* under the headline "California Overtakes Oklahoma as State with Most American Indians" (see Hubner 2001). This change was due to increased migration of primarily Mexican indigenous people to California—a trend that began to take off in the 1980s but was not widely recognized until the 1990s.

The overall 2000 census data on the Native American population in the United States showed dramatic growth nationwide, due in part to their increased self-identification. Among those who identified as "American Indian," persons who *also* identified themselves as "Hispanic" grew dramatically as well. The census reported that the Native American population grew 21 percent nationwide over the 1990s, and in California the population of American Indians of Hispanic origin grew by 146 percent. Those who chose both categories became known, in census terms, as "Hispanic American Indians." The growth in this combined racial/ethnic category was made possible in part by changes in the census categories that resulted from past public debates over how the census could better facilitate self-identification. This chapter will review the 2000 census findings to describe the reported geographic distribution of "Hispanic Native Americans" within California and the United States.

Race has long been a contentious part of the census process, and official racial categories have both influenced and reflected more widely used social categories.[1] Despite the widespread racialization of ethnic–national origin categories such as Mexican American or Puerto Rican in the United States, according to the U.S. census, Hispanics can be of any race. Officially, the category is based on cultural legacy and language rather than race. In practice, the ways in which people of Latin American origin in the United States have identified racially have varied widely, both over time and across social and national groups.[2] More generally, the civil rights movement taught many lessons about the importance of recognizing the cultural dimensions of identity, both to facilitate popular mobilization and to allocate the public resources necessary to address the social needs of distinct groups in culturally appropriate ways.

The Bureau of the Census publication "Overview of Race and Hispanic Origin: A Census 2000 Brief" details how "Hispanic-origin status" is derived and has been influential to our understanding of the term (Grieco and Cassidy 2001). The term was included for the first time in the 1980 census as a direct result of the adoption of Directive No. 15 in 1977. The directive defined Hispanic as an ethnic category, which made it compatible with various possible one-race categories (though mestizo is not one of the racial category options in the U.S. census). Widespread lack of response to the Hispanic ethnicity question in the 1990 census questionnaire led to a change in the order of the questions. The Bureau of the Census believed this omission was due to confusion caused by the sequence of the questions on race and ethnicity, in which the questionnaire form asked the race question first and the Hispanic-origin question second. Census analysts believed that respondents mistakenly interpreted Hispanic origin as a racial category. The Bureau of the Census's solution was to rearrange the order of the questions on the 2000 census questionnaire, to oblige respondents to answer the Hispanic question before reporting their racial identification.[3]

---

[1] For a history of the census treatment of Latinos, see Rodríguez 2000. For further analysis of racial census categories, see Nobles 2000.

[2] The concept of Hispanic itself is a relatively new invention, created by the federal government as a social policy tool that brought together different national-origin groups. In response, civil rights groups promoted "Latino" as an alternative umbrella term. See, among others, Oboler 1995.

[3] This approach had mixed results in 2000, when 5.5 million California residents identified as "some other race" and 99 percent of them were Latino. Both in 1990 and in 2000, 51 percent of Latinos answered the race question with "some other race." A recent study concludes that this is evidence that respondents are treating "Latino" as a de facto racial category. See Tafoya 2003.

When referring to "Hispanic-origin status" the census uses the terms "Hispanic" and "Latino" interchangeably. In order to maintain consistency, the term Hispanic will be used here since that is the dominant usage in the federal government. The Hispanic-origin status question is structured to provide only two answers: whether one is of Hispanic origin or not. The federal government's Office of Management and Budget established six all-inclusive categories for the race question: White, Black or African American, American Indian/Alaskan Native, Asian, Native Hawaiian/Pacific Islander, or "Some Other Race."

The nature of the question determines the possible answers or, more precisely, the choices for self-identification. Therefore, looking at the 2000 census questionnaire will help us understand how the racial and ethnic categories are determined and how the Hispanic American Indian category is derived. The 2000 census's initial question dealt with identity in the following manner: "Is this person Spanish/Hispanic/Latino?" The prescribed options were: "No, not Spanish/Hispanic/Latino" and "Yes," with options to specify Mexican, Mexican Am., Chicano, other Spanish/Hispanic/Latino, Puerto Rican, and Cuban. In the next question, race was asked in the following manner: "What is this person's race?" The response choices were: White; Black, African Am., or Negro; American Indian or Alaska Native. This is the framework within which respondents can identify as Hispanic American Indian (see figure 10.1 for a sample view of the census questionnaire).[4]

The option for identifying as American Indian also left a space to indicate a specific "tribe." According to the Bureau of the Census, American Indian or Alaska Native status is determined by tribal affiliation or community recognition. However, this reflects North American usage of the term "tribe," a concept that is not used by most Latin American native peoples. As a result of this cultural difference, it is not surprising that preliminary census data suggest that only a small fraction of those who identified as Hispanic American Indian also reported membership in a specific "tribe."

Because of persistent problems of census undercount, especially in migrant communities, the 2000 census data for this population must be

---

[4] Note that the combination of American Indian (a racial category) and Hispanic (an ethnic category) does not refer to the new option of choosing multiple races, which has produced reports of a growing multiracial category. In other words, the category "Hispanic American Indian" as used here refers exclusively to people who identify as indigenous only, rather than as of mixed race.

**Figure 10.1. Sample Page of the 2000 U.S. Population Census, Showing the Choice Options That Render an Identification as Hispanic American Indian**

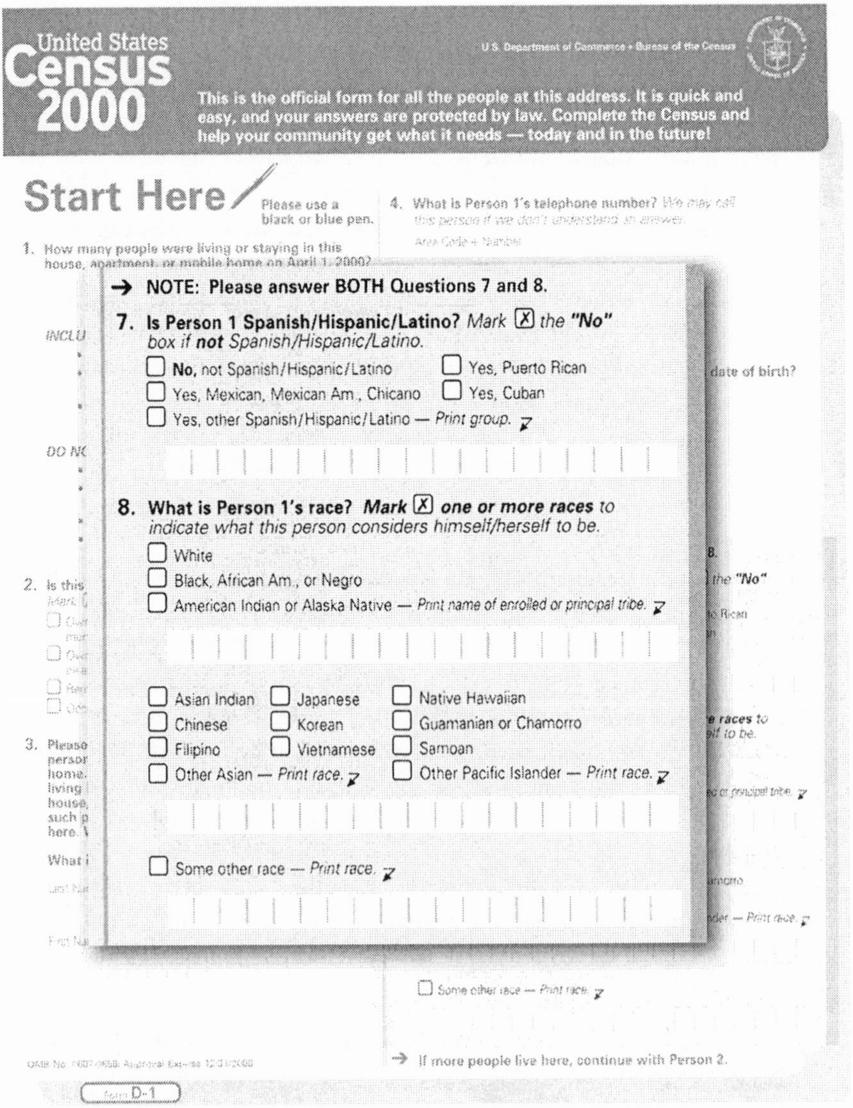
United States Census 2000

U.S. Department of Commerce • Bureau of the Census

This is the official form for all the people at this address. It is quick and easy, and your answers are protected by law. Complete the Census and help your community get what it needs — today and in the future!

Start Here Please use a black or blue pen.

1. How many people were living or staying in this house, apartment, or mobile home on April 1, 2000?

4. What is Person 1's telephone number? *We may call this person if we don't understand an answer.*

→ **NOTE: Please answer BOTH Questions 7 and 8.**

**7. Is Person 1 Spanish/Hispanic/Latino?** *Mark* ☒ *the* ***"No"*** *box if* ***not*** *Spanish/Hispanic/Latino.*

- ☐ **No,** not Spanish/Hispanic/Latino
- ☐ Yes, Puerto Rican
- ☐ Yes, Mexican, Mexican Am., Chicano
- ☐ Yes, Cuban
- ☐ Yes, other Spanish/Hispanic/Latino — *Print group.*

**8. What is Person 1's race?** ***Mark*** ☒ ***one or more races*** *to indicate what this person considers himself/herself to be.*

- ☐ White
- ☐ Black, African Am., or Negro
- ☐ American Indian or Alaska Native — *Print name of enrolled or principal tribe.*
- ☐ Asian Indian
- ☐ Japanese
- ☐ Native Hawaiian
- ☐ Chinese
- ☐ Korean
- ☐ Guamanian or Chamorro
- ☐ Filipino
- ☐ Vietnamese
- ☐ Samoan
- ☐ Other Asian — *Print race.*
- ☐ Other Pacific Islander — *Print race.*
- ☐ Some other race — *Print race.*

→ If more people live here, continue with Person 2.

Form D-1

taken as suggestive rather than definitive; that is, the numbers should be understood as minimum estimates rather than absolute figures. Because of the changing and geographically uneven nature of the undercount, it is also likely that the distance between the reported and actual numbers varies across and within states. For example, the undercounting problem was probably much more serious in regions of relatively new arrivals, such as Florida and New York, than in some regions of California, where significant efforts were made to reach out to communities and overcome problems of undercounting during the 1990s.[5]

Nationwide, the 2000 census reported a Hispanic American Indian population of just over 407,000 (table 10.1). Because of problems of undercounting and the possible perceived ambiguity of census categories, this figure should be treated as a minimum estimate. Most of those who identified as Hispanic American Indian are predominantly of Mexican and Guatemalan origin, including Mayan, Mixtec, Zapotec, Triqui, and P'urépecha peoples. Most come from home communities in rural areas and supply low-wage labor in agriculture and the urban service sector throughout the United States, with the most notable concentration in California. In order to observe the broad trends in the growth of Hispanic American Indian populations in the nation, we have broken up the data into easily recognized regions of the United States (see table 10.1; see also figure 10.2). At first glance, we see that the West is home to the largest population of Hispanic American Indians, with a reported population of 232,110, or 57 percent of the U.S. total. The region with the second highest number of Hispanic American Indians is the South, with a total population of 88,382 (primarily in Texas and Florida). The Northeast comes in third with a total population of 49,171 (primarily in New York).

The data reported in this category show that California was home to the largest population of Hispanic American Indians in the United States, with 154,362 reported. It was followed by Texas, with 49,503 (one-third of the California total). In our analysis of California census data, we have also organized the data by regions (San Francisco Nine-County Region, San Joaquin Valley, Central Coast, northern California, and Southern California; see table 10.2). Figure 10.3 shows all the counties in California and the total population of Hispanic American Indians in each county.

---

5 Kissam and Jacobs, this volume; interviews with Lucas Benítez, organizer for the Coalition of Immokalee Workers, Florida, March 2003, and Gaspar Rivera-Salgado, March, 2003; and email correspondence with Alex Stepick, director of the Immigration and Ethnicity Institute at Florida International University, March 2003.

**Table 10.1. U.S. Population of Hispanic American Indians, by State and Region in 2000 U.S. Census, Summary Tape File 1**

| Region | U.S. States/Regions[a] | Total Population | Total Population of Hispanic American Indians |
|---|---|---|---|
| All U.S. Regions | West Region | 63,197,932 | 232,110 |
| | South Region | 100,236,820 | 88,382 |
| | Northeast Region | 53,594,378 | 49,171 |
| | Midwest Region | 64,392,776 | 37,410 |
| | Total U.S. population | 281,421,906 [b] | 407,073 [b] |
| Western Region | California | 33,871,648 | 154,362 |
| | Arizona | 5,130,632 | 22,509 |
| | Colorado | 4,301,261 | 15,259 |
| | New Mexico | 1,819,046 | 12,023 |
| | Washington | 5,894,121 | 7,905 |
| | Oregon | 3,421,399 | 5,081 |
| | Nevada | 1,998,257 | 5,023 |
| | Utah | 2,233,169 | 3,021 |
| | Idaho | 1,293,953 | 1,856 |
| | Montana | 902,195 | 1,642 |
| | Alaska | 626,932 | 1,538 |
| | Hawaii | 1,211,537 | 996 |
| | Wyoming | 493,782 | 895 |
| | Western regional subtotal | 63,197,932 [b] | 232,110 [b] |
| Midwest Region | Illinois | 12,419,293 | 12,774 |
| | Michigan | 9,938,444 | 5,058 |
| | Wisconsin | 5,363,675 | 3,248 |
| | Minnesota | 4,919,479 | 2,958 |
| | Kansas | 2,688,418 | 2,614 |
| | Ohio | 11,353,140 | 2,501 |
| | Indiana | 6,080,485 | 2,161 |
| | Missouri | 5,595,211 | 1,774 |
| | Nebraska | 1,711,263 | 1,436 |
| | South Dakota | 754,844 | 1,295 |
| | Iowa | 2,926,324 | 1,034 |
| | North Dakota | 642,200 | 557 |
| | Midwest region subtotal | 64,392,776 [b] | 37,410 [b] |

| Region | State | | |
|---|---|---|---|
| Southern Region | Texas | 20,851,820 | 49,503 |
| | Florida | 15,982,378 | 11,183 |
| | Oklahoma | 3,450,654 | 7,072 |
| | North Carolina | 8,049,313 | 4,218 |
| | Georgia | 8,186,453 | 4,067 |
| | Virginia | 7,078,515 | 2,576 |
| | Maryland | 5,296,486 | 2,111 |
| | Louisiana | 4,468,976 | 1,348 |
| | Tennessee | 5,689,283 | 1,332 |
| | Arkansas | 2,673,400 | 1,106 |
| | South Carolina | 4,012,012 | 953 |
| | Alabama | 4,447,100 | 812 |
| | Kentucky | 4,041,769 | 677 |
| | Mississippi | 2,844,658 | 428 |
| | Delaware | 783,600 | 407 |
| | West Virginia | 1,808,344 | 150 |
| | Southern region subtotal | 100,236,820 [b] | 88,382 [b] |
| Northeastern Region | New York | 18,976,457 | 29,962 |
| | New Jersey | 8,414,350 | 8,154 |
| | Massachusetts | 6,349,097 | 3,751 |
| | Pennsylvania | 12,281,054 | 3,444 |
| | Connecticut | 3,405,565 | 2,372 |
| | Rhode Island | 1,048,319 | 940 |
| | New Hampshire | 1,235,786 | 266 |
| | Maine | 1,274,923 | 187 |
| | Vermont | 608,827 | 95 |
| | Northeast region subtotal | 53,594,378 [b] | 49,171 [b] |

[a] Puerto Rico and Washington D.C. are not included in the regions: Puerto Rico, total population 3,808,610, total population of Hispanic American Indians 12,773. District of Columbia, total population 572,059, total population of Hispanic American Indians 439.
[b] The U.S. census calculates the totals for each region and the nation differently; they are not an aggregate of states. These totals can be found at American FactFinder, U.S. Census data Web site, http://factfinder.census.gov.

Figure 10.2.

# United States -
## Total Population of Hispanic American Indians in 2000

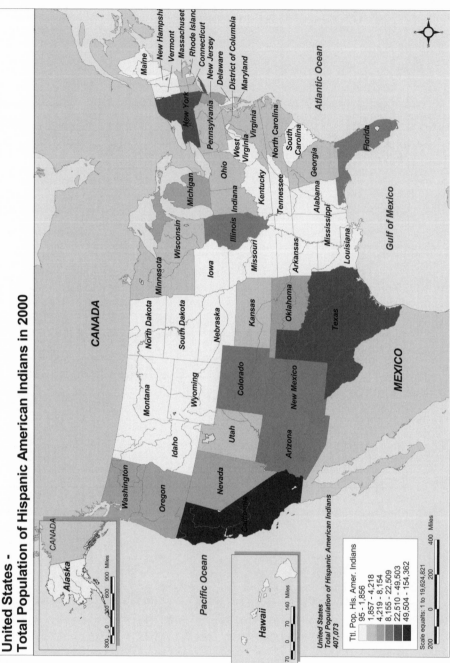

Ttl. Pop. His. Amer. Indians
95 - 1,856
1,857 - 4,218
4,219 - 8,154
8,155 - 22,509
22,510 - 49,503
49,504 - 154,362

United States
Total Population of Hispanic American Indians
407,073

Scale equals: 1 to 19,624,821

U.S. Census Bureau. "P8, Hispanic or Latino by Race - Universe: Total population." Census 2000 Summary File 1 (SF 1) 100-Percent Data. <http://factfinder.census.gov>.

The data show that the Southern California region, which includes the five counties with the largest numbers reported, is home to the largest concentration of Hispanic Americans—a total population of 94,958. Los Angeles County ranks first, with a total population of 51,379. Although the Los Angeles data include a significant number of Mayans of Guatemalan origin, the vast majority of Hispanic American Indians elsewhere in California are of Mexican origin.

With the use of geographic information systems (GIS), we were able to create a series of maps showing the geographic dispersion of Hispanic American Indians in California by county and then on a more micro-level by census tracts. We chose to represent the data using six breaks or clusters that represent finer gradations in the data. This enables us to show on the maps the locations of extremely low and high population concentrations of Hispanic American Indians (figures 10.3 through 10.14).

In the context of the preliminary research findings on the industries that use Hispanic American Indian labor, the census data open a window on where this new group of immigrants is settling in the United States.[6] It is also important to keep in mind the powerful role of census data in determining the pattern of allocation of public resources and services for poor communities. For Hispanic American Indians to gain effective access to basic rights and services, local, state, and federal officials need to have efficient and precise enumerating techniques that also recognize diversity and facilitate self-identification. Moreover, accurate counts are important for underrepresented social groups to be able to use census data and statistical analysis to articulate and legitimize their civic, social, and political goals.

The 2000 census made advances toward improved data collection in three clear ways: by allowing for multiracial identification, by clarifying the confusion in the Hispanic-origin question, and by incorporating the Hispanic American Indian category. While it is too soon to assess the scope and impact of these changes with precision, it is clear that the Hispanic American Indian category helps to make a previously invisible group more visible.

---

[6] See the chapter by López and Runsten (this volume) on the contrasting settlement patterns of Zapotec migrants, who tend to work in urban services, and Mixtecs, who are found in agriculture, especially in California's Central Valley. The census data confirm that urban Los Angeles hosts one of the major concentrations of indigenous Mexicans in the United States.

Table 10.2 California Population of Hispanic American Indians, by County and Region in 2000 U.S. Census, Summary Tape File 1

| | County | Total Population | Total Population of Hispanic American Indians |
|---|---|---|---|
| All of California | | 33,871,648[a] | 154,362[a] |
| Northern California | Sacramento | 1,223,499 | 4,289 |
| | Yolo | 168,660 | 788 |
| | Mendocino | 86,265 | 665 |
| | Butte | 203,171 | 571 |
| | Humboldt | 126,518 | 519 |
| | Placer | 248,399 | 512 |
| | Shasta | 163,256 | 503 |
| | Lake | 58,309 | 359 |
| | El Dorado | 156,299 | 294 |
| | Sutter | 78,930 | 285 |
| | Yuba | 60,219 | 263 |
| | Del Norte | 27,507 | 177 |
| | Tehama | 56,039 | 170 |
| | Nevada | 92,033 | 151 |
| | Lassen | 33,828 | 145 |
| | Colusa | 18,804 | 123 |
| | Siskiyou | 44,301 | 121 |
| | Glenn | 26,453 | 113 |
| | Plumas | 20,824 | 86 |
| | Modoc | 9,449 | 58 |
| | Trinity | 13,022 | 48 |
| | Mono | 12,853 | 42 |
| | Alpine | 1,208 | 40 |
| | Sierra | 3,555 | 11 |
| | Approximate regional subtotal | 2,933,401[b] | 10,333[b] |
| San Francisco Bay Area Nine-County Region | Santa Clara | 1,682,585 | 6,080 |
| | Alameda | 1,443,741 | 3,840 |
| | Contra Costa | 948,816 | 2,182 |
| | Sonoma | 458,614 | 1,912 |
| | San Mateo | 707,161 | 1,594 |

| Region | County | | |
| --- | --- | --- | --- |
| | San Francisco | 776,733 | 1,438 |
| | Solano | 394,542 | 916 |
| | Marin | 247,289 | 431 |
| | Napa | 124,279 | 403 |
| | San Francisco SMSA | 7,039,362[a] | 20,077[a] |
| Central Coast | Santa Barbara | 399,347 | 2,649 |
| | Monterey | 401,762 | 2,420 |
| | Santa Cruz | 255,602 | 1,281 |
| | San Luis Obispo | 246,681 | 845 |
| | Approximate regional subtotal | 1,303,392[b] | 7,195[b] |
| San Joaquin Valley | Fresno | 799,407 | 6,567 |
| | Kern | 661,645 | 4,114 |
| | Tulare | 368,021 | 2,726 |
| | Madera | 123,109 | 1,518 |
| | Merced | 210,554 | 1,395 |
| | Kings | 129,461 | 874 |
| | San Benito | 53,234 | 337 |
| | Inyo | 17,945 | 124 |
| | Mariposa | 17,130 | 72 |
| | Approximate regional subtotal | 2,380,506[b] | 17,727[b] |
| Southern California | Los Angeles | 9,519,338 | 51,379 |
| | Orange | 2,846,289 | 11,492 |
| | San Bernardino | 1,709,434 | 10,111 |
| | San Diego | 2,813,833 | 9,084 |
| | Riverside | 1,545,387 | 8,033 |
| | Ventura | 753,197 | 3,929 |
| | Imperial | 142,361 | 930 |
| | Approximate regional subtotal | 19,329,839[b] | 94,958[b] |

[a] The U.S. census calculates the totals for each metropolitan area and the state separately, and does not aggregate the totals of each county. These totals can be found at American FactFinder, U.S. Census data Web site, http://factfinder.census.gov.

[b] This is an approximation of the total population for these regions; the census does not give totals for these specific regions.

Note: SMSA = Standard Metropolitan Statistical Area.

**Figure 10.3.**

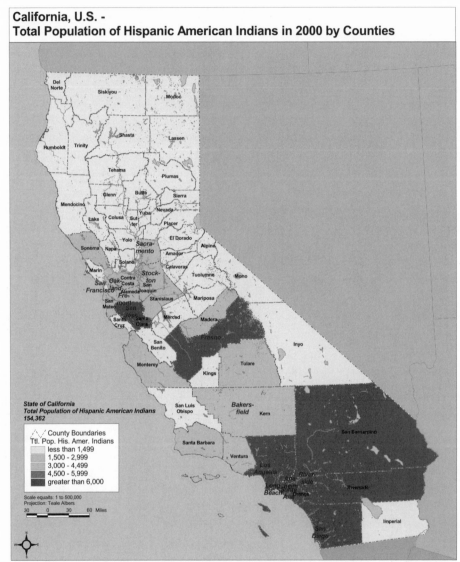

California, U.S. -
Total Population of Hispanic American Indians in 2000 by Counties

U.S. Census Bureau. "P8, Hispanic or Latino by Race - Universe: Total population."
Census 2000 Summary File 1 (SF 1) 100-Percent Data. <http://factfinder.census.gov>.

Figure 10.4.

# San Francisco Greater Bay Area, California -
# Total Population of Hispanic American Indians in 2000 by Census Tracts

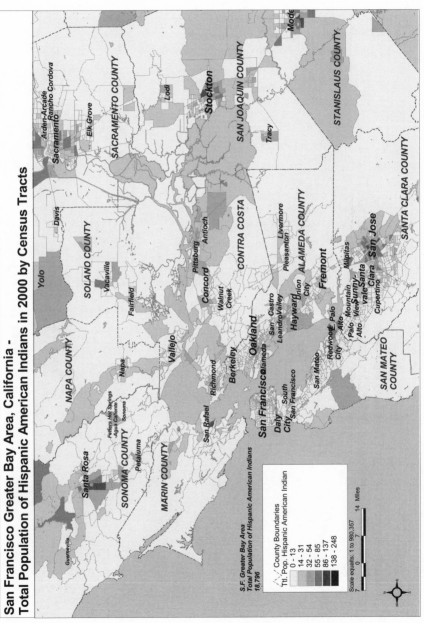

Figure 10.5.

# The North Bay of the San Francisco Bay Area, California -
# Total Population of Hispanic American Indians in 2000 by Census Tracts

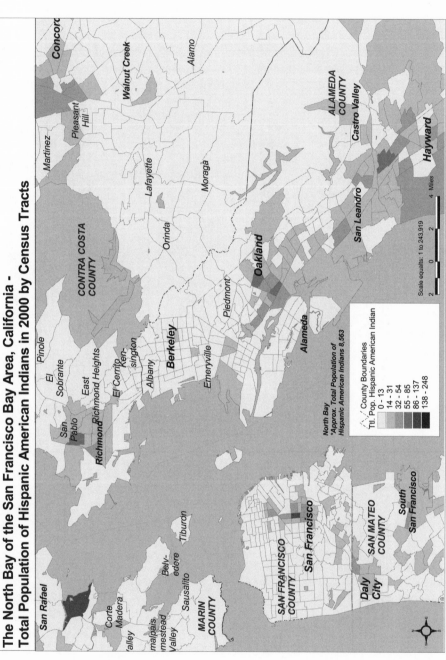

Figure 10.6.

# The South Bay of the San Francisco Bay Area, California - Total Population of Hispanic American Indians in 2000 by Census Tracts

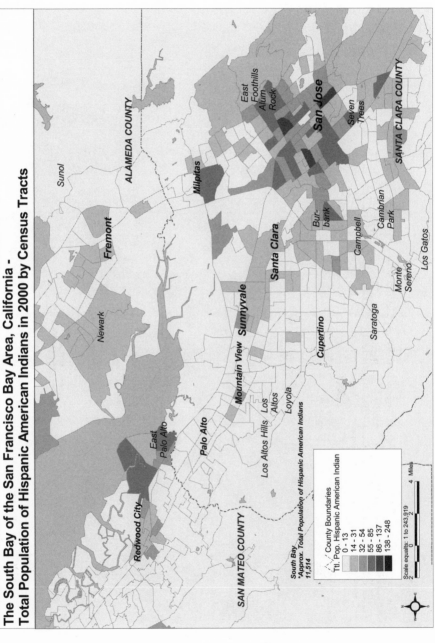

South Bay
*Approx. Total Population of Hispanic American Indians
11,514

County Boundaries
Ttl. Pop. Hispanic American Indian
0 - 13
14 - 31
32 - 54
55 - 85
86 - 137
138 - 248

Scale equals: 1 to 243,919
0        2        4   Miles

Figure 10.7.

## San Joaquin Valley, California -
## Total Population of Hispanic American Indians in 2000 by Census Tracts

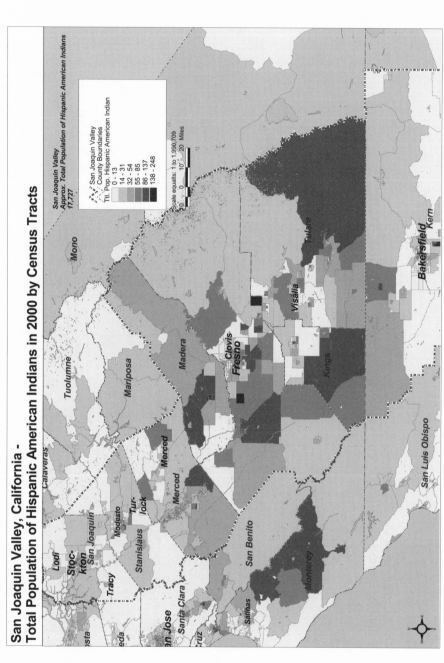

U.S. Census Bureau. "P8, Hispanic or Latino by Race - Universe: Total population." Census 2000 Summary File 1 (SF 1) 100-Percent Data. <http://factfinder.census.gov>.

Figure 10.8.

# Fresno County, California -
# Total Population of Hispanic American Indians in 2000 by Census Tracts

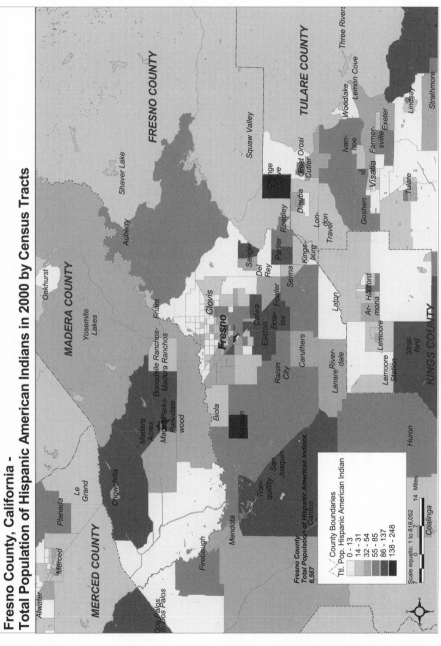

U.S. Census Bureau. "P8, Hispanic or Latino by Race - Universe: Total population." Census 2000 Summary File 1 (SF 1) 100-Percent Data. <http://factfinder.census.gov>.

Figure 10.9.

# Kern County, California –
## Total Population of Hispanic American Indians in 2000 by Census Tracts

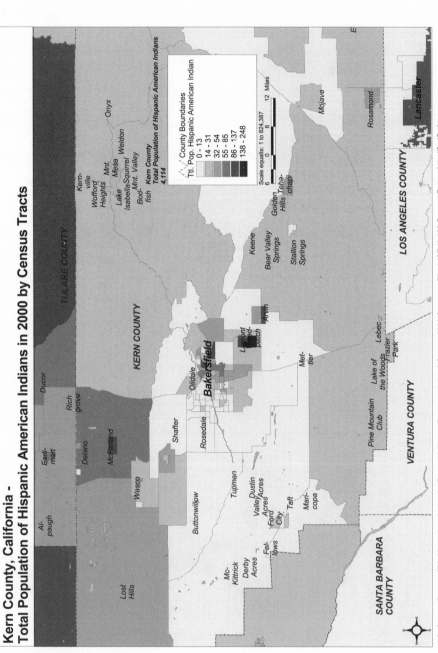

Figure 10.10.

# Los Angeles Metropolitan Area, California -
# Total Population of Hispanic American Indians in 2000 by Census Tracts

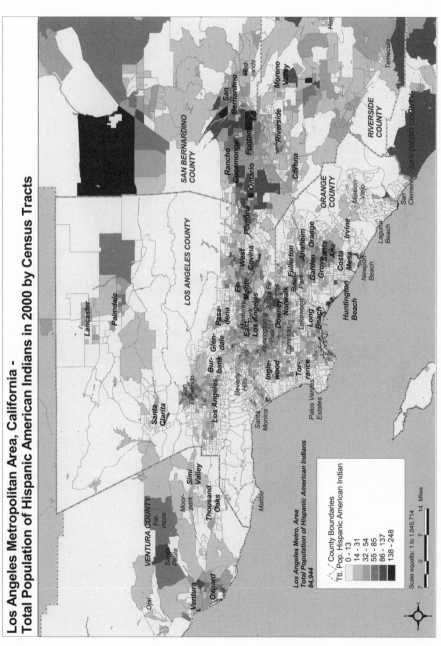

Los Angeles Metro. Area
*Total Population of Hispanic American Indians*
84,944

```
County Boundaries
Ttl. Pop. Hispanic American Indian
    0 - 13
   14 - 31
   32 - 54
   55 - 85
   86 - 137
  138 - 248
```

Scale equals: 1 to 1,045,714

7    0    7         14 Miles

U.S. Census Bureau. "P8, Hispanic or Latino by Race - Universe: Total population." Census 2000 Summary File 1 (SF 1) 100-Percent Data. <http://factfinder.census.gov>.

Figure 10.11.

## Los Angeles County, California -
## Total Population of Hispanic American Indians in 2000 by Census Tracts

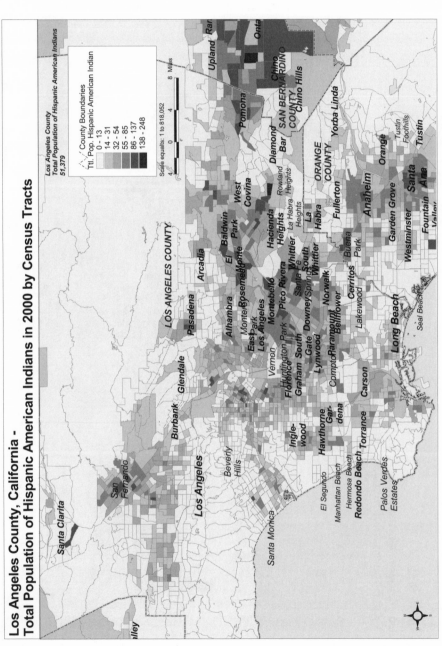

U.S. Census Bureau. "P8, Hispanic or Latino by Race - Universe: Total population." Census 2000 Summary File 1 (SF 1) 100-Percent Data. <http://factfinder.census.gov>.

**Figure 10.12.**

## Orange County, California -
## Total Population of Hispanic American Indians in 2000 by Census Tracts

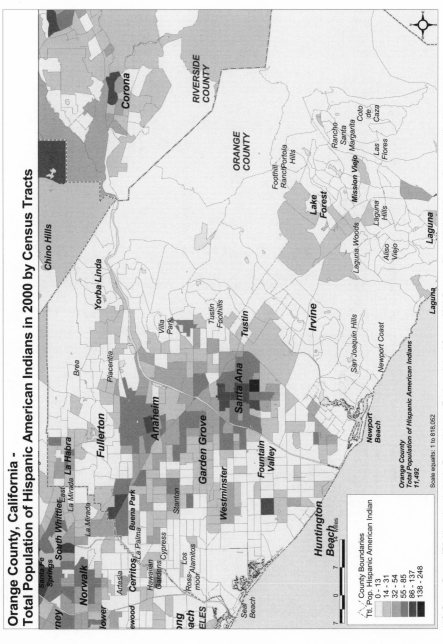

U.S. Census Bureau. "P8, Hispanic or Latino by Race - Universe: Total population." Census 2000 Summary File 1 (SF 1) 100-Percent Data. <http://factfinder.census.gov>.

Figure 10.13.

## San Diego County, California - Total Population of Hispanic American Indians in 2000, U.S. Census 2000 Summary Tape File 1

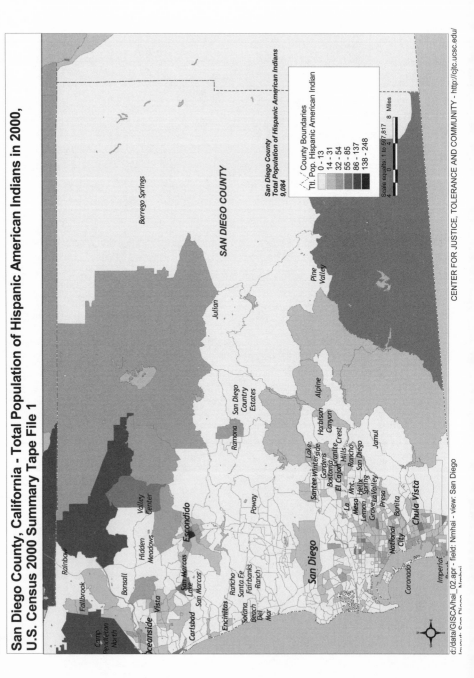

**Figure 10.14.**

## San Diego Urban Areas, California -
## Total Population of Hispanic American Indians in 2000 by Census Tracts

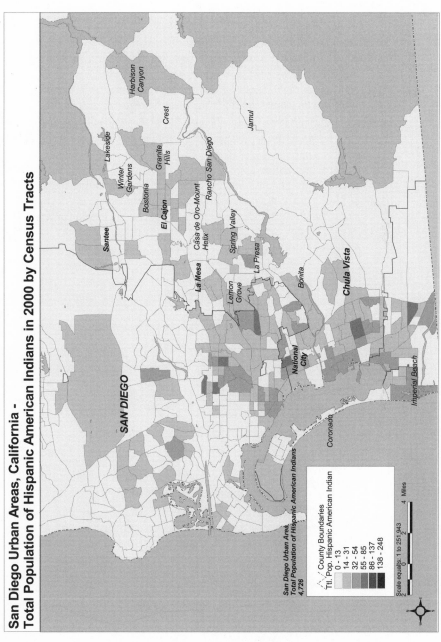

U.S. Census Bureau. "P8, Hispanic or Latino by Race - Universe: Total population." Census 2000 Summary File 1 (SF 1) 100-Percent Data. <http://factfinder.census.gov>.

## References

Grieco, Elizabeth M., and Rachel C. Cassidy. 2001. "Overview of Race and Hispanic Origin," *Census 2000 Brief*. Washington, D.C.: Dept. of Commerce, Economics and Statistics Administration, U.S. Census Bureau, March.

Hubner, John. 2001. "California Overtakes Oklahoma as State with Most American Indians," *San Jose Mercury News*, August 4.

Nobles, Melissa. 2000. *Shades of Citizenship: Race and the Census in Modern Politics*. Palo Alto, Calif.: Stanford University Press.

Oboler, Suzanne. 1995. *Ethnic Labels, Latino Lives: Identity and the Politics of (Re)presentation in the United States*. Minneapolis: University of Minnesota Press.

Rodríguez, Clara. 2000. *Changing Race: Latinos, the Census, and the History of Ethnicity in the United States*. New York: New York University Press.

Tafoya, Sonya. 2003. "Latinos and Racial Identification in California," *California Counts* (Public Policy Institute of California) 4, no. 4, May, at www.ppic.org.

# 11

## Practical Research Strategies for Mexican Indigenous Communities in California Seeking to Assert Their Own Identity

EDWARD KISSAM AND ILENE J. JACOBS

In this chapter we examine the role that data play in the efforts of communities of indigenous Mexicans to forge and assert their own identity, and we describe several practical strategies we believe will enhance these communities' abilities to prevail in a policy-formation and program-planning environment that is increasingly "technical." We believe that it will be important for indigenous organizations to build their capacity to carry out applied research projects. We are not, in any sense, apologists for the status quo, where ethnocentric policy analysis and program evaluation all too often becomes the "gold standard" for public dialogue and decision making about our collective future as communities, as a state, or as a nation. We see the syntax of public dialogue in contemporary America being distorted, where "technical" expertise often is professional narrow-mindedness based on tabular data which characteristically displaces the old-fashioned processes of governance in which decision makers actually had to listen to their constituents and respect their insights.[1]

---

[1] We are no more than interested observers of indigenous communities' modes of governance, but we have no doubt that the community processes of dialogue and decision making under the system of "usos y costumbres" more closely approximate traditional ideals of democracy than the processes of contemporary technocracy. For example, neither city managers nor school superintendents interviewed

We have observed with dismay the spread of a bureaucratic culture that gives ritual homage to "data" in almost magical terms, without understanding how data are generated, and then uses these magical "data" primarily as a negotiating tool in establishing and perpetuating information gaps between "haves" and "have-nots." These concerns escalate for practical social-policy and service-planning issues that affect indigenous communities in California because they are minorities among minorities, "outliers" for better or worse, whose perspectives, concerns, priorities, and needs are obscured by the power of large numbers, where regression to the mean rules supreme, making California's indigenous immigrant populations "marginal" to policy development and civic dialogue about our collective priorities.

We do not believe that new applied research capacity will necessarily make indigenous community organizations "better"; however, it will be useful for them and their advocates to speak the lingua franca of bureaucracy, to have the analytic and communication tools to engage in dialogue and debate—for example, to comment on public agencies' rule making, contest misplaced priorities, correct thoughtless assumptions based on false stereotypes, suggest more innovative and effective social programs, compete for funding, and, where necessary, litigate to assure equitable access to more responsive public services.

In order to do this, we argue, indigenous communities of Mexican and Guatemalan origin will need to articulate their own research agenda and priorities, effectively critique and correct the inaccuracies of conventional wisdom and standard datasets, undertake their own research initiatives using appropriate and affordable research methodologies, and deploy the findings from more authentic research programs in a strategic fashion in order to leverage change in inequitable policies and ineffective social programs.[2] We suggest initiatives through which California indigenous immigrant communities can take the first steps toward research autonomy, an important strand of self-liberation in a society and economy where information rules.

---

by Kissam in his research on the Central Valley Partnership were very eager to hear from their constituents.

[2] Indigenous immigrant communities in the areas of rural California that we know best are primarily of Mexican origin, but these issues are important also for Guatemalan indigenous communities in urban California and in other farmworker areas of the United States such as Florida.

## THE CAUSES AND CONSEQUENCES OF DISTORTED DATA

We present here our analyses of the deficiencies of decennial census data and similar datasets as an empirical foundation for systematically addressing the social program needs of communities of indigenous-origin immigrants in California and the nation.

### Why Focus on Census Data

Data from decennial censuses are, in many circles and official contexts, considered the gold standard for applied social science research, the foundation for community needs assessment, and the framework for social planning. We focus on the problematic "case" of 2000 U.S. Census of Population and Housing data in five rural California communities where we have a fairly good understanding of the causes and consequences of distorted census data on indigenous Mexican immigrants and their families. There are several reasons why we focus on this case even though there are many examples of flawed data that are nevertheless widely used as the basis for decision making in the California context.[3]

The first reason we focus on census data is because they are the basis for developing a wide range of other data series at the state, county, and local levels. Census data have primary use in political representation and federal program planning and funding decisions, but these data are used even more widely by the state, counties, and local communities for a variety of decisions. For example, these data provide the baseline for California Department of Finance population projections throughout the decade, development of local housing elements, and planning related to community development.

The second reason is that the census methodology and data are so respected. Census methodology provides the paradigm for survey research methodology (because it is highly reliable in homogeneous communities

---

[3] Examples of fundamentally flawed data widely used but disastrously ethnocentric include standard data on unemployment (which has been known for decades to have serious problems relating to definitions of "labor force" and methods for measuring numbers of persons seeking employment) and STAR data on educational achievement in California's schools where there is a very high proportion of limited-English students. We have for more than five years sought to convince the Census Bureau to address very basic problems stemming from ethnocentricity — the assumption that employed persons have a single, stable "job" (seldom true for immigrants or, for that matter, researchers) and the assumption that few households have more than six people living together.

and for traditional data needs), yet it epitomizes the ethnocentric assumptions and methodological limitations of standard applied research techniques for generating data on nonstandard populations such as indigenous Mexicans living in California. In the words of the National Academy of Science, the goal for Census 2000 was to be a "mirror which reflects America," but this mirror distorts. A critical problem is that the mirror is used widely as the basis for centralized, "cookie cutter" approaches to social planning. "Minor" flaws in developing an overall snapshot of America — that is, the invisibility of a few hundred thousand farmworkers or a few hundred thousand indigenous immigrants — are considered to be inconsequential at the national level, but they become huge and serious barriers to forging reasonable responses to widespread community problems at the regional or local level.

The third reason is that census data are the "800-pound gorilla" that drives crucial funding decisions by public agencies.[4] A good example is the state Community Development Block Grant program (CDBG), where the funding allocation formula includes a term about the relative number of persons in poverty and another term about the number of overcrowded housing units. Other key data elements in important social programs include number of children in poverty, persons with less than a high school education, and per capita income. Half (thirteen of twenty-five) of the major programs analyzed by the U.S. General Accounting Office (GAO) — including a variety of compensatory education, employment training, health care, and social service programs — rely on such population profile data in addition to population counts for allocating funding.

Table 11.1 lists several programs of particular importance to California communities of Latino immigrants of indigenous origin that are affected due to sample bias when differential census undercount skews California's population profiles. This table also lists the specific funding formula elements where undercount of immigrant farmworkers, and particularly indigenous immigrants, would result in significant funding losses for programs that provide crucial services for their well-being. A full analysis of the social impact of greater or lesser financing for each of these programs is beyond the scope of this chapter. It is clear, however, that many of these

---

[4] Census data have a two-stage process impact on funding: first, they determine the amount of funds flowing from federal programs to state, county, and local community jurisdictions; and second, they determine the activities and projects funded by agencies with the discretion to grant the funds to community-based organizations or various projects.

**Table 11.1. Federal Programs of Importance for Indigenous-Origin Latino Immigrants Impacted by Differential Undercount in the Decennial Census**

| Program Name | National Funding Level, 1998 | Key Element(s) in Funding Formula |
|---|---|---|
| Title I grants to local educational agencies | $7.5 billion | % of children ages 5 to 17 in poverty |
| Medicaid | $104 billion | Per capita personal income |
| WIC | $3.0 billion | # children in families < 185% of poverty level |
| Maternal Child Health Services block grant | $0.6 billion | # children under age 18 in poverty |
| Child Care and Development block grant | $1.0 billion | Per capita income; Population < 5 years of age |
| Community Development Block Grant-entitlement | $2.7 billion | Poverty; # overcrowded housing units |
| Community Development Block Grant – state program | $1.2 billion | Poverty; # overcrowded housing units |
| Home Investment Partnerships program | $1.4 billion | # rental units occupied by poor # problem rental housing units # families in poverty Per capita income of 3-person family |
| JTPA Title II-A and B/WIA | $2.0 billion | # economically disadvantaged individuals ages 22 to 72 with family income below LLSIL |
| EL/Civics (within WIA) | $.07 billion | 10–year growth in LPR immigrants 3–year growth in LPR immigrants |
| WIA/Adult Literacy Act | $.46 billion | # persons aged 16+ without high school diploma |
| Vocational education | $1.0 billion | Population aged 15 to 19 |

*Source:* GAO 1999.

*Note:* Not included are programs in which the only census-driven funding formula element is the state's or local jurisdiction's share of the national population.

WIC = Women, Infants, and Children; TPA = Job Training Partnership Act; WIA = Workforce Investment Act; EL = English Language; LPR = legal permanent resident; LLSIL = lower living standard income level.

programs play a key role in rural California immigrants' ability to live in anything better than marginal, substandard circumstances. It also should be understood that census data drive state, regional, and local planning and resource allocations; accurate census data are as important for these purposes as they are for the allocation of federal funds.[5]

When assessing the potential impact of census undercount on rural communities with high proportions of immigrants and on the social integration of immigrants in general, it is particularly important to recognize the significance of federal formulas that allocate funding to impacted counties or local communities. Although a census undercount tends to "smooth out" in larger units, the small communities where immigrants are concentrated and which have the highest relative proportion of immigrants are likely to have the deepest "pockets" of "mega-undercount" (when the undercount exceeds 10 percent of total population).

The systematic bias that affects the reliability of census data for numbers of children and characteristics of children in communities with high concentrations of indigenous-origin immigrants is one of our primary concerns. Our concern arises in part because programs for children are so important to immigrant families but also because census data on children are particularly vulnerable to systematic undercount (an issue discussed in more detail below).

Title I funding is of particular consequence, both because of the importance of compensatory education as a mechanism for supporting educational services to immigrant children (both Migrant Education and "regular" Title I services) and because of the specific provisions of the funding formula. Title I funding includes Basic Grants plus a subprogram of Concentration Grants and Targeted Grants that direct funding to the most seriously disadvantaged counties in the country. Virtually all California children of indigenous origin should be served by programs that are supported entirely or primarily with Title I funding.

Funding for child and maternal health is another important issue. There continue to be serious constraints on indigenous immigrants' access to

---

[5] A good example of the ways in which the census data affect state funding is in the county-administered programs for families with preschool-age children that receive annually about $500 million in state funding ($492 million in 2001–2002). County commissions have funding discretion, but their decisions about which groups to fund are in principle determined by data that provide indicators of the need to serve various identified subpopulations, such as Mixteco-origin families in Madera County.

Medicaid (Medi-Cal), which is restricted to citizens and legal permanent residents. Nevertheless, federal funding for this program and other maternal and child health services remains important to the degree that these programs support service provision for all California-born children, including children born to nonresident mothers.

Several programs with census-driven funding formulas (such as CDBG) fund community infrastructure as well as programs that directly affect the well-being of individuals and families in a particular population. The negative impact of systematic bias in decennial census data in communities with high concentrations of indigenous-origin immigrants is likely to be particularly severe because the crowded and substandard housing that is so prevalent in these areas contributes in an important way to the census undercount.

Approximately $700 million in annual funding for programs serving migrant and seasonal farmworkers (Migrant Education, Migrant Health, Workforce Investment Act–funded employment training) can be affected by census profile data, even though their funding formulas do not rely primarily on census data.

## Causes of Differential Census Undercount—Theoretical Framework

It was not until the 1970s that serious attention was given to understanding the causes of census undercount. And only in the past fifteen years has adequate attention been paid to what might be termed the *structural* causes of undercount—that is, ways in which the decennial census research methodology interacts with contemporary social systems to give an undercount. Our contribution to the field of applied policy research on census undercount has been to recognize and demonstrate that, in the context of extremely divergent social and economic conditions, the interaction among these multiple factors would yield what we call "mega-undercount"—the underrepresentation of immigrant, particularly farmworker, communities that fall not into a "debatable" range of 3 to 7 percent undercount, but rather into a range of 10 to 50 percent. Not only does this range of undercount lead to problems in quantifying the numbers of persons in a community of migrant and seasonal farmworkers, but it also grossly distorts the population and community profile (Kissam, Gabbard, and Martin 1993; Kissam, Padilla, and Jacobs 1996; Jacobs and Kissam 2001). This structural analysis of undercount is extremely important for California's indigenous immigrants and the communities in which they live, because their census participation is negatively affected by a broad range of social factors:

- quality of U.S. Postal Service address lists/Census Bureau address lists;

- housing conditions (low visibility, illegal, subdivided, "unusual");

- housing conditions (crowded);

- housing segregation ("linguistically isolated");

- limited-English ability and limited literacy;

- prevalence of recent immigration;

- prevailing patterns of employment and working conditions;

- quality of census operations (recruitment/hiring and training);

- quality of census operations (non-response follow-up, NRFU); and

- quality of census operations (procedures for enumerating migrant labor camps).

## Causes of Census Undercount: Immigrant Communities as Extreme Cases

Our initial work in the late 1980s on census undercount of migrants and seasonal farmworkers recognized that the structural causes of undercount, which had been acknowledged for urban areas, are also present in rural areas. This recognition was perhaps easier in California, where "farming" is less about American folklore and more about the factories in the fields described by Carey McWilliams more than fifty years ago, less a matter of finding remote residences and more a matter of dealing with communities that Michael Kearney and others describe as part of a global phenomenon of "peripheralization of the core" (see Kearney and Nagangast 1989; Sassen 1991).

We adopted a theoretical model of census undercount stemming from the work of David Fein (Fein 1989; Fein and West 1988) and a team of Census Bureau researchers. The model was based on data collected in the "Causes of Undercount" Survey (CUS) as part of the 1986 Los Angeles Test of Adjustment-Related Operations (TARO, a large-scale test census that took place in inner-city areas of Los Angeles). Fein's research showed very deep pockets of undercount of Hispanics in East Los Angeles—on the order of 20 percent, or four to five times greater than reported at the national level. We recognized that the structural (social system) analysis of the causes of undercount demonstrated by Fein had particular relevance for understanding the undercount of immigrants in general and the undercount of farmworkers in particular. In their 1993 analysis, Kissam, Gabbard, and Martin used Fein's logistic regression model to generate the "synthetic estimate" of approximately 50 percent probability of census omission for the typical California farmworker household. We then compared this synthetic estimate to actual farm labor data from the 1990 census (Public Use Microdata Samples; PUMS) and labor market data (Unemployment Insurance Records; UI). When adjusted for migrant and seasonal farm worker (MSFW) migrants not in California on Census Day, the estimates and extant data sources were in close agreement, showing that less than half of California farmworkers were identified in the decennial census.

## Components of the Census Undercount of Immigrants in Rural Communities

We discuss below the distinct factors implicated in census undercount in both inner-city neighborhoods with high concentrations of immigrants and in rural communities where indigenous immigrants to California are concentrated. This discussion provides a conceptual map demonstrating the cascade of events that generate the "mega-undercount."

Component 1 of the rural California undercount of indigenous immigrants originates in the reliance on a March "snapshot" for generating community profiles. What is needed to provide a full portrait of the population is a "movie" showing migration patterns throughout the year. Transnational migration patterns indicate that a significant number of back-and-forth migrants are in Mexico at the time of the census snapshot. Ironically, among Mixtec farmworker populations, the subgroup of transnational migrants that is most likely to disappear from the census snapshot comprises earlier cohorts of immigrants who adjusted their status under the Immigration Reform and Control Act of 1986 (IRCA) and are now able to travel more easily between California and their home villages.[6] Although we have limited data on this, our research showed that 26 percent of the farmworkers in Parlier were out of the country when the 1990 decennial census took place (Griffith, Kissam, et al. 1995).

---

[6] This is a good example of an area of research where indigenous communities are better prepared than outsiders to investigate the proportions of individuals and families who are not in the United States during the census time frame. The National Agricultural Worker Survey sample provides a good basis for estimates of proportions of farmworkers who are not in the United States in March, but it does not have a large enough subsample of indigenous farmworkers to make such analysis possible.

Component 2 of the undercount stems from Census Bureau problems in assuring that census forms are received by persons living in "low-visibility" crowded housing in rural California communities and that delivered forms are returned. Specific reasons identified for missing entire housing units include factors that relate to census implementation (address list omission, erroneous deletion of real addresses) and factors that relate to the social context of hard-to-count populations (physical characteristics that affect unit visibility, such as hidden housing and illegally subdivided housing).

Our census evaluation research revealed that these problems vary greatly from community to community. Some communities with substantial concentrations of Mixtecs—such as Arvin—have little "low-visibility" housing, while somewhat similar communities—such as Parlier—with significant populations of Mixtec and Triqui residents have a good deal of "low visibility" housing (Jacobs and Kissam 2001; Sherman et al. 1997). An extreme case of low-visibility housing resulting in census undercount is a North San Diego County encampment well known to Oaxacan migrants who have come to California over the past fifteen years. Although California Rural Legal Assistance (CRLA) had brought this encampment to the attention of local census office staff, it never was enumerated. The "social cause" component of census undercount distorts the sample of persons so that the census underrepresents the most economically and socially marginal populations, such as recently arrived transnational migrants from minority communities in indigenous areas of Mexico and Guatemala. These migrants include, for example, Chatinos and Amuzgueños (one of the groups residing in the hidden camp the CRLA enumerated).

Traditional census research tends to attribute undercounts to census respondents; our research, however, has emphasized systemic causes. One area in which respondents do contribute to census enumeration problems is in language ability; a respondent who has little or no English-speaking ability and little schooling has difficultly completing the English-language and highly formatted census form.[7] This problem surely contributed to some households' failure to complete and return the census forms, but this should have triggered non-response follow-up by a Census Bureau enu-

---

[7] Forms' formatting conventions present special difficulties for low-literate respondents. Low-literate readers have difficulty understanding procedural directions for forms completions even when the Spanish terms, such as *renglón*, are correct.

merator.[8] We were disappointed to discover in Census 2000 in rural California that some households that were apparently *in* the census sampling frame (houses to which a census form had been mailed) but did not return the form were not enumerated because of a failure in the local census office non-response follow-up procedures.[9]

Component 3 of the undercount stems from difficulties in listing everyone who lives in the housing unit on the census form. Previous census researchers had suggested that the main problem was that census respondents "forgot" persons, such as newly born infants. Our research in Census 2000 showed that the main problem was that the census form, which secured information on up to six persons in the housing unit, did not permit otherwise willing census respondents to list all of their family members or members of another family who shared their house, apartment, or trailer.

Component 4 of the undercount involves the design of the census form, in which bureaucratically defined concepts of "race," "Hispanic origin," and "ethnicity" gave rise to such an extraordinarily strange survey instrument design that tabulation for rural communities might be worthless.[10] We are not yet certain that we know the full dynamics of census efforts to represent ethnic minorities among rural Latinos, but it appears that in most of the rural communities where indigenous immigrants are settled, the census data make it impossible to recognize four out of five indigenous households.[11]

---

[8] A good deal of Census Bureau research has shown a correlation between high rates of non-return of forms by mail and census undercount, generally believed to stem from not fully understood modes of system breakdown in local office operations.

[9] This was very surprising because the mailback rate was relatively good even in rural communities; we believe this stems in part from the fact that so many of the "hard to count" households were omitted from the census address lists. In cases where there was a contact by a Census Bureau enumerator, most, but not all, respondents we talked to were pleased with the help they had received in completing the form. Problems with enumerators simply stemmed from cases where enumerators did not speak Spanish.

[10] Hispanic respondents' confusion about the census question for "race" resulted in absolutely useless breakdowns of census respondents listing their "race" as "White" or "other." Arvin, a community where we know that almost all Hispanics are of Mexican origin, had 40 percent of the Hispanic respondents list their race as "White," while about 60 percent listed their race as "other."

[11] We know that Arvin has a significant concentration of Mixtecs and a well-established network of immigrants from San Juan Mixtepec, but census data suggest there are only 280 persons living in households that speak Mixtec or another

## Census Undercount in Rural California Communities with High Concentrations of Indigenous Immigrants

This section focuses on findings in five communities examined as part of CRLA's research on Census 2000 in rural California. All of these communities—Oxnard, Arvin, Madera, Parlier, and Santa Maria—are known to have relatively high concentrations of Oaxacan indigenous immigrants, most of whom are farmworkers. The 1991 California Institute for Rural Studies (CIRS) survey of Oaxacan village networks in California enumerated more Oaxacan immigrants in Madera than in any other California community (2,444, or more than a third of all *oaxaqueños* enumerated in rural California). Santa Maria was recorded as having 365 *oaxaqueños*, Arvin, 240, and Parlier, 33. Surprisingly, only 11 *oaxaqueños* were found in Oxnard (Runsten and Kearney 1994).

The variations in undercount by community suggest that in some cases efforts by census personnel and local partner organizations served to mitigate problems of undercount. Our finding that undercount varies substantially from community to community underscores how problematic census quality problems can be for data users. This problem stems from the recognition that a single adjustment factor cannot be easily applied to all of these communities, although they might be considered to fall into a single stratum—"rural farmworker communities."[12] Table 11.2 reports our estimate of undercount in the five case study communities with high concentrations of indigenous immigrants.

The extent of undercount varies substantially among the communities, as do the components of undercount—that is, the relative contribution of total and partial household omission to the overall undercount. Varying patterns of undercount are an important consideration when assessing the reliability of census data at the local community level because each undercount pattern gives rise to a different bias. Low census quality in the Oxnard sample block, for example, stems entirely from the failure to secure information on persons aged 7 through 15 in large, complex, and crowded households. The Parlier undercount, in contrast, stems primarily from

---

indigenous language—about 2.5 percent of the Hispanics (we believe the actual proportion is at least 10 percent).

[12] The strategy needed to yield "best estimates" of the actual population and population characteristics of persons in each community would be to generate synthetic estimates using multivariate regression models such as the one developed by David Fein (1989) on the basis of the Causes of Undercount Survey in the 1986 Census Test.

omission of low-visibility housing. The Parlier community contains more "back houses," which long-term settled farmworkers rent to transnational migrants and socioeconomically peripheral residents, while in Oxnard these peripheral subpopulations share crowded single-family dwellings with the "primary" family unit.[13] Arguably, the variations in housing accommodations that affect the nature of census undercount stem in large measure from differences in the mix of migration networks in each community, as well as the history of each network's migration and its success in coming to control housing resources.

**Table 11.2. Extent and Type of Census Undercount in CRLA Case Study Communities**

| Community | Study Block Population | Overall Undercount in Study Block (N) | Not Enumerated, Total Household Omission (N) | Not Enumerated, Partial Household Omission (N) |
|---|---|---|---|---|
| Oxnard | 161 | 34.1% | 9.3% | 24.8% |
| | | (55) | (15) | (40) |
| Santa Maria | 128 | 10.9% | 8.6% | 2.3% |
| | | (14) | (11) | (3) |
| Arvin[a] | 109 | 13.8% | 6.4% | 7.4% |
| | | (15) | (7) | (8) |
| Parlier[b] | 170 | 37.6% | 27.6% | 10.0% |
| | | (64) | (47) | (17) |
| Madera[c] | 157 | 19.8% | 15.3% | 4.5% |
| | | (31) | (24) | (7) |

*Source:* Jacobs and Kissam 2001.

[a] Excludes five unresolved households, two due to refusals and three due to non-availability of residents after multiple visits.

[b] Excludes four unresolved households due to refusals. The analysis also includes four "ambiguous" households in which there were inconsistencies but where we considered it possible to impute census status. We tabulated two of these households as having been enumerated and two as not having been enumerated.

[c] Assumes that seven in-movers who arrived after the questionnaire had been returned had actually arrived after April 1. Thus the analysis excludes these in-movers from the sample as they were not and should not have been enumerated.

---

[13] In Parlier, the majority of the landlords are mestizo former farmworker families from Guanajuato or Michoacán, while the majority of the transnational migrants are *oaxaqueños*.

PARTIAL HOUSEHOLD OMISSION

The CRLA community case studies show two causes of *partial* household omission, neither of them related to household residents' "forgetting" to list persons living there, as some census researchers have suggested. The first and most serious source of partial household omission is the fact that the census form has space to provide population profile information for only six persons living in the housing unit. This meant that in any household with more than six persons—in the study communities and in other communities with crowded housing—some persons were at risk of not being enumerated. We specifically asked all respondents in the study blocks whether they had returned a census form and, if they lived in a household of more than six persons, whether someone from the Census Bureau had come to ask for information on the people for whom no personal characteristics had been reported. We heard of no case in which there was follow-up to determine the characteristics of the missing persons.

The second type of household omission is related to the prevalence of "complex" households occupied by several distantly related families, unrelated families, or "unaccompanied male transnational migrants." Census forms were typically filled out to reflect the composition of the primary family unit—for example, a couple and their two children. The secondary family unit was totally omitted in some of these households, even if the primary family unit numbered fewer than six persons. We are less certain about the circumstances in households consisting entirely of unaccompanied male migrants, but it is possible that in these households (which also have an internal social structure based on smaller social/economic units of men clustered on the basis of extended family or village network ties) some of the residents were omitted.[14]

TOTAL HOUSEHOLD OMISSION

There are also two types of *total* household omission in the community case studies. The first and more systematic pattern of total household omission occurred when the housing unit appeared not to have been in the Master Address File in the first place. These dwellings included backyard trailers, shacks used as "back houses," housing quarters that were structurally part of a single-family home, with their own entrance ("*cuartitos*"), camper shells, and sheds. These omissions systematically skew the com-

---

[14] We have tabulated these households as being partial household omissions only when there were more than six persons residing in the dwelling.

munity profile to make the most economically and socially marginal portions of the overall community "invisible" in census data. The second type of total household omission arises when there is mail delivery and a census form is delivered to a dwelling, but it is not returned and there is no non-response follow-up. We know little about the dynamics of this component of undercount except that it appears to be fairly random. Non-response follow-up was much better in some communities (such as Arvin and Santa Maria) than in others (like Oxnard), but we know only that this type of census problem arises from some breakdown within census operations.

## Bias in Community Profiles as Result of Census Undercount

Our primary concerns about census data have centered on the problems that arise when differential undercount systematically skews the population profile of low-income communities. These concerns are real and practical. Flawed census-based population profiles create substantial problems for local jurisdictions seeking to secure equitable access to program funding targeted to provide services to the very subpopulations that are underrepresented in the census-based population profile, as well as creating problems for program managers who are seriously attempting to adapt program designs to respond to community needs.

Table 11.3 shows the kinds of sample bias associated with each type of census omission observed in the CRLA case study communities. The most serious consequence we have observed is the notable underrepresentation of children, which occurs when householders in large families systematically list persons on the census form, beginning with the couple filling out the form and then, usually, list children in decreasing order of age.

## Differential Undercount within Rural California Communities

The sample blocks in the CRLA case study communities of census undercount were chosen because community researchers believed they were "at risk" for possible census undercount. There appears to be an even higher risk of undercount for farmworkers than for other types of families in predominantly immigrant neighborhoods. Not all farmworkers are of indigenous origin, but farmworker undercount remains a serious problem for indigenous Mexican immigrants in rural California because they are concentrated in farmwork.

In the Causes of Undercount Survey in Los Angeles, neighborhoods with more recent immigrants had the most serious undercount, but even

**Table 11.3. The Impacts of Differential Undercount on Indigenous Immigrant Community Profile and Social Program Funding**

| Type of Omission | Types of Persons Typically Left Out | Impact on Social Program Funding |
|---|---|---|
| Total household omission; dwelling not in Master Address File | Transnational migrants, unaccompanied males | Moderate downward bias in estimates of prevalence of households in poverty |
| | Transnational migrants, young families | Strong downward bias in estimates of *extremely* poor individuals and families; for example, < 40% of poverty guidelines |
| | Very poor families | |
| | Indigenous persons not linked to locally dominant network (such as Mayas) | Strong downward bias in estimates of educationally disadvantaged; for example, % of population with < high school |
| Total household omission; failure of NRFU | Settled immigrants with very limited literacy or English ability and their dependents | Slight downward bias in estimated prevalence of crowded housing |
| | | Slight downward bias in estimates of educational attainment |
| Partial household omission; large nuclear family | Underrepresentation of preschool and elementary school–age children | Strong downward bias in estimates of number of low-income children, children targeted in compensatory education, preschoolers |
| | | Moderate downward bias in estimates of prevalence of crowded housing |
| Partial household omission, complex household | Underrepresentation of recent immigrants, especially *arrimados* (non-relatives) | Substantial underrepresentation of preschool and elementary school–age children, especially those with limited English |
| | | Downward bias in community-level estimates of prevalence of crowded housing |

among recent immigrants, undercount probably varies greatly.[15] Based on hundreds of discussions with recently arrived teenage migrants, we know that different sending villages have more or less developed networks and that persons in established networks have better access to housing than others. This probably skews the census profile of different indigenous networks. For example, migrants from communities with long migration histories—such as Juxtlahuaca, San Juan Mixtepec, Tlapa, or Santa María Tindu—may be better enumerated, while migrants from more remote areas with more recent migration are less well enumerated, thereby skewing the cultural-linguistic profile of indigenous migrant communities in California. Table 11.4 reports the demographic composition of the community case study blocks and the extent of farmworker undercount in each.

Table 11.4 shows that even within communities at high risk of census undercount—due to widespread prevalence of low-visibility and crowded housing, recent immigration, limited English-speaking ability, and low literacy—census undercount is concentrated primarily in the farmworker population. Even in households where farmworkers' dependent children are U.S. citizens and fluent in English, their parents' status as farmworkers means that these children will have a higher risk of undercount than other similar children, primarily because they tend to live in more crowded, low-visibility housing.

## The Case of Two Informal Labor Camps, California Destinations for Indigenous Migrants

This section examines case studies that were done of two labor camps, both illegal encampments controlled by San Diego County tomato producers known to rely primarily on transnational migrants to make up their labor force.[16] The CRLA notified the local census office about these camps, but

---

[15] It is assumed that the very high levels of census undercount in neighborhoods and communities with high levels of recent immigration stem primarily from fear of government authorities. We believe that substandard housing conditions, low literacy, and language problems have more to do with undercount in these neighborhoods than respondent refusal. The Los Angeles CUS was not designed to determine which immigrant networks were represented in the study area nor to explore the relationship between migration network maturity and undercount.

[16] CRLA consultant Anna García first became aware of these encampments in the course of field research she was conducting for the Center for U.S.-Mexican Studies at the University of California, San Diego in the mid-1980s. Two of the CRLA community researchers had lived in these camps in the 1980s when they first came as migrants from Oaxaca to California.

Table 11.4. Demographic Profile of Case Study Community Sample Blocks and Extent of Farmworker Undercount in Each

| Community | Oxnard | Santa Maria | Arvin | Parlier | Madera |
|---|---|---|---|---|---|
| Percent Hispanic | 94% | 95% | 98% | 100% | 91% |
| Percent limited-English-proficiency adults | 78% | 43% | 78% | 65% | 41% |
| Mean years of schooling (adults 18+) | 5.4 | 8.1 | 5.3 | 8.2 | 6.6 |
| Mean household size | 5.9 | 5.8 | 3.9 | 4.6 | 4.0 |
| Number of farmworker households in block (percent of total) | 16 (55%) | 19 (73%) | 17 (61%) | 20 (49%) | 23 (55%) |
| Number of farmworker households totally or partially omitted (percent of total) | 6 (37%) | 5 (26%) | 5 (38%) | 11 (55%) | 6 (26%) |
| Problem households in block that are farmworker households (percent) | 6/9 (67%) | 5/6 (83%) | 5/5 (100%) | 11/12 (92%) | 6/7 (86%) |
| Ratio of problem farmworker households to problem non-farmworker households | 1.4:1 | 1.8:1 | — | 11.5:1 | 4.1:1 |

Source: Jacobs and Kissam 2001.

the camps were never properly enumerated with the procedures designed for "special places-migrant camps." The encampments could not be enumerated using standard procedures because they were hidden and had no mail delivery. Because the populations living in these camps and similar concealed housing tend to be recently arrived indigenous transnational migrants, the failure to enumerate them has very serious consequences for data users interested in the growing ethnic diversity of California. Table 11.5 provides a summary profile of the ethnic/linguistic and demographic composition of the two encampments.

**Table 11.5. Profile of Nonenumerated Residents of Two Hidden Labor Camps in San Diego County**

| Characteristics | Camp 1 (N = 69) | Camp 2 (N = 39) | Overall (N = 108) |
|---|---|---|---|
| PRIMARY LANGUAGE | | | |
| Spanish only | 9% | 18% | 12% |
| Mixteco | 54 | – | 35 |
| Triqui or Amuzgo | 7 | 82 | 34 |
| Mixteco, Triqui, Amuzgo, and Spanish | 29 | 48 | 19 |
| Limited Spanish | 72 | 33 | 58 |
| EDUCATIONAL ATTAINMENT | | | |
| 3 years of school or less | 70 | 28 | 55 |
| 4–6 years of school | 23 | 67 | 38 |
| 6+ years of school | 7 | 5 | 7 |

*Source*: Jacobs and Kissam 2001.

## Census Long-Form Data on Mexican Immigrants of Indigenous Origin

Ambiguities in the SF-3 tabulations[17] of Census 2000 long-form data on the five CRLA case study communities that we know have high concentrations of Latinos of indigenous origin show that the decennial census "mirror" provides only a blurred outline of the true picture of these communities. This review shows that the fourth component of census undercount (misidentification) provides an additional and important source of error in profiles of indigenous Mexican populations in rural California. Table 11.6

---

[17] Summary File 3 data include information on household income, occupation, education, and mode of travel to work.

Table 11.6. Summary File 3 (SF-3) Data from Census 2000 as Basis for Profile of Mexican Indigenous Immigrants

| Case Study Community | Number of Hispanics Aged 5 and Above | Number of Persons Aged Five and Older in Household with Amerindian Language (percent of Hispanics five and older)[a] | Number of Possible Indigenous Ancestry (percent of total Hispanic)[b] | Number of Recent Immigrants (1995–2000) | Recent Immigrants as Percent of Hispanics |
|---|---|---|---|---|---|
| Arvin | 10,046 | 281 (2.8%) | 1,717 (13.3%) | 1,508 | 13.2% |
| Madera | 25,667 | 471 (1.8%) | 6,838 (15.8%) | 3,469 | 11.8 |
| Santa Maria | 40,469 | 382 (0.9%) | 12,391 (27%) | 5,527 | 12.0 |
| Oxnard | 101,235 | 440 (0.4%) | 24,365 (21.5%) | 12,439 | 11.0 |
| Parlier | 9,725 | 93 (1.0%) | 1,722 (15.9%) | 933 | 8.6 |

[a] Tabulated based on "other" languages as tabulated in SF-3, that is, non–Indo European, non–Asian Pacific Islander, non-English.
[b] Tabulated based on ancestry being listed as unclassified or not reported.

reports our tabulations of relevant data for the case study communities from the CRLA study.

The problems that compromise the reliability of the census data presented in table 11.6 provide a striking example of the problems inherent in ethnocentric research within the context of California's ethnically and linguistically diverse rural communities. The tabulations of languages spoken at home list "other" as the closest classification for any Amerindian language of Mexico or Guatemala. "Other" language is defined as non-European, non-Asian, Pacific Islander, and non-English, so we can assume with some certainty that most persons in households where some "other" language is spoken are speakers of Mixteco or another Oaxacan language.[18] In Oaxacan indigenous households, where the languages spoken at home usually include Spanish and a native indigenous language, we cannot consider "language spoken at home" as a reliable indicator of the ethnicity of the household since it is very likely that many of these households were classified as Spanish-speaking households.

The Census 2000 data on "ancestry" (the Census Bureau's closest approximation of ethnicity) provide a similarly uncertain picture of indigenous *mexicanos* in our rural case study communities because no classification exists for indigenous Mexican ethnic groups and because "unclassified and not reported are tabulated together" in reports on specific ancestry. Although the classified "ancestries" include such esoteric categories as "Carpatho Rusyn," "Celtic," "Bermudan," and "Pennsylvania German," Mexican and Guatemalan ancestries are not tabulated, neither at the level of linguistic-cultural identification (such as Triqui, Tzeltzal) nor at the regional/pan-linguistic level (Oaxaqueño, Maya). Based on census data, therefore, we have no certain idea how many Mixtecs, Triquis, or other Mexican indigenous immigrants there might be in these communities.

In the case of Arvin, we know (from census data) that the lower bound for numbers of Mixtecs is 281 and the upper bound is 1,717; this is the range for the count of persons 5+ years of age speaking a non-Asian, non-European, non-English language.[19] Given what we know about the propor-

---

[18] Other possible speakers of Amerindian languages might be U.S. or Canadian American Indians, but the data on race and country of birth suggest that most of these "other" language households are indeed Mexicans of indigenous origin.

[19] While the California Department of Education language census generally provides sound, up-to-date information often useful in profiling populations, there appear to be problems in identifying households such as Mixtec households. (Only eight Mixteco-speaking children are identified in the latest data on the Arvin Elementary School District from the California Department of Education, and

tions of Mixtecs in the farm labor force, the ratio of farmworker dependents to farmworkers, and the local economy of Arvin, it is very unlikely that there could be fewer than 1,000 persons of Mixtec ethnicity in this community.[20]

The CIRS Survey of Mixtecs identified 2,444 Oaxacans in Madera in 1991, and the Census 2000 data suggest a lower bound of 471 and an upper bound of 6,838; the ambiguity introduced by the Census Bureau's ethnographic incompetence is extremely unfortunate. Based on what we know about international migration networks, the increasing representation of farmworkers from Oaxacan networks in the California farm labor market, and Madera's key role as an upstream migration node in Pacific Seaboard networks, we consider it extremely unlikely that there were fewer than 4,000 Oaxacan-origin immigrants in Madera in 2000. Recent survey work by Kissam in the Madera area suggests that *at least* 31 percent of low-income *mexicanos* in the Madera area are of Oaxacan indigenous origin.[21] This would yield an estimate of approximately 3,600 indigenous-origin *mexicanos* in Madera. However, using birthplace as an indicator of ethnicity, it would seem that an even higher proportion of Spanish-speaking households in Madera are of indigenous origin.[22]

---

only sixty-two speakers of Mixteco are identified in Madera Unified School District.)

[20] Kissam's "New Pluralism" research team recently completed a household survey of Arvin that includes detailed information on languages spoken in the 119 surveyed households.

[21] This tabulation is based on information about indigenous languages spoken at home. Listed languages include Mixteco, Zapoteco, and Triqui. Data were collected as part of the California Endowment/Tri-Valley Tobacco Survey conducted for Radio Bilingüe (Kissam, Intili, and García 2003). The analysis presented here is based on a subsample of eighty-five survey respondents interviewed at the Madera swap meet in June–July 2002.

[22] Listed birthplaces elicited in the survey which we know to be Oaxacan indigenous villages included San Juan Copala, Huajuapan de León, Juxtlahuaca, Nochixtlán, Magdalena Loxxicha, Miahuatlán, Ometepec, Putla de Guerrero, San Agustín Atenango, San Miguel Tlacotepec, San Sebastián del Monte, San Sebastián Ixtapa, Santa Catarina Yutandu, Santa María Tindu, Santa María Tlacotepec, Santa Rosa Caxtlahuaca, Santiago Naranjas, Tlaxiaco, Tequesquitlán, and Tlaxiaco.

## Overall Assessment of Census 2000 Data on Mexican Immigrants of Indigenous Origin Living in Rural California Communities

Our research on Census 2000 operations in five communities in rural California with higher-than-average concentrations of *mexicanos* of indigenous origin, primarily *oaxaqueños*, suggests that a cascade of failures in research methodology (components 1 through 3 of census undercount) and reporting (component 4) makes the available data on indigenous *mexicanos* in these communities highly unreliable. Overall undercount in neighborhoods where most indigenous immigrant individuals and families live ranged from 11 to 38 percent. The flawed methodology for identifying indigenous-origin Mexican immigrants further compromises reliability of the official data. Our review of Census 2000 long-form data in communities that we know have concentrations of indigenous-origin immigrants suggests that the most conservative estimates of numbers of indigenous-origin immigrants—if we trust the SF-3 data—fall midway between the flawed possible indicators of indigenous Mexican ethnicity (that is, household language classified as non-European/non-Asian/non-English, and ancestry not reported or classified). Although Census 2000 data indicate that indigenous-origin persons constitute somewhere between 3 and 13 percent of Arvin's population and between 2 and 16 percent of Madera's population, more precise estimates of indigenous-origin residents are around 8 percent for Arvin and 10 percent for Madera.

Because total and partial household omission skew the profile when the indigenous population is enumerated in different ways, the divergent modes in which census methodology fails in rural communities make it very difficult to generate reliable "synthetic estimates" to correct sample bias in the census profile of indigenous *mexicanos*. It is possible to make qualitative statements about the types of sample bias that result from ethnocentric census research methodology (such as underrepresentation of younger and more recently arrived transnational migrants, underrepresentation of the youngest children in the large, complex households in which the poorest indigenous immigrants live). A review of the SF-3 data reveals that what should have been easily avoidable definitional problems in fact present the greatest threats to the integrity of census data on indigenous Mexican populations in rural California.

What we know about the Madera case suggests that improvement in the severely flawed census data is both possible and necessary. Even imperfect (but affordable) research methodologies can be used to generate population profiles that, despite their technical limitations, compete favorably with the grossly distorted profiles of indigenous-origin immigrant populations that emerge from the technically sophisticated but theoretically flawed research that gives rise to decennial census data. This, in turn, suggests that indigenous community groups might be able to initiate their own research programs to generate a faithful image of their communities, an authentic mirror of their own lives. The next section of this chapter describes options and promising strategies to turn this possibility into reality.

## REPAIRING THE FLAWED CENSUS 2000 MIRROR

What are the steps to improve the distorted profile of indigenous communities of Mexican and Guatemalan immigrants in California? We believe the most challenging yet most important next step is for indigenous communities to identify their own research priorities and define their own research agenda. Such an agenda should be cognizant of relevant "mainstream" research agendas, on the one hand; but on the other, it should not be unduly influenced by externally identified priorities. The resulting research agenda should be "authentic"; it should truly reflect concerns within the indigenous immigrant community. Such an agenda should prove attractive to the more sophisticated philanthropic institutions and public-sector agencies.[23]

### Processes for Developing an Authentic Research Agenda

Applied research is too important to be left to experts and funders, though neither experts nor potential funders should be ignored. They control resources that are key for the success of such a research agenda, and they are legitimate stakeholders in the outcomes. It would be wise to articulate and implement a structured and broad-based process of community consultation to define the agenda, its priorities, and its sequence.

We believe that the basis for a successful community consultation process is to recognize that "ordinary people" are very good at *qualitative* assessments of their lives and the social dynamics of their communities (though they would be hard-pressed to provide *quantitative* estimates of

---

[23] One policy perspective is that part of the value of investments in community-based organizations stems not simply from the activities that such funding permits but from the "value added" by such organizations' knowledge of the environment in which they are working and the difficult-to-measure contribution of their commitment to their organizational mission.

even widely observed "issues" such as the arrival rate of new migrants to California, prevalence of substandard housing, extent of underemployment in a given community, or problems in accessing competent health care). The community consultation processes must tackle real problems so that the guidance the "community" provides is not simply a generic ratification of fairly evident priorities and so that the full and diverse range of community interests and opinion can be heard.

## Articulating a Practical, Community-Oriented Research Agenda

There are many practical questions about how best to implement a community consultation process in order to provide the foundation for indigenous organizations to further refine and "market" such an agenda. We do not address these here; however, we recommend exploring five conceptually distinct research agendas:

### BASIC POPULATION RESEARCH ON INDIGENOUS IMMIGRANTS

Basic research is critically needed, both to correct the distorted picture of California's rural and urban indigenous immigrant communities and to fill in key gaps in the picture. Based on our census research, we strongly recommend priorities such as improving estimates of the number of children in families of indigenous origin and determining key issues relevant to social policy, such as the proportions of undocumented, legal permanent resident, and citizen children in these families. The ultimate research priorities should be set by the indigenous communities.

There is a broad spectrum of competing "basic research" priorities, due in part to the gaping holes in census research. It would be very useful to understand the ethnic diversity of indigenous immigrants to California. There is consensus that the diversity of indigenous immigrants coming to California is increasing, yet there is little sense about which village networks and languages are represented. These questions boil down to asking whether a community-defined research agenda should include the full range of "standard" data items collected in a survey like the census (such as grandparents who care for children),[24] irrespective of immediate rele-

---

[24] The criterion for including or dropping questions from Census 2000 was articulated narrowly in terms of legislatively mandated questions and comparability with earlier data series, rather than priorities based on the utility of the resulting data for sound program planning. This is the source of the questions on grand-

vance to current issues. Or should indigenous community organizations' research agendas focus on addressing basic questions that are *not* asked by the census but *are* important in community life (such as information on the multiple types of economic activities households carry out to survive in low-income communities and information on the frequency and duration of returns to Mexico, whether to carry out *cargos* or to participate in the *tequio* or to deal with family problems)? We believe that the indigenous "basic research" program should drop particularly American preoccupations (such as the specific sources of public assistance income, type of fuel used for cooking) and add new items and analyses (such as information on limited-Spanish/limited-English persons in indigenous-origin immigrant households).

## TARGETED RESEARCH ON ISSUES/PROBLEMS INDIGENOUS IMMIGRANTS FACE

Targeted research is the area where community research will be crucial because of the existence of legitimate competing agendas. For example, standard data sources do a very poor job of distinguishing the problems of settled immigrants from those faced by recently arrived, predominantly male, and predominantly young transnational migrants. Should understanding these young men's needs be a priority? Are these immigrants really willing to forgo decent housing (as agricultural employers argue) in order to maximize their earnings and remittances? How often do they migrate, and what key problems do they face in the course of migrating? How often do they go without access to health care and why? Is exposure to HIV a major problem (as some researchers fear)? Might it be wiser to focus on the problems facing immigrants of indigenous origin who are in the process of settling in California? Do indigenous-origin children and youths face ethnic discrimination in their schooling, and if so, to what extent? To what extent does the language barrier compromise the health care of indigenous-origin women from communities where Spanish is not spoken, and what are the most prevalent problems?

The answer is that we need multifaceted research, and the process of collectively identifying, articulating, and prioritizing research questions is a potentially rewarding undertaking. One promising possibility of a community-initiated program of targeted research is that it provides a welcome

---

parents caring for children (legislatively mandated) and types of fuel used at home (comparability with previous data series).

antidote to the poorly articulated "cookie cutter" research agendas identified in the research programs of mainstream institutions (often designed to be comparable with questionable prior research). Perhaps more important, community research can provide the practical basis for mounting social policy and program responses that are not narrowly confined within the guidelines of a single bureaucracy, but are instead designed as across-the-board responses to problems over a broad spectrum of programmatically defined "populations" (such as parents with preschool-age children).[25] It should be noted that the "fuzzy" lines between "basic" and "targeted" research present opportunities, such as a chance to insist on special procedures to assure that indigenous communities are not left out of the picture or to insist on improved definitions of basic variables in the research (such as ethnicity) so that indigenous communities do not blend into the background of research on "Hispanics."

## OPPORTUNISTIC/ENTREPRENEURIAL FUNDER-DRIVEN COMMUNITY-BASED RESEARCH

A fundamental reality of the world of applied policy research is that funders define the research agenda, often with minimal consultation with those who best understand the populations being studied or those who may ultimately use the research findings. We do not recommend that community-based organizations adopt a "purist" stance and forgo funders' invitations to explore issues that affect their communities—even if this does somewhat shift their own priorities. We recommend that community-based organizations engage in dialogue at every opportunity and nudge funders' research agendas and designs in ways that are more productive from their perspective, broadening research driven by a fairly narrowly defined set of research interests to encompass a wider range of critical issues.

The current boom in funders' interest in program evaluation presents an opportunity for community-based research on indigenous Mexican and Guatemalan immigrants in California, at least to the extent that program

---

[25] Research conducted by Kissam and his colleagues (Anna García, Anna Rodríguez, Jo Ann Intili) for Radio Bilingüe makes it clear that in the minds of parents of preschool-age children in Fresno and Tulare counties, the problems they faced related to family life in general, not to the more narrowly defined "target population" for programs funded by Proposition 10—that is, children 0 to 5 years of age.

evaluation can be shaped to incorporate sound research. Prior emphasis on process-oriented evaluation left little room for sound research, but the new emphasis on evaluation and program outcomes makes sound research feasible, but only if strategies are in place to ensure that indigenous immigrants are included in the research population and are adequately identified once they are included.

The California Endowment's commitment to solid community research is an impressive component of its multiyear, multimillion-dollar Agricultural Worker Health Initiative. This applied research effort—which is being designed to track individual, family, neighborhood, community, and systemic outcomes—presents many opportunities to improve basic understanding of indigenous immigrants' lives and most pressing community needs, at the same time that it generates information on "best practices." Indigenous community organizations need to persistently assert their own research interests, their insights about the basis for sound program design, and oversight to ensure consistent attention to their experiences as a "subpopulation" among farmworkers.

### Opportunistic/Entrepreneurial Issue-Driven Research

Community-based organizations of indigenous immigrants and their allies must also shape their research agenda to respond to new policy opportunities, new legislation, and new regulations. Here, too, there are many legitimately competing priorities. To what extent should research be designed to explore issues for which a policy solution or legislation may be urgently needed? To what extent should research seek to generate information on "best practices"—that is, on what works best for which group of potential beneficiaries who may be poorly served by existing program designs or institutions? Both uses of research findings are legitimate and might bring practical improvements in community well-being. An entrepreneurial approach that actively seeks opportunities to advance certain areas or priority research questions as part of an overall long-term agenda has great promise.

A good example of such opportunities is the emerging interest in the "mainstream" policy and program planning agenda regarding questions relating to the cultural and linguistic competency of service providers. Recent regulations from the Department of Health and Human Services regarding patients' rights to health care services in their own language have given rise to a burgeoning policy debate as to whether the mandated program designs are actually needed. (For example, a prominent physician suggested that children's translations for their parents are adequate and that interpreters would make health care delivery unaffordable.) The California Endowment's overall strategy for improving health care in California rests on various initiatives to improve the cultural competency of health care providers. This provides an opportunity—and, arguably, an obligation—for community-based organizations serving indigenous immigrants to assess the cultural and linguistic barriers to adequate health care and to explore issues relating to possible solutions, such as what would be required to recruit and train Mixteco- and Triqui-speaking paraprofessionals to function as cultural interfaces between physicians and their patients.

Similarly, passage of the AB 540 California Nonresident Tuition Exemption, which allows immigrant students to be considered California residents for the purpose of determining tuition fees at state institutions of higher education, also presents an opportunity and an obligation. Questions to be answered involve how well the current provisions function for youths from indigenous-origin families—whether these young people are graduating from high school, have equitable access to courses that satisfy the A-G requirements to enroll in the University of California system, and will be able to afford in-state tuition fees. Negative answers to these questions would strengthen the argument for passage of federal legislation (the DREAM Act) to provide a special program of immigration status adjustment for in-school students.

## COLLABORATIVE RESEARCH ON IMPROVING CENSUS BUREAU METHODOLOGY

Community-based organizations advocating on behalf of indigenous immigrants cannot afford to abandon efforts to improve Census Bureau research. They should join in the collective efforts of a wide range of organizations representing minority populations adversely affected by census undercount. CRLA, the Mexican American Legal Defense and Educational Fund (MALDEF), and Asian American and Native American tribal groups have all been actively involved in efforts to improve census methodology and operations. While progress has been slow, indigenous immigrants should be heard; their insights for improving census methodology will be crucial in the coming decade as a new national data effort, the American Community Survey, takes shape and efforts continue to improve census-style national surveys such as the Current Population Survey. Indigenous immigrant organizations should present themselves as collaborators with the federal government and be recognized as such.

## FINAL REFLECTIONS ON ARTICULATING A COMMUNITY-DRIVEN RESEARCH AGENDA

The five research subagendas we articulate above are not irrevocably separate categories of research. Rather, they represent strands that should be woven together in ongoing strategic planning to develop the indigenous immigrant community's research agenda. Advocacy from indigenous community–based organizations can shape emerging "mainstream" research agendas, blending "basic" research with "targeted" research as the basic research agenda comes to include an increasing proportion of research questions that reflect the interests and priorities of indigenous communities. Recognition of "issue-oriented" research opportunities can provide the basis for shaping funders' interests so that the gap between funder-driven research agendas and community-oriented research agendas diminishes.

It is entirely appropriate for community-based organizations to look to potential allies as they begin to implement initiatives to make mainstream research more responsive to community priorities and needs. A number of important philanthropic institutions in California clearly recognize the diversity of Latino immigrants and understand their importance for California. These institutions are potential allies in efforts to forge a well-articulated research agenda by and for indigenous communities. The "targets" of a campaign to redefine research should be the public institutions at the local, county, state, and federal levels that, in their preoccupation with disparities in equity among different racial groups, consistently ignore the disparities that exist *within* racial groups (or pseudo-racial categories such as "Hispanic"). Even marginal improvements will help ameliorate the current situation.

### Appropriate, Affordable Methodologies for Research

It is crucial, both from a research perspective and from the pragmatic perspective of community activists, to understand that no currently affordable research methodologies provide the "ideal" research tool for applied research on populations of indigenous Mexican immigrants. Pursuit of perfection and reliance on "conventional wisdom" is the archenemy of sound research on minority populations. Our experience suggests that the best research on "hard-to-research" populations asks relevant, useful questions and has a "toolbox" of field research techniques from which to select the best approach for answering the central research questions on a study-by-study basis.

Several methodologies have been used to address the problems inherent in conducting sound research in the rural communities where many of the indigenous immigrants to California live and work. We believe that all of these methodologies should become part of the inventory of research tools that indigenous immigrants' organizations can use to explore their own research agenda. High-quality, multi-stage random sampling is very expensive; the more affordable research strategies we describe below have the advantage of allowing community field researchers to draw on their stores of social capital and funds of knowledge of community life to elicit more accurate information than is collected through better-funded and technically superior research that is ethnocentric in the modes it uses to communicate with survey respondents.

## NETWORK-BASED "SNOWBALL" SAMPLING AND ETHNOGRAPHIC RESEARCH

Some of the most useful research on California immigrants in rural communities has been based on snowball sampling. Richard Mines and Michael Kearney used snowball sampling in 1982 in their groundbreaking study of rural immigrants' health care needs in Tulare County. Mines and Philip Martin used a similar approach in a 1986 study, sponsored by the Employment Development Department (EDD), that provided the first profile of California farmworkers recognizable as corresponding to the actual working conditions and population profile of farmworkers.[26] The CIRS research "survey" of Oaxacan village networks in California agriculture (Runsten and Kearney 1994), which used this technique, is a good example of the practical utility of affordable, albeit imperfect, research methodology, as well as of the need to provide appropriate explanations about the limitations of the research.[27]

The advantages of snowball sampling in ethnographic research relate not simply to reliability but to the researcher's ability to elicit important

---

[26] Many of the interviewers in this study were former farmworkers employed by the California Monitor Advocate's Office. The profile of farmworkers in the Mines and Martin report (1986) is likely to have much more closely approximated the true profile of the 1985 California farmworker population than did the 1980 census, which was the basis for grossly inequitable national distribution of funds for farmworker programs.

[27] The principal investigators, David Runsten and Michael Kearney, were, for example, clear that the study did not seek to estimate numbers of Mixtecs from Guerrero or Puebla and that the original focus had been on enumerating Mixtec and Triqui persons, resulting in an underestimate of Zapotecs.

insights in the course of the research. The value of such methodologies is evident in the utility of the research carried out using this approach—most notably the work of Michael Kearney and Bonnie Bade (Bade 1999), but also the excellent research by Fred Krissman. Bade's ethnographic work has done more to highlight critical issues regarding indigenous immigrants' access to health care than much more costly research designs, including the California Agricultural Worker Health Survey (CAWHS) conducted by CIRS. Bade's research was better designed to address priority issues than was the "generic" research approach of the CAWHS.[28]

Kissam is using ethnosurvey strategies in his case study research on social dynamics and civic life in two communities with concentrations of Mixtecs: Arvin, California (with a population of about eight thousand immigrants), and Woodburn, Oregon (with a population of perhaps six thousand immigrants). We have discovered that network-based snowball sampling is feasible in communities of this size because the networks are not so large nor are there so many networks to explore that costs skyrocket out of control.

## SERVICE POPULATION STUDIES

Service population studies have merit in certain circumstances. For example, Census Bureau researchers have conducted excellent research on the potential of using school-based counts of children to assess the extent to which the decennial census failed to enumerate school-age children. The methodology is convincing, and the selection bias is not serious when the population is limited to elementary school–aged children.[29] If indigenous community-based organizations could convince local school districts to conduct a "special census" of immigrant students developed specifically with the goal of determining the extent of ethnic and linguistic diversity within the population and designed specifically to overcome the problems with the existing language census, such research could have a positive impact on the schools' ability to respond to their students' needs and educational experiences.

---

[28] Interestingly, the CAWHS "rediscovered" a number of farmworker health issues that had been highlighted by the California Raza Health Alliance in 1979—more than twenty years earlier.

[29] Selection bias would become an issue if a school-based study of middle school students' and teenagers' educational needs or overall perspectives were needed.

Admittedly, there would be sample bias affecting the reliability of certain research findings from studies of service populations of indigenous immigrants to California, but appropriately conditioned studies might have utility. For example, using hometown associations' membership lists as the basis for a variety of exploratory research efforts seems quite useful, even though, by definition, the membership represents a self-selected network.

## HOUSEHOLD SAMPLES IN THE CONTEXT OF COMMUNITY CASE STUDIES

A common methodology for applied research in contemporary contexts is random-digit-dialing phone surveys. We have opposed such an approach in research on California immigrants because a significant proportion of the rural California immigrant population (18 to 30 percent of the population universe) do not have listed phone numbers. This bias in samples of persons with phone numbers is sufficiently serious as to make the exercise unproductive.

The intermediate-cost approach we have used is to conduct household-oriented community case studies where the initial sampling frame is purposefully chosen—for example, persons living in Arvin or Parlier. This is a particularly responsible approach in rural California farmworker communities because the diversity *within* a community can approximate the diversity *between* communities. We prefer to present reliable information about the diversity of immigrants within Farmersville or Arvin than to present an unreliable picture of rural immigrant communities based on a phone survey of Spanish-surname persons, a universe that would disproportionately represent U.S.-born Hispanics and long-term settled immigrants while underrepresenting recently arrived, predominantly indigenous transnational migrants.[30]

This intermediate-cost approach is not cheap, and there is the possibility of sample bias due to refusals. However, our experience using these techniques in Parlier (Farm Labor Supply Study), in Long Beach, Redwood City, and Sanger (Survey of Limited-English Latinos' Adult Education Needs), and in Lindsay and Winters (Central Valley Partnership Evalua-

---

[30] Our mention of Farmersville is purposive since it is in this community that Fred Krissman's dissertation research revealed at least two major networks in the community, Mixtecos and Zacatecanos, and, within these networks, a broad spectrum of migration patterns and living circumstances (Krissman 1996). In Arvin a similar situation exists, with major differences between long-term migration networks of Guanajuatenses and more recent Mixtec networks.

tion Community Survey) is that refusals did not seriously jeopardize the research.[31]

The CRLA research on census undercount in rural farmworker communities used a community case study approach. What worked well in this study was that CRLA community workers, several of whom were Mixtecs, relied on their local knowledge of the communities to identify study blocks that would be at risk of census undercount and subsequently to establish rapport with persons in the block to secure detailed information on their experience in Census 2000.[32] The methodology's drawback in this context is that we did not have the resources for a multi-stage random sample of study blocks in the case study communities, and thus cannot definitively demonstrate the overall rate of undercount in the community (although the at-risk blocks were not noticeably different than adjacent blocks).

## INTERCEPT SURVEYS

Intercept survey techniques are widely used in market research because they are affordable and yield rapid turnaround. The sampling frame for intercept surveys is really a venue frequented by a cross-section of the study population. Typically, intercept studies interview people outside supermarkets, in shopping malls, and so on. There are two key concerns regarding the reliability of this strategy. The first is to correctly understand and describe the overall population frequenting the venue and to assess the extent to which this population is representative of the desired study population. The second concern is to ensure that the survey techniques do not result in unacceptable sample bias so that significant subgroups in the study population are omitted from the survey sample.

As part of research for Radio Bilingüe, Anna García explored the use of intercept interviews in research to assess the prevalence of smoking among transnational migrants (Kissam and García 1998). García wisely chose public parks as the venue for her intercepts of transnational migrants and conducted interviews in summer during the late afternoon. This sampling approach worked well because few in this population have any other place

---

[31] A critical practical issue relates to procedures for replacing nonresponding households.

[32] Of the five communities we focus on here, research in three was conducted by Mixtec community workers Antonio Flores (in Oxnard), Jesús Estrada (Santa Maria), and Fausto Sánchez (Arvin).

to "hang out" and because, with time on their hands, virtually all were willing to participate in an interview—if it was not too formal or burdensome. In 2002 we moved this approach forward by conducting one component of a large-scale audience research project for Radio Bilingüe[33] in a variety of *remates* (swap meets) in Fresno, Madera, and Tulare counties, relying heavily on Mixtec-speaking interviewers.[34] This strategy is very promising for community research because the population of immigrants who frequent swap meets seems to represent a good cross-section of the population of low-income immigrants that interests service providers who seek to improve the lives of rural California immigrants.

Kissam, García, Mullenax, and their research team used a version of the intercept survey technique in combination with ethnographic research as the basis for a study of the living and working conditions of teenage farmworkers, most of whom turned out to be of indigenous origin. Although the methodology constrained the team's ability to generalize from the research, a more formal approach would not have yielded any practical insights about the sorts of interventions that would have an immediate positive impact on their well-being (Kissam et al. 2001). The venues for "intercepting" and interviewing the teenagers included several versions of street-corner labor markets—a drive-by bakery where *pinqueros* congregated to pick up workers, the "bus station" where *troqueros* picked up workers, a convenience store parking lot in Arizona used extensively by transnational migrants, *coyotes*, and *raiteros*, and "El Parque de los Negros" in Madera. Each venue has its unique challenges, but taken together they provide a more accurate picture than formal multi-stage sampling in exploring the living conditions of this population.

## Feasibility of Using Appropriate Research Methodologies

Those who believe that policy decisions and program planning are best made on the basis of empirical data need to articulate and implement research agendas that generate reliable insights. The search for research perfection is a wild goose chase, as even a superficial perusal of the history of science will demonstrate. The true value of empirical research lies, in large

---

[33] Findings of the TVT/TCE Survey are presented in Kissam, Intili, and García 2003.

[34] Both of these interviewers, Rafael Flores and Jorge San Juan, are associated with the Oaxacan Indigenous Binational Front (FIOB). Their ability to establish rapport with interviewees and successfully elicit in-depth candid responses was even more important than their language abilities.

measure, in articulating and systematically exploring hypotheses and, in a practical vein, policy issues of practical importance. The idea that universities or other august research bodies are the only institutions with the "capacity" to do sound research is a dangerous one. This is particularly true if community-based organizations accept this assertion and leave it to "others" or "outsiders" to conduct research that might be crucial in identifying more effective or novel strategies to address the problems their communities face. At the same time, community-based organizations concerned about the well-being of indigenous immigrant communities in California must work diligently to generate the systematic research findings that will complement the first-hand knowledge and anecdotal evidence about what goes on in these communities, what are the most pressing community problems, and what solutions look most promising.

Researchers and community activists alike need to work to build effective applied research collaborations. The work by CRLA and the Aguirre Group/Aguirre International on immigrants and farmworkers (Kissam et al. 2001), as well as Kissam's research as part of Radio Bilingüe's audience research program (Kissam 2000), gives us first-hand knowledge of the benefits of working in collaboration with community leaders and activists from California indigenous communities to conduct relevant research on community issues. We face serious challenges in pursuing a long-term research agenda because our support comes in the form of "soft money." It would be naive to think that indigenous community organizations will not face similar challenges, but this only heightens the need for advocacy and, ultimately, insistence on the principle that indigenous communities are key stakeholders in social science research on their communities. We look forward, individually and institutionally, to working as partners to better understand indigenous immigrants' experiences in their individual, family, and community lives in California.

Our hope is that improved understanding will result in improved responsiveness of social programs and institutions. This entails confronting challenges, analyzing the implications of available research, and advocating for increasingly "customized" social programs and policies in order to leverage significant impacts in Latino communities that are, despite their apparent homogeneity, tremendously diverse in terms of ethnic, cultural, and linguistic composition, not to mention immigration status. There is much more work to be done. We all need to be patient and to persevere.

## References

Bade, Bonnie. 1999. "Is There a Doctor in the Field? Underlying Conditions Affecting Access to Health Care for California Farmworkers and Their Families." Presented at the California Program on Access to Care, California Policy Research Center, Sacramento, September.

Fein, David. 1989. "The Social Sources of Census Omission Rates in Recent U.S. Censuses." PhD dissertation, Princeton University.

Fein, David, and K.K. West. 1988. "The Sources of Census Undercount: Findings from the 1986 Los Angeles Test Census," *Survey Methodology Journal* 14, no. 2.

GAO (General Accounting Office). 1999. "Formula Grants: Effects of Adjusted Population Counts on Federal Funding to States," February.

———. 2003. "Decennial Census: Lessons Learned for Locating and Counting Migrant and Seasonal Workers." GAO 03-605, July.

Griffith, David, Edward Kissam, et al. 1995. *Working Poor: Farmworkers in the United States*. Philadelphia, Penn.: Temple University Press.

Jacobs, Ilene, and Edward Kissam. 2001. "Census 2000 Undercount of Immigrants and Farmworkers in Rural California Communities." Report to the California Endowment, August.

Kearney, Michael, and Carole Nagengast. 1989. "Anthropological Perspectives on Transnational Communities in Rural California." Working Paper No. 3. Sacramento: California Institute for Rural Studies.

Kissam, Edward. 2002. "Community Reflections on Radio Bilingüe's Service: Alternative Approaches to Audience Research on Program Impact," Latino Public Radio Summit, September.

Kissam, Edward, Susan Gabbard, and Philip Martin. 1993. "The Impact of Migrant Travel Patterns on the Undercount of Hispanic Farm Workers." In *Proceedings of the Bureau of the Census Research Conference on Undercounted Ethnic Populations*, Richmond, Virginia, May.

Kissam, Edward, and Anna García. 1998. "Strategies for Radio Bilingüe's Programming to Influence Transnational Migrants' Smoking Behavior." Research report submitted to Radio Bilingüe and the Tobacco Control Section, California Department of Health Services, August.

Kissam, Edward, Jo Ann Intili, and Anna García. 2003. "Spanish-Language Community Radio as a Resource for Health Promotion Campaigns Targeted to Farmworkers and Recent Immigrants," *California Journal of Health Promotion* 1, no. 2: 183–97.

Kissam, Edward, Philip Martin, and Susan Gabbard. 1993. "The Impact of Migrant Travel Patterns on the Undercount of Hispanic Farm Workers." In *Proceedings of the 1993 Research Conference on Undercounted Ethnic Populations*. Washington, D.C.: Bureau of the Census.

Kissam, Edward, José R. Padilla, and Ilene Jacobs. 1996. "2000 Census Advisory Committee Position Paper Submitted by Member Organization California Rural Legal Assistance on Behalf of Migrant and Seasonal Farmworkers." White paper circulated to the Secretary's Advisory Committee on the Decennial Census, May.

Kissam, Edward, et al. 2001. "No Longer Children: Case Studies of the Living and Working Conditions of the Youth Who Harvest America's Crops." San Mateo, Calif.: Aguirre International.

Krissman, Fred. 1996. "California Agribusiness and Mexican Farm Workers (1942–1992): A Bi-national Agricultural System of Production/Reproduction." PhD dissertation, University of California, Santa Barbara.

Mines, Richard, and Michael Kearney. 1982. *The Health of Tulare County Farmworkers*. Sacramento, Calif.: Farmworker Health Services Section, Tulare County Department of Health Services.

Mines, Richard, and Philip Martin. 1986. *A Profile of California Farmworkers*. Giannini Foundation Information Series, no. 86-2. [Calif.]: Giannini Foundation of Agricultural Economics, University of California.

Runsten, David, and Michael Kearney. 1994. "A Survey of Oaxacan Village Networks in California Agriculture." Davis: California Institute for Rural Studies.

Sassen, Saskia. 1991. *The Global City: New York, London, Tokyo.* Princeton, N.J.: Princeton University Press.

Sherman, Jennifer, et al. 1997. "Finding Invisible Farmworkers: The Parlier Survey." Davis: California Institute for Rural Studies.

# PART IV

# Comparative Perspectives: Ethnic and Geographic Diversity

# 12

# Yucatecos and Chiapanecos in San Francisco: Mayan Immigrants Form New Communities

## Garance Burke

In 2000, community organizers and health professionals began noticing that the demographics of the Mexican immigrant population in San Francisco were changing. Patients from southeastern Mexico were coming in with health problems similar to those of other Latino immigrants, but they did not speak Spanish as a first language. Although immigrants from the Mexican states of Michoacán and Zacatecas have decades-long traditions of working seasonally in the Bay Area, in recent years more than ten thousand immigrants from Yucatán and Chiapas—many of whom grew up speaking Maya or Tzotzil—have flocked to the Bay Area. Largely undetected by local governments, these ethnically distinct populations have come from regions that do not have strong traditions of migration, to seek work in northern California. Despite their precarious position in the local labor market, the *yucatecos* and *chiapanecos* have already made an impact in San Francisco. For the purposes of this essay, I will narrate these incipient communities' stories through Santos Nic. In Mexico, Nic, fifty-one years old, was a bilingual elementary schoolteacher. Since his arrival to the United States ten years ago, he has assumed a new role as an unofficial leader of the Mayan community in San Francisco's Mission District.

"When I first got to San Francisco in 1988, there was no one here from the Yucatán," said Nic, sipping a cup of sweet coffee a few doors down from what he calls San Francisco's "Mayan corner." "At most, there were twenty of us who spoke Maya, but a few years ago all the *muchachos* started leaving town to come up here."

A pedestrian might not notice the half-dozen young men speaking in Maya on the corner of Mission and 16th streets on any given afternoon. Most come from a village called Oxkutzcab, near the pyramids of Uxmal in northwest Yucatán. The majority have not completed high school and speak Spanish only as a second language—and English as a distant third.

While the Mayan community might be under the radar of many San Franciscans, the growing numbers of indigenous immigrants from the Yucatán Peninsula have made an impact in the halls of justice, in community health clinics, and in the city's informal labor market. San Francisco's Mexican consulate estimates the current Mayan population in the Bay Area at ten thousand, noting that thirty thousand new indigenous Mexicans arrive in California each year.

Ethnically, linguistically, and culturally distinct from other Mexican migrants, the *yucatecos* have made this corner their hub. As they circulate through shelters and shared apartments, this strip of pavement has become a place to keep in touch with their communities while on the move.

"All my friends from Oxkutzcab are here now," said Enrique, who, like many new immigrants, spoke accented Spanish and declined to give his full name. They are coming for the reasons that motivate most immigrant journeys—to seek opportunities to make a better life. As one young Mayan man explained, he could no longer bear to watch the crops of bitter oranges native to the Yucatán rot in the orchards because there is no market for them. "They used to work on the land at home," Enrique said, "but now they're up here, just trying to make money to send home to the family."

Mayans from the Yucatán are not the only indigenous newcomers to the Bay Area. In recent years, they have been joined by at least a thousand migrants from the state of Chiapas, where low-intensity warfare and economic isolation have dislocated indigenous communities. The *chiapanecos* in San Francisco, many of whom speak Tzotzil and Tzeltal (also within the Mayan family of languages but remotely related to Yucatec Maya), confront a different set of challenges than their Yucatecan counterparts, but they share similar histories of communally based, agricultural societies.

Even though labor differentiation among migrants may separate them into different specialties in the Bay Area—Mayans have carved out a niche in the restaurant industry, while *chiapanecos* are largely working as day laborers—the political and economic factors that brought both groups to

California are markedly similar. Both Yucatán and Chiapas will be re-shaped by Mexican President Vicente Fox's Plan Puebla Panamá (PPP), an ambitious US$20-billion development project aimed at integrating Meso-america into the global marketplace. Most are first-time immigrants who left home because they were economically displaced by Mexico's entrance into the global economy, and they come without benefit of preceding gen-erations' knowledge of how to live a seasonal life that crosses the border.

If they follow the pattern of other Mexican immigrants, such as the eighty thousand Oaxacan Mixtecs now living in California, they may even-tually form their own hometown associations or grassroots political groups like the Oaxacan Indigenous Binational Front (FIOB). Traditionally, such hometown associations have provided an infrastructure that helps channel members' earnings back to Mexico and leads to greater cohesion among immigrant communities in the United States. Such groups are gaining political clout with the government of President Fox, who is considered more enlightened than previous administrations on the subject of migrant communities in the United States.

In Oxkutzcab, Nic explained, "People borrow money to get [to San Francisco]. So if things don't work out right away, they get stuck here for a while." He smiled, as if to say he was still trying to understand how he ended up as a dishwasher after twenty years working as an adviser for the Mexican Education Ministry. In his fourteen years in the United States, Nic has worked picking lettuce in Soledad, as a prep cook on Valencia Street, and as a college speaker on Mayan culture. Customarily attired in the light linen shirt typical of the Yucatán, Nic is known to newcomers as *el profesor*.

"This guy knows more than any of us," said a man on the corner, wear-ing a baseball cap and orange shorts. Jorge, aged thirty-two, is from an-other small village, near Tecax, where a garment-assembly plant paid him $3 per day to sew jeans for the export market. He left Tecax after complet-ing junior high school to work in Cancún. He said he hopes to take English classes but has had trouble finding a steady job.

> We came to mine for gold here in California. But without *el profe*, we wouldn't keep it together. He tells us stories about home. A lot of *yucatecos* are here in San Francisco and in San Rafael, or up in Oregon picking onions. Others are in Florida. We speak Maya among ourselves and if somebody needs a translator, then we help out. Those who don't know how to read or speak Spanish hang out with a buddy who does, in order to find a job.

As with most immigrant networks, the indigenous newcomers are seeking out linguistic and financial support from established members of their communities. Several *chiapanecos* stated that they were staying with family and acquaintances in San Francisco, some of whom had come from regions as remote as Marqués de Comillas, which borders Guatemala. (In the case of the *chiapaneco* population discussed here, however, the community is still too small to allow us to draw broad conclusions about the ways in which newcomers are using their linguistic and ethnic ties to support one another. As one of the fastest-growing immigrant groups in the city, however, this matter merits further research.)

Nic sees it as his duty to keep the Mayan identity alive in the United States and makes a point of reminding younger Mayan immigrants of their ancestors' cultural practices. "Even when the Mayan people were persecuted, they went underground to venerate their gods. They knew how to ask their gods for protection, and the shamans always stood by them," he said.

Nic applied the same principle when he was teaching in the Yucatán in the 1970s, sometimes traveling for days to reach remote schoolhouses. At a time when the Mexican government was pushing for the assimilation of indigenous groups, he used the bilingual curriculum to teach his pupils how to read in Spanish and how to understand the legends and traditions of their Mayan forebears. "As a bilingual teacher, my role was to keep our culture alive, so that Mayans would not be ashamed to say where they come from or to say their last name if it sounded too Indian," he said. "We need to maintain our traditions, because our Mayan culture is the most beautiful thing we have."

Nic eventually navigated through the Mexican Education Ministry to become a national adviser on bilingual education. When an automobile accident wiped out his savings, however, he found he could not live on his $30-per-month teaching salary. He felt he had no choice but to come north to earn back the money, and he now pays $200 per month in rent to share a crowded Victorian apartment with his two sons and seven other men.

The surroundings have changed, but Nic still plays the role of teacher: cultural arbiter, interpreter, even surrogate father. He recounts stories about the planting cycle and the rain god, Chaac, as a way to keep his *paisanos*—some of whom were once his students—connected to their traditions. His English is faulty, but his Spanish is eloquent, salted with the soft "sh" of the Mayan language. "A lot of people have told me that I should form some sort of hometown association or support group," he said, "because people don't know how to get through the bureaucracy here. Bosses take advantage of them, and they need someone to give them a moral orientation."

Officially or not, Nic has contributed just that. "I've helped a lot of people go to City Hall or to the Mexican consulate. When someone's relative dies here, we pool our money to send the body back. It costs between $5,000 and $6,000, but we feel it's important that our people be buried at home, so their souls can rest."

From 300 to 900 A.D., Mayan civilization flourished throughout the Yucatán Peninsula and in Guatemala, El Salvador, Belize, and Honduras, achieving unparalleled advances in astronomy, mathematics, architecture, and the arts. Archaeological wonders are still being uncovered throughout the region, revealing the empire's sphere of influence. While tourist guidebooks typically focus on the Mayan civilization's glorious past, Mayan culture today dominates the entire southern region of the Yucatán Peninsula, where most families live in extreme poverty.

The Bay Area has always been a magnet for Spanish-speaking immigrants from northern and central Mexico, but it only became a common destination for *yucatecos* when construction jobs in Yucatán's tourism economy started to ebb in the late 1990s. After an initial boom in job creation, the development of Cancún ceased to bring prosperity to the greater Yucatán Peninsula. Tourism flagged considerably after September 11, 2001, when resort occupancy rates fell to an all-time low and hotel owners cut ten thousand jobs.

"We have noticed an important increase in the number of people coming here from the Yucatán Peninsula; people from those states never used to leave their hometowns," said Georgina Lagos Dondé, the Mexican consul general in San Francisco. "People are coming here from Chiapas, too, some from the conflict zone and others from agricultural areas."

Of all the Mexican nationals her consulate serves, Lagos says Yucatecan Mayans are the fastest-growing group, closely followed by *chiapanecos* and immigrants from the state of Guerrero. In the case of Chiapas, at least twelve thousand people have fled their homes since the Zapatista uprising began in 1994, according to the UN Secretary General's special representative on internally displaced persons, Francis Deng, who visited Chiapas in August 2002. Much of the displacement, both internal and external, is the result of the ongoing conflict and paramilitary violence, although the big migration boom began in Chiapas in 1998, when heavy storms and floods buried towns and destroyed the state's agricultural economy.

A recent study by Mexico's National Population Council (CONAPO) states that Chiapas now accounts for 13 percent of the nearly 500,000 residents of seven southern Mexican states who have fled north in the past five years. (Initial studies and community reports demonstrate that *chiapanecos* have also begun to establish communities in the Los Angeles metropolitan area, as well as in Oregon and Florida.)

"The networks of communication between people who are here and their relatives in Mexico are incredibly impressive," said Lagos. "People don't come to the United States simply looking for work; they go where they know someone, and that someone has told them there is work. When there is work to be had, people start coming here immediately."

Such seasonal work patterns have long played an unacknowledged role in the California economy, but the debate around immigration has taken on a more serious tone over the past two years. In September 2001, Presidents Bush and Fox were close to hammering out a plan for legalizing the three million undocumented Mexican nationals estimated to be living in the United States, a proposal supported by Senate Majority Leader Tom Daschle. While the events of September 11 put immigration policy on the back burner, they have not stopped the "pull effect" that lures new generations of migrants across the 2,000-mile U.S.-Mexico border.

The number of *yucatecos* requesting consular identification cards—or *matrículas consulares*, now a valid identification for undocumented Mexican immigrants in eight hundred U.S. cities—has grown exponentially in recent years, according to the Mexican consulate. Consul René Santillán reported that 15 percent of all the ID cards he processed in 2001 went to people from the Yucatán who have settled in San Francisco, Redwood City, San Rafael, and Fruitvale.

Mayan men have also become regular customers at Mission District Western Union outlets. And many storefronts feature hand-lettered signs advertising Oxkutzcab as a primary destination for paychecks wired home.

At the Mission Neighborhood Health Clinic, director of patient services Dolores Ramírez has noted the growing indigenous immigrant community. Her organization is a major health care provider for Latino immigrants, a population she said now includes about 10 percent Maya speakers. The numbers have been growing, she said, "and a lot of these people are too frightened to seek out help, so they cure themselves with herbs until they have a health problem so bad they have to go to the doctor."

Countywide, officials are aware that the composition of the immigrant population is changing. But despite a need for more translators in various

Latin American indigenous languages, the system is too strapped to deal with the situation. To learn English, newcomers must first improve their fluency in Spanish, a situation that can invite discrimination from mestizo immigrants. The San Francisco Day Labor Program reported that 40 percent of the immigrant laborers they work with are indigenous, and they come from communities suffering acute poverty and political discord.

For the deputy director of community programs at the San Francisco Department of Public Health, María X. Martínez, it is a question of institutional blindness to the demographic reality. "Generally speaking, the institutional culture says, 'They all look Latino, so they're all going to have the same epidemiological problems.' Indigenous Mexicans are a much larger percentage of migrant workers than ever before, and they may have different health needs," she said.

Last year, Ventura County hired trilingual interpreters to help the thousands of Mixtecs living in the area get access to social services. At present in the Bay Area, no services are specifically targeted for indigenous Latino populations. Martínez noted that institutional culture will be more likely to respond with funding for services if this generation of migrants keeps its identity intact—and if numbers grow significantly. "We have six or seven categories for Asian languages—Mandarin, Cantonese, Vietnamese, Tagalog, and so on—and then we have just one term for all the people who come here from Latin America: Spanish," Martínez said. "The client base doesn't fit into that category, but services won't move beyond the generic term 'Latino' until the communities rise up and say: 'This is biased, our numbers are growing, you are not meeting your clients' needs.'"

Day Labor Program director Renée Saucedo said one of her program's most popular components is the mental health clinic, where clients are often treated for depression, loneliness, or, in the case of many immigrants from Chiapas, the legacy of violent conflict. Saucedo described the process as being one of "triple translation and acculturation." "Depending on where they come from, a lot of the Mayan communities in southern Mexico bring their cultural norms and values with them," Saucedo said. "You're talking about people who have arrived here where the culture is a lot more individualistic and hostile to them. For the newly arrived folks, that can be very despairing, but what's amazing is that most of them maintain this sense of hope—that this will improve life for their families."

Saucedo added that the economic situation is particularly dire for campesino immigrants from Chiapas, who have been hard hit by the global fall in coffee prices and by the liberalization of the Mexican agricultural sector.

Such is the case of Pablo, a 27-year-old immigrant from the village of Limonares, outside Ocosingo, who said he speaks Tzeltal, Tzotzil, and *un poco de español* [a smattering of Spanish]. He arrived in San Francisco in spring 2002 and since that time has earned $7 per hour working as a roofer, painter, and doing odd jobs.

"We were still growing our corn and beans, but we could only get a few pesos for every kilo we sold. A bag of soap costs 12 pesos, and a pair of pants costs 100 pesos," he said, standing on the corner of 26th Street with other new arrivals from Guerrero and Oaxaca. "How were we going to survive like that? That's why we came here. Here at least if you work for a day, then you have some money left over to save."

Now living with cousins in San Francisco's Mission District, Pablo said the ongoing tensions between rebel groups and the Mexican army pushed him to leave his village, much of which sympathizes with the Zapatista Army of National Liberation (EZLN). "They kept on bringing more and more government soldiers into the area. After the massacre at Acteal, we started collecting corn and beans for those communities that were affected. The army was introducing guns into the communities so people would kill one another," he said.

Like many immigrants from southern Mexico, Pablo crossed the border by paying a *coyote*. Increasingly, however, the legacy of Operation Gatekeeper has encouraged immigrants from areas that lack well-established migration patterns to cross in remote, dangerous areas in the desert. In August 2002, four young men from Chiapas were found floating in the All-American Canal, just a hundred feet from U.S. soil, near the California town of El Centro.

Some California politicians have begun to take notice. Elmy Bermejo, the San Francisco district representative for state senator John Burton, takes a personal interest in the development of indigenous immigrant communities. A native of Oxkutzcab, Bermejo came to San Francisco as a child. She is now a powerful force in the state Democratic Party, and she was the first Latina and first woman to be appointed to two state commissions by former California Governor Gray Davis (including the Commission on the Status of Women, which she chairs).

Bermejo's father, Tomás, came to California as a guestworker under the Bracero Program and brought his entire family here by the late 1960s. After spending her formative years in Oxkutzcab, Bermejo found it difficult to assimilate. "I still think of my first identity as being a *yucateca*. Yucatán is a very special place, and if you are born there your heart is from Yucatán," she said. "I was ten years old when I came here, and we didn't speak English, so we just went to school with everyone else. Kids didn't understand why you couldn't talk to them, and from that experience I realized that you become victimized if you don't know English or Spanish. Other Latinos take advantage of you, and you're dependent on others to do everything for you."

In part as a result of her own experiences (and due to the influence of her family's rigorous work ethic), Bermejo has become an influential promoter of Latino political participation. As a member of the California Complete Count Committee for the 2000 census, Bermejo helped direct some $24 million from the California state budget to ensure that the immigrant population was counted as part of the state population.

Bermejo sees the immigrant community as "an underclass, a hidden society that does not trust the government."

> I've been really amazed at how many *yucatecos* are in San Francisco. People are coming here to get a job, save money, and then go back. I don't see people who want to stay here forever, and a lot of them don't have papers.... People say they can't get used to the lifestyle here, and there isn't the extended family.

For many new Mayan immigrants, Bermejo's father Tomás *is* the extended family. In 1965, he opened his Geary Boulevard restaurant, Tommy's, where his children grew up serving plates of the banana leaf–wrapped dishes common to the peninsula. As Tomás's success story circulated in Oxkutzcab, family and friends began to drift northward. In addition to his wife and four children, one brother, six cousins, twenty nieces and nephews, and countless acquaintances have followed him to San Francisco. Over the years, he has provided occasional jobs and an informal safety net for dozens of friends who have come to northern California to start a new life.

Tomás grew up speaking Maya, and in every other sentence he muses about returning to the home he has built for himself in Mérida. A self-made entrepreneur, he jokes that with the incursion of American-style values and business practices, *yucatecos* "don't need to speak Maya anymore; they're more civilized."

Juanita Quintero, one of the Bermejo family's distant cousins, shares their commitment to supporting the *yucateco* community, but she has taken a different tack. One of the first women from the region to arrive in San

Francisco in the early 1960s, she said it was not until she began raising her son in the Mission District that she realized how isolated she felt from her family's traditions. In recent years, she has been exploring Mayan traditions through Grupo Maya, a small community group that meets in members' homes in Oakland. Mayan political refugees from the Guatemalan civil war formed Grupo Maya in the late 1980s, but the organization has since come to include Mayans from several countries.

In view of her own struggle to find a place as a transplant to San Francisco, Quintero hopes newly arrived immigrants to California will find strength in their roots. "Many people don't say they're Mayan when they get here; they just say they're *mexicano*. There's still discrimination against the culture even in the Yucatán," she said. "There's this idea that the Mayans were really intelligent and they built all of these amazing temples, but that civilization is over now and now we are nothing. That's how I started going to Grupo Maya. I just started thinking about the rituals that my grandfather used to do, the festivals for new corn and for the rain. We need to understand that we're part of that, too."

Every nine months, Grupo Maya cosponsors a sunrise ceremony to celebrate the day when, according to the Mayan calendar, the creator shaped human life. Quintero said that participating with Grupo Maya has allowed her to make contact with other Mayans from Guatemala and El Salvador, whose languages differ from her own Yucatec Maya but who share similar cultural customs. Her knowledge of the language comes in handy in her work assisting patients at General Hospital and when she is called to moonlight as a trilingual court interpreter for immigrants entangled in the city's justice system.

Initial findings suggest that immigration and assimilation have already made an impact on *yucateco* culture. Professor William Hanks, of the University of California, Berkeley, began studying the Yucatec Maya language in Oxkutzcab in 1977. According to Hanks, cultural transformation has occurred at both a material level, in that increasing numbers of two-story cement houses have been built through migrant remittances, and on a linguistic level, in that English words have become part of the regional patois in southern Yucatán.

"*Yucatecos* have been in contact with foreigners for a very long time, and they're very creative at absorbing other things and making them Maya," he said. "Even if Yucatecan people do not generally reproduce their tradition by rejecting what is outside, I think the most obvious change is the number of California license plates there now. There's quite a presence of California in Oxkutzcab."

Nic is concerned that Oxkutzcab's migratory odyssey means that the younger generation is more likely to talk about Sony-brand stereos than their ancestors' legendary battles against cultural domination. Mayan resistance to the Mexican government meant that the peninsula was not fully pacified until the early 1900s, when Mayan rebel fighters relinquished control. Nic—whose father was born into indentured labor in 1898, when most Mayans were still working under slave-like conditions on the colonial plantations that defined the power bases of the Yucatán—equates forgetting this history with denying his own roots.

By the time Nic was born, land reform had reshaped some of the region's great inequities, but by and large, national development has not been of significant benefit to the Mayan population. Statistics from the Mexican government's Social Development Ministry (SEDESOL) indicate that 15 percent of the population in southern Yucatán is illiterate, and the bilingual education program Nic once led has floundered under the Fox administration.

While many *yucatecos* have hopes for improvement of socioeconomic conditions under President Fox, Nic fears that the current development model hinders indigenous self-determination. The *maquiladora* system that boomed along Mexico's northern border in 1994 after trade restrictions were relaxed under the North American Free Trade Agreement (NAFTA) now lures poor, rural workers to foreign-owned factories in Yucatán, where wages have stayed low compared to the northern border region.

More changes are soon to come: southeastern Mexico is poised to receive hundreds more assembly plants, as well as billions of dollars in investment projects, as part of Plan Puebla Panamá. The 25-year project is now the Inter-American Development Bank's highest priority for the region. The bulk of the funding thus far has been earmarked for transportation projects, many of which would cut through indigenous lands, an issue that is especially contentious in Chiapas. In the Mexican government's $697.4-million budget for the PPP in 2002, 82 percent of funding was reserved for transportation projects, while "social development" and health projects merited just 2.9 percent.

Particularly following the widespread destruction wrought by Hurricane Isidore in September 2002, few critics would argue that transportation projects are dispensable in Yucatán. Yet as it becomes increasingly difficult for campesinos in southern Mexico to sustain locally based agricultural economies, immigration patterns northward are only likely to increase. For community leaders like Santos Nic, maintaining strong ties to Oxkutzcab will be key to navigating what is to come.

"A lot of people confuse us with the other migrants, but every town, every state has its own way of being, its own way of thinking and living," he said. "If you go to Chichén Itzá, every spring you can witness the birth of a new life. Three days after the equinox, the snakes shed their skins and the fields are filled with flowers. The sun falls, and the shadow of a snake appears to crawl down the side of the pyramid. The Russians and the French and even the Americans tried to recreate that symmetry. But no one other than the Mayans could achieve that perfection."

# 13

## P'urépecha Migration into the U.S. Rural Midwest: History and Current Trends

Warren D. Anderson

This chapter draws on an ethnographically based case study that examines the transnational migration patterns of one group of indigenous Mexicans. In the tradition of cultural anthropology's abiding interest in the empirical wealth embedded in the praxis of local communities, the study is anchored quite tightly in the events and trends of two specific sites, identifiable spaces in a migratory circuit that spans the roughly 2,000 miles between the Mexican state of Michoacán and the U.S. state of Illinois. This circuit represents much more than a pathway between two disconnected, discrete spaces with well-defined boundaries; rather, the migratory circuit herein described may be likened to a single body's circulatory and nervous systems, through which flows the very life of a unified, living whole. The effects of globalization require a "reorganization of the bipolar imagery of space and time" (Kearney 1995), and nowhere is this more evident than in the complexities of nation-state and local community interconnectedness engendered by transnational labor migration.

Knauft (1996) contends that modern anthropological practice runs the risk of abandoning the traditional focus on localized field sites in favor of other modes of investigation. The intricacies of globalization make such abandonment an inviting prospect, streamlining the research process and affording more sweeping propositions about the nature of transnational phenomena. I believe with Knauft, however, that a key strength of cultural anthropology lies in its unwavering commitment to empirical studies in the field. They contribute to what he claims is one of the twin ethical goals of modern cultural anthropology: "to document and valorize the richness and diversity of human ways of life" (1996: 48). In short, ethnographic case studies are crucial to a balanced cultural anthropology, exposing questions of cultural practice and disciplinary methodology that merit theoretical attention.

My purposes in this essay are three: to provide a reasonably comprehensive portrait of two towns (one in Mexico and the other in the United States) profoundly affected by transnational labor migration; to examine relevant migration theory and its applicability to observed patterns of migratory behavior; and to highlight specific characteristics of this particular migration circuit that merit further theoretical and empirical attention.

## THE CHERÁN-COBDEN "LABORATORY"

The following discussion centers on the P'urépecha[1] residents of the town of Cherán, Michoacán, and their journeys into the small southern Illinois village of Cobden. Relevant characteristics of each place are explored in detail later, but for now it is significant to note that, in terms of absolute numbers of participants, this migration circuit is very small. This is not to say that it is unusual, however. Given that the overwhelming majority of Mexican labor migrants have traditionally found employment in the U.S. agricultural sector, it would not be surprising to find that Cobden, far from being unique or atypical, is actually quite representative of a significant proportion of Mexico-U.S. wage labor migration. The difficulties inherent in conducting detailed observations of multiple sites like Cobden in the United States and Cherán in Mexico may eclipse the value such localized studies have for wider comparative purposes in the quest to understand human migratory behavior.

The Cherán-Cobden connection invites investigation for a variety of reasons, several of which give it what might be termed laboratory-like characteristics. While by no means offering a set of "controlled variables," it does provide a well-defined window into the vitality of migration that the complexities of large-scale, urban, industrialized, long-term scenarios may make difficult to comprehend.

---

[1] The P'urépecha are commonly known as Tarascans. The origin of the word's use has various interpretations, but most agree that it is a Hispanicized derivation of a P'urépecha word and became the name by which the people were called by the Spanish in the sixteenth century.

Among the topics of interest to contemporary social science, few are more dynamic than international migration, especially as it has manifested itself in recent years. Hence, the danger that the theoretical apparatus used to apprehend migration may lag behind its actual evolution becomes all the greater (Portes and Böröcz 1989: 606).

In short, the "actual evolution" of the Cherán-Cobden migration is susceptible to theoretical apprehension largely because of its controlled characteristics. Among those characteristics we find that: (a) it is recent and short; (b) it is rural and therefore limited in the types of employment offerings available to migrators and employers alike; (c) the two towns involved are small, making their specific relevant features relatively simple and easy to highlight; (d) the numbers of people who participate are limited, facilitating comprehensive knowledge on the part of informant and researcher alike; and (e) it is between two towns with coincidental, albeit interesting, similarities. This collection of controlled features cuts two ways, however, because the limited temporal and numerical scale of Cherán's migration into southern Illinois raises questions about its representative value for discussions of the larger picture of transnational labor migration between Mexico and the United States. Nevertheless, a brief review of some of the characteristics of this particular labor migration circuit will make explicit both its limitations and its attractiveness.

## Temporal Limits

Contact between the P'urépecha of Michoacán and Cobden began no earlier than 1959. The limited time scale of forty years, with no previous history of contact between the two towns, makes for clean and comprehensive longitudinal investigations. By 1962, nearing the end of the Bracero Program, the orchards around Cobden hosted probably no more than eight young Mexican migrant workers, all males and all from Cherán. Of that original group of *cheranecos*, six are still in the Cobden area, now all grandfathers, in varying conditions of health, some still actively working forty and more hours a week. They have seen firsthand the myriad changes in migration over their four-decade tenure. As will be made clear in the following discussion, their experiences and memories are neither unique nor of more value than elderly immigrants from other times and places. However, the fact that they all share the same cultural and geographic background, came and stayed and raised families in one small town, and have witnessed the panorama of migration between two villages provides a richness to their narrative and gives them an "ownership" to those events that might be lacking in more transient or complex circumstances.

## Rurality

Traffic between Cherán and Cobden is essentially rural-to-rural migration. Cherán is an agrarian community, with strong ties to the land and ample territorial resources in the forested mountains of north-central Michoacán. It is a community of farmers, participating in the same economic base and with the same methods that have traditionally sustained the Meseta (Beals 1946; Carrasco 1952; Castile 1974; Aguirre Beltrán 1952; field interviews with local farmers). Surrounding communities are known for crafts (such as woodworking, pottery, and leatherwork), but Cherán has been consistently characterized by its primary dependence upon agriculture. Traditionally, a mixture of farming and another occupation forms the basis of the household economy, and few families are dependent entirely upon crop production, although some combine animal husbandry (the second most common source of income in the region), forest exploitation, and agriculture (Beals 1946; Maturana Medina and Sánchez Cortés 1970). Current land use practice in Cherán can be traced to aboriginal land inheritance rules among the pre-contact P'urépecha, rules that, for a variety of reasons, were never overridden by colonial dictates (Foster 1948; Aguirre Beltrán 1952; Friedrich 1970).

Cobden shares many geographical and rural similarities with Cherán. Nestled deep in a forested agricultural region of southernmost Illinois, it lies approximately 90 miles south of St. Louis, Missouri, and 175 miles north of Memphis, Tennessee. County populations in the region are sparse, and agriculture is the rule. In addition to horticulture (primarily apples, peaches, and strawberry and blueberry production), animal husbandry (cattle and sheep) and fairly small-scale row crop operations all carve out their niches among the hilly woodlands of the Shawnee National Forest, which covers southern Illinois from the Mississippi to the Ohio River.

In the agrarian community of Cherán, residents live in town but are closely tied to agriculture, walking to their fields, forest plots, or cattle pastures each day. Their lives in Cobden reflect the same arrangements. Until recently, the nearly exclusive employment arena was local agriculture, primarily in the apple and peach orchards that surround Cobden and in commercial strawberry and blueberry operations. Vegetable crops have been phased into the orchard operations to offer more steady employment between April and October, and thus stabilize the workforce available to local growers.

## Small Towns

Cherán, though of significant size for an "indigenous" community, is not a large urban center. Its population of 12,000 to 15,000 is densely packed into a hub that requires no more than 45 minutes to traverse on foot. The influx of migrant dollars and the surging growth of its population in the last fifteen years have diminished, but not eliminated, the village feel of the place. The entire population is served by one Roman Catholic church staffed by two priests. Until recently there was no bank and no hotel. There are two gas stations. Only in the year 2000 did the town open its own community clinic. Dirt and cobblestone streets in areas away from the center are slowly being paved. More than a third of its population is bilingual P'urépecha-Spanish, and P'urépecha is commonly heard in the streets, weekly markets, work *faenas*, and other community events.

Cobden is much smaller. The village's official population is 1,090. Its consolidated school district (serving a large rural area) boasts a K–12 population of less than 700. Two gas stations, one bank, and a variety of small businesses serve its residents. The owner of the sole grocery store closed his operation in 1999, and the town's only food store is La Mexicana, owned by a Hispanic resident and catering to Mexican food tastes. Many Cobden residents earn their living in other towns, specifically Anna, 9 miles to the south, and Carbondale, 20 miles north.

## Numerical Limits

The smallness of scope within which migrants have moved between Cherán and Cobden allows not only for manageable survey methods but also for well-rounded native knowledge of entire migrator groups. Many people in both communities are acquainted with the majority of the migrants in their area, whether they are Anglos who come into regular contact with *cheranecos* in Cobden, or natives of Cherán who are well informed about their migrating cohort.

Neither Cobden nor Cherán can any longer be described as a closed corporate community in the traditional senses of the phrase. Nevertheless, given the limited population sizes, the agricultural economic base for many of their residents, and the leisurely economic development in the regions surrounding them, the two towns offer a certain demographic homogeneity that is lacking in faster-moving economies and urban centers with more transient populations.

## Similarities

Finally, in a curious way, the two towns share a bond in terms of their respective migration histories.[2] Cherán's long experience sending its workers abroad for seasons of agricultural labor is complemented by Cobden's history of receiving outsiders for temporary help in the orchards and berry fields. Seasonal migrant labor has been a part of the village's history at least since the American Civil War (Cole 1919: 374–75; Bogart and Mathews 1920: 76–77; Dexter 1994). Prior to the arrival of the *cheranecos* in the Cobden area, fruit and berry harvest was accomplished by local residents and by seasonal black and white migrant workers from Tennessee, Arkansas, Louisiana, and Mississippi. A 1956 report by the Cobden Community Council made mention of "some 1,500 migratory workers who come for the berry and vegetable harvests and another 1,100 for fruit picking" (Holter 1971: 10). Significantly, in a region marked by racial discrimination, segregation, violence (for example, the Cairo, Illinois, riots of the 1960s), and ambivalence about issues of slavery in the mid-nineteenth century (Adams 1994; Evers 1964; Dexter 1994), Cobden's history of in-migration seems to have created in this tiny village a tacit tradition of tolerance for the presence of outsiders and people of color (Perrin 1883).

The limited scope of nearly all aspects of the migratory relationship between Cherán and Cobden offers the researcher opportunities to "see" migration from its infancy, through its robust years, and, as will be seen later, on into what might be considered its twilight. It affords the researcher an enviable position in the center of a very accessible array of social relations. Few residents of Cherán are not touched by migration, and

---

[2] Although not advantageous for research reasons, it is interesting to note that Cobden and Cherán both have received attention in the media and government organs that belies their size and relative significance on the Mexico-U.S. migration scene. A 1997 feature on Mexican labor migration on the National Public Radio program *All Things Considered* featured Cherán and mentioned Cobden as one important destination for its migrants. The current Web site of Mexico's National Indigenous Institute (INI) also makes mention of Cobden (spelled "Cobde" on the site). The March 10, 2002, *New York Times Book Review* mentions the village in a review of Rubén Martínez's *Crossing Over*. Cobden, despite its diminutive size, is not lost in the thinking of Cherán migrants when queried about significant destinations in the United States.

the names of the growers around Cobden are as familiar to many of them, even those who have never left Michoacán, as they are to the Anglo residents of Cobden itself. It is a very tightly woven circle, making data corroboration a straightforward task for the fieldworker in Cobden and Cherán alike.

Smallness presents dilemmas as well. As I mentioned earlier, the generalizability of research findings is in question. Cherán migrants journey to many places but few as small as Cobden.[3] And despite its size, this hosting community offers to incoming Hispanics a cluster of attributes, discussed below, that research suggests bear significant effects on migratory behavior. Whatever its generalizability to other small receiving communities, Cobden's characteristics clearly place it near the opposite pole in many respects from the migration phenomena exemplified by areas such as Los Angeles, Chicago, or Houston, urban centers with extensive infrastructural development, long histories, associated mixtures of peoples and origins, and the dynamic of competing identities. To what degree the migration of the P'urépecha people into rural Cobden may be indexical of migration phenomena in large U.S. urban centers is unclear.

## MIGRATION THEORY: SEARCH FOR INTERMEDIATE CAUSES

The voluminous literature engendered by the search for causality in transnational migration has become increasingly intricate in its theoretical formulations and rigorous in the ways that it puts those theories to the test. No attempt is made here to survey or critique that research, but only to sample fragments of it that hold promise for further understanding the localized migration phenomena described in this chapter. Certainly a healthy trend in the last two decades has been the attempt on various fronts to explore less exclusive, less polarized theoretical positions as explanations are sought for migration. Empirical work with transnational migration shows it at once anchored both to the daily-life ways of thinking, calculating individuals and to the greater socioeconomic and political forces beyond their control or knowledge. This dual anchorage is so strong that to adopt one exclusionary theoretical stance or another is to discover

---

[3] Throughout the 1980s and into the 1990s, migrant workers from Cherán consistently reported five places in the United States (in addition to Cobden) in which they and their fellows sought work: pine reforestation in north-central Arkansas; mushroom work outside of Reading, Pennsylvania; Christmas tree farms near Raleigh, North Carolina; and services and industry in the Chicago area and in Los Angeles.

immediately that the observable realities of transnational migration easily escape the conceptual containment of unidimensional approaches.

Traditional anthropological fieldwork has centered on "the micro-level phenomena of a single culture within a relatively circumscribed time" (Dewalt and Pelto 1985: 6). Macro-level phenomena—often described in historical, structural, world systems, and even urban (as opposed to village) studies—feature suprasystems and more global relationships of economics, transformation, and social relations. Giddens, in gently rejecting the dichotomy altogether, observes that:

> the distinction between micro- and macro-analysis is not a very useful one in social science, at least in some of the ways in which it is ordinarily understood. It is especially misleading if seen itself as a dualism—where "micro-situations" are those to which a notion of agency is appropriate, whereas "macro-situations" are those over which individuals have no control (Giddens 1993: 7).

A variety of what have been termed "integrationist schools" has developed in response to this difficulty. Common to these researchers is the concern that neither the micro-level nor the macro-level phenomena are lost in analyses of labor migration. Massey (1990) formulates a model that posits migrant networking as a central intermediate object somewhere between the individual and society. Stark (1991; see also Stark and Levhari 1982) contends that the most viable (for analytic purposes) linkage between micro and macro phenomena is the household. The focus on extended, decentered, multi-local households and renewed interest in the internal structure of the household are now commonplace in discussions of migration (Ilcan 1994; Stonich 1991; Shields 1995; Agesa and Kim 1999; Little 2000; Young and Fort 1994; Lawson 1998; Cohen 2001). Fawcett's (1989) "systems approach" views the interconnectedness of systems (the larger socioeconomic systems, as well as the individual's systems of family and social networks) as of crucial importance in the understanding of labor migration.

Beyond a generalized integration of the micro and macro poles, another research dimension has emerged that makes use of extensive statistical and field research designed to test the validity and applicability of leading migration theories to the issues of Mexico-U.S. migration (see Durand and Massey 1992; Espenshade 1990; Massey, Goldring, and Durand 1994; Massey et al. 1994). In a comprehensive evaluation of migration theory specifically oriented to Mexico and the United States, for example, Massey and Espinosa (1997) use empirical surveys to test the predictors of various theories (neoclassical economics, social capital theory, the new economics of migration, segmented labor market theory, and world systems theory) against actual occurrences of migration from twenty-five Mexican communities. The ultimate purpose of their study is to provide "theoretical understanding [permitting] a clearer evaluation of policy options for the United States" (Massey and Espinosa 1997: 990).

The development of integrated perspectives, with their resulting emphases on phenomena intermediate between the macro and micro levels, coupled with the rich empirical critiques of the field studies provide a framework for understanding current trends in the Cherán-Cobden migration. A useful by-product of the Massey and Espinosa study is the development of a set of general characteristics of the towns, economies, family structures, and demographic factors that lead to differential probabilities of migration to the United States. Migration patterns from the P'urépecha region, mapped against the resulting generalized profiles, make it evident that the transnational migration originating in Cherán is driven by events and conditions common to much of Mexico. First-time undocumented migrants are likely to come from agrarian communities, particularly where there is some degree of economic transformation in the community and surrounding countryside. They are likely to be young and unmarried. The likelihood of migration is increased significantly with the possession of social capital (contacts and support) at the destination point. Repeat migration is engendered by experience, increasing social and human capital, and the presence of children after marriage (with the accompanying expenses of a household). Family members in the United States with documents increase the probability of migration for all categories. None of these comparisons is particularly surprising, and all of them place at least the initial phases of P'urépecha migration between Cherán and Cobden into a typical scheme for most migrant-sending regions of Mexico.

## THE MIGRATION CONTEXT OF COBDEN AND CHERÁN
### Cobden

Cobden is located in north-central Union County, in deep southwestern Illinois. The county is rural, with striking vistas of forested hills and valleys, the meeting place of the old mountain systems of the Ozarks and Ouachitas to the south and west. It has a total population of only 17,000, only one town with more than 4,000 inhabitants, and three villages of approximately 1,000. The forested and hilly terrain has successfully prohibited urban and industrial development of any employment significance. Virtually all locally generated employment comes either from agriculture or from whatever services can be sustained by the small urban centers. Union County is bordered to the south and east by counties even less developed, to the west by the Mississippi River, and to the north by Jackson County, relatively more prosperous and populous. In Jackson County, the city of Carbondale (population 25,000) and Southern Illinois University provide significant employment avenues for residents of surrounding counties. Carbondale has also been a magnet for Hispanics through the years.

Cobden, founded in 1852 as South Pass (the Central Illinois Railroad surveyed its north-south line through the hills at this point), is in the middle of a region that has seen extensive peach, apple, and strawberry production since the mid-nineteenth century. Early in the 1900s, Cobden was surrounded north and south by peach and apple orchards. Since World War II the number of farms has diminished greatly, and the majority of those remaining are to be found north of Cobden around the village of Alto Pass (population 340). It is these orchards that have formed the catalyst for Cobden's experiences with migrants from Cherán.

Cobden is in many ways typical of any town whose geographic position and small size have kept its economic and demographic growth (as well as its manifest desire for such growth) to a minimum. The few businesses it has cannot employ its inhabitants, making it a de facto "bedroom" community. Malls and other such urban amenities are a twenty-minute drive from town. The village is far from dying, however. The close of peach harvest brings with it the Annual Peach Festival, celebrated since 1929. Parades, carnivals, queen contests, and so on provide a homecoming atmosphere at the end of summer that attracts visitors from all over the region. Other festivals throughout the year cement the community identity. A recent bond referendum launched an ambitious high school building project. The lingering pride of a 1964 run at the state high school basketball tournament, coupled with the self-image of a healthy and safe place to live, helps maintain a palpable pleasantness within the village and surrounding area.

Concrete and verifiable counts of migrant workers are, of course, difficult to come by, but those who work with this particular population estimate the numbers to have stayed steady since the early 1980s at around

1,500 to 2,000.[4] Such numbers reveal the significant proportion of the county's total population that is of Mexican migrant origin. This is in a part of the country that, prior to 1960, had no recent experience with a "foreign-born" population.

## Cherán

Cherán is located in the north-central part of the state of Michoacán known as the Sierra P'urépecha, one of four distinctly P'urépecha zones. The state is home to four indigenous groups, of which the P'urépecha are the most numerous and well organized, constituting 82.5 percent of all indigenous-language speakers in the state. The P'urépecha have higher levels of literacy, primary education, and household amenities (indoor plumbing, electricity, finished floors) than other indigenous groups, although their levels are still far below nonindigenous levels (INEGI 2002).

The blurring of the distinctions between the modern and the traditional notwithstanding (Kearney 1996), the Sierra owns a long-standing reputation for its cultural and linguistic conservatism, and Cherán exemplifies those attributes. Both residents of the town and observers from without have found its conservative character remarkable. Its isolation, conservatism, resistance to change from within and to influences from outside, and the strength of its reputation in the surrounding area have been consistently noted by nearly every author familiar with the town. Cherán, whether fairly or not, has long been susceptible to generalized portrayal as a conservative, homogeneous, isolated community. Much of that, however, is changing with the tides of migration that have engulfed it. Nevertheless, Cherán maintains a historical homogeneity with regard to settlement patterns and population movement. Aguirre Beltrán (1952) mentions that in 1742 non-P'urépecha inhabitants (creoles, mestizos, mulattos) numbered eleven in Paracho, two in Aranza, and five in Nahuatzen—all towns within close proximity to Cherán. There were no non-P'urépecha living in Cherán. In 1940, when Cherán had a population of 5,000, Beals recorded only eight people who had moved into the town "in recent years," and reported that while "there is no bar to purchase of land by outsiders ... if land is for sale,

---

[4] This and other figures used in this discussion represent informal estimates by those who work with the population, a group that includes researchers, legal advocates, health care outreach workers, growers, local clergy, educators, and other social service providers. The general consensus among them is that this population is undercounted in the official census.

owners are expected to offer it first to local residents" (1946: 98). The president of Cherán told me in February 1994 that, to his knowledge, there were no landowners in Cherán who were not born in the village. "It is a very homogeneous population. Property is sold within the community." Such reports of demographic autonomy are not universal among all residents, some claiming that over the last twenty years "all sorts" of different people have come to settle in the community.

Today's P'urépecha are young, with an average age of 23.5 years and with over 43 percent of the population under 15 years of age (CONAPO 1999). Anecdotal evidence would suggest, however, that despite its youth, the population as a whole still values and to some degree propagates a variety of traditional practices, including community endogamy, bride capture, and witchcraft, along with traditional healing arts, cuisine, dress (particularly for females), and dancing. The *pirekua*, the traditional musical style of the Sierra, is heard not only in the streets but on the local radio station as well. Another traditional characteristic whose vigor apparently remains unchecked is the system of *compadrazgo*. "Among the P'urépecha, this institution [*padrinazgo* and *compadrazgo*] of Hispanic origin has been adapted to the point of transforming it into something sophisticated, by the number of godparents and affinal relatives that an individual can end up having throughout his life cycle, in addition to the exceedingly elaborate ritual behavior which is put to use for the occasion" (INI 2002).

Hand in hand with its conservatism and homogeneity goes Cherán's "indigenous" character. Beals noted that, "although white admixture certainly exists in the town's population, there are virtually no acknowledged Mestizos" (1946: 12). Brand's (1952) and Foster's (1948) studies of neighboring Quiroga and Tzintzuntzan, respectively—both mestizo towns according to Stanislawski (1944)—categorize Cherán as "Indian." It is still, according to one current researcher in the area, the only indigenous *municipio* in the region (Roth Seneff, El Colegio de Michoacán, personal communication, February 1994)—measured subjectively. Informal observations abound regarding the tenacity of Cherán's ethnicity despite the pressures of general Mexican mestizo culture, as well as the influences carried home by the multitudes of migrants who annually work in the United States and return with dollars, vehicles, clothes, and ideas from the north.

## MIGRATION HISTORY

In November 1993, after some months of waiting and searching, I made my initial encounter with Pedro Herrera, the unwitting instigator of a four-decade migrant flow, the very first man ("*el mero primerito*," as he was described to me) to make it to Cobden from Cherán. He came to the door of his home in Cherán after a summons by his wife upon her hearing the words "Cobden" and "Illinois." Never having left the region of her birth, she recognized the two names immediately and decided it would be all right to let me speak to her husband. There at his doorstep, I unfolded my mission to him, and at the mention of Cobden and Union County, so far away from him in space and time, his face broke into the nostalgic grin of recalled journeys and life-changing adventures, and he bade me sit down and visit with him. He related his story, piecing it together as he made the passage again in his mind, as much for himself as for me. I sensed that he enjoyed hearing the narrative again.

> I don't remember but I think it was around 1959 or 1960 when I left Cherán for the first time. I was on foot mostly — a little bit by bus and some on a truck. I went to the border because there wasn't any work at home and I was young [laughing] and curious and wanted adventure. I swam across the Río Bravo alone at night and nobody saw me and I spent some time wandering around the streets and alleys of Laredo, in Texas. I was on the "other side" now. I remember how hot it was the next day and I was thirsty and hungry and I was scared, but I thought that trying to go back home would be worse than staying in Texas and working. So I stayed. I didn't have any money. I didn't know any English. I found a railroad yard and an open car and climbed in. I was cold now and really hungry. In fact I thought I was going to die and that my trip to the north was a stupid idea. I don't remember how I lived in that train car, with no food and only a little water. I really don't remember. But it started to move and I stayed in it for three or four days.[5]

Neither did he recall when the train left the border heading north and what route it took to reach its destination along the Mississippi River at Chester, Illinois. Four days after departing Laredo, he tumbled out of the

[5] This bit of oral history is taken from field note transcriptions of my informal interviews and conversations at Pedro Herrera's home in Cherán, Michoacán, in the fall of 1993. The transcription provided here is not verbatim but is an amalgam of significant bits and pieces in the narration, many of them prompted by specific questions (such as "How many days were you in the train car?").

car along some siding, certain that he was still in Texas somewhere near Laredo. He was completely lost and alone, with no resources in a part of the United States that, at that time, had no experience with Mexicans. Only thanks to the attention, gestures, and curiosity of some unnamed farmer in Missouri did he eat his first meal in many days, bathe, and learn of the distance he had traveled. This same farmer brought him to one of the orchards in Illinois north of Cobden, where he was put to work and stayed, slowly learning the craft of horticulture and, most importantly, earning enough to feed himself. After about two years he returned to Cherán with the expressed purpose of fulfilling his boss's desires and bringing up more people "who can work like you do." And return he did, with the first group of young men to enter the southern Illinois agricultural workforce from Michoacán.

From the mid-1960s, after Herrera's group had established itself with a single grower north of Cobden, the fame of the Mexican workers simply spread under its own power, from one grower in the area to the next. Seasonal fruit harvest was carried out at the time by white and black migrant labor, much of it originating in Tennessee and other southern states. The memory of those first years, when domestic migrant labor worked side by side with Mexicans, leaves many orchard men virtually at a loss for words to describe the magnitude of difference between the two groups in production, responsibility, and cooperation. A new "machine" had been discovered. It spoke Spanish, rarely complained, and could complete a harvest cleanly in a fraction of the time and with a fraction of the problems of the old machine of domestic migrant labor. There was much to learn about this new agricultural device, by now tried and proven in other parts of the United States but relatively unknown in southern Illinois. By the mid-1970s, the conversion to Mexican field labor was all but complete in all the orchards around Cobden.

The decade of the 1980s saw the stabilizing of the migrant workforce in Cobden, some through the normal socializing channels of children in school and the relative economic and social security stemming from the accumulation of social and human capital. Efforts by the Illinois Migrant Council, with a branch office located 20 miles north of Cobden in Carbondale, to arrest the migrant cycle and to get individuals and families out of the migrant stream through better housing, children in schools, and steady, nonagricultural work began to bear fruit. A spate of home buying began in the mid-1980s and lasted until the early 1990s, culminating in 20 percent of homes in Cobden and the neighboring hamlet of Alto Pass (population

340) being owned by Hispanics. Leaders among the homebuyers were immigrants from Cherán. At the time, Cobden's only bank processed many of the loans, and the chief concern of the bank's loan officer was that Hispanic homebuyers not purchase houses or properties near one another, creating a racial ghetto (personal communication, January 1990).

## THE P'URÉPECHA COMMUNITY IN COBDEN

The Hispanic population is now a solid demographic fixture in Cobden. It is comprised of P'urépecha from Cherán, along with mestizos from Guanajuato (mostly from the community of Salvatierra), Jalisco, Central America, and scattered places in Mexico, including Guerrero, Chiapas, and, recently, Veracruz. The migrants from Cherán still probably constitute the single numerical majority of any specific origin, and they are arguably the most cohesive Hispanic group as well. Though their housing is scattered in and about Cobden (in nearby migrant labor camps, low-rent housing, and mobile homes throughout the surrounding countryside), a question about the location of virtually anybody's residence will generate a confident answer. Their families and extended families are anchored in the village, and robust biological kin networks are augmented by the extensive and intricate fictive kin relations of *padrinazgo* and *compadrazgo*. Information networks (both factual and gossip) about the community and between Cobden and Cherán are of easy access, up to date, and usually accurate.

The general Mexican presence in Cobden is noticeable but not overwhelming. Pedestrians on the streets, patrons at the gas stations or bank, parents at school functions, and visitors at community events constitute the bulk of their presence inside the village. Much migrant housing is located in the orchards and countryside outside of town, and the housing occupied within the village limits is not remarkable in appearance or location. The central park in Cobden, however, presents quite another story. It is an important gathering place on Saturday and Sunday evenings for many from Cherán, clearly a surrogate plaza for the one back home. Its playground equipment, benches, and picnic tables offer places to visit and watch the ever-ongoing basketball game taking place on the park's one court every weekend evening that weather permits. Coolers of sodas and sports drinks are pulled from pickup trucks and the beverages are set out for sale; the home cookers sell their tamales, breads, and other culinary creations; and the occasional would-be merchant displays his rack of cassette tapes. Music thumps from the woofers of cars parked nearby. Only on the very fringes of this gathering will one find Hispanics who are not from

Cherán, and very few at that. This park tradition has a twenty-year history, with as many as 150 to 200 Cherán natives gathering on any given Sunday evening, much to the consternation of some resident Anglos.

## Formal Political and Social Organization

In Michoacán, Cherán residents may participate in a variety of formal civic and political organizations. La Nación P'urépecha, first appearing publicly in 1991, represents the widest formal political and social organization oriented to the concerns of this particular ethnic group.[6] The organizations, coalitions, and alliances run the gamut from community groups based on barrio affinity to intercommunity linkages and regional organizations with very focused agendas (such as the Organización Ribereña contra la Contaminación del Lago de Pátzcuaro). Cherán itself claims the Sociedad de Solidaridad Social de la Meseta P'urépecha, a group dedicated to issues of cattle production and pasture conservation.

Despite the variety of political and social organizations to which *cheranecos* may belong, no evidence of any formal organization within the P'urépecha community exists in Cobden. Nor is it evident that expatriate leadership has any interest in forming such organizations. The early 1990s saw attempts by outsiders (neither *cheranecos* nor Cobdenites) to "organize the people"—something vaguely along the lines of the United Farm Workers of America. But insufficient interest from the Mexican community left these attempts withering in the face of Anglo apathy and opposition, and most of the would-be organizers have since left the community. Certainly nothing resembling the Frente of the *oaxaqueños* of California (see Kearney 2001) has ever existed. The occasional church function or school event may draw together many interested Hispanics of all origins, but the organization of such activities is generated from outside the Cherán community.

This lack of formal organizations stands in stark contrast to the highly organized community structures that guide the social life of the P'urépecha in Cherán. Some of those structures made their way along the migration paths and continue to play a part in the lives of Cherán natives in Cobden, but with far less rigidity and weight. Elsewhere I have documented the long reach of barrio relations (Anderson 1999) beyond the bounds of Cherán. Significant life events, such as retirement, weddings, grave illnesses, and

---

[6] The Frente Estatal Indígena de Michoacán, of fairly recent creation, claims to represent the interests of all four indigenous groups in the state—the P'urépecha, Nahuas, Otomís, and Mazahuas.

death, often leave migrants dependent upon each other through the relationships structured by civic organizations back home. Raffle tickets sold around Cobden to benefit physical improvements to the church building in Cherán are not an uncommon occurrence, fellow *cheranecos* trusting each other to actually deliver the cash and communicate with the lucky winners.

Beyond such incidental events, however, the involvement of P'urépecha migrants in the civic life of Cobden or Cherán is so insignificant as to be imperceptible. The idea of a migrant in Cobden, even one away only a few months each year, occupying any type of municipal or religious position in Cherán is met with puzzlement and amusement. How could a migrant know enough about events in Cherán to be trusted with authority? People would not put them into office knowing they would likely be gone. These attitudes are bolstered by the apparent abundance of nonmigrants in Cherán who are willing and able to serve in civic and political capacities. Despite the fact that *ayuntamiento* (municipal government) estimates put the number of those who leave annually at around 25 percent of Cherán's population, out-migration has, in the experience of a former president of Cherán, never resulted in the inability to fill a civic or political post (personal communication, February 1994). Each city block requires a *jefe de manzana*, and each of the town's four barrios requires a *jefe de barrio* and fourteen *comisionados*, a different set of the latter selected every six months to organize the town's two large religious festivals.

In Cobden, interest in such activities is uniformly weak, as the following two cases will show. Basketball games in the Cobden park represent the only semblance of ongoing formal organization to have developed among the P'urépecha community. For most of the season, these are little more than pick-up games for whoever has the energy to play. In 1993, however, three Cherán natives formed the "Hispanic Sports Committee." This committee organized basketball tournaments at regular intervals during the migration season, encouraging teams from different orchards to suit up and compete. Complete with referees, scorekeepers, entry fees, cash awards, and trophies, these tournaments attracted perhaps a dozen teams, some from neighboring Kentucky and Tennessee. Organization was by word of mouth and occasionally by Xeroxed flyers. I am not aware of a single participant during the several years of the Hispanic Sports Committee's existence who was not from Cherán.

In 1993 an eclectic group of interested parties formed a local chapter of the Illinois Interagency Committee on Migrant Affairs (IACOMA). In attendance at the first organizing meeting were eight Hispanics (one from

Cherán) and five Anglos. One result of this group's efforts was the organization of a Mexican Independence Day celebration at Cobden's park. This first festival of its kind in Cobden, and subsequent festivals spawned by its initial success, revealed unmistakable fissures in the Hispanic community which had remained, until that time, quite well concealed. Cherán natives were at the center of the divisions and strife. Their principal antagonism was against a group of nearly equal size (but less cohesive because of its more scattered origins in Mexico) from Guanajuato. The details of the conflict are beyond the scope of this discussion, they being fairly typical of intergroup tensions in a small community. One result of the open division was the declaration by the *michoacanos*, in comments and behaviors both public and private, of what it meant to be P'urépecha. History, common territory, language, blood, *cabeza*, the first rights of the "pioneers" into Cobden, and a host of other attributes were implicitly and explicitly invoked to justify the *cheranecos'* position in the discord. In a turn reflecting the linguistic reappropriation described by Kearney (2001), the term *indio* took on a less than pejorative meaning in informal conversations around town, this most likely to distinguish the P'urépecha from their mestizo rivals. Public aspersions and private critiques contributed to the diminished influence of the Hispanic (read "Cherán") Sports Committee and the increasing marginalization of the local IACOMA group. A few interested "members" of the latter continued to meet, but for all practical purposes the organization was defunct and nobody was paying attention.

These two cases are offered here to demonstrate the low level of interest for participation in public organizations of any kind. No group of migrants in Cobden is sufficiently integrated into the life of the Anglo community to offer a candidate for the village or school boards.

## Religious Practice

Cherán today is unquestionably and ardently Roman Catholic in its general orientation. Small non-Catholic endeavors (Baptist, Jehovah's Witnesses, and others) in the town have a history that dates to the 1930s (Aguirre Beltrán 1952: 325; Castile 1974: 95; Friedrich 1970: iii), but Protestant doctrine has had little to no effect in Cherán, even by admission of a missionary with fifty years of labor there (personal communication, December 1993). While the sheer numbers of devout Catholics in town and the religious festival system which still constitutes a vital part of community life keep Cherán a bulwark of Catholic belief and practice, the town is awash with migrants returning from the United States with ideas about religious tolerance, informed perceptions about Protestant beliefs (as well as a non-Mexican perspective on Roman Catholic practice), and religious eclecticism and cooperation. The major elements of Tarascan beliefs are of Roman Catholic origin (Carrasco 1976), and the religious festivals and observances draw migrants home on a regular basis. So strong is the pull, in fact, that during apple harvest — arguably the most "lucrative" time for fruit workers to be away from home — growers in southern Illinois are often hit with a mass departure of Cherán workers heading home for the town's patron saint festival, not to return until March or April. Cherán's Roman Catholicism is easily transported to Illinois. The priest of Cobden's Catholic church is a Mexican native from Toluca, making a linguistic and cultural connection to migrant workers that only strengthens the already hearty attachment to the Catholic Church that they bring with them.

## Labor Shift

In the early 1990s, a single event sparked a labor shift out of the orchards around Cobden and into nonagricultural industrial sites, some as far as two hours away and none closer than a half-hour drive from Cobden. The Illinois Migrant Council (IMC) local office managed (after years of trying) to secure contractual arrangements for Mexican laborers in two industrial plants, one approximately 50 miles north of Cobden and another 85 miles south, in Kentucky. As had been the case with local migration in the first place, natives of Cherán were the first Mexican group to take advantage of the new options. While the initial effect of these two employment alternatives amounted to little more than several dozen workers leaving the farms, the long-term effects proved to be far-reaching. As more people learned of the advantages of full-time, nonseasonal work, with vacation time and health benefits built in, the natural comparison to the grueling, seasonal, minimum-wage work in the orchards engendered more interest in off-farm work and increased efforts by the IMC and others to secure stable, nonagricultural employment. The result has been profoundly beneficial to workers in general and difficult for some growers around Cobden.

With new avenues opened up for wage labor, the thirty-year grip of horticulture as the sole employment option was, in a matter of eighteen months, effectively broken. Within two years of the first group leaving Cobden orchards for industrial-type work, it was common to find carloads of day laborers on their way to a cereal plant (50 miles distant), pasta-packing factory (30 miles), diaper manufacturer (30 miles), ceramic and brick works (40 miles), chicken-processing plant (85 miles), and aluminum boat manufacturer (50 miles). The number of sites continues to grow. The scattering of workers is significant, not for where they went but for where they chose to stay. Beyond work in the orchards, Cobden has virtually no employment to offer its migrant guests, yet no more than a mere handful of families relocated.

## MIGRATION THEORY AND POPULATION MOVEMENT

Standard theories of migration, though variably focused on different dimensions of the phenomenon, coincide in their view that transnational migration's basic engine is fueled by economic interests (Massey et al. 1994). Despite the fact that migration theory increasingly points to the household and social networks intermediate between the macro and micro levels as crucial to an understanding of the dynamics of migration, gainful employment is unquestionably at the root of virtually all transnational movement out of Cherán. In twenty years of fieldwork with this population, I have never encountered or interviewed a male migrant who offered any reason but employment for his move north. (Women, children, and the elderly often give family reasons for migrating.) The accounts are remarkably similar and fit Massey and Espinosa's (1997) profiles with precision.

Characteristic of historical processes of migration the world over, "migration flows, once established, tend to continue with relative autonomy" (Portes and Böröcz 1989). This is particularly exemplified by the Mexico-U.S. case. The establishment of migration networks through kinship ties and other social institutions was noted early on as a key feature of the historical process of Mexican migration to the United States (Ranney and Kossoudji 1983; Bean and Tienda 1987; Portes 1989). This microstructural building of financial safety nets may engender migrational trends that seem at odds with larger economic patterns (Portes and Böröcz 1989). Such would appear to be the case with the P'urépecha in Cobden. Despite the shift in labor patterns, informal counts of Cherán natives in and around Cobden show their numbers apparently unchanged. Home ownership and occupancy have not increased significantly since the late 1980s, but neither have they declined, as might be expected with a local loss in employment opportunities.

As with all else concerning the Cherán-Cobden migration dynamic, evidence is obtained on a painfully small scale. In 2000, a Mexican food store (named La Mexicana but known somewhat affectionately by many local Mexicans as "La Kroger"), owned by a family from Cherán, opened up in an old historic building across from the park in the center of town.

Fully stocked and busy with customers, it does a brisk business, almost exclusively with Hispanic patrons. The owner is unconcerned that many workers make their living elsewhere. In a more urban, densely populated area, the presence of a single store would go unnoticed. In Cobden, however, the significance of the store's success is seen in the fact that La Mexicana is the *only* grocery store of any kind in the village. Time will tell of the store's success or failure, but as is common to many immigrants, multiple avenues of employment are cobbled together in a sixty-to-eighty-hour workweek (Raijman 2001), and the owner of La Mexicana is no exception. Despite his seeming lack of worry, his investment in the store is ponderous and risky. The case of this little store is important for two reasons. Its presence in Cobden constitutes perhaps the only infrastructural development internal to the P'urépecha community in Cobden, and the owner's attitude is representative of many who continue to live in the village.

If economic reasons are at the base of initial migratory moves, how might we account for the tenacity with which *cheranecos* have stayed in Cobden, despite its current inhospitable economic climate? And what might such an account teach us about other similar locales in the United States and the transnational in-migration they experience? The answer to such questions leads to a detailed inspection of what Cobden specifically offers the P'urépecha migrants from Cherán and how these offerings correspond to the needs and expectations of people from this specific origin. It will be seen that, beyond the general profile of migrants and the dynamic of the household and social networks, specific linkages may play an important role in determining the holding power of a specific destination. The Cherán-Cobden connection suggests that yet another dimension of migration merits examination: the idiosyncratic conditions and similarities beyond social networks that bind migration terminals and regions together. A brief review of conditions in Cobden sets the stage for such an examination.

## Hedonic Factors

In addition to the similarities between the two towns already described, the historical presence of intact families from Cherán has lent stability to Cobden. Social networks have traditionally driven hiring in the area as well, holding a *contratista* system at bay. The isolated conditions in the village make for a sense of security for its inhabitants, both Anglo and Hispanic. Finally, a comparatively high rate of poverty and low educational levels in the county ameliorate somewhat the socioeconomic contrasts that could, under other circumstances, easily be interpreted as racial or national divisions. Hedonic migration theory (Shields 1995) holds that such conditions play a significant role in migration decisions and that the "amenities of a region [can be] treated as goods which can only be consumed by households if they reside in that region" (Shields 1995: 117). Framed around the questions of employment and regional economic equilibrium as conceptualized within the U.S. working population, hedonic migration theory nevertheless offers provocative investigative avenues for transnational migration as well. Cobden indeed offers some special amenities, particularly for households with children, that make it, for lack of a better term, "special." Such concepts are nearly impossible to measure and thus fall beyond the realm of hardcore empirical scrutiny.

Through the years I have made the question of why P'urépecha migrants end up at a place like Cobden—and stay there—a consistent focus of my interactions with Cherán natives. Besides the predictable influences of social capital, the responses range from whimsical ("we like the water" or "the basketball court") to more thoughtful responses about safety, landscape (very similar to Cherán's), pace of life, and likeable qualities of the area's growers. I have not attempted to "measure" these intangibles, but I am convinced they play a significant role in many migrants' decisions to come and to stay, even in the face of undesirable employment conditions.

P'urépecha migrants in Cobden, having been the earliest to arrive and to bring families, have established a multigenerational presence. Elderly *cheranecos*, most still unable to communicate in English (and some only poorly conversant in Spanish), ply their parental trade with grandchildren in many households. The tight connections between grandparents and grandchildren, so common in Cherán, are part and parcel of many lives in Cobden as well. Their residences serve as geographic anchors for their offspring, who continue to migrate, albeit only regionally, from industrial job to industrial job and back and forth across the Mexico-U.S. border. Weekends and vacations find the middle generation returning to Cobden, visiting others of their age, displaying their new offspring, making sure the elders are doing well, and continually nourishing the migratory patrimony that they have embedded in this village.

These features of P'urépecha life in Cobden form a cluster of amenities that, with effort, could be re-created elsewhere—but not without time and a sedentariness that runs counter to migrant cycles. Despite the brief relationship between Cherán and Cobden, there is much to suggest that hedonic migration theory bears further attention as it relates to rural, small-scale migration patterns.

## Bilingual Services and Education

There are two other, less ethereal amenities in Cobden as well: Spanish language services and a local bilingual school program. The Union-Jackson Farm Workers Camp, built in 1966 two miles north of Cobden, houses offices and facilities for a migrant Headstart daycare program (one of only seven in the state), a health clinic, playground and basketball and volleyball courts, and legal services. Virtually all services are offered in Spanish. Over the decades of its existence, the camp evolved beyond a simple collection of dwellings; it has served as community center and a place of social focus as well. The traffic of visitors and users of its facilities is constant during the months when it is open. Moreover, since its inhabitants are concentrated spatially, unlike the Hispanic residents of Cobden, the visiting done each evening out on the stoops, in the parking lots, and in the kitchens lubricates informational networks and gossip currents to the degree that many who are not even residents spend their evenings at the camp to visit and keep informed about the community.

The Cobden Consolidated School District (K–12), through the efforts of a series of district superintendents and bilingual teachers, has created a grant-based bilingual education and English as a Second Language (ESL) program which operates twelve months out of the year. The program has developed over two decades to include all grade levels and has expanded to reach the preschool levels, as well as to recruit students beyond the high school years for summer language training and GED work. One of the strengths of the Cobden program is its structured involvement of parents. The controversial nature of such programs and the political and linguistic firestorm that generally surrounds them are, for all practical purposes, lost on the participants of the programs. What is important is the programs' presence in the lives and education of migrant children.

I would suggest that the importance of Cobden's bilingual program has two dimensions for P'urépecha migrants. The first is the obvious and immediate value of education (homework materials, bilingual teachers and aides, program announcements, and so on) provided in a language the entire family understands. A second, however, is directly traceable to the bilingual roots in the Sierra P'urépecha of Michoacán; P'urépecha residents are firsthand observers of both sides of the bilingual education debate in Mexico. As in all regions of Mexico with significant indigenous populations, public education takes two forms in Michoacán: the federal system and the bilingual or indigenous system. The federal school system is by far the more extensive, well funded, and well staffed. The indigenous system employs teachers who have been certified by the state as possessing sufficient knowledge of P'urépecha to be able to manage a classroom containing children whose primary home language is not Spanish. In contrast to the relatively well funded federal system, the indigenous schools tend to be located in colonias on the outskirts of larger population centers or in isolated, smaller communities of clear P'urépecha character. Differences in the funding, administration, and physical plants between the two systems are stark. Indigenous schools containing multilevel classes are housed in one-room clapboard shacks outside of town (where contact with families is easier), while up the road a few kilometers, federal school students enjoy multiple-room facilities, with courtyards, gymnasiums, windows, uniforms, and a full complement of teachers in the various subject areas. Since Cherán sits in the center of a P'urépecha-speaking region, the outlying area is dotted with schools whose curricula and faculty are bilingual, at least in theory.

This dual educational system and the philosophies behind it are rife with the contentious divides that characterize much of the debate over bilingual education in the United States. Many P'urépecha parents in Cobden, far from being naïve recipients of a language program they do not understand or appreciate, come to the table fully cognizant of the costs and the benefits such a program entails, for they have seen it already from both sides.

## Religious Participation

A limited amount of research suggests that involvement in a religious congregation that makes social as well as spiritual demands on individuals and families has a suppressive effect on migratory movement (Myers 2000). This research, too, had its origins with questions about U.S. population mobility and social capital accumulation (Bibby 1997; Sandomirsky and Wilson 1990; Stump 1984). As with hedonic migration theory, theory about religious involvement and geographic movement holds potential for application to transnational migration as well, particularly given the specifics of the Cobden community.

> It is generally assumed that migration is less responsive to variables like religion—that is, to variables that are more about ideology and less about material standard of living. However, religion occupies a central role in the lives of most Americans (Myers 2000: 756).

Cobden's sole Catholic priest, assigned in the 1980s, is from Mexico (Toluca) and has managed to keep his congregational efforts well balanced between the Anglo and Hispanic parishioners. He has had personal contacts with a succession of priests in Cherán through the years, garnering respect and appreciation from his P'urépecha congregants. His contact with them is to be expected, for such, in their eyes, is the work of a priest. Something of a religious novelty for *cheranecos*, however, emerged in the 1980s with the development of a large Protestant (United Methodist) congregation on property north of Cobden. From small beginnings in a storefront in the village, the church—through a succession of Mexican pastors and seminary students working as evangelical missionaries out of institutions in Monterrey, and with the backing of the United Methodist Church hierarchy—acquired twenty-two acres and erected a group of structures to house a growing congregation (in fact, one of the larger United Methodist congregations in southern Illinois). No other non-Catholic religious group has marshaled the resources necessary to maintain a presence like that of the United Methodists. Thus Hispanic migrants of either Roman Catholic or Protestant persuasion have access to faith-based communities reflecting familiar cultural and linguistic practices.

Cherán natives were very slow to embrace the Protestant congregation; in fact, they were the last group of Mexican migrants to venture in (various personal communications with the pastor). Such tardiness is not surprising given the religious climate in Cherán itself, described in earlier sections. Nevertheless, congregational participation on the part of P'urépecha believers from Cherán has grown over the years to the point where many hold leadership positions within the church. Child care, financial support, employment contacts, temporary housing, and a host of services (carpentry, cooking, and auto mechanics, among others) provided by church members to their fellow congregants come bundled in the package of spiritual commitment.

Myers contends that "location-specific religious capital is a very distinct form of social capital and contains unique aspects not present in social capital" (2000: 760). Religious capital, for example, generates "nonreligious outputs" which are nevertheless "still situated in a socio-religious context." In fact, religious capital in this view entails far more than mere ideology. Migration separates individuals not only from the comfort of fellow believers but also from concrete material goods that, given the context in which they were generated, would require significant investment to reestablish. Hispanic churches with robust spiritual and community life are the exception rather than the rule in the multi-state region surrounding Cobden. The pastor and individual leaders from the congregation have been asked to travel as far as 300 miles in order to help found similar operations. For those who are committed to this congregation, migration away from its benefits, both spiritual and material, represents potentially intolerable risks.

## CONCLUSION

Logic would suggest that the aforementioned characteristics are all advantageous to the stability of a migratory population. They should not be construed, however, to indicate that Cobden is particularly progressive with regard to cultural or racial issues. It is an isolated, historically European-American village that has found a number of ways, albeit sometimes grudgingly, to deal with an onslaught of people different from its own. Although the growers of the surrounding farms hold positions of influence and power in the community, the village itself has neither invited nor rejected the presence of P'urépecha migrants or Hispanics in general. It has tolerated and coped. Cherán, too, moves along its path in a very pedestrian fashion. There is scant evidence of any premeditation or planning, for good or ill, that the community has put into dealing with the exodus of its many members. Like Cobden, it has neither invited nor rejected the effects of migration. Cherán's priest once remarked that the people of the Sierra "*es muy aguantadora*" (put up with a great deal). The P'urépecha of Cherán tolerate and cope. The residents of the two spaces are neither adversaries (although some see it that way) nor "brothers." They are, however, fellow copers.

This discussion, admittedly of an often "thick" and anecdotal nature, highlights a crucial aspect of transnational migration that is frequently lost in studies whose aim is more theoretical or whose focus is on the patterns of larger populations. Indeed, the very label "transnational migration" is apt to obscure the important fact that it is about humans—humans moving out of familiar surroundings and discovering ways to make new surroundings somewhat like home. Those new surroundings into which migrants move are, of course, constituted by more than neatly analyzable socioeconomic structures. They are spaces that other groups have invested in and made familiar, part of a "multidimensional global space with unbounded, often discontinuous and interpenetrating sub-spaces" (Kearney 1995: 549). One of the objectives of this chapter has been to look closely at the thick interplay between familiar spaces as they are woven together by the actions of P'urépecha migrants and those in Illinois who receive them.

The warp of P'urépecha life in Michoacán and the weft of village life in southern Illinois combine intricately, yet systematically, to form a fabric that, although difficult to comprehend fully, nonetheless invites inspection and admiration. A portion of this fabric has to do with the individual agency that migrants exercise as they confront the choices and obstacles that circumstances throw their way. Another portion is fixed, not by their agency but by the households, community associations, and other intermediate social structures of which they are a part. Finally, of course, much of their behavior is constrained by the macro-level forces of global sociopolitical, historical, and economic relations between the various political entities occupying the spaces through which they travel.

It is not likely that the individual features Cobden holds for migrants—the availability of social services, the ready option of both Protestant and Roman Catholic ministries in Mexican Spanish, the full-fledged bilingual program at the school, relative isolation and security, and the employment conditions—are particularly unique to this village. Virtually any community of reasonable size can marshal such resources. The diminutive scale on which these features play out for indigenous migrants may make this particular case unusual, however. Its uniqueness, or lack thereof, may be determined with more comparative studies and survey work of other small towns.

It is not clear that the small fibers making up this particular tapestry could have nearly the same stabilizing effect on a large and shifting urban population. Nevertheless, the way in which Cobden's particular array of attributes intertwines with the cultural and social characteristics that the P'urépecha migrants bring with them—intact families, extensive biological and fictive kin networks, an implicit appreciation for bilingual schooling, a strong sense of ethnic solidarity, an informal civic organizational structure (sports) that draws minimal attention from potential interlopers—should prompt an examination of migratory behavior with careful focus on the many cultural resources upon which migrants may draw and the serendipity with which those resources may be linked across a single migratory space.

## References

Adams, Jane. 1994. "1870s Agrarian Activism in Southern Illinois: Mediator between Two Eras," *Social Science History* 16, no. 3: 365–400.

Agesa, Richard, and Sunwoong Kim. 1999. "The Determinants of Household Migration Patterns in Kenya," *Atlantic Economic Journal* 27: 239.

Aguirre Beltrán, Gonzalo. 1952. "Problemas de la población indígena de la Cuenca del Tepalcatepec," *Memorias del Instituto Nacional Indigenista,* vol. 3. Mexico City: Instituto Nacional Indigenista.

Anderson, Warren D. 1999. "Familias tarascas en el sur de Illinois: la reafirmación de la identidad étnica." In *Fronteras fragmentadas,* edited by Gail Mummert. Zamora: El Colegio de Michoacán.

Beals, Ralph. 1946. *Cherán: A Sierra Tarascan Village.* Washington, D.C.: Institute for Social Anthropology, Smithsonian Institution.

Bean, Frank, and Marta Tienda. 1987. *The Hispanic Population of the United States.* New York: Russell Sage Foundation.

Bibby, Reginald. 1997. "Going, Going, Gone: The Impact of Geographical Mobility on Religious Involvement," *Review of Religious Research* 38: 289–307.

Bogart, Ernest L., and John M. Mathews. 1920. "The Modern Commonwealth 1893–1918." In *Centennial History of Illinois,* vol. 5. Springfield, Ill.: Illinois Centennial Commission.

Brand, Donald D. 1952. *Bosquejo histórico de la geografía y la antropología de la región tarasca.* Anales del Museo de Michoacán, No. 5. Morelia.

Carrasco, Pedro. 1952. *Tarascan Folk Religion.* New Orleans: Tulane University Press.

————. 1976. *El catolicismo popular de los tarascos.* Mexico City: Secretaría de Educación Pública.

Castile, George Pierre. 1974. *Cherán: la adaptación de una comunidad tradicional de Michoacán.* Mexico City: Instituto Nacional Indigenista/Secretaría de Educación Pública.

Cohen, Jeffrey H. 2001. "Transnational Migration in Rural Oaxaca, Mexico: Dependency, Development, and the Household," *American Anthropologist* 103: 954–67.

Cole, Arthur C. 1919. "The Era of the Civil War, 1848–1870." In *Centennial History of Illinois,* vol. 3. Springfield, Ill.: Illinois Centennial Commission.

CONAPO (Consejo Nacional de Población). 1999. *Población de los municipios de México, 1950–1990.* Mexico City: CONAPO.

DeWalt, Billie R., and Pertti J. Pelto, eds. 1985. *Micro and Macro Levels of Analysis in Anthropology.* Boulder, Colo.: Westview.

Dexter, Darrel. 1994. *A House Divided: Union County, Illinois 1818–1865.* Anna, Ill.: Reppert.

Durand, Jorge, and Douglas S. Massey. 1992. "Mexican Migration to the United States: A Critical Review," *Latin American Research Review* 27: 3–42.

Espenshade, Thomas. 1990. "Undocumented Migration to the United States: Evidence from a Repeated Trials Model." In *Undocumented Migration to the United States: IRCA and the Experience of the 1980s,* edited by Frank D. Bean, Barry Edmonston, and Jeffrey S. Passel. Washington, D.C.: Urban Institute Press.

Evers, Joseph Calvin. 1964. *The History of the Southern Illinois Conference of the Methodist Church.* Nashville, Tenn.: Parthenon.

Fawcett, James T. 1989. "Networks, Linkages, and Migration Systems," *International Migration Review* 23, no. 3: 671–80.

Foster, George M. 1948. *Empire's Children: The People of Tzintzuntzan.* Washington, D.C.: Institute of Social Anthropology, Smithsonian Institution.

Friedrich, Paul. 1970. *Agrarian Revolt in a Mexican Village.* Englewood Cliffs, N.J.: Prentice Hall.

Giddens, Anthony. 1993. *New Rules of Sociological Method: A Positive Critique of Interpretative Sociologies.* Stanford, Calif.: Stanford University Press.

Holter, Sandra. 1971. "Cobden: Fruit Center Becomes a Bedroom Community," *Southern Illinoisian,* January 31.

Ilcan, Suzan M. 1994. "Peasant Struggles and Social Change: Migration, Households and Gender in a Rural Turkish Society," *International Migration Review* 28: 554–79.

INEGI (Instituto Nacional de Estadística, Geografía e Informática). 2002. "Aspectos sociodemográficos: Michoacán de Ocampo," August 25. At http://mich.inegi.gob.mx/sociodem/html.

INI (Instituto Nacional Indigenista). 2002. "Diagnóstico de los pueblos indígenas de Michoacán." At http://207.248.180.194/bibdf/ini/perfiles/purhepecha/04%20identidad/htm.

Kearney, Michael. 1995. "The Local and the Global: The Anthropology of Globalization and Transnationalism," *Annual Review of Anthropology* 24: 547–65.

———. 1996. "La migración y la formación de regiones autónomas pluriétnicas en Oaxaca." In *Coloquio sobre Derechos Indígenas: Migración Indígena.* Mexico: Instituto Oaxaqueño de las Culturas, Fondo Estatal para la Cultura y las Artes.

———. 2001. "Struggle and Difference: The Jujitsu of Transnational Indigenous Resistance and Domination." In *History in Person: Enduring Struggles and Identities in Practice,* edited by D. Holland and J. Lave. Santa Fe, N.M.: School of American Research Press.

Knauft, Bruce M. 1996. *Genealogies for the Present in Cultural Anthropology.* New York: Routledge.

Lawson, Victoria A. 1998. "Hierarchical Households and Gendered Migration in Latin America: Feminist Extensions to Migration Research," *Progress in Human Geography* 22: 39–53.

Little, Stephen E. 2000. "Networks and Neighborhoods: Household, Community and Sovereignty in the Global Economy," *Urban Studies* 37: 1813–25.

Massey, Douglas S. 1990. "The Social and Economic Origins of Immigration," *Annals of the American Academy of Political and Social Sciences* 510: 60–73.

Massey, Douglas S., Joaquín Arango, Graeme Hugo, Ali Kouaouci, Adela Pellegrino, and J. Edward Taylor. 1994. "An Evaluation of International Migration Theory: The North American Case," *Population and Development Review* 20: 699–751.

Massey, Douglas S., and Kristin E. Espinosa. 1997. "What's Driving Mexico-U.S. Migration? A Theoretical, Empirical, and Policy Analysis," *American Journal of Sociology* 102: 939–99.

Massey, Douglas S., Luin P. Goldring, and Jorge Durand. 1994. "Continuities in Transnational Migration: An Analysis of 19 Mexican Communities," *American Journal of Sociology* 99: 1492–1533.

Maturana Medina, Sergio, and José Sánchez Cortés. 1970. *Las comunidades de la meseta tarasca.* Mexico City: Centro de Investigaciones Agrarias.

Myers, Scott M. 2000. "The Impact of Religious Involvement on Migration," *Social Forces* 79: 755–83.

Perrin, William Henry, ed. 1883. *History of Alexander, Union and Pulaski Counties, Illinois.* Chicago: O.L. Baskin and Co.

Portes, Alejandro. 1989. "Del sur de la frontera: las minorías hispánicas en los Estados Unidos," *Revista Mexicana de Sociología* 51: 263–90.

Portes, Alejandro, and Jozsef Böröcz. 1989. "Contemporary Immigration: Theoretical Perspectives on Its Determinants and Modes of Incorporation," *International Migration Review* 23: 606–31.

Raijman, Rebeca. 2001. "Mexican Immigrants and Informal Self-Employment in Chicago," *Human Organization* 60: 47–55.

Ranney, S., and S. Kossoudji. 1983. "Profiles of Temporary Mexican Labor Migrants in the United States," *Population and Development Review* 9: 475–93.

Sandomirksy, Sharon, and John Wilson. 1990. "Process of Disaffiliation: Religious Mobility among Men and Women," *Social Forces* 68: 1211–29.

Shields, Michael P. 1995. "Time, Hedonic Migration, and Household Production," *Journal of Regional Science* 35: 117–34.

Stanislowski, Dan. 1944. "Historical Geography of Michoacán." PhD dissertation, University of California, Berkeley.

Stark, Oded. 1991. *The Migration of Labor.* Cambridge, Mass.: Basil Blackwell.

Stark, Oded, and D. Levhari. 1982. "On Migration and Risk in LDCs," *Economic Development and Cultural Change* 31: 191–96.

Stonich, Susan C. 1991. "Rural Families and Income from Migration: Honduran Households in the World Economy," *Journal of Latin American Studies* 23: 131–61.

Stump, Roger W. 1984. "Regional Migration and Religious Commitment in the United States," *Journal for the Scientific Study of Religion* 23: 292–303.

Young, Gay, and Lucia Fort. 1994. "Household Responses to Economic Change: Migration and Maquiladora Work in Ciudad Juárez, Mexico," *Social Science Quarterly* 75: 656–70.

# 14

# The Blossoming of Transnational Citizenship: A California Town Defends Indigenous Immigrants

PAUL JOHNSTON

This is an account of a vigorous community response to a U.S. Immigration and Naturalization Service (INS) raid in the town of Greenfield, California, in the spring of 2001. The raid targeted a small population of indigenous Triqui migrants from southern Mexico. The case is of interest because of the ethnic focus of the INS roundup, because of the sexual fears cited as cause for action, and because of the apparent effectiveness of local response in defense of the Triqui. The analysis offered here argues that the last of these was a product of citizenship development among longtime residents of Mexican descent, itself stimulated by controversy over the status of recent Mexican immigrants since the mid-1990s and by a long history of labor movement activity in this region.

On April 6, 2001, a team of Immigration and Naturalization Service agents arrived in the town of Greenfield, a small agricultural community in the Salinas Valley on the California coast. They descended upon three apartments occupied by indigenous Triqui immigrants from Oaxaca State, in southern Mexico. Breaking open doors without displaying warrants, they moved through the homes, arresting all the men. The agents pursued some of the men out of the houses and into the surrounding streets, where they fanned out and apprehended any male with the slight frame and distinctive features of the Triqui.

Over following weeks, controversy raged in the Salinas Valley as unions, community groups, and local elected officials criticized the INS and the county sheriff whose staff had invited the raid. In response, both the INS representatives and the county sheriff raised the specter of "sexual predators," arguing that the officials' actions had been necessary to protect the children of Greenfield.

Despite this most stigmatizing charge against this most marginalized group, the strength of community opposition led the INS to reverse course. Three weeks later, when INS agents picked up a group of Triqui again, the regional director of the INS ordered the detainees released. Six months later the still-recalcitrant sheriff announced he would not seek reelection. At this writing, both finalists in the sheriff's election — vying for the vote of new citizens — vow never to repeat the episode.

As the Ashcroft Justice Department steadily hardens its approach to interior immigration enforcement, more local communities may be challenged to respond to INS raids. If so, the strength of local community response will be of increasing interest to all concerned.

One way to explain the strength of the local response in Greenfield would focus on the strategies that participants employed. Those strategies, however, were not particularly complex and are fairly self-evident in the account that follows. Of greater interest is the historical process that produced political circumstances conducive to those strategies — and produced political actors willing and able to employ them. Accordingly, after an account of the raid and local response, I offer a brief historical argument that seeks to identify the developments that produced those essential circumstances and actors.

Perhaps because it is based on research that predates the pivotal final years of the twentieth century, recent research on the "Mexicanization of rural communities" has been by and large a "social problems" literature, stressing "disturbing underclass conditions" (see, for example, Allensworth and Rochín 1998), variously attributed to the effects of federal immigration policy (Taylor, Martin, and Fix 1997, among others) and to globalization and the structure of corporate agriculture (Palerm 1997). In contrast, without denying the significance of such factors, some urban scholars have over the past decade placed greater emphasis on public institutions and urban regimes (Elkin 1985, 1987; Stone, Orr, and Imbroscio 1991) and on the continuing significance of race (Fainstein and Fainstein 1986; DiGaetano and Klemanski 1993). In that vein, this study examines an episode of racialized conflict over the status of indigenous immigrants in one small rural community, offers an analysis that centers on the significance of political factors, and traces the effects of unions and labor movements on those institutions.

Recent research on the emergence of citizenship among immigrants focuses narrowly on the formal naturalization process, stressing, moreover, factors that include changes in public policy, rate of return migration, language and education, and economic circumstances (Liang 1994; DeSipio 1987; Yang 1994). In contrast, this study employs a more sociological concept of citizenship as our relationship to public life (Johnston 2001), affirming classical accounts that stress, again, the impact of workers' movements and labor unions (Hobsbawm 1968; Thompson 1974; Montgomery 1993).[1]

In brief, I argue that controversy over the status of recent arrivals has expanded naturalization by longtime legal immigrant residents, increased identification with Mexican ancestry and the immigration experience, and stimulated voter registration among unregistered U.S. citizens of Mexican ancestry, producing a significant shift in the balance of political power. In the case of Greenfield, moreover, both political participation and support for recent immigrants were intensified by the influence of labor movements and labor unions.

## THE TRIQUI IN GREENFIELD

Greenfield is a town of around 13,000 inhabitants in Monterey County. It lies in the fertile Salinas Valley, just south of Silicon Valley, and opens onto Monterey Bay. Despite its geographic isolation, the town is closely linked by labor markets, regional government, commuter traffic, and family ties to the surrounding region, including King City to the south and Salinas to the north. The economy of the town and surrounding region is dominated by corporate agriculture.

The town's population consists of layers of immigrants and their descendents, with scarcely a trace remaining of the indigenous inhabitants of pre–gold rush days. As is the case in California as a whole, most individuals or their parents were born outside the state.[2] So also as in most Califor-

---

[1] Elsewhere I offer evidence that gender and family arrangements also appear to have been a significant factor in the recent emergence of citizenship among Mexican immigrants (Johnston 2001).

[2] The 1990 census found that 54 percent of California's population was born either outside the United States (22 percent) or in other U.S. states or territories (32 percent) (U.S. Census of Population and Housing, 1990).

nia towns, Greenfield society is repeatedly reconstituted as waves of new residents become a majority and enter public life.

According to the 2000 census, 88 percent of the residents of Greenfield are "Hispanic," an increase from 67 percent in 1980 and 77 percent in 1990.[3] Most of this growth has come as immigrants from rural Mexico came north to work in the fields of the Salinas Valley, eventually settling there.[4] Many of the Anglos[5] of Greenfield were themselves migrant farmers who came to the valley from the rural U.S. Midwest in dustbowl days, or are children of the dustbowl migrants. The most recent arrivals — at this writing, nearly 10 percent of the town's population — are indigenous immigrants, mainly from Oaxaca, including an estimated two hundred Triqui.

Most of the Triqui residents of Greenfield are more fluent in their native tongue than in Spanish. Many are related by complex ties of kinship. Three large extended families are centered on three west-side apartments that serve as gathering places for the larger community. Interviewed at one of these sites, an elderly man commonly known as "grandfather" said, "I prefer life in Oaxaca because here everything costs money. But when there is no work, how can we live?"

The risk of family separation due to U.S. immigration enforcement is an ominous threat to Triqui families. According to several informants, the Triqui make their way to the Salinas Valley through a border crossing that requires walking for "a day and a night" through open desert. "Our biggest fear is that we will be sent back to Mexico," said Ignacio, a younger man accompanied by his wife and newborn child. "Not only because it is so hard to cross. We fear they will send us all the way to Oaxaca, which is very far away, and our families will be here alone."

Among our main informants is Digna, a young woman who was among the first Triqui to settle in Greenfield, just five years ago. Two months prior to this writing, she returned to Mexico by Greyhound bus to care for her dying father. Accompanied by her husband and youngest child, she left two older children (aged 3 and 4) in the care of relatives in Greenfield. Two weeks ago, burdened by the baby while trying to return

[3] The larger region shows similar trends, at 26, 34, and 47 percent in the county of Monterey, and 19, 26, and 32 percent in the state of California in 1980, 1990, and 2000, respectively (U.S. Census of Population and Housing, 2000).

[4] According to the 1990 census, 95 percent of "Hispanics" in Greenfield were of Mexican origin.

[5] "Anglo" is the term commonly used to refer to non-Latinos of European origin in the region. While some people speak of Chicanos and Chicanas and of Mexicanos and Mexicanas, "Anglas" are unknown.

through the desert, the family fell behind their guide. Wandering for three days and nights, they became increasingly dehydrated before finding water at a station provided by a border rights group. There they were apprehended by the INS and deported, penniless, to Hermosillo, 165 miles south of the border. At this writing, they had again set out to cross the border, and family and friends were awaiting news of their fate.

## THE INS RAID

In the spring of 2001, the San Francisco regional office of the INS launched an investigation of alleged sexual harassment of schoolchildren by Triqui men loitering outside a pool hall and convenience store on the streets of Greenfield. According to their account, after observing some of these men calling and making suggestive gestures to girls as they left a nearby school in the mid-afternoon on March 30, INS agents arrested six men for deportation.[6]

One week later, on April 6, a larger INS team arrived in town. They sealed off the pool hall and convenience store, accosted those within, and swept the surrounding area, apprehending several unauthorized immigrants. Then they moved to a neighborhood where the main concentration of Triqui was known to live. Acting without warrants, they forcibly entered three homes. "They pounded on the door and then they broke it open," said Digna. "They ran into all the rooms and shouted at us, and the babies were crying and we were all afraid."

The INS agents ignored the women and children. They apprehended all the men in the apartments and others observed fleeing from the area. In a departure from the normal practice of holding detainees for a period in U.S. incarceration centers, the agents immediately deported a total of thirty-nine men to Mexico. Fearing that the INS agents would return, a group of women and children fled the town to hide under a nearby bridge.

The Greenfield raid was an exception for INS activity in this region. As everyone—from the INS regional director and the area's congressional representatives through local newspaper publishers and law enforcement—

---

[6] Alarm about the sexual threat represented by "alien" men is, of course, a familiar theme in U.S. race relations. Though this theme is not reported, to my knowledge, in other local responses to the recent stream of indigenous immigration, local experience suggests the Greenfield case is not unique. A year after the Greenfield episode, a mini-movement among Anglos in nearby Carmel Valley calling for INS enforcement against day laborers appealed to concerns that the men might prey upon young boys.

knows full well, the area's economy is heavily dependent on the labor of undocumented farmworkers like the Triqui. As a result, not only immigrants and their advocates but also most employers oppose INS enforcement efforts against otherwise law-abiding unauthorized immigrants. In fact, in a policy brokered by the region's congressional representative, enforcement is limited to the deportation of persons convicted of serious felonies.

The charge of sexual harassment seemed to give good reason, however, for INS agents to make an exception to standard practice in Greenfield. Following the publication of a sympathetic newspaper article profiling the new Triqui community in nearby Salinas, the INS received several inquires and complaints from local residents. In the public debate that followed the Greenfield raid, INS representatives stated that their action had been triggered by a complaint made through informal channels by a county sheriff's deputy. Later, Greenfield's local police chief stated that his department had been aware of a "loitering" problem but had received no complaints of sexual harassment. For his part, the sheriff would acknowledge that his staff had been the source of the complaint, and also that they had not passed the same allegations on to the Greenfield police but had instead taken them directly to the INS.

Over the weeks that followed, Greenfield city council meetings became a forum for debate about the episode. The county sheriff attended the second of these meetings, alongside representatives of the INS. Both the sheriff and the INS representatives spoke at length of the possibility that the Triqui might be sexual predators, and they expressed concern for the safety of the children of Greenfield. The local media focused on this charge, and the story was eventually picked up in papers around the United States.

The remaining Triqui, meanwhile, repeatedly expressed their bewilderment at the charges directed against them. Uniformly, they observed that nearly all of the men who had been apprehended had just returned from work in the fields, while the alleged harassment of schoolchildren had occurred hours earlier, in the mid-afternoon.

Pursuing a theme similar to the sexual predator allegations, an INS media spokesperson described an incident in which a Triqui man was said to have disrobed in public, adding that the agency believed "a tragedy may have been narrowly avoided." The local police later clarified the story of "the disrobing man." In the local laundromat, a recent arrival from rural Oaxaca with no other clothes than those he wore removed them for washing, wrapping himself in a burlap sack. Called to the scene by a scandalized witness, an officer had lectured the man on standards of dress in his new community.

## GREENFIELD RESPONDS

Considering the nature of the accusations against the men, INS officials had expected to receive local community support for the raid. They were surprised when, instead, hundreds of community members turned out at two subsequent Greenfield city council meetings at which INS critics vastly outnumbered supporters.

In fact, community support for the Triqui surfaced instantly. At the moment of the raid, a neighbor involved with Líderes Campesinas, a farmworker women's activist network, reported the incident to a member of that group who was also involved with the Citizenship Project, an immigrant rights group sponsored by the Teamsters Union. Citizenship Project activists arrived on the scene within an hour. Later that night, they would escort the women and children hiding under the bridge to the home of a Teamsters Union representative, where they took shelter for the night.[7]

Three days later a large group of local residents, including around twenty Triqui men, women, and children, assembled at the city council meeting to protest. On the same day, a representative of the Mexican consul arrived from San Jose, California, to take statements from witnesses and to prepare a protest on behalf of those who had been deported. Following that meeting, members of the Triqui community gathered to meet with him and with activists from the Citizenship Project at the United Farm Workers (UFW) union office. Over the following weeks, Citizenship Project organizers provided food, funds, clothing, and personal support to the affected families.

Two weeks after the first city council meeting, a second meeting drew what was (according to the recollection of attending city officials) the largest crowd in city history. Some fifty Triqui attended. Over thirty people spoke, including two Triqui. Only six of the speakers were Anglos. All the Mexicano/as and Chicano/as and half of the Anglos criticized the INS and the county sheriff.

The citizenship status of speakers ranged from undocumented recent arrivals to lifelong residents. A Triqui woman whose husband and grand-

---

[7] The Citizenship Project is a local product of collaboration between the Teamsters Union and an action-research project by the author, who observed the developments described here in his role as a participant in that organization.

father had both been deported spoke in very limited Spanish. She described the INS agents' forced entry into her home and the fear of her family members. A Chicano Vietnam veteran, a native of Greenfield, followed. Speaking without a trace of Spanish accent, he described how he himself had been stopped by the INS because of his Latino appearance, and he asserted that the deported Triqui were victims of the same mentality:

> I remember not long after I got back from 'Nam, I was out driving in my truck up by San Andreas and an officer stopped me. He asks me, "*hablas inglés?*" and I say, "Man, I speak English just as good as you do." He stopped me just because I'm Mexican, even though my family's been here 50 years. Now they call that "driving while black or brown."...
> It sounds to me like it should be called driving while black or brown ... or Triqui.

Another criticism focused on the INS's involvement in a matter that could have been handled by local law enforcement agencies. Critics pointed out that without a separation between local law enforcement and immigration enforcement, unauthorized immigrants would be afraid to report crimes and would become even easier targets for muggers and other predators. Along the same lines, others protested the involvement of school district staff in summoning the INS, suggesting that now undocumented parents would be afraid to come to the school or perhaps might even keep their children away. This criticism was echoed in an editorial in the *Salinas Californian*, the region's main newspaper (*Salinas Californian* 2001), and by congressional staffers communicating with the INS.

At this second meeting, a city council member introduced a strongly worded resolution, jointly drafted by the Teamsters, the UFW, and the Citizenship Project, that criticized the INS. Among other points, the resolution asked the INS to refrain from taking such action within the city limits in the future, directed that local law enforcement activities be conducted separately from immigration enforcement, condemned ethnically targeted immigration enforcement, and directed the chief of police to notify individual council members immediately if he learned of any such planned activity. The measure narrowly passed on a 3–2 vote that pitted the mayor (a retired Mexican American police officer) and a conservative Anglo small businessman against three younger and more recently elected Mexicano/as.

In the week following the city council's action, the regional director of the INS met with a group of local elected officials and union and community representatives. He expressed chagrin over fallout from the raid, and he promised that the agency would refrain from similar activity in the Salinas region for the foreseeable future.

Days later, however, INS agents conducted another raid, this time at a farm outside town. They apprehended five men, all Triqui, who had been deported in the raid described above and had since returned. None of them had been accused of any inappropriate sexual behavior. Within an hour, the regional director of the INS began receiving calls from the local representatives to whom he had given his personal assurances. He acted to rein in his staff, directing them immediately to release the men involved. That afternoon all five were removed from detention in San Jose and driven by INS agents 100 miles south to their homes in Greenfield. There they were released, with an admonishment to leave the country within thirty days. Over a year later, one of those involved recalled the episode with some bemusement:

> When they put me in that car they didn't say where we were going. I thought I was going back to Mexico. But they took me home. And they said, "see, we didn't even charge you for your ride!"

In sum, despite their portrayal of the Triqui as sexual predators, the INS and the county sheriff failed to win local and regional political support for their raid. The INS beat a hasty retreat—and even took the extraordinary step of releasing a group of undocumented immigrants who had been apprehended for deportation.

In contrast, the county sheriff remained unrepentant. Six weeks after the raid, an informal group of Chicano/a and Mexicano/a labor and political activists assembled to plan a campaign to elect a new sheriff. Among the challengers was a second-generation Mexican immigrant whose father had come to the United States as an undocumented worker. Three months later, the incumbent sheriff announced he would not seek reelection. In a primary election in March 2002, two Anglo candidates qualified for a run-off. Both pledged to vigorously oppose any further INS raids.

## WHAT IS NEW

What is new in this episode is not the emergence of cross-border social and economic networks, long a central part of the fabric of life in southwestern U.S. towns like Greenfield. Rather, I argue, the significant new feature is the expansion of citizenship with the entry of first-generation Mexican immigrants into public life. A brief historical sketch will suggest the processes that triggered this development.

As a major center of corporate agriculture in California, the Salinas Valley has long been a focal point of labor struggles by Mexican immigrant workers (and by dustbowl migrants in the 1930s and IWW-led migrant workers and Japanese and other immigrant workers in decades past). A key moment in local history was the eruption of the United Farm Workers strikes in the 1970s, commencing with the general strike in agriculture in the Salinas Valley in the summer of 1970. At that moment, the farmworker movement exploded out of the population of predominately U.S. citizen workers in the grape industry and into the increasingly undocumented workforce in the rest of California agriculture (Johnston 2001; Wells 1995).

The UFW strike, directed against an alliance between valley growers and the Teamsters Union, was mainly an assertion of workers' right to elect their own union representatives. Over time, this movement unfolded into a series of statewide political campaigns through which the union sought to win labor rights for farmworkers. Those movements inspired today's Mexicano/a and Chicano/a labor and other community leaders in the valley (and also this Anglo writer) in their own youth. And although the UFW's role in the Salinas Valley declined sharply in the 1980s, Greenfield remains the site of the union's headquarters for the south valley.

Also during recent decades, a rank-and-file union reform movement led by Chicano/a and Mexicano/a residents of Greenfield and nearby King City (many of them former UFW members, and many employed at the Basic Vegetable Products plant in King City) won leadership in the big Teamsters Union Local 890, inaugurating an era of more amicable relations between the two major unions in this part of rural California.

More recently, triggered by the passage of California's Proposition 187 in 1994, a naturalization movement surfaced among longtime legal permanent residents. In Greenfield as elsewhere, the volume of applications for U.S. citizenship exploded in 1995 and 1996, subsiding by mid-1997 (Johnston 2001). Also in response to Proposition 187, activists in the reformed Teamsters local launched a grassroots organization—the Citizenship Project referred to above. That organization led the naturalization movement in Greenfield and elsewhere in the Salinas Valley, and then broadened its work to organize and help defend immigrants in a variety of citizenship statuses (Johnston 2004a).

In sum, a long current of social movement activity—solidly rooted among undocumented workers and legal residents, and expressed in labor movements and struggles for union democracy—shaped and fashioned the UFW and the Teamsters Union, as well as the latter's Citizenship Project and their constituents in the Salinas Valley. With the eruption of controversy over the status of recent immigrants in the mid-1990s, these groups and their constituencies were poised to respond.

Not surprisingly, the naturalization movement of 1995–1997 produced a sharp change in the ethnic composition of the Greenfield electorate. According to the author's tally of voter registration records, in late 1994, 57 percent of the town's registered voters had Spanish surnames. Six years later, in 2000, the figure had risen to 76 percent. All of this increase was attributable to the number of Mexico-born naturalized citizens who had registered to vote, which had gone from 10 percent to 31 percent of the electorate over the 1994–2000 period.

The visible shift in the balance of political power in Greenfield began in November 1998, when Mexico-born registered voters reached 20 percent of the electorate, double the 1994 rate. In that year, two young second-generation immigrant men were elected to the town council. One was the son of a longtime local UFW leader. Still, the majority remained Anglo and conservative.

Then in 1999 came a bitter and highly politicized strike by 750 mostly Mexican immigrant Teamster families at the Basic Vegetable Products plant in nearby King City. (The strike had lasted for twenty-two months and was continuing at the time of these events.)[8] The strikers conducted a voter registration campaign that added hundreds of new voters to the Greenfield and King City electorates. Those years produced another sharp increase in voter registration among Mexico-born naturalized citizens. In November 2000, Mexico-born family members (a spouse and a sister) of Basic Vegetable Products strikers were elected to council seats in both Greenfield and King City. With this election, three young Latino leaders came to form a new city council majority in Greenfield.[9] This change in

---

[8] Five months later, surprising many participants and observers, the Basic workers won their strike. See Johnston 2004b for an account and analysis of this strike.

[9] Also in the late 1990s, a reinvigorated United Farm Workers launched a high-profile organizing drive among Mexican immigrant workers in the strawberry industry in the Salinas and nearby Pajaro valleys. That campaign (steered by the new leadership of the AFL-CIO) deliberately avoided issues of immigrant rights, and so failed to tap the power of the citizenship movement.

Greenfield's electorate is visible in figure 14.1, drawn from the Monterey County voter records.

Figure 14.1 shows the sharp jump in the proportion of Mexico-born registered voters between late 1994 and late 1996 — years in which the barrage of attacks on immigrant rights triggered the naturalization movement described above. The first jump, then, displays the voter registration movement's success among already naturalized but unregistered Mexican immigrants that accompanied the naturalization movement among legal permanent residents of the same period, both triggered by controversy that Prop. 187 raised over the status of undocumented immigrants.

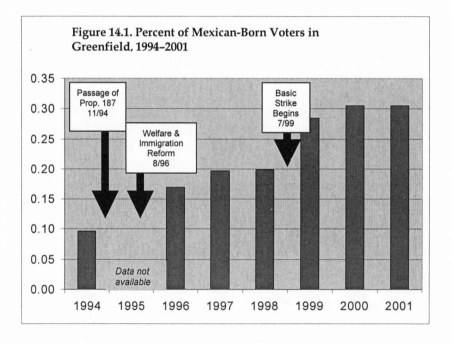

Figure 14.1. Percent of Mexican-Born Voters in Greenfield, 1994–2001

Due to the time lag between date of application and date of approval for naturalization, most participants in this naturalization movement became eligible to register to vote between early 1997 and late 1998. Interestingly, however, the proportion of Mexico-born voters did not rise as newly naturalized citizens joined the pool of persons eligible to vote in 1997 and 1998. Nor did it level off in 1999 as the growth of that pool slowed. Instead, the proportion of Mexico-born registered voters remained level from 1996 through 1998, jumped at the end of 1999 (six months after the outbreak of the Basic Vegetable Products strike), and then held fairly steady thereafter.[10]

Second-generation members of immigrant families provide much of the public leadership in episodes such as those described above. As they find themselves relying upon more recent immigrants as their political constituents, their heritage has become politically salient. Thus they respond simultaneously as both Mexicans and "Americans." The more or less "Anglified" identity of the Mexican-ancestry candidate for county sheriff shifted, for example, as he sought to identify through his familial heritage with the cross-border migrants of today.

This identification with the experience of recent immigrants is evident not only among Mexican American politicians but also among ordinary citizens. Consider again the words of the Chicano veteran who spoke at the Greenfield council meeting, quoted above. In his statement, he reminded himself and his audience of his Mexican identity, drew a parallel between his treatment by the police and the INS's selective targeting of the Triqui, and objected to that targeting in terms that appealed to the color-blind norms of U.S. civic culture. In everyday life, as well as in formal political practice, it appears that controversies regarding the treatment of the continuing stream of new arrivals serve to replenish Mexican identities among longtime residents, who respond in terms that assert the universal relevance of basic civil rights.

To what extent do the Triqui share this sense of political entitlement? Over a year after the INS raid in Greenfield, we explored this question with a group of Triqui in one of the homes targeted by the INS. We were interested, first, in the extent to which the Triqui were aware that the elected city government had taken their side against the INS and, more generally, in their perception of their own status and rights.

The group of twelve was evenly divided between persons who had been in Greenfield at the time of the INS raid (most had attended the decisive city council meeting) and more recent arrivals. The recent arrivals had heard that something had happened that led to people being released by the INS, but they knew none of the details. Of those present during the earlier period, none recalled the city council vote. Those most involved said, "The Citizenship Project protected us."

---

10 Significant increases in new voter registration would normally be expected to have occurred in 1998 and 2000 due to the even-year cycle of major elections in local, state, and federal government (and in 1998, due to a California proposition abolishing bilingual education), rather than in odd years like 1999.

In response to a direct question, those present emphatically denied that they had rights. When asked why they felt this was the case, they spoke exclusively about selective law enforcement based on their appearance. They focused, however, not on INS actions but on traffic stops by local police. In terms strikingly similar to the words spoken by the Chicano veteran quoted above, one man said,

> He sees me driving the other way and I was doing nothing wrong, but he turns around and stops me and he says, "I can tell you are illegal." He just looks at me and he says, "I can tell you have no papers." And so he takes my car and now I have a record. It is not correct. Other people also have no papers, but he does not stop them. Only us, because we look different.

For the recently arrived migrant without papers, employed in an industry where undocumented status is the rule, the main point of contact with public authority appears to be the traffic officer. "Driving while Triqui" carries a threat of citation, confiscation of autos, and imposition of fines that typically escalate to the status of warrants. In the absence of INS immigration enforcement, this is the most tangible denial of basic civil rights—in this case, to freedom of movement in public spaces—that accompanies undocumented status.

Nonetheless, in this bitter assertion that "we have no rights," we can also hear the assertion of the right to have rights. Though he was identified—correctly—as an undocumented migrant on the basis of his appearance, the speaker claims the right to be treated without regard to his appearance. His demand for due process suggests that Greenfield may yet prove fertile soil for the emergence of citizenship among her most marginalized and most recently arrived residents.

## References

Allensworth, Elaine, and Refugio Rochín. 1998. *The Mexicanization of Rural California*. East Lansing: Julian Samora Research Institute, Michigan State University.

DeSipio, Louis. 1987. "Social Science Literature and the Naturalization Process," *International Migration Review* 78, no. 21 (Summer): 390–405.

DiGaetano, Alan, and John S. Klemanski. 1993. "Urban Regimes in Comparative Perspective: The Politics of Urban Development in Britain," *Urban Affairs Quarterly* 29: 54–84.

Elkin, Stephen L. 1985. "Twentieth Century Urban Regimes," *Journal of Urban Affairs* 7, no. 2: 11–28.

———. 1987. *City and Regimes in the American Republic.* Chicago: University of Chicago Press.

Fainstein, Norman, and Susan Fainstein. 1986. "New Haven: The Limits of the Local State." In *Restructuring the City: The Political Economy of Urban Redevelopment*, edited by Susan Fainstein, Norman Fainstein, R. Carter Hill, Dennis Judd, and Michael P. Smith. Rev. ed. New York: Longman.

Hobsbawm, Eric J. 1968. *Labouring Men: Studies in the History of Labour.* London: Wiedenfeld and Nicolson.

Johnston, Paul. 2001. "The Emergence of Transnational Citizenship among Mexican Immigrants in California." In *Citizenship Today: Global Perspectives and Practices*, edited by Thomas Aleinikoff and Douglas Klusmeyer. New York: Sage.

———. 2004a. "Organising Citizenship at Local 890's Citizenship Project: Unleashing Innovation through an Affiliate Organisation," *Development in Practice* 14, nos. 1–2 (February).

———. 2004b. "Outflanking Power, Reframing Unionism: The Basic Strike of 1999–2001," *Labor Studies Journal* 28, no. 4 (Winter): 1–24.

Liang, Zai. 1994. "Social Contact, Social Capital, and the Naturalization Process: Evidence from Six Immigrant Groups," *Social Science Research* 23: 407–37.

Montgomery, David. 1993. *Citizen Worker: The Experience of Workers in the United States with Democracy and the Free Market during the Nineteenth Century.* New York: Cambridge University Press.

Palerm, Juan Vicente. 1997. "A Farm Community Update, 1995–1997." Presented at the conference "Poverty amid Prosperity: Immigration and the Changing Face of Rural California," University of California, Davis, October 9.

*Salinas Californian.* 2001. "Immigration Issue Is Here to Stay," editorial, May 5.

Stone, Clarence, Marion Orr, and David Imbroscio. 1991. "The Reshaping of Urban Leadership in U.S. Cities." In *Urban Life in Transition*, edited by Mark Gottdiener and Chris Pickvance. Newbury Park, Calif.: Sage.

Taylor, J. Edward, Philip Martin, and Michael Fix. 1997. *Poverty amid Prosperity: Immigration and the Changing Face of Rural California.* Washington, D.C.: Urban Institute Press.

Thompson, Edward P. 1974. *The Making of the English Working Class.* Hammondsworth: Penguin.

Wells, Miriam. 1995. *Strawberry Fields: Politics, Class and Work in California Agriculture.* Ithaca, N.Y.: Cornell University Press.

Yang, Phillip. 1994. "Explaining Immigrant Naturalization," *International Migration Review* 28: 429–47.

# 15

# Heritage Re-Created: Hidalguenses in the United States and Mexico

## ELLA SCHMIDT AND MARÍA CRUMMETT

This essay examines the causes and consequences of a relatively new migratory pattern linking communities in Mexico and the United States. Our research focuses on Ixmiquilpan, Hidalgo,[1] and Clearwater, Florida. Located in the semi-arid Mezquital Valley northwest of Mexico City, Ixmiquilpan, with a population of approximately 100,000 people, is home to Mexico's fifth largest indigenous group, the Hñahñu (Otomí). Over the past ten years, approximately one-fifth of Ixmiquilpan's residents, the vast majority of them Hñahñu, have migrated to Clearwater, a tourist city located on Florida's gulf coast. Issues of ethnicity, entrepreneurship, and cultural capital provide a rich framework upon which to understand processes that are re-created and transformed as migrants build communities extending across international borders.

Our research suggests that transnational migration patterns and their impacts on cultural and social processes go beyond traditional economic analyses of migration, which focus on push forces (poverty and lack of opportunities in Mexico) and pull forces (labor demand in the United States) to explain population movements across international borders. Rather, this research places economic and social processes within a cultural

---

[1] The municipality of Ixmiquilpan is located in the west-central region of the state of Hidalgo. The municipality includes 110 communities, including the city of Ixmiquilpan, where the municipal headquarters are located.

context in which civic expectations and participation are based on a strong sense of community present in the migrants' projects in both the sending and receiving communities. Based on primary field research in Ixmiquilpan and Clearwater, our approach addresses how community traditions and civic responsibility craft themselves into migrants' economic, social, and cultural strategies for cross-border cooperation and economic development.[2]

Most important, our research in Clearwater and Ixmiquilpan underscores the fact that migrants are agents of change in economic, cultural, and civic life in both their sending and receiving communities. The changes the migrants effect are a result of their understanding of civil society and their perceptions of their role in it. Key to this understanding are the opportunities migrants identify and seize upon to become active citizens, in their own cultural terms, in the communities that host them (Golte and Adams 1990). In this case study, the community of origin, Ixmiquilpan, rooted in an indigenous culture, shapes migrants' understandings of their rights and obligations as members of a transnational community. A history of strong community organizing around issues of ethnic identity and social and economic justice at the community and regional levels has had social and political impacts on local governments. In Clearwater, this effect spills over into the international arena through organizing that mirrors that of Ixmiquilpan. Indeed, the cultural and social capital accumulated in Ixmiquilpan before migration becomes key to resolving and negotiating a range of issues present in Clearwater and in Ixmiquilpan, thus allowing for the creation of a community that fosters new ways of understanding transnational connections at the economic, social, and cultural levels.

Three major issues have been identified in order to analyze the transformation of both Clearwater and Ixmiquilpan that has been brought about by international migration. First, this essay analyzes the impact of migration on civic participation in both home and host communities as a systemic whole, one that creates responses and processes that cannot be understood in isolation from each other nor outside of the current context of

---

2 The fieldwork for this research began in the fall of 2001 with interviews with members of the migrant community in Clearwater, Florida. In the summer of 2002 the authors spent six weeks visiting communities in the Mezquital Valley. Two additional weeks were spent in Hidalgo in the summer of 2003. The authors gratefully acknowledge the Globalization Research Center of the University of South Florida for its financial support of this research.

globalization and social, cultural, and economic integration. Second, it examines the ways in which transnational communities emerge, flourish, and transform civic life, including local economies, governments, and cultures. And third, it addresses how the principles of community, civic participation, and economic savoir faire—that is, the cultural and social capital that migrants bring with them—re-create themselves such that new "transnational social formations" (Goldring 1998; Guarnizo and Smith 1998) and cultural redefinitions emerge in communities in Hidalgo and Florida.

For the purposes of this analysis, the chapter is divided into five sections. The first examines the nature and extent of the migration pattern linking Hidalgo and Clearwater. Next, attention is given to alternative theoretical approaches that address the formation of migrant communities in the context of transnationalism. In order to understand how "transnational social spaces" emerge in the case of Clearwater and Ixmiquilpan, the third section provides a brief historical overview of the Hñahñu. The fourth section addresses how cultural identity and citizenship are re-created and transformed as migrants build communities extending across international borders. Tentative conclusions of the study are presented in the final section.

## THE HIDALGO-CLEARWATER CONNECTION

Although undocumented migration from Mexico has been a dominant feature of many U.S. cities for generations, particularly in the Southwest and destinations in the Northeast and the Midwest (Cordero-Guzmán, Smith, and Grosfoguel 2001; Andrade Galindo 2003), the migratory pattern linking Hidalgo and the United States is striking in several respects. First, large-scale out-migration from Hidalgo to the United States dates to the mid-1990s, with the largest contingent of migrants heading to nontraditional destinations for Mexican migrants, such as Florida (Clearwater), Nevada (Las Vegas), Georgia (Atlanta), and North Carolina (Hickory). By 2000, Hidalgo had emerged as the state with the second highest rate of growth of out-migration from Mexico to the United States (Granados Alcantar 2001). Second, the Hñahñu, Mexico's fifth largest indigenous group, have played a pivotal role in supporting and defending migrant workers' rights in the United States and Mexico. At the same time, the Hñahñu culture, centered on family and collective responsibility, has been at the forefront of channeling migrant remittances into community development projects such as roads, water systems, municipal buildings, rural schools, and churches. Finally, the nature and extent of the migratory process between Hidalgo and Clearwater have led to the development of strong institutional and civic linkages that transcend national borders.

Migration from Hidalgo to Clearwater began in the early 1980s.[3] The 1990s witnessed the greatest increase of people from Hidalgo (*hidalguenses*) into Clearwater; census data indicate that the Hispanic population experienced a threefold increase between 1990 and 2000, rising from 2.92 percent of the local population to 8.97 percent. The largest percentage of this increase is attributable to migrants from Hidalgo. In 2003, unofficial estimates placed Clearwater's *hidalguense* community at closer to 15 percent of the city's population, or approximately 20,000 people.[4]

Economic conditions in Clearwater have enabled migrants to play a vital role in the city's transformation. First, the exodus of downtown dwellers in the 1970s vacated one-third of the business and residential spaces. Second, the explosive growth of the hotel and related tourist industries in the mid-1980s created a need for a low-wage, reliable, and flexible labor force. Together, these factors created a favorable environment for Mexican migrants, who are injecting new economic and cultural life into Clearwater. There are now over fifty Mexican-owned businesses in Clearwater, making migrants a significant force in revitalizing neighborhoods in deteriorating sections of the downtown area. Migrant entrepreneurs are opening grocery stores, bakeries, restaurants, music stores, and money-wiring establishments; the latter not only cater to the migrant community (and, increasingly, other population groups), but they also serve as sources of employment for recent immigrants (Headrick 2000).

The migrants' presence has not been ignored by the city of Clearwater, which has programs in place to organize Mexican immigrants into neighborhood associations, recognizing the importance of engaging them civically as their economic and demographic importance grows (Clearwater Neighborhoods 2000). Migrants not only contribute to the local economy as workers in the expanding service sector and as small business owners; they are also crafting a space for dialogue with city, school, and social service agencies.

The *hidalguenses'* rapid economic integration in Clearwater contrasts sharply with the slow pace of integration of Mexican immigrants in other

---

[3] Authors' interview with Robin Gómez, City of Clearwater auditor, fall 2001.

[4] The estimate for 2003 comes from the city of Clearwater and Hidalgo State's Office in Support of Hidalguenses in Their Home State and Abroad (Coordinación General de Apoyo al Hidalguense en el Estado y Extranjero).

areas of Florida. Mexican farmworkers in Dade City, for instance, came to the area in the late 1960s, responding to restrictions in the hiring of Jamaican contract pickers. Yet only within the last four years have Mexican-owned small businesses started to appear in Dade City, catering to the more than 10,000 farmworkers that live in the area. Writing for the *Tampa Tribune*, Juliet Greer (2000) noted the presence of eight Mexican-owned stores and restaurants "serving a culture that was largely forgotten by the city's more mainstream merchants."

Migrants' socioeconomic and educational backgrounds, civic participation, and migratory patterns can explain differences between migrant communities in Dade City and Clearwater. Any explanation, however, must also encompass the circumstances these migrants left in Mexico and those in their host communities. In Dade City, Mexican farmworkers tend to live in marginal neighborhoods that mirror the broader socioeconomic, cultural, and political distances that this population experiences vis-à-vis mainstream U.S. residents (Schmidt 2000).

## TRANSNATIONAL COMMUNITIES AND MIGRATION

Several scholars have argued that the transnational movements of peoples represent a new phenomenon, in both scope and nature (see, for example, Suárez-Orozco 1998). In response to these claims, Sidney Mintz (1998) has argued that transnational movements of peoples are not new. By the end of the nineteenth century, for example, some hundred million people were living far from their birthplace. One hundred years later, a 1992 International Labour Organization report indicated that there were one hundred million people living, once again, outside of their countries of origin— because of war, poverty, and widespread unemployment (Kearney 1995). The increasing complexity and speed with which different global communities are coming into contact with each other and the accommodations and negotiations that these contacts entail have been addressed by scholars such as Saskia Sassen (1998). Sassen has focused not only on people's involvement in these processes but also on how different systems of thought, behavior, and social interactions—and their contradictions—are forced to coexist, in many instances for the first time.

The uniqueness of these contacts requires a focus on "transnational communities." These communities demonstrate how the specificities of the local are connected to global forces as new cultural and economic arrangements emerge across international borders. Numerous studies have addressed these arrangements from a top-down perspective by examining, for example, the roles that nation-states play in directing and controlling migrant remittances and the potential of political support.[5] Other studies (Portes 1999; Roberts, Frank, and Lozano-Ascencio 1999) have focused on the types of communities migrants come from in an effort to analyze the differences between rural and urban sending communities and the strength of the migrants' relationships once they have settled in their host communities. Roberts, Frank, and Lozano-Ascencio (1999) and Guarnizo and Smith (1998), for example, cite research from Guadalajara, Mexico, indicating that urban migrants tend to act in more individualistic patterns that ignore their communities at both ends of the migration stream, thus discouraging the formation of transnational ties.

Yet the Hñahñu from Ixmiquilpan exhibit high levels of ethnic cohesiveness and solidarity both in Hidalgo and in Clearwater. They maintain their traditional social and kinship ties, and use these ties to help migrating relatives and neighbors find employment in the United States and, generally, as a social, cultural, and economic support network. These ties and the transactions that emerge from these relationships are fundamentally transnational in nature (Glick Schiller, Basch, and Blanc-Szanton 1992).

Several other migrant ethnic groups demonstrate similar patterns of engagement. The Kanjobal Mayan community in Los Angeles, for example, uses its religious heritage and ritual customs to solidify ties among those who have settled in the United States as well as those who have remained in Mexico (Popkin 1999). Otavalans in the United States and Europe use their culturally transmitted sense of entrepreneurship to achieve greater economic success than their more educated mestizo counterparts from Ecuador (Kyle 1999).

However, our research suggests that the Hñahñu's sense of identity and solidarity cannot be reduced to a reactive ethnicity utilized to protect them from hostile environments encountered in their host communities, as is the case for Mayan migrants in Los Angeles (Popkin 1999) or Salvadorans in Los Angeles and the Virginia-Maryland area (Landolt, Autler, and Baires 1999). According to the Hñahñu, their sense of identity is the result of centuries of political, cultural, and economic struggles against conquering forces—beginning with the Toltecs and followed, in turn, by the Aztecs, the Spaniards, and the Mexican government. Their understanding of themselves as members of an ethnic minority with a history of

---

[5] For examples of this body of research, see Goldring 2002; Levitt 2001; Mahler 1998; Smith and Guarnizo 1998; Guarnizo 1998; Basch, Glick Schiller, and Szanton-Blanc 1994; Kearney 1995.

struggle—but also with a sense of entrepreneurial flexibility and opportunity—is what informs their dealings in both their host communities and their communities of origin.

## THE HÑAHÑU: CONQUEST, RESISTANCE, AND INTEGRATION

The Hñahñu, builders of the ancient city of Tula while under Toltec domination, have been present in the Mezquital Valley since around 250 BC. Actively resisting conquest by the Aztecs and Spaniards, among others, the Hñahñu decided to retreat to the valley's most arid and desolate areas. This strategy imposed serious limitations on their participation in the region and promoted their exploitation as cheap and submissive labor by caciques who settled in the area with the aim of concentrating available irrigated land into large landholdings. The Hñahñu, like many other ethnic minorities, lived their lives in isolation, ignored by the great majority of Mexicans.

In 1948, in an effort to bring indigenous communities into the twentieth century and integrate them into the Mexican nation-state (Aguirre Beltrán 1955), the Mexican government created the National Indigenous Institute (INI) amidst an *indigenista* discussion that could not decide whether the "indigenous problem" was based on cultural or biological differences. Only a few years later, in 1951, the Indigenous Patrimony of the Mezquital Valley (PIVM) was created by presidential decree at the strong recommendation of several social scientists and consultants to the presidency like Manuel Gamio, who combined efforts in order to draw attention to the problems of the desolation and abject poverty to which the Otomí population had been endemically subjected (Gamio 1952).

Created to promote the development and economic integration of the valley's indigenous population, the PIVM fell into the hands of the local caciques who owned extensive property holdings in the Mezquital's highly productive irrigated sections, especially Ixmiquilpan. This situation began to change with the naming of Maurilio Muñoz, a Hñahñu anthropologist, as director of the PIVM in 1970. This move proved to be of crucial importance to the region's indigenous communities. In an effort to restore dignity and a sense of agency to the Hñahñu, Muñoz changed the nature of their interactions with the PIVM. The paternalist and clientelist transactions that PIVM representatives had imposed on the indigenous population were replaced by more egalitarian ones in an effort to recognize rural communities as active partners in the development process. But probably more important to this research, in addition to supporting the bilingual teacher program that the INI promoted at the national level, Muñoz developed leadership training programs for communal leaders, recognizing them as the legitimate representatives of their communities of origin, with the right to negotiate as equals with government representatives and other political agents. These community leaders were, in many instances, rural teachers trained in bilingual indigenous schools founded by President Lázaro Cárdenas during the 1930s and whose mission was to promote their ethnic cultural and indigenous languages in their own communities (Baumann 1975; Kugel 1996). The social prestige that teachers gain by virtue of their position and their regular transactions with the institutional world helped these rural teachers to be seen as an indigenous elite that could negotiate between two worlds (Kugel 1996).

Many people opposed Muñoz's work in support of the indigenous population. Indeed, attempts were made on his life. However, his indefatigable efforts to win fair and equal treatment for indigenous communities made him an almost mythical personage, and rural teachers in the Mezquital Valley today invoke his name as an inspiration in the advancement of the Hñahñu people.

Rural teachers' association with leadership positions was a discovery we made during our fieldwork with members of the Hñahñu Supreme Council (Consejo Supremo Hñahñu) in Ixmiquilpan.[6] Almost all official positions in the council (president, secretary, and so on) were filled by rural teachers who had either retired or were on professional leave at the time of our visit.

The mystique that Muñoz inspires among rural teachers and members of the Supreme Council in Ixmiquilpan is equally present in Clearwater, and it continues to serve as a guide to the Hñahñu's redefinition of themselves, this time in a transnational context. Many of the most active mem-

---

[6] This council is one of fifty-six supreme councils created by President Luis Echeverría in the 1970s to give representation to ethnic minorities while simultaneously ensuring that the central government could control them. Even though the ties with the Institutional Revolutionary Party (PRI) are obvious, the Hñahñu Supreme Council in Ixmiquilpan has made an effort to distance itself from the traditional political machine and maintain a degree of independence. For instance, in the 2000 presidential election, some council members supported candidate Vicente Fox of the National Action Party (PAN) over PRI candidate Francisco Labastida. Choosing not to focus on party affiliations, the council members stressed their interest in advancing their own political, social, and economic agendas and the need to have the support of whichever candidate was most likely to win the presidency (authors' interview with Celedonio Botho, summer 2002).

bers of the Mexican community in Clearwater are professionals (account-ants and technicians) or teachers who work in the service sector in Clear-water or own small businesses. These individuals were the ones who con-tacted Clearwater officials a short time after their arrival and asked to be recognized as an emerging community within Clearwater.[7] They continue to be the organizational and promotional force behind the sports leagues, the Mexican celebrations in Clearwater that attract thousands of *hidalguen-ses* living in the area, and other civic and social activities.

## HERITAGE RE-CREATED: REAPPROPRIATING CULTURAL IDENTITY AND CITIZENSHIP

Dismissed by some scholars and members of the Mexican elite as having been "invented" by the federal government's National Indigenous Insti-tute, the Hñahñu illustrate a powerful instance of reappropriation of cul-tural symbols (Dening 1986) and social and cultural space. Their history— rich with struggles for cultural, social, and economic advancement dating back to precolonial times—serves as the context for the ways in which migrants from Ixmiquilpan negotiate their social and economic environ-ment in the United States and Mexico.

The Hñahñu have played a pivotal role in supporting and defending migrant workers' rights in the United States and Mexico. The Hñahñu Supreme Council, a civic/political organization funded by the Hñahñu in Mexico and the United States, is one of the few supreme councils that con-tinues to be active. It provides services such as supplying identification for migrants returning to Mexico, providing legal documentation for migrants seeking dual citizenship, and contacting appropriate government agencies in the event of a migrant's imprisonment or death. Based on our inter-views, we learned that the council's leadership role among Hñahñu mi-grants led to the creation of the Office in Support of the Hidalgo Commu-nity in Their Home State and Abroad (Coordinación General de Apoyo al Hidalguense en el Estado y Extranjero), an office that reports directly to the Hidalgo state government and was one of the first institutions of its kind in Mexico.

At the same time, the Hñahñu culture, centered on family and collec-tive responsibility, has been at the forefront of channeling migrant remit-tances into community development (Bada 2003; Goldring 1998). Indeed, the Hñahñu's code of ethics, based on defining the individual as a citizen

---

[7] Authors' interview with Robin Gómez, spring 2003.

of the community, is strongly associated with active community participation. *Faenas*, or civic responsibilities, require individual commitments to the community on a weekly basis, in terms of either labor or financial contributions. Migrants in the United States must either find someone in the community to undertake their role in a specific project or remit money to cover the costs of the *faena*, whether it is constructing a municipal building, installing water canals, or paving roads. The Hñahñu definition of "citizen," then, carries a strong communal commitment defined by active participation in community *faenas* and community offices—a trait common in indigenous communities throughout Latin America which has little to do with legal definitions of citizenship in nation-states (Castles 2000; Castles and Davidson 2000) but that informs their transactions with various political and civic spheres in Hidalgo and Clearwater.

This notion of citizenship, however, has not kept the Hñahñu from understanding the benefits of becoming politically active. In Hidalgo, for example, several Hñahñu hold key political posts in state and local government, enabling them to advance economic, cultural, and social agendas that impact them directly. In the federal legislative elections in July 2003, the district with the highest concentration of Hñahñu in the region elected a Hñahñu to the federal Congress.[8] In Clearwater, the Hñahñu's ethnic identity and political savoir faire guide them in their interactions with city officials.

The Mexican Council of Tampa Bay (Consejo Mexicano de la Bahía de Tampa), a civic organization founded by the city's Hñahñu population, is a leader on issues related to civic participation, education, health care, and immigrant rights (mirroring the activist role played by the members of the Supreme Council in Ixmiquilpan). In November 2002, the Tampa Bay council hosted representatives from the Mexican consulate in Orlando. It also coordinates the athletic leagues with the city's Parks and Recreation Department and provides significant support to the police department's Hispanic Community Outreach Program, a program that has earned national recognition (Weiss and Davis 2002).

The nature and extent of migration between Ixmiquilpan and Clearwater have led to the development of strong linkages that transcend national borders. For example, since 2000, representatives from the Hidalgo state government, including the Office in Support of the Hidalgo Community,

---

[8] A rural bilingual teacher, PRI candidate Roberto Pedraza scored his second win as federal deputy. He had previously served as mayor (*presidente municipal*) of Ixmiquilpan and as secretary of public works for the state of Hidalgo.

have visited Clearwater regularly to discuss immigration issues with city officials, police, immigrant organizations, and social service and faith-based groups. In February 2003, Hidalgo's Governor Miguel Ángel Núñez Soto made his first official visit to Clearwater; he returned in May to inaugurate the Cinco de Mayo festivities organized by the Mexican consul. Clearwater city officials have also traveled to meet with their counterparts in Hidalgo. Numerous civic and ethnic organizations, in place before mass out-migration from Hidalgo, have become transnational in character. Through the Mexican Council of Tampa Bay, the Hñahñu Supreme Council, for example, maintains a base of support and communication linking the Hñahñu communities in Ixmiquilpan and Clearwater.

Recognizing the need to engage the migrants civically, the city of Clearwater has implemented an impressive array of programs to address migrant issues and concerns. In 1999 the city created the Hispanic Task Force which comprises representatives from city offices, social service agencies, and Mexican organizations, including the Mexican Council of Tampa Bay. The task force spearheaded efforts with the Clearwater Police Department to develop a unique program, Joining Hands: Operation Apoyo Hispano, that includes the appointment of a Hispanic outreach officer, training a civilian force of bilingual interpreters, recruiting bilingual officers, community education and crime prevention programs in Spanish, and basic Spanish classes for officers (Weiss and Davis 2002). The city's Neighborhood Services Program produces a quarterly bilingual newsletter, and its bilingual staff supports neighborhood groups undertaking a variety of social and cultural activities.

In November 2002 the city, in conjunction with the YWCA, inaugurated the Hispanic Outreach Center (Centro de Apoyo Hispano) to bring Hispanic residents in contact with city services. The center, located near the police department, houses a bilingual child care center, office space for the Hispanic outreach officer, victim advocacy and interpreter programs, and an office for a representative of the Mexican consulate. In the summer of 2003 the Mexican consulate in Orlando sponsored two teachers from Hidalgo to teach Spanish and Mexican culture to over forty-five Mexican American children, ages five to twelve, at the Hispanic Outreach Center. At the end of the two-month program, Mexican businesses in Clearwater sponsored a graduation ceremony for the children and over four hundred of their family members and friends.

Ixmiquilpan, especially its Hñahñu community, has also experienced a dramatic transformation. Remittances — estimated at between US$2 million and $4 million a month from Clearwater to Ixmiquilpan—have promoted economic development and generated local employment opportunities. New rural development programs, originating from the Hñahñu communities themselves, include eco-tourism, indigenous handicrafts (textiles and woodcarvings), and the manufacture of lotions, shampoos, and sponges from the maguey and salvia cactuses.

Significantly, women, many with husbands, sons, and other relatives in the United States, are at the forefront of these economic development activities. In El Alberto, for example, over two hundred Hñahñu women in the Women United cooperative (Mujeres Reunidas) produce sponges from maguey fiber which are sold in Europe and the United States through The Body Shop, Inc. Women's cooperatives are also prevalent in the production of other items derived from the maguey cactus and of traditional handicrafts. Women in the cooperatives understand the precarious nature of remittances: their partners may be laid off, fall ill, or abandon them. Yet these women's ability to generate income and interact with local, state, and even global institutions enhances their economic and social standing with the community at the same time that it helps them transform gender hierarchies that act as barriers to their self-development as full members of their home and host communities.

## CONCLUSIONS

Our research details the processes in which migrants engage while trying to build new channels of transnational support and communication. In Clearwater, migrants are not necessarily perceived as a burden on local education, health, and law enforcement services (Camarota 2001). Rather, migrant workers are vital components of the city's service sector and tourism industries. Migrant entrepreneurs are opening businesses that cater to the migrant community and other local residents alike, and that also provide employment opportunities for recent immigrants. In addition to their economic integration, the Hñahñu's integration into Clearwater's social and cultural fabric allows them to be viewed as members of the community with legitimate claims to social and economic services.

In conclusion, the migration between Clearwater and Ixmiquilpan reveals the migrants as agents of change in both their communities of origin and their host destination. We find this agency to be the result of two interrelated factors: (1) the migrants' understandings and perceptions of the roles they have played and continue to play in their home communities; and (2) the opportunities that migrants identify and seize upon to become active citizens—on their own terms—in the communities that host them. Our research stresses that migrants' civic experiences, sense of belonging, perceptions of economic and social opportunities, and understandings of their rights and obligations as members of a community are shaped by their experiences in both their communities of origin and the communities that host them. Once engaged in a migratory process, migrants bring the cultural, social, and economic capital of their ethnic identity with them. And when rebuilding their lives in a new locale, they call on those understandings to create a context that makes cultural sense to them (Golte and Adams 1990).

The Hñahñu base their interactions on cultural and social capital that is the product of centuries of resistance to and negotiation with dominant forces and imposed integration. This cultural and social capital informs them in their construction of spaces that go beyond geographical, economic, political, and cultural boundaries. By the same token, the Hñahñu concept of citizenship—based on a commitment to their communities and ethnicity—fosters the maintenance and development of transnational linkages that allow them to be part of a social and cultural space that is more than the sum of Ixmiquilpan and Clearwater.

## References

Aguirre Beltrán, Gonzalo. 1955. "A Theory of Regional Integration: The Coordinating Centers," *América Indígena* 15: 29–42.

Andrade Galindo, Jorge. 2003. "Tonatico, Illinois: una comunidad transnacional." PhD dissertation, Escuela Nacional de Antropología e Historia.

Bada, Xochitl. 2003. "Mexican Hometown Associations," *Citizen Action in the Americas* (Interhemispheric Resource Center ) 5 (March).

Basch, Linda, Nina Glick Schiller, and Cristina Szanton-Blanc. 1994. *Nations Unbound: Transnational Projects, Postcolonial Predicaments and Deterritorialized Nation-States*. Basel, Switzerland: Gordon and Breach.

Baumann, William. 1975. "Economic Development and Culture Change in an Otomí Village: A Critical Analysis." Master's thesis, Goddard College.

Camarota, Steven. 2001. *Immigration from Mexico: Assessing the Impact on the United States*. Washington, D.C.: Center for Immigration Studies.

Castles, Stephen. 2000. *Ethnicity and Globalization: From Migrant Worker to Transnational Citizen*. Thousand Oaks, Calif.: Sage.

Castles, Stephen, and Alastair Davidson. 2000. *Citizenship and Migration: Globalization and the Politics of Belonging*. New York: Routledge.

Clearwater Neighborhoods. 2000. *Neighborhood Services Working for You!* Summer.

Cordero-Guzmán, Héctor C., Robert C. Smith, and Ramón Grosfoguel. 2001. *Migration, Transnationalization, and Race in a Changing New York*. Philadelphia, Penn.: Temple University Press.

Dening, Greg. 1986. "Possessing Tahiti," *Archeology in Oceania* 21, no. 1: 103–18.

Gamio, Manuel. 1952. "Consideraciones sobre el problema del Valle del Mezquital," *América Indígena* 12: 217–22.

Glick Schiller, Nina, Linda Basch, and Cristina Blanc-Szanton, eds. 1992. *Towards a Transnational Perspective on Migration: Race, Class, Ethnicity, and Nationalism Reconsidered*. New York: New York Academy of Sciences.

Goldring, Luin. 1998. "From Market Membership to Transnational Citizenship? The Changing Politization of Transnational Social Spaces," *L'Ordinaire Latino-Americain* 173–174 (July–December): 167–72. Reprinted in *Red Internacional de Migración y Desarrollo*. At http://www.migracionydesarrollo.org, and as Working Paper No. 23 of the Chicano Latino Research Center, University of California, Santa Cruz.

———. 2002. "The Mexican State and Transmigrant Organizations: Negotiating the Boundaries of Membership and Participation," *Latin American Research Review* 37, no. 3: 55–99.

Golte, Jurgen, and Norma Adams. 1990. *Los caballos de troya de los invasores: estrategias campesinas en la conquista de la gran Lima*. Lima: Instituto de Estudios Peruanos.

Granados Alcantar, José Aurelio. 2001. "La emigración de hidalguenses hacia E.U. en los años noventa." Presented at the "Primera Jornada sobre Migración," Pachuca de Soto, Hidalgo, August.

Greer, Juliet. 2000. "At the Storefront of Change: Mexican Business Owners Are Thriving as They Carve Out Their Niche and Fulfill Dreams," *Tampa Tribune-Community Focus Pasco*, February 11.

Guarnizo, Luis E. 1998. "The Rise of Transnational Social Formations: Mexican and Dominican State Responses to Transnational Migration," *Political Power and Social Theory* 12: 45–94.

Guarnizo, Luis E., and Michael Peter Smith. 1998. "The Locations of Transnationalism." In *Transnationalism from Below*, edited by Michael P. Smith and Luis E. Guarnizo. New Brunswick, N.J.: Transaction.

Headrick, Christina. 2000. "A Mexican Flavor: Businesses Catering to Clearwater's Growing Immigrant Population Continue to Grow and Adapt with Their Clientele," *St. Petersburg Times*, October 8.

Kearney, Michael. 1995. "The Local and the Global: The Anthropology of Globalization and Transnationalism," *Annual Review of Anthropology* 24: 547–65.

Kugel, Veronica. 1996. "Les instituteurs: Formation d'une nouvelle elite indienne? (Valle del Mezquital, Méxique)." PhD dissertation, Université de Toulouse-le-Mirail.

Kyle, David. 1999. "Otavalo Trade Diaspora: Social Capital and Transnational Entrepreneurship," *Ethnic and Racial Studies* 22, no. 2: 422–46.

Landolt, Patricia, Lilian Autler, and Sonia Baires. 1999. "From Hermano Lejano to Hermano Mayor: The Dialectics of Salvadorean Transnationalism," *Ethnic and Racial Studies* 22, no. 2: 290–315.

Levitt, Peggy. 2001. *The Transnational Villagers*. Berkeley: University of California Press.

Mahler, Sarah. 1998. "Theoretical and Empirical Contributions: Toward a Research Agenda for Transnationalism." In *Transnationalism from Below,* edited by Michael Peter Smith and Luis E. Guarnizo. New Brunswick, N.J.: Transaction.

Mintz, Sidney. 1998. "Localization of Anthropological Practice: From Area Studies to Transnationalism," *Critique of Anthropology* 18, no. 2: 117–33.

Popkin, Eric. 1999. "Guatemalan Mayan Migration to Los Angeles: Constructing Transnational Linkages in the Context of the Settlement Process," *Ethnic and Racial Studies* 22, no. 2: 267–89.

Portes, Alejandro. 1999. "Conclusion: Toward a New World – The Origins and Effects of Transnational Activities," *Ethnic and Racial Studies* 22, no. 2: 463–77.

Roberts, Bryan R., Reanne Frank, and Fernando Lozano-Ascencio. 1999. "Transnational Migrant Communities and Mexican Migration to the US," *Ethnic and Racial Studies* 22, no. 2: 238–66.

Sassen, Saskia. 1998. "Spatialities and Temporalities of the Global: Elements for a Theorization," *Public Culture* 12, no. 1: 215–32.

Schmidt, Ella. 2000. "Dreams from the Fields: Farmworker Lives, Cultural Reckoning, and American Realities." PhD dissertation, University of California, Davis.

Smith, Michael P., and Luis E. Guarnizo, eds. 1998. *Transnationalism from Below*. New Brunswick, N.J.: Transaction.

Suárez-Orozco, Marcelo M., ed. 1998. *Crossings: Mexican Immigration in Interdisciplinary Perspectives*. Cambridge, Mass.: David Rockefeller Center on Latin American Studies, Harvard University.

Weiss, Jim, and Mickey Davis. 2002. "Clearwater's Operation Apoyo Hispano," *Law and Order* 50, no. 4 (April).

# 16

# Expressions of Identity and Belonging: Mexican Immigrants in New York

## Liliana Rivera-Sánchez

This chapter explores ways in which Mexican immigrants organize in New York City, focusing particularly on the role that the Catholic Church has played in incorporating new immigrants through the Tepeyac Association. I first describe the main characteristics of Mexican immigration to New York and discuss the immigrants' organizational processes. I then outline the organizational structure of the Tepeyac Association, highlighting the profound impact it has had on New York's Mexican community. I also offer some insights into how the Tepeyac Association articulates two basic ideas as its organizational resources: Catholic beliefs — specifically the practices of traditional Mexican religiosity — and the "immigrant condition." Both resources reinforce a project of raising the public visibility of Mexican immigrants in New York. This strategy can also be interpreted as an effort to symbolically re-create an image of the Mexican nation and a national identity, even as migrants are in the midst of being displaced. In other words, it is an image of an incipient diaspora.

The initial phase of the research reported here was done as part of the project "Religion and Immigrant Incorporation in New York," coordinated by Professors Aristide Zolberg and José Casanova of the International Center for Migration, Ethnicity, and Citizenship, at the New School for Social Research. An earlier version of this essay was presented at the conference "Religion and Immigrant Incorporation in New York," at the New School in May 2002. Translation by Stuyvesant Bearns and Odette León Martínez.

The objective of this study is to analyze some of the relationships be-tween organization, mobilization, religiosity, and ethnicity in the lives of Mexican immigrants in the United States, with New York City as our spe-cific study case. This analysis suggests that recent immigrants are develop-ing new ways to establish themselves in U.S. society, as well as forming different relationships with their communities of origin, although these relationships do not necessarily imply assimilation, incorporation, or accul-turation into the new community.

## FROM THE SIERRA TO THE CITY OF SKYSCRAPERS

Mexican migration to the United States has developed new routes, pat-terns, and forms of settlement at destination points. The flow of Mexican immigrants to the New York City area is relatively recent, in contrast to traditional Mexican migration patterns (Gonzales 1999).

By 1997, estimates of the Mexican population in New York City ranged from 230,000 to 330,000, accounting for at least 3 percent of all Mexico-born immigrants in the United States.[1] By 2002 the Tepeyac Association esti-mated that the number of Mexicans living in the area had climbed to 500,000.[2] New York's Mexican population has burgeoned through new arrivals, through internal migration from other U.S. states such as Califor-nia, and through the high fertility rate of Mexican immigrant families. Between 1990 and 1996, 29,000 children were born to Mexican parents in New York City, or 3 percent of total births during that period.[3]

Mexican immigration to New York began in the 1950s,[4] but it only reached notable levels in the late 1970s and the first half of the 1980s. Ac-cording to U.S. population censuses, the number of Mexican migrants in New York rose from about 7,000 in 1970 to over 21,000 in 1980, over 61,000 in 1990, and 187,000 by 2000 (see also Bada-García 1998). In other words, the Mexican population in New York grew by 185 percent between 1980 and 1990 and by 203 percent in the following decade. Today Mexicans are the third largest Hispanic group in New York, behind Puerto Ricans and

---

[1] These data are drawn from the archives of the Tepeyac Association.

[2] See www.tepeyac.org.

[3] Department of City Planning 1999: 25. Among migrant groups, only Dominicans and Jamaicans surpassed Mexicans in number of births.

[4] According to Robert Smith, director of the Mexican Migration Project at Columbia University, the first Mixtec migrant to reach New York crossed the border on July 6, 1943 (Smith 1995).

Dominicans. Moreover, these numbers are probably an undercount, given that many Mexicans living in New York are undocumented and hence do not come forward to be counted by census takers.

It is difficult for someone to immigrate alone. Therefore, most immigration flows to places where there is already an established contact and where the possibilities for employment have been explored. Immigrants who go to New York use previously established networks of people already residing in the city and who are from the same community of origin in Mexico. These people can be family, *compadres* (fictive kin), friends, or neighbors. Before September 11, 2001, the traditional arrival points for Mexican immigrants in New York were the John F. Kennedy and Newark airports. The common pattern was for their contact to pick them up and then provide accommodation until they had settled into their new community. Approximately 30 percent of arriving immigrants already had a job waiting for them (Magallán 1999). The most common forms of employment were (and remain) jobs in restaurants (as dishwashers, bus-persons, delivery people, and cooks); as vendors in fruit, vegetable, and flower stands; as clerks and stockers in grocery stores; in dry cleaners; as care providers for children, the sick, and the elderly; as house and office cleaners; in car washes; and as workers in the garment industry and construction.

Causes of the high influx of immigrants can be found both in New York and in the Mixteca Sur,[5] the region of origin for most Mexicans living in the New York greater metropolitan area. These immigrants are mostly from rural zones such as Izúcar de Matamoros, Tulcingo de Valle, Acatlán de Osorio, Tecomatlán, and Tehuitzingo in Puebla, or from the neighboring region of Huajuapan de León in Oaxaca. They also come from the Tlapa area in the Montaña region of Guerrero, the Valle de Atlixco in Puebla, and Ciudad Nezahualcoyotl in the state of México. The Mixteca region was among those hardest hit by the Mexican economic crises of the 1980s and the trade liberalization policies initiated in 1986.[6] Implementation of the North American Free Trade Agreement (NAFTA) in 1994 exacerbated the situation; the financial crisis it sparked reverberated throughout the Mixteca Sur, spurring out-migration from the region (Binford and D'Aubeterre 1999).

---

[5] The Mixteca Sur is a region in south-central Mexico that comprises parts of three states: Puebla, Guerrero, and Oaxaca. It is a predominately rural, indigenous area that revolves around seasonal agricultural activities—mostly the farming of corn, beans, squash, and watermelon, along with livestock raising.

[6] Mexico's trade opening began with its entry into the General Agreement on Tariffs and Trade (GATT) in 1986.

New York's labor market, meanwhile, experienced a rising demand for unskilled workers. Between 1980 and 1990, immigrant workers as a share of New York's workforce increased from 22 to 33 percent. Within the context of high demand for unskilled labor, young immigrant workers found themselves an attractive niche in New York (Smith 1996, 1998). Of the migrants from Puebla, 60 percent were between the ages of fifteen and twenty-four, and most had, at most, a ninth-grade education.[7]

Puebla has a long tradition of out-migration. In 2000, 7 percent of all *poblanos* living in Puebla had lived outside of their hometown, and 41 percent of these had lived for at least some time in the United States. Of the migrants who had spent time in the United States, those from the southern region of Puebla showed a greater propensity to migrate northward, with 57 percent of people from this area having lived in the United States at some point. In terms of gender differences in migration patterns and final destination points, 34.4 percent of all migrants were women, and 20 percent of them had spent time in the United States. Migrant men, on the other hand, showed a higher inclination to migrate across the border, with 36 percent having spent time in the United States (Cortés 2002).

If we observe migration from southern Puebla more closely, we see that the Mixteca region constitutes the main sending area. Although the most important and traditional migration circuits have experienced an increase in both male and female migration, this increase has not had much of an effect on the ratio between genders in the migrant stream, and two men still migrate for every woman migrant. In the communities of the Mixteca Poblana, 25 percent of women have migrated at some point in their lives, versus 50 percent of the men (Cortés 2002).

The healthy economy in New York (and in the United States more generally) prior to September 11, 2001, was an incentive for Mexicans to venture out in hopes of finding better living conditions. In addition, family reunification was facilitated by amnesty programs, particularly the Immigration Reform and Control Act of 1986 (IRCA), which gave legal status to undocumented workers who had lived at least ten years in the United States. IRCA paved the way for the immigration law of 1990, which granted "legalization of dependents" (or other family members) to those who had gained legal status in 1986. Some Mexicans in the New York area were able to legalize their situation under these amnesties. However, the

---

[7] INEGI 2000. In 1995, 25.9 percent of all people living in the Mixteca region did not read or write, a figure that represents one of the highest illiteracy levels in Mexico, where the median is 9.5 percent.

great majority were new immigrants who lacked the required residency period in the United States and hence were forced to remain in the "undocumented worker" category and to suffer the resulting consequences in the labor market: excessively long workdays, no social benefits, pay below minimum wage, and the constant threat of being reported to immigration authorities.

## ORIGINS OF THE TEPEYAC ASSOCIATION

The Tepeyac Association is a network of nongovernmental, nonprofit organizations whose mission is to promote social welfare and human rights, primarily those of New York's undocumented immigrants. It informs and educates immigrants and their families about their rights and available resources, and it currently serves over ten thousand members in the five boroughs and some areas of upstate New York.

It began by drawing on preexisting Guadalupano Committees as its base groups.[8] These committees' activities include veneration of the Virgin of Guadalupe and celebrations of important religious holidays in their parishes, especially the annual celebration of the Virgin of Guadalupe on December 12.[9] In 1997 twenty Guadalupano Committees in the greater New York metropolitan area joined together and formed the Tepeyac Association; by 2003 the Association included forty committees.

Several factors had combined to accentuate the new migrants' sense of exclusion in New York—the dramatic growth of the Mexican immigrant community, their vulnerability in the labor market and in their neighborhoods, the presence of Mexican religious groups that felt discriminated against by more established migrant groups in their Catholic parishes, the differences between the Mexican immigrants' religious practices and those of other Latino groups, and the shortage of Spanish-speaking priests and priests from Mexico. These conditions led members of the Archdiocese of New York to create a new group to assist the Mexican community, that is,

---

[8] Guadalupano Committees have existed since 1983. These committees closely resemble the Christian base communities that spread throughout Latin America in the late 1960s and the 1970s. These small religious groups are created in Catholic parishes by pastoral bishops, priests, nuns, and laypeople, most of whom were influenced by Jesuit training and try to connect their religious studies with everyday life. See Mainwaring and Wilde 1989: 5–6.

[9] Author interview with José Antonio Laguna, consul at the Mexican consulate in New York, December 2000. These committees had received moral support from the Mexican consulate since the early 1990s.

to address the specific needs of Mexicans within the Catholic Church of New York.

During the last three decades, the Catholic Church has witnessed increasing Hispanic diversity in its parishes—similar to the pattern in society in general—especially along lines of nationality, class, and race. New waves of immigrants from Latin America have posed challenges to Puerto Ricans, Cuban Americans, and Mexican Americans (the most established Latino groups) for a space within their churches. In some cases, newer arrivals are not always welcome in community churches and are made to feel like outsiders in their own neighborhoods. The existence of multiple nationalities in a single parish sometimes leads to other types of tensions as well. Since there is a close link between the construction of nationhood and local forms of traditional Catholicism, each Latino nationality brings its own way of celebrating collective identity, including particular Catholic rituals and beliefs (Bishops' Committee 1999).[10]

For these reasons, differences between national origin groups lead some migrants to affiliate with particular apostolic movements (Assumptionists, Cursillistas, Maristas, and so on). The result is competition between national groups and/or increasing tensions between pastoral approaches. Sometimes the Catholic Church itself, through some churches and priests, has polarized conflicts among parishioners by denying that the tensions exist, arguing that "we are all Catholic." This tension between unity and multiplicity has contributed to the recent recognition of the diversity among Hispanics in the Catholic Church. The response has been to style different types of ministries for Catholic groups of different ethnicities and nationalities, taking into account the fact that the recent immigrants' experience of belonging simultaneously to two worlds—their home community and their host community in the United States—gives rise to many kinds of conflict (Bishops' Committee 1999).

A few priests in the South Bronx noted the growing number of Mexicans, many of whom were not being welcomed in the churches, not even those who had organized into religious groups. These groups were defined primarily by areas of origin in Mexico, and it was clear that the new immigrants were using them to assemble themselves into various groupings within the parishes. They would, for example, organize in Guadalupano Committees (or a committee for the respective patron saint of their hometown), in *mayordomías* (civic-religious posts), or in festival committees for

---

[10] For background, see www.usccb.org/hispanicaffairs/encuentro.htm.

their patron saint. Fathers Patrick Hennessy, John Grange, and Francis Skelly were pioneers of the project to incorporate the new immigrants; they were among the first to bring attention to this new group within the Catholic Church in New York. They observed that the Mexicans did not participate in preexisting groups, something that constituted a challenge for the Hispanic Catholic Ministry in the United States.

Father Hennessy, who noted that newly arrived Mexican immigrants tended to seek refuge near his parish in the Bronx, had made it possible since 1988 for the faithful of Christ the King Church to venerate the Virgin of Guadalupe (priests in other parishes probably have done so as well). Father Grange, who had received many immigrants from the Mixteca region, decided to extend a public invitation to Saint Jerome's Church. He placed a large statue of the Virgin of Guadalupe outside the church to welcome Mexican immigrants to the neighborhood, whose Latino community was mostly Puerto Rican and Dominican.[11] Father Skelly, of the Immaculate Conception of the Virgin Mary Church in the South Bronx, had also noticed the growing presence of this new group of parishioners and their unusual religiosity. One December, he saw a group of Mexicans enter his church for the first time and, with guitars in hand, sing "Las Mañanitas" (a traditional Mexican birthday song) to the Virgin of Guadalupe, whose image was housed in the church.

In 1994, after communicating with Fathers Grange and Skelly about this new group, Father Hennessy initiated conversations within the Archdiocese of New York to find ways to inform, protect, and educate the new immigrants and to address their sacramental needs. He sought the help of Cardinal O'Connor and Father Neil Graham, the manager of Hispanic affairs within the archdiocese, suggesting that they contact the archbishop of Puebla in Mexico and request that he send priests and monks to better serve the migrant community in New York. When the response finally came, it was less than encouraging. Although priests came from Tulcingo de Valle, Chila de la Sal, Progreso, and Tianguismanalco to offer masses in the Bronx and Brooklyn, it was not enough. More work was needed with the Mexican migrant community, especially ongoing efforts to inform them of their basic rights, which were being violated by employers, neighbors, landlords, and immigration lawyers.

---

[11] Author interview with Father John Grange, parish priest of St. Jerome's Church, New York, October 2001.

## Making Headway

In the summer of 1995, Father Hennessy visited Tulcingo de Valle, the home community of 90 percent of the Mexican immigrants of Christ the King parish.[12] He was received by Fathers Lucino Flores and José Luis Bautista in the Church of San Gabriel Archangel. These two priests took him to meet others throughout the Mixteca Poblana, including in the Valle de Atlixco and the foothills of Popocatepetl.[13] Hennessy's aims were to learn about the organizational structures in his parishioners' hometowns, to understand their religiosity and religious practices, and to establish an institutional relationship with the churches in the Mixteca region, principally in Puebla but also in other "new" immigrant hometowns.

Father Hennessy returned from this visit convinced of the need to create a pastoral council, or consulate, for the Mexican community in the city—to aid them spiritually but also to help them through the learning process as they entered a different culture and to help them defend their basic rights in the knowledge that "justice is, without a doubt, the best translation of the Catholic faith."[14] In conjunction with Fathers Grange, Skelly, and Graham, Father Hennessy contacted Mario Paredes, executive director of the American Northeastern Region of the Hispanic Catholic Center, seeking his support for the mission and asking him to formally request Mexican clergy for the New York Archdiocese.

In early 1996 Paredes asked Father Enrique González Torres, a Mexico City–based Jesuit, to attend meetings of the recently formed Grupo Timón (steering committee), which was created to carry out the project with the Mexican community in the Archdiocese of New York. Father González then asked the Educational Studies Center in Mexico City to help conduct a study of the Mexican community in New York and to design some educational programs for them. The director of this center, Luis Morfín, S.J., arranged for Brother Joel Magallán, S.J. to be placed in charge of evaluating the New York parishioners' situation and needs.[15] In May 1996 Brother Magallán moved from Chicago to New York to undertake his assignment.

After meeting with bishops and parishioners, Brother Magallán set out to visit Mexicans in all the churches in New York's boroughs, even those

---

[12] Father Hennessy had polled the faithful at weekly mass and found that the majority were from the same region in the Mixteca Poblana. The members of his congregation gave him the names of their family members in Tulcingo.

[13] Author interview with Father Lucino Flores, Tulcingo de Valle, March 2002.

[14] Author interview with Father Patrick Hennessy, the Bronx, January 2002.

[15] Author interview with Brother Magallán, New York, May 2002.

churches that already had Guadalupano groups and/or *mayordomías*. The churches he visited reflected the Mexican presence in the city. Their migrant parishioners were mostly Mixtecs (the majority from Puebla), although there were also people from Oaxaca, Guerrero, Morelos, and Mexico City. The immigrants welcomed Brother Joel and told him about their hometowns and family members who had stayed behind. They talked about their struggles to survive and about their life and work expectations in their new home. Brother Joel also visited groups that were organizing civic festivities in the city and owners of the various area soccer leagues.

The priests and secular leaders of the Hispanic Ministry of the Archdiocese of New York met in 1995 and 1996 to plan their work with the Mexican community.[16] Toward the end of 1996, a decision was made at one of these Grupo Timón meetings to ask Brother Magallán's help in developing a preliminary plan. His first task was to learn about the new immigrants' home communities and to identify the migrants' main points of entry to the United States and their major concentrations in the New York area.

Brother Magallán's trip to the Mixteca and the Valle de Atlixco was guided by the concerns of the migrants in New York and by information that Father Hennessy had gathered during his 1996 visit.[17] Brother Magallán—hoping that some diocesan priests would come to officiate pastoral services for the Mexican community, at least during key celebrations like those of the Virgin of Guadalupe and other especially important patron saints—met with the archbishop of Puebla and the bishops of Tehuacan, Puebla; Huajuapan, Oaxaca; and Tlapa, Guerrero. Father Sotomayor offered to accompany Brother Joel during his travels, and Father Rodríguez offered him an introduction to the region's traditional religious and organizational practices.[18]

---

[16] Participating priests included Peter Precourt, the Assumptionist Father of the Virgin of Guadalupe Church in Manhattan; Bishop Patrick J. Sheridan, vicar general of the archdiocese; Father Flynn of Saint Martin's Church in the Bronx; Father James Joyce, of the Jesuit Province of New York; and priests, monks and laypeople from Fordham University, among others.

[17] He was received in Puebla by some of the same priests Father Hennessy had met in 1996 and who were anxious to participate in the project. They included Fathers Lucino Flores and José Luis Bautista of the Tulcingo de Valle parish, Father Marcos Sotomayor of the Tianguismanalco parish, and Father Gustavo Rodríguez of the Santa Clara Ocoyucan parish.

[18] Author interview with Father Marcos Sotomayor, Puebla, August 2002.

## First Steps

Based on these experiences, Brother Magallán and others were able to develop an empowerment plan for New York's Mexican community that centered on creating community leaders in the various parishes. Brother Magallán's inquiries had identified the distinctive ways in which new immigrants organized, worked, experienced their spirituality, and practiced their religion. This knowledge permitted the archdiocese to better respect their particular traits and to work with them on a project to organize the community and to defend their human rights, especially their labor rights. Another outcome was that some community leaders were able to establish contact with one another, which enabled them to contribute early on to the formation of their own organization.

The Tepeyac Association was born on September 6, 1997, during a Grupo Timón meeting in the cafeteria of Saint Jerome's Church. The meeting included the members of the steering committee itself, the twenty Guadalupano Committees in the city (present at the invitation of parish priests and representatives), and people Brother Joel had invited by going door to door. The Association's leaders decided that they would meet on the last Sunday of every month to ensure that the organization was on track, and from that point forward the organization began to grow. For the first four months, the office equipment consisted of Brother Magallán's backpack, beeper, and daybook.

An important meeting took place in November 1997, when Association members presented Cardinal O'Connor with a proposal for the development of a Mexican organization with specific goals and activities. The Association also determined on that day to make a formal request for office space. As a result of this meeting, the Tepeyac Association gained financial support from the Archdiocese of New York through the Catholic Charities program, as well as use of an older building on 14th Street to house the offices of what was then called the Centro Guadalupano. The founding members, together with Brother Magallán and Esperanza Chacón (who headed "urgent affairs" for the Association until June 2003), remodeled and painted the building's first floor.

The Centro Guadalupano offices were inaugurated on December 12, 1997. Many clergy members, including Bishop Patrick Sheridan, were present, but the majority of attendees were community leaders from the city's Mexican neighborhoods. The center began with a single desk and three paid staff: Brother Joel, whom Cardinal O'Connor had appointed director of the project (and later of the Association); Esperanza Chacón; and Azucena

Véliz, technically a receptionist but de facto administrator of the recently formed Tepeyac Association.[19] Catholic Charities covered basic services (electricity, telephones) and the salaries of two employees; Brother Joel's salary was paid by the archdiocese. The plan was for the organization to become self-supporting through foundation grants and individual donations, but with most support coming from the Mexican community itself.

The primary objective had been to create a social organization to defend the human rights of Mexican immigrants, especially those who had just arrived and had no information about their rights or available social services. The nascent Association tried to serve as a meeting place in which Mexicans could feel part of a community and rebuild their sense of belonging. One of the project's initial priorities was to train community "animators."[20]

During the Association's first assembly, members decided to stage a demonstration of solidarity on behalf of César Díaz, a Mexican waiter who had been beaten by his employers at Panarella's Restaurant. This protest, on September 8, 1997, was the first show of unity among Mexican leaders in New York, now joined in the Tepeyac Association. It was also the first time that the struggles of Mexican people living in New York appeared in the city's media.

The Association planned all its actions according to the traditional organizational approach followed in Mixtec communities, where all social and religious matters relate to the days of local patron saints. All the events the Association carries out revolve around the Virgin of Guadalupe, the patron saint of Mexico, which means that the Guadalupano Committees offered an optimal way to establish communication and good relations with church-going Mexicans. Therefore, the strategy adopted was to form a Guadalupano Committee in every church that counted Mexicans among its faithful.

Some community leaders and Brother Magallán (already named director of the Association) began to see problems with this system. Instead of addressing social and political issues that were affecting them as a community, some Guadalupano Committees were concerned solely with prayer and veneration of the Virgin of Guadalupe. According to the Tepeyac Association's action program, animators were to include discussion of

---

[19] Author interview with Brother Magallán, May 2002.

[20] "Animator" was used rather than "leader" to refer to a community leader or member of a Guadalupano Committee in order to avoid the negative connotations associated with the latter term in Mexican history.

problems affecting the community in their meetings. This would support the integral development of the community through the dissemination of information to members, educating them and empowering them to identify problems affecting them and then devise solutions.

Resolving the tension between a project focused exclusively on the liturgy and one tied to social justice became an important challenge for many Guadalupano Committees. After witnessing the positive results for the community that came out of the Association's first collective actions, however, more Guadalupano Committees became involved in discussions about issues that affected them. Through a learning process that was both collective and religious (drawing from bible stories that had relevance for the migrants' daily lives), members learned about their rights and about recent events in Mexico and in their communities of origin. Members soon felt represented and supported by the organization and, as a result, began to identify with it. These groups then, following a Jesuit pattern, began to establish themselves as community-based committees in their neighborhoods and parishes. By linking faith with justice (and later with community action), the committees' focus changed from primarily prayer and conversion to embrace a concern with broader social issues as well.

This last feature makes the Tepeyac Association distinct from other organizations. Although it emerged from the initiative, creativity, and integrity of a group of priests and laypeople who built a path for the Mexican community within the Catholic Church, the Tepeyac Association is now a project that transforms and develops itself inside city neighborhoods — often against the will of parish priests and among hostile immigrant groups with a longer history in New York. The Tepeyac Association has come about as the result of this community's need to make a space for itself, not only within the confines of its churches but also in its neighborhoods and places of employment. This was achieved as a result not only of members' celebrations and religious rituals, but also of their recognition by employers as a dedicated workforce.

In this context, the Tepeyac Association became a community-based organization concerned with the integral development of the Mexican community. Because its appearance coincided with the passage of new laws affecting immigrants,[21] the Association's immediate task became the

---

[21] The legislation included the Immigration Reform and Control Act of 1986 (IRCA), the Illegal Immigration Reform and Immigrant Responsibility Act of 1996 (IIRIRA), and the Personal Responsibility and Work Opportunity Reconciliation

defense of undocumented workers and their families in New York's greater metropolitan area. Its main objective, however, remained one of community building by emphasizing a sense of belonging to an ethnic community with inviolable traditions and beliefs, and by promoting ways in which the community could make these rights matter.

The following section outlines briefly what Tepeyac means for Catholic Mexicans and how the Association's name and devotion to the Virgin of Guadalupe have served as powerful organizational resources.

## TEPEYAC'S MEANING FOR MEXICAN IMMIGRANTS

The Virgin of Guadalupe is the patron saint of Mexico and the most important religious icon of Mexican Catholicism. According to legend, in 1531 (ten years after Spaniards had conquered the Aztec Empire) a dark-skinned Virgin Mary appeared three times to an Aztec peasant named Juan Diego. This Virgin told Juan Diego that she loved and would protect Mexico's indigenous peoples, as well as their Spanish conquerors. What is interesting is that this story managed to create a syncretism between the two cultures by combining elements of European Catholicism with elements of the native people's beliefs. The dark-skinned, dark-haired Virgin declared herself the protector of Mexicans at a moment when the Mexican nation did not yet exist and Catholicism was just beginning to gain a foothold in the Americas. The apparition of a native Virgin symbolized the incorporation of Catholic beliefs into traditional indigenous beliefs and festivities in the newly conquered land. From that moment forward, the image of the Virgin of Guadalupe became the mother figure to Mexican Catholics.

During one of their encounters, the Virgin of Guadalupe asked Juan Diego to have the Catholic Church build a temple to venerate her image in the exact location where she had appeared; this would later become the home of Mexican Catholicism. Juan Diego and the Virgin of Guadalupe met on a hilltop (Tepeyac, now encompassed within Mexico City), and this is where the Basilica of the Virgin of Guadalupe was built.

The Virgin became an even more powerful symbol of Mexican national identity after she "led the struggle for Independence in 1810." Her image adorned the banner Miguel Hidalgo carried when he declared war against

---

Act of 1996 (PRWORA), which place heavy fines on employers who knowingly hire undocumented workers.

Spain and gave the *grito de guerra* (battle cry) against oppression and injustice. The Virgin's image is therefore linked, according to Catholic versions of Mexican history, with the arrival of a new era—the independent Mexican nation. The name also recalls the hope that the Virgin announced for the people when she appeared on the hill named Tepeyac. The Tepeyac Association of New York has retrieved these two elements of Mexican Catholicism and used them as symbols of the organization.

Brother Magallán's discourse uses the image of the Virgin of Guadalupe as a symbol of hope for the Mexican immigrant community:

> The Virgin, to the majority of Mexicans, represents a connection with our country and our home.... We say that we are more Guadalupano (devotees to the Virgin of Guadalupe) than Mexican. We say that the Lady of Guadalupe is our symbol, our identity. Our Lady of Guadalupe has more strength in the United States because she is the mother of oppressed people, of people who are being discriminated against. She is the protector. When we are feeling desperate and suffering in New York City, she becomes the strongest symbol we can follow.

The Virgin of Guadalupe represents the guardian, and the name Tepeyac, according to the Association's leaders, symbolizes a starting point from which to invigorate a new Mexican community in exile and help it form an identity outside of Mexico.

The name Tepeyac Association was the unanimous choice of participants at the organization's constitutive assembly. The Association has followed a strategy based on liberation theology, drawing parallels between biblical stories and the immigrants' current situation, as well as between the significance of the Tepeyac site as a "place of hope" and the organizational space of the Tepeyac Association.

As the organization's symbol, the Virgin of Guadalupe has served to create a sense of community belonging. The annual Virgin of Guadalupe celebration is in fact a diasporic moment for Mexicans in New York since it is celebrated by Mexicans throughout the world. This is the Tepeyac Association's most important event; it reconnects people with their home country and national identity. The dual process of "remembering" and "not forgetting" enables the migrants to bring together elements of their past, drawing lines of continuity that nourish their feeling of socio-territorial belonging.

## GUADALUPANO COMMITTEES IN THE NEIGHBORHOODS

The Tepeyac Association comprises a network of forty Guadalupano Committees throughout the city and other parts of New York.[22] Each one elects three representatives (president, treasurer, and secretary) who become part of the Association's highest decision-making body, the General Assembly (see figure 16.1). The assembly meets twice a year to develop plans and determine which programs will be implemented during the upcoming six months. Decisions are reached by secret ballot.

**Figure 16.1. Organizational Chart of the Tepeyac Association of New York, 2000**

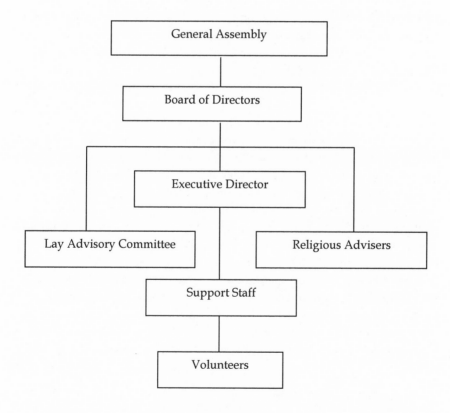

---

[22] Brooklyn has three committees; Queens has two. Northern Manhattan, particularly the Bronx, accounts for the vast majority, followed by Staten Island.

Guadalupano Committees are grouped by region (there are currently eight) and arranged according to size and location. The representatives of each committee elect one regional representative, and these representatives make up the Board of Directors, which is the intermediary before the General Assembly. The Board of Directors is charged with bringing proposals from the regions they represent as well as contributing substantially to project development. They also frame the organization's stance on specific problems or political issues such as, for example, the treatment of migration issues in the Mexican Congress.

The committees have support staffs of religious and secular consultants and volunteers, who also form part of the Tepeyac Association. They plan and carry out various Association projects, but only after the General Assembly and Board of Directors have approved them. These individuals have moral authority only; they can speak but not vote in assembly meetings (they generally do not attend). Brother Magallán, executive director of the Association, falls into this category; he has moral authority and significant influence in the Association, but he does not have the right to vote.

The Centro Guadalupano, the administrative office of the Tepeyac Association, has few paid staffers and operates thanks to the dedication and support of volunteers. One Association objective is collective learning, training immigrant workers to staff the organization's office; some immigrant volunteers have gone on to become part of the paid staff as a result of their excellent work.[23] The Association also counts on the support of students at Jesuit universities in Mexico, who spend a semester supporting Association projects with the Mexican community.[24] The group of volunteers also includes housewives, construction workers, graduate students, and professionals (psychologists, teachers, engineers, designers, and photographers, to name but a few).

The institutionalization process has passed through several evolutionary stages. The Association's organizational structure was established at the first meeting, in September 1997. On March 29, 1998, the General Assembly approved its first statutes and named the first Board of Directors. On April 15, 1998, the New York City government recognized Tepeyac as a

---

[23] The Proyecto Calmecac trains promoters in the development of the Mexican community in New York. It was approved at the Association's VI General Assembly on January 30, 2000.

[24] Two of these universities—the Instituto Tecnológico y de Estudios Superiores del Occidente (ITESO) in Guadalajara, and the Universidad Iberoamericana Puebla (UIA)—are particularly supportive.

civil association. On August 3, 1998, a Board of Consultants was formed, and finally, on January 26, 1999, the Tepeyac Association was approved as a nongovernmental, nonprofit, 501c organization.

## Internal Dynamic

Beyond the Tepeyac Association's formal structure and institutionalization, there is also a process of consolidation of the Mexican community across New York City. The differentiations in internal dynamics between Guadalupano Committees depend on the size of their membership, whether their members are old or new immigrants and documented or undocumented, and whether some sort of autocratic leadership is already in place. Their dynamics are also contingent on their representatives' leadership and mobilization capacity, the types of relations that have been established between committee members and their parish priests, the size of the Mexican population in the parish, and the presence of Spanish-speaking priests. Other factors that affect committee strength and character include the level of tolerance within each congregation for ceremonies that are specific to Mexican religiosity and any tensions that may exist between members who emphasize the sacraments and those who focus on social struggles.

Consolidation of the Guadalupano Committees has followed a lengthy process of negotiation among representatives of these base groups and the priests, members of Guadalupano Committees and other religious groups, and Mexicans and people of other nationalities within the church. Before the establishment of the Tepeyac Association, many Guadalupano Committees found it difficult to practice their religious traditions and to hold their celebrations in the church. Some priests and monks would refuse to celebrate *quinceañera* masses for girls reaching their fifteenth birthday or presentation masses for three-year-olds. The Tepeyac Association and the archdiocese's Grupo Timón suggested to these priests that they hold these services, which offer opportunities to get close to the Mexican community and make them feel welcome in the churches. These achievements have spurred Mexicans to unite and form Guadalupano Committees in churches where they previously did not exist. The presence of images of the Virgin of Guadalupe and the opportunity to venerate her have undoubtedly encouraged community-based organization.

Animators have served as a link between parishes and the Mexican community. At the same time, however, they have been responsible for some committees operating as *closed* organizations, with, for example, a membership limited to people from a particular town in Mexico. Thus, beyond the external problems that Guadalupano Committees face in winning social recognition in their parishes, the committees also face leadership problems. Some examples would be conflicts between recently arrived and earlier immigrants, competition among individuals to reclaim identifications they may have had in the community of origin, bad blood between families, and so on. On some occasions, infighting has been an obstacle to recruiting new members. Such conflicts arise because of the prestige that being a representative of a Guadalupano Committee confers in the imagined context of the Mexican community in New York.

Guadalupano Committees function in much the same way that Christian base committees operate within the Jesuit tradition. They organize weekly meetings in which members of neighborhood committees share news from the Centro Guadalupano about cultural events, protests, marches, or collective activities that require their participation. In addition, the group discusses immediate problems facing their community, evaluates the advances made toward their goals, and plans new activities. These meetings are often popular events, with members and their families sharing food, practicing regional dances, and talking late into the night in the church basement.

Each committee has its own internal dynamic. Some organize rosaries and masses on the twelfth day of every month in anticipation of the great celebration in December. A main activity of these groups has been to carry out the "Guadalupana mission," visiting all homes in their neighborhood with Mexican immigrants in the household and encouraging them to join their group and regain their closeness to the Church. During these visits, members carry a statue of the Virgin of Guadalupe through the neighborhood and pray a rosary to her at each stop. They ask her to help in bettering their employment and health situation in the city, to give them hope of one day seeing those they left behind, and to watch over them while they wait.

The Guadalupano Committees are basically community meeting spaces for discussing problems and possible solutions. Discussions address topics such as improving English and computer skills, folkloric dances, and so on. The goal of the meetings is to organize the civic and religious festivities and, above all, to ensure that the children know their roots and that families, upon leaving mass, can re-create the shared public space that existed in their towns. The committees usually meet in spaces loaned by the church—a backyard, gymnasium, or classroom—but they are not dependent on the availability of these spaces. When committees are unable to convince their priest to lend a space, they meet in homes or public parks. In fact, many Guadalupano Committees have no meeting space in their church but they continue to function in their neighborhoods nonetheless.

The committees also organize festivities in which people can dance to traditional music and eat traditional foods. The objective goes beyond entertainment; these events allow people to meet one another, and they also help attract funds to support the group's operation and the continuation of celebrations, as is done in their communities of origin. Just as these activities represent an attempt to reclaim space left behind, there are "afternoon schools" at which teachers from the Centro Guadalupano teach Mexican history and the Spanish language to elementary schoolchildren who were born in New York and only know about their parents' hometowns through the reminiscences of their elders. Neighborhood animators also participate in this program and quickly learn to be educators in their own neighborhoods, often replacing the teacher as the group's guide in recovering their Mexican sociocultural roots.

The next section highlights some important actions undertaken by the Tepeyac Association, especially the mobilizations in defense of Mexican immigrants' human rights and activities in support of a general amnesty for all immigrants in the United States. Particular attention is given to the Association's success in mobilizing people who were formerly almost exclusively dedicated to religious worship but now participate in demonstrations and protests, carrying placards calling for "Amnesty now, because we make this country rich."

## FROM PRAYER TO ACTION

In a mere three years the Tepeyac Association registered over ten thousand members. Its primary means of communication with the membership is its bulletin, *El Popocatepetl*, whose monthly run of five thousand copies cannot meet demand in many migrant areas of New York. The bulletin uses bible stories to draw parallels to the current situation of the immigrants, illustrating the items with cartoons of *paisanos* speaking in vernacular about their day-to-day struggles in the city. This strategy has proved effective in involving Mexican families and workers in nonreligious activities, in accord with the Tepeyac Association's determination that "the Catholic faith translates into action against social injustice."

*El Popocatepetl* addresses problems that the Mexican community faces in New York. Stories constantly reinforce the value of belonging to an organization, a community. The bulletin covers a wide range of topics, from news about the latest amnesty negotiations to health, sexuality, and financial advice. There are tips on how to defend the rights of workers regardless of their legal status, and about migration procedures and laws. There are articles by young people discussing their drug and alcohol addiction; articles on problems that arise due to prostitution and gang membership; and stories about immigrants infected with HIV. News stories include accounts of Mexicans arrested by the U.S. Immigration and Naturalization Service, deportations and immigration sweeps, and relevant political debates occurring in Mexico. The news also covers natural disasters in the immigrants' communities of origin and announcements of local festivities, dances, neighborhood parties, carnivals, and other community events. There are invitations to participate in the Association's English, computer, and dance classes; soccer games; free psychological counseling; and afternoon schools. The bulletin prints announcements about festivals the Guadalupano Committees will carry out in neighborhood churches. *El Popocatepetl* is also the medium used to call its readers to mobilize and, in general, to promote all Association activities. Its main purpose, however, is to serve as an informational vehicle for the immigrant community.

The Guadalupano Committees have distributed *El Popocatepetl* in the neighborhoods since the first issue was published on September 6, 1997. Since then the bulletin has also provided space to share personal or family stories with the community. The bulletin's writers and editorialists are members of the organization, as are the people who print, edit, and bind it in the basement of the Association's building.

In addition to its informational role, the Tepeyac Association aims to fulfill the following activities and goals:

- To organize the Mexican community living in New York in order to preserve their cultural roots through religious and traditional celebrations, as well as civic festivities such as Mexican Independence Day (September 16) and the Day of the Dead (November 2).

- To help Mexicans who have been arrested in immigration sweeps and/or are being held in detention centers.

- To ensure that unscrupulous immigration attorneys do not take advantage of vulnerable and uninformed Mexican immigrants.

- To denounce employers who violate labor rights. For example, the Association may negotiate with employers to recover an immigrant worker's unpaid wages, file suit against an employer and testify at trial, and hold protest demonstrations in front of a workplace (restaurant, store, factory) that has violated a worker's rights.

- To streamline support procedures (ranging from legal assistance to psychological help) for workers whose human and labor rights have been violated and to educate Mexicans on their labor rights through meetings and labor clinics in their churches.

- To promote self-employment by creating community-based businesses and cooperative societies, both in the United States and in Mexico.

- To fight for a new general amnesty for all undocumented immigrants by lobbying political leaders and members of Congress, by organizing protests and religious demonstrations, and by building nationwide networks of undocumented workers who find themselves in the same situation.

- To inform the Mexican immigrant community about agreements and negotiations between the Mexican and U.S. governments that affect them, and to consult with the immigrants on their needs so as to demand that both governments respect the immigrants' right to work and to live with dignity.

- To press for an officially sanctioned Virgin of Guadalupe holiday on December 12. Employers and other ethnic groups would respect this day as one of celebration for Mexican Catholicism, similar to other ethnic holidays already on the calendar, and no Mexican employee would have to work in New York on that day.

The Tepeyac Association has built a large network of civil, religious, and political organizations, unions, churches, foundations, and social service institutions. It has also allied itself with the National Coalition for Dignity and Amnesty, which comprises 160 organizations throughout the United States.[25] In collaboration with some of these organizations, the Association has promoted a series of support programs for the Mexican community and for Latin American communities more generally. These programs consist of helping people with health problems, legal issues, English classes, and computer instruction, among other needs. With regard to labor rights, the Association has worked closely with the Latino Worker

---

[25] For a history of the Tepeyac Association's organizational collaborations, see Rivera-Sánchez 2001.

Center and many other organizations in New York's greater metropolitan area and other U.S. cities.

The Guadalupano Committees, which are involved in all these activities, call on the Association's central office to organize workshops and meetings. Committees frequently request legal advice from the Association regarding labor and immigration rights, and through *El Popocatepetl* they receive excellent monthly reports about the ways in which a general amnesty could change their quality of life in the United States. Members of the Tepeyac Association have become active in public demonstrations in favor of an amnesty, participating in New York and also traveling en masse to Washington, D.C., to demonstrate before Congress. They have also participated in mobilizations in defense of human rights and against police brutality.

Emergency situations reveal the ties that exist between the immigrant community and their communities of origin in Mexico. This was the case when the Popocatepetl volcano erupted in December 2000. The Tepeyac Association and a radio station in Puebla combined their resources to broadcast live from Mexico directly into the Association's office via telephone. For all of December this broadcast reported on the situation in the communities endangered by the eruption. Anyone seeking information about family members in Mexico could come to the Association's office and ask their questions live on the air. In 1999 the Association rallied the immigrant community to provide financial assistance to people hurt by the severe storms that hit Puebla, Tlaxcala, and Hidalgo. The funds collected in New York were delivered by Guadalupano Committee members directly to the affected communities in Mexico. Such solidarity has been a central element in the effective operation of the neighborhood committees and in the maintenance of strong ties with the immigrants' communities of origin.

The terrorist attacks of September 11, 2001, wounded New York's Mexican community to a degree that is difficult to comprehend. Many immigrants lost family members in the World Trade Center. Calls poured in from remote areas of Mexico and other Latin American countries from people desperate for news of their loved ones. The Tepeyac Association shouldered the task of helping all families who asked for their services, processing some 110 missing persons reports in the office. The Association organized search efforts; provided legal, psychological, and emotional support; and raised funds for surviving children, adolescents, and elderly who were left alone. It also aided the more than eight hundred workers who found themselves unemployed after the tragedy, helping alleviate both their financial worries and the psychological aftereffects common to survivors of tragedy. Some of these victims were ineligible to receive government help because of their undocumented status.

The Association displayed impressive solidarity with the Latin American community, working energetically on behalf of those not helped by the agencies deployed to assist victims. Sadly, the Federal Bureau of Investigation closed many of the missing person cases for migrant workers, arguing a lack of evidence because these workers' names did not appear on any payroll records. The lack of documentation could be due to many factors; often family in Mexico lacked precise information about a migrant's address or workplace, and migrants sometimes worked under someone else's name. The Tepeyac Association is seeking help for these invisible victims of the World Trade Center bombings and justice for the families still awaiting news or the remains of a father, brother, or child.

These emergencies have strengthened the community-based organizations by testing their capacity to react in a crisis. Through its work with victims of September 11, the Tepeyac Association has extended its influence in the United States and become known throughout Mexico. Its efforts in the struggle for an amnesty for undocumented workers have also brought it increased recognition.

The following section outlines how rituals and celebrations allow New York City's Mexican community to join together to re-create the culture and local traditions of their hometowns, even as they create a new Mexican community in the United States.

## CREATING A SENSE OF COMMUNITY

The Tepeyac Association encourages respect for the way that each Mexican group in New York organizes and celebrates its festivities, but it also organizes festivities that bridge these differences and bring families and young people from the various groups together through the network of Guadalupano Committees. Along with moments of crisis and problems affecting the entire migrant population in New York, commemorations, rituals, religious celebrations, and civic festivities are also important elements with which the Mexican community of New York has been able to establish some cohesiveness.

A primary characteristic of the demonstrations in support of a general amnesty is the mix of national symbols and religious icons—including the Mexican flag and representations of the Virgin of Guadalupe—that Mexicans display on placards as they march through the streets of New York demanding amnesty, respect for their human rights, and improved labor conditions. These public demonstrations allow Mexicans to affirm their presence in the city, reinforcing a community identity and an emerging cultural project.

There are three moments during these events at which Catholic faith and Mexican nationalism come together: origin (structured around traditions), settlement (configured with a concern for continuity), and the immigrant condition (which is connected to identity and difference; see Fortier 2000). These interconnected moments allow us to anticipate some of the ways in which Mexicans will incorporate into their host societies. It is the idea of identity as an umbrella, a deterritorialized community that extends beyond the geographical limits of the nation-state.

The Tepeyac Association has contributed substantially to the process of reconfiguring identities and settlement patterns by means of discourses, celebrations, and festivities. Part of this success has come about by employing collective strategies of remembrance and reference narratives to create a *community in continuity*. The next section will consider this incorporation method, but the following few paragraphs may provide an initial understanding of how symbols of Mexican-ness are re-creating the cultural repertoires of Mexican immigrants in New York.

The celebration of the Virgin of Guadalupe on December 12 at Saint Patrick's Cathedral has become the most significant and solemn moment in which to ask the Virgin for the miracle of a general amnesty. The day's sermons have been used to rally Mexicans to the defense of their human rights, both as undocumented workers and as "workers who enrich this country." At the last such celebration, a direct call was issued to the Mexican community to participate in the mobilization for an unconditional amnesty for all immigrants in the United States.

The December 12 celebration and the Stations of the Cross on Good Friday are the two events that hold most resonance for members of the Tepeyac Association. On Good Friday, a parallel is drawn between the crucifixion of Jesus and the migrants' long journey—first as they cross the border, and later as they experience exclusion, discrimination, exploitation, and humiliation in their day-to-day life in the city. The metaphor of suffering is applied to the collective suffering inherent in the condition of immigrant communities. Sacrifice is a recurring image for Mexican immigrants, but, like all sacrifices, it implies redemption. The idea of sacrifice reminds the immigrants to press forward; it becomes an element in a cohesive

Mexican identity outside of the home country. As one immigrant noted, "We become more Mexican in the United States."

The idea of sacrifice is also present in the Day of the Dead celebration on November 2. According to Joel Magallán, "The vigil reminds us of the hundreds of immigrants who, because they were needed as cheap manual laborers in the United States, have died attempting to cross the border. Some were attacked by racists; some succumbed to cold, heat, or thirst; others drowned in their attempt to cross the border." Redemption could take the form of an amnesty for the family, friends, and neighbors of those who died.

With regard to the day of the Virgin of Guadalupe, the Tepeyac Association has been the annual sponsor of this celebration since 1997, with a mass followed by a pilgrimage through Manhattan. Participants are met at the end by busses that take them back to their individual churches. Members of the respective Guadalupano Committees carry torches to symbolize the Mexicans' faith, taking turns in accordance with a longtime Mexican tradition and eventually carrying the flame from "the Mother Church to their own churches." The torchbearers strengthen the identity of the faithful in their neighborhoods because the fire they bring to their own churches symbolizes the heritage and faith of their ancestors. It also serves to announce this faith to the city of New York, thereby symbolically representing the strengthening of Mexican identity and declaring, as noted by Joel Magallán, that "from this day forward they will celebrate a day without work, as do all nationalities in New York." Festivities begin the preceding evening when Mariachis and trios sing "Las Mañanitas" to the Virgin; the music continues into the early morning as immigrants offer traditional songs to the "brown Virgin" in their respective neighborhoods.

In addition to the historical reasons for this celebration's community impact, one key to decoding its meanings and influence is to observe the effort made to re-create a communal reference within the context of the migrant condition. This is also a means of re-creating a national identity without using Mexico as a referent; in fact, this identity is forged in opposition to the Mexico referent. In other words, some Mexican immigrants feel alienated from their home country and express hostility toward its representatives, especially with regard to the Mexican consulate in New York. There remains, nevertheless, a prominent national current in the discourses, practices, and celebrations of the Tepeyac Association and the Guadalupano Committees. Thus the Virgin of Guadalupe, as a deterritorialized symbol of Mexican-ness, enables migrants to break geographic barriers and particular identities, at least during her celebration. For this reason, to be a Guadalupano, as interpreted by the Tepeyac Association, is to recognize the Virgin of Guadalupe as an unequivocal symbol of the uniqueness of Mexican religiosity. It is, in fact, the only element that could generate a mobilization. The Virgin has become a symbol of protest and unification for Mexicans who find themselves both *here* and *there*.

The annual celebration of the Virgin of Guadalupe establishes a connection with the immigrants' country of origin and national identity, but it also connects them with their local community and identity. The celebration may serve to reconstruct the *myth of the nation* and build a sense of shared homeland outside the nation-state, where the burden of the "immigrant condition" is too heavy to bear alone.

## DIFFERENT MIGRATION PATTERNS, NEW WAYS OF INCORPORATION

How are new Mexican immigrants incorporating in relation to their migration patterns? Field observations in New York City revealed a complex interaction between newly arrived immigrants and their host society. My perspective on the condition of Mexican immigrants was mediated by the experience of people affiliated with the Tepeyac Association, and my observations should be understood in that context. Below I summarize some of my findings and explain how my theoretical conclusions evolved.

Contemporary international migration theory offers many insights into the settlement and incorporation methods of new immigrants in the United States. Some of the most important findings are by Massey, Goldring, and Durand (1994). Also important is Piore's classic work on segmented labor markets (1979). In short, analyses of migration flows and of the migration process as such provide principles for discussing multiple forms of immigrant settlement and incorporation. With his "birds of passage" image, Piore noted that for various communities the migration process was one of seasonal work cycles. Over the course of years, the seasonal cycle became a way of life; economics forced workers to migrate to the United States and placed them on the lowest rung of the job ladder. The United States needed this unskilled labor force to fill jobs that local workers will not take but which are essential for the functioning of the economic system (Piore 1979; Sassen 1991; Smith 1996). This dynamic between countries that send manual labor and those that receive it has generated varying sociocultural logics in the migration process of the sending communities and affected the migrants' settlement and incorporation behaviors at the destination points.

Drawing from international migration theory and adopting a perspective of social networks and transnationalism, we can reach some conclusions about new forms of immigrant incorporation, especially as these exist in Mexican immigrant communities. For members of some communities in Mexico, the move northward in search of better employment opportunities is almost a rite of passage. In effect, the process of transnational migration becomes self-reinforcing and increasingly independent from its original stimulus (Massey, Goldring, and Durand 1994). Various theoretical positions concur that the social capital migrants accumulate through their movement between the United States and their communities of origin reduces the costs and risks of migration—and hence eliminates the selectiveness of the process. The migrants' particular experiences and knowledge gained become part of the accumulated knowledge of the community. Over time this knowledge produces differing migration strategies and new migration patterns. I suggest that these new migration patterns also represent new forms of incorporation and settlement—not necessarily assimilation into the new community but a kind of socio-spatial stretching of the home community's symbolic referents across the border (Rouse 1996).

The new migration patterns are based on the constant movement of people, goods, information, and images. Immigrants' deep ties to their communities of origin spur them to establish communities in the societies of their destination countries (Rouse 1996). Their objective is to re-create an ethnic neighborhood through social organizations with a local reference, as, for example, a soccer team or a Guadalupano Committee whose members are from the same town in Mexico. Most Mexican immigrants who come to the United States see their stay as transitory; they plan to return to their communities of origin (Massey, Goldring, and Durand 1994). This characteristic, which is common among Mexican immigrants in New York, is an important sociocultural barrier to the migrants' permanent settlement in the new society.

There is an apparent contradiction between living in a host society and simultaneously keeping solid ties with one's community of origin—between practices that promote the creation of ethnic communities/neighborhoods and forms of sociocultural appropriation that produce new methods of settlement and incorporation. These new forms are not a product of synthesis; they are a *re-creation of significance* of their condition as immigrants. The circulation of all types of symbolic goods (money, people, information) allows a community to be extended to a variety of sites—what Roger Rouse has called "transnational migration circuits." These new forms also encompass incorporation into the context of a global system, a form of incorporation that is precisely the product of a globalized society and an outcome of the *translocal* transformation of socio-spatial relations, as well as a form of settlement for the new communities of Mexican immigrants.

The processes of incorporation, assimilation, and settlement in a global society cannot be understood in terms of national or local cultures that are defined strictly in spatial terms (Rouse 1996). The image of an extended community, as Rouse notes, implies the re-creation of symbolic references and socio-spatial transformations in which "separated worlds are now juxtaposed." This is the imagined community of Benedict Anderson (1991) and closely resembles the Tepeyac Association's project to organize Mexican immigrants in New York City.

The Tepeyac Association highlights this circuit of transmigrants, emphasizing incorporation through the images of extended community and diaspora. The Association also reinforces the circuit by opening and broadening channels for the circulation of symbolic goods, such as the images of community. This is done through the re-creation of festivities, rituals, carnivals, and religious celebrations, allowing a local-global connection with the communities of origin. The organizational strategies of "remembering" and "not forgetting" also strengthen collective memory, thereby reinforcing the principal basis for the formation of identity. This identity, however, can only be constructed in the local-global logic of the migratory circuit.

Guadalupano Committees operate as new forms of socio-spatial relationships for immigrants in their neighborhoods, where the local adopts a new symbolic content. Mexican immigrants are grouped together in traditional organizations within their churches, but at the same time they are enriching their cultural repertoires through day-to-day interactions with people of other nationalities in the workplace and elsewhere. While these migrants' repertoires of rituals and celebrations show signs of having been enriched by their encounters with the "other," these celebrations serve first and foremost to reinforce a sense of belonging to an ethnic community outside the home country, a sense of belonging that is supported by the Tepeyac Association as it educates new immigrants about their rights in their new home.

Tepeyac encourages coherence across the various channels of the Mexican migration circuit. An example is the Association's weekly radio program that provides information in both Puebla and New York. Its *El Popocatepetl* bulletin informs migrants about happenings in their hometowns, thereby establishing a new agenda in the life of the immigrant. More broadly, the Guadalupano Committees' symbols of struggle, faith, and devotion serve as a link between the migrants' situation in New York, on the one hand, and their prior experiences in their home communities and family members still in Mexico, on the other. This dual reality is also present in the public visibility project of the Tepeyac Association as a new *extended community* form of incorporation.

## References

Anderson, Benedict. 1991. *Imagined Communities: Reflections on the Origin and Spread of Nationalism*. Rev. ed. London: Verso.

Bada-García, Xochitl. 1998. "Mexican Population Living in New York City." New York: New School for Social Research. Manuscript.

Binford, Leigh, and Maria Eugenia D'Aubeterre, eds. 1999. *Conflictos migratorios transnacionales y respuestas comunitarias*. Puebla: Instituto de Ciencias Sociales y Humanidades, Benemérita Universidad de Puebla.

Bishops' Committee on Hispanic Affairs. 1999. *Hispanic Ministry at the Turn of the New Millennium*. Report of the Bishops' Committee on Hispanic Affairs, United States Conference of Catholic Bishops, November.

Cortés, Sergio. 2002. "Migration by Residents of the State of Puebla in the Decade of the 1990s." Presented at the conference "Haciendo Historia: The Development, Organization, and Mobilization of Mexicans in New York," CUNY Graduate Center, New York, September.

Department of City Planning. 1999. *The Newest New Yorkers, 1995–1996*. New York City: The Department.

Fortier, Anne Marie. 2000. *Migrant Belonging: Memory, Space, Identity*. Oxford: Berg.

Gonzales, Manuel. 1999. *Mexicanos: A History of Mexicans in the United States*. Bloomington: Indiana University Press.

INEGI (Instituto Nacional de Estadística, Geografía e Informática). 2000. *Censo Nacional de Población*. Mexico: INEGI.

Magallán, Joel. 1999. "Apostolate Report with the Mexican Community." Unpublished document, Archives of the Asociación Tepeyac.

Mainwaring, Scott, and Alexander Wilde. 1989. "The Progressive Church in Latin America: An Interpretation." In *The Progressive Church in Latin America*, edited by Scott Mainwaring and Alexander Wilde. Notre Dame, Ind.: University of Notre Dame Press.

Massey, Douglas, Luin Goldring, and Jorge Durand. 1994. "Continuities in Transnational Migration: An Analysis of Nineteen Mexican Communities," *American Journal of Sociology* 99, no. 6: 1492–1533.

Piore, Michael. 1979. *Birds of Passage: Migrant Labor and Industrial Societies*. New York: Cambridge University Press.

Rivera-Sánchez, Liliana. 2001. "The Mexican Community Living in New York: The Case of Tepeyac Association as an Organizational Network." Report to the Pew Project, New School for Social Research.

Rouse, Roger. 1996. "Mexican Migration and the Social Space of Postmodernism." In *Between Two Worlds: Mexican Immigrants in the United States,* edited by David Gutiérrez. Wilmington, Del.: Scholarly Resources.

Sassen, Saskia. 1991. *The Global City: New York, London, Tokyo.* Princeton, N.J.: Princeton University Press.

Smith, Robert C. 1995. "Los Ausentes Siempre Presentes: The Imagining, Making and Politics of a Transnational Migrant Community between Ticuani Puebla, Mexico and New York City." PhD dissertation, Columbia University.

———. 1996. "Mexicans in New York: Membership and Incorporation in a New Immigrant Community." In *Latinos in New York,* edited by Gabriel Haspil-Viera and Sherrie L. Baver. Notre Dame, Ind.: University of Notre Dame Press.

———. 1998. "Transnational Localities: Community, Technology and the Politics of Membership within the Context of Mexico and U.S. Migration," *Comparative Urban and Community Research* 6, special issue edited by Michael Peter Smith and Luis E. Guarnizo.

# PART V

# Migrants' Social and Civic Participation in Their Hometowns

# 17

# Oaxacan Municipal Governance in Transnational Context

## MICHAEL KEARNEY AND FEDERICO BESSERER

The rapid growth of circular and permanent migration from Oaxaca into northern Mexico and to the United States that has taken place since the late 1960s is now well documented (see, for example, Besserer 1989; Kearney 1986; Rivera-Salgado 1999a, 1999b; Runsten and Kearney 1994). As Oaxacans have moved into these northern regions, they have brought with them social and cultural resources that have served to maintain considerable social cohesion and cultural continuity, even as their society and culture has been transformed in the north, as in Oaxaca, which has been profoundly affected by this extensive migration.

Among the most notable social and political innovations associated with Oaxacan migration has been the formation of a broad spectrum of transnational associations and regional organizations designed to promote the well-being of Oaxacans throughout their diaspora. Beginning in the early twentieth century, Mexican migrants in the United States began to form self-help hometown associations. In the 1980s and 1990s, many innovations were made on these community-based organizations as they joined to form regionally based and interethnic organizations (Velasco Ortiz 2002). Also, while the original community-based organizations dealt with immediate material needs — such as collecting funds to send the bodies of deceased migrants home for burial and improving roads and schools in their home

We are grateful to Jonathan Fox and Gaspar Rivera-Salgado for helpful comments and suggestions on earlier drafts of this essay and for ongoing productive dialogue.

communities—the more recent migrant organizations have taken on many other responsibilities that are both cultural and political in nature.

The original migrant self-help organizations were based on an association of migrants who had a single community of origin in Oaxaca; by contrast, the newer organizations tend to incorporate various communities' organizations into larger coalitions. As these organizations have grown and joined into larger alliances, they have created a broad spectrum of Oaxacan organizations of organizations, such as COCIO, ACBJ, ORO, FIOB, and so on (Rivera-Salgado 1999c; Velasco Ortiz 2002). In California, this development of Oaxacan migrant organizations culminated in the formation in 2000 of the Oaxacan Federation of Indigenous Communities and Organizations in California (FOCOICA). Considerable institutionalization of these organizations has taken place as they have legally incorporated as not-for-profit entities in the United States and as civil associations in Mexico.

The highly dispersed and deterritorialized transnational associations, organizations, and informal networks of Oaxacan migrants and immigrants that radiate across expanses of Mexico and the United States are based in discrete territorial geopolitical entities—*municipios*—in Oaxaca. In what follows, we focus on Mixtec communities to argue that the spectacular growth of the transnational Oaxacan popular organizations has been made possible because of the sociocultural and political resources inherent in these bounded home communities in the Mixteca region.[1] These *municipios* are the bedrock of contemporary transnational Mixtec society, in all its variations.

The transnational organizations and associations have received considerable attention from the media, scholars, private foundations, and government agencies. Less noticed, however, are the *municipios*, which we see as the most important foundation of Oaxacan transnational social, cultural, and political life. We call attention to the importance of the *municipios* of Oaxaca as the foundation of the diasporic Oaxacan communities and their

---

[1] The Mixteca region occupies approximately the western third of the state of Oaxaca. The reader unfamiliar with the distinctive history of Mixtec rural communities and their extraordinary social and cultural resources, as they have been inherited from pre-Columbian times and shaped by the colonial period, the Reforma, and postrevolutionary developments, is referred to the work of Ronald Spores (1967, 1984), Rodolfo Pastor (1987), Robert Ravicz (1965), and John Monaghan (1990, 1995). These works provide a basis for comprehending the distinctive social, cultural, economic, and political features of not only present-day Mixtec *municipios* but also the transnational communities, organizations, and associations based on them.

transnational migrant organizations.[2] A primary concern is the future health of municipal governance within the transnational context. The distinctive features of Mixtec civic governance have developed over many centuries in what, until fairly recently, were relatively local communities. Some degree of circular migration within and beyond the Mixteca has been present since pre-Columbian times. But since the latter half of the twentieth century, permanent and circular out-migration has severely stressed the distinctive systems of governance prevalent in the region. The future well-being of these communities is currently at risk, as are also, therefore, the greater extended transnational communities and organizations that are based on them.

## OAXACAN MUNICIPIOS

Municipal governments — *municipios* — are the first level of government in Mexico, the other two being the federal and the state. The state of Oaxaca is unusual in the degree that it is fragmented into 570 *municipios*, 23 percent of all *municipios* in Mexico. Furthermore, most *municipios* are broken down into *agencias*, which are smaller territorial and administrative units. This abundance of *municipios* and *agencias* in Oaxaca is a reflection of the state's ethnic and geographic diversity and of the citizens' intense identification with their local communities, which are often distinct social, cultural, and political universes. Indeed, 418 communities are governed by their own customary law (*usos y costumbres*), a legal form now legally recognized by the constitution of the state of Oaxaca as amended in 1995. Most of Oaxaca's *municipios* tend, however, to share some common structural features typical of the region and which derive from their indigenous heritages as they were modified in the colonial and subsequent periods.

Relationships between *agencias* and *municipios* vary considerably. Whereas some *agencias* are highly subordinated to and dependent on their municipal *cabeceras* (head towns), other *agencias* function with considerable autonomy. In our research sample, San Jerónimo Progreso is a good example case of the latter situation. One of the apparent reasons that the citizens of San Jerónimo zealously guard their autonomy is the fact that their municipal *cabecera*, Silacayoapam, is a predominantly mestizo town, while the residents of San Jerónimo are notably indigenous in their identity, lan-

---

[2] Mutersbaugh (2002) also focuses on Oaxacan "sending community agency" as compared with the more prevalent concern in the literature with transnational communities, organizations, and associations.

guage, and institutions, and as such perceive a certain discrimination by and exploitation from the *cabecera*. The situation is quite different, for example, in the *municipio* of San Juan Mixtepec, where there is less ethnic differentiation between *cabecera* and *agencias*.

In most of Oaxaca's *municipios* and *agencias*, local citizens fill public offices as a requirement for membership in the community. Typically these offices are *presidente, alcalde, juez, comisario de bienes comunales, comité de bienes comunales, comandante de policía, topiles, alguaciles, secretario,* and so on, plus any number of special committees. Most of these offices also have a *suplente* (second or vice officer). And in some towns, religious offices such as *sacristanes* of the local church are chosen in the same manner. Often *regidores* or *principales*—venerable older men (*pasantes*) who have completed their formal community service and preside as a council of elders— guide the younger men responsible for actual day-to-day governance.

Elections and important problems of the community are often discussed and solved in communal assemblies. Here we also find variations which we can illustrate with the cases discussed above: Whereas the *principales* are the most important political reference in the community of San Jerónimo Progreso, in San Juan Mixtepec the office of *principales* has almost disappeared while the importance of the general assembly in the political dynamics of the community has grown considerably.

Another basic institution in many Oaxacan communities is the *tequio*, which with variation from community to community is a form of communal labor in which citizens, led by the town authorities, participate in work projects ranging from construction and maintenance of basic infrastructure (roads, bridges, buildings, potable water and irrigation systems, and so on) to general town upkeep. As with civil and religious *cargos*, participation in *tequios* is a requirement of town membership for all male citizens who are, usually, under sixty years of age. In many Oaxacan communities, land tenure, except for homes and house plots, is communal, and use of it for agriculture, pasturage, and access to its other resources (woods, water, game, minerals) is restricted to community members in good standing, a basic condition of which is fulfillment of public and ceremonial offices and other obligations as ordained by custom.

## MUNICIPAL GOVERNMENTS UNDER STRESS

In most of the *municipios* and *agencias* of Oaxaca, municipal offices are filled by local citizens as a requirement for membership in the community. Typically in the *agencias* and smaller *municipios*,[3] persons who fill civil and religious offices do not receive a salary; indeed, they finance their own expenses and forgo other primary means of income during their term of office, which may last from one to three years. In many towns, holding of office entails major ceremonial expenses as well, often amounting to thousands of dollars. In some communities, such ceremonial obligations are assigned apart from civil office.

In recent years, high rates of permanent and temporary migration have strained the capacity of many Oaxacan *municipios* to fill offices. It is now common for citizens of Oaxacan communities residing in the north to be recalled to serve, and for the most part they do, but often at considerable expense and hardship for their families.[4] High rates of migration also seriously challenge the ability of the communities based in Oaxaca to fill municipal offices to maintain effective governance. What is at stake here is the viability of an ancient, time-tested form of essentially democratic community governance.

Out of concern for the future of governance in Oaxacan communities with high rates of migration, we formed a research team composed of ourselves and nine undergraduate students in the Anthropology Department of the Universidad Autónoma Metropolitana–Iztapalapa, in Mexico City. The task of this team is to ethnographically investigate and document patterns of and variations in municipal governance in a sample of six Mixtec communities that have high circular and permanent migration rates.[5]

---

[3] Herein, unless there is need to distinguish them, we will refer to both *municipios* and *agencias* as *municipios*.

[4] See Velasco Ortiz 1995 for the ways in which families are affected by and, with hardship, adapt to maintaining residences in both Oaxaca and the border area. Besserer (1999a) discusses more general aspects of citizenship in the transnational context.

[5] We wish to thank our research assistants who worked in the towns in Oaxaca, noted below, and among migrants from those towns at various places in the United States and northern Mexico. In the Distrito de Silacayoapam, René Robles and Fabiola González worked in San Jerónimo Progreso; Ariana Estrada in Ixpantepec Nieves; and Estefanny Espinoza in Santiago Asunción. In the Distrito de Juxtlahuaca, Alma Reyes, Julio Morales, Yuribi Ibarra, and Adriana Zaraté worked in the towns of San Miguel del Progreso, San Juan Mixtepec, and Santa Cruz, Mixtepec in the large municipio of Mixtepec.

The primary reasons for selecting these study communities were existing databases and ethnographic background, and working relations that served as a platform for this research. Also, each community functions with considerable autonomy with respect to internal governance and collective identity, and as such is typical of hundreds of other Oaxacan communities.

This research is documenting and analyzing the extent to which community governance in the study communities is performed by migrants who, at their own expense, return to their hometowns to fulfill their civic and ceremonial obligations. We are also assessing positive and negative impacts of these patterns on communities and families. We assume that procedures and customs having to do with community governance are changing under the new conditions, and we propose to document these trends. Special attention is given to the stresses placed on communities and their families as they struggle to adapt to these new and complex ways of living and governing. A goal of this research is to develop policy recommendations for appropriate agencies of the municipal, state, and federal governments to assist these communities and families adapt to these new, deterritorialized transnational contexts (see the section on policy relevance, below).

## THE CONTEMPORARY CONTEXT

In recent years, the rates of migration from Oaxaca, especially to northern Mexico and the United States, have increased dramatically. Indeed, many Oaxacan communities are now de facto deterritorialized "transnational communities," or TNCs (Besserer 1989, 2003, n.d.; Kearney and Nagengast 1989; Rivera-Salgado 1999a, 1999c). In an extreme case of the governance of a town being displaced abroad, Robert Smith (1994) describes a pattern in which a Mixtec community in Puebla is effectively governed by town authorities living in New York City.

In our previous research (for example, Besserer 1999b; Kearney 1986; Kearney and Nagengast 1989) we became acutely aware of how the new residence patterns strain municipal governance and impose great hardship on migrants who retain their citizenship in their home communities but who must return to fulfill their civic and ceremonial obligations to do so. Thus it is now common for citizens of a community who are residing elsewhere in Mexico or in the United States to be called to fulfill an office in their hometown. These appointments usually require that the new officeholders leave their work in the north for one to three years and relocate to the home community for the period of service. In some cases, arrangements are made for intermittent return trips to the north to attend to per-

We also appreciate the help of Konane Martínez, who facilitated work in Ixpantepec Nieves and in San Diego County, California, and Ernesto Reyes for assistance in Santiago Asunción. And we are grateful to UC MEXUS, of the University of California, and to CONACYT in Mexico for funding to support this research.

sonal matters. This pattern of governance represents a new moment in the history of Oaxacan communities in which municipal governance and citizenship are increasingly dependent on the service of return migrants and the taxes of immigrants living "in the north."

As citizens reside in ever more dispersed networks, governance is becoming increasingly deterritorialized. Two contrary trends are thus evolving. On the one hand, communities are weakened by migratory dispersion. But on the other, they are now able to tap and accumulate greater financial resources—essentially taxes—from citizens living and working temporarily or permanently in the north. For example, the authorities of San Jerónimo Progreso (see below) maintain committees among concentrations of its citizens who reside in Tijuana, Nogales (Sonora), Southern and Central California, and Arizona. One of the duties of these committees is to collect *cuotas* (taxes) from each head of household in their respective area and remit the money to the town authorities, who allocate the funds for public works. Note, however, that these monies are not used to pay salaries for the town authorities.

## CHALLENGES TO TRANSNATIONAL MUNICIPAL GOVERNANCE

As noted above, *municipios* and *agencias* are the cores of the TNCs. Whereas the transnational organizations and associations are typically highly deterritorialized and dispersed, the home communities in Oaxaca are territorially based and have strong symbolic meaning and emotional significance to their "sons" and "daughters," in Oaxaca and abroad. Legally, most of the communities in Oaxaca are *comunes* in which land and other major resources are owned by the community at large. In many communities, these resources include extensive areas of land and the resources on them, such as forests, minerals, and water. As such, they contrast with the other two principal forms of land tenure in Mexico: *ejidos* (collectives) and *pequeñas propiedades* (private property). Membership in a commune is acquired primarily by birth to parents who are members; also, outsiders occasionally become members by marriage to a member. Due to the communal land tenure and limitations on outsiders becoming members, there is virtually no market for real estate in the communes. Land is transferred primarily by inheritance.

Many *municipios* and *agencias* in Oaxaca can trace their continuity back to pre-Columbian times, and there is thus a considerable continuity of basic institutions and patterns of governance in these communities. The recognition of this continuity and the vitality of this de facto situation was the basis for the recent state constitutional changes to give the communities the legal authority to govern their internal affairs in accord with their own local customary laws. But in the last decade, many of Oaxaca's *municipios* have been experiencing population decline within their territorial limits, and this trend is projected to continue indefinitely in some of them. Although no firm data exist, it can be safely assumed that while many Mixtec *municipios* are losing local residents, their actual overall membership is increasing when the total numbers of citizens who live outside of their territorial boundaries are taken into account.

## The Impact of Migration on the Ability to Govern

At this moment in the history of the Mixteca, a major concern of ours is the future well-being—and indeed the continued social, political, cultural, and economic existence—of the *municipios* and *agencias* as viable self-governing communities. At present, many *municipios* and *agencias*, not only in the Mixteca but throughout Oaxaca, are losing local residents even though, as noted above, the sum total of their members may be growing. Thus, as migration to the north increases, the demographic center of gravity is shifting away from the actual bounded communities and into the greater, widely dispersed populations of the TNCs. The greater deterritorialized TNCs remain anchored in the territorially based communities in Oaxaca, but increasingly their members are dispersing away from the territorially based home community.

Before the present high rates of migration, most officeholders lived within their communities of origin and were more or less able to maintain normal economic and family activities during the period of their obligation. But with so many community members now living elsewhere in Mexico and in the United States, many *municipios* and *agencias* are having trouble filling municipal offices, and it is now common for community members elected to municipal office to leave their jobs in the north for a year or more to fulfill their obligations. The penalties for a migrant's failure to return to fulfill municipal obligations vary from community to community. In some communities it is possible to arrange for substitutes, while other towns are stricter in requiring the elected person to return. Indeed, failure to fulfill civic obligations can, and at times does, result in loss of membership in the community, confiscation of land and home, loss of rights to reside in the community, and loss of access to its economic, legal, and social resources. Excluded members may also be denied the right to be buried in the town's graveyard.

The fact that some communities are imposing such strict sanctions for failure to assume elected and appointed offices is an indication of the stress that their civil governments are experiencing. Indeed, there is much reason to be concerned about the ability of communities to staff offices and deliver basic services, maintain and improve infrastructure, maintain law and order, and preserve communal ceremonial and religious life and identities. In other words, nothing less than the survival of many Oaxacan communities is at stake. Similarly, the well-being and continuity of the greater TNCs and their organizations and associations is also at stake insofar as they are outgrowths and extensions of the *municipios*.

## Impact on Migrant and Immigrant Families

In most Oaxacan communities, the main *cargos*, which are filled by men, typically involve extensive ceremonial obligations centering on religious events and feasting, in which the preparation of food and hosting are central. Thus, when men are called from the north to return to fulfill public obligations, their wives are often required to accompany them (Velásquez C. 2002). In such cases, women must also leave their work in the north, and children must be taken out of school and be left behind with relatives or fend for themselves. Thus we are also concerned with aspects of household maintenance, family cohesion, and impact on children. Of concern as well are the attitudes of children of citizens who live in the north and their dispositions to carry on the traditions of their parents. Quite relevant in this regard are the changing patterns of marriage. The integration and solidarity of Mixtec communities are due in large part to a deep sense of common membership, which is reinforced by high rates of community endogamy. However, as Lestage (1999) demonstrates, community exogamy tends to increase among migrants in the north. It is reasonable to assume that, as migration out of Oaxaca continues, this increasing exogamy will impact the construction and exercise of citizenship within the TNCs as well as relationships among them.

## Democratization of Municipal Governance

Jonathan Fox cites a World Bank report that notes, "The poor indigenous communities of Oaxaca have a notable participatory tradition" (2002: 102).[6]

---

[6] Our translation. This report also notes that the high level of participatory governance present in Oaxaca is relatively absent in Chiapas, which is the other major state in Mexico populated by indigenous peoples.

But within this extensive grassroots democracy there are many exceptions and considerable variation in the forms and bases of power and decision making. Indeed, our current research reveals that the actual loci of power vary considerably among the Oaxacan *municipios* (see also Fox and Aranda 1996). In some, major decisions are made by general meetings (*asambleas*) of male citizens, while in others the de facto power is held by what Laura Velasco Ortiz (2002) refers to as a gerontocracy of elder men, who in effect direct communal political and ceremonial life. These "*principales*," as they are often called, have gained their status and power by having passed through a series of major *cargos* and ceremonial obligations. They also tend to be the richer and more politically powerful men of a community. In some instances, the power and prestige of the *principales* fades into forms of *caciquismo*. But under the contemporary conditions of extensive migration, a common pattern is for younger, more affluent migrants and immigrants to return to their home communities and propose alternative forms of governance and ceremonial life.

There is reason to assume that, in some communities, changes in governance introduced by returnees are leading to more democratic forms and practices. Indeed, in some communities the power of caciques has been challenged by return migrants who organized, became empowered, and instituted certain reforms (Besserer 1999b). Important here, but as yet little understood, is the impact of the dispersion of political power from the territorially based *municipios* into the greater deterritorialized spaces of their extended TNCs. One example of the expansion of the political power of the municipality is when municipal presidents act in favor of members of the community who live outside its territorial boundaries, as reported in cases of natural disasters (Besserer 1999b). Another instance of empowerment of the transnational community is when citizens of a *municipio* in Oaxaca engage in negotiations with authorities of the state of Oaxaca in U.S. territory, as has been reported in the context of visits by various authorities of Oaxaca to the state of California (Besserer 2003). Furthermore, the working relations between hometown associations in northern Mexico and the United States, on the one hand, and the authorities of *agencias* or *municipios*, on the other, have generated a demand for transparency and accountability in expenditures, electoral processes, and political negotiations with federal and state levels of government. Indeed, a working assumption of the present research is that this dispersion of residence and governance is having positive impacts on social justice and human rights (see Nagengast, Stavenhagen, and Kearney 1992).

## Impacts on Indigenous Identity, Law, and Gender

Elsewhere we have described and documented the emergence of organized expressions of Mixtec ethnicity under the seemingly improbable conditions of long-distance migration to northern Mexico and the United States (see Besserer 1990, 2000a, 2000b; Kearney 2000, 2001, 2003; Nagengast and Kearney 1990). These new political forms and identities are being imported back to Oaxaca and elaborated within the new state constitutional framework—and also in the context of new federal constitutional reforms, should they come to pass. Thus, although migration from Oaxaca erodes many aspects of traditional local identities, at the same time it is creating and reinforcing other expressions of ethnicity and regionalism, which are visible in the many Oaxacan organizations and associations that have been formed in the north. These organizations and associations articulate with municipal governments in varied and complex ways. To some extent municipal governance is being displaced into these nongovernmental organizations (NGOs), but at the same time the NGOs often provide considerable financial, material, and symbolic support for the municipal governments.

For example, the ceremonial and symbolic life of Mixtec towns is typically largely a responsibility of the local government and/or local individual and group sponsors. But increasingly, town fiestas and ceremonial life in general are being augmented by migrants and immigrants in the north, who have greater financial resources than those in the home community. In some cases these increased expenditures are encouraged, even demanded, by the stay-at-home elders and *principales*, and they have become a point of tension. But regardless of the tensions over sponsorship, these changing patterns toward larger town fiestas are socially and symbolically significant for maintaining community identity, cohesion, and governance.

Because of difficulties in filling some of the traditional male *cargos*, women are now occasionally named to some of these municipal posts, and women are increasingly performing *tequio* duties.[7] As is true in many "traditional" societies, Mixtec women have been largely excluded from participation in municipal governance, especially in the more rural contexts. There are, however, indications that the transnational migration experience, whereby women enter into new and diverse economic and social spheres, has prompted greater participation of women in civic affairs, a trend that in turn has promoted greater recognition of women as "citi-

---

[7] See Besserer 2000b for further discussion of the changing roles and identities of women within the transnational context. Also see the chapter by Velásquez in this volume.

zens." The generally higher rate of male migration, as compared to that of women, has also affected gendered identities and roles. Although not in the Mixteca, the Zapotec *municipio* of Yatzatchi El Bajo in the northern Sierra offers an example. Due to the high rate of male migration from Yatzatchi, some women are now elected to the office of *policía*. Women so named patrol the town at night with wooden clubs (*macanas*), which are the major symbol of this traditionally very male office.[8] But despite such notable changes, as María Cristina Velásquez notes (this volume), indigenous women are still largely excluded from municipal government in rural areas. But Velásquez does find some positive trends that are revealed in her detailed study of Oaxacan communities governed by customary law. Indeed, Velásquez found that out of a sample of 418 *municipios*, women vote and serve in various offices in 248 — and that, in addition to voting, they are creating other ways to participate in civic governance. Also, a new pattern is the emergence of women's committees dedicated to aspects of community maintenance and governance. One example comes from San Jerónimo Progreso, where circular migrant women from the town have formed an association dedicated to civic beautification.[9]

Particularly relevant is the presence of women in the *cargos* created by TNCs to establish community mechanisms for transferring remittances from the United States to Mexico.[10] The emergence of female small entrepreneurs in Oaxaca, who have invested savings resulting from their own migration or family remittances, has also created economic strongholds that often translate into female positions of political leverage in moments of elections.[11]

These new trends of female participation in the political life of TNCs are related not only to the pattern of predominantly male migration that we find in some communities (Runsten and Kearney 1994) but also to the political spaces won by women in their own processes of migration (Besserer 2000a; Velasco Ortiz 2002). It is an empirical question if they are in fact conducive to an increase in women's participation and power in municipal governance.[12]

---

[8] Personal observation, Michael Kearney, 1991.

[9] Personal observation, Michael Kearney, 2001.

[10] We are grateful to Yuribi Ibarra, the member of our team who explored remittances from California to Mixtepec.

[11] We are grateful to Julio Morales, the member of our team who explored this theme in Mixtepec and its satellite communities.

[12] At present, seventeen *municipios* in Oaxaca have elected women municipal presidents, who have formed a network to coordinate their interests. This remarkable

## National Citizenship, Immigration Law, and Municipal Governance

Recent changes in Mexican law have made it possible for Mexicans who become U.S. citizens to retain Mexican nationality, and it is possible that this law will be extended to include Mexican citizenship (see below). A question that arises, then, is how such new legal identities would affect Mixtecs' ability and willingness to retain their memberships and rights in their home communities and participate in their governance. Also, because many Oaxacans are in the United States as unauthorized immigrants—and given the present tightening of the U.S.-Mexico border—the frequency of their return visits to Oaxaca appears to have been greatly reduced. The conditions affecting the legal status of Oaxacans in the United States and changing U.S. immigration law and policy are influencing the ability and willingness of Oaxacans in the north to participate in hometown governance, and it remains to be seen what the impact will be on the well-being of municipal governance.

Our research has shown that, because of the increasing difficulties for cross-border mobilizations, municipal *cargos* in Oaxaca are increasingly fulfilled by "legal" immigrants to the United States. Individuals who have not regularized their stay in the United States tend to make other kinds of contributions to their communities from the U.S. side of the border, thus hoping to delay having to return to Mexico.[13] Thus a result of the recent strengthening of U.S. border controls is that offices in the Oaxacan territorial community are increasingly being held by male members of the deterritorialized community who are able to travel back and forth.[14] Additionally, active participation in the diaspora is encouraged for those who left Mexico most recently and are less financially equipped to travel back.

Therefore, we assume that one likely outcome is that decreased cross-border migration will promote ongoing dispersion of municipal governance into the greater deterritorialized space of the TNCs (see Kearney 1996). Additionally, the combination of legalization of the Mixtecs residing

---

pattern appears to be due to the difficulty of recruiting men to fill the major *cargos*, under conditions of extensive out-migration (personal communication from Sergio Robles Camacho). For a detailed discussion and analysis of the relationships between gender and ethnicity within the transnational context, see Velasco Ortiz 2002.

13 We are grateful to our team members Ariana Estrada and Estefanny Espinoza for fieldwork on this theme in Ixpantepec Nieves and Santiago Asunción, respectively.

14 René Robles reports that transmigrants who return to fulfill cargos in the community of San Jerónimo Progreso are often supported for part of their term by their wives who remain in the United States and become the economic mainstay of their families—and thus, indirectly, of the municipal system of governance (Robles 2003).

in the United States with a tightening of border-crossing control systems will strengthen informal citizenship and allegiance to the TNC (which differs from formal municipal citizenship and national citizenship).

## POLICY RELEVANCE

The trends in Oaxacan *municipios* noted above are also being affected by several important policy developments in Mexican society and constitutional law that are associated with the new post-PRI (Institutional Revolutionary Party) administration of President Vicente Fox and the ongoing neoliberal reforms of "the New Federalism," which promote more direct articulation between the federal and the municipal governments and more municipal powers and autonomy. Furthermore, at this moment Mexico is rethinking the status and roles of Mexican nationals living abroad. Thus, shortly after assuming office, President Fox signaled an intent to extend dual citizenship (in addition to dual nationality) to Mexicans living in the United States. Also, Mexico recently launched the "Programa Paisano" and "Peso por Peso" (Goldring 1999), two policy initiatives designed to maintain state hegemony over Mexican nationals abroad and to control their potential for financing community infrastructure projects. To date, these two programs have focused on migrants from the states of Zacatecas and Guanajuato, which, like Oaxaca, have histories of strong migrant organizations in the United States. With the technical and financial assistance of the federal government, the migrant organizations in these two states were brought together to coordinate their efforts with federal financial assistance for community development projects in which the federal government matches community development funds raised by migrants from different towns for local projects. Hence the designation Peso por Peso.

Recently a similar project was proposed to President Fox by representatives of FOCOICA when he met with them in Fresno, California, in 2000. The proposed program, based on the Peso por Peso concept, is being referred to as "Tres por Uno," because the plan is for the government of Oaxaca to also contribute funds to match those of the migrant associations and the federal government.

### "Pesos por Servicio"

At the meeting in Fresno referred to above, Mr. Rufino Domínguez presented President Fox with a proposal devised by one of the authors of the present essay. This proposal is patterned on the Peso por Peso and Tres por

Uno programs and is tentatively referred to as Pesos por Servicio. The aim of this proposal is to establish a program to help defray the personal costs of Oaxacan migrants who return to fulfill government service. The rationale for such a program is that the migrants are filling government administrative offices and delivering vital government services at their own expense, and often with severe financial and social impacts on themselves and their families. These expenses and hardships are exacerbated in the case of return migrants by the costs of return and lost income, the impact of taking children out of school in the north, and the separation of families during the long periods of service.

## CONCLUSION: MIGRATION AND THE FUTURE OF MUNICIPAL GOVERNANCE

In large part because of the impact of the Zapatista uprising in Chiapas in 1994, indigenous peoples and indigenous issues are now in the foreground of national politics and policy concerns. In the San Andrés Accords, signed in 1996, autonomous regions were created in Chiapas and a series of *consultas* (consultations) was called for to explore the possibilities for and parameters of creating autonomous regions elsewhere in Mexico. Due to the high degree of ethnic diversity in Oaxaca, a special *consulta* was called for this state, in which we drew attention to the need to take into account the high rates of migration from Oaxaca to the north in discussions about the formation of autonomous regions — and about local governance in general (Kearney 1996). This research is in large part a follow-up to this concern. Furthermore, we have been predicting that the Oaxacan migration pattern will be followed by migrants from Chiapas, and we argue that this research will be relevant to it and to other areas of Mexico from which large numbers of rural people migrate.

The research and perspectives discussed above are designed to generate data to advance discussion on the Pesos por Servicio proposal described above. A major challenge that we foresee, should this policy be implemented, is the equitable distribution of such assistance and the avoidance of the invidious comparisons and destructive competition for such resources that could ensue in the application for allocation of these resources and in their administration. Also, it is to be expected that such assistance to migrants who are returning to fulfill municipal obligations will further alter their political and economic status vis-à-vis the traditional, nonmigrating power holders and elites in the home communities, thereby contributing to ongoing socioeconomic and political changes in the home communities as well as in the greater TNCs of which they are the nuclei.

One thing is certain: transnational migration is profoundly affecting the form and functioning of municipal governance in Oaxaca. The concepts and work reported on here have as their major goal to contribute to the successful adaptation of these remarkable institutions to the realities of the rapidly accelerating trends of deterritorialization, transnationalization, and globalization that are reshaping them.

## References

Besserer, Federico. 1989. "Mixtecos errantes," *México Indígena* 1 (October): 16–18.

———. 1990. "Filemón López, dirigente mixteco de la Asociación Cívica Benito Juárez," *México Indígena* 13 (October): 40–43.

———. 1999a. "Estudios transnacionales y ciudadanía transnacional." In *Fronteras fragmentadas*, edited by Gail Mummert. Zamora: El Colegio de Michoacán.

———. 1999b. *Moisés Cruz: historia de un transmigrante*. Culiacán: Universidad Autónoma de Sinaloa/Mexico City: Universidad Autónoma Metropolitana–Iztapalapa.

———. 2000a. "Política cuántica: usos de la radio por comunidades transnacionales," *Nueva Antropología* 25 (August).

———. 2000b. "Sentimientos (in)apropiados de las mujeres migrantes: hacia una nueva ciudadanía." In *Migración y relaciones de género en México*, edited by Dalia Barrera Bassols and Cristina Oemichen Bazán. Mexico City: GIMTRAP-UNAM.

———. 2003. "Contesting Community: Cultural Struggles of a Mixtec Transnational Community." PhD dissertation, Stanford University.

———. n.d. *Topografías transnacionales: hacia una geografía de las comunidades transnacionales*. Mexico City: Universidad Autónoma Metropolitana/Plaza y Valdés. Forthcoming.

Fox, Jonathan. 2002. "La relación recíproca entre la participación ciudadana y la rendición de cuentas: la experiencia de los Fondos Municipales en el México rural," *Política y Gobierno* 9, no. 1.

Fox, Jonathan, and Josefina Aranda. 1996. *Decentralization and Rural Development in Mexico: Community Participation in Oaxaca's Municipal Funds Program*. La Jolla: Center for U.S.-Mexican Studies, University of California, San Diego.

Goldring, Luin. 1999. "El Estado mexicano y las organizaciones transmigrantes." In *Fronteras fragmentadas*, edited by Gail Mummert. Zamora: El Colegio de Michoacán.

Kearney, Michael. 1986. "Integration of the Mixteca and the Western U.S.-Mexican Border Region via Migratory Wage Labor." In *Regional Impacts of U.S.-Mexican Relations*, edited by Ina Rosenthal-Urey. La Jolla: Center for U.S.-Mexican Studies, University of California, San Diego.

———. 1996. "La migración y la formación de regiones autónomas pluriétnicas en Oaxaca." In *Coloquio sobre Derechos Indígenas*, edited by Coordinación General de Asesores del Gobierno del Estado de Oaxaca. Oaxaca: Instituto Oaxaqueño de las Culturas.

———. 2000. "La comunidad rural oaxaqueña y la migración: más allá de las políticas agraria e indígena," *Cuadernos Agrarios* 19–20: 11–23.

———. 2001. "Struggle and Difference: The Jujitsu of Transnational Indigenous Resistance and Domination." In *History in Person: Enduring Struggles, Contentious Practice, Intimate Identities*, edited by Dorothy Holland and Jean Lave. Santa Fe, N.M.: Oxford /School of American Research Press.

———. 2003. "Valor, clase y espacio en las comunidades mixtecas transnacionales," *Universidad de México* 620.

Kearney Michael, and Carole Nagengast. 1989. "Anthropological Perspectives on Transnational Communities in Rural California." Davis, Calif.: California Institute for Rural Studies.

Lestage, Françoise. 1999. "Diseñando nuevas identidades: las uniones matrimoniales entre los migrantes mixtecos en Tijuana." In *Fronteras fragmentadas*, edited by Gail Mummert. Zamora: El Colegio de Michoacán.

Monaghan, John. 1990. "La desamortización de la propiedad comunal en la Mixteca: resistencia popular y raíces de la conciencia nacional." In *Lecturas históricas del Estado de Oaxaca*, vol. 3, *Siglo XIX*, edited by María de los Ángeles Frizzi. Mexico City: Instituto Nacional de Antropología e Historia.

———. 1995. The Covenants with Earth and Rain: Exchange, Sacrifice, and Revelation in Mixtec Sociality. Norman: University of Oklahoma Press.

Mutersbaugh, T. 2002. "Migration, Common Property, and Communal Labor: Cultural Politics and Agency in a Mexican Village," *Political Geography* 21, no. 4.

Nagengast, Carole, and Michael Kearney. 1990. "Mixtec Ethnicity: Social Identity, Political Consciousness, and Political Activism," *Latin American Research Review* 25, no. 2.

Nagengast, Carole, Rodolfo Stavenhagen, and Michael Kearney. 1992. *Human Rights and Indigenous Workers: The Mixtecs in Mexico and the United States*. La Jolla: Center for U.S.-Mexican Studies, University of California, San Diego.

Pastor, Rodolfo. 1987. *Campesinos y reformas: la Mixteca, 1770–1856*. Mexico City: El Colegio de México.

Ravicz, Robert. 1965. *Organización social de los mixtecos*. Mexico City: Instituto Nacional Indigenista.

Rivera-Salgado, Gaspar. 1999a. "Welcome to Oaxacalifornia," *Cultural Survival Quarterly* 23, no. 1 (Spring).

————. 1999b. "Migration and Political Activism: Mexican Transnational Indigenous Communities in a Comparative Perspective." PhD dissertation, University of California, Santa Cruz.

————. 1999c. "Mixtec Activism in Oaxacalifornia: Transborder Grassroots Political Strategies," *American Behavioral Scientist* 42, no. 9.

Robles, René. 2003. "San Jerónimo Progreso: migración y remesas. Un sistema político sustentado por ellas." Master's thesis, Universidad Autónoma Metropolitana–Iztapalapa.

Runsten, David, and Michael Kearney. 1994. *A Survey of Oaxacan Village Networks in California Agriculture*. Davis: California Institute for Rural Studies.

Smith, Robert C. 1994. "'Los Ausentes Siempre Presentes': The Imagining, Making, and Politics of a Transnational Community between Ticuani, Puebla, Mexico and New York City." PhD dissertation, Colombia University.

Spores, Ronald. 1967. *The Mixtec Kings and Their People*. Norman: University of Oklahoma Press.

————. 1984. *The Mixtecs in Ancient and Colonial Times*. Norman: University of Oklahoma Press.

Velasco Ortiz, Laura. 1995. "Migración femenina y estrategias de sobrevivencia de la unidad doméstica: un caso de estudio de mujeres mixtecas en Tijuana." In *Mujeres, migración y maquila en la frontera norte*, edited by Soledad González Montes. Mexico City: El Colegio de México/Tijuana: El Colegio de la Frontera Norte.

————. 2002. *El regreso de la comunidad: migración indígena y agentes étnicos, los mixtecos en la frontera México-Estados Unidos*. Tijuana: El Colegio de la Frontera Norte/El Colegio de México.

Velásquez C., María Cristina. 2002. "Discriminación por género y participación en los sistemas normativos de gobierno indígena: contrastes y paradojas." Unpublished.

# 18

# Migration and Return in the Sierra Juárez

SERGIO ROBLES CAMACHO

## REASONS FOR MIGRATING

Out-migration from towns in the Sierra Juárez of Oaxaca stems from many factors, among which two are preeminent. The first was an agreement between the U.S. and Mexican governments that aimed to reverse the shortage of agricultural workers in the United States (mostly in the southern states) during World War II and the postwar period. Labor shortages have spurred sustained and increasing migration in regions and communities where it has long been an alternative for people in poverty. Today, labor migration is becoming an increasingly common option in many additional areas, including urban areas, that are facing worsening living conditions. Official statistics report that 54 million Mexicans currently live in poverty.

A second factor that influences migration is people's search for alternative means of personal, family, and community development, which is based on the Juárez tradition of leaving one's village to study and prepare oneself to build a better life. This pattern reflects the lack of educational opportunities outside major cities, a lack that encourages people to migrate not only to Oaxaca City and elsewhere in Mexico but also abroad.

These two processes are not independent of one other. They are interconnected and have multiple impacts in the migrants' lives and in their towns of origin. Among the myriad impacts of migration, remittances—and their far-reaching economic effects—have generated substantial re-

Translation by Naomi Adelson.

search interest. However, little has been documented about how migrants apply the skills and knowledge they acquire during migration to the development of alternative projects to improve living conditions in their hometowns.

In many important migrant-sending regions, only older adults remain today. This means that there are few citizens available to fill local community posts or to provide community labor (*tequio*). Our towns have no musical groups, and we have no more youths to send as migrants. The dismaying question we are asking ourselves is whether, in a few years' time, our towns will have become ghost towns. In exploring this possible eventuality, I will describe my experience as a migrant returning to his hometown as municipal president and president of the Union of Communities from Zoogocho (Unión de Pueblos del Sector Zoogocho) in the Sierra Juárez of Oaxaca.

## MY HISTORY

Our parents tell us that it was in the 1940s that the people of our indigenous communities first heard the words "hiring," "wave of labor," and "Empalme, Sonora." The hearts and heads of the grandparents and women were filled with worry. They went to the church to ask God to take care of their loved ones and bring them home safe and sound. That was how it was with the first braceros—those hired under the Bracero Program to work in the United States. When these workers returned, they were transformed; they came back with other experiences, speaking broken Spanish, some forgetting their native tongue, wearing cowboy boots. Their *huaraches* (traditional sandals) and white cotton pants had been left behind in the agricultural fields of the United States. On the other hand, the dollars these migrants brought back temporarily improved community and family economies.

Migration from our region only became extensive in the 1970s, when it was very difficult for rural Mexicans to achieve food self-sufficiency. One could say that poverty emigrated, because the dollars that began to arrive created a new dynamic in the social and economic life of our towns. However, this economic boon also created a loss: today the children of many of the migrants are *cholos*, and their families and communities feel they have lost them forever. Today's migrants think about returning to their towns to educate their younger children. They also recognize that, because of their many years away, they may be called upon to serve in all of the municipal posts in which they could not serve while abroad. They are caught in a dilemma: on the one hand, they suffer when they see their children losing their ethnic identity, but they also worry knowing that they will only be able to return to their land if they bear the costs of occupying the religious and civil posts that await them.

The first organizations of indigenous migrants living in Oaxaca City and Mexico City formed in the late 1950s, as the migrants found they could only adapt to their new living conditions in a hostile space if they enjoyed the mutual support and solidarity of their own people. These migrants also had responsibility for supporting their communities of origin; at the time, all community projects—roads, schools, and municipal buildings—had to be built with community labor and citizens' donations because the government provided no support. In the mid-1970s, indigenous migrant organizations began to appear in Los Angeles as well. Today they are the economic force that enables indigenous towns to build public works and hold community celebrations. Their support is especially important because community members who remain in Mexico are seeing their ability to contribute support erode as unemployment increases, salaries are frozen, and the peso loses purchasing power.

The indigenous migrant organizations respond to their communities' most basic needs and, in receiving regions, to the migrants' need for mutual support. They have also gained the attention of the Mexican government and the political parties. Thanks to umbrella organizations, fronts, and federations of Oaxacans living in California, people now speak of migrants as citizens. With these political developments, the indigenous migrant organizations have grown beyond their original purpose and have found new ways to defend migrants in a changing society and vis-à-vis a government that only a few years ago had forgotten them.

Democracy is a cornerstone of our communities; it is the people who directly elect individuals to core community positions. The political parties do not participate because indigenous communities operate under customary law (usos y costumbres). People who are elected serve without pay; they serve for the honor of being chosen, having known lifelong that this is their duty. The community greets the birth of a boy with the words, "the municipal president has been born." When the baby is a girl, they say, "the wife of the municipal president or of the town councilor has been born." This clearly demonstrates their hope that the children will grow up to serve their communities.

Ever since migrant organizations began to gain a presence in our towns, they elected migrants to municipal posts, for at least two reasons. First, migration has severely reduced the number of available citizens, so migrants must be included in the pool of eligible position holders. Second, this change is a reflection of modern life, in which new kinds of knowledge are required to administer the financial resources the government allocates to municipalities, knowledge that migrants can provide. However, this situation generates another dilemma for the migrant: if he accepts a post, he will please his community but sacrifice his family and family economy. If he does not accept the post, he feels that he loses moral claim to return to his town and fears that the community may expropriate his property. Even if his property is untouched, the community may hold him in poor regard if he returns.

Many migrants who receive social security payments from the U.S. government have returned to their homes in Mexico to occupy municipal posts, and thus compensate their home communities somewhat for their years away. The towns often take advantage of the migrants' experience by appointing them to posts for up to three years. Migrants who continue to work abroad, and thus cannot return to occupy posts, are asked for in-kind contributions.

A migrant who has never supported his community and has never participated in his hometown association is a migrant who has lost his community rights. He even loses the right to have the church bells rung for him when he dies.

## A MIGRANT'S VISION: AN ALTERNATIVE FOR FAMILY AND COMMUNITY DEVELOPMENT

I mentioned above that migration from the Sierra Juárez has two basic causes. Through luck or destiny, I migrated for the second reason: education. My father was a businessman and leader in our Zapotec community, well known throughout the region. When I was in secondary school he told me, "Son, you have to study a profession so that tomorrow you can guide our people down the path of peace and harmony with neighboring communities. Through the lens of your profession, you will be able to see through the economic, social, and political injustices the government has imposed on us." I admired my father and have tried to carry out the task he gave me.

That is how, with a significant sacrifice on the part of my family, I went to Mexico City to study communications engineering. I was a student at the National Polytechnic Institute (IPN) in 1968, at the time of the student protests and the government's violent repression of them. My participation in the student movement marked my first political experience.

We indigenous people are incensed to see Mexico's jails filled with our innocent compatriots whose only "crime" is that they fought for their rights. There is no law, meanwhile, to punish the officials, the politicians, the bankers that steal millions of pesos from the country. Such are the injustices against our people that shape us and make us stand together to seek alternatives for community development, to clamor for justice in the indigenous countryside, and to defend migrants as they migrate and in their receiving communities.

In 1970 Mexico's Institutional Revolutionary Party (PRI) nominated Rodolfo Flores Alavez, a Mixtec, to the state congressional seat from the Sierra Juárez. His nomination provoked local outrage, and the region proposed my father as their candidate and Flores's opponent. During the campaign that followed, we heard people, full of pain, making their demands. Here, for the first time, I saw democracy crushed in the cradle of Juárez.

## SERVING MY PEOPLE

In 1984, when I was a technical coordinator in the Telecommunications Department, we installed the first satellite telephone in Zoogocho. This link allowed us to communicate with our compatriots in other places and also benefited our entire region.

I soon became involved in various organizations, always with the aim of helping my town and my region. When someone called a meeting in Oaxaca on local community problems and grassroots participation in negotiations with the government for town improvements, I always participated regardless of who organized the meeting. That is how I became the founder and a leader of the Center for Indigenous Regional Development (CEDRI). CEDRI is a local Mixtec-Zapotec organization based in Oaxaca. It was founded as an affiliate of the Mixteco-Zapoteco Binational Front (FM-ZB), with the same principles and objectives—to support community development in the places migrants work and in receiving regions—taking into account that migrants are often defenseless, lack basic labor rights, live in unhealthy conditions in crowded barracks, and are otherwise seriously exploited.[1]

---

[1] Nearly a year later we fired the Front's general coordinator, who lacked the skills to coordinate activities, failed to acknowledge our work, and did not support us.

Working with CEDRI gave me the opportunity to visit the Benito
Juárez Civic Association (ACBJ), based in Fresno, as well as a foundation in
San Francisco. In 1994, I returned to Fresno to participate in a meeting of
Mixtec and Zapotec organizations with Diódoro Carrasco Altamirano,
governor of Oaxaca. Carrasco Altamirano was the second Oaxaca governor
to visit communities of migrant Oaxacans in the United States to discuss
their situation, provide updates on public works under way in Oaxaca, and
receive petitions for projects to be implemented in their communities of
origin—though he was clearly acting more in his political persona than out
of genuine concern for the poverty affecting the indigenous communities.

Through CEDRI, we got the government to support a project to provide
fifteen pigs to Social Integration Center No. 8 (a boarding school for indigenous children). This enabled the children to learn how to care for and
breed these animals as part of their education and training.

Since 1994 I have also participated in the meetings and activities of the
Organization of Authorities and Peoples of Zoogocho (Organización de
Autoridades y Pueblos del Sector Zoogocho). In 1997 the state government
announced that, because of a lack of resources, the last 10 kilometers of the
highway to San Bartolomé Zoogocho could not be paved. We pressured
the government through the Organization of Authorities and succeeded in
getting the highway paved all the way to the town.

In 1998 a company working on this road did not want to pay one of our
communities for river materials used in the paving process. Once again the
Organization of Authorities interceded, holding government officials and
company employees hostage until the company paid. Broad participation
has made the Organization of Authorities more dynamic, and that has
enabled us to hold workshops on the situation of our migrants, our environment, reforestation, and the recovery of our lands and springs that are
being polluted with agrochemicals, plastics, and wastewater. We are also
discussing how to support our crops, since products from other states are
invading our markets.

In the same year, 1998, at a meeting of the towns of the Sierra Juárez, I
was nominated for a deputyship in the state legislature. In order to participate in the election, however, we had to ally ourselves with the Party of the
Democratic Revolution (PRD) to gain a party affiliation. This was the case
because, then as now, indigenous organizations created through customary
law are not legally recognized for state legislative posts. In the end, the PRI
government was able to impose its candidate.

By 1999, I had retired and returned to live in my home community. In 2000, I began to organize groups of people in the community to support projects for local artisans, butchers, and greenhouses. Working with other groups, we cleaned up the nonbiodegradable trash left after the weekly (Thursday) market. And we started talking about crop irrigation to decrease our dependence on unpredictable and irregular rainfall. I got involved in efforts to improve Social Integration Center No. 8, which schooled Mixes, Chinantecs, and Zapotecs. I was also deeply involved in community assemblies, consulting with municipal authorities on their dealings with the state government. At the same time, we began to discuss line items in the budget that we learned we could access; we had not claimed these monies previously because we did not know that these funding sources were available to us. My reincorporation into the community was smooth because trust already existed; since the 1980s people had asked me to support their efforts in my interactions with municipal authorities.

By 2001 I was serving as municipal president and, simultaneously, as president of the Organization of Authorities of Zoogocho, an organization that for nearly ten years has used its political influence to obtain communications, education and health services, productive projects, and nature conservation. As municipal president I ensured that the community's access roads and main potable water line were maintained. I also had the main road out of town paved so that the adjacent houses would not be filled with dust kicked up by passing vehicles. We did maintenance work on some municipal buildings, and we also began reforestation, putting in 10,000 plantlets and adopting organic fertilizers and a new method of soil preservation. We had to lobby for government resources to support all of these activities. A lot of work remained to be done since, according to customary law, the municipal president serves for only one year.[2]

I always maintained good relations with neighboring towns in order to strengthen the Organization of Authorities. At the same time, I maintained deep relationships with the organizations of migrants in Los Angeles, Mexico City, and Oaxaca City.

In 2001, when I was president of the Organization of Authorities of Zoogocho, we created a regional fund to support productive projects. We also planned an event to mark the organization's tenth anniversary, with

---

[2] Despite all of these efforts, much remained to be done when I stepped down. This is virtually inevitable given that, according to customary law, a municipal president is restricted to one year in the post.

the aim of exchanging experiences and identifying new ways to collabo-rate. Many sister organizations attended the anniversary event, including Zapotecs from the valley and Cuicatecs and others from the coast. We concluded this event by issuing the "Zoogocho Declaration."[3]

## REPRODUCING OUR CULTURE

In the annual celebration to honor our patron saint, we welcome musical groups from other towns and hold a reception at our town's entrance. We speak of peace, love, and fraternity between our peoples. Then we march into town as bells ring, fireworks go off, and bands play. During all of the days of the celebration, several kinds of dances are performed and all of the *compadres* (fictive kin) and friends from neighboring communities stay as guests in our homes. It is during these celebrations that migrants return home to be with their families. These are the periods when we spend the most time together, and they provide us with great spiritual renewal.

Migrant organizations have been very successful at transposing this cultural reproduction to new sites, especially given that some 90 percent of our musicians are migrants. Towns like Zoogocho, Xochixtepec, Yalálag, Zoochina, Yatzachi El Bajo, and Yatzachi El Alto all have bands in Los Angeles. The musicians' presence has enabled us to hold our celebrations in Los Angeles, complete with our music, tamales, mole, tortillas, mescal, and our festival dances. These celebrations, coordinated by the migrant organizations in receiving areas, empower us to reaffirm our indigenous nationalism. They allow us to analyze our situation and our community's situation, thus strengthening our organizations.

We who have been or are migrants also gain grounding in our indige-nous identity by learning to listen to our elders; we need to link our migra-tion experience with our elders' advice so that we can form a good munici-pal government. The council of elders and former presidents are today's representatives of a resource we have inherited from our ancestors — a core of citizens who have faithfully filled significant civil and religious posts, and thus should be able to transmit their knowledge and to advise the community on the road of good and harmony. We should take advantage of their experience; there is no other school that teaches us how to fill our posts and fulfill the mandates of our laws and community customs.

---

[3] *Editors' note:* See http://www.trasparencia.org.mx/Deczoog.pdf.

## A MIGRANT AND AN ELECTED AUTHORITY

One year before filling their posts, all individuals elected to positions of municipal authority must ask the council of elders on what day they should go to church; this should be in the early morning of a November day during the new moon. On this day, all members of the municipal council bring flowers, candles, incense, and oil to the church. Their families also attend. The oil is poured into glasses that contain wicks; these glasses will later substitute for the candles. The leader of the elders blesses the candles and flowers and assigns them to the various council members. He also indicates the saints to which they should bring their offerings. The municipal president is directed to the town's patron saint, and the other council members to other saints, according to a hierarchy of the council members.

This rite allows the elders to bring the elected municipal authorities before the altar of the patron saint and to ask God and the saints to keep them in good health and to keep the evil spirits away so that they can fulfill the responsibilities the people have given them. The elders also ask God to assure that there be no accidents during the days of community labor. They ask God to grant their sons, who will be municipal authorities in the future, the ability to implement justice (and keep them from temptation), serve the people with humility, and understand their people. Between supplications, they pray to God the Father and say the rosary.

At the conclusion, fireworks sound and bells are rung to signal that the rosary has ended. Participants are then invited to drink mescal and have a smoke. The first cup of mescal is given to the lead elder; he accepts it and raises it to the sky while reciting an "Our Father." When he finishes, he offers the mescal to Mother Earth while making the sign of the cross and he places two cigarettes where the mescal has fallen. The elders then begin to drink and smoke, together with the elected municipal authorities. During this celebration, they determine the dates on which they will go to church during their time in government. The elders talk of their successes and failures, of difficult and important decisions they have made in their private lives and as municipal authorities. These life stories are lessons delivered person to person. Because the elders are not literate, they have developed an oral tradition that holds the memory of the people.

According to our customs, during the afternoon of December 31 the town's men, women, children, band, and new council meet in the home of the municipal president-elect. The people gain the opportunity to spend time with the new government, and the incoming government gains confidence for the great responsibility they will soon shoulder. After drinking three or four cups of mescal and eating some food, the council of elders, the people, and the band march to the church to leave flowers and candles on the altar of the patron saint. They then enter the church to wait.

The outgoing authorities leave the municipal palace at 11:30 p.m. for the church, where the people are assembled with the incoming municipal government. The two groups of municipal authorities greet one another ceremoniously, and all march to the municipal palace, accompanied by the band and the people. When the clock strikes midnight, the change of municipal authorities begins. The outgoing government passes the *bastón de mando* (staff of command) to the new municipal government. The bells toll, the fireworks thunder, and the band plays *dianas*. Leading townsmen thank the outgoing authorities for fulfilling the mandate of the people and tell the new authorities in which direction they should lead the town, thereby helping the new authorities define their mandate.

Once the incoming municipal authorities have presented themselves before the main altar of the church and asked for permission to begin their activities, they must go from house to house every night—to the homes of the elders, former presidents, and others—to speak and to listen to the people's advice on how they should serve and make important decisions in government. Every night, different teachers pass on profound lessons about how they served as presidents and how they fulfilled the duties required for public works and service. The following discussion includes details of some of these lessons.

- Gentlemen of the 2001 Council, in the first minute in front of the town hall, the municipal auditor will tell the staff major [who is head of the *topiles*, the community watchmen who guard the town at night] and a *topil* that they should remain on duty until the guard duties and roles of the *topiles* have been assigned. At 3 a.m. on the first day of the month, the body of elders will come to the municipality to accompany you to the religious procession. At each stop on the procession [there are four], each council member will offer copal incense at the place where the monument to José Jacinto y Santiago is located.[4]

---

[4] José Jacinto was a leader from Zoogocho who, from 1710 to 1715, struggled to establish a regional market. He conducted negotiations with the viceregal government in Mexico City, traveling the eight days from Zoogocho to Mexico City carrying *totopos*, *chintesle*, and rocks of salt to eat on the way. A few days before the José Jacinto market was inaugurated, Jacinto suffered a fatal fall while attempting to mount his horse in the marketplace.

There, you will offer copal to José Jacinto and ask him for his wisdom as a leader, for his patience as you guide and implement demands that benefit our people of Zoogocho, and, above all, for the knowledge to oversee our regional market. And promise him that the people will always take care of the market he left to us.

On January 1, the old and new municipal governments will hold a ceremony to take charge of the town's goods and property. This is done with care to detail because, if errors are committed, the new authorities will be responsible for them.

The collectors who charge merchants for their market stalls will be told what to charge, depending on whether the sellers are merchants or compatriots who have come to sell their products. They will also be instructed to be polite when charging people. If the merchant has not sold anything or does not have correct change, the collector should tell them that they can pay the second or third time the collector comes around. The collectors will also be told not to raise prices for the merchants and to support them in any way they can. They will be reminded that the markets in Yalálag and Talea de Castro failed because they did not provide such support, and those markets, along with the one in Zoogocho, were the largest in the region since the 1800s.

- On January 2, the Council should be in permanent session to elect the guards—eight *topiles* organized into pairs—and assign them roles. Then the Council, along with the two staff majors and the *topiles*, will be told of their duties. The *topiles* will be assigned their cleaning areas and told that when on guard duty they should wait at the main road of the town to receive instructions at any moment. They will also be told that they should present themselves 10 minutes before shift change, and that shift change will occur at 7:00 p.m. Nobody should leave until he has been relieved, and the *topiles* should do the cleaning on Wednesday before the market and on Thursday after the market. The collectors, watchmen, and auditor should ensure that there are no animal droppings in the area during the market. If there is any animal waste, the *topiles* on shift will be responsible for cleaning it up. Both the watchmen and the staff majors will be told to be respectful to their leaders and to all of the municipal authorities. Any disobedience will be punished. The municipal policemen will also be told their functions and responsibilities. This is when the municipal auditor is told that he will lead all community works and will be responsible for administering and leading the townspeople. He will also be told that he shall assign tasks and work areas to each citizen according to their age, physical strength, and knowledge. He will be told that the people like to see a hard-working, entrepreneurial auditor, and that if the auditor is lazy, the people will not perform community work and he will lose command. Finally, the auditor will be informed that he should check on Wednesday to be sure the market area is clean and be on guard at night. Additionally, together with the police and *topiles*, he should supervise the market from 4:00 a.m. on Thursday until the market closes, to avoid incidents.

- Gentlemen of the 2001 Council, today the people have joined you to one another for a year. Inside the municipal palace you should act like a family and try to understand each other and coordinate your activities. Additionally, each Council member should understand that the team has only one objective: to serve honestly and responsibly in order to guide the people down the road of development and progress. After the daily *tequio*, you will assemble to discuss the day's events and tomorrow's tasks. That is how the municipal government makes its decisions. During the year, you should be aware that the people's commands are God's commands. If you do not follow these guidelines, you will have negative outcomes, and the government that turns over bad accounts to the people never has a voice in the assembly again. That is the lesson from municipal authorities who have failed. The people got their revenge by selling off these bad citizens' property.

- During the year that you serve as a municipal authority, you do not have the people's permission to work and plant your lands, nor to conduct any personal or family activities that infringe upon these rules. It is frowned upon, and you will be seen as irresponsible and you will not be able to give advice or speak in town assemblies. Either you serve the people full time or you had better not serve.

- It is very important to travel throughout the community territory to learn where the conflict zones are or where lands have been invaded. Your findings should be presented to the people in order to be considered in later discussions and meetings with the counterpart or neighboring town. You should check the access roads to town and the roads and paths within the town to assess their physical state and to schedule maintenance. You also have a responsibility to visit the educational facilities to observe the state of school buildings and to learn about the education problems in our community. At the same time, you should visit the health center to familiarize yourself with its operations and its difficulties.

- You should maintain good relations with the migrant organizations from Zoogocho based in Los Angeles and be respectful of them. You should not view them merely as a source of dollars.

- You should take advantage of the elders' experience and wisdom to protect our culture and plant our fields. Familiarize yourself with reforestation and the best way to cut trees. Take advantage of the moon's energy, learn how animals signal rain and earthquakes, and so on.

- Council members should be tightly united throughout the year if they are to maintain their authority over the people. They should also be united before the *topiles* and the police; otherwise these groups become uncontrollable when they realize that there is no understanding among the Council members.

- In hard times and when making important decisions, the municipal president should consult with the council of elders first, and then with the town assembly, where final decisions will be made.

- The people are good and noble when the municipal government is intelligent and knows how to guide and consult with the citizens.

- To retain your authority, you must not drink alcohol within the municipality. The president and auditor should not offer alcohol to those below them in the Council hierarchy, or their authority will suffer. When the *topiles* and police clean the roads and highways or conduct some extraordinary activity, you need to provide incentives for them, such as sodas and food. Other types of drink are acceptable as long as they are served in some other special location.

- The municipal government–elect should not make any precipitate promise to construct public works projects or undertake impetuous actions. It should only carry out the assembly's dictates delivered at the offering of flowers in January, when the town assembly becomes a congress and hears the activities and public works report on revenues and spending from the municipal and ecclesiastic government of the previous year. There, before the people, the exiting authority turns financial resources over to the incoming government. Later, the municipal government in office proposes three public works projects and the assembly approves what it considers to be the priority. If none of the three proposals is approved, the town assembly decides which public work or works will be built over the year. It is in this assembly that the outgoing government is put on trial; the people judge if its actions were good or bad. If money is missing, the people oblige the transgressors to make restitution, with specified payment schedules. If they cannot pay immediately, their property is confiscated and sold in the public plaza. The law of the people is as follows: the town's money and property are sacred; he who attacks them shall be subject to the punishment of God and the people.

In June, the municipal government goes to the church with the elders to thank God for the blessings he has given them during the first part of their mandate. They give thanks that the community work is in process and that they are at peace at home. When the religious ceremony ends, the municipal government meets with church authorities to discuss the celebration of the patron saint on August 24 and to program the series of activities. These festivities need to be organized; a band must be hired in some Zapotec or Mixe community, and the festival commission of men and women must be named. The men will set up the festival spaces, welcome the bands and attend to them during meals, and register all citizens who bring their contribution of bread, tortillas, and chocolate drink. The women will be in charge of the kitchen during the week of the festival. During the meeting they will review the list of migrants who have donated one or two cows, those who donated fireworks towers, and those who want to pay for a band. Also in the meeting they name the dance committee, which is responsible for choosing the dances to be performed, organizing the youth dancers, finding a dance teacher, and coordinating rehearsals at the dates and times the teacher sets. The women should also try to identify bands that would like to participate voluntarily or in the same manner as in the Guelaguetza.

## THE IMPACTS OF MODERNIZATION, GLOBALIZATION, AND POLITICAL MANIPULATION

It is important to recall that we indigenous peoples have been marginalized, forgotten, manipulated, and deceived by those in power for more than five hundred years. During this entire time, they have refused to recognize our most fundamental rights. Today you ask what is happening with Mexico's Indians, and I answer that the Indian is in his shack laid out like a corpse, dying of hunger, and with no medicine to cure him. The pain he feels is the government's indifference and contempt—more than five hundred years with no recognition of his rights and repression of all his demands. We cannot conceive how it is possible that in our country the privileged enjoy all the wealth while 54 million of us live in extreme poverty.

Already stooped low under the weight of our burdens, we now must confront the new burdens of modernization, neoliberalism, and globalization that the government has loaded onto the bare and bloody back of the Indian. Foreign capital is plundering our riches, invading our lands and environment, without bringing any hope of an improved living standard for the people. With globalization, our riches will be turned over to foreign capital, with no regard for our culture and development. That is how our false government will waive our right to sovereignty and abandon us along with our wounded land.

The only thing we can do is organize and raise our people's political and civic awareness. We must find the strength to remove the bandages from our eyes and defend our indigenous territory and reclaim our rights. We need to promote the sustainable development of our lands, and for that we need to reintegrate our migrants and reap the benefit of their experiences and knowledge.

Migrant, you who fled from misery and death only to arrive in a nightmare land of racism, pain unites us again in the trenches. Together we can defend our indigenous nationalism with dignity.

# 19

## Migrant Communities, Gender, and Political Power in Oaxaca

MARÍA CRISTINA VELÁSQUEZ C.

The phenomenon of women occupying public positions in Oaxacan communities—in the absence of their husbands or sons—is often attributed to the state's high out-migration rate. This is especially important because, apart from the fact that Oaxaca has one of the highest migration rates in Mexico,[1] it is also a state in which the systems of government and the political and social organizations of indigenous communities appear to "exclude" women. If migration is transforming the citizen status of indigenous women or the quality of their participation in local decision making, we

The author would like to thank UC MEXUS, Dr. Jonathan Fox, the women's working group of the Oaxacan Indigenous Binational Front (FIOB) and, in particular, their leader, Centolia Maldonado, as well as Anabel López Sánchez and Aline Castellanos for their collaboration. Many of the ideas expressed here draw from the views shared by the women of FIOB who participated in a workshop held in Juxtlahuaca, Oaxaca, on September 20, 2002, as well as from a survey carried out in the Mixteco municipalities of Santiago Yucuyachi and San Francisco Tlapancingo, and a brief comparative study of the Chatino municipality of San Juan Quiahije, Juquila. Special thanks go to Memo Zavaleta Rojas. Translation by Adam Critchley.

[1] In 1995 Oaxaca occupied sixth place nationwide as a sending region for indigenous labor; it placed first in the number of migrants from one ethnic group. The group with the highest number of migrants is the Zapotecs, followed by the Mixtecs from Oaxaca, Guerrero, and Puebla. Third are the Otomís, from Hidalgo, México, Querétaro, Puebla, and Veracruz (Rubio, Millán, and Gutiérrez 2000).

could be witnessing an important change in the cultural and political traditions of Oaxaca's indigenous communities and municipalities. Nevertheless, we must carefully examine the evidence for these propositions.

## MIGRATION AND COMMUNITY ORGANIZATION

The process of migration encompasses myriad social, cultural, economic, and political changes experienced by hundreds of thousands of people, groups, and villages. But in Mexico it also speaks of indigenous men and women's struggle to survive and to continue the social reproduction of an identity that is caught between the traditional and the modern, between custom and innovation.

In Oaxaca, the traditional profile of community obligations within social systems—based on networks of relations prescribed by customs and internalized values, of socialization processes and ingrained functions that tend to reproduce themselves in a stable manner—has been transformed in recent years. Migration has been a factor in this change.

The way in which migration has shifted the structures of indigenous social and political organization has several facets, each of which has a specific impact. First, besides being an obvious alternative to the economic situation of extreme poverty, migration represented and continues to represent a way of temporarily avoiding or postponing obligations, responsibilities, and community services, as well as the assumption of positions designated by the assembly, which are generally pro bono and imply expenses and an often unsustainable economic sacrifice.[2]

This facet of *migration as a form of avoiding community obligations* is perhaps in part responsible for the emergence of alternative mechanisms that allow migrants to comply with their obligations: making payments in lieu of services, fulfilling community obligations through economic contributions for the collective benefit, or, if the option exists, bringing one's contributions "up to date" upon return to the community. This facet of migration points to a change in the local laws governing social and political organization, as it obliges the traditional system of norms to adapt to the migratory

---

[2] I am currently compiling statistics on electoral conflicts in 1995 in municipalities that were declared part of the *usos y costumbres* (customary law) system. In many such municipalities, there were recurring issues with extraordinary assemblies due to local elected leaders' decision to migrate for economic reasons or because they were unable to pay the costs associated with serving in a post.

phenomenon so that migrants can retain their rights despite not being physically present in the community.

With this change in the rules, not only is a migrant anchored to the native community due to familial economic obligations and the values and symbols that provide an identity as a member of a cultural, linguistic, and territorial community. The new customary mechanisms also conscientiously bind the migrant to a political community through a legal responsibility. Compliance with this legal system will now be required for a migrant — and the migrant's family — to continue enjoying a status that allows them to take part in collective decisions. Failure to comply with this responsibility could be costly, including the loss of rights as a citizen and landowner, or even social exclusion.

Under these conditions — and given the systematic increase in migration from some regions of Oaxaca, such as the Mixteca, the Central Valleys, and the northern Sierra — the traditional structure of community positions and services begins to depend substantially on how the citizens distribute or redistribute their obligations and rights according to the migratory cycles or seasons. From another perspective (perhaps the opposing perspective), another facet takes shape in which migration ceases to be a mechanism of legal evasion — or a risk of destabilizing the system — to become a means of *restructuring the social and political organization of the community.*

Depending on the type of migration — circular, haphazard, or multiple-season — the migrant has several ways in which to satisfy his community service responsibilities within this legal framework. In the case of *tequio* or *faena*,[3] for example, a migrant can hire a substitute community member to do the work, make a cash contribution directly to local government, or make a donation to maintain public spaces such as the church or town benches.

Another form of repaying community service that has acquired special importance is through collective contributions, that is, through the committees or hometown associations that have emerged in recent years. Payments from these groups are usually channeled to public works or traditional festivities. This mechanism has proved effective because it not only organizes and facilitates the collection of remittances to satisfy the migrants'

---

[3] *Tequio* is defined as obligatory community service for the collective benefit. It can include diverse activities such as road maintenance, cemetery cleanup, weeding community land, and working without pay as a complement to labor for government-financed social infrastructure projects. This practice is legally acknowledged in Oaxaca's state constitution.

obligations, but it also becomes a system of community protection, of solidarity among residents, and of exchange and reinforcement of cultural identity.

Although these norms exist for community services, this is not the case for public leadership positions, which are independent of the roster or hierarchical structure. The migrant must at minimum occupy the position of *topil*, or local policeman. These obligations are imposed by custom and are sanctioned by the collective, which generally meets in a community assembly. Unlike the *tequio*, in some villages migrants cannot pay for substitutes to take their place in these positions, and in any case the economic cost would be onerous.

Even though this facet of migration as a mechanism for the continuation of tradition continues to carry weight in community life, new factors have emerged that are changing not only the rules of organization but also the norms of access to political power. Migration is ceasing to be a process that reproduces the system and is becoming *an agent of sociopolitical change*. This proposition is based on various factors that cause changes in the perspective, interest, and actions of the migrant regarding the political reality of the home community.

For example, serving in community-designated leadership positions has ceased to represent the sacrifice of unpaid labor. The Mexican government now channels resources (wages or per diems) to individuals who serve as municipal authorities, making such positions much more attractive. In fact, if migration previously represented an escape from such "obligations," today's migrants who return home to serve in such positions — and receive some payment for doing so — are less resentful over the loss of their wages in dollars. In other cases, migrants have earned money through their work outside their community that allows them to pay for a substitute.

No less important is the fact that both migrants and residents are increasingly organized. There are several explanations for migrant committees', networks', or organizations' growing interest in local and even regional politics. One important motive is the desire to oversee remittances donated to cover community obligations. Another is the migrants' interest in launching productive, development, or cultural projects. Naturally, migrant organizations have a legitimate interest in contributing toward improved living standards in their home communities. The development projects they support can help counterbalance the inequalities that migration generates.

The recognition of customary law (the system called *usos y costumbres*) as a legal means for holding municipal elections in Oaxacan indigenous communities has also been a watershed for organized migrants.[4] This electoral legislation, based on a concept of legal pluralism, has allowed the values and norms that sustain the social and political organization of the communities to be accepted and respected. This includes those communities' own concept of citizenship and, in the case of migrants, signifies their inclusion as active citizens in the election process and the selection of local authorities. At the same time, this legislation has opened up the spectrum of political participation to citizens' groups that do not belong to any particular political party in the mainly indigenous municipalities in which this system is applied. In the case of migrants, this legislation not only facilitates recognition of the migrant's citizen status, but it also favors the organized participation of migrants as a group interested in exercising local government functions.[5]

It must be noted, however, that the migrants' political and electoral participation has had the strongest impact in situations of community conflict or in local elections when assemblies are undergoing democratization. In a context of strong electoral competition within the *usos y costumbres* system—as the 2001 municipal electoral process demonstrated—alliances of hometown associations with the different political factions in conflict have the potential to change electoral outcomes.

Last but not least, the diminished male population in some villages with high out-migration and, in particular, the exhaustion of the legal mechanisms to oblige migrants to return and comply with their community obligations have opened the door for women to substitute for men in

---

[4] This electoral system was legally recognized by the state of Oaxaca in 1995. Currently, 418 out of the state's 570 municipalities, mostly indigenous municipalities, are governed by customary law. Theoretically, this electoral system is based on collective values of political representation and favors consensus for electing or designating someone to a position. This is unlike the system of political parties in which election is determined by competition among two or more political parties. However, the conflictive social nature of some municipalities means that even within the framework of customary law, groups or political currents are formed and disputes arise over municipal power. In the same way, under customary law, the voting procedure varies and tends to be public and not secret.

[5] The FIOB was the first migrant organization to submit a request to participate as a group in a municipal election under customary law—for the municipal electoral process in Calihualá in 1998.

these posts or services. However, this pattern is variable, and it must be remembered that it does not always represent changes in the position of women regarding possibilities for decision making or access to political power. We must also consider the inherited customary laws and the status that women have within them.

## WOMEN AND CUSTOMARY LAW IN OAXACA

Although traditional normative indigenous systems based on customary law are often perceived to be associated with high levels of gender subordination and discrimination, there are important nuances in the context of two simultaneous trends. On the one hand, there are many communities and municipalities in which women do not have spaces of public participation, have no vote, and cannot develop processes of self-government. On the other hand, however, in some communities and in increasing numbers of municipalities, women not only occupy positions within the framework of services and community cooperation, but they are organized and hold political positions in their local governments.

Preliminary data on the female population living under customary law systems in Oaxaca reveal the following trends within the 418 municipalities considered to be within this electoral regime. In 10 percent of them, women do not exercise their right to vote in internal elections, and their public participation is low or null; in 9 percent they do not vote, but they do hold community positions; in 21 percent they vote, but the trend of public participation is low or null; and, finally, in 60 percent they vote, hold positions, and participate in the public life of the community.[6]

Regarding government positions, the statistics show that for the 1998–2001 three-year municipal period, thirty-two town counselors were named (including five female municipal presidents) in twenty-seven municipalities; for 2002–2004, fifty-four town counselors were elected, belonging to forty-one municipalities (including six female municipal presidents). That is, on average, in 8.5 percent of the customary law municipalities, there are women who hold positions in local government.[7] As regards services and

---

[6] This information is based on a research project coordinated by the author to produce a statewide catalogue of systems of customary law (Velásquez 1997). The data need to be updated.

[7] While these statistics are considered an indicator of the variable participation of women inside indigenous normative systems in Oaxaca's state context, a census

lesser posts, although women participate in public life in most municipalities ruled by *usos and costumbres*, they are not subject to the same level of obligations as men regarding their compliance with services and positions.

There are conflicting opinions regarding decision making. Some observers claim that indigenous women are "totally excluded" and that they live under authoritative and coercive systems. Others assert that women communicate their opinions to their husbands or sons and exercise their citizens' rights through them. This last pattern is not considered to be a synonym for exclusion from public life or a restriction that condemns women to the domestic world. Still other observers report that indigenous women influence their husbands so that couples make their decisions together, with the woman accompanying her husband and serving as the "guardian of his public image." This last perspective is similar to ideological positions that claim that an indigenous woman need not participate personally or actively in public life—since she does so through her husband or son—and that attempt to justify her failure to exercise her vote by arguing that it is a "family vote," one that reflects a kind of gender equality based on "non-Western" cultural patterns.

There is a relationship between the structure of public power and family, the notion of "exclusion" is inaccurate, the role of women in social processes is greater and more complex than is usually acknowledged, politics impregnates both the public and private worlds, and women participate via reproduction and social transformations. It must be emphasized that indigenous women live in a context that is broader than the domestic sphere. This context has an impact on the generally accepted gender roles, and it questions the supposed harmony between the sexes and the patterns of decision making after marriage.

There are several channels for indigenous women's public participation and their participation in community life. First, while the community hierarchical system is largely honorific, *women are also assigned roles according to the positions held by their husbands*. For example, the president of the local Family Development Agency (DIF) is the wife of the municipal president.

Second, the government's public policies stimulate the participation of women, principally in local health and education committees. Despite the

---

conducted by Mexico's National Institute of Statistics, Geography, and Informatics (INEGI) in 2000 reports that 31.4 percent of people working in government activities are women, but only 2.1 percent are government officials or occupy posts in the head of government.

fact that the government encourages *female participation in community development* and considers it an advance in the promotion of "gender equality," in practical terms such participation raises questions for the women themselves. One relates to the mechanism by which women are elected; designation by the authorities, by community groups, or by the assembly itself highlights the sometimes involuntary character of participation. Women also note that these positions could represent an increase in their daily workload. Some organizations fear that these community female jobs will contribute to the continuation of gender stereotypes. No less important is the criticism that this participation is "passive" in the sense that, although women will hold the positions, those making the health and education decisions are the state or federal government officials or the male teachers or doctors.[8]

Third, we can observe *women's participation in religious and festive spaces*, where they may be in charge of religious activities.

Fourth, *processes of productive organization* have played an important part in the public roles that women assume. However, there is a difference between organizational processes that emerge from governmental promotion and those that are autonomous and do not just follow proposals and policies developed by institutions. The autonomous case involves a political stance and a gender and identity awareness in the organizational work. Female participation has arisen in particular out of the efforts of social organizations, technical teams, and even the Church. This space—even when it focuses on improving the material conditions of women rather than transforming the gender roles that subordinate them—constitutes a key space for the promotion of women's equality and women's leadership at the local or regional level.

Fifth, we can observe the space for *the organization of public power*, in which women's participation, though low, is not nonexistent. Indigenous women's very limited participation in elected positions is related not only to the difficulties men have in "sharing power" but also to the fact that these women do not have the educational background or skills to carry out the functions the state expects of them. In the same way, women's domestic work, in their productive and reproductive roles, hinders their ability to accumulate experience that would be useful in these roles.

---

[8] Author interview with Romualdo Juan Gutiérrez, state coordinator of the Oaxacan Indigenous Binational Front.

The exceptions are women who have attended school, have a natural flair for leadership, and have no children or are beyond their childbearing years. Those who hold elected posts do so as town councilwomen or as members of party committees. It is difficult for indigenous women to be chosen as municipal presidents because, according to local gender values, "it is not customary for a woman to want to rule a village." An ongoing investigation by Margarita Dalton suggests that women who serve as municipal presidents are often named as a result of a political conflict (personal communication, 2002).

## CAN WE SPEAK OF WOMEN'S POLITICAL EMPOWERMENT?

If we add the impacts of male out-migration to a contextual understanding of women's participation in public spaces, the remaining question is not just whether women are occupying more posts than before; the issue is not simply replacing a man in a position of public power. Instead, the questions must be, what are the characteristics of this situation? Is this participation voluntary? And, in particular, are men accepting the fact that women are making decisions? In the same way, questions must be asked about the women who have migrated and returned to their communities.

Despite the fact that migration is independent from the electoral regime, the participation of women is conditioned by the electoral system that prevails in their community. The transitional process toward women's participation in the public and political life of migrant-sending communities is taking place at a much more accelerated rate in municipalities and communities that have a plebiscite system for access to power (of the *usos y costumbres* variety) than in those that have a party-based electoral system.

This is due to more than demographic or ethnic factors.[9] The public participation of women in migrant communities governed by customary law is *necessary* to meet the needs of a hierarchical social order. In this sense, women can be obliged to carry out the functions of a given post even though a man may be the official holder of the position. Women can also be required to pay for certain services or the community labor that an absent man would normally provide. For example, women have to pay the

---

[9] In general, the system of customary law is applied in communities with low demographic indices and that have a majority indigenous population, where the impact of migration is significant in percentage terms and where its effects are felt more than in municipalities with larger populations.

local government so that the municipal president or another authority "can identify and pay" someone to fulfill the *tequio* responsibilities; otherwise, women would have to participate in the community labor directly.

The disadvantage is that this situation fails to stimulate women's civic participation. It creates a sense of manipulation, as well as a burdensome workload as women add to their household duties by taking on community obligations or filling local positions in the name of a male relative. Some women take on these positions or "commitments" as a gesture of solidarity with their husband or sons who migrate. In this way, *the indigenous woman concedes her citizen status to a man*. In other words, in this system men must comply with their public obligations and functions, but they can do so via a woman—meaning that *the male assures his citizen status thanks to the woman*. The perception that the women have of this situation oscillates between positive—because it represents well-being for the village and the children—and negative—"a lot of work and responsibilities."

Furthermore, local society—including the women—and local authorities find it more logical within the defined gender roles to fill a post with a man who is absent than with a woman who is present. The vision of a woman occupying a government post generates contradictory feelings that, on the one hand, elevate the woman's status but, on the other, ridicule the capacity of the men. In the worst of scenarios, "if a male mayor is not obeyed, a woman mayor will be less so—only if she has a lot of authority." In addition to the weight of the cultural change involved, on a practical level, women note, "the post is a lot of work; even the men can't do it. Where will one find the time?"

The lack of recognition given to women—and their own lack of self-recognition—is such that in some cases women serve as mute witnesses who legitimize the decisions of the men who remain in the village, even though the women may bethe majority in community assemblies. In fact, assemblies are sometimes interrupted suddenly so that the women can telephone their absent male relatives to consult on how they should vote.

In municipalities or communities where access to power is through party structures, women's participation is less visible, mainly because they will only participate if they identify with the governing group or party. On the other hand, the fact that they choose to participate in politics voluntarily, rather than in response to a social or normative demand that obliges them to concede their status in the name of a man, facilitates a more active participation than that found in more traditional municipalities and communities.

Clearly the homogenized vision of municipal and political reality in Oaxaca must be changed. There is a wide range of behaviors and norms that define women's legal status, their rights and obligations, the quality and scope of their public participation, and the ways in which they exercise governmental positions under customary law. Further, the exercise of political and electoral rights cannot be evaluated solely based on the parameters in place for a society where power is defined by political parties or for a society where those rights find their basis in the concept of individual liberties — the right to vote, to be elected, to participate in government, to enjoy free political association, to petition.

A system of collective obligations is what defines people's right to take part in collective affairs, so for all intents and purposes this system of obligations has more weight than the law. In this sense, women's political participation is conditioned not only by differences in electoral systems but also by differences within the customary law electoral system, in which socioeconomic conditions or processes like migration can have much less weight than the values, attitudes, and concepts that define representation. The fundamental problem here is that women are having to assume a third role as they fulfill their husbands' community obligations, but nobody is substituting for the women's productive or reproductive obligations.

In the specific case of women who have migrated, there are other differences at play as well, and these merit closer examination. It is clear that their experiences outside the community, their ability to move about in the Spanish- or English-speaking world, and the transformations at work in terms of their self-presentation all give women migrants a new image within the community, one that jeopardizes their acceptance back into the community. Women who have migrated are sometimes severely criticized. If they display interest in participating publicly, the value of their opinions is downplayed because "they are not aware of the community's problems" or because "they no longer share socially accepted customs."

Despite a discouraging outlook for the recognition of women's status as citizens, it may well be that social and productive organizations provide a more effective space for women's political participation and action than does the legal and political framework of the community. This hypothesis is based on the fact that voluntary, visible, and recognized participation within organizations has an effect not only on the quality of participation but also on self-esteem.

If organizations can promote collective reflection and become spaces for individual learning, they can offer women greater freedom to express their needs or to advance personal or community interests. These organizations have the additional advantage of not endangering the citizenship of migrant families. In fact, some women have indicated that they are more interested in participating in locally based organizations than in assuming a public post. This is due largely to the fact that an organization is viewed as a safe space.

Such participation also yields more direct benefits than those offered by city hall or the local government. Many women believe that federal resources should go directly to women, not only for development or basic infrastructure projects but also to address family problems stemming from a husband's absence, such as drug abuse among a community's youth.

Women run a risk, however, when participating in social organizations in party-driven political contexts. If the organization is perceived to be associated with a particular political party, the women can be denied a voice if the municipal government is of the opposing party and acts arbitrarily to exclude the organization's membership.

Despite many organizations' obvious achievements in the promotion of gender equality, designing strategies to reconcile the duality of public and political participation distributed between the local normative framework and social and productive organizations remains a challenge. This challenge goes hand in hand with the transition mentioned at the beginning of this essay: the growing participation of migrants and their organizations in the political life of their home communities.

Much remains to be done to create a new model for women's participation in organizations. As women join these organizations in order to gain access to productive resources, the newly created spaces must be designed to serve several needs simultaneously: they must enable women to gain awareness about gender and sexual roles, they must enable women's participation in decision making, and they must teach how to control and deploy that participation to promote balance between men and women in the context of their governmental and electoral systems.

## References

Rubio, Miguel Ángel, Saúl Millán, and Javier Gutiérrez, eds. 2000. *La migración indígena en México*. Mexico City: Instituto Nacional Indigenista/Programa de las Naciones Unidas para el Desarrollo.

Velásquez, María Cristina. 1997. *Catálogo municipal de usos y costumbres*. Oaxaca: Instituto Estatal de Oaxaca/Centro de Investigaciones y Estudios Superiores en Antropología Social.

# 20

## "Now We Are Awake": Women's Political Participation in the Oaxacan Indigenous Binational Front

### CENTOLIA MALDONADO AND PATRICIA ARTÍA RODRÍGUEZ

> *The organization has helped us to reflect upon and understand our problems.... Now we are awake.* — Olga Quiroz, of San Miguel Tlacotepec
>
> *It has cost us a great deal as women to have a voice and a vote at the assembly meetings since they were previously limited exclusively to men. Women who attended were present solely to listen and bring back the information to their husbands.* — Centolia Maldonado, of Agua Fría

This chapter documents transformations that have taken place in one area of the Mixteca region of Oaxaca. Over the last decade, the absence of men due to migration has allowed for the emergence of new practices of political participation among the women who remain in the communities. This essay reflects upon the authors' organizational experiences working with and supporting the indigenous women of the Oaxacan Indigenous Binational Front (FIOB). Our aim is to identify conditions that facilitate or limit the achievement of our goals. This involves analysis that will permit us to critically assess, question, and learn from our current practices, to be able to develop new gender equity proposals in support of indigenous women.

---

Translation by Emma E. Lukin and Stuyvesant Bearns.

We have taken on the challenge of writing with "two voices," attempting to build a bridge of dialogue between us—Centolia, a Mixtec activist of the FIOB, and Patricia, an anthropologist interested in the spaces for political organizing among indigenous women. For me, Patricia, this writing experience has created an opportunity to cross borders between the academic and nonacademic worlds. The teachings of indigenous women have nourished the perspective from which I think and speak, compelling me to constantly question the frameworks that guide my writing.

For me, Centolia, being able to focus on the women's organizing process has allowed me to reflect on the advances made, step by step, during my many years of active participation in different settings, both as a member of the community and as a leader within the organization. In describing one's personal experience it is necessary to create a space for reflecting on what has been achieved and on future challenges, and also to acknowledge the bad experiences, which teach valuable lessons as well, especially for those of us who work closely with our communities.

In the first of the following sections, through the voices of some women members of the FIOB, we examine the repercussions they experience as a result of their participation, the conquering of their fears, their travels beyond their communities, and their service in positions of community leadership. We cannot avoid addressing the costs involved in these processes. By pointing out the household and community obstacles facing women who choose to participate in the FIOB, we demonstrate the continuity of their collective action. This involves uncovering a history of struggle as well as tracking their multiple resistance strategies, not only in terms of their participation in the FIOB but also by taking into account the pressures that each individual faced. This choice involves recognizing the value of personal experiences as knowledge that is shared through struggles and contradictions, in which the women do not merely reproduce discourses that come from outside but rather construct meanings from their own contexts.

It seemed timely to rescue these changes and put them into words. These changes generally do not fit into classic ethnographic studies nor into social movement analyses because they tend to occur in the private sphere, which is typically not considered to be a space for political action. Each personal biography and family micro-history was constantly changing, as women gathered at workshops, traveled outside of their communities, participated in marches, gained skills, and negotiated their husbands' and fathers' permission to participate.

Listening to the voices of Olga and Centolia in the following pages is an effective means by which to illustrate their efforts to reclaim themselves as historical subjects and to contest the "invisibility omission" of indigenous women in studies of social movements and political participation. This "anthropological texture" permits a deeper and more direct understanding of the parallels found within social relations of life experiences of the past and the present, thus re-valorizing the meaning of subjectivity and of the collective and individual experience (Massolo 1992).

In the following section, using the narrative of Centolia Maldonado—a native of Agua Fría and the FIOB's coordinator of culture and sports, as well as a women's leader in the Mixteca—we relate the history of the weakening of local boss rule (*cacicazgo*).[1] Her story will help us understand the collective context, giving us a sense of the past in order to better understand the present.

The diversity among groups of women within the FIOB is a result of their different individual needs and motivations. Women in some communities have organized because they have been excluded from community assembly meetings and government social programs. The only women allowed to participate in these programs are those whose husbands or sons are recognized as active citizens. Within indigenous communities, "citizens" are males between eighteen and fifty years of age who participate in *tequio* (collective community work), *mayordomías* (religious/cultural festivals), and *cargos* (rotating community leadership duties). For a family to retain its social status within the community, the male members must carry out these duties and pay their *cuotas* (community membership dues). Failure to fulfill these obligations results in sanctions against the families, so when the men are absent, the women must pay someone else to carry out these duties in their absence. In communities where women's *tequio* work is not yet recognized, women are denied access to government social programs, a situation that has spurred them to seek assistance from the FIOB.

Another reason women participate in the FIOB is to learn about resources available from the municipal government and to inform their local village leadership about these funds. This logic tends to appear in communities that finance their public works solely with community funds. Since the municipal authority (*presidente municipal*) in the head town often pays little heed to village representatives (*agentes municipales*), the latter are

---

[1] *Editor's note*: As coordinador of culture and sports, Maldonado serves on the FIOB's Binational Commission, a body that is elected by delegates from Oaxaca, California, and Baja California at binational assemblies held every three years.

blocked from gaining access to the government programs—except during election campaigns. By using the FIOB's regionwide networks to communicate with women in other communities, however, the women come to understand that the FIOB brings direct benefits not only to their families but to the local village government as well.

## THE BEGINNINGS OF PARTICIPATION

Women's involvement in the FIOB began with their participation in protest marches and demonstrations (*plantones*) that called on the Oaxacan state government to open communication with the FIOB and to serve the needs of the communities. This initial participation led to the idea of having a space dedicated to the development of community productive projects geared specifically to women. As Olga Quiroz, a pioneer in the organizing work of the women of San Miguel Tlacotepec, relates:

> Our participation began in 1994, when we took part in some demonstrations; it was there that we were told that we had the same rights as men. The mayor and everyone else in the town used to tell us that we didn't have the same rights as men and couldn't go to the meetings because we didn't have [the right to] a voice or a vote because being a woman wasn't as valuable as being a man. And then during the demonstrations we began to help ... with a little coffee, the food, whatever we could do to help the folks who were in the action. Afterwards, they invited the women to the community assembly, and we said, "let's go to the assembly." Some said, "how, if the leaders don't want us to?" But for the first time we went to the assembly; all the women showed up.[2]

Quiroz's account also demonstrates that the beginning of women's participation within the movement did not come about without conflicts or tensions—with husbands, fathers, village leaders, and even within themselves.

> There are many "macho" men here who said, "there are lots of men there, you are not going." They are needed but some-

---

[2] This and following quotatations are drawn from an interview with Olga Quiroz, San Miguel Tlacotepec, Oaxaca, September 2002.

times their husbands don't allow them to attend the meetings.

To slowly leave the private sphere and overcome their fear of speaking out, to share longings and frustrations, to say "I think" and "I want" changed gender relationships. This process also allowed us to feel the "need to be somebody, to feel like somebody, that men and women are equal, that no one is more or less," a feeling of strength, power, and solidarity with women. "I did it! I did it! I was able to make a change, we, as women, do serve a purpose; we were able to get the thought that we were 'good for nothing' out of our head." The information conveyed in the training workshops transforms and changes the perception of some spaces, such as the domestic space.

Once I learned what the work was all about and all those other types of things, thoughts started to enter my head. After participating in so many workshops and all, I decided that it is important to learn things other than housework, that it is important that we have the opportunity to keep learning. When someone guides us, we learn.

The "seeing one's self" or "awakening" that Olga speaks of also forces women to question those traditional elements that serve to exclude and marginalize them. "There are so many customs that we are trying to reflect on, such as those differences that hurt men and women." Gradually, however, each personal story was changing as women participated in workshops, marches, or demonstrations, leaving their communities and heading to the city, negotiating permission with their husbands or fathers, going to training sessions and sharing their newly acquired knowledge with other *compañeras*. To leave their homes, overcome their fear of speaking, and find other women who shared their same problems and dreams led them, as Olga states, to:

learn many things. Women used to be treated very badly here. We don't let that happen anymore since we joined the organization. Now we don't let them hit us. Before, we used to be ignorant; we believed that all paths were closed to us. Since we joined the organization many mothers do not allow the abuse to continue. Now we women are awake.

What was learned in the training sessions, demonstrations, and marches enabled the women to reflect, and it changed their perception of some traditional practices, such as domestic violence, male alcoholism, and child abuse, which used to remain hidden behind closed doors. As Olga said, they were "never talked about." In this context, the public-private dichotomy becomes very clear; after participation, issues that were considered to belong to the private sphere began to be questioned, transforming the personal into the political. Just as this has redefined the division between the "public" and "private" spheres, it has also broadened the sense of what "politics" embraces and brought to the surface topics that—forgotten, ignored, or silenced—had previously been confined to the private realm of the intimate.

Throughout our work we have seen a tension between the demands of family life as mothers and wives and being women who care about problems of their communities. Again Olga sheds some light:

> We had to cook and clean the house, because if we didn't get the housework done our husbands wouldn't allow us to leave. Now that our husbands give us permission, we have to be responsible for both [our public and home responsibilities]. We can't abandon one or the other.

Participation does not relieve women of their household responsibilities or other chores that are considered "women's work" ("*propias de su sexo*"). Moreover, the men's migration results in extra burdens of domestic work that must be picked up by the women.

> Whether it is as mother or daughter, we women within a family have a commitment to help out with the household chores.... We have to negotiate our schedule with the rest of the family in order to fulfill our duties both at home and in the community.[3]

The women of the FIOB have made significant gains in finding ways to improve their well-being and to advance their social, economic, and political rights. After a long journey, the women have begun to create and enter spaces where they can exchange experiences, speak their minds, and gradually build leadership. Likewise, they have initiated many kinds of

---

[3] Centolia Maldonado, manuscript, October 2002.

community-based income-generating projects such as savings clubs (*cajas de ahorro*).

The family economy suffers when the male head of household migrates and the woman must assume his role in terms of the support, education, and care of the children, as well as his commitments to the community. In their search for alternatives, the women of the FIOB used their own contributions to create the savings clubs in 1999. The idea came out of the workshop "The Woman Who Builds, Advances," in which women whose husbands had gone as migrants reflected about migration. These women were forced to turn to lenders and pay exorbitant interest rates on the money they borrowed: As Olga Quiroz observed:

> There is no work here for women, but as long as our sons are there we can count on their help. If I don't have the money to pay for my daughter's school, I have to do something. If I just sit here with my arms crossed, my family does not move ahead.[4]

The beneficiaries of the savings clubs are low-income women who are heads of household and do fieldwork and street vending. Some of them buy and sell vegetables; others set up small family businesses (selling *tamales* or *pozole*, starting a little store, farming, or selling produce and artisan crafts). Currently there are twelve savings clubs in operation, with approximately 155 women.

We view this experience as very positive. In economic terms, the funds have grown as interest charges have been added to the start-up capital, enabling the women to meet their educational and community commitments. The clubs also produce cultural capital; as they take on responsibilities in the clubs, the women acquire an increased knowledge of official documents and gain the skills to manage and administer their accounts. The savings clubs have made it possible for communities to count on the women as a means of economic support in times of need. The presence of indigenous women in these processes demonstrates how the problems of their communities have brought them together and, in some cases, incorporated them into new spaces of participation, beyond those that relate to family or community.

---

[4] Interview with Olga Quiroz, September 2002.

## "LISTEN UP, DON'T ASK QUESTIONS: THIS IS MEN'S BUSINESS!"
## The Story of a Cacicazgo as Told by Centolia Maldonado

As noted above, within indigenous communities citizens are defined as males between the ages of eighteen and fifty. For their families to have social status within the community, these men must fulfill *cargo* service, carry out *tequio* work, and pay community membership dues.

One indigenous woman who had been attending assembly meetings for months did not understand how the *cuotas* were used, and she asked for information in the assembly so that she could explain the reasons for the payments to her husband. The response she received was, "Listen up and don't ask questions, because you don't know anything; this is men's business!" The woman continued to pay the fees and never again asked a question. As Elena Maldonado Morales recalls, "Since that time, I regret to say, I feel that it is not worthwhile to participate. I would rather stay home and take care of my family."

This became the routine; decisions were controlled by the eight Maldonado brothers, four who continued to migrate and four who stopped migrating and remained in the village. The brothers called assembly meetings only to tell people how much they owed in dues and to assign shares in communal tasks. The situation worsened over time; the brothers began refusing to recognize the community labor of the elderly as payment on behalf of their migrant children and grandchildren. The brothers also demanded a full day's wage to cover the costs of a replacement worker who took over a migrant's community labor responsibility, even if the replacement worker only needed to work two or three hours to complete the task. Worse, the brothers used these payments to buy alcohol for the heavy drinking sessions that followed each communal labor task. The women of the community grumbled among themselves, but they did not call for accountability.

The four Maldonado brothers who remained in the village year-round covered the *cargos* corresponding to themselves and also those of their brothers and nephews living in the United States. During this period they made no attempt to obtain resources for the community from the government, but only from candidates of the ruling Institutional Revolutionary Party (PRI) during campaigns. Even then they would only get a sound system or a typewriter; although these donations were never worth more than ten thousand pesos, the brothers presented them as a great bounty and a sign of the PRI's generosity and favor.

When the migrants returned home at the end of the season and their wives informed them of what had occurred during their absence, they voiced their disagreement in heated community assembly meetings. But since the migrants reside in the community only six months of the year and because the Maldonado brothers controlled all the information with which to legitimate their actions, the brothers always carried the day in these debates. There was nothing anyone could do to change the situation.

I learned about these issues during weekend visits. In 1994, I decided to return to the house next to my parent's home in the community. Very soon after my arrival I accompanied my father to an assembly meeting—just to listen—and I was surprised to see more than thirty women standing in for migrant citizens. What was worrisome was that the women were present only to receive orders.

This was during the time when the town's yearly celebration was being planned; the eleven men that were presiding had already decided how many tortillas each woman had to donate and how much they had to pay for the ingredients for the food. Everything seemed fine; no one protested. But after the meeting the women began whispering among themselves: "it's too much chile and too much meat; everything will go to waste! Who decided to buy so much? I think it was Juaño; no, it was Fausto." I only listened. But then they noticed I was watching them and they said to me, "These men are in the habit of asking for money just for the sake of asking." I answered, "it is only because you allow it; this will only stop when you decide it has to stop." They responded, "Oh, child, it's obvious you don't know them," to which I replied, "Yes, I do know them because my father and mother have told me about them, but we'll see what happens."

At the next assembly meeting, the community health program was discussed. The local health organizer sheepishly asked for the community's help in providing a place to store medicines and in establishing their own health committee. The government was pressuring communities to provide space to house the program—or risk the loss of the health program altogether. The Maldonados self-assuredly said, "let them take it. So what? We don't use it anyway because it's useless." I could not contain myself and I shot out a question to the women: "Do you want to lose your community health program?" They responded,

> No! We *do* use it—for vaccinations and when we have the flu,
> or when one of our children gets hurt, we go running to Tía
> Chave [the local health promoter]. There are days when we

don't have enough money for bus fare to get to the clinic in town, much less to buy the medicine we need. They [the Maldonados] can pay because they're well off.

Tía Chave added, "There are women who do not even come to the meetings, yet they are the ones who come to me most often for medicine." I said, "Tía, can you continue to lend your house for the program if the women agree to give you their support?" Her reply was, "I've been doing it for two years, but the supervisor wants the program to work through the township." Even with that explanation the men informed us that there was no locale that could be used for the program. To this I replied, "Well, what if we secure some funds and build our own building?" They responded, "Are you crazy? We don't even have the land!" That is when my mother said, "I will donate the land, but who will work on it?" In the end, there wasn't enough will to move forward.

After the meeting, Tía Chave asked me, "Where you work, they provide a great deal of support to the women of Chayuco. How do they do it?" I described the process, and she suggested organizing a meeting in her home to discuss this further. I asked her to invite women who do not usually attend assembly meetings, and in two days we had a group of fifteen women, led by a local committee of five, ready to participate. The following week the health supervisor and Tía Chave came to ask for my assistance in naming members to the health committee. Since the local government was not willing to call another meeting to deal with the health program, it became our responsibility to fill these positions. The health supervisor explained to us what the responsibilities would be, but no one was willing to accept the position for fear of reprisals from the Maldonados. In this situation, I agreed to become the head of the committee; the rest of the women agreed at most to fulfill their duties and to participate in the assembly meetings when needed.

As soon as the Maldonados found out, they accused me of dividing the community and of introducing a new political party in the village. Fausto Maldonado used his influence to convince the new local authorities (migrants who had just returned to serve their three-year civic duties) not to sign any document relating to me. At this point I asked the women of the community to refrain from making any comments that could provoke more problems, and I found out everything I could about my rights from the leaders of the FIOB and I asked my mother for advice.

I clearly remember the words of advice I received: "May prudence be on your side, not theirs. Keep the authorities informed of what you are doing; if they don't support you, that is their problem." And that is what I did. I asked the committee to keep the local authorities informed; we gave them copies of all authorizations we received for resources. The committee and I turned to the mayor in the head town, who treated us well and signed the documents the government agencies needed in order to deliver the resources we requested. The first benefits we received were the installation of a local phone booth and a check for 50,000 pesos with which to buy lambs to be raised by the families of the fifteen women in the committee. Today the health clinic is located next to the office of the local government authorities (the *agencia municipal*), which signs all documents relating to the clinic and to the women's organization.

In the last two years, the local authorities (returned migrants) have sought my advice on how to negotiate for resources from the government and for information about the government programs that are operating in the community. The women members of the FIOB have made donations from their projects to the local authority (cement, fencing materials for the cemetery, some economic support) in recognition of their efforts and un-conditional support. Women—including the wives of the Maldonado brothers—are now openly active in the community (with or without their husbands) and participate in diverse activities, government projects, and educational programs that aid women, children, and the elderly.[5]

Centolia's words reflect the transformations and conflicts that indige-nous women are experiencing as they begin to participate at the local level. These actions speak to the mechanisms of inclusion and exclusion they must navigate within a traditional system of governance that is based on customary law (*usos y costumbres*).[6] In this system, elections occur by gen-eral consensus in the assembly, and the *cargos* are mainly assigned to men. However, in areas of high out-migration of men, as in the Mixteca, the community is left with mostly women, children, and the elderly—that is, without "citizens" to fill the roster of leadership positions and to carry out the *tequios*. The prolonged absence of men from these communities has brought changes in the family, with women taking on new community responsibilities that were previously limited to men and making decisions that affect the collective well-being of the village.

---

[5] Centolia Maldonado, manuscript, November 2002.

[6] The system of *usos y costumbres* was legally recognized by Oaxaca's state government in 1995. Of Oaxaca's 570 municipalities, 418 are governed by customary law.

As Centolia explained, migration to the United States is more than the crossing of a geographic border. It is also a social practice with widespread impacts. Migration simultaneously involves large-scale changes and redefines social networks, while also transforming intimate daily routines. Within families, the redefinition of roles generates tensions and adaptations, bringing together many dreams, longings, and individual stories with local and international political narratives.

Centolia's story describes how the women of Agua Fría confronted the Maldonados' *cacicazgo* and slowly ceased being passive, unquestioning followers of the decisions that the men made. The result has been the appearance of new female leadership roles that challenge a core idea of the patriarchal system—that only men have the ability to exercise power in the public sphere. This challenge then allows for a questioning of the stereotypes that have been ascribed to each gender (Lagarde 1999)—even though such questioning still carries repercussions, from public stigma to gossip. As Centolia states:

> We faced criticism from the community in order to break with tradition since, in an indigenous community, a good woman is a woman who is submissive to her husband or father and dedicates herself to caring for her children.[7]

When women began to participate and advance the concept of "what should be," other meanings begin to emerge regarding what it means to be a "woman" and a "man." This opened up a new arena of conflict, bargaining, and agreement, which allowed for a new construction of what are considered acceptable attributes for a woman. This is not just a new form of participation; it also involves opening up new spaces where women like Olga and Centolia "leave" the participatory spaces they have been assigned and begin to occupy others, mainly tied to the "public" and the "political" (Barrera Bassols and Oehmichen Bazán 2000). The emergence of new leadership has paved the way for the acquisition of new skills, insights, and knowledge.

> Migration has permitted women to participate in new spaces. They now participate in assembly meetings. Before they did

---

[7] Centolia Maldonado, manuscript, , Santa Cruz, November 2002.

not even use the telephone or go to the bank. Now women
have to take leadership to do things.[8]

The women's voices belie the idyllic view of pre-Hispanic cultures and
challenge the pattern of gender inequalities that silences both female and
male dissidents in the interests of "preserving the ideology of harmony."
This ideology subordinates women's interests to community goals that
emphasize social peace and downplay internal community inequalities.
The resulting tensions and conflicts illustrate an innovative change that
transforms women into their own agents, agents who can accept, reject, or
negotiate different situations at the same time that they question homogenous and essentialist visions of indigenous customs and normative systems. Seeing indigenous women as something more than passive victims of
history, war, or politics means understanding them as social actors. This
opens up another facet of their history—as actors with their own trajectories, who produce their own outlooks on change and who until now have
been invisible to classic ethnographic studies (Artía 2001).

It is interesting to observe, in light of the political situation in Agua
Fría, how women are struggling within their communities and their organizations to change those elements of tradition that exclude and oppress
them. One example is how, in the name of tradition, the exclusion of
women from the public sphere was justified as the norm. "Agua Fría is one
of so many communities where injustices and political tyranny were part
of *usos y costumbres*."[9] The women's own words contradict the vision that
the customary law of indigenous villages is harmonious, untouched by
power relations and gender inequality.

We observed that these women's leadership is based on deep commu-
nitarian roots, corroborating the findings of scholars who have researched
women's participation in other environments (see, for example Barrera
Bassols 1999). Olga's and Centolia's experiences coincide in that both have
become leaders because of their deep roots and participation in the community, which gives them "credibility" with the people. They are deeply
committed to their communities and, as a result of this sense of
responsibility, they take their calling as leaders more as an obligation than
a privilege.

---

[8] Personal communication, Centolia Maldonado, November 2002.

[9] Manuscript, Centolia Maldonado, November 2002.

The majority of the women who are local community leaders in the FIOB are the same ones who are members of the health and school committees as well as the local organizers for Progresa[10] and other government programs.[11]

## FINAL REFLECTIONS

Today's world is in the midst of profound transformations that challenge our analytical categories, our imagination, and our ability to create and innovate. As a result, for us, this essay has involved proposing new types of questions as well as different kinds of answers.

The voices presented here are but a small example of the women who participate in the space opened up by the FIOB. As these narratives have shown, different personal experiences enrich the organization's arena. The local political environment is encouraging these stilled voices to emerge, reminding us that more is involved than just the willpower of a few individuals or isolated incidents. The central question that guides our final reflections, then, is, "what has participation in the FIOB brought to the women we have worked with?"

In relation to the social costs — and there have been many, within households as well as in the community and organization — we have tried to avoid envisioning indigenous women as victims or heroines as they confront patriarchal powers. To do so would prevent us from viewing them as actors who have rejected or negotiated these practices at different historical moments, and it would not recognize the spaces women have found for strengthening themselves through discussions, demonstrations, and workshops. Even though there have been limitations to women's participation, we have tried to shed light on the ways in which their everyday lives and personal stories have changed and how these women have adapted as they integrated themselves into their organizations. These spaces then transform themselves into appropriate places from which to question the customs and traditions that exclude women from political as well as communal and household decisions. From this questioning of the supposed equilibrium of their cultures and out of their interactions with others (as they lose their fear of speaking out and become able to say "I

---

[10] *Editor's note*: Progresa, now known as Oportunidades, is the Mexican government's flagship program for education and health in low income rural communities. Government payments are given to mothers to encourage children's school attendance and participation in health programs.

[11] Centolia Maldonado, manuscript, November 2002.

think" or "I want"), they cross the borders of their culture by considering it as neither immutable nor ahistorical.

The women's trajectories and testimonies destroy the notion of indigenous women as mere victims of wars, exploitation, or patriarchal powers. They enable us to see the possibilities the women have to act in response to power relations and in the struggles to achieve their goals. As Hernández Castillo proposes (2001), this involves recognizing their social agency without denying the domination they face, which further implies that we cannot essentialize or victimize the women. We recognize that, although subordination creates oppression, it also creates opportunities.

Migration allows us to imagine new geographies of equality and solidarity, which have led many women to assume functions that were traditionally held by men and have prompted them to reflect upon gender roles and to question the stereotype of the passive, submissive woman. The men's absence has made it possible for women to assume a greater role in the public lives of their communities and has redefined gender relationships. What is new here is that previously silenced voices burst onto the local political scene, asking for a turn to speak and to be heard as women calling for the full exercise of their political rights.

These achievements have led women to cross borders—not geographical borders but cultural borders (Rosaldo 1991). By questioning the customs and traditions that exclude them from participatory spaces, these women have crossed cultural borders in the political arena but also in the private sphere of the household, where the women have spoken out against domestic violence and alcoholism. We believe it is crucial to recall that this all began with the questions women asked about their communities' *usos y costumbres*. It was only after meeting like-minded women over this issue that they lost the fear of speaking out and dared to cross one of the most solid borders that exists—that of culture. These border crossings are one example of the struggles indigenous women are undertaking in many different community, regional, national, and international arenas (Artía 2001).

While significant political questioning has emerged from women's participation in marches, forums, and meetings, what previously remained quietly restricted to the private sphere is also coming to light, leading women to question everyday practices in the domestic sphere as well. Participation in the FIOB has also become a space for political learning, a process that required new understandings which have now become part of these women's cultural capital. The women had to learn how to make alliances and how to negotiate with diverse authorities.

To recognize the contributions that indigenous women have made to the development of their communities, as well as their achievements in the area of more equitable participation, requires a look at the social actors — men and women — who, by participating in different struggles for rights and by taking on the issues of exclusion and inclusion in their specific contexts, extend and link these issues to the regional and to the global level.

## References

Artía, Patricia. 2001. "Desatar las voces, construir la utopías: la Coordinadora Nacional de Mujeres Indígenas en Oaxaca." Master's thesis, Centro de Investigaciones y Estudios Superiores en Antropología Social, Mexico City.

Barrera Bassols, Dalia. 1999. "Mujeres y gobiernos municipales en México," *Revista Cuicuilco* 17.

Barrera Bassols, Dalia, and Cristina Oehmichen Bazán, eds. 2000. *Migración y relaciones de género en México*. Mexico City: Instituto de Investigaciones Antropológicas, Universidad Nacional Autónoma de México.

Hernández Castillo, Rosalva Aída. 2001. *La otra frontera, identidades múltiples en el Chiapas poscolonial*. Mexico City: Centro de Investigaciones y Estudios Superiores en Antropología Social/Miguel Ángel Porrúa.

Lagarde, Marcela. 1999. *Una mirada feminista en el umbral del milenio*. Heredia, Costa Rica: Instituto de Estudios de la Mujer, Universidad Nacional.

Massolo, Alejandra. 1992. *Por amor y coraje: mujeres en movimientos urbanos de la ciudad de México*. Mexico City: Programa Interdisciplinario de Estudios de la Mujer, El Colegio de México.

Rosaldo, Renato. 1991. *Cultura y verdad*. Mexico City: Conaculta/Grijalbo.

# Acronyms

| | |
|---|---|
| ACBJ | Asociación Cívica Benito Juárez / Benito Juárez Civic Association |
| ACNR | Asociación Cívica Nacional Revolucionaria / Revolutionary National Civic Association |
| AGB | Asamblea General Binacional / Binational General Assembly |
| CAWHS | California Agricultural Worker Health Survey |
| CBDIO | Centro Binacional para el Desarrollo Indígena Oaxaqueño / Binational Center for Indigenous Oaxacan Development |
| CCB | Consejo Central Binacional / Central Binational Council |
| CCPM | Comité Cívico Popular Mixteco / Mixteco Popular Civic Committee |
| CDBG | Community Development Block Grant program |
| CEAMO | Coordinación Estatal de Atención al Migrante Oaxaqueño / State Coordinating Office for Oaxacan Migrant Affairs |
| CEDRI | Centro de Desarrollo Regional Indígena / Center for Indigenous Regional Development |
| CIOAC | Central Independiente de Obreros Agrícolas y Campesinos / Independent Central of Agricultural Workers and Peasants |
| CIRS | California Institute for Rural Studies |
| COCIO | Coalición de Comunidades Indígenas de Oaxaca / Coalition of Indigenous Communities of Oaxaca |
| CONAPO | Consejo Nacional de Población / National Population Council |
| COR | Confederación de Obreros Revolucionarios / Confederation of Revolutionary Workers |
| COTLA | Comunidad Tlacolulense en Los Angeles / Tlacolula Community in Los Angeles |
| CRLA | California Rural Legal Assistance |

| | |
|---|---|
| CROC | Confederación Revolucionaria de Obreros y Campesinos / Revolutionary Confederation of Workers and Peasants |
| CROM | Confederación Regional Obrera Mexicana / Mexican Regional Labor Confederation |
| CSC | Centro de Servicios para Campesinos / Farmworker Service Center |
| CSUSM | California State University, San Marcos |
| CTM | Confederación de Trabajadores de México / Confederation of Mexican Workers |
| CUS | "Causes of Undercount" Survey |
| DIF | Sistema Nacional para el Desarrollo Integral de la Familia / Family Development Agency |
| EDD | Employment Development Department |
| EZLN | Ejército Zapatista de Liberación Nacional / Zapatista Army of National Liberation |
| FILT | Frente Independiente de Lucha Triqui / Independent Front for the Triqui Struggle |
| FIOB | Frente Indígena Oaxaqueña Binacional / Oaxacan Indigenous Binational Front |
| FM-ZB | Frente Mixteco-Zapoteco Binacional / Mixteco-Zapoteco Binational Front |
| FOCOICA | Federación Oaxaqueña de Comunidades y Organizaciones Indígenas en California / Oaxacan Federation of Indigenous Communities and Organizations in California |
| GAO | U.S. General Accounting Office |
| GATT | General Agreement on Tariffs and Trade |
| IACOMA | Illinois Interagency Committee on Migrant Affairs |
| IMC | Illinois Migrant Council |
| IMSS | Instituto Mexicano del Seguro Social / Mexican Social Security Institute |
| INEGI | Instituto Nacional de Estadística, Geografía e Informática / National Institute of Statistics, Geography, and Informatics |
| INI | Instituto Nacional Indigenista / National Indigenous Institute |
| INS | U.S. Immigration and Naturalization Service |
| IPN | Instituto Politécnico Nacional / National Polytechnic Institute |
| IRCA | Immigration Reform and Control Act of 1986 |
| LAIPA | Los Angeles Indigenous People's Alliance |

| | |
|---|---|
| MALDEF | Mexican American Legal Defense and Educational Fund |
| MEChA | Movimiento Estudiantil Chicano de Aztlan |
| NAFTA | North American Free Trade Agreement |
| NAO | Nueva Alianza Oaxaqueña / New Oaxacan Alliance |
| NAWS | National Agricultural Workers Survey |
| NGO | nongovernmental organization |
| NRFU | non-response follow-up |
| OPAM | Organización Pro-Ayuda a Macuiltianguis / Organization for Macuiltianguis Community Support |
| OPEO | Organización del Pueblo Explotado y Oprimido / Organization of Exploited and Oppressed People |
| ORO | Organización Regional de Oaxaca / Oaxacan Regional Organization |
| PAN | Partido Acción Nacional / National Action Party |
| PCM | Partido Comunista Mexicano / Mexican Communist Party |
| PCME | Programa para Comunidades Mexicanas en el Exterior / Program for Mexican Communities Abroad |
| PCUN | Pineros y Campesinos Unidos de Noroeste / Northwest Treeplanters and Farmworkers United |
| PIVM | Patrimonio Indígena del Valle del Mezquital / Indigenous Patrimony of the Mezquital Valley |
| PRD | Partido de la Revolución Democrática / Party of the Democratic Revolution |
| PRI | Partido Revolucionario Institucional / Institutional Revolutionary Party |
| PRONJAG | Programa Nacional de Jornaleros Agrícolas / National Agricultural Day Laborers Program |
| PSUM | Partido Socialista Unificado de México / Unified Socialist Party of Mexico |
| PUMS | Public Use Microdata Samples |
| RIIO | Red Internacional Indígena Oaxaqueña / International Indigenous Network of Oaxaca |
| SAW | Special Agricultural Workers program |
| SEDESOL | Secretaría de Desarrollo Social / Social Development Ministry |
| SHCP | Secretaría de Hacienda y Crédito Público / Treasury Ministry |

| | |
|---|---|
| SINGOA | Sindicato Gremial de Obreros Agrícolas Similares y Conexos / Trade-Union Syndicate of Agricultural Workers |
| SRE | Secretaría de Relaciones Exteriores / Mexican Foreign Ministry |
| TNC | transnational community |
| UCSO | Unión de Comunidades Serranas de Oaxaca / Union of Highland Communities of Oaxaca |
| UDMO | Unión de Mujeres Oaxaqueñas / Union of Oaxacan Women |
| UFW | United Farm Workers |
| WIC | Special Supplemental Food Program for Women, Infants, and Children |
| WVIP | Willamette Valley Immigration Project |

# Contributors

**Warren D. Anderson** is assistant professor of anthropology at Southeast Missouri State University. He and his wife and daughters make their home in the peach- and apple-growing region of southern Illinois. The orchards, many established in the nineteenth century, began attracting migrant laborers from Mexico in the 1960s. Anderson's ethnographic and oral history work among the P'urépecha of Michoacán dates from the late 1970s and continues to evolve with the changes and challenges that the migrants themselves face with each new season.

**Patricia Artía Rodríguez** is a native of Montevideo, Uruguay, where she received her BA in social anthropology. Her undergraduate research centered on sexual and reproductive rights from a gender perspective. She migrated to Mexico four years ago, where she obtained her master's degree from the Centro de Investigaciones y Estudios Superiores en Antropología Social (CIESAS) with the thesis titled "Desatar las voces, construir las utopía: la Coordinadora Nacional de Mujeres Indígenas en Oaxaca." She is currently a member of the ongoing seminar on "Gender, Ethnicity, and Multiculturalism," and is a PhD candidate at CIESAS. Her dissertation is on the spaces of political participation of the women of the Oaxacan Indigenous Binational Front (FIOB) in the Mixteca Oaxaqueña and in California.

**Bonnie Bade** is a medical anthropologist whose work focuses on farmworker health, health care, California agriculture and farm labor, transnational migration, ethnomedicine, indigenous Mexico, ethnobotany, and Mixtec communities in California, the San Diego–Tijuana border region, and Oaxaca. Dr. Bade teaches at California State University, San Marcos and earned her PhD in cultural anthropology at the University of California, Riverside in 1994. Her dissertation is entitled "Sweatbaths, Sacrifice, and Surgery: The Practice of Transnational Health Care by Mixtec Families in California." She attended the same university for her bachelor's degree, which was in biology and history. In 2000 she was coinvestigator of the first statewide farmworker health study in California. Titled "Suffering in Silence," the study was conducted by a team of investigators from the California Institute for Rural Studies and the University of California, Davis, and was funded by the California Endowment. The results can be found at www.calendow.com.

**Federico Besserer** is a professor in the Department of Anthropology and vice dean of the School of Social Sciences and Humanities at the Universidad Autónoma Metropolitana, Unidad Iztapalapa, in Mexico City. He holds a PhD from Stanford University. His primary research interest is the study of social inequalities in transnational contexts. He has done multi-sited field research in mining enclaves of transnational corporations in Mexico and in transnational indigenous communities. He has published (with V. Novelo and J.L. Sariego) *El sindicalismo minero en México 1900–1952* (1983); *Moisés Cruz: historia de un transmigrante* (1999); and *Topografías transnacionales: hacia una geografía de la vida transnacional* (in press). He has recently completed the manuscript "Contesting Community: Cultural Struggles of a Mixtec Transnational Community."

**Garance Burke** is a northern California correspondent for the *Boston Globe*. For five years she worked and lived in Mexico City, Oaxaca, and Chiapas, where she wrote on politics, migration, and indigenous communities for the *Washington Post* and *El Financiero*. Her scholarly work is included as a chapter in *Forjando matrias*, a three-part edited volume on Mexican women's history. Burke has a BA in anthropology from Brown University and a master's degree in journalism from the University of California, Berkeley.

**Isidro Cerda** was born in Mexico and received a bachelor's degree from the University of California, Santa Cruz, with a double major in global economics and Latin American and Latino studies. His current interests are in cross-border relationships between the United States and Mexico and related public policies.

**María Crummett** is director of the Center for International Business at the University of South Florida. Dr. Crummett's areas of interest include macro-economics and economic development in Latin America, with particular emphasis on Mexico and Costa Rica. She has written on gender and economic development, international migration, and protective legislation. Her current research focuses on regional trade agreements in the Americas and Mexico-U.S. migration. She has worked as a consultant to numerous international development agencies, including the U.S. Agency for International Development, the International Labor Organization, the Food and Agriculture Organization, the United Nations Development Programme, and the Development Fund for Women. She received her BA in Latin American studies from Stanford University and her PhD in economics from the Graduate Faculty, New School University.

**Yolanda Cruz** is an independent filmmaker and the founder of Petate Productions. She is currently the women's action coordinator for the Federation of Oaxacan Indigenous Communities and Organizations in California (FOCOICA) in Los Angeles. She is a native of the Chatina community of San Juan Quihije, Cieneguilla, Oaxaca. She received her BA in liberal arts from Evergreen University in Olympia, Washington, and an MFA from the University of California, Los Angeles, with an emphasis on film production and direction. She participates in diverse community organizations in Oaxaca and Los Angeles, with a focus on women's rights. Her films have been shown at film festivals and community centers in both Mexico and the United States. She is currently editing a film about the Mixtec women of Oaxaca and is producing a documentary funded by the Rockefeller Foundation about Chatino and Mixtec migration.

**Guillermo Delgado-P.** is an anthropologist of Andean origin who actively defends concepts of human rights. He received his PhD from the University of Texas at Austin and has been a member of the Latin American and Latino Studies Department at the University of California, Santa Cruz since 1988. He writes about indigenous movements, particularly the new transnational strategies that are created by them. In collaboration with John Schechter, he has recently finished compiling a volume entitled *Quechua Expressive Art*, forthcoming in the BAS (Bonner Amerikanistische Studien) collection in Germany. Delgado is the editor of the online magazine www.bolivianstudies.org and writes for *Ojarasca* newsmagazine in Mexico City. He is also a member of IRCA (Indigenous Research Center of the Americas), an initiative organized by the Indigenous Studies Department at the University of California, Davis.

**Rufino Domínguez Santos** is the current general coordinator of the Oaxacan Indigenous Binational Front (FIOB) and executive director of the Binational Center for Indigenous Oaxacan Development, Inc. (CBDIO), both organizations based in Fresno, California. He is a native of the community of San Miguel Cuevas, Juxtlahuaca, Oaxaca, in the Mixteca Baja region. By invitation of Mexican President Vicente Fox, he participated in the creation of the Indigenous Development Council. Since 2001 he has been the host of the radio program titled *Nuestro Foro* (*Our Forum*) on KFCF 88.1, a show that is coproduced by the FIOB. He received the Leadership for a Changing World award from the Ford Foundation, the Advocacy Institute, and the Robert F. Wagner Graduate School of Public Service at New York University, as well as the Local Hero of the Year award from Valley Public Television and Union Bank of California. He currently resides in Fresno, California.

**Luis Escala Rabadán** is a sociologist who completed his doctorate at the University of California, Los Angeles. His research interests bring together the sociology of culture and the sociology of migration. His past work has included the study of transnational communities and the political participation and the human rights situation of Mexican migrants in the United States. He received his PhD in sociology from the University of California, Los Angeles and is currently on the research faculty of the Department of Social Studies at El Colegio de la Frontera Norte in Tijuana, Baja California.

**Jonathan Fox** is professor in the Latin American and Latino Studies Department (LALS) at the University of California, Santa Cruz, where he has taught since 1996. At UCSC he works with the Chicano-Latino Research Center, the Hemispheric Dialogues project, and the Summer Institute on Social Change across Borders, and he recently completed a term as chair of LALS. He also works with several public interest groups, including the Oaxacan Indigenous Binational Front (California, Baja California, and Oaxaca), Bank Information Center (Washington, D.C.), the Interhemispheric Resource Center (Silver City, New Mexico), and Trasparencia (Oaxaca). His books include: *Demanding Accountability: Civil Society Claims and the World Bank Inspection Panel* (coedited, 2003); *Cross-Border Dialogues: U.S.-Mexico Social Movement Networking* (coedited, 2002); *The Struggle for Accountability: The World Bank, NGOs and Grassroots Movements* (coedited, 1998); *Decentralization and Rural Development in Mexico: Community Participation in Oaxaca's Municipal Funds Program* (coauthored, 1996); *The Politics of Food in*

*Mexico: State Power and Social Mobilization* (1992); and *The Challenge of Rural Democratization: Perspectives from Latin America and the Philippines* (edited, 1990). His recent articles have been published in *Foro Internacional, Latin American Research Review, Development in Practice, Revista Mexicana de Sociología, Política y Gobierno, Policy Sciences, Nonprofit and Voluntary Sector Quarterly,* and *Global Governance.* He can be reached at jafox@cats.ucsc.edu.

**Ulises García** is currently vice president of the Oaxacan Federation of Indigenous Communities and Organizations in California (FOCOICA), based in Los Angeles. He has also served as president of the Union of Oaxacan Highland Communities (UCSO). This coalition of Los Angeles area residents from five mountain communities organizes one of the largest basketball tournaments in the Oaxacan community; in 2003, sixty-five teams of Oaxacan migrants participated in the tournament held in the Sereno Recreational Center in Los Angeles. García was born in Santa María Jaltianguis, Ixtlán District in Oaxaca's northern Sierra.

**Javier Huizar Murillo** received a bachelor's degree from the University of California, Santa Cruz, with a double major in Latin American and Latino studies and global economics. His final project for his Latin American and Latino studies major was a documentary on Mexican student movements. He subsequently worked as a postgraduate researcher for the Center for Justice and Tolerance at UCSC. Javier is currently a community organizer with Congregations Organizing for Renewal. He is a longtime resident of the Bay Area.

**Ilene J. Jacobs** is director of litigation, advocacy, and training for California Rural Legal Assistance, Inc. (CRLA). Ms. Jacobs has devoted her thus far twenty-year legal career to advocacy for the housing and civil rights of minority, farmworker, homeless, and other low-income communities in the urban and rural United States. She formed the California Rural Fair Housing Working Group and has worked with federal and state housing and fair housing officials to provide fair housing training to state housing and community development staff. Ms. Jacobs is cochair of the CRLA Housing Task Force; project director for the CRLA Rural Fair Housing Center targeting farmworkers, recent immigrants, indigenous persons, hate crime victims, and other minority communities; founder of the statewide California Rural Fair Housing Working Group; serves on the board of directors of the California Coalition for Rural Housing and the RCAC Agricultural

Worker Health and Housing Advisory Committee; presented and published "Farmworker Housing in California" for the *La Raza Law Journal* symposium on housing discrimination, Boalt School of Law, 1996; and presents seminars to local government, real estate industry, and tenants. She recently was appointed to the national steering committee of NABRE (Network of Alliances Bridging Race and Ethnicity), a project of the Joint Center for Political and Economic Studies in Washington, D.C.

**Paul Johnston** is a sociologist who serves as executive officer of the Monterey Bay Central Labor Council and has a research appointment at the University of California, Santa Cruz. After working for twenty years in labor and other social movements, he received his PhD from the University of California, Berkeley in 1988. From 1989 to 1997 he was assistant professor and then associate professor of sociology at Yale University, where he also served as director of the organizational behavior program in sociology and as research fellow at the Institute for Social and Policy Studies. In 1995 Johnston launched an action-research project examining labor movement response to the assault on immigrant rights in California. That effort led the development of the Citizenship Project, a model union-based immigrant workers center in the Salinas Valley that was the focus of a case study in Joe Feagin and Hernan Vera's *Liberation Sociology* (Westview, 2001). In addition to numerous journal articles and book chapters on labor relations, urban affairs, citizenship, and immigration, Johnston's publications include *Success while Others Fail: Social Movement Unionism and the Public Workplace* (Cornell Institute for Labor Relations Press, 1994). Johnston is currently at work on a book tentatively titled *Citizens of the Future: Labor, Citizenship and Social Change in California*. He can be contacted at johnston@mbclc.org.

**Michael Kearney** is professor of anthropology at the University of California, Riverside. He works with Oaxacans whose lives span the Mexico-U.S. border. His primary interest and concern is with how migration and life in two nations shape the formation of transnational communities and changing patterns of class relations, ethnicity, nationality, and the violation and defense of human rights within this binational context. The practical dimensions of his work deal with the reshaping of municipal institutions and the creation of effective transnational indigenous organizations to meet the political and civil administrative challenges of self-governance in the binational context. These practical challenges have also stimulated him to work on reshaping basic concepts and organizational features of anthropology, so that it may better comprehend and serve the needs of transnational communities, as they are shaped by yet larger global dynamics.

**Edward Kissam** is a senior research associate at Aguirre International/The Aguirre Group, where he works on a range of applied research projects addressing issues related to farmworkers and other Latino immigrants. His social policy and program planning interests include: adult education, K–12 education, employment training, immigrant civic engagement, Latino public radio, and community health. He is currently directing a national study, sponsored by the Fund for Rural America, on the ways that immigration is transforming rural communities and strategies for responding to this social transformation. Kissam is the coauthor (with David Griffith) of *Working Poor: Farmworkers in the United States* (Temple University Press, 1995) as well as major research studies on migrant and seasonal farmworkers for the U.S. Commission on Agricultural Workers and the Department of Labor. He is currently working on a book manuscript, *Here To Stay*, about rural Mexican immigrants' civic involvement.

**Felipe H. López** is currently a PhD student in the Department of Urban Planning and Regional Development at the School of Public Policy and Social Research of the University of California, Los Angeles. He is the coauthor of the first Zapotec-English-Spanish dictionary. His research focuses on the role of Oaxacan immigrant organizations in development in the state of Oaxaca. He has served on various Oaxacan immigrant organization boards, such as the Federación Oaxaqueña de Comunidades y Organizaciones Indígenas en California, Consejo Indígena Binacional de Los Valles Centrales de Oaxaca, and Red Internacional Indígena Oaxaqueña. He also worked as a consultant to the Food and Agriculture Organization (FAO) of the United Nations.

**Filemón López** hosts the radio program *La Hora Mixteca* on the Radio Bilingüe network every Sunday. The program is bilingual in Spanish and Mixteco and is broadcast in California, Baja California, and Oaxaca. In 1984 he helped to found the Benito Juárez Civic Association (ACBJ), based in Fresno, California, one of the pioneer organizations in the movement for the rights of indigenous migrant workers. He was born in the community of Río Timbre, in the municipality of San Juan Mixtepec, in the Mixteca Baja region of Oaxaca. His migration experience began in 1971, and he has lived in many places, including Sinaloa, Sonora, Baja California Sur, Mexico's Federal District, Chiapas, Florida, Oregon, and California. He currently resides in Fresno, California.

**Centolia Raymunda Maldonado Vásquez** is a leader of the Oaxacan Indigenous Binational Front, working at the local, regional, national, and transnational levels. At the FIOB's 2001 Binational Assembly she was elected to serve on its Binational Commission. She was born in Santiago Juxtlahuaca, Oaxaca. As a migrant to Mexicali, she was able to earn a degree in business administration. She then returned to her home community, which is on the overlapping border of the Mixteco and Triqui regions. In addition to her work with the FIOB, she has also worked with Mexico's National Indigenous Institute (INI) as well as with local nonprofit social service organizations. Her community organizing work includes promoting community-based initiatives such as savings clubs and programs run by teenagers for development of children's needs within the community. She participated in the UCSC/LALS Summer Institute on Social Change across Borders in 1999. She returned to UCSC in the fall of 2002 to participate as a visiting action-research fellow in the Hemispheric Dialogues project. Recently her community development work has focused on support for the FIOB's growing network of women's community-based savings clubs.

**Jesús Martínez-Saldaña,** a native of Michoacán, is assistant professor in the Department of Chicano and Latin American Studies at California State University, Fresno. His research focuses on the transnational political activities of Mexican immigrants. He is coauthor, with Leticia Calderón Chelius, of *La dimensión política de la migración mexicana* (Instituto Mora, 2002). Other recent publications include: "Los Olvidados Become Heroes: The Evolution of Mexico's Policies towards Citizens Abroad," in *International Migration and Sending Countries: Perceptions, Policies and Transnational Relations* (Palgrave, 2003); with Nayamín Martínez Cossío, "La lucha por el voto de los mexicanos en el extranjero," in *Siete experiencias migratorias en América Latina* (Escuela de Estudios Panamericanos, Consejo Superior de Investigaciones Científicas, 2002); and, with Raúl Ross, "Suffrage for Mexicans Abroad," in *Cross-Border Dialogues: Lessons from Mexico-U.S. Social Movement Networking* (Center for U.S.-Mexican Studies, UCSD, 2002). Current projects include the Mexican right-to-vote movement, politics in California, and *michoacano* migration to the United States.

**Alejandra Ricárdez** is the cofounder and current project manager of the Coalition of Indigenous Communities of Oaxaca (COCIO), based in San Diego, California. She is also a member of the leadership of the Oaxacan Women's Union (HUDMO), based in Los Angeles. She is a native of the community of Agua Blanca, in the municipality of Santa Ana Tlapacoya in the District of Zimatlán, Oaxaca. She received her BA in sociology from San Diego State University and an MA in urban planning from the University of California, Los Angeles, with an emphasis in international and regional development. She currently resides in Los Angeles and San Diego, and works as an agricultural mental health analyst for North County Health Services in San Diego County, California.

**Gaspar Rivera-Salgado**, who received his doctorate in sociology from the University of California, Santa Cruz, is an adviser to several migrant organizations in California, including the Binational Center for Oaxacan Indigenous Development (CBDIO), the Oaxacan Federation of Indigenous Communities and Organizations in California (FOCOICA), and the Oaxacan Indigenous Binational Front (FIOB). From 1999 to 2003 he was assistant professor of sociology and American studies and ethnicity at the University of Southern California, were he taught courses on international migration, Latino politics, and race relations in the United States. Currently he is an independent consultant on transnational migration and Mexican economic development. His most recent publications include book chapters in *Cross-Border Dialogues: U.S.-Mexico Social Movement Networking* (Center for U.S.-Mexican Studies, UCSD, 2002) and *Immigration Research for a New Century: Multidisciplinary Perspectives* (Russell Sage Foundation, 2000). He also writes for the newspapers *El Oaxaqueño* and *La Jornada* (in the Sunday newsmagazine *Masiosare*).

**Liliana Rivera-Sánchez** received her BA in sociology from the University of Veracruz and her MA in social sciences from the Facultad Latinoamericana de Ciencias Sociales (FLACSO) in Mexico City. She is currently a PhD candidate in sociology at the New School for Social Research in New York City. She was also a professor and researcher at the Centro de Investigación y Docencia Económicas (CIDE) in Mexico City. She has done research for the International Center for Migration, Ethnicity and Citizenship at the New School for Social Research in New York. She has also served as a consultant for various nongovernmental organizations, such as the DEMOS Foundation and the Tepeyac Association of New York. She received the award for best postgraduate thesis (in the Master of Sociology category) from the Mexican Science Academy and the National Council of Science and Technology, and the Ibero-American Award for the best research paper on ethnicity and religion from the Latin American Association of Religious Studies (ALER) in Spain.

**Sergio Robles Camacho** was born in the Zapotec community of San Bartolomé Zoogocho, Villa Alta, Oaxaca. He received his degree in telecommunications engineering from Mexico's Instituto Politécnico Nacional and worked for twenty-seven years in the Telecommunications and Transport Ministry. Since the late 1970s he has also been active in many hometown community development projects in San Bartolomé Zoogocho, and in 1994 he was named community adviser. In 1994 he also became a founding member of the Center for Indigenous Regional Development (CEDRI), a binational community development organization related to the Frente Mixteco-Zapoteco Binacional. In 1996 he was named community adviser to a broader coalition of communities in the Sierra de Juárez, the Organization of Authorities and Communities of the Zoogocho Sector. In 2001 he was chosen through the customary law process to serve as the municipal president of San Bartolomé Zoogocho. That same year he was also named president of the Organization of Authorities and Communities of the Zoogocho Sector, which includes eighteen Zapotec communities in the Sierra Juárez.

**David Runsten** is associate director of the North American Integration and Development (NAID) Center at the University of California, Los Angeles. He administers the Center and conducts research on rural development and migration in Mexico, California, and Central America. He has done research on agriculture in all three NAFTA countries, focusing on fruit and vegetable production and the potential for small-scale producers to participate in high-value markets. He was director of research at the California Institute for Rural Studies for six years, where he created the Farm Labor and Rural Poverty Program, which carried out research in association with a variety of community organizations, labor unions, and farmworker service providers, and included several studies of the Mixtec community in California. He is also currently a research consultant for the Los Angeles Alliance for a New Economy (LAANE), where he is conducting a survey of the impacts of living wages in Los Angeles, as well as working to create an Equity Impact Analysis tool for local development projects.